CANADA'S AR

Waging War and Keeping the Peace, Second Edition

The first edition of *Canada's Army* quickly became the definitive history of the Canadian army. The intervening years, however, have seen major changes in the way Canadians think about their military, especially in the context of the Afghan War and increased federal funding for the Canadian Forces. In this second edition of *Canada's Army*, J.L. Granatstein – one of the country's leading historians – brings his work up to date with new material on the evolving role of the military in Canadian society, along with additional sources and illustrations.

Canada's Army traces the full three-hundred-year history of the Canadian military from its origins in New France to the Conquest, the Revolutionary War and the War of 1812; through South Africa and the two world wars to the Korean War, contemporary peacekeeping efforts, and the War in Afghanistan. Granatstein points to the inevitable continuation of armed conflict around the world and makes a compelling case for Canada to maintain properly equipped and professional armed forces.

Canada's Army offers a rich analysis of the political context for the battles and events that shaped our understanding of the nation's military. Masterfully written and passionately argued, this book has been lauded as 'belong[ing] on all concerned citizens' bookshelves.'

J.L. GRANATSTEIN is the former director and CEO of the Canadian War Museum and taught Canadian history for thirty years.

CANADA'S ARMY

Waging War and Keeping the Peace

Second Edition

J.L. GRANATSTEIN

UNIVERSITY OF TORONTO PRESS
Toronto Buffalo London

© J.L. Granatstein 2011
Toronto Buffalo London
www.utppublishing.com
Printed in Canada

First edition published 2002; paperback edition (with new introduction) published 2004
Second edition published 2011

ISBN 978-1-4426-1178-8

Library and Archives Canada Cataloguing in Publication

Granatstein, J.L., 1939–

Canada's army : waging war and keeping the peace / J.L. Granatstein. – 2nd ed.

Includes bibliographical references and index.
ISBN 978-1-4426-1178-8

1. Canada. Canadian Armed Forces – History.   2. Canada – History, Military.   I. Title.

UA600.G7 2011   355.00971   C2010-907472-6

Cover illustration: Soldiers in training. Reproduced with the permission of the
Minister of Public Works and Government Services, 2010.

University of Toronto Press acknowledges the financial assistance to its publishing program of
the Canada Council for the Arts and the Ontario Arts Council.

 Canada Council **Conseil des Arts**
for the Arts   du Canada

 ONTARIO ARTS COUNCIL
CONSEIL DES ARTS DE L'ONTARIO

University of Toronto Press acknowledges the financial support of the Government
of Canada through the Canada Book Fund for its publishing activities.

For Tess

CONTENTS

Contents

Illustrations follow page 288

PREFACE

I am the product of demographic good luck. I was born in 1939 at the tail end of the Great Depression and the beginning of the Second World War. I grew up in a Canada that was prosperous as never before, and, through good fortune rather than good management on my part, university education in the late 1950s, good jobs in the 1960s, and a reasonably priced house at the end of that decade were my lot.

Because of when I was born, again through the sheer accident of timing, I was too young for the Second World War and for Korea. When I joined the army in 1956, I encountered what now seems part of a half-century of peace, though it was the heart of the Cold War. My ten years of military service were wholly uneventful: a good university education at Le Collège Militaire Royal de Saint-Jean and the Royal Military College in Kingston, desultory training at Camp Borden, and uneventful service in Ottawa, until I left the armed forces in 1966 to go into university teaching. I never heard a shot fired in anger and, except for the one occasion when I accompanied my platoon sergeant to blow up an unexploded hand grenade, I was never near danger.

Virtually everything I know about the army therefore comes from academic study, not hard experience. I am ultimately a dabbler and a dilettante, a scarred campaigner of the university wars, but not the real kind. Yet I do not doubt that my time at RMC was the definitive factor in shaping me. I was a feckless seventeen-year-old when I went to military college and a driven and organized Type A personality when I left. Ever since, I have made my career out of the organizational skills I learned while trying to balance RMC's demanding academic schedule with military duties.

RMC shaped me in other ways too. The central staircase in the college's main building is a shrine to those hundreds of ex-cadets killed on active service, and the recently restored Memorial Arch at what used to be the college entrance commemorates them as well in resonating wording: 'Blow out ye bugles over these rich dead ...' RMC's auditorium, Currie Hall, honours every unit of the Canadian Corps of the Great War along with its great commander, General Sir Arthur Currie, and there are monuments, plaques, and the artifacts of wars past and present everywhere.

Those who attended the college came away imbued with a sense of service. Not to have that attitude required almost a conscious effort of will, and my will certainly was not strong enough to resist. But this commitment did not mean that every graduating cadet stayed in the armed forces; most throughout RMC's 125 years of history did not. Nor did it mean that every graduate believed in the military. For long periods I had doubts about the rightness of Canadian Forces' policies and about our alliances, and I sometimes still do.

Yet I am certain that everyone who went to RMC Kingston left with the sense that ordinary Canadians had done extraordinary deeds in the past and would do so again in the future, the classic definition of nationhood laid down decades ago by historian Frank Underhill. The evidence was all about the college that this confidence was justified – from Currie Hall to the bust of Harry Crerar, the commander of First Canadian Army in the Second World War, to the weaponry of the Cold War and peacekeeping on the grounds. The army had been the nation in arms in the two world wars, and the graduates of the college had helped lead the efforts that did so much to make Canada a nation and preserve the freedom of the world. In the Cold War and the peace that followed it had been the same, and it still is in a new millennium that is as dangerous as any other time in the last century.

This history of Canadians and their army is written in this spirit, but with an admixture of what is, I trust, constructive criticism. It is gratefully dedicated to all those Canadians who served their country in war and peace, and especially to those who did not survive their service to return to what is, thanks to their sacrifice, this best of all nations.

I should explain what this book is about and what it is not. It is a history of the Canadian Army, of organized bodies of Canadians fighting, training, and serving their nation in peace and in war. It is not a history of every war fought on Canadian soil, nor is it the story of Canadians who served as individuals in other armies. This organization explains why the text moves quickly through the seventeenth, eighteenth, and nineteenth centuries: very simply, the Canadian Army scarcely existed before the dawn of the twentieth century. It also explains why I have omitted the Nile Voyageurs of the 1880s and the Mackenzie-Papineau Battalion that fought on the Loyalist side in the Spanish Civil War. I must also add that I have not followed today's practice of converting all measurements into metric: when soldiers fought for yards of ground and their vehicles ran on gallons of gas, the imperial system is employed.

Canada's Army is an extended argument for military professionalism. The military profession, much like any other, is based on expertise, a sense of corporate identity, and responsibility. The soldier has specialized skills learned and mastered through study and practice; he belongs to a self-regulating and exclusive organization distinct from civil society; and, in Canada, the soldier accepts that his profession makes him responsible to the civil authority, a servant of the government. Because the soldier controls deadly force, the sense of responsibility to the state, one firmly based on an ethical foundation, is crucial. But a professional soldier, unlike a doctor or an engineer, has one trait that marks him as different and special. As General Sir John Hackett put it, there is an unwritten clause of unlimited liability in his contract. 'It requires of a man that he be prepared to surrender life itself if the discharge of his duty should demand that. This is not often evoked in peacetime,' Hackett continued, 'but its existence lends a dignity to the military condition which is difficult to deny.' Civilian soldiers in huge numbers did their wartime duty for Canada, and more than a hundred thousand died in the process. But the professional has the obligation to give his life in peacetime too if so required. Many have.

Although I do not believe that history repeats itself, preparing this manuscript persuaded me that Canadians have replicated their military mistakes far too often. In peace we almost always underfunded the professional military and relied on the militia, the ordinary citizenry in arms. When war came, the people expected that great victories would be won at once, demanded that all officers be strategists of Napoleonic calibre, and insisted that every soldier had a field marshal's baton hidden somewhere in his knapsack. The result of this utter naivety has been needless casualties while the army learned its trade in battle. And then, as soon as victory was won and peace came, the government disbanded the army, and the nation resumed its faith in the militia myth that every Canadian was, by definition, a natural soldier. In Canada no professionals were needed, except, perhaps, for the training of the militiamen.

Twenty years after the end of the Cold War, ten years after al Qaeda's attack on the United States, and a decade after Canada first sent troops to Afghanistan, Canada's Army is in a better condition than it has been in decades. The Army's junior leadership and many of its senior commanders have proven themselves in battle, and this will shape the Army of the future. Since 2005, both Liberal and Conservative governments have provided new funding and invested in new equipment and in some (but still too few) additional men and women for the Army's battalions and regiments. Just as important, for the first time since the Second World War, the Army stands high in the public mind, and the war in Afghanistan, while unpopular with much of the public, has greatly increased the esteem in which the nation's soldiers are now held in every province. This is a change of historic proportions, and it suggests that the Canadian people may be willing to see those in uniform well provided for in the coming years. They should be because the costs of the nation's professional armed forces are the insurance premiums on which Canada's security ultimately depends. The equation is and always has been very simple: we pay now in dollars for a competent military or we pay later in dollars *and* with our sons and daughters.

ACKNOWLEDGMENTS

As always, in writing this book I have benefited from the advice and admonitions of friends and colleagues, some of which I have actually accepted. I have been struck by the fact that my close friends and former students occupy the high ground in Canadian military history, and their expertise has been of great value to me. My friends and former students Jock Vance and Patrick Brennan offered sage counsel. My closest colleagues at the Canadian War Museum, Roger Sarty and Dean Oliver, read chapters for me, as did Pat Brennan, David Bercuson, Des Morton, LCols Ike Kennedy and J.P. McManus, Bill McAndrew, and Norman Hillmer. Roger Sarty, Bill Young, Jerry Tulchinsky, and Major Doug Delaney shared documents with me. With great generosity, Terry Copp and Bill McAndrew, distinguished military historians both, let me use interviews they had conducted, and they, Major Delaney, and Patrick Brennan, whose work on the Canadian Expeditionary Force will change many preconceptions, let me read some of their yet unpublished work. So too did Lieutenant-Colonel Jack English, my RMC and Duke classmate who continues to challenge Canadian military historians with his interpretations. The Chief of the Land Staff, Lieutenant-General Mike Jeffrey, gave me copies of some of his papers and speeches and talked with me about the present condition and future of the army. Lieutenant-General Henri Tellier graciously allowed me to use some of his material on the Royal 22e Régiment. The Department of National Defence gave me permission to use the superb maps produced by the Directorate of History and Heritage at National Defence Headquarters, and I am most grateful to Dr Serge Bernier for his help in this matter. My cousin Carol Geller Sures let me use the Major Harry Jolley letters, a fine, sensitive collection from the Second World War, and then graciously donated them to the Canadian War Museum. Jack Saywell allowed me to use his father's Great War letters and memoir, and also presented these materials to the museum.

While I was at the War Museum from July 1998 to June 2000 I had the opportunity and privilege of meeting and coming to know many veterans of the Second World War, Korea, and peacekeeping, as well as many serving members of the Canadian Forces. These encounters have greatly enriched this book. So too did my dealings with the museum's staff and Friends, a very knowledgeable group indeed. In addition to Roger Sarty and Dean Oliver, I must single out Serge Durflinger, Laura Brandon, Harry Martin, Dianne Turpin, Rachel Poirier, Jim Whitham, Leslie Redman, Colonel Jerry Holtzhauer, and General Paul Manson for their patience and perseverance in teaching me so much about military history, military artifacts, and war art. Leslie Redman greatly facilitated the photo research in the War Museum's all but untouched collections, research ably done for me by Gabrielle Nishiguchi. My friend LCdr Jacques Fauteux helped me get photographs of current Canadian Forces operations.

Linda McKnight, my longtime literary agent, continued her work on my behalf with great effect. Len Husband was a pleasure to work with at the University of Toronto Press. Rosemary Shipton edited this book, not the first of mine she has tackled, and any stylistic grace and coherence it may have must be credited to her. Any errors that remain are, of course, entirely my fault.

Over the years I have learned much from my good friends Desmond Morton (forty-six years now in his case), Norman Hillmer, Robert Bothwell, William Kaplan, Michael Bliss, Jack Saywell, Jerry Tulchinsky, Peter Neary, and David Bercuson, and I am unfailingly grateful to them all. My immense scholarly debt to Des and David will be apparent from the references to their many works in the notes. Even where I knew these colleagues to be wrong, I have doubted my own judgment, so highly do I esteem theirs! My academic and personal debts to Jack Saywell, in particular, extend over more than four decades and are very great indeed.

My dear wife, Elaine, has borne this book through its gestation as readily as the others. Carole and Eric and, especially, Tess keep me optimistic for the future. As always, Michael makes me wish that the past could have been different.

MAPS

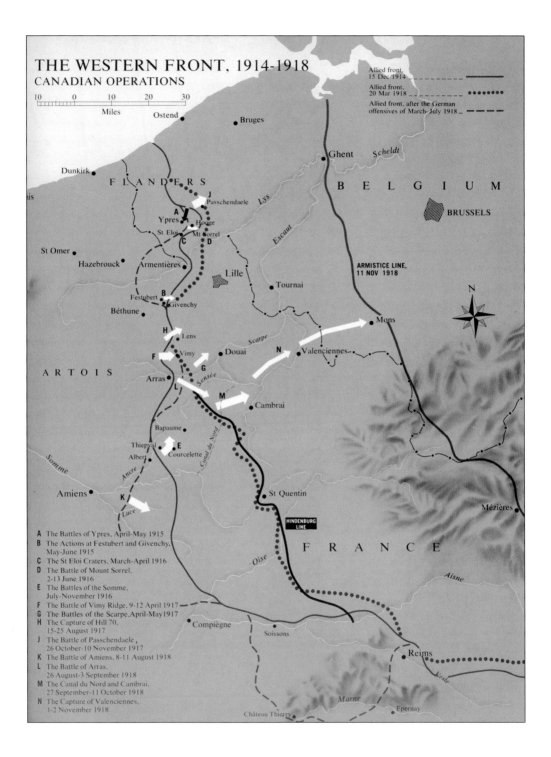

THE WESTERN FRONT, 1914-1918
CANADIAN OPERATIONS

Miles
10 0 10 20 30

Allied front,
15 Dec 1914 ————————
Allied front,
20 Mar 1918 ●●●●●●●●●
Allied front, after the German
offensives of March-July 1918 ————————

Ostend

Bruges

Dunkirk

F L A N D E R S

Ghent   Scheldt

B E L G I U M

BRUSSELS

J
A
Ypres   Passchendaele   Lys
Hooge
St Eloi
Mt Sorrel   Escaut
C   D

St Omer

Hazebrouck   Armentières

Lille

Tournai

ARMISTICE LINE,
11 NOV 1918

Festubert
B
Givenchy
Béthune

N

H
Lens   Mons
F   Vimy   Douai
Scarpe
A R T O I S   Valenciennes
Arras   G
L   Sensée

M   Cambrai

Bapaume
Thiepval   E
Albert   Courcelette

Somme
Ancre

Amiens   K
Luce

St Quentin

HINDENBURG
LINE

F R A N C E

Oise

Aisne

Mézières

A The Battles of Ypres, April-May 1915
B The Actions at Festubert and Givenchy,
   May-June 1915
C The St Eloi Craters, March-April 1916
D The Battle of Mount Sorrel,
   2-13 June 1916
E The Battles of the Somme,
   July-November 1916
F The Battle of Vimy Ridge, 9-12 April 1917
G The Battles of the Scarpe, April-May 1917
H The Capture of Hill 70,
   15-25 August 1917
J The Battle of Passchendaele,
   26 October-10 November 1917
K The Battle of Amiens, 8-11 August 1918
L The Battle of Arras,
   26 August-3 September 1918
M The Canal du Nord and Cambrai,
   27 September-11 October 1918
N The Capture of Valenciennes,
   1-2 November 1918

Compiègne

Soissons

Reims

Vesle

Marne
Château Thierry   Epernay

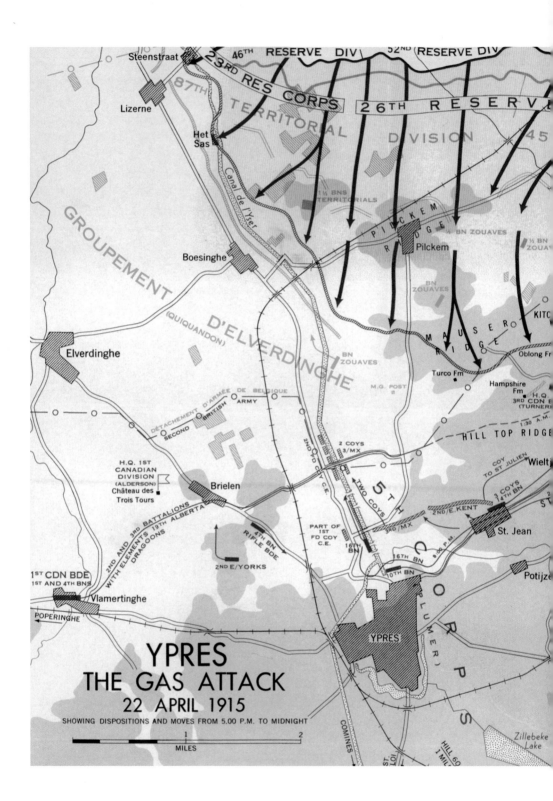

YPRES
THE GAS ATTACK
22 APRIL 1915
SHOWING DISPOSITIONS AND MOVES FROM 5.00 P.M. TO MIDNIGHT

1   2
MILES

RESERVE

Poelcappelle

POELCAPPELLE RIDGE

2ND

POELCAPPELLE DIVISION

Lekkerboterbeek

13TH BATTALION RESERVE ERSATZ BRIGADE

26TH RESERVE CORPS

38TH LANDWEHR BRIGADE

27TH

RESERVE

15TH BATTALION

3RD CDN BDE

1ST CDN BDE

STROOMBEEK RIDGE

Stroombeek

8TH BATTALION

5TH BATTALION

Passchendaele

CANADIAN DIVISION

2ND CDN BDE

(8)

(5)

53RD RESERVE DIVISION

ROULERS

aere

COY 2/E KENT AND ELEMENTS 15TH BN.

(15)

2ND CDN DIVISION

COY 7 BN

GRAVENSTAFEL RIDGE

Locality "C"

(8)

BERLIN WOOD

Gravenstafel

85TH BRIGADE

DIVERSIONARY ATTACKS 11.00 P.M.

10TH BATTERY C.F.A.

A COY 15TH BN

Boetleer's Fm

Haanebeek I

St. Julien

2ND CDN BDE (CURRIE)

Pond Fm

COY 7TH BN

28TH DIVISION (BULFIN)

COY 5TH BN

BN

GUN AREA

COY 5TH BN

ZONNEBEKE RIDGE

84TH BRIGADE

Broodseinde

Fortuin

Zonnebeke

Zonnebeke

CORPS

Frezenberg

FREZENBERG RIDGE

83RD BRIGADE

EWAARDE IDGE

Bellewaarde Lake

POLYGON WOOD

POLYGON WOOD BRIGADE

54TH RESERVE DIVISION

Becelaere

Hooge

DIVISION (SNOW)

80TH BRIGADE

81ST BRIGADE

39TH DIV

M CORPS

MENIN

SANCTUARY WOOD

27TH

Canadian & British | French & Belgian | German

Positions occupied at 5.00 p.m.

Positions subsequently occupied

Secondary defence lines

Small elements of Canadian battalions identified thus .... (8)

Military bridges

Gas cloud

Contours indicated by layer tints: 20, 30, 40 metres

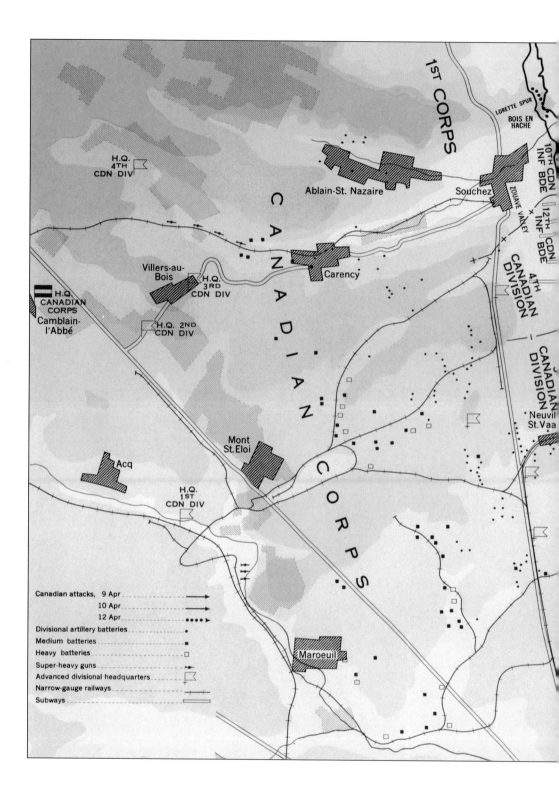

1ST CORPS

LORETTE SPUR
BOIS EN HACHE

10TH CDN INF BDE

12TH CDN INF BDE

ZOUAVE VALLEY

4TH CANADIAN DIVISION

3RD CANADIAN DIVISION

H.Q. 4TH CDN DIV

C A N A D I A N

Ablain-St. Nazaire

Souchez

Villers-au-Bois

H.Q. 3RD CDN DIV

Carency

H.Q. CANADIAN CORPS

Camblain-l'Abbé

H.Q. 2ND CDN DIV

Neuvil St. Vaa

Acq

Mont St. Eloi

C O R P S

H.Q. 1ST CDN DIV

Canadian attacks,	9 Apr	——→
	10 Apr	
	12 Apr	•••• ►
Divisional artillery batteries		•
Medium batteries		■
Heavy batteries		□
Super-heavy guns		
Advanced divisional headquarters		
Narrow-gauge railways		
Subways		

Maroeuil

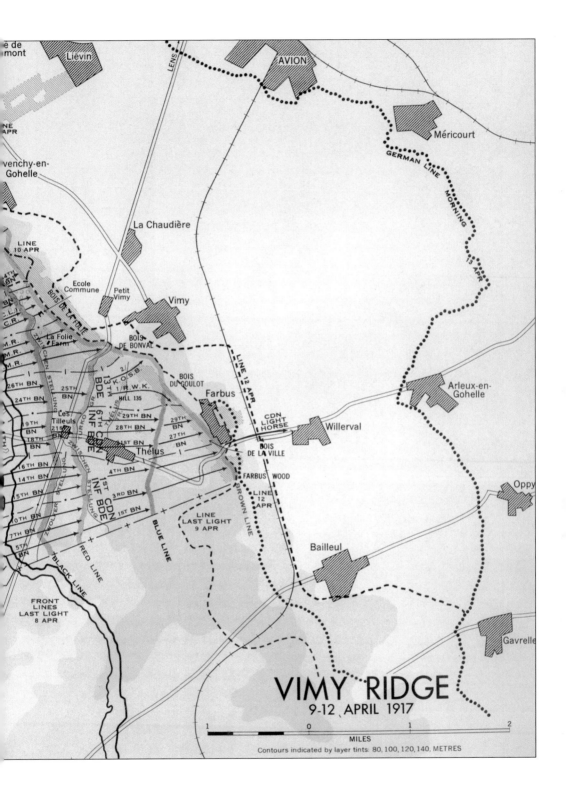

VIMY RIDGE
9-12 APRIL 1917

1   0   1   2
MILES
Contours indicated by layer tints: 80, 100, 120, 140, METRES

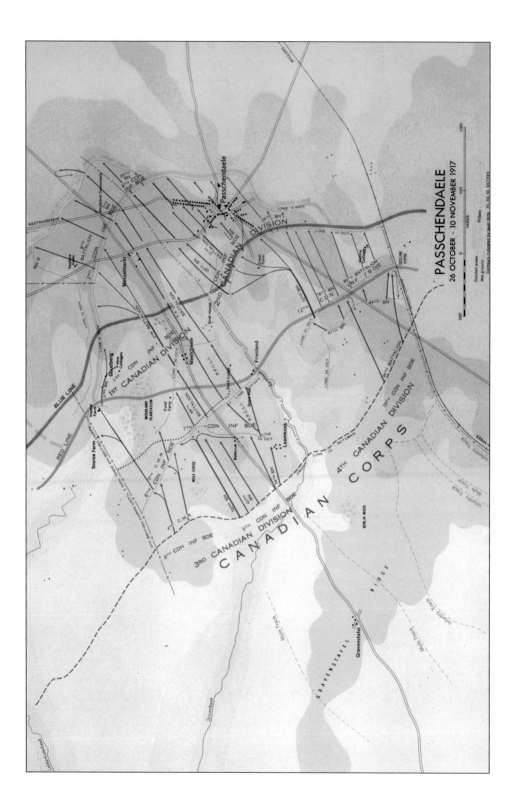

PASSCHENDAELE
26 OCTOBER - 10 NOVEMBER 1917

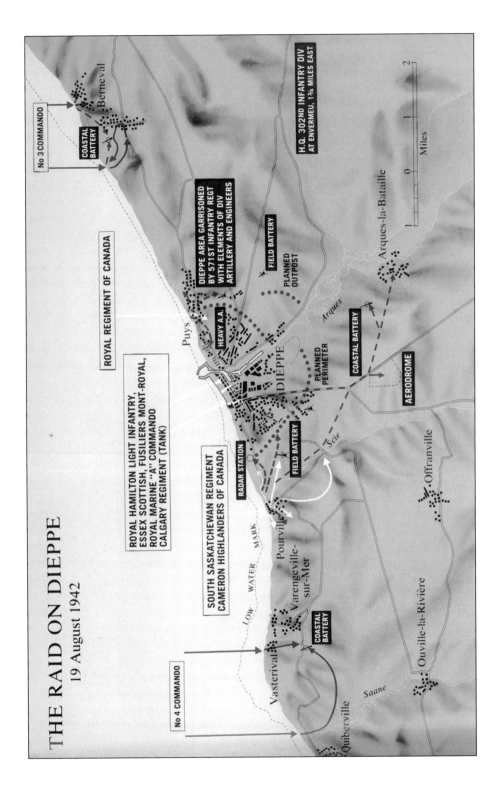

THE RAID ON DIEPPE
19 August 1942

No 4 COMMANDO

SOUTH SASKATCHEWAN REGIMENT
CAMERON HIGHLANDERS OF CANADA

ROYAL HAMILTON LIGHT INFANTRY,
ESSEX SCOTTISH, FUSILIERS MONT-ROYAL,
ROYAL MARINE "A" COMMANDO
CALGARY REGIMENT (TANK)

ROYAL REGIMENT OF CANADA

No 3 COMMANDO

DIEPPE AREA GARRISONED
BY 571ST INFANTRY REGT
WITH ELEMENTS OF DIV
ARTILLERY AND ENGINEERS

H.Q. 302ND INFANTRY DIV
AT ENVERMEU, 1¾ MILES EAST

COASTAL BATTERY

FIELD BATTERY

PLANNED
OUTPOST

HEAVY A.A.

PLANNED
PERIMETER

COASTAL BATTERY

AERODROME

RADAR STATION

FIELD BATTERY

COASTAL
BATTERY

Berneval

Puys

DIEPPE

Arques

Scie

Arques-la-Bataille

Offranville

Pourville

Varengeville-
sur-Mer

Vasterival

Ouville-la-Rivière

Saane

Quiberville

Low WATER MARK

Miles

0   1   2

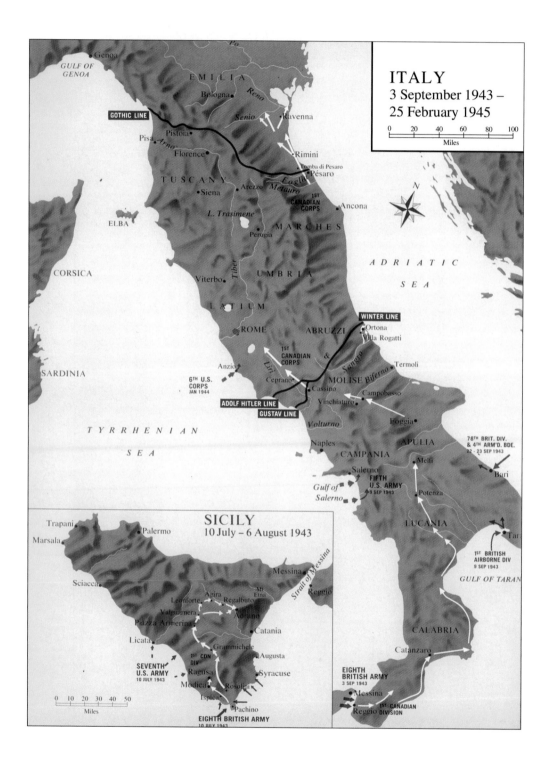

ITALY
3 September 1943 –
25 February 1945

0   20   40   60   80   100
Miles

GULF OF GENOA

Genoa

EMILIA

Po

Bologna   Reno

Senio   Ravenna

GOTHIC LINE

Pistoia   Rimini

Pisa   Arno

Florence   Foglia   Tomba di Pesaro   Pésaro

TUSCANY   Arezzo   Metauro

Siena   1ST CANADIAN CORPS   Ancona

L. Trasimene

Perugia   MARCHES

ELBA

CORSICA   ADRIATIC

Viterbo   Tiber   UMBRIA   SEA

LATIUM

WINTER LINE

ROME   ABRUZZI   Ortona
Villa Rogatti

1ST CANADIAN CORPS   &

Anzio   Liri   Sangro   Termoli

Ceprano   Biferno

6TH U.S. CORPS   JAN 1944   Cassino   MOLISE   Campobasso

SARDINIA   ADOLF HITLER LINE   Vinchiaturo

GUSTAV LINE   Volturno   Foggia

Naples   APULIA   78TH BRIT. DIV. & 4TH ARM'D. BDE.   22 - 23 SEP 1943

TYRRHENIAN   CAMPANIA   Melfi   Bari

SEA   Salerno   FIFTH U.S. ARMY   8-9 SEP 1943

Gulf of Salerno   Potenza

LUCANIA   1ST BRITISH AIRBORNE DIV   9 SEP 1943

Tar

GULF OF TARAN

SICILY
10 July – 6 August 1943

Trapani   Palermo

Marsala   Messina   Strait of Messina

Sciacca   Reggio

Mt Etna   CALABRIA

Agira   Regalbuto

Leonforte   Adrano   Catanzaro

Valguarnera

Piazza Armerina   Catania   Messina

Licata   EIGHTH BRITISH ARMY   Reggio   1ST CANADIAN DIVISION

Grammichele   3 SEP 1943

1ST CDN DIV   Augusta

SEVENTH U.S. ARMY   Ragusa   Syracuse

10 JULY 1943   Modica   Rosolini

Ispica

0 10 20 30 40 50   Pachino

Miles   EIGHTH BRITISH ARMY

10 JULY 1943

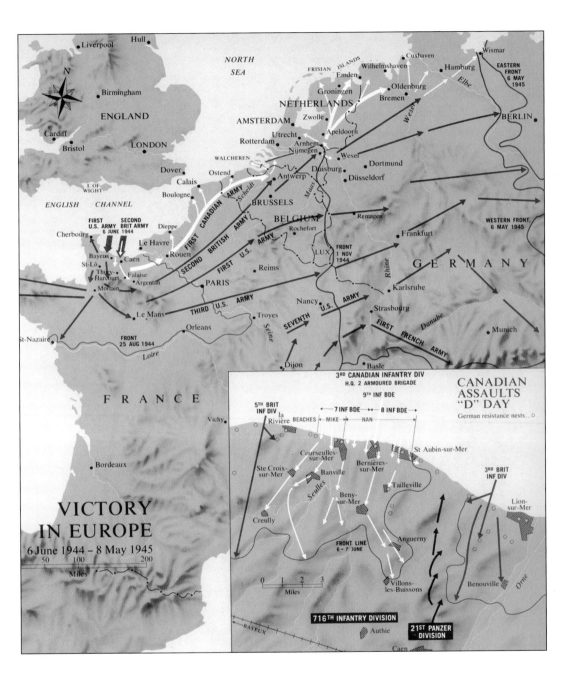

VICTORY
IN EUROPE
6 June 1944 – 8 May 1945

50   100   200
Miles

CANADIAN
ASSAULTS
"D" DAY

German resistance nests...

3RD CANADIAN INFANTRY DIV
H.Q. 2 ARMOURED BRIGADE
9TH INF BDE

7 INF BDE   8 INF BDE

716TH INFANTRY DIVISION

21ST PANZER
DIVISION

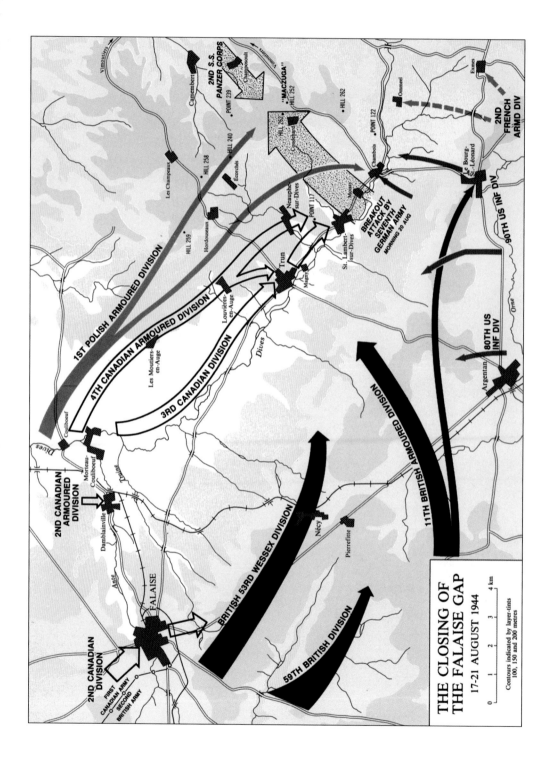

THE CLOSING OF
THE FALAISE GAP

17-21 AUGUST 1944

Contours indicated by layer-tints
100, 150 and 200 metres

0   1   2   3   4 km

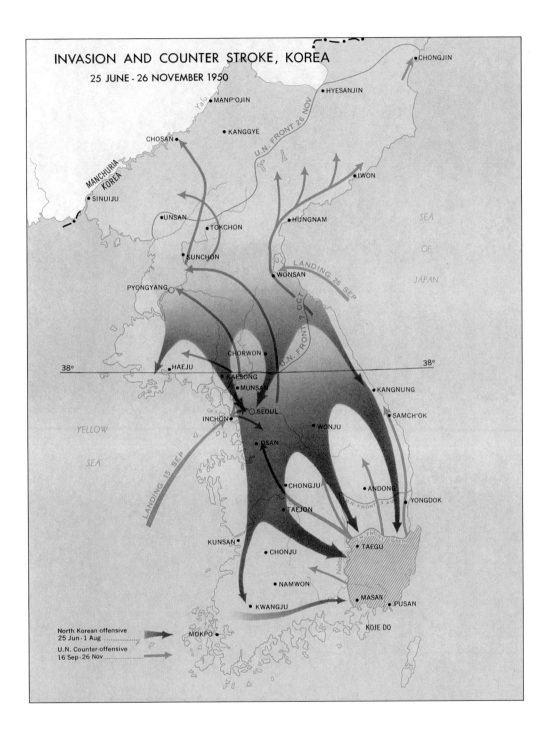

INVASION AND COUNTER STROKE, KOREA

25 JUNE - 26 NOVEMBER 1950

• CHONGJIN

• HYESANJIN

• MANP'OJIN

• KANGGYE

CHOSAN •

U.N. FRONT 26 NOV

MANCHURIA
KOREA

• IWON

SINUIJU •

• UNSAN

• TOKCHON

• HUNGNAM

SEA

SUNCHON •

LANDING 26 SEP

OF

• WONSAN

JAPAN

PYONGYANG ◦

U.N. FRONT 7 OCT

38°   38°

CHORWON •

• HAEJU

• KANGNUNG

KAESONG •
• MUNSAN

• SAMCH'OK

INCHON •   ◦ SEOUL

YELLOW

• WONJU

• OSAN

SEA

LANDING 15 SEP

• CHONGJU

• ANDONG

• TAEJON

U.N. FRONT 5 AUG

• YONGDOK

KUNSAN •

• TAEGU

• CHONJU

• NAMWON

• MASAN

• KWANGJU   • PUSAN

KOJE DO

North Korean offensive
25 Jun - 1 Aug ....

MOKPO •

U.N. Counter-offensive
16 Sep - 26 Nov ....

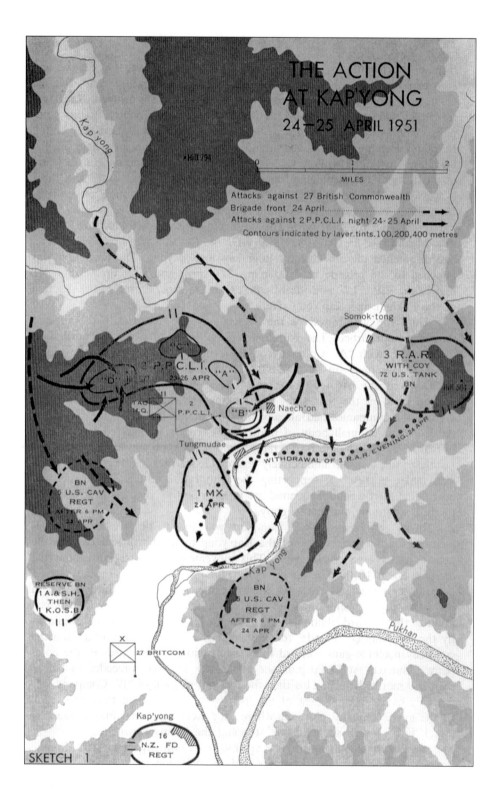

THE ACTION
AT KAP'YONG
24–25 APRIL 1951

Hill 794

0   1   2
MILES

Attacks against 27 British Commonwealth
Brigade front 24 April........................
Attacks against 2 P.P.C.L.I. night 24-25 April
Contours indicated by layer.tints.100,200,400 metres

Kap'yong

Somok-tong

"C"

2 P.P.C.L.I.
23-26 APR

"D"

"A"

3 R.A.R.
WITH COY
72 U.S. TANK
BN

Hill 504

TAC
H.Q.

2
P.P.C.L.I.

"B"

Naech'on

Tungmudae

WITHDRAWAL OF 3 R.A.R. EVENING, 24 APR

BN
5 U.S. CAV
REGT
AFTER 6 PM
24 APR

1 MX
24 APR

RESERVE BN
1 A.& S.H.
THEN
1 K.O.S.B.

Kap'yong

BN
5 U.S. CAV
REGT
AFTER 6 PM
24 APR

Pukhan

X
27 BRITCOM

Kap'yong

16
N.Z. FD
REGT

SKETCH 1

CANADA'S ARMY

Waging War and Keeping the Peace

one

THE MILITIA MYTH: CANADIAN ARMS TO CONFEDERATION

'I had foreseen almost everything accurately,' wrote George T. Denison of the Fenian raid in the spring of 1866, 'but on one point I had absolutely failed. The idea never entered my head that the authorities would send infantry without any cavalry whatever ... I do not blame myself for not foreseeing this, for I was still a young man, only twenty-six, and I had not then that confidence in the average stupidity of officials which, through long experience, I have since acquired.'[1] The militia officer, the man of the people, always knew best.

The central myth in the history of Canadian arms is, and always has been, that the colonists and citizens provide their own defence. Professional soldiers are not necessary so long as the people, organized into a militia, received the minimal training required to protect the country. In New France, after all, the *habitants*, from teenagers to greybeards, had rallied to their elected captains to fend off marauding Indians and incursions from the hated Americans or English. In Upper Canada the sturdy yeomanry, their flintlocks at the ready, had formed a military force-in-being, quick to serve their leaders in war against the republic to the south or enemies of the crown. And the South African War, the Great War, the Second World War, and Korea were all fought and won by militiamen. There are elements of truth in this myth, to be sure, but Canada has survived in war more because of good luck than the military skills and ferocity of her militias. The myth, however, has power, though it never served the best interests of Canada or its army.

The militia myth took shape in Upper Canada during and after the War of 1812, and it continued to harden into gospel truth before and after Confederation. According to its tenets, as laid down by the main creator of the myth, the Anglican cleric John Strachan, Upper Canada had been saved from the Americans by the exertions of the local citizenry. Yes, the British regulars had been involved, but it was the Upper Canadians who had truly carried the load. Egerton Ryerson, writing in 1880, expressed this fairy tale in its grandest terms: 'The Spartan bands of Canadian Loyalist volunteers, aided by a few hundred English soldiers and civilized Indians, repelled the Persian thousands of democratic American invaders, and maintained the virgin soil of Canada unpolluted by the foot of the plundering invader.'[2]

Ryerson and Strachan between them turned myth into history. As early as November 1812, when the first American attacks had just been repulsed, Strachan noted proudly that 'the Province of Upper Canada, without the assistance of men or arms, except a handful of regular troops, repelled its invaders, slew or took them all prisoners, and captured from its enemies the greater part of the arms by which it was defended.' Never, Strachan said later, 'never, surely, was greater activity shown in any country than our militia has exhibited; never greater valour, cooler resolution, and more approved conduct; they have emulated choicest veterans, and they have twice saved their country.'[3] There was little truth in this account, but that was beside the point. Truth never does matter in the creation of myth.

Strachan continued his efforts as the war went on, its fortunes fluctuating. To him, British commanders were often weak and vacillating, too willing to retreat, too ready to give up territory. He lived in the town of York, twice taken by the invaders,[4] and he intemperately denounced Lieutenant-General Sir George Prevost, the British Captain-General and Governor-in-Chief in British North America, for having 'abandoned the Loyalists to be bound hand and foot to their fate.' Prevost's tactics were governed by 'imbecility,' said Strachan, and his successor in 1814 in Upper Canada was worse, a commander 'destitute of that military fire and vigour of decision, which the principal commander in this country must possess in order to preserve it.' In an open letter, the cleric and his supporters offered their prescription: 'A new commander and more troops.'

Strachan, an armchair general, was partially correct in the severity of his judgment: the incompetence of some British commanders was matched, if not exceeded, by that of the Americans. But he overstated matters dramatically when he claimed that only the 'astonishing exertions of the militia' had saved the situation in 1814.[5] The British had repeatedly bumbled, he argued, but the local companies had done the job – and kept Canada British. The love/hate relationship with an empire that could hardly manage its affairs, but to which Canada must belong if it was not to be Americanized, was all too evident. The fear that London would sell out British North America if that were in its interests was also palpable. Most important for the creation of myth, if the country boasted a militia of proven bravery, there was no need for a standing army with high-caste officers, tremendous expenses, and potential danger towards the state.

Powerful as the militia myth was for the locals, sensible leaders in both New France and Upper and Lower Canada recognized that these citizen armies were fundamentally untrained, ill-disciplined, and equipped with a variety of incompatible weapons. The shrewder among them understood that militiamen sustained the local economy and produced much of the food that both the professional soldiers and the militias needed to march or fight. Removing these men from their farms for any length of time could be disastrous. At the same time, the leaders knew that militiamen would fight hardest to protect their own homes and families, but much less willingly for broader geopolitical interests that might take them anywhere up to 50 or 500 miles away from their hearth. The eighteenth-century world wars between France and England concerned the *habitant* only to the extent that they directly affected him. The War of 1812, whatever Strachan might say, similarly affected primarily the Loyalist farmers in southwestern Upper Canada and the 'late Loyalists' who came from the United States after the revolution, as American armies headed east from Detroit through Upper Canada. Would these men fight? Would they opt out and hope for the best? Or would they join the American 'liberators'?

The idea that Canada's defence had been provided primarily by the local militias was taken as a given by both *Canadiens* and Canadians, who did not always, in times of peace, look with a kindly gaze on the regular troops who were garrisoned on their lands, chased their daughters, and caused fights in their taverns. In war, however, those same locals demanded that more men, more weapons, more everything, be provided for their defence. The colonial masters overseas had their own reasons for holding Canada, but those interests were not always the same as the settlers'. The imperial governments wanted the riches of North America, the furs, timbers, and fish, for London or for Paris, and they wanted to deny those riches to the other. The colonists, in contrast, wanted a good life for themselves and their children, their share of the bounty of the land, and peace. The interests on both sides might converge, but they were not always the same.

To protect their North American holdings, the governments across the North Atlantic sent regiments to Canada, usually infantry, artillery, and, very occasionally, cavalry. The numbers involved were always small, and the battles of the colonial era tended to be confused struggles between a few thousand troops caught up in a vast wilderness. Against the aboriginal peoples, the French with their firearms initially had huge advantages in the conflicts after contact. The first firing of Samuel de Champlain's quadruple-shotted arquebus in 1609 killed two Iroquois and mortally wounded a third, stunning the rest of the large war party into defeat and flight.[6] But against other regular forces, drawn up in European formation or sheltering behind European-style wooden battlements, the advantage went to the commander able to seize the key ground and keep the troops disciplined and motivated.

Those troops soon included native allies. Through strategic calculation, as well as gifts, bribery, and political and commercial promises almost always destined not to be kept, the various native tribes forged their alliances with the French or the English. The chiefs negotiated with the white leaders, trying to preserve as much of their lands as they could against the encroachments of settlement. They hoped to play one side off against the other, but, inevitably, they were caught up in the struggle between the imperial forces. As a result, natives served as scouts, as skirmishers, and as vital adjuncts in battle. The difficulty was that the Indians were not always reliable allies for either empire: they persisted in acting as though they had their own ways of warfare and their own tribal and commercial interests, as they did. But when they fought, they usually fought well, their simple presence on a battlefield frequently enough to terrify enemy soldiers and force them to look to the protection of their own scalps.

The Indian warriors provided an element of savage terror that could demoralize all who faced them. In June 1813, for example, the Americans tried to take on a British infantry company at Beaver Dam in the Niagara peninsula. Warned by Laura Secord of the coming attack, or so the story goes, Lieutenant James Fitzgibbon was ready, and he had four hundred Mohawk and Caughnawaga in place to harass the enemy rear. As Fitzgibbon later reported: 'Not a shot was fired on our side by any but the Indians. They beat the Americans into a state of terror, and the only share I claim is taking advantage of a favourable moment to offer them protection from the tomahawk and the scalping knife.'[7] The Americans' fear was understandable: despite the best efforts of white commanders, the Indians routinely tortured and killed those they captured in battle. Nor were women and children spared their depredations.

From the beginning of their alliances with the newcomers, the Indians regularly launched raids against civilians with the active connivance of either the French or the English. These slaughters and abductions made frontier life terrifying for the *habitants* and for the settlers in the American colonies.[8] Not averse to savagery of their own, the militiamen preferred to defend their homes and lands – the place where, in their opinion, they were most needed. The Indians, in contrast, could be very effective in long-range raids, where they were often led by white officers. In the early days of the Seven Years' War, for example, French-led raiders ventured as far south as Virginia, spreading terror wherever they went. Using Fort Duquesne as a base and carefully keeping their Indian alliances in good repair, the French disrupted the British and Americans' war preparations. Guerilla warfare was inexpensive for the attackers, but very costly for those trying to beat it down.[9]

The natives also forced tactical changes on the European armies that were fighting in the new world. In Europe it sometimes made sense to send serried ranks marching through the countryside with flags flying and bands playing. In the trackless wilderness that was North America, it never did, especially after the Indians adapted to the use of gunfire. The Iroquois, for one, quickly realized that their old tactic of massing large groups of warriors made no sense in fighting against the French and their arquebuses. Instead, even after they acquired firearms of their own, the two-thousand-strong Six Nations warriors developed and mastered guerilla tactics, applying the techniques of the hunt directly to warfare. Concealment, harassment, ambush, and dispersion were their new watchwords in what the French came to call *la petite guerre*, and surprise became the Indians' primary principle of war. 'They come like foxes in the woods,' reported the *Jesuit Relations*. 'They attack like lions. They flee like birds.'[10] The European armies regularly blundered into disaster, lured into the forest where the advantages conveyed by gunpowder were limited, if not neutralized.

The wiser among the British and the French commanders gradually learned these lessons. The development of light infantry by the British, for example, was directly attributable to North American conditions of warfare.[11] Even more quickly, the colonial militias learned from the Indians. Very few *Canadiens* were well-trained militiamen or voyageurs, attuned to quick travel by canoe and knowledgeable about the natives. Their strength was that they knew much more about the Quebec countryside than the French regulars did, and, as they lacked the parade-square discipline and willingness to accept high casualties that had been pounded into the regular troops by the knout and the lash, they instinctively understood that, when muskets were firing, the proper response was to drop to the ground and fight from cover. It always made sense to use the ground, not to defy it. To the Quebec militia, the tactics of war on the frontier suggested that it was best to lie concealed until the moment came to strike, and then to fall back.[12]

The French and British commanders who led the armies usually failed to take the militiamen's adaptation of Indian tactics into account. On the Plains of Abraham in September 1759, for example, when the Marquis de Montcalm and General James Wolfe faced off for control of North America, the *habitant* militia, interspersed among the regular regiments, enthusiastically ran at full tilt towards the British line a half-mile away as soon as they heard the order to advance. This response defied the French way of war, with its measured advance of carefully dressed lines of infantry, and disrupted the regular regiments. Montcalm's difficulties compounded when, after the first ineffective French volley at Wolfe's lines, the regulars stopped to reload, standing upright as they had been trained to do. When the militia dropped to the ground or took cover, the shaky cohesion of Montcalm's 4500-strong army dissolved into a nothingness that was blasted to pieces by the first devastating British volley, delivered at a range of 40 yards.[13] The militia and the natives who had the most detrimental effect on the British were the snipers on the flanks, hidden in woods or cornfields. Those in the line only contributed to the defeat by their 'ill discipline,' as defined by French army standards. The militia did, however, hold up the advancing British long enough to allow the fleeing French to cross the St Charles River and reach their camp at Beauport. Quebec surrendered on September 17, and New France followed the next year.[14]

Skilled commander though he may have been, Montcalm had unaccountably failed to grasp the fundamental differences in attitude and approach between regulars and militia. His overall strategic plan, which had served him well in 1757 and 1758, was no longer sustainable after the capture of Louisbourg by the British effectively cut New France's sea links to the home country. The strategy that might have worked in 1759 was, as one option, to remain within the walls of Quebec, avoid a pitched battle, use New France's Indian allies to the fullest extent, fight with surprise, and simply outlast Wolfe, whose supplies were dwindling as winter approached.[15] This protracted guerilla war, the strategy proposed by the Marquis de Vaudreuil, the governor general of New France in 1759, just might have succeeded where the direct confrontation with Wolfe's ten battalions of disciplined regulars failed. Unfortunately for Paris, unfortunately for the French Canadians, Montcalm followed his own strategy and New France succumbed.

Vaudreuil understood that Canada was indefensible in a conventional war both then and later. The fact that it was also invulnerable was a paradoxical situation that continues to the present. Without aid from abroad, the French Canadians had no chance against the invading English or Americans, who had bigger armies, greater resources, and, with their nearby American colonies, shorter supply lines than did New France. The Royal Navy also controlled the seas, cutting New France off from succour. Similarly, without aid from overseas a half-century later, the Loyalists had no chance of resisting an American invasion in the War of 1812. But General Weather and Colonel Wilderness were always on the side of the defenders of Canada, and, for European and American armies, the campaigning season in New France and British North America was short. Once the St Lawrence and the Great Lakes' harbours froze, once the snows fell and the thaw turned roads into gumbo, the movement of armies and fleets ceased, and soldiers struggled to survive on bad meat and mouldy biscuit in the harshest of climates. Could invaders remain in Canada if they were surrounded by a hostile population and subject to harassing raids by Indians and militia? Even if they did, there was always the chance to destroy them later. Alternatively, everything lost could be regained if men and supplies arrived from overseas. In any case, the discussions in far-away peace negotiations might restore what had been lost on the battlefield.

These discussions were always conducted by leaders appointed by Paris or London or Washington. Strategy was the province of the imperial masters, not the Canadians, whether French- or English-speaking. John Strachan's complaints about British generalship, right or wrong, were at root a cry for Upper Canada's needs to be decided by Upper Canadians. His successors down through the next two centuries were no more likely to be heeded. Strategy was not for Canadians to decide; tactics, perhaps, but strategy, never.

In a curious way, therefore, the militia myth was true. The regular troops of both France and England were simply passing through, fighting their European dynastic battles in what was almost always a sideshow in North American fields. The settlers, the *habitants*, the Loyalists, and the earlier and later immigrants to what became Canada had the fate of their country, their home, in their hands while London and Paris dealt with the broader, bigger issues of empire. Indefensible their country might be, but they would still have to fight to protect it. Whether they would fight, and whether they could fight effectively, were less certain.

Still, the militia myth was just that, a myth. In every war fought in North America until the American Civil War, the brunt of the fighting was borne by regular troops, French, British, or American. Regular officers planned the campaigns, husbanding their resources of trained men. Militias were sometimes useful, sometimes critically so, but militiamen fresh from the farm or the shops of the towns would not and could not stand up to the rigours of the battlefield. Their training was minimal: in Upper Canada in early 1812 the Militia Act provided that regiments parade one day a year. Companies had to meet at least twice a year, but no more than four times in all.[16] Only disciplined troops could hold steady in the face of a volley of musket fire or a hail of cannon shot, and the militia had no discipline. There was nothing wrong with the quality of British North Americans, French or English. Militia could be trained to become good soldiers, but that took time. Without training, they could play administrative roles or help extend the line, as they had done for Montcalm in 1759 and as they would do against the Americans during the War of 1812. But they could not tip the balance in a serious battle or a protracted struggle.

Nonetheless, there were more elements of truth in the myth. In Lower Canada, even more than in Upper Canada in 1812, there was no desire to be taken over by the Americans. Bad as the British rule might be, at least the religion and language of the *Canadiens* were relatively safe; with the Americans, who knew? Although almost all the *Canadiens* had sat on their hands when the Americans invaded at the outset of the Revolutionary War,[17] in the War of 1812 Quebec's militia served with at least as much assiduity as did Upper Canada's. Indeed, at Châteauguay, Lower Canada, in October 1813, a mixed force of regulars and militia numbering perhaps 1700 men in various states of training forced the retirement of a superior but ill-led American force of 3000–4000 after a short, sharp engagement that saved Montreal. Even more to the point, the defending force of about four hundred that did most of the fighting was commanded by Lieutenant-Colonel Charles de Salaberry, a thirty-five-year-old French Canadian who had been a British regular officer for twenty years. De Salaberry had the usual ragtag *milice* under his command, but he also had the Voltigeurs, a volunteer unit 'worthy of the ancient warlike spirit of the country' that he himself had trained for several months to a high standard.[18] In the judgment of Dr William 'Tiger' Dunlop, who passed units of the *Canadien* militia on their way to meet the invaders, they 'presented a serviceable effective appearance – pretty well drilled, and their arms in perfectly good order, nor had they a mobbish appearance.'[19] True, the victory was won because the American commander blinked and his men were reluctant to fight, but the lesson was clear enough: the *Canadiens* could fight well and *la milice*, with sufficient training time and good leadership, could be turned into good soldiers.*[20]

---

* It is worth noting that half the officers and one-fifth of the men in the Voltigeurs were anglophones. See M.F. Auger, 'French Canadian Participation in the War of 1812,' *Canadian Military History* 10 (summer 2001): 28–9.

The question of how best to train, equip, and employ the militia of the Canadas was one that greatly concerned the British high command. The defensive-minded Sir George Prevost may not have been John Strachan's favourite commander, but he was vigorous and clear sighted in the way he tackled the problems he faced in 1812. The key question was what the *Canadiens* would do in the event of war. They formed the bulk of the militia of 60,000, but the men were 'ill-armed and without discipline' and their loyalties were thought suspect.

Soon after he assumed political and military command in late 1811, as war with the United States seemed likely, Prevost set out to try to solidify the province's support. He placed three *Canadiens* on the Legislative Council and two more on his Executive Council, and he bolstered the position of the Roman Catholic bishop in Lower Canada. More directly, Prevost had the Legislative Council pass a new Militia Act in April 1812 that provided for selection by ballot of two thousand bachelors between the ages of eighteen and twenty-five to receive ninety days training in each of two successive summers or, in the event of war, their retention in service for two years. This Select Embodied Militia had the potential to be of use. Even more so was the all-volunteer Provincial Corps of Light Infantry, the Voltigeurs, which Prevost raised for service during the 'apprehended war' with the United States.[21] To judge by the results at Châteauguay, Prevost's efforts had paid off handsomely. Similarly, the Volunteer Incorporated Militia in Upper Canada, an almost regular unit of 300 men by the end of the war, performed well in the battles of 1814.

In Upper Canada, where Prevost's able and energetic subordinate, Major-General Isaac Brock, commanded when the war began, the problems were similar but different. The problem here was not the *Canadiens* but the recent American settlers, who outnumbered the Loyalists four to one. The militia in the province was estimated to number at most 11,000 to 13,000 men, 'of which it might be prudent to arm [no] more than 4,000.' Brock began the process of raising flank companies of volunteers from each of the *Sedentary* Militia battalions – a wonderful phrase that perfectly captured the military worth of most of the militia – and, while he hoped to enrol two thousand men, they were to train only for three days a month.[22]

The remainder of the Upper Canadian Sedentary Militia, organized around the community and county in which they lived, nominally comprised every fit male between sixteen and sixty years of age. Some militia units, especially those from the Niagara area that had first fought at Queenston Heights in October 1812, had been called out for service so often by 1814, said Donald Graves, that the ones who responded to the call for service had become reasonably effective in the field. Others were at best 'very cautious civilians.'[23] Another scholar, George Sheppard, noted that 'most Upper Canadian males, although obligated to fight, did not do so. The squads of volunteers and those forced to do their duty, while sometimes useful, could rarely be relied upon for more than a few days at a time.'[24] In 1812, in fact, militia in the southwest of Upper Canada had frequently refused to respond to call-up orders; some treated with the invading enemy, eagerly offering their paroles as a guarantee that they would not have to fight again; and many who did report left for home as soon as they possibly could.[25] Yet, as J. Mackay Hitsman observed, 'the sedentary militia satisfactorily performed the principal roles expected of it – transporting supplies, building roads and fortifications, guarding prisoners, and providing mounted couriers – necessary tasks that could be performed by men who had little or no military training.'[26] The low casualty rate of militiamen – 157 pensions were awarded families of deceased militiamen, of whom only twenty-six had been killed in action[27] – suggested that Hitsman's description of the militia role was the correct one.

In New Brunswick, where the Militia Act of 1810 had replaced the primitive organization of Loyalist times with one based on contemporary British army practices, the militia of 4000 was in a pathetic state. In 1812 there were 437 weapons on hand, of which only 253 were serviceable, and the provincial Assembly refused to agree to efforts by the British local commander to improve militia training; instead, it reduced the number of training days from ten to two. The war against the Americans, of course, was not really New Brunswick's affair, except for the opportunities it offered to make money by supplying provisions.[28] The same could be said for Nova Scotia and Prince Edward Island.

The British had also tried to raise regiments of more reliable troops in British North America after 1803.[29] The shortage of regular regiments, thanks to the demands of the long war against Napoleon, meant that local men could be enlisted into units that were, in effect, regulars in all but name. Originally intended for local defence, regiments of Fencibles could be required to serve anywhere in British North America. Their equipment and discipline did not differ dramatically from that of British troops. Recruiting was difficult everywhere, for the army offered a hard, brutal existence, without great appeal in a colony where land and opportunities were ample. The Regiment of Canadian Fencible Infantry managed to raise only 124 men in its first three years. By 1808, thanks to bounties paid to recruits, strength had risen to 400, still hardly an indication of enthusiasm for military service. Recruiting efforts for Fencible regiments in New Brunswick and in Upper Canada similarly met with difficulties, though the Upper Canadian Glengarry Light Infantry Fencibles raised 730 men in 1812.[30] They fought effectively enough as skirmishers in many of the battles of the War of 1812.

The British had some success in whipping the volunteers and the militiamen chosen by lot for extended service into useful units. In Lower Canada a bewildering array of units – Embodied Militia, Canadian Light Dragoons, Provincial Royal Artillery Drivers, Commissariat Voyageurs, Frontier Light Infantry, and Independent Militia Volunteers – served for varying periods of time, much like the Voltigeurs. In Upper Canada, with a smaller population and more American sympathizers, recruiting for Volunteer Incorporated Militia battalions was slow, despite attractive cash bounties and the promise of land grants. Even so, there was a volunteer troop of Dragoons, a Militia Artillery Company, and a troop of Provincial Royal Artillery Drivers, all serving for eighteen months or the war's duration.[31] The Upper Canada Incorporated Militia Battalion, commanded by a regular officer, was not long off the farm, but its men were volunteers, equipped with British flintlocks, and uniformed and trained much like the regulars.[32]

The War of 1812 ended in an overall stalemate, but for the Canadas it was a great victory. They had survived, and the expansionist ambitions of the United States had been denied. The narrowness of that outcome might have been expected to lead to efforts in Upper and Lower Canada to rectify the flaws in militia organization and training that had been so clearly revealed, but it was not to be. Once the fighting ceased, military matters all but disappeared from the scene as men turned their thoughts to expanding settlement, building roads and canals, and making money. In 1816 the Lieutenant-Governor of Upper Canada had pointed to wartime experience to urge the formation of flank companies of militia, able to serve with the regulars, as they had done during the war. But nothing was done and, when the Militia Act came up for revision in 1823, the necessary clauses for the creation of such companies were omitted. All that remained was the Sedentary Militia, in effect every able-bodied male in the colony, and an Active Militia, those who agreed to accept a day or two of training each year. J. Mackay Hitsman, the ablest historian of nineteenth-century defence policy, observed dryly that, as the United States army was so small, 'there was some basis for the general belief that an annual militia muster, even if it degenerated into a drunken brawl, was all the preparation for war that Canadians need make.'[33] The British helped in this attitude by maintaining troops in British North America roughly equal in size to the United States Regular Army. In the colonists' view, one Canadians of later generations would continue to cherish, defence was not necessary in the foreseeable future, and government funds were better spent elsewhere.

In such circumstances, the British government took the defence of the Canadas far more seriously than the local citizenry did. After the War of 1812 there were several tours of inspection by senior officers, and the Duke of Wellington, serving as Master General of the Ordnance, pressed defensive construction forward. The Rideau Canal between Kingston and Bytown was completed in 1832, Fort Lennox took form south of Montreal, and citadels were built at Halifax and Quebec. Royal Engineers completed substantial work at Kingston's Fort Henry, but it was the only one of six forts there to be finished. These fortifications did not make Canada defensible, but it was a start. Significantly, embarrassingly, it was the British taxpayer who paid the bills.

The United States government had little interest in threatening Canada, so absorbed were Americans in westward expansion and growth. But there were threats to the established order from within the Canadas and from American sympathizers. The rebellions of 1837 were largely serio-comic affairs, especially in Upper Canada, but the good citizens of both provinces feared the worst. In Upper Canada in November, William Lyon Mackenzie's motley, ill-armed rebels, many without firearms, tried to advance on Toronto to take over the militia's weapons stored there. They fled at the sight of local volunteers, equally motley and ill-armed. A rebellion in western Upper Canada the next month also failed in the face of the militia.

In Lower Canada, *patriotes* who had fortified two stout buildings engaged in a pitched battle with British troops at St Denis and drove them off after a five-hour engagement, but, a few days later, the rebellion in the Richelieu valley died in a sharp skirmish at St Charles. The next month 1200 regulars attacked the rebels at St Eustache and crushed them, leaving some seventy dead, though three-quarters of the locals had fled before the gunfire even began.[34]

Rebels who fled south of the line continued their fulminations and drew the support of individual Americans, but not their government, which turned a blind eye to their cause of liberating British North America. Again the British took matters seriously, dispatching regular regiments to the colonies. In Upper Canada the militia was called up for duty along the Niagara frontier and elsewhere. The troubles of 1838 included an abortive attack on Amherstburg, an American ship seized by militia in southwestern Upper Canada, a retaliatory burning of a Canadian steamer by Americans, a militia attack on rebels gathered on Point Pelee, and a fierce battle at Prescott in the eastern part of the province. There 'Hunters,' as the American supporters called themselves, staged an invasion and were eventually crushed by artillery in a windmill where they had made their stand. The British regulars and militia, newly raised as provincial troops, suffered eighty casualties; the Hunters, fifty. The surviving invaders were taken prisoner and their leader was hanged.[35]

In Lower Canada, where ten thousand militia were called out, a handful of rebels crossed the border in November 1838 and rallied several thousand *patriotes* to their cause. British regulars and English-speaking militia, including some from Upper Canada, smashed the rebellion on December 9. Savage justice followed, including the execution of twelve men and the exiling of fifty-seven to Australia.

The fear of another Anglo-American war led to continued alarums along the border. The British had more than 10,000 regulars along the boundary and, over the winter of 1838–9, 21,000 provincial militia remained on continuous service. (A handful of provincial troops, including the Coloured Corps, composed largely of slaves escaped from the United States, continued in service to 1850.)[36] For once, the troubles spread to the usually immune east and, along the Maine–New Brunswick border, there was a threat of war as American loggers demanded a rectification of Maine's border. Regular and militia troops took position on both sides of the international boundary, but the troubles cooled and, eventually, a border commission fixed the line.

In the years before Confederation united most of the British North American colonies into the Dominion of Canada, there was a succession of war scares between Britain and the United States. Most were not serious – just incidents that hotheads used to rail against the perfidious British or the republican United States. Canada was almost never the cause of the ructions. As was to happen so often, Canada, the closest British possession, located on the northern border of the United States, and a colony with no power to control its own foreign affairs, was always at risk if the war of words between London and Washington turned hot. Even so, Canada's relations with the United States were improving, and north-south trade was growing.

The British, reasonably enough, resented the expense they had to bear to defend British North America. Very simply, the United States, bigger, more populous, and much more prosperous, was vastly more important to the future than Canada. Trade, investment possibilities, and the shared heritage of the two nations made an Anglo-American alliance a dream that many in London, if few in the United States, were beginning to contemplate. In such circumstances, Canada was something of a liability, both for what it cost now and what it might harm in the future.

British North Americans might have been expected to anticipate this change as Britain began pulling out troops through the 1840s and 1850s, but the legislatures did almost nothing to create reliable militias, let alone raise professionals. In the 1840s, for example, New Brunswick had a reasonably proficient militia artillery, but efforts to create reliable infantry failed as the legislature refused to credit the possibility of war. Now that the Canadas had achieved responsible government, Lord Grey, the Secretary of State for War and the Colonies, argued that 'they ought also to pay all its expenses, including military protection.'[37] The Governor General, Lord Elgin, did not agree:

> Canada has a special claim for protection beyond any other Colony because it
> is the fact of her connexion with Great Britain which exposes her to hostile
> aggression – She has no enemy to dread but the States, and they would cease
> to be dangerous to her if she were annexed ... What You really want then is a
> sufficient body of troops to occupy the forts, to form a nucleus around which

a great force composed of militia may be gathered in case of regular warfare, and to give the peaceful residents on the frontier who have the misfortune to dwell in the vicinity of a population combining the material force of high civilization with the loose political morality & organization of barbarous hordes, a reasonable security against marauding incursions.[38]

The belief that the Americans were a lower form of life was clearly not limited to the United Empire Loyalists. Even so, Elgin eagerly sought reciprocal trade with the United States and achieved it in 1854. For a brief time, good feelings prevailed across the line.

During the Crimean War in the mid-1850s, the colonies burst forth in military fervour, raising men to guard posts vacated by British regiments recalled to fight the Czar. In the Canadas, in particular, there seemed some hope of taking genuine steps for defence. Following a commission report on the best means of reorganizing the militia and providing an efficient system, the legislature passed a new Militia Act in 1855 that was intended to last three years. The new post of Adjutant-General of Militia went to a half-pay British colonel, and new volunteer regiments of riflemen, artillery, cavalry, and artillery won authorization. In his first report, the Adjutant-General was optimistic: 'The persons who have joined this Force are not the dissolute and the idle, but they are, on the contrary, the respectable Mechanics of the several Towns and Villages where the Companies of this Force are located.'[39] The volunteers in this Active Militia elected their own officers and paid for their own uniforms. For a time, many of them trained far more days than the number authorized and paid for by the legislature. In 1856, £25,000 had been allocated for the militia, a small sum compared with the £280,000 Britain spent for upkeep of its small forces in the Canadas. Volunteer officers immediately developed great skill in jockeying for preferment, an early indication that the militia was a political force much more than a military one.[40] In any case, the initial enthusiasm could not be sustained and most of these well-dressed militia volunteer units soon sank into a decay matched by that of the Sedentary Militia. Even so, their organization demonstrated that the Sedentary Militia could no longer be considered the main defence of the colonies. Some training, some equipment, and some leaders who might know what they were about was at last seen as a necessity.

The Civil War that tore the United States apart for four years after April 1861 forced a renewed interest in defence upon the colonies. In the eyes of the Lincoln administration, Britain's neutrality seemed tilted towards the Confederacy. That perceived bias increased tensions along the border, especially when Confederate agents were found to operate in Canada and, in 1864, when Confederate soldiers sheltered behind the border after a raid on St Albans, Vermont. Tensions had first mounted in November 1861 when a United States Navy warship stopped a British mail vessel, the *Trent*, and removed two Confederate diplomats. War seemed a real possibility.[41] At the same time, many British North Americans also feared that, when the war finally ended and regardless of the winner, the huge American armies might turn north. A decisive and victorious campaign against Canada could reunite the North and the South, fulfil America's manifest destiny, and poke a sharp stick in London's eye.

The difficulties of defending British North America were the same as they always had been: distance, a small population, and a reluctance by Britain – or the colonies – to spend enough funds to create a credible force. The British dispatched three regiments of infantry and a battery of artillery in May 1861, but this influx increased the strength of the regular force to only 5100 in the Canadas. The militias of the colonies were utterly pathetic, Major-General Sir Hastings Doyle complained to London. Nova Scotia between 1859 and 1862 implemented increased training for its militia, using officers and sergeants from the British garrison. This attention made small progress, he said, but New Brunswick was more typical: the militia 'exists alone on paper, & altho' nominally officered, they are generally speaking too old for service (in some cases from 60 to 90 years of age) entirely unacquainted with their duty, totally ignorant of Drill, & without Adjutants or Staff.' Worse, the legislature – and New Brunswick was not alone – has 'repeatedly refused to provide money for the purpose of Defence.' At the same time, the Adjutant-General in New Brunswick reported that commanding officers of the Sedentary Militia battalions could not be persuaded to take much interest in their units, 'nor to find Company Officers at all acquainted with drill, or willing to seek even the most rudimentary instruction.'[42] If there was a war, or a serious threat of war, this attitude might change.

The *Trent* affair stirred the colonies. John A. Macdonald, joint leader in the Canadas, became the colony's first Minister of Militia, and his government agreed to embody 38,000 of the Sedentary Militia, many of whom turned out to drill in this crisis, apparently ready to fight should the need arise. The volunteer units formed during the Crimean War revived and, after a visit by the Lieutenant-General Commanding in North America to survey the situation, defences were strengthened. Another 11,000 British regulars arrived in British North America, as did large quantities of weapons and ammunition for the volunteer units of the Canadian militia. This militia now numbered a credible 14,000, most of whom were to be found in urban areas.

A parliamentary commission reported in 1862 that the Canadas needed an Active Militia of 50,000 and a reserve force of similar size. The active force, consisting of the existing volunteers as well as men selected by ballot from the Sedentary Militia, was to drill for fourteen to twenty-eight days a year. This plan, if implemented, might have laid the basis of a real militia. But the government bill to implement the commission recommendations met defeat in the legislature after fifteen francophone government supporters defected and Macdonald's government resigned. There were many reasons for the defeat of the defence bill, but, not for the first time or the last, Canadians had refused to accept responsibility for their own defence. 'Leave it to the British and trust the Americans to behave responsibly' seemed to be the message.

In London, not unexpectedly, government ministers grumbled furiously. Why defend British North America if its inhabitants persistently refused to contribute? Why alienate the Americans, who were far more important for the future? The newspapers in Britain fulminated against the colonies, and the Colonial Secretary instructed Lord Monck, the Governor General, to investigate the possibility of a uniform militia system for all the British North American colonies. When Monck put this suggestion to the new Canadian government, the predictable answer came back in late 1862. There would be no standing army, no broadly based militia: the volunteer units were the way in which 'the military spirit of the people must find vent in a period of peace.' Above all, any attempt to enforce compulsory militia service on the population would only cause discontent.[43]

The government of John Sandfield Macdonald passed a new Militia Act in 1863, but it allowed for only twelve days of drill per year for 10,000 volunteers. The act authorized merit as the criterion for promotion of officers, and officers in turn had to satisfy minimum educational requirements. Prospective officers were required to take a three-month course before commissioning at new schools of instruction that were run by British officers. Battalion commanders required an additional three-month course. The schools were a great success and brought a small measure of professionalism to the militia – for the six years of their existence.

As the Civil War continued to devour armies, the British colonies were beginning to consider the possibility of Confederation. The potential threat from the United States actively spurred this movement, though it was only one of the main causes. New tensions with Washington, created this time by the St Albans raid and the release of the raiders and the money they had looted from a bank by a Montreal magistrate, frightened the colonies in 1864. The Americans were furious, and rightly so, as Congress abrogated the Reciprocity Treaty of 1854. Rattled, New Brunswick assembled a thousand militia selected by ballot for an unprecedented twenty-four-day 'camp of instruction' in July 1865.[44] The Canadian legislature, indicating a willingness to spend money on defence at last, offered to pay for fortifications to defend Montreal, devoted $1 million to the militia, and called up thirty companies of volunteer militia. In April 1865 it filled the long-vacant post of Adjutant-General of Militia, just as the Confederacy surrendered. If the Americans now chose to fight Britain and to fulfil the Union's manifest destiny, their time was ripe. The Canadian government, like New Brunswick's, authorized a militia summer camp of instruction at Laprairie in 1865 and, after the Fenian scare, a camp of 'observation' at Thorold on the Niagara frontier in 1866, both of which were commanded by Colonel (later Field Marshal) Garnet Wolseley.

In fact, the United States government did not wish to fight. Some Americans, however, did, most notably Irish Americans forming the Fenian Brotherhood. Their object was to free Ireland by striking at British power in Canada, a slightly farfetched goal, but, as most of the Fenians were experienced veterans of the Union Army, not one that could easily be ignored – especially as Washington sometimes seemed to be whispering cautious encouragement to Fenian activities. With British North America heading towards Confederation, with some provinces still reluctant, and with militias everywhere ill-trained and ill-equipped, defence became a key element of the ongoing discussions.

In late 1865 and early 1866, while the British reinforced their North American garrisons, the Canadas called up the militia to defend the border against expected Fenian attacks. The Fenians were badly divided, so the attacks did not materialize, but an abortive raid on Campobello Island, New Brunswick,[45] and additional and more serious threats in April 1866 helped convince that colony of the virtues of Confederation. By the end of May, Fenians under self-styled 'General' John O'Neill had begun to mass at Buffalo, New York, bringing together 800 well-armed men. On the morning of June 1, some 600 of the invaders came ashore in Canada, just north of Fort Erie. Once again, the Niagara Peninsula was to be the scene of fighting.

By this time, the militia of Canada West was in the field across the breadth of the province. Approximately 14,000 had been called up on May 31, and 6000 more two days later. Pathetically, the militia had no administrative organization to provide shelter or food for the called-up troops, and the men had to beg for the assistance of the local citizenry. George Denison, of Toronto's militia cavalry, described the shambles:

> The want of organization or preparation in view of the long threatenings seems almost incredible. I had to take my corps on a campaign without the carbines I had asked for, but with revolvers for which we had only some four or five ten-year-old paper cartridges for each. We did not know whether they would go off or not. We had no haversacks, no waterbottles, no nose bags. Some of us had small tin cups fastened on our saddles. We had no canteens or knives or forks, or cooking utensils of any kind, or valises. We had no clothes except those on our backs ... We had no tents and no blankets.[46]

The only troops at hand in the Niagara area were a battery of British artillery and two batteries of militia artillery, subunits of two British infantry regiments, four militia infantry battalions, and a troop of militia cavalry.[47] At Port Colborne, at the Lake Erie entrance to the Welland Canal, the Queen's Own Rifles, a Toronto unit that also 'had neither haversacks nor water bottles,'[48] and the 13th Battalion from Hamilton formed the bulk of the Canadian force, with 810 men all told. In a confused and confusing situation, with estimates of the Fenian numbers and morale wildly variant, the militia at Port Colborne moved eastward towards the tiny village of Ridgeway, where the Fenians had taken position. With much more battle experience than the militiamen, who were 'deficient in nearly everything except enthusiasm,'[49] the Fenians' plan was to hold a good defensive position and lure the Canadians into attacking. Better trained from their Union army service, the Fenians could fire four rounds a minute; the Canadian militia, using similar weapons, could not match that rate of fire.

The two forces met about 8 a.m. and firing broke out. Very soon, with the Fenians pulling back their skirmishers to their main position, a ridge rising 30 feet above the surrounding country, the militia began running low on ammunition.[50] No reserve was available. A misplaced fear that Fenian cavalry was about to attack led the Canadians to form square, the classic tactic to defend against a mounted attack. For a brief time the Fenians had an easy target in the massed militiamen. The order was quickly countermanded amid much confusion, the Fenians chose that moment to advance, and the Canadians wavered and withdrew. The retreat turned into a near rout and the militia officers were unable to stop the flight. The Fenian commander observed later that his men 'gave them a volley and then charged them, driving them nearly three miles through the town of Ridgeway.'[51] There were nine dead and thirty wounded among the militia. The Fenians rightly feared that another column of troops, this time including British regulars, was drawing near, and through further Canadian bungling, the enemy successfully made its way back to the American side of the line. There the American authorities duly interned General O'Neill for violating American neutrality.

This debacle should have provided two clear lessons. In the words of Brian Reid: 'First, wishful thinking and amateurism disguised as ardour are no substitutes in combat for detailed preparation, hard training and clear-headed thinking. Second, and more important, a government that structures its defences to achieve social and political, not military, ends should not be surprised when its forces fail the test of war.'[52] But the Fenian invasions petered out after Ridgeway. The Irish Americans raided Canada East in 1866 and 1870 with small numbers and mounted an attack against Pembina, Manitoba, in 1871, but nothing on the scale of the Niagara invasion was ever attempted again. As the inquiries about the militia defeat at Ridgeway proceeded and as recriminations against and between commanders mounted, Nova Scotia, New Brunswick, and the Canadas joined together on July 1, 1867, to create the Dominion of Canada. The opportunity to remedy the deficiencies of the colonial militia systems was at hand – if only Canadians chose to act.

two

MAKING AN ARMY: BEGINNINGS

The Governor General was delighted. Writing to the Colonial Office in July 1908, Earl Grey spoke of the great spectacle that had been the Quebec Tercentary, the national celebration of the 300th anniversary of Champlain's arrival in Canada. What impressed him most was, of all things, the Militia: 'the smartness, smoothness and precision of the movements of the Canadian militia and the excellence of their horses were a source of great satisfaction to His Royal Highness, a surprise to Lord Roberts, and a revelation to all.'[1] If only it had been so.

—⁂—

The constitution of the new Dominion of Canada, the British North America Act, gave the federal government control over all aspects of defence. The Militia Act, passed in May 1868, laid down the outlines of a defence scheme. The Sedentary Militia now became a Reserve Militia in which all fit males between eighteen and sixty years of age had an obligation to serve. The Reserve was enumerated once in 1869 – and thereafter ignored. The only force in being was the existing Volunteer Militia, which could have a maximum of 40,000 men receive sixteen days' paid training each year. Those volunteers in service at the time of Confederation had to re-enrol if they wished to continue in uniform. The government divided the country into nine Military Districts – four in Ontario, three in Quebec, and one each in New Brunswick and Nova

Scotia. Because Canada continued to depend on the British Army, there was no provision for a permanent force of professional soldiers.

This assumption was quickly seen to be a mistake. In 1869 Britain's Prime Minister, William Gladstone, declared his government's intention to withdraw all its forces from Canada the next year – except for a small garrison at Halifax (and at Esquimalt, British Columbia, not yet part of Canada). Ottawa protested to no avail, and the last British regulars departed in November 1871. Their departure had been delayed by the outbreak of rebellion on the Red River and by the Fenian raids of 1870. In 1869 Canada had purchased Rupert's Land from the Hudson's Bay Company. The dominion now owned the West, but, as the rebellion showed, its hold was far from firm.

Led by the able and charismatic Louis Riel, the Métis rebellion was taken seriously in Ottawa. There were fears of American meddling and concerns that the entire West could be lost. Fortunately for the new dominion, London agreed to a joint Anglo-Canadian expedition under the command of Colonel Garnet Wolseley, an able officer who had served in Canada since 1861. Wolseley's force was to consist of two composite battalions of militia, recruited from both Ontario and Quebec, and almost four hundred troops from the dwindling British garrison, men of the King's Royal Rifle Corps. Included were a battery of artillery, some engineers, and ancillary troops.

The expedition's real challenge was to reach the Red River. For political reasons, Wolseley's little army could not ride the railway through the United States. Instead, it moved by rail and steamer to the head of the Great Lakes and then struck out overland and by river through the rough country between Lake Superior and the Red River. For thirteen weeks it hauled its equipment and boats on endless portages, battling the country and finally overcoming it. The little force arrived at Fort Garry on August 24, 1870. Prepared to fight, fearful that Riel might resist, Wolseley instead discovered that the Métis leader had fled minutes before.[2] After a small celebration to mark the bloodless victory, the troops settled in to recover from their arduous journey. Most were frustrated to have come so far without even a skirmish, and discipline collapsed in drunken revelry the first night. Colonel Wolseley was disgusted.

Wolseley and the British regulars soon returned to their post in central

Canada to prepare for their withdrawal from the country,* but the militiamen remained on the Red River over the winter. The territory, now a minuscule Province of Manitoba, soon had its own Militia units and designation as a Military District. When Fenian raiders menaced Manitoba the following year, Ottawa dispatched a 200-man militia force westwards, in winter, to assist the new Manitoba units. This 'Dominion Force on Service in Manitoba' reached Winnipeg in twenty-eight days, an astonishing feat. It would remain there for six years, all but forgotten.

At the same time, with the British finally departing, the government decided that it had to create two batteries of garrison artillery, primarily to take care of the artillery and stores left by the British Army at the fortresses of Quebec and Kingston and to run artillery schools for the Militia. On October 20, 1871, 'A' and 'B' batteries were established. They were commanded by British officers and initially manned by militiamen on call-out, though their ranks were stiffened by retired gunners of the Royal Artillery. In 1873 the batteries' gunners went on a full-time, regular basis and became the foundation of Canada's Permanent Force. It was all makeshift. When Lieutenant-Colonel Thomas Bland Strange, the British officer who had agreed to take the command in Quebec City, arrived in Canada, he found that no uniforms, rifles, ammunition, or accommodation had been provided for his battery. Even the Citadel's guns had been dismounted so the gun platforms could be repaired. Strange soon whipped his bilingual unit into shape, but the lack of preparation would prove to be typical.[3]

As the threat from the United States and the Fenians receded and as Canada's economic prospects worsened in the 1870s, the defence appropriations declined. Money problems forced cuts in Militia training, and uniforms and equipment soon became threadbare and obsolete. The infantry weapon, for example, was the Snider-Enfield, a 3-foot-long muzzle-loader converted into a single-shot breech-loader that fired a huge .57-calibre round. This weapon was both clumsy and out of date. Summer camps fell off to alternate years for rural

---

* Wolseley's career flourished and he ended as Commander-in-Chief of the British Army. In 1884, remembering his Canadian service, he engaged four hundred voyageurs from Canada to help ferry supplies up the Nile in the expedition for the relief of General Gordon in Khartoum. For my purposes, this was not a military campaign and it is not covered in this book. See Roy MacLaren, *Canadians on the Nile, 1882–1898* (Vancouver, 1978).

regiments, most of which scarcely existed between camps except for a cadre of officers. Urban units, unless they were well provided for by benevolent patrons, were cut back everywhere. In any case, the camps were little more than drunken play-acting at soldiering. All the Militia was really good for was to support the civil power – appearing at Irish Catholic-Irish Protestant confrontations, for example, or at violent strikes, where they invariably upheld the interests of capital against the workers. The few regulars were little better in their effectiveness.

At this low point, in 1875, Ottawa named a British officer, Major-General Edward Selby Smyth, as the first General Officer Commanding (GOC) the Canadian Militia. He was in the forefront of the many British officers given local general officer rank to advise the Canadian government on military matters. Selby Smyth, like most of his successors, would try to impose reform on a patronage-ridden institution but inevitably fail.

The only bright spot in a bleak time was the creation in 1876 of the Royal Military College in Kingston. Though the object of the college was to train officers for the Militia or, secondarily, the Permanent Force, the best four graduates each year received offers of commissions in the British forces. By 1894, however, only ten graduates had joined the Permanent Force, while eighty-four had signed up with different imperial units. RMC was tiny, yet it provided a mix of military and academic courses heavy on engineering and modelled itself on the United States Military Academy at West Point. Only eighteen cadets enrolled in the first class. Standards were not high, and, initially, they had to be reduced further still to encourage applications.[4] Even so, it was a beginning, a recognition that a nation had to train its military officers to professional standards.

Further recognition came in 1883 when a new Militia Act authorized the establishment of a regular troop of cavalry and three regular companies of infantry. These forerunners of the Royal Canadian Dragoons and the Royal Canadian Regiment were to serve as a Cavalry School and an Infantry School. At the same time, the two batteries of artillery were renamed the Regiment of Canadian Artillery. Canada's little standing army, not to exceed a strength of 750 officers and men, was at last in existence. Two years later, a School of Mounted Infantry opened in Winnipeg. In 1887, amid fears of an Anglo-Russian war and the prospect of tsarist cruisers attacking Victoria, the Department of Militia and Defence established a third battery of artillery in Esquimalt to defend the Royal Navy's base there.

Slowly, very slowly, professionalism had begun to make its way into the Canadian Militia, but the process suffered from that bane of Canadian politics: patronage. The Minister of Militia and Defence, Adolphe Caron, appointed the Permanent Force's first officers almost wholly on the basis of political acceptability, social connections, and regional representation. True, Lieutenant-Colonel W.D. Otter of the Queen's Own Rifles was believed to be efficient (and he had lobbied very hard for the position), and six RMC graduates received Permanent Force commissions, but nine of the officers named had no military experience at all, while others had failed in Militia posts. The GOC, Major-General R.G.A. Luard, was appalled, but the best he could do was to get the Prime Minister to agree that none of the appointments could be confirmed until the officers had passed their qualifying examinations.[5]

Still, it was a beginning, and none too soon, for in 1885 the Militia faced its first real test of arms in the North-West. Métis and Indian unrest at increasing white settlement and at the decline of the buffalo had been building for years and, over the winter of 1884–5, it burst into flame. Louis Riel, called back from his long American exile by his people, again led a rebellion against Canada. At Duck Lake his men defeated a party of North-West Mounted Police and volunteers and forced its retreat. This news caused near panic in Ottawa. There were almost no military resources on the prairies west of Winnipeg, except for the NWMP's thin and not very efficient ranks, and the difficulties of moving a force from central Canada were forbidding. The government quickly authorized an expedition under the new GOC, Major-General Frederick Middleton, a portly fifty-nine-year-old British officer who had served with courage in New Zealand but was no high-flier. Middleton proceeded west at once, leaving the raising of the force to Caron, who was obliged to bludgeon an understaffed and less than competent department into action. In peacetime, there were only four military officers on the Ottawa staff, including Middleton. All the administrative duties fell to a small corps of civilian officials, who seemed most reluctant to overexert themselves during a crisis.

This time Canada would quell the rebellion itself, except for Middleton and a few British staff officers. In a force of some 6000 officers and men, all but 363 regulars came from the Militia, with more than 3000 drawn from eastern Canada, 1200 from Manitoba (where new battalions were formed pell-mell), and 800 from the North-West. The government's paramilitary force, the NWMP, also provided virtually its entire complement to the conflict. There was no shortage of volunteers. Walter Stewart, who joined the Midland Battalion on March 31 and was appointed a staff sergeant on April 1, wrote in his diary that he was 'delighted at the prospect of being able to take part in defending our country.'[6] Many others felt the same way.

Equipping the Militia battalions was a challenge. One private in the Midland Battalion, a unit put together from untrained Ontario rural battalions, noted that the first uniform he received 'was as poor a fit as you can imagine. Some of the men had never drilled or soldiered before, and knew nothing of order or discipline. Most of us had been "smelling the cork," and as a result there were quite a few that had to be put in the guard room for the night. The next day we were furnished with brand new uniforms from head to foot.'[7]

With the Canadian Pacific Railway still under construction, getting to the North-West over snow more than 3 feet deep was half the battle. 'Wish you to travel night and day,' the Minister telegraphed, sounding almost Napoleonic. 'I want to show what Canadian Militia can do.'[8] The troops from the east had to march over stretches of rough terrain on the north shore of Lake Superior, where the rail line was incomplete, all the while suffering under an administrative and supply system that was rudimentary at best. They did so without losing a man, though some troopers were said to have contemplated suicide because of the cold and the conditions. On the rail line, most of the troops rode on open flatcars while their officers kept warm in heated cabooses. The artillerymen had to manhandle their 9-pounder muzzle-loading guns on and off the flatcars and over the impossible terrain.[9]

If the move to the West was a credible feat, the fight against Riel was much less so. Middleton divided his force into three columns, the most westerly under former British regular Major-General T.B. Strange from Quebec City. Strange, who had two understrength francophone units from Quebec as well as local militia, led his men north from Calgary to Edmonton and then east to Fort Pitt. The centre column, led by Lieutenant-Colonel Otter, the commanding officer of the Infantry School Corps at Toronto, headed north from Swift Current to

Battleford. Middleton's own column proceeded north from Qu'Appelle to Batoche, Riel's stronghold, aiming to strike the rebels at their heart.

The militiamen struggled to move through the spring mud and suffered from shortages of critical supplies. There was no grass for the horses to eat so early in the season, and forage had to be transported. 'When you get to be 200 miles from your base,' Middleton complained, 'the team horses nearly eat what they carry.'[10] Desperate and frustrated, Middleton arranged for a steamer to move his men and their supplies forward.

The Métis, led militarily by Gabriel Dumont, were potentially a tough opponent. The men were skilled horsemen and used to privation, but, armed with a variety of weapons and fiercely individualistic, they were unlikely to respond well to orders, despite Dumont's efforts to tighten discipline. There were perhaps a thousand Métis fighters in all. A skilled tactician and natural commander, Dumont understood his people's strengths and limitations. He realized they could not stand up to the Militia either in their numbers or in their artillery and just-acquired hand-cranked Gatling guns. He sensibly relied on ambush where possible. When forced to stand and fight, his men did so from well-sited bunkers and rifle pits, and they exacted their toll. Hampered by an interfering Riel and his apocalyptic visions, Dumont did well with the resources he had.

The Indians were the unknown factor in the campaign: if the Blackfoot and the Cree joined the rebellion *en masse*, many in Ottawa and the West fretted, all could be lost. It was, after all, only a few years since Custer's 'last stand,' just south of the international boundary. There was great concern among the settlers and much fear of scalping. The Canadian force had to consider this political factor, even though the military value of native fighters may have been overrated.

The Indians could fight, however, if they chose to join the fracas. When a few hot-head Cree from Poundmaker's band plundered Battleford, Otter foolishly ignored Middleton's orders to leave the Indians alone and led his column to Cut Knife Hill, west of Battleford. There Poundmaker forced the Militia to retreat, despite its artillery (rendered all but useless when the rotted gun platforms fell apart) and its single Gatling gun. After Dumont's defeat at Batoche, Strange's Alberta Field Force, a tiny column of 220 men, confronted Cree led by Big Bear and Wandering Spirit at Frenchman's Butte. Although the force was initially checked, Big Bear surrendered on July 2. The Indians could count the number of men Canada had put in the field and most sensibly stayed out of the rebellion.

In effect, Middleton's little army lost all the battles but the crucial one at Batoche. Cut Knife Hill and Frenchman's Butte were defeats, and Middleton's column bumped into an ambush from 150 of Dumont's men at Fish Creek. The Militia suffered fifty-five casualties there – dead, wounded, or missing – but it moved on to Batoche. 'We got no sight of the enemy' defending Riel's capital, wrote Staff Sergeant Stewart of the Midland Battalion on May 9; 'they were well hidden in their rifle pits.' The soldiers were puzzled by this tactic: 'This was a rather different way of fighting from what we expected. We calculated on seeing the enemy anyway. We were all fully under the impression that in aiming our rifles we would have something to aim at in the shape of human forms.' Worse, Stewart said, 'they were in prepared positions, well protected, while we were in the open working forward to take theirs away from them.'[11] On May 12, while Middleton delayed, some of the Militia colonels seized the initiative. 'I have not received any orders to do what I am going to do,' Colonel Williams of the Midland Battalion said, launching his men at the Métis and Indians. 'Firing as we went in rushes,' Stewart wrote, the infantry exchanged heavy rifle fire with their enemy, then 'the whole line with a rush advanced across the open and plowed field right through and around the stores and houses and for a half mile ... The village was ours.'[12]

The Métis, their ammunition depleted, had inflicted thirty casualties and pulled back. There are no accurate counts of their casualties at Batoche or elsewhere during the rebellion. Three days later, Riel surrendered and Dumont was en route to an American exile. Soon after, Middleton accepted Poundmaker's surrender and moved on to Prince Albert. His men occupied themselves by looting every Métis house they came across.

So ended the rebellion. The Canadian government and the press treated it as a famous victory, a great feat of arms. It wasn't. The Canadian force had the advantage of numbers and armaments; Dumont's troops had the great disadvantage of Riel. In all, the Militia suffered 26 dead and 103 wounded in a campaign that was neither well directed nor well planned. Middleton had little use for his inexperienced Canadian commanders, and he relied on his British staff officers. He believed, rightly enough, that the Militia lacked training and discipline. Canadian militiamen resented these slurs, though they had no real reason to do so. The militia myth was alive and well in 1885, and it led to bickering during and after the campaign. Militia colonels, such as the Midland Battalion's A.T.H. Williams, a Tory MP, damned Middleton up and down before, during, and after the action at Batoche.[13] After the rebellion, Middleton even found himself accused of theft, and he was effectively driven out of Canada.

More important for the future were the inefficiencies exposed by the campaign. The logistical difficulties Middleton faced could have brought the expedition to a halt, but, fortunately for all concerned, the CPR improvised brilliantly, the Hudson's Bay Company provided supplies from its posts, and the United States permitted Canada to move men and goods through its territory. At the same time, patronage prevailed in war as in peace. Caron chose units for the force because they had good Conservative commanding officers, and his department routinely awarded contracts for provisions to the party faithful. The Minister had shown energy in putting the Militia force together, but patronage could – and would – be a fatal flaw. Still, Canada had won, the rebellion had been crushed, and the unfortunate Louis Riel was hanged at Regina. The army had made the West safe for settlement.

There ought to have been lessons for the government in the second Riel rebellion. None of the infantry battalions were even remotely ready for action, new units had to be created to fill gaps, and there was no supply and transport organization, no medical service, no engineers. Beyond unready infantry, cavalry, and artillery, there was nothing. The Permanent Force (PF) units, artillery, infantry, and cavalry, had performed satisfactorily, but there were too few of them to matter.

The Militia viewed the Permanent Force as a threat. If it ever became numerous and efficient (unlikely as both attributes may have seemed), this regular force would pose a threat to the existence and role of the country's part-time soldiers. Yet PF officers such as Otter knew that partially trained, ill-disciplined Militia simply could not do the job – even against irregular Fenians and Métis. Militia stalwart Sam Hughes, a Lindsay, Ontario, newspaper owner and aspiring Tory politician, opposed any such reformist attitude. To Hughes and his cronies, citizen soldiers were the heart of the nation, the first line of its defence, while the regulars 'were all right for police purposes in times of peace and for training schools, but beyond that they are an injury to the nation.'[14] A standing army was only a drain on the nation's resources, nothing more. Regulars were men who had failed at everything they tried and had found the Permanent Force as their employer of last resort. Even then, Hughes complained, they could not succeed without the assistance of a patron.[15] Sadly, there was substantial truth in such complaints, given the way the PF's initial cadre of officers had been appointed. But for efficient officers such as Otter, Hughes's arguments verged on madness.

First, the Militia, even more than the Permanent Force, remained a swamp of patronage. The new GOC, Major-General I.J.C. Herbert, reported to London in late 1891 about the 'abuses' he found: 'Men were brought to camp who were quite unfit for service, & put on the pay lists, though it was never intended that they should do a day's drill. Officers absented themselves without leave, and their places were taken by others without any authority, & frequently persons holding no commissions at all were entered on pay lists in place of those absent without leave.' It was not that the quality of the militiamen was poor. 'They are all full of a fair, manly spirit,' Herbert added, 'full of zeal and the very stuff that makes fine soldiers.' The problems were politics and patronage, officers who were political hacks, and city regiments that had become 'political organizations on the model of the United States militia.'[16] Herbert would try his best to overcome political resistance and to make the Militia more efficient by rooting out the aged and the infirm.

There were PF problems that troubled Herbert too. There were too many British officers in the Permanent Force who had not kept up with their profession. Pay was too low, about half what an American officer of similar rank received. Militia officers, almost wholly unqualified, could get rapid, politically assisted promotions, while PF officers were forced to use all the political influence they could muster just to survive. The infantry and cavalry schools, scattered in small packets across the country, not only were rife with jealousies and desertions but taught and trained differently – something that horrified Herbert, who had grown up in the family atmosphere of British regiments. Herbert decided to boost morale by reorganizing the Permanent Force, and he set to work with a will. 'C' Battery in Esquimalt was withdrawn when British Columbians, lured by high wages elsewhere, refused to enlist. After failing to recruit locally, the Militia Department posted gunners from King-ston and Quebec City to the Pacific – only to discover that they, too, deserted at the earliest opportunity, leaving 'C' Battery completely dysfunctional. Eventually the problem was solved by replacing it at Canadian expense with a garrison of Royal Marines.[17] The savings that ensued permitted a complete field battery to be established in Kingston, and a skeleton battery, along with garrison artillery, at Quebec. These Kingston and Quebec units formed the Regiment of Canadian Artillery. The cavalry and mounted infantry schools became parts of a regiment of dragoons, and the four infantry schools became companies in a regiment of infantry. Within months, the regiments had the right to call themselves 'Royal,' and officers could be posted from one regi-mental station to another. All these reforms meant that the differences between the Permanent Force and the Militia had been accentuated. This gulf was made even more apparent when Herbert insisted that PF units be trained as units, and that PF personnel not simply be used as instructors in corps schools to teach the Militia. In 1894 the four infantry companies, the Royal Canadian Regiment of Infantry, trained together at Lévis, Quebec, for the first time.[18]

In an era when imperial defence was attracting interest in Britain and in Canada, General Herbert was thinking of the future, of a time when Britain might need Canadian soldiers to help fight the empire's battles. Better to have regulars, who operated efficiently with British tactics and equipment, than only militiamen, who would need long training. Herbert was not alone in his thinking. At the Colonial Conference of 1897 the British government tried to push the new Liberal Prime Minister, Sir Wilfrid Laurier, in this direction. Many English-speaking Canadians, including some who detested the Perma-nent Force, agreed that Britain might need assistance to protect the empire. The Americans, moreover, were always obstreperous, and in 1895 a dispute over the boundary between Venezuela and British Guiana had come close to a war that likely would have been fought on Canadian soil. The then-GOC, General W.J. Gascoigne, discovered to his horror that no plans existed for countering a Yankee invasion.[19] The French challenged British control in Africa, and the Russians followed suit along the Indian borders. Then there were the Germans, their industries booming, whose Kaiser seemed resentful of British pre-eminence. Canadians were part of the greatest empire the world had ever seen, and some were prepared to pay the price for that privilege. All too soon, they would have their chance.

Yet another reforming General Officer Commanding had arrived in Canada in 1898. The officers taking the post must have been apprehensive – all but one had left Canada before completing his term. But Major-General E.T.H. Hutton was confident, clever, and capable, and he intended to press the government for change. Laurier's Militia Minister, Dr Frederick Borden, initially seemed to be in full agreement. Borden was a Militia supporter, one who expected that the Permanent Force's main task should be to teach the citizen soldiers, not to play at 'real' soldiering. Hutton shared this view to a substantial extent. He wanted a 'national army,' an integrated force of regulars and militia capable of rapid mobilization in an emergency. This was an idea whose time had come, but Hutton set out, like Herbert before him, to attack patronage. Borden interpreted this move as a direct assault on his prerogative, one intended to enhance the GOC's own importance. Hutton was British, of course, and nationalists believed that he served imperial interests before Canada's; moreover, he was responsible to the Canadian government, they claimed, and civil control of the military required that he know his place. Hutton's time in Canada was destined to be brief.

Just at this time, however, there were crises where military advice – and the military – were needed. In 1896 gold had been discovered in the Yukon, sparking an extraordinary rush of prospectors, speculators, prostitutes, and hangers-on into the sparsely populated territory. Dawson, for example, went from a few souls to 30,000 in a twinkling. There had been only a handful of Mounties at the site, but more went north as soon as word of the gold strike reached Ottawa. With Americans in Alaska, riches in the ground, and 80 per cent of the Yukon's population American, fears developed quickly that the United States might have designs on the territory. Had not Washington already begun to press its claims along the Alaska Panhandle?

Soldiers seemed necessary to bolster Canada's position. In the spring of 1898 the government created the Yukon Field Force from its regular force. PF soldiers from the Royal Canadian Regiment of Infantry, the Royal Canadian Artillery, and troopers from the Royal Canadian Dragoons, 203 officers and men in all, set out for the Yukon in May with artillery and machine guns and close to 60 tonnes of supplies. In September they arrived in the Yukon after an epic 180-mile trek from Glenora, the end of navigable water, to Fort Selkirk. Their presence, the first use of PF troops in an independent military role, calmed the situation.[20] The Canadian military, the Permanent Force, actually seemed to have some utility in freezing a situation until diplomacy could determine the border, though the arbitration award in 1903, giving the United States almost everything it had sought, left Canada outraged. Half the Field Force withdrew in the autumn of 1899; the remainder departed in June 1900. There was a real war under way in South Africa, and Canada was in it.

The trouble in South Africa between the Boers' Orange Free State and Transvaal and British 'uitlanders' (foreigners) was long-lived. Just as in the Yukon, it had been exacerbated by recent rich discoveries – of gold and diamonds in this case. This dispute should not have troubled Canadians, situated thousands of miles away, but it did. British justice, the rights of free men, and the oppression exercised by 'a horde of ignorant Dutch farmers' (as the *Vancouver Province* put it) could not be tolerated by the British Empire. In the Orange Free State, under the autocratic president, Paul Kruger, British settlers and miners had no rights and their children had to attend Boer schools. In such circumstances, how could free Britons not want to liberate their compatriots? In an era of jingoism, such attitudes could press nations into war. Had the United States not fought a war against Spain after the USS *Maine* blew up – from unknown causes – in Havana harbour. 'Remember the *Maine*' had been a powerful slogan to yellow journalists. The South African situation gave the yellow press in Canada and imperial-minded politicians and soldiers the same opportunity to get Canada into a war.

Laurier had no desire to fight in South Africa, but many English-speaking ministers in his Cabinet did. So too did many militiamen. The GOC, General Hutton, had been pondering what Canada should do if – or more likely when – war came. His plan, presented as Canada's plan to offer a regiment for service in South Africa, appeared in the *Montreal Star* on September 29, 1899. The Colonial Office had asked the Governor General, Lord Minto, in July if Canada might make a spontaneous offer of troops. Minto knew that Laurier would allow no such offer, so he asked Hutton to prepare a plan. Hutton did so at once: his scheme called for a 1200-man force of infantry, cavalry, and artillery, along with the names of the officers who should command the force. Most of the officers were from the Permanent Force – bad as it was, the force at least had some competent trained officers, unlike the Militia. Neither Minto nor Hutton advised the Prime Minister or the Militia Minister of this plan in July, though Hutton did tell Borden in early September. He also told the *Montreal Star* and other newspapers, along with his supporters in military and imperialist circles in Ottawa, Montreal, and Toronto. For its part, the Colonial Office, hiding its smile behind its hand, thanked Canada for its offer of troops.

The political and military fat was now in the fire. Minto, Hutton, the Colonial Office, and the press had mousetrapped Laurier. In vain he argued that the Militia Act did not permit Canada to send troops overseas. Moreover, Parliament was not in session, so no money could be voted for an expeditionary force. Laurier was right, but English Canada wanted its war, even though South Africa was still at peace. That condition was rectified when Krueger declared war on Britain on October 11. The outbreak of war, together with pressure from his English-speaking ministers, forced Laurier's hand. The British government initially wanted Canada to send 500 infantry to serve with British regiments and be paid by the War Office. Minto and Hutton decried this pittance and urged London to ask for an infantry regiment of 1000 officers and men. Stunned by the jingo opinion in the country and the Cabinet, and worried by the hostile response in French Canada, Laurier had no choice other than to agree. His government decided to put up the $600,000 to equip and transport the regiment to South Africa; once there, the costs of pay, rations, and transport back to Canada were to be borne by Britain. At least Canadians would serve in a regiment under their own commanders, not broken up into pennypackets under imperial officers. Nonetheless, the strictures of the Militia Act and Parliament's right to be consulted were forgotten. Very simply, Britain's representatives in Canada had hustled the government into participating in a war.[21]

Once in, Canada had to find the troops. The Department of Militia and Defence called for men for a year's service, forming 125-man companies from most of the major cities between Halifax and London, Ontario. Everywhere except London and Quebec City there were more recruits than places, and high medical standards, marksmanship skills, and previous military experience were used to winnow the numbers down. The French-speaking recruits from Quebec, New Brunswick, and Ontario went to 'F' Company, whose officers and half of the non-commissioned officers (NCOs) were francophones. To command the regiment, called the 2nd (Special Service) Battalion of the Royal Canadian Regiment of Infantry, or, more popularly, the Royal Canadian Regiment (RCR), Borden and Hutton selected Lieutenant-Colonel Otter, now fifty-six years old but arguably the best Canada could provide. A skilled trainer of troops, but a dour, humourless man with no capacity to inspire, Otter had more than thirty years' experience. He had some political skills, as well he might after a generation of playing patronage and political games to get and hold his positions, so he wisely let ministerial suggestions shape his selection of officers. There were forty-one, for a start, rather than the thirty-one a battalion usually had. There was a French-speaking lieutenant-colonel and supernumerary officers, including medical officers, chaplains, a commander of a machine-gun section, a historical recorder, and four nursing sisters – the first women to go overseas from Canada.[22] Although the key positions in the contingent went to PF officers, few were particularly competent at their trade. 'There are a good many good officers and some who are useless,' the *Globe* correspondent with the troops wrote privately to his editor in Toronto. 'That, of course, was to be expected; the govt really seems to have done the best it could.'[23] The 2nd Royal Canadian Regiment was made part of the Permanent Force for its service abroad.

The men of the Royal Canadian Regiment were not untypical Canadians of the era. In the first place, more than 70 per cent were Canadian-born, with another quarter coming from Britain. The vast majority were English-speaking city residents, and only 5 per cent hailed from rural districts. There were only a small number of Québécois, as the war against the Boers, a people much like the *Canadiens*, was highly unpopular in Quebec.[24] ('There are a lot of the boys,' wrote Private Tom Wallace, son of Tory Member of Parliament N. Clarke Wallace, to his mother in Woodbridge, Ontario, '[who] think a lot of these "Quebec people" are as bad as the Boers.')[25] The men seemed motivated by a desire for adventure, but also by imperial patriotism. Private George Shepherd of Paris, Ontario, said he wanted to 'show the world the unity of the Empire, and to show that if one part of the Empire is touched, all are hurt.'[26] That may have been a positive factor, but Colonel Otter would have preferred a few more experienced soldiers. Only one in twelve of the men listed his occupation as soldier, but Otter soon realized that most of his regiment had no military experience whatsoever. Even the officers, including those from the Permanent Force, knew little beyond parade-square drill.

The difficulties Otter faced were compounded by the process of equipping the men. Some equipment would not be ready until the regiment arrived in South Africa; the field uniform was made of stiff canvas duck that chafed; and the leather Oliver equipment – the belts and packs – was a distinctive Canadian design, but no more satisfactory for that. To distinguish the troops, their badge was a crown superimposed on a maple leaf, with Canada below the crown's base. Still, with only sixteen days to equip a thousand men, the Militia department had performed creditably, though the soldiers complained that equipment issued at Quebec City was frequently stolen within hours.

Another, more serious, problem was that the *Sardinian*, the ship chartered to transport the regiment, turned out to be a converted cattle boat with too little room for the men – and the gifts of fruit, tobacco, sardines, cocoa, and other comforts pressed on the unit. Otter had hoped to use the voyage for training, but the cramped space, bad weather, and an outbreak of dysentery put paid to those plans, except for some marksmanship exercises. Private G.R.D. Lyon noted in his diary on November 2 that it was 'pretty rough ... was on deck for a while but could only bring up blood which came up for over half an hour.'[27] The regiment arrived in Capetown on November 30, 1899, to discover that the war was going badly for the British – so badly that, on December 16, London announced it would accept a second contingent from Canada.

The Royal Canadian Regiment moved inland to train, thereby missing 'Black Week,' when British armies met a succession of disasters. The regiment's Commanding Officer rapidly became unpopular as he tried to whip his men into shape through parade-square drill, patrolling, outpost duty, route marches, and testing out new manoeuvres to combat those that the Boers' sharpshooters and machine guns had forced on the British. As the *Globe's* correspondent reported, these tactics were the new way of war: 'A succession of thinly extended lines advance upon the enemy, one line behind another, each so extended as to present the minimum target. As the objective point is reached the rear "waves" come up and join the "wave" in front, thus feeding the firing line and developing its fire with gradually increasing intensity.' Volley fire was gone forever and, because the Boers' sharpshooters picked off the officers, rank badges and gold buttons disappeared as well.[28]

The first taste of action failed to lessen the soldiers' complaints. On New Year's Eve a company of the Royal Canadian Regiment joined British and Australian troops on a hunt for a Boer encampment. On January 1 they found, attacked, and took it. Tom Wallace wrote home that 'the English colonel gave us great praise for the part we took in the engagement.' Unfortunately, the other companies, he added, 'try to belittle what we did.'[29] The RCR was full of grumblers, bitching about Colonel Otter as well as each other. The searing heat and sand wore out the troops, and disease, frequently typhoid or enteric fever, reduced the regiment's strength. In fact, Otter had done a wondrous job of training his raw recruits and, on February 12, 1900, the regiment joined in a large British advance towards Magersfontein, where the troops of the elderly General Piet Cronje were laying siege to Kimberley.[30]

Seeing trouble coming quickly towards him, Cronje slipped away, only to be caught by his pursuers in mid-February on the Modder River at a place named Paardeberg Drift. The RCR, well back in the British force, reached Paardeburg at 5 a.m. on February 18 after a long, gruelling, dry march. Their orders were to cross the 20-metre-wide river and attack Cronje's laager. Getting across the swift river was difficult, as some companies hauled themselves over by rope, and others formed fours and marched into the flow, the taller holding the shorter above the water. 'I put my book and my papers in my hat,' wrote Private Albert Perkins, 'and in that way have kept them dry.'[31] With enemy fire whistling overhead, Otter and his men advanced in short rushes towards the Boer positions until, unable to proceed any further, they took cover and waited for orders. 'Here we lay all day,' wrote Douglas McPherson of Dutton, Ontario, 'with the bullets whistling and cracking all around us and no cover except the ant hills, which were far too scarce.'[32] Wounded men could not be reached with medical assistance, and the heat and lack of drinking water began to take its toll. A heavy downpour made matters worse.

There were still no orders when, at 5:15 p.m., a British battalion came through the RCR position and charged the Boer lines. Many of the Canadians, hearing the order to advance, rose with the British and, like them, were cut down. The RCR, in its first day of real action, had lost twenty-one killed and sixty-three wounded. At nightfall, Otter withdrew to a bivouac on the Modder to lick his wounds and curse the high command.

For the next ten days the siege of Cronje's laager went on. The weather was miserable with rain and wind. British supply arrangements were hopelessly inadequate, thanks in part to raids by Boer commandos against the supply columns, and the rations frequently failed to arrive at the front. On February 21 Perkins noted that 'we got a drink of weak tea and a piece of biscuit. It seems to be very poor management.' Five days later he added, 'We are still weaker and there is nothing to eat.'[33] There was scant potable water either, for the Modder was polluted by the dead bodies of men and horses. The only solace was that the surrounded Boers, many of whom had their wives with them, were suffering even more.

Finally, on February 26, the RCR went back into the line, facing Cronje's main position. The order was to attack in the early hours of the 27th in two lines. It was pitch dark and most of the men held hands to prevent their straying out of line. For thirty minutes they were undetected; then intense Boer fire fell upon them, killing and wounding many. Private Frederick Lee wrote home about the night: 'It was simply awful ... we advance on to about 25 yards from the trenches without being fired on but as soon as we got within that distance the Boers sent volley after volley right in amongst us.'[34] The right flank of the RCR could return fire, while the others, pinned in the open, had to keep their heads down. Someone shouted to retreat and, leaving their dead and wounded, most of the regiment did.

'G' and 'H' Companies, 'the brave Easterners' on the right, had not heard the order and, as a result, they stayed put, working hard to improve their trenches. When daylight finally came, the 120 or so Canadians in these two companies discovered that their position commanded almost the whole of Cronje's lines and, when they opened fire, the Boers quickly realized the game was up and surrendered. The RCR's Roman Catholic padre, Peter O'Leary, told the *Montreal Star* that the Boers raised the white flag. 'One of our officers stood up to indicate that it had been seen by us. Fearing treachery, one of the superior officers ordered him to lie down until a definite move in our direction had been made.' The desired move soon followed, and a Boer officer 'stepped over the earthworks, and advanced towards our position. He was received by a Canadian Officer to whom he said he wished to surrender with all his men ... It was not very many moments before white flags were up in all directions. I myself counted sixteen.'[35] Cronje surrendered with 4200 of his men, 'as degenerate a looking rabble as any person could wish to see,' observed a Canadian war correspondent.[36] Paardeberg was the first important British success in a war that had been a long succession of disasters.

Canada had won its first battle on a foreign field. Despite the confusion and panic inherent in a night attack by an untested unit, the regiment had performed well. But Otter could not forget the humiliating unplanned and precipitate withdrawal. The victory 'was not quite as satisfactory and complete as we had hoped for,' he wrote to his wife.[37] When the plaudits began to come in, Otter was commended for his coolness under fire. The British commander, Lord Roberts, rode over to offer his praise. Immediately, Paardeberg became heralded as a great Canadian victory. And so it was, though there was a price: thirteen killed and thirty-seven wounded.

Meanwhile, Canada's second contingent was on the way to South Africa. Instead of infantry, the dominion sent four squadrons of mounted infantry and three batteries of artillery. Organized into two two-squadron battalions, the Canadian Mounted Rifles (CMRs) had recruited from members of the North-West Mounted Police, PF, the militia, and the public. The artillery batteries, called the Royal Canadian Field Artillery in South Africa, drew heavily on the Permanent Force and on Militia artillery units. At the same time that these units were formed, Lord Strathcona, the Canadian Pacific Railway millionaire who was also Canada's High Commissioner in Britain, put up the cash (an astonishing $550,000 in 1900 dollars) to raise a regiment of mounted riflemen and get it to the war. Lord Strathcona's Horse drew heavily on the Mounties and on Prairie and British Columbia cowboys. Canada also raised an infantry battalion (3 RCR) to relieve the British garrison in Halifax for service in South Africa. The mounted infantry arrived in South Africa in time to join the march on Pretoria.

There was one more task at home for the government to clean up. The GOC, General Hutton, had pushed and prodded Canada into the war with the assistance of the Governor General, who had unquestionably acted improperly. Minto could not easily be touched, but Hutton was vulnerable, and Laurier demanded his recall. Minto initially blew the matter up into a constitutional crisis, telling the Prime Minister that he should replace Frederick Borden and, amazingly, adding that the Minister had no right to interfere with the Militia.[38] London rescued the situation by appointing the tactless, foolish Hutton to a post in South Africa (where he ended up commanding a brigade that included the two units of Canadian mounted infantry).

If the war in Ottawa was temporarily over, the war on the veldt went on. The RCR participated creditably in the advances against the Orange Free State capital of Bloemfontein and the Transvaal capital of Pretoria. At Israel's Poort, in April, they ran into a Boer ambush. Under heavy fire, the Canadian ranks wavered and men began to retreat, until Colonel Otter stopped them with curses and threats. Otter suffered a wound in the neck, but he had saved the day.[39] As a senior officer, Otter could refuse to be treated in the military hospitals, which he apparently thought had changed little since Florence Nightingale's time in the Crimea; instead, he found shelter in a private house and made use of the RCR surgeon, Dr Eugene Fiset.

Recovered by the end of May, Otter led the regiment in its final days in South Africa, but the RCR was shrinking. C.F. Hamilton of the *Globe* wrote to Toronto that he doubted 'if it could place more than 450 rifles in the firing line. Death and wounds, about 150; sickness of one sort & another (including a peculiar disease known locally as Mauseritus, & possessing many & various symptoms & one cause) perhaps 650. That's war & our regiment has shot its bolt. That's volunteers,' he added, 'good as the best for 6 months – after that, not so good.'[40] When he was asked by Lord Roberts to persuade his men to extend their one-year commitment, Otter dutifully tried. Some 300 agreed to stay on, but 17 officers and 385 of the RCR opted to return to Canada in September, refusing to stay at war more than the year they had agreed to. In November the remaining RCR left for England for presentation to Queen Victoria; in December they returned to Canada to cheers and public plaudits.

By any criterion the Boers, with their cities occupied, ought to have surrendered. Instead, they turned to guerilla war, using their commandos on horseback to hide, strike hard, and hide again in country they knew well. In response, the British developed anti-guerilla tactics that were brutally effective. Troops, including Canadians, cleared women and children off the Boer farms and put them in fetid concentration camps, where 20,000 of the 100,000 or so who were locked up died of disease. Farmhouses were looted and burned, and the Canadians did their share of the damage. Blockhouses and barbed wire quartered the countryside. The two battalions of Canadian Mounted Rifles, one now called the Royal Canadian Dragoons, and the Strathconas worked hard in this campaigning and they frequently outran their supplies. As one RCD trooper wrote, 'We manage to make up by commandeering from the Boers.'[41] Armed with Lee-Enfield rifles and Colt revolvers, the mounted riflemen were quick and capable. The Strathconas won the first Canadian Victoria Cross of the war in a small action at Wolve Spruit, where Sergeant Arthur Richardson, a member of the NWMP, rode through a Boer crossfire to rescue a wounded comrade. Led by Colonel Sam Steele, the Strathconas earned a reputation for fierceness and the nickname 'The Headhunters.' The guerilla war had inevitably turned into a brutal struggle, but later investigation cleared the Strathconas and their colonel of all charges.[42]

The Royal Canadian Dragoons won their first VCs at Leliefontein in November 1900. The RCDs and two 12-pounder guns of 'D' Battery of the Royal Canadian Artillery formed a small rearguard for a large British force. When 200 Boers came out of nowhere and charged, Lieutenant H.Z.C. Cockburn put his troop between the Boers and the guns, giving the RCD time to escape. Cockburn's command was lost to a man, and only the wounded officer got away. Later, the Boers struck again, this time running into Lieutenant Richard Turner's troop. Turner and a dozen men held off a Boer charge, saving the guns a second time. His sergeant, Edward Holland, kept the RCD's air-cooled Colt machine gun firing and, when the Boers were all but on him, was said to take the hot gun by the barrel and to safety. All three RCDs received the empire's highest award for gallantry.[43] Lieutenant E.W.B. Morrison, who was commanding the guns, should perhaps also have received the award. The RCD, the CMR, the artillery batteries, and the Strathconas returned home in early 1901.

The struggle was winding down. Canada sent a second regiment of Canadian Mounted Rifles in early 1902, along with a field hospital. On March 31, 2 CMR suffered heavily at Boschbult when a twenty-one-man rearguard from the regiment fought several hundred Boers. Seventeen of the troopers were killed or wounded, and the survivors threw their rifle bolts away or broke their rifles before they were captured. Four additional regiments of CMRs were raised in 1902, though they all arrived in the field after the Boer capitulation in May 1902. An additional 1200 men volunteered in Canada to serve in the

South African constabulary, a quasi-military force, and Steele became a colonel in the new organization.

In all, Canada's first overseas war had seen 8372 men volunteer for service, a number that included the Halifax garrison unit and the constabulary. Of this total, 89 died in action, 135 succumbed to disease, and 252 suffered wounds. They had done well by virtually every standard. Colonel Otter was not one to brag about his own service, but there was more than a little bitterness when he said privately that the war had been 'blood and sand and everything that is disagreeable all for a bit of riband and a piece of silver.'[44]

The South African War alarmed the British Army, the government, the media, and the public because of the weaknesses it exposed in tactics, training, equipment, and leadership. Wholesale reform followed, and Canada found itself caught up in the process. Hutton's successor but one as GOC, Major-General the Earl of Dundonald, spearheaded the reform. With Frederick Borden's encouragement and agreement, Dundonald established Permanent Force engineer, signals, ordnance, and army service corps units. The GOC also created a medical staff and, two years later, it formed a Nursing Branch in which members held officer status. A rudimentary Intelligence Branch took shape in Ottawa, with a Corps of Guides to assist in the field. Artillery strength was increased, and the name of the batteries trained to work with cavalry changed to the Royal Canadian Horse Artillery. Some cavalry regiments were converted into mounted infantry, and additional mounted infantry regiments were created. Once these reforms were in place, Canada could theoretically put a force in the field and maintain it. But better training facilities were needed, Dundonald argued, and the government acquired land at Petawawa, Ontario, for this purpose. Dundonald pressed for the establishment of a system of officer education, as he sent PF junior officers on courses and laid down criteria for the appointment of future officers. All this cost money, and Borden, who was still Minister, secured $1.3 million a year after 1903 to purchase arms and equipment.

Dundonald also took serious steps to eliminate favouritism and patronage from the Permanent Force. To improve the PF's professional standing, he began the practice in 1903 of sending officers to the British Army's Staff College at Camberley. By 1914, twelve officers had passed the course. In 1908 his successor created a Militia Staff Course that, within six years, had trained 124 officers.[45]

Like so many of his predecessors, Dundonald wanted to eliminate patronage from the Militia, too, but that was against the Canadian tradition. His first report on the state of the Militia was blunt, detailing every flaw he could find, including the lack of training. The GOC told a Montreal dinner that too many in Canada 'believed that in order to keep transgressors out ... all Canadians had to do was to stick up a notice board "This is Canada."' The General indicated that his preference was to have men with rifles behind the notice board. Later, he complained to the Conservatives about Liberal patronage appointments.[46] In 1904 inevitably the government sacked him.[47]

A new Militia Act in that year eliminated the requirement that the GOC be a British officer; henceforth, Canada would have a Chief of the General Staff and a Militia Council, responsible to both the Minister and the government. The act also gave Canadian officers equal status with British regulars of the same rank. In wartime, however, 'when the Militia is called out for active service to serve conjointly with His Majesty's Regular Forces,' it continued, 'His Majesty may place in command thereof a senior General Officer of His Regular Army.' The 1904 act established a Militia Council with wide powers under the Minister and appointed an Inspector-General to advise on the Militia's readiness for war. At the same time, the Permanent Force's authorized strength was increased to 2000. These were major, long-overdue changes and, when added to Dundonald's reforms, they left Canada better prepared for war than it had ever been. The reforms were also nationalist in their effect, though not quite as nationalist as they have frequently been painted.[48] Sir Frederick Borden tried manfully – and with substantial success – to make the new system work. He also supported the Permanent Force as best he could, even though it, unlike the Militia, had no political constituency.

While these changes took hold, public opinion in Canada became increasingly militaristic. The growing power of Germany, the system of alliances in Europe, the increased spending on arms by the Great Powers – all these developments made Canadians who were proud to be part of the British Empire aware that they might have to go to war. Pacifism had its supporters, as did those who urged Canada to spend as little as possible on the military and armaments. In the decade before the Great War, however, those who advocated preparedness and training had the upper hand, though the support for militarism waxed and waned depending on the overseas news. The Canadian Defence League, formed in 1909, called for universal military training, and many of its members urged that schoolboys receive cadet training. Sir Frederick Borden in 1908 persuaded Nova Scotia, his home province, to ensure that every male teacher had military training and qualifications to teach physical fitness and drill. By 1911 six provinces, including Quebec, had subscribed to a similar scheme and, two years later, 40,000 boys trained as cadets. Cadets learned discipline and grew up to be manly, not ruffians, or so right-thinking Canadians believed.[49] One historian greatly overstated the result of all this militarism: 'It is not too much to claim that, by 1914, most aspects of young men's lives were oriented towards the military ... co-opted by the state to ensure the production of manly patriotic men who would willingly go to war.'[50] In truth, the tiny Canadian state had no such powers.

The support for the cadet movement was only one sign of Ottawa's increasing efforts to bolster the country's military forces. The key event was the British government's transfer of Halifax and Esquimalt to Canadian control in 1905–6. Whitehall was interested in cutting costs, but this economizing was also a de facto recognition that the United States was no longer considered a potential threat to Canada. The British departure obliged Canada to raise its defence spending so it could increase the garrisons on both coasts to 1200 men in Halifax and 100 in Esquimalt. The Royal Canadian Regiment provided 600 of the troops for Halifax and, for the first time, had the makings of a genuine infantry battalion permanently on the ground in one place in Canada. The artillery also benefited by taking over the modern British guns in Halifax. The Canadian engineers expanded there as well, as did the Army Medical Corps, which began to operate the base hospital. Nationalism had its benefits for the Permanent Force, but, still, long-service British soldiers were encouraged to remain in Canada as part of the Permanent Force.[51]

The first Chief of the General Staff, Major-General Percy Lake, was one such British officer with Canadian connections and long service in Canada. He began to create a tiny General Staff and to plan for mobilization. Both initiatives meant more permanent staff and more complaints from the Militia in and out of Parliament, but Sir Frederick Borden persevered. Borden, however, did not go along with efforts in London to make Canada's General Staff a section of the Imperial General Staff, even when W.D. Otter, now a Major-General and the first indisputably Canadian CGS, suggested it in 1910.[52] Nationalism had arrived at the Department of Militia and Defence. Directed by Otter, who was no dominion separatist, and led by Lieutenant-Colonel W.G. Gwatkin, a British officer, the notion of and planning for the dispatch of a large expeditionary force – a division of infantry and a brigade of cavalry – took shape.

Through all these developments, the Permanent Force and the Militia remained at loggerheads. If the PF trained separately, it inevitably came to think of itself as a standing army; if it trained only the Militia, it could not itself be well trained. The dual-purpose PF was doomed to be inefficient until Otter's successor as CGS, Major-General Colin Mackenzie, proposed to Borden that the PF should be split in two: an instructional cadre and a tiny standing army. This solution worked, and it remained in place for a generation.[53]

By 1913, with the Conservatives in power and Sam Hughes as Minister of Militia and Defence, there was no shortage of disputes between the government and the CGS.[54] Reports in 1910 and 1913 by senior British generals on tours of inspection in Canada criticized many Militia and PF shortcomings, though General Ian Hamilton in 1913 found matters much improved since 1910.[55] They all agreed, however, that stockpiles for mobilization were wholly inadequate, training was spotty, and patronage still ruled in the Militia.

Despite Sam Hughes's belief in the militia myth and his low regard for professional soldiers, or 'bar-room loafers' as he called them, the PF's strength in 1913 was some 3100 members, with 793 infantry, 346 cavalry, 910 artillerymen, 314 signallers and engineers, 164 army service corps men, and 101 medical corpsmen and nursing sisters, as well as a number of specialists.[56] Hughes's prized volunteers, the Militia, numbered 74,000 at their peak, though they had a huge annual turnover – something that hampered training severely (and still does). Nonetheless, in that year 55,000 men trained during the summer, while the department's budget was $11 million – a huge increase over the $1.6 million before the Boer War, and a very substantial sum in a time of economic depression. The Militia had also been organized into a six-division structure (except in the West). Though largely untrained in tactics beyond the smallest of subunits and vastly understrength in efficient officers and NCOs, the Militia was better than it had ever been. The Canadian Army had come a long way since Confederation.

One critical gap remained, however. Canadian officials had grappled with the question of French Canada and the Militia for years.[57] The calculus was simple enough: in 1759 and 1812 the Quebec militia had been a significant factor in the military struggle. In 1775 it had not joined in, and in 1837–8 the militia had largely sat out the rebellion or sided with the *patriotes* in Lower Canada. Some francophones had served against the Fenians, but most had not. If Canada was to be defended successfully, if the Canadian militia was ever to become a genuine national force, some way had to be found to bring French Canadians willingly into its ranks.

Despite the best efforts of ministers and generals, this problem could never be resolved. The military structure of the new Dominion of Canada, confirmed in the Militia Act of 1868, modelled itself on that of the Canadas – and that model was bilingual in its operation. The senior military officer in Canada East, the Deputy Adjutant-General, had always spoken French, and two of the three new Military Districts in the Province of Quebec were, for all practical purposes, unilingually French-speaking, with room for command and staff appointments for French Canadian officers. There were French-speaking volunteer regiments, and Militia training courses could be offered in French for their soldiers. In the tiny Permanent Force, created in 1872, a good portion of the artillery battery stationed in Quebec City was French-speaking. When the PF expanded in 1883, one of the infantry schools was designated to serve the French-speaking militia. The force created to put down Riel's 1870 rebellion had a Quebec battalion, and the force used in the second Riel rebellion of 1885 included two Quebec battalions. In addition, the Ministers of Militia and Defence were frequently Québécois, as, almost invariably, was the deputy minister, the senior civil servant in the Militia department. Some ministers – Sir George-Étienne Cartier, for example – had substantial political clout in both Quebec and Ottawa. All ministers, French- or English-speaking, Liberal or Conservative, enjoyed the patronage that lay under their control in Militia and Defence.

So what was the problem with Quebec? All too often the reality was different from the paper statistics of duality. At the first enrolment of Militia volunteers after Confederation, Quebec produced a respectable third of the dominion's 37,000 men; unfortunately, almost half of this number originated in Quebec's one English-speaking Military District.[58] During the Fenian raids of 1870, the call-up of Militia generated about one-third of those Québécois on the rolls. The Quebec battalion sent to Red River in 1870 was about one-fifth French-speaking. Francophone regiments seemed to fold for lack of interest more frequently than English-speaking regiments, and one of the battalions employed in 1885 had to scramble to fill its ranks on call-up. Moreover, the French-speaking regiments in the province were relatively few. Desmond Morton noted that, in Montreal, there was only one such regiment, compared with five English-speaking ones; in Quebec City there was one unit for each language group; and in the rest of the province there were only fourteen francophone units, compared with ten anglophone ones. Given the province's relatively small English-speaking population, the imbalance was striking.

The Militia was effectively a voluntary organization, and some military politicians (and one or two historians since) have argued that this attribute was part of the problem: Québécois, they said, preferred the compulsory system of the ballot that had been employed in New France and that existed, more honoured in the breach than the observance, through most of the British regime. There is scant evidence for this claim. More seriously, English-speaking units in Quebec and elsewhere in Canada modelled themselves on British regiments, following their traditions and adopting their uniforms. For obvious reasons, this aping of the Guards and Rifle regiments struck no chord in Quebec, though those regiments that existed followed suit. And when, between 1868 and 1870, more than 500 young francophones went off to Italy to fight for the Pope as Papal Zouaves in peculiar mock-Algerian baggy pants and kepis, the British military authorities in Canada and London in the late 1870s flatly refused to permit the formation of a Militia battalion with a similar uniform.[59] That mock-Algerian pantaloons were as relevant to Canadian conditions as *faux*-British bearskins and redcoats cut no ice with Ottawa and London.

Perhaps that uniform business was a sign of something bigger. Thereafter, the English-speaking tide began to batter against the French-speaking Militia. When the Royal Military College came into being in 1876, its courses paid scant attention to bilingualism and made no concessions to French-speaking applicants writing the entrance examinations. As a result, no one could have been surprised that, between 1876 and 1914, only thirty-nine out of a thousand RMC cadets were francophones.[60] And when, in 1880, the two Permanent Force artillery batteries switched station, the Quebec City gunners of 'B' Battery found themselves posted to resolutely unilingual Kingston, Ontario. Unhappiness and desertions soon followed.

The 1885 Riel rebellion, a conflict that quickly pitted French against English public opinion in Canada, did further damage. The Quebec Militia battalions that mobilized for the North-West were seriously understrength, and there seemed to be scant support for them in the local media. Both battalion commanders were Conservative MPs, and one left the West as quickly as he could, until he was forced back to duty by the mockery of the English-speaking press.[61] The Ontario newspapers sneered at Quebec's military effort in the rebellion, and the expedition commander, General Middleton, unfairly developed an absolute contempt for his Québécois troopers. Riel's execution and the furore it created in Quebec unquestionably left many members of *la milice* believing they had betrayed their province by serving in the Anglos' army.

Another dampening effort came when General Herbert, the GOC, tried to enhance Militia efficiency at the beginning of the 1890s. A bilingual Catholic, Herbert spent time with the Quebec Militia, visiting units and camps. The old and unqualified were his special targets across Canada, but, as Morton noted dryly, 'the scourge of Herbert's reforms seemed to fall more heavily on the French-speaking if only because there were more old, unqualified and unsuitable officers to be removed and fewer young enthusiasts to be replaced.'[62] Understandably, perhaps, many francophones believed that the efforts at reform targeted them.

Under the Laurier government, renewed efforts began to build up Quebec's Militia participation. There was more money for training, for one thing, and the GOC, Major-General Edward Hutton, another bilingual British officer, worked hard to encourage Québécois to serve, using church parades and church notables to this end. Summer camps were opened to the public, and the mock battles that closed these concentrations were popular showpieces. Hutton also encouraged choral competitions among Quebec units, another welcomed measure. The GOC even went so far as to order that bilingualism be a requirement for English-speaking staff officers. The response in Quebec was positive and in the rest of the country, frigid; when Hutton departed in 1900, he went unmourned in English Canada – for this and many other reasons. The order that officers be bilingual was not put into practice for another seventy years. Unfortunately, none of these efforts had much success, and Quebec's contribution of men to the South African War was minimal.

Governmental efforts to bind Québécois to the Militia effectively ceased when the Conservatives won the 1911 election and Sam Hughes became Minister of Militia and Defence. Hughes was an Ontario Tory and Orangeman who had little time for Roman Catholics and their church parades, particularly those of the Québécois. Militia units were forbidden to parade under arms in church processions, and some units with too many Liberal officers were closed down. The 86th Three Rivers Regiment, more than forty years old and with 200 officers and men training in a new armoury, was summarily ordered disbanded in the spring of 1914 for just this reason, though no one said so openly. It was 'le vengeance hypocrite' of a partisan minister and government, proclaimed a Trois-Rivières Liberal newspaper.[63]

All this was serious business, especially when the numbers were examined. In 1914 there were one hundred infantry battalions on the Militia List; only fifteen were French-speaking and most of these were grossly understrength. There was no francophone cavalry unit, and only one such battery of artillery. Only seven francophones had passed the Militia Staff Course to train for staff positions. Permanent Force officers numbered 254 in 1912, but only 27 were French Canadian.[64] When war broke out in August 1914, statistics such as these became increasingly important.

three

A MILITIA UNDER ARMS:
SAM HUGHES'S ARMY

'You are not going across, Frank, are you?' said Ethel.

'If I can. There is very strong competition between both officers and men. I have been paying little attention to soldiering for a year or so ... But now things are different. If I can make it, I guess I will go.'

'Oh, Frank, *you* don't need to go,' said Ethel. 'I mean there are heaps of men all over Canada wanting to go. Why should you?'

'The question a fellow must ask himself is rather why should he stay,' replied the young officer.[1]

—m—

Canada went to war on August 4, 1914, buoyed by an enthusiasm and dutiful sense of responsibility much like that Ralph Connor described in his hugely popular novel *The Major*. There was no separate declaration of war, for the dominion, as a colony, was bound by Britain's decision to fight Germany and the Austro-Hungarian Empire. Few dissented, and, almost everywhere, there were cheering crowds and genuine displays of enthusiasm. Other than the sure belief in a British victory, no one knew what to expect. The sole reference point for Canadians was the South African War.[2]

The man who was to define and shape the Canadian war effort was Sam Hughes, the Minister of Militia and Defence in Sir Robert Borden's government. Hughes was an Ontario Orangeman, newspaper publisher, businessman and railway speculator, longtime Member of Parliament, and militia enthusiast. He had hoped to lead the Canadian contingent to South Africa, but was obliged to make his own way to the battlefields once the General Officer Commanding, Major-General E.T.H. Hutton, denied him that role. He wrote begging letters for employment to everyone of note in South Africa, and, in early 1900, became supply and transport officer on the lines of communication supporting the advance on Bloemfontein and Pretoria. As the war turned into a struggle against Boer commandos, Hughes did well, and he was put in charge of intelligence and scouting for a column of British troops operating south of the Orange River. He succeeded for a time and showed courage in action, but was forced out of South Africa in July 1900 when he failed to obey orders. He had also written indiscreet letters, which were widely published. Hughes's constant propagandizing on his own behalf offended almost everyone,[3] as did his loudly trumpeted claim that he was entitled to not one, but two, Victoria Crosses for his exploits. There was an element of mad buffoonery about Sam Hughes that did not bode well.

As militia critic for the opposition during the Laurier government, Hughes had supported Sir Frederick Borden, the Minister of Militia, in his effort to foster the development and production of a rifle in Canada. The Ross rifle, manufactured in a factory conveniently located in Laurier's own Quebec City riding, was the result. Nominally a .303-calibre weapon (but frequently unable to fire the standard British .303 cartridge without jamming), the Ross was fine when used on a rifle range; it would not prove as effective on active service despite many modifications. Hughes was a Ross partisan, a true believer in this Canadian weapon that would free the Canadian Militia from dependence on British sources of supply. His refusal to adopt the Lee-Enfield, despite ample evidence of the Ross's failure in action, cost Canadian lives until 1916, when the Canadian Corps leaders and soldiers finally acted on their own and made the switch.

Once appointed Minister of Militia and Defence, Hughes continued to believe in what was now 'his' rifle and 'his' Militia. He also built armouries at a furious pace, expanded the Militia to a peak strength of more than 70,000, and insisted that it receive both more funding and more training time. The Boer War had confirmed Hughes in his opinion that all regular officers were incompetents and that a citizen soldier and militiaman was, by definition, a better soldier. Canada's defence, he held, should be provided by a people in arms. This fixed attitude guided his policies.

Hughes's vigour was impressive, even if he directed some of his energies against the Chief of the General Staff, with whom he continually sparred. Nonetheless, staff planning for the dispatch of a contingent for overseas service in the event of a major war was in hand. While still a relatively unready nation, Canada was infinitely better prepared for war than at any previous time in its history. All too soon, Sam Hughes's army would have the opportunity to show the world what it could do.

The first thing the world saw was chaos, if anyone outside Canada was watching the dominion mobilize. The day after the British declaration of war, Hughes announced that Canada would send an infantry division of some 25,000 officers and men. Mobilization plans for such an expeditionary force had been drafted in 1911 by the able Major-General W.G. Gwatkin, the officer who became Chief of the General Staff in 1913. His plan called for composite units drawn from all the regions of Canada and for concentration of the force at Petawawa, the large camp north of Ottawa.[4] A major modification of the plan, drafted in 1914 by Lieutenant-Colonel G.C.W. Gordon-Hall, Gwatkin's replacement, called for mobilization using existing Militia units.[5] Hughes's first act on the outbreak of war was to scrap both mobilization plans. Instead, he sent the 226 Militia unit commanders a 'call to arms' by telegram, asking them to forward to Ottawa the names of men willing to serve overseas with the status of British regulars. There was no shortage of recruits from within the units as well as from the streets and farms. Men wanted to fight: some lied about their age to get accepted; others persuaded recruiters to let them sign up. In Edmonton, on the day Britain declared war, 2000 volunteers marched from the United Services Club, led by a veteran on horseback and accompanied by the Citizens' Band playing 'Rule Britannia,' 'La Marseillaise,' and the Czarist anthem. In Lethbridge, Alberta, volunteers left for Valcartier on August 19, cheered on their way by the largest crowd ever assembled in the town.[6] Hughes's call had been eagerly, almost jubilantly, received.

But there were errors nonetheless. Hughes had shut down the 86th Regiment in Trois-Rivières months before, yet the last commanding officer received one of the telegrams. Lieutenant-Colonel Louis-Philippe Mercier replied that, regretfully, since his regiment no longer existed, he had no one to send. As a result, Trois-Rivières dispatched all of five men, two of them French-speaking, to the First Contingent.[7]

The volunteers, Hughes directed, were to concentrate at Valcartier, north of the embarkation point of Quebec City, where no camp yet existed. Hughes himself would directly control the appointment of officers, though it was traditionally a government patronage plum. In every respect but the appointments, Hughes's description of the process he followed was absolutely correct: it was 'different from anything that had ever occurred before.'[8] At Valcartier, contractors feverishly carved a camp out of the bush. Rifle ranges, sewers, water, tent lines, latrines, roads, and rail links to Quebec City – all were in place within thirty days. This was an amazing, if wholly unnecessary, feat.

The first of the eventual 32,665 men of the Canadian contingent arrived in the third week of August, well before construction had finished. Men continued to arrive by special trains until September 8, while, over in Europe, the German armies, following the Schlieffen Plan, marched through Belgium and deep into France. 'It is the real soldier's life, alright,' Private Roy Macfie wrote home to his family on a farm near Parry Sound, Ontario, on August 23; 'the first night we were here there was fourteen men slept in each of those little round tents.'[9] There was initially no fixed organization for the division, its battalions, or its artillery batteries, and, although orders poured forth in a steady stream from Hughes, he almost always countermanded them at once, imposing new organizational structures. Hughes was working in the dark, for there were no firm directives from the War Office and no one really knew what kind of war Canada was facing. Even so, Hughes repeatedly compounded the chaos. The Minister was most interested in the infantry and the cavalry – the other units tended to be left alone long enough to get their structure sorted out – and he placed men into provisional battalions holus-bolus, organized them into brigades, and then reorganized them again. Wearing his colonel's uniform, Hughes created new units at whim – a motor machine-gun unit, for example – spoke freely to the press, and completely dominated the process he had set in train.

At the same time, Captain Hamilton Gault of Montreal, a businessman with wide holdings in manufacturing and real estate, offered $100,000 towards the cost of raising an independent infantry battalion. Recruited primarily from British reservists or ex-soldiers, the Princess Patricia's Canadian

Light Infantry mustered in Ottawa and prepared to sail for Britain on August 28, while the Canadian Division was still in process of gathering in Valcartier. Admiralty orders, however, held up the embarkation, and the PPCLI left for Britain in convoy with the First Contingent, though not part of it. Its initial service in France would be with the British 27th Division.[10]

Ultimately, a Canadian divisional organization took shape in the dust of Valcartier. There were three brigades of field artillery, each with eighteen 18-pounders. There were four infantry brigades, each with four battalions of one thousand men, and a seventeenth battalion of surplus infantry. The battalions were numbered from one through sixteen, and the historic names of the Militia units of which Hughes had been the patron and great supporter were not used. Militiamen and officers, the backbone of the contingent that had been created by the efforts of Militia unit commanders, were furious, but Hughes was impregnable to argument. And, since almost all the battalions were formed from many different Militia units, there was some rationale for his decision.

The First Contingent (subsequently deemed to include all those who proceeded overseas by March 31, 1915) numbered 36,267 in all. Of these, 23,211 were born in Britain and only 10,880 in Canada, including 1245 French-speaking Canadians.[11] From the start, the trends of enlistment that prevailed throughout the war were clear. The British-born, the most recent arrivals in the dominion, felt the call to arms, the call of the blood, most strongly and responded most willingly. Native-born Canadians, a generation or more away from Europe, were initially slower to respond; and francophones, three hundred years in Canada, were slower still. There was only one French-speaking company in the First Contingent. Hughes was widely perceived as prejudiced against French and Catholic Quebec and the province's Militia, and this factor contributed to an enlistment of less than 3.5 per cent in that quarter. Still, only 30 per cent of the contingent was Canadian-born, itself an astonishing statistic and explicable only if the British-born men were those most likely to have previous military experience and the first selected by commanding officers. 'It seems a very funny thing this is supposed to be a Canadian Contingent,' Private Macfie of the 1st Battalion wrote, 'and I think that two thirds of the men that are here are Old Country men.' More than two-thirds of the officers, however, were Canadian-born, most coming from the Militia or the Permanent Force.[12]

The selection of officers posed both an opportunity and a problem for the minister. Hughes's Cabinet colleagues had their favourites to promote. All good Tories expected, indeed demanded, preferment; and the scrapping of the mobilization plan left a surplus of unit commanding officers in a rage as Hughes cobbled new battalions together. The Minister believed that he knew who was capable and who was not, so he promoted and demoted at will, not even listening to the demands of his Conservative colleagues. One provisional battalion had four commanding officers at Valcartier; another had none.[13] Hughes's son Garnet became a staff officer. The Adjutant-General at Militia headquarters in Ottawa, a man presumably critical in the mobilization process and what must follow, went to Valcartier and then proceeded overseas. He was not replaced for months.

Despite this confusion, the senior posts in the contingent, the four brigade commanders, somehow went to relatively competent Militia officers. Hughes gave the 1st Brigade to Lieutenant-Colonel M.S. Mercer, the 2nd to Lieutenant-Colonel Arthur Currie, the 3rd to Colonel R.E.W. Turner, VC, and the 4th to Lieutenant-Colonel J.E. Cohoe. Turner was a Boer War hero who had been running his family's grocery business in Quebec City. Mercer was a Toronto lawyer, the holder of a commission in the Queen's Own Rifles since 1885. Cohoe, whose brigade was subsequently made the reinforcement depot for the division in yet another reorganization to a three-brigade division, had long service in the Militia on the Niagara peninsula. Currie, a Liberal, a real estate and insurance broker, a large fat man who did not fit the popular image of a commander, proved to be the most inspired choice. He had one major advantage: he was a friend of Garnet Hughes, who had served with him in Victoria, British Columbia, thought highly of him, and persuaded him to go to Valcartier. In Sam Hughes's army, that was enough to get the man who would become the nation's greatest military commander a senior post.[14]

The requirements demanded of junior officers were minimal: an officer had to be at least eighteen years old and 5 feet 4 inches tall, with a minimum chest measurement of 33 inches. He needed a Militia commission and the approval of a Militia commanding officer. Naturally, social or political connections helped, as did the completion of various training courses. Most officers were likely to have come from business or the professions, at least initially; as the war went on, good soldiers, selected by their officers and promoted from the ranks, went to officer training schools. What all would need was personal courage, honesty, and constant care for their men's needs. Many would perform brilliantly; others would not. And both kinds of officers would be killed in the battles to come.[15]

The question of command of the division had yet to be settled. Hughes naturally hoped and half-expected that he would lead his boys into action, and the Prime Minister seemed willing to agree. Fortunately, the War Office told the Canadian government that it would be a mistake to change the Militia Minister at this juncture. Hughes, who was soon to be made a Major-General, had, in fact, been contemplating both commanding the division and remaining Minister.[16] In the end, Lieutenant-General E.A.H. Alderson, a British officer who had commanded Canadian troops in South Africa, became General Officer Commanding the Canadian Division. Alderson was a close friend of General Hutton, the man Hughes had clashed with during the South African War. He was to replicate his friend's problems in spades.

The Permanent Force, as we have seen, was no favourite of Sam Hughes, and the early plans for the contingent omitted PF units entirely. When the British asked for an infantry unit to go to Bermuda to relieve one of their regular regiments for service at the front, Hughes offered the Royal Canadian Regiment, the nation's only PF infantry regiment. This was utter stupidity, a decision motivated by ministerial prejudice and one that deprived the Canadian Division of experienced instructors. Nonetheless, some PF officers had good connections to Hughes and they received posts in the division. Indeed, more PF officers and men than might have been expected made their way past Hughes's blockade. Thanks to a request from the Governor General, the two PF cavalry regiments, the Royal Canadian Dragoons and Lord Strathcona's Horse, were included in the contingent, as was the PF artillery, the Royal Canadian Horse Artillery (RCHA). The division Signal Company made good use of PF personnel, as did the field ambulances and the two stationary and two general hospitals created to provide medical services for both the division and the British Army's lines of communication. The other PF arms and services provided some officers and men to the contingent, even though, as the 1938 official history noted, 'they could ill be spared from their duties in Canada.'[17] The men and horses at Valcartier had been fed and watered, to give but one example, and the Army Service Corps, with more than a decade of experience in managing militia summer camps, deserved credit for this achievement. This experience was similarly essential overseas.

The division had to be equipped for overseas service – a major problem as there were insufficient stocks of everything a division of men needed. Militia-men had traditionally provided their own boots, shirts, and underwear, for instance, and there were only small quantities of the field service uniforms, weapons, and stores required to outfit and to maintain a large force overseas. Hughes was equal to the task – after a fashion. Without waiting for the Cabi-net to agree or money to be allocated, he instructed the Quartermaster Gen-eral to place orders for, among other things, 50,000 uniforms to be delivered no later than September 21. Boots and harness were ordered in quantity. The Ross rifle factory worked overtime to equip the infantry battalions with the Mark III rifle (one unit had the Mark II), and the need for Colt machine guns was partly met from American sources. The Minister's agents bought horse-drawn vehicles and trucks, and the trucks, armoured cars, and Colt .30 machine guns for the 120-man Motor Machine Gun Brigade came from the United States. A total of 8150 horses were purchased, including more than a few spavined nags, and the MacAdam shovel, an entrenching tool designed to serve simultaneously as a shield with two loopholes for firing and seeing, was issued to each man. A device patented by Hughes's young secretary, Ena Mac-Adam, the shovels proved unable to stop bullets or to be an effective imple-ment for digging. They were later scrapped.

So too was much of the equipment Hughes ordered in the rush of August 1914. The boots proved unable to withstand wet English weather and almost literally melted.* The Oliver equipment, its belts and packs hated by Canadi-ans in South Africa, was carried overseas by all but five battalions. There it was dumped because it could not carry as much ammunition as the newer British web pattern, which was also much more comfortable. The Canadian-made trucks were mainly scrapped in England because spare parts could not readily be found overseas. The horse-drawn Bain wagons were found to be too flimsy to carry ammunition and less manoeuvrable than British models, so were soon

---

* William Peden of the 8th Battalion remembered that 'our nice soft Canadian brown shoes quickly took on the appearance of soggy moccasins with turned up toes.' It was all the fault of 'this stupid Bastard into whose care the Canadian people had entrusted the lives of some 30,000 men' – Sam Hughes (available at www.My Docu~1\WorldW~1.html, 'World War I').

jettisoned.[18] Contracts for artillery ammunition, issued later in 1914, turned into an appalling scandal, with both profiteering and sloppy workmanship creating difficulties for Hughes and the government.

Hughes's rush to equip the force ran into entirely predictable difficulties. The August 1914 contracts, like too many others that followed, went to Hughes's political cronies. Before long, many of these men were wearing newly issued officers' uniforms of high rank, and waste and graft added to the inevitable problems of haste. Canadian-pattern equipment and Canadian-produced munitions simply were not up to standard, at least not in the first years of war.

Hughes's intention had always been to transport the Canadian Division to Britain as quickly as possible and to complete its training there. In fact, virtually no training was accomplished at Valcartier, so chaotic was the situation and so short the time. Troops fired their rifles on the ranges – 'I want, first of all, men who can pink the enemy every time,' Hughes proclaimed – and field engineer units got some practice throwing pontoon bridges across the local river. The field artillery gunners and some infantry units did small-scale tactical exercises, most did route marches, and there were formal parades. That, aside from rifle and parade-square drill, was about all that was accomplished in Canada. And, since many men of the contingent had enlisted without even militia training, precious time had been squandered.

Still, the contingent was in place, the units had been created, and the men were champing at the bit to get overseas and have a crack at the Hun before the war was over – in the six months that all optimists agreed the conflict would last. The pessimists thought it might take a year for the Allies to march into Berlin. All that remained was to load the ships – itself a colossal task that Hughes bungled when he again scrapped the preparatory planning. The government had decided to send all the fit men massed at Valcartier – some 31,300, not just the 25,000 that was the complement of a division – and the troops, their horses, and their equipment proceeded to Quebec City to board the transports. Aboard ship, they received a printed farewell address from the minister. Entitled 'Where Duty Leads,' it continued: 'Soldiers! The world regards you as a marvel ... Every man among you is a free will volunteer ... Soldiers! Behind you are loved ones, home, country, with all the traditions of Liberty and loyalty ... May success ever attend you, and when you return rest assured a crowning triumph will await you.'[19] The troops jeered at the mock-

Napoleonic address, and even the Prime Minister, hitherto impressed with his Minister's energy and accomplishments, had the grace to blush.[20]

The First Canadian Contingent left Quebec City on October 2 and arrived in Britain twelve days later. The troops began unloading on the 15th, and command of the division now fell to General Alderson. It required nine days to unload the division and its stores, jammed onto the ships without much rationality. Then the units moved into tents on Salisbury Plain, a British Army training camp located near the prehistoric Stonehenge monument.

Although the weather was splendid when the first Canadians arrived at their new camp, the rains that began on October 21 soon turned the area into a muddy morass. The wettest autumn and winter in two generations made the training period a misery and spread disease among both men and horses. The leaking tents were sodden and cold, the winds high, and there were barracks for only a small proportion of the men. Trying to help, the War Office soon resorted to billeting troops in the small villages around the Plain. This dispersal likely increased the incidences of drunkenness and venereal disease, of which 1249 cases were reported in the months before the division went to France. 'There seems to be about half this contingent bums,' grumbled Private Macfie. 'They think of nothing but drinking and getting into all the trouble they can.'[21]

Training in these conditions of miserable weather was strictly limited – the artillery did not get to fire their guns until the end of January 1915[22] – and it was disrupted further by repeated War Office alterations to the divisional organization. When, in early February 1915, the division prepared to move to France, it was still an ill-trained, if high-spirited, force. Its officers and non-commissioned officers knew almost nothing of conditions on the front and had only the vaguest idea of the difficulties of command in battle. The artillery, engineers, and signallers, just as much as the supporting services, understood their duties in the field not at all. The Canadians were as green as they could be.

The Canadian Division's organization and almost all its equipment, except for its Ross rifles, were now identical to those of a British infantry division. There were three brigades, each with four battalions of infantry and four companies in each battalion; three brigades of field artillery, each with four batteries of four guns each; and the requisite signallers, engineers, service corps units, and field ambulances. The new divisional establishment was 610 officers and 17,263 other ranks.[23] Meanwhile, the cavalry units and the RCHA (with the addition of a British cavalry regiment) now formed the Canadian Cavalry Brigade. The Fort Garry Horse, hitherto the 6th Battalion, became the cavalry depot and was replaced in the 2nd Brigade by the 10th Battalion.

The war in France and in Flanders, meanwhile, had not been proceeding to either the Allies' or the Germans' plan. The British and the French had expected to check the Germans at the frontier and then move rapidly eastward. The Germans, however, had moved into Belgium in early August and sent a massive force in a giant wheeling movement that aimed to sweep beyond Paris. The small but effective British Expeditionary Force had met the enemy at Mons, imposed a brief check on the advancing Germans, and then retreated westward. The French too were staggered by the Germans' advance, and their retreat halted only on the Marne in early September. The Germans, exhausted by their extraordinary exertions, stalled and soon began to fall back. The war of movement turned into a war of entrenchments, as each side tried to outflank the other and to reach the sea. Trenches had been used in sieges for centuries, and they had also been employed in the American Civil War, to protect soldiers from the weight of enemy fire, and again in the Russo-Japanese War. Nowhere, however, had trenches been used as they would be in the Great War. By the middle of the autumn of 1914 the trench lines stretched from the North Sea to Switzerland. Already, casualties on both sides had been huge, the power of machine guns and artillery to slaughter infantry had been demonstrated, and the need for deep trenches to provide shelter for the troops against enemy fire was evident. This was the war the Canadian Division found awaiting it.

The Canadian Division's first taste of warfare came between February 17 and March 2, 1915, when the three brigades did a week's familiarization with British front-line units. Officers and men each paired off with an experienced Tommy for two days of individual instruction. Then platoons manned a stretch of the line for twenty-four hours, while artillerymen worked with British gunners. On March 3 the division took over 6400 yards of trench in the Armentières area. The trenches with a high water table were shallow, and breastworks were constructed of sand bags to provide some protection. In March, conditions were miserable, damp, cold, and muddy. The line was quiet for a week, but on March 10 the British launched an attack on Neuve Chapelle. The Canadians received orders to hold themselves ready to participate in a breakthrough and, in any case, to provide fire support to the attackers. The British had initial success, but failed to solidify their gains, as the Germans plugged the gaps faster than the British could exploit them. Over two days, each side lost 12,000 men, including about a hundred Canadians – 'no more than the normal wastage for that period in the line,' the official history noted. Macfie observed on March 19, 1915, that 'our battalion has lost quite a few,' but 'I have only heard one bullet whistle by me yet.'[24] This was not a war like the one in South Africa, where casualties had been limited.

Once its first stint in the line was over by March 27, the Canadian Division moved north into the area of Ypres, the Belgian city that had become the centre of a salient jutting into the German line. While British troops were taking over most of the line, there were French troops, colonial troops from Algeria, and Belgians in the area as well. Ypres, or 'Wipers' as the British called it, had not yet been totally smashed by the fighting, but the war would complete that task over the next three years. The Canadians moved into the six-division-strong line at Ypres between April 14 and 17, relieving a French division. Their front was 4500 yards in length, with the left flank joining the 45th Algerian Division and their right, the British 28th Division. The key points under Canadian control were the hamlets of St Julien and Wieltje, and Gravenstafel Ridge to the rear of the line.

The Canadians were not happy with what they found in their trenches. The French, their huge casualties notwithstanding, still believed in preserving the spirit of the offensive, and their generals felt that constructing good trenches helped to create defensive attitudes. Moreover, the French, unlike the British, thought in terms of a defence in depth, and they relied on artillery and reserves to halt German attacks. As a result, their trenches were scarcely connected, very shallow, and, the Canadians claimed, full of dead bodies and human excreta.[25]* Their use of barbed wire, too, was strictly limited. At once, the Canadians set to work to bring their position up to 'British standards.'

---

* Some Allied soldiers would eventually prepare a mental list of the cleanest troops, a matter of some importance when trench reliefs occurred. The British poet Robert Graves's list was 'English and German Protestants; Northern Irish, Welsh and Canadians; Irish and German Catholics; Scots ... Mohammedan Indians; Algerians, Portuguese, Belgians, French. We put the Belgians and French there for spite,' he added: 'they could not have been dirtier than the Algerians and Portuguese.' *Goodbye to All That* (New York, 1998), 182.

They did not have sufficient time. It was sheer bad luck that the division took its place at Ypres just as the Germans launched an attack, one aimed to test the use of gas as an offensive weapon. The Germans had unsuccessfully used artillery shells filled with gas against British troops in October 1914 and January 1915, and against Russian troops early in 1915. Now they had refined their experimental techniques and, in an attack code-named Operation Disinfection, had 5730 cylinders of chlorine waiting for the right winds to carry the heavy gas over the Allied lines. So far as is known, gas warfare had never before been tried on this scale.

On April 22 the Canadian Division began its day in normal fashion. There had been warnings of the possibility of a gas attack, but no one knew what kind of gas, the possible effects, or how to counter them. The commanders largely ignored the warnings. Thus, the 2nd and 3rd brigades were holding the line while the 1st Brigade trained for possible action as part of a British attack on Hill 60, a high rubble mound that overlooked the salient. A heavy German bombardment on the neighbouring Algerian division's positions began in the late afternoon. At 5 p.m., with the winds at last blowing to the northeast, the enemy released 160 tons of chlorine, which drifted towards the Allied lines. The gas threw the Algerians and a French territorial division into a panic, and the survivors fled, gasping, vomiting, and choking, their faces purple. Major Andrew McNaughton, a battery commander, wrote that the Algerians 'came running back as if the devil was after them, their eyeballs showing white, and coughing their lungs out – they literally were coughing their lungs out; glue was coming out of their mouths.'[26] The gas had not hit the Canadian line, but the division's left flank was now fully exposed and the German infantry were advancing into the breach in the line. Worse yet, the entire British Second Army's left flank was exposed for a distance of almost 5 miles, and the Canadian Division was literally all that lay between the Germans and an Allied rout.

The next few days became a confused scramble to survive. Staggering from lack of sleep, Canadian commanders hurriedly moved battalions, platoons, and companies to the left flank, where they found surviving French colonial infantry resisting the enemy. British reinforcements began to move forward. The Germans, startled by their success, had not fully prepared themselves to exploit their gains on April 22. Had they been ready, they might have put the whole Second Army – and the Canadians – in the bag. Still, the situation was desperate, and casualties mounted as the Allies struggled to re-form the line.

Brigadier-General Turner's 3rd Brigade, ordered to counterattack towards Kitcheners Wood in the centre of the Canadian front, launched 1500 men at the enemy without knowing the ground and with no 'prearranged plan of objectives, consolidation, or disposition.'[27] Canon F.G. Scott, the division's senior padre, was with the attacking troops. 'I passed down the line and told them that they had a chance to do a bigger thing for Canada that night than had ever been done before. "It's a great day for Canada, boys," I said. The words afterwards became a watchword, for the men said that whenever I told them that, it meant that half of them were going to be killed.'[28] The position was taken, then abandoned, and only five hundred survivors of the 10th and 16th battalions, both primarily from western Canada, were left to dig in just south of the wood. Another 3rd Brigade attack met mixed results, but, with the assistance of one of Arthur Currie's battalions, established a continuous, if very shaky, line over all but 1 mile of the initial breach. A 1st Brigade counter-attack with the 1st and 4th battalions, and additional British support on Mauser Ridge at 5:25 in the morning of the 23rd, met a hot reception. This hasty counterattack and those that followed later in the day – ill-planned, largely unsupported with artillery, and clearly the product of desperation – produced predictable results: heavy losses and scant gains. The 1st Canadian Battalion from Ontario had lost 404 men; the 4th, again from Ontario, 454, including its Commanding Officer. The worst was yet to come.

The Germans now planned to send their new terror weapon – and, indeed, it did create a psychological terror – against the Canadian positions in order to capture St Julien and reach into the heart of the salient beyond Gravenstafel Ridge. They assigned a fresh division and three brigades, perhaps three times the strength of the defending Canadians, to the task, which began at 4 in the morning of April 24. The cloud of greenish-yellow gas rolled forth on a 1200-yard front against the positions held by the 8th Battalion of Currie's 2nd Brigade and the 15th of Turner's 3rd. Some of the Canadians had cotton bandoliers and were told to urinate on them and hold them over their noses in the event of a gas attack, a crude and not very effective way of countering chlorine; others in desperation peed on their handkerchiefs or their unwrapped puttees. Lieutenant-Colonel George Nasmith, a 4-foot-6-inch-tall chemist who had persuaded

Sam Hughes to let him take a mobile laboratory to France to test drinking water, was the first to identify the gas and to recommend the emergency measures that helped save lives. Nothing much could be done for those soldiers who had breathed deeply of the chlorine. They either died where they fell or in casualty clearing stations, where they were brought because the medical officers had no idea how to treat them.[29]

More immediately, the effect of the gas was devastating on the affected companies in the two battalions hit. Puking, gasping men, their eyes running, struggled to breathe and to see, knowing that the enemy infantry, wearing crude respirators, walked forward just behind the slowly drifting gas cloud. Remarkably, artillery fire, rifle and machine-gun fire from flanking companies unaffected by the gas, and those men in the gas but somehow able to fight, still hammered the Germans. Supporting the 8th Battalion, the 7th Battery fired 'over open sights down to eight or nine hundred yards with shrapnel ... waiting for them to line up so that we could get the greatest number of people in the line of fire,' the battery commander noted.[30]

Meanwhile, the infantrymen's wretched Ross rifles with their five-round magazine required frequent reloading and repeatedly jammed. In rapid fire their bolts became too hot to grasp, and the bayonets had a tendency to fall off. At Ypres, cursing soldiers hammered at the bolts with their boot heels, and wounded men tried to pass loaded magazines to their comrades.[31] Whenever they could, Canadians threw away Sam Hughes's Ross rifles and picked up Lee-Enfields from dead Tommies. There were plenty of those.

Well supported by the guns, the 8th Battalion's Winnipeggers held, though 119 were killed and 172 taken prisoner. Without any artillery support and, given the configuration of the trenches, without flanking fire, the 15th broke. A 700-yard gap in the line opened up.* The unit, largely based on Toronto's 48th Highlanders, sustained 647 casualties in one day, including 257 taken

---

* The story persists that a 48th Highlander, Sergeant Harry Band, was captured by the enemy and cruci-fied with bayonets to a barn door on April 24. A recent wrinkle, published in the *National Post* (April 14, 2001, B7), attributes the atrocity to the killing of German prisoners of war by Canadian troops retaliat-ing for the gas attack. While it is always possible that some POWs might have been killed, very few Germans were captured by the Canadians before or on April 24. The Germans were taking Canadians prisoner, not the reverse. This crucifixion story, which sprang up during the war and was much discussed then and later, and even commemorated in a sculpture (which showed the Highlander in trousers) and presented in a film, is most likely a myth. Certainly the Germans persistently denied it.

prisoner, and was all but eliminated. The battalion's colonel, J.A. Currie, was later found drunk, well to the rear, while his men fought for their lives. Colonel Currie, like many others, discovered that war was vastly different from what he had expected. Gallantry, courage, and leadership were still part of battle, but, blanketed in gas and with men choking and dying horribly all around, it was sometimes hard to remember what to do and how to act, especially for officers with no training or experience.

At the same time as they followed the gas, the Germans attacked the remainder of the 3rd Brigade's position on the northwest of the Canadian line. The Canadians repulsed the first assaults, but then heavy and accurate artillery fire pounded the shallow Canadian trenches, and the surviving defenders received orders to pull back. 'It is funny how calm you get,' one soldier recalled. 'A man falls beside you, and you just heave him out of the way, like a sack of flour.'[32] Repeated infantry assaults interspersed with artillery fire followed, and the Canadians gave up more ground in a fighting withdrawal. Soldiers in companies that failed to get away in time died or became prisoners, depending on the mood of the Germans. 'At the finish,' the official history noted, 'there was no ammunition and almost every rifle bolt had stuck.'[33] St Julien itself was now under attack from three sides. It fell after Turner misinterpreted a confusing order from division headquarters and reinforced the so-called GHQ line rather than the beleaguered hamlet. The fog of war and the lingering whiffs of gas made misunderstandings all too easy, but Turner and his Brigade Major, Sam Hughes's son Garnet, seemed unable to cope with the building crisis and frequently provided misleading reports to the other brigades and division headquarters. This did not help General Alderson, whose grip on the battle seemed weak and who was frequently out of contact with his brigadiers, often through no fault of his own: German shelling cut telephone lines repeatedly.

Brigadier-General Mercer's 1st Brigade, south of St Julien, bore the brunt of the German attack in the afternoon of April 24. Five times the Germans attacked, their ranks cut down by Canadian Field Artillery guns firing over open sights and by rifle and machine-gun fire. A British counterattack by two battalions smashed the last German effort, but not before the surviving remnants of the 2nd and 3rd battalions, both Ontario units, had been overrun by a German brigade.

Meanwhile, Arthur Currie's 2nd Brigade continued to hold onto most of its original front line, but, under increasing German pressure, its position was worsening. An attack on the right flank and front of the 7th Battalion on the morning of April 24 made significant progress until the battalion's machine-gun officer, Lieutenant Edward Bellew, and his sergeant, each operating a weapon, checked the Germans. Many of the Colt machine guns with which the division was equipped were faulty and hard to keep clean in action, and Bellew had previously complained about them. This time, however, the guns worked well.[34] Attempts to send reinforcements to Bellew's position failed, but the lieutenant and the sergeant decided to fight it out. Soon the sergeant was killed and Bellew wounded, but the thirty-two-year-old officer manned the Colt until it was out of ammunition. The Germans then rushed his position, but Bellew smashed his gun, seized a rifle, and fought the Germans until he was taken prisoner. Six officers and 260 men of his battalion marched into captivity; he, alone of the 7th, won the Victoria Cross.[35]

At this juncture, with his brigade's lines crumbling under the German pressure and in constant danger of being outflanked, Currie decided to leave his headquarters to go to the rear to seek out reinforcements for his men. A commander's task was to remain where he could direct the battle, and Currie's decision was unusual. Ever after, his actions opened him up to unfair and scurrilous charges of implicit cowardice and of abandoning his men.[36] Inexperience was most likely the reason he behaved as he did. Even so, he had made an error in judgment that could have resulted in his removal and deprived the CEF of its most successful commander. His explanation that a brigadier-general's requests for support might be better received than those from a subordinate was, while correct, not wholly convincing. But when Currie could not succeed in persuading British commanders to lend him assistance, he rounded up about 300 survivors of the 7th and 10th battalions and brought them back to his lines. He also found that his brigade Major had cajoled two battalions of the British 28th Division to dig in on the left of the brigade position.[37] That the 2nd Brigade held as long as it did was arguably the most impressive Canadian feat of the battle, and Currie, his battalion commanders (especially Lieutenant-Colonel Louis Lipsett, a British regular who commanded the 8th Battalion), and his westerners, such as Lieutenant Bellew, deserved the credit. On April 25, nonetheless, the brigade had no choice but to withdraw, so thin were its ranks, so fearful the enemy pounding. As Currie wrote to General Alderson, his 7th and 10th battalions had been 'simply blown out of their trenches by Artillery fire.'[38]

For all practical purposes, the Canadian Division's part in the battle had ended, though artillery units supported British counterattacks that were mostly futile and the 2nd Brigade had to go back into the line for two days. The PPCLI, part of the 27th Division, did play a substantial role in subsequent British attempts to restore the line. The regiment was all but destroyed: its strength on May 8 after the battle of Frezenberg Ridge was just four officers and 150 men.

The Germans had made substantial gains of up to 3 miles in some places in the Ypres battles, but the salient had been successfully defended and the enemy's opportunity for a decisive breakthrough had been squandered. In the first three days of the struggle, the Canadians had literally saved the day. With the whole of the British left flank in disarray, the raw battalions had fought and died, choking on the gas, reeling under constant infantry and artillery assault. That they had held as long as they did was magnificent and, in this new kind of war, such courage would be needed again and again. 'The Germans,' wrote Private Albert Roscoe of the 5th Battalion from Saskatchewan, 'thought we Canadians would run because we were not like the English troops, but they found out to their sorrow we did run but the wrong way to their liking ... we mowed them down like a mowing machine mows down hay.'[39] Roscoe and his comrades had done well, and British writer Richard Holmes described their performance as 'an early indication of the quality of Canadian troops.'[40] Similarly, senior officers like Currie, Lipsett, and Mercer had proven themselves. Others, like Turner, Garnet Hughes, and J.A. Currie, had failed the test. Many junior officers and NCOs, too, had shown great courage, while others broke under the strain. The survivors knew who had done well, but there were few enough who survived. The young lieutenant or brave NCO rallying a platoon all too often died in the effort. The casualties numbered more than 6000 in the division, including thirty-nine officers and some 1250 men taken prisoner – a dreadful price for a few days in action.[41]

'Two of our little bunch are gone,' Macfie of the 1st Battalion wrote home on May 7; 'there was six of us that have stuck together ... now there are only four of us, one was killed and the other badly wounded and one of the others scratched a little all by the one shell.'[42] In fact, half of the division's infantry had been killed, wounded, or captured.

At home, the first press reports of the struggle at Ypres did not convey many of the details or spell out the cost of the action, though Canadian heroism featured prominently. 'Then came the first casualty list,' wrote Grace Morris Craig many years later. 'Beneath a banner headline, "Canada Forever and Forever," were the names of the gallant men who had fallen in battle. In Pembroke the long list was posted in the window of the telegraph office on Main Street. People stood in the street to read it. There was silence and deep sorrow.'[43]

With casualties like those at Ypres, more men would be needed, and they were already in the pipeline from factories and farms across Canada to Britain and on to the Continent. The government had authorized a Second Contingent of 20,000 men on October 6, 1914, just after the First had set sail from Quebec City. Before any detailed requirements had been received from the War Office, orders went out from Ottawa to begin the new mobilization. By the time London had responded, fifteen new infantry battalions were well along in the process of creation. This time, at the Prime Minister's insistence, the Gwatkin mobilization plan took over: four battalions were to be recruited in Ontario, one each in the western provinces, one each in Nova Scotia and New Brunswick, and two in Quebec – including the 22nd Battalion, wholly francophone, and raised with a $50,000 contribution from Dr Arthur Mignault, a pharmaceuticals manufacturer.[44] Units organized in their home region and began their training there, reinforcing ties to town and city. Arms and services units similarly took shape across the country.

The Second Contingent, soon to become the Second Canadian Division, effectively had the men it needed before the end of 1914. In April 1915, partially trained, it embarked for England to work up in the Shorncliffe area under the command of the seventy-six-year-old westerner Major-General Sam Steele, whose claims to command had been promoted by the Minister of Public Works, Robert Rogers. Its brigades were the 4th, 5th, and 6th, its battalions numbered (with a few gaps) from the 18th to the 31st. Before long, the War Office objected to Steele on the wholly reasonable grounds of age and lack of battle experience, and Hughes had to give way. Others objected to the officers selected by the Minister. Lieutenant-Colonel J.J. Creelman, a militiaman commanding an artillery brigade, complained that the battalion COs in the Second Division were officers who had been refused captaincies in the First Contingent because they lacked experience.[45] Two of the brigade commanders also had to be replaced, including Brigadier-General J.P. Landry, a French Canadian.[46] The case for his replacement was a good one, but the effect on recruiting in French Canada was not helpful. The Second Canadian Division went to France in September 1915 under the newly promoted Major-General R.E.W. Turner. Its brigadier-generals were David Watson, promoted from commanding the 2nd Battalion in France; H.D.B. Ketchen, who had been named in Canada; and Lord Brooke, a British officer and son of an earl with some experience of the Canadian Militia in 1913 and 1914.

Even before the Second Contingent left Canada, Hughes had begun to authorize colonels to raise battalions for future contingents. John Saywell, a teenager in Broadview, Saskatchewan, noted in his memoirs that his town was a recruiting centre for the 227th Battalion. 'The Colonel was A.B. Gilles, M.P. for Moosomin constituency. He was the least likely candidate for a soldier's life ... Many of his officers were men around town ... some of them were good Conservatives.' Although under age, Saywell soon enlisted, his parents agreeing he could go because his friends were joining up and they knew the officers.[47] Before long, however, the flow of men began to slow and recruiters set out to enlist Americans into an 'American Legion,' despite U.S. neutrality laws and the Governor General's concern that 'American citizens do not always make the best of soldiers.'* Efforts to enlist blacks and Indians ran into predictable problems. Hughes feared that Indians might not receive the 'privileges of civilized warfare,' whatever that might mean,[48] and General Gwatkin fretted that 'the civilized Negroe [sic] is vain and imitative ... the average white man will not associate with him on terms of equality.'[49] Eventually, pressures for men destroyed most such barriers.

In June 1915 the government declared an authorized strength of 150,000 for the Canadian Expeditionary Force, as the units overseas and those in-

---

* Five battalions by mid-1916 were recruiting Americans, but enough men for only one battalion enlisted. The 97th Battalion went overseas in mid-1916, but the authorities broke it up for reinforcements. Ronald Haycock, *Sam Hughes: The Public Career of a Controversial Canadian, 1885–1916* (Waterloo, 1986), 218–20.

tended for service there had come to be called. Borden arbitrarily raised that figure to 250,000 in October and, on New Year's Day 1916, to 500,000. No one knew if Canada's population of 8 million could sustain a CEF of that size. If casualties such as those at Ypres were to be the norm, British calculations suggested that reinforcements of up to 20,000 men a year would be required by each division, and, in Canada, the government was creating new battalions in wholesale. The CGS, General Gwatkin, sensibly warned that 'reserves must be maintained. You cannot put every available man into the firing line at once. Casualties must be replaced. It takes 3,000 to place 1,000 infantrymen in the field and to maintain them there in numbers and efficiency for a year.'[50] Borden had nonetheless made a commitment that soon had the force of holy writ.

After the departure of the Second Division, Britain and Canada had agreed that Canada would dispatch as many men as it could. Divisions would be formed in England out of the battalions and partial battalions that arrived. By June 1915 CEF strength was 100,247; by the end of 1915, 218,000 had enlisted. The first half of 1916 saw recruiting successes as well: 28,185, 26,638, 33,960, 20,200, 14,572, and 10,059 enlisted in the months from January to June,[51] by which time there were 150,000 men overseas out of a total enlistment of 312,000.

With such numbers serving, firm control and clear lines of authority were critical. Unfortunately, they did not exist. The men overseas served at the disposal of the War Office, but they were also Canada's army, paid for and administered by Ottawa. In effect, the senior officer at the head of the First Division and then the Canadian Corps was simultaneously responsible to the British high command and to the Canadian government. Alderson, a British officer unwise to the ways of the Canadian Militia and Sam Hughes, suffered terribly as he tried to satisfy his two masters. But he had no choice other than to accept the instructions from Canada on everything except battle planning; even here, Hughes's insistence on retaining the Ross rifle long after its failure had been documented came very close to impinging on the operational side of the equation. Complicating matters further, Hughes had dispatched his friend Colonel John Carson to England as his special representative to oversee the administrative arrangements for the CEF. Soon calling himself 'Vice-Minister of Militia,' Carson dealt with the War Office as though he had Hughes's blessing over everything, including promotions and appointments. Unfortunately for Carson, Hughes still insisted on approving all decisions himself. Command of the troop training in England was similarly confused, as some commanders resisted the authority of Brigadier-General J.C. MacDougall as GOC troops in England. By the end of 1915, with chaos reigning among the Canadians in Britain, something had to be done.

As this farce played out in Ottawa and London, it was suddenly becoming harder at home to persuade men to enlist. English Canadians universally pointed the finger at French Canada, which, despite the 22nd Battalion, was undoubtedly underrepresented in the ranks. The Vingt-deux proved to be the first and the only wholly francophone battalion in the Canadian Corps, and, although other battalions raised in Quebec made it to England, none went to France. Most, but not all, of the francophones enlisted went to the 22nd as reinforcements.

There were many reasons for this reluctance. The failure for years before the war to foster the Militia in Quebec was one explanation, but there were others as well. There was widespread political resentment at the Borden government's policies in the province; Ontario's 'make-them-learn-English-in-school' Regulation 17 was a sore point with francophones everywhere; *nationaliste* leader Henri Bourassa quickly lost his initial enthusiasm for the war; and, while the church hierarchy professed support for the war effort, the parish priests were lukewarm at best. Moreover, Québécois married earlier, had larger families needing support, and, because of poverty, bad food, and too much sugar in their diet, they were thought more likely to be physically unfit than their English-speaking compatriots. Most important, public pressure in French-speaking Quebec was *not* to enlist.[52]

Fingers pointed elsewhere in Canada too. The Maritimes had been slow to send men, rural Ontario was lagging, and only westerners and the large cities seemed enthusiastic. Men enlisted for many reasons, and imperial patriotism and a sense of duty were but two. Of those who joined up, some sought adventure or a free trip home to Britain; others wanted to escape family obligations, debts, unemployment, or a boring job. What was most striking, however, was the point the First Contingent had already demonstrated: the British-born were disproportionately eager to volunteer to fight for King and Empire. The number of years in Canada was a decisive variable, with those here longest – the Québécois and the Maritimers – proving most reluctant to serve. The 1911 census had shown that there were 804,000 British-born in the Canadian population of 7.2 million, some of whom were too young or too old for military service. Over the entire war, the CEF recruited 619,636 men, of whom 228,174 were immigrants from the United Kingdom, while only 318,705 were born in Canada. The disparity in the percentage of men enlisting was extraordinary, with just 51 per cent of the entire CEF born in Canada – and this figure was swollen by conscripts in 1918.[53]

There are, unfortunately, no clear or accurate data on the total of French-speaking enlistments. Quebec made up 27 per cent of the population, but provided only 14.2 per cent of CEF enlistments, the lion's share undoubtedly coming from the province's English-speaking minority. On June 25, 1917, Parliament was told that, in the spring of that year, the CEF had 14,100 French Canadians, 8200 of whom were from Quebec. After conscription came into force, the usual guesstimate, almost certainly too generous, is that 50,000 francophones served during the war, a number that would include volunteers and conscripts, Québécois, Acadians, Franco-Ontarians, and French-speaking westerners. There was much history to be overcome and there were undoubtedly errors in the management of Quebec recruiting, but, however apologists then and later massaged the data, francophones had not given their 'share' to the war.[54]

The pressures in English Canada for a greater effort mounted as 1915 turned into 1916. Clergymen asked their male congregants why they were not in khaki, now 'a sacred colour,' and provided names of men who should enlist to the Methodist Church's Army and Navy Board, a recruiting organization. The newspapers and opposition politicians pointed to the higher numbers in percentage terms that had enlisted in Britain and France or in Australia and New Zealand. In English Canada fit men were sometimes harassed on the street by women who pinned white feathers on their lapels.[55] Hughes responded to the political heat by authorizing yet more colonels to recruit units. In all, 265 battalions received authorization to recruit, and 179 of them were raised by private individuals, usually local notables.[56] Naturally, some were more successful than others, but virtually every one of these battalions had a full complement of officers and NCOs, all jealous of their ranks and positions. Moreover, Hughes had guaranteed that these officers could keep their ranks, and none were obliged to revert when they went overseas.[57] When the battalions, or more likely part-battalions, proceeded to England, they trained there in depot battalions and later as reserve battalions, of which there were twenty-three. These battalions grouped up to 2000 men from a geographic area (Central Ontario, British Columbia, Quebec) and provided reinforcements to Canadian Corps battalions. The 10th Reserve Battalion, for example, took men originally from the 41st, 57th, 69th, 150th, 163rd, 178th, 189th, and 258th battalions, all raised in Quebec, and reinforced the 22nd Battalion. In March 1917 the system was further refined on a territorial basis. The nominal 'Alberta Regiment,' for instance, recruited in Military District No. 13 in Alberta, trained there in the 1st Depot Battalion of the Alberta Regiment, trained in England in the 21st Reserve Battalion, and provided reinforcements to the 10th, 31st, 49th, and 50th battalions, all originally formed from Alberta, in France.[58]

Wherever they trained, officers and men underwent a rather simplistic initiation. By 1917 the fourteen-week course included drill, map-reading, rifle and bayonet practice, bomb throwing, sanitation, gas warfare, and section and platoon tactics. Officers, mainly provided by Canadian Officers Training Corps at the country's universities, went to the Canadian Training School for Officers and the School for Infantry Officers, if that was their corps.[59] Although this training was vastly superior to that given to officers of the First Division, the majors, lieutenant-colonels, and senior NCOs in the battalions sent to Britain by Hughes were no better trained than their men and were nearly all without battle experience. They were almost never allowed to go to France in the existing ranks they brought with them from Canada. The battalions fighting in France wanted reinforcement lieutenants and privates, not unit or company commanders who knew nothing of the front.

Hughes's system of sending whole or part battalions to England predictably created a great deal of bitterness. Harold Becker, an NCO in the 91st Battalion in July 1916, described how it felt in his memoirs: 'We had learned that the possibility of our going to France intact was remote ... It appeared that the C.O. with the most pull with old Sir Sam Hughes had the best chance to keep his command and as our C.O., Col. Green, was never given to cringing and kow-towing to the war time brass hats, he, of course, was not one of the favored ones.'[60] The favouritism was certainly there, but Becker was simply unaware of the resistance from the corps in France to taking green officers.

The result, after the creation of reserve battalions, was that the privates went to the front in composite units in the new divisions or as reinforcements for battalions already there, while the lieutenant-colonels, majors, and company sergeant-majors often piled up in England, complaining to their MPs or to Hughes, drawing their pay, and feeling much too embarrassed to tell the folks at home what had happened to them. The mess, for mess it was, was another of Sam Hughes's many gifts to Canada.[61]

In August 1916 Borden seized control of recruiting from the Militia Minister. He insisted that a Director General of Recruiting be installed at Militia headquarters, with directors in each Militia District. The Director General, Montreal businessman Sir Thomas Tait (who soon altered his title to Director General of National Service), was told to secure the maximum number of men for the army, but with due regard for Canada's industrial and agricultural requirements. At last there was some realization that a skilled die-maker might be of more use in a munitions factory than in France, or a wheat farmer more productive on his fields than in Flanders. By September, National Service had escaped the Militia Department and now was run wholly by civilians. By October, Tait had been replaced by Calgary Tory MP Richard Bedford Bennett, and the National Service Board began to prepare for a registration of men – the first effort to determine how many fit men Canada had left. The registration, stupidly made voluntary and therefore much less worthwhile than it could have been, did not commence until January 1917.

If the government was finally becoming serious about systematizing recruiting, one major task remained to be tackled before Canada's military effort could begin to approach efficiency. Sam Hughes had to go. The break between Prime Minister and Minister took a long time to occur and, when it finally did, it was because of Hughes's unweening ambition and his inability to organize matters rationally.

In March 1916, during one of his visits to Britain, Hughes had created a council to sort out the chaotic administration of the Canadians abroad. Simultaneously in Ottawa, Prime Minister Borden had begun to draft his own plan. After persuading Borden to give his organization a chance, Hughes watched his council fall apart in squabbling over responsibilities. By September 1916 Hughes had created the Acting Sub-Militia Council for Overseas Canadians, with John Carson, now a Major-General, as its head, in open defiance of Borden's demand that an order-in-council creating this body be approved first. In response, Borden established a Ministry of the Overseas Military Forces of Canada and selected Sir George Perley, the Canadian High Commissioner in London, as the Cabinet Minister responsible. In effect, just as Borden had taken control of recruiting from Hughes, he now overrode Hughes's control in Britain. These farcical but very serious events provoked the final break between a patient, frustrated Borden and his Militia Minister. Outraged, Hughes denounced Borden in his usual intemperate language, and Borden then demanded Hughes's resignation. On November 11, 1916, Hughes was gone, as his resignation letter put it, with 'much satisfaction.'[62] At Canadian Corps headquarters and in the field, the officers cheered. 'The Mad Mullah of Canada has been deposed,' wrote Lieutenant-Colonel J.J. Creelman. 'The Canadian Baron Munchausen will be to less effect ... The greatest soldier since Napoleon has gone to his gassy Elbe, and the greatest block to the successful termination of the war has been removed. Joy. Oh Joy!'[63]

Hughes had confounded the war effort from August 1914. He had raised the First Contingent with speed, but in conditions of chaos. He had put his friends in positions of authority over war contracts, but scandals were the only real product. He had installed cronies in London to interfere with the CEF's operations in Britain and France, but almost always with damaging effect. He had refused to recognize the failings of the Ross rifle, though they were apparent to every soldier in France. And he had simply been unable to grasp that locally based recruiting could not conjure up full-strength battalions at will. Hughes's replacement was Sir Edward Kemp, a Toronto industrialist who, while no organizational or political genius, had the virtue of being sane. Hughes, however, remained in the House of Commons, perpetually defending his record and denouncing his legions of enemies.

Meanwhile, the war continued to swallow regiments in France and in Flanders. The First Canadian Division had to be rebuilt after its exertions at Ypres, and men of the 4th Brigade, which had been disbanded in January 1915, along with three battalions from Canada, provided the necessary reinforcements. New men needed time to be integrated into their platoons, while new junior officers had to be taught their duties by their NCOs. Two weeks after the conclusion of their first battle – far too little time to absorb the new men – the Canadians were deemed ready to return to the fighting in Artois, south of the Ypres salient, where the British and the French had launched a major offensive.

The initial attacks on May 9, 1915, had foundered, so strong were the German defences. Barbed wire was arrayed in belts at least 50 feet deep; soon key German positions would be protected by up to ten belts, creating all but impassable obstacles for soldiers with flimsy wireclippers that could cut British wire, but not the thicker and stronger German product. The machine guns covered the wire with fire, creating pre-planned killing zones. The German trenches were almost always deeper, more solidly constructed, mutually supporting, and arranged in two or three lines to achieve defence in depth. After the first day's heavy losses, the First British Army's commander, General Sir Douglas Haig, now decided that heavy artillery preparation was essential before an attack. The Canadian Division, scheduled to participate in the assault at Festubert along with British and Indian troops, fired one hundred thousand rounds over two-and-a-half days from an artillery concentration of 433 guns. Those numbers would be dwarfed as the war went on, but in May 1915 they were huge. The impact, however, was less than it might have been. The gunners were not yet very accurate, the high explosive shells for the 18-pounder were too light to destroy enemy positions or to cut the barbed wire, and shrapnel was effective only against exposed troops.[64]

Turner's 3rd Brigade, attached to the British I Corps, went into action on May 18 after successful attacks two days before had pushed the Germans back 3000 yards. The 14th Battalion went over the top in the late afternoon and was cut to pieces by machine-gun and artillery fire after a gain of 400 yards. The troops dug in, soon joined on their right by Currie's brigade. On May 20 the two brigades attacked once more. The 3rd advanced in full daylight into a hail of machine-gun fire and made some progress. The 2nd Brigade attack, its artillery support reduced, made it to the enemy's communication trench, then stalled. The next day, Currie, following orders despite the failure of his efforts to postpone the attack to permit further reconnaissance and preparation, attacked once more in daylight, made some progress, and then had to pull his men back under heavy artillery fire. The German artillery was more accurate than the British and the Canadian, and it caused losses wherever it fell, breaking up attacks and supporting counterattacks. The enemy machine guns, mortars, and grenades were also more effective. This German superiority put the attackers at a serious disadvantage, greater than the threat that faced any troops who attacked strongly defended, well-wired positions. It was also true that the Germans were far better trained and much better led than the Canadians at this stage of the war. Courage would have to carry the day, if courage alone could do it.

Nonetheless, the orders came to attack again, and Currie's weary battalions leapt off at 2:30 a.m. on May 24 and took their objective, a German redoubt known as K5. The division's efforts had advanced the line some 600 yards on a mile-long front, but at a cost of almost 2500 casualties. Elements of the Canadian Cavalry Brigade, 1500 officers and men who had volunteered to serve as infantry and one squadron of which had received only a single day's training in the trenches, then threw themselves at the Germans on May 25. Using gas bombs (the first time they were employed), the Canadians reported making headway. Regrettably, their maps proved unreliable, an all too common failing, and they missed their objective.

The Canadian Division had a respite of a few weeks to bind up its wounds and make good its losses. The high command grappled with the task of defending the armies against the Germans' new poison-gas weapon, and makeshift gas masks, bulky devices that restricted vision and reduced men's ability to fight, began to be distributed. Officers and men received training in anti-gas techniques, but the masks themselves were claustrophobic and frightening, heightening the psychological effect of the gas weapon. Still, training was the key to overcoming terror *and* gas. The men listened and learned, but with the division based in the area of Givenchy, a place where the trenches were blessedly dry and the countryside still intact, it all seemed a bit unreal. After the shattered horror of Ypres, few could contemplate a return to such conditions of warfare.

The idyll came to an end when orders were received for the division's 1st Brigade to attack the German positions on June 15. For once, there was time to prepare. The artillery intended to cut the enemy's wire defences – and it succeeded. It aimed to destroy the enemy's forward machine guns, and Brigadier-General H.E. Burstall, commanding the Canadian Division's artillery, had three 18-pounders brought into the front lines to blast the enemy positions. Two of the 18-pounders destroyed three machine guns, but were, in turn, neutralized by enemy artillery; the third was so badly sited that it could not be fired without hitting the Canadian troops forming up for the attack. The 1st Battalion, the 1st Brigade unit selected for the attack, ran into difficulty when a 3000-lb mine blew up part of the enemy position and some of the Canadian attackers. The battalion made some gains, but had to fall back when the German counterattack hit it. Casualties were heavy, including twenty officers. Fresh men went forward to reinforce defeat – always a bad practice – and they, too, suffered heavily.

After two months of action, the Canadian Division scarcely resembled the contingent that had assembled at Valcartier. The division's infantry of 11,000 had suffered 9413 casualties. Most of the wounded might return after weeks or months of recovery, but the battalions had to reform around the few survivors. Fortunately, Givenchy was the last major action for the division for many months, a period that allowed for the Second Canadian Division to arrive in France in September 1915 and for the Canadian Corps to be established. Alderson became GOC of the corps, Turner got the Second Division, and the First went to the newly promoted Major-General Arthur Currie.* Currie's 2nd Brigade went to Louis Lipsett, formerly CO of the 8th Battalion. Mercer, of the 1st Brigade, was promoted to command the corps troops, and Garnet Hughes, hitherto the GSO 1 (senior staff officer) to Turner, took over his brigade. Politics had played a major role in these appointments. Mercer and Currie received their promotions on merit. Even if he was not completely beloved by the Minister, Turner had not. And almost everyone viewed Garnet Hughes's promotion to Brigadier-General as politically inspired.

At the same time, the expanded ranks of the corps demanded more senior staff officers than could be supplied by Canadians, very few of whom had attended the British Army Staff College. Despite Sam Hughes's best efforts, British officers took the key staff appointments at corps headquarters and in the divisions. It took time to make staff officers and, for example, the role of Brigadier-General General Staff, in effect the corps' chief operations officer, could only be filled by an officer of great experience and training – something

---

* Roy Macfie of the 1st Battalion wrote that Currie had visited his unit. The new GOC 'seems to be a fine fellow, he walked down the horse lines, and asked a lot of us where we came from, and what we used to work at. You wouldn't catch the English generals talking to men like that.' Unfortunately, most men of the CEF found the new GOC aloof and cold. Macfie, *Letters Home*, 59.

no Canadian had as yet. As E.L.M. Burns, a signals officer in the 4th Division, later wrote in his memoirs, 'this resembled the Prussian system, under which a senior but somewhat obsolescent general would nominally command a formation, but the real control would reside in a younger member of the Great General Staff.'[65] This hierarchical approach may have been the case in the Fourth Division, where the GSO I was Lieutenant-Colonel Edmund Ironside, later a Chief of the Imperial General Staff and a Field Marshal, but it most certainly was not true in the First Division when Currie commanded it. Currie made no bones about relying heavily on his British staff officers and he fought to keep them; nonetheless, he commanded.

Over the winter of 1915–16, while the war in France continued in its stalemated way and Allied initiatives elsewhere, as in the Dardanelles, ran into terrible difficulties, the Canadian Corps took its turns in the line. It became expert in trench raids, an invention of the PPCLI, which had launched the first such attack at the end of February 1915.[66] Trench raids aimed to keep the enemy on edge, to take prisoners, and to force reinforcements to be brought forward – so artillery could pound them. Ordinarily, they were platoon or company sized, often they were formed from well-rehearsed and trained volunteers, and sometimes they worked. Wire-cutters, bombers, and riflemen all operated in a choreographed pattern, if everything went according to plan. The first large raid by the 2nd Brigade occurred on November 17; one element went nowhere, but another caught the Germans by surprise, inflicted thirty casualties, and returned to the Canadian lines with a dozen prisoners. The hastily summoned enemy reinforcements were duly plastered by artillery fire, likely causing more casualties.[67] The Canadians wanted to dominate No Man's Land, the area between the opposing sides' front-line trenches, and they could often do so. But trench raids provoked heavier artillery attacks by the Germans, and this response increased casualties. Some soldiers doubtless preferred a live-and-let-live philosophy to prevail, but this was not the attitude of the corps or division headquarters.

Meanwhile, the troops tried to survive winter in the line. It was cold, wet, and miserable, much like Salisbury Plain except that enemy gunfire and sniping inflicted a slow, steady drain of casualties. In the first three months of 1916, battle casualties numbered 546 killed, 1543 wounded, 3 gassed, and 1 prisoner of war. There were also 667 non-battle injuries, including 20 fatalities.[68]

Staying healthy was always a problem. Macfie wrote home: 'We are having a fierce time of it now with mud and rain, mud everywhere, in our hut and even the blankets are muddy, it just takes a fellow up to about the boot tops all around our lines.'[69] The trenches filled with water, and there never seemed to be enough rubber boots to go around. Trench foot was a perpetual threat, so much so that officers had to conduct daily foot inspections. Trench fever was a constant peril, and fit young men developed rheumatism. Illness took more soldiers out of the line than battle casualties, primarily because warmth was impossible to achieve under a sodden greatcoat, and only rarely could fires large enough to provide any warmth be lit in the front lines. Even the blessed rum ration provided only a brief once-a-day fillip – and upset temperance organizations in Canada and a few teetotalling commanders at the front.[70] In the line, food was usually cooked by small groups of soldiers over alcohol burners. It was then eaten from the pot or slopped into mess tins, often cold when the last man got his share. The daily rations were heavy on meat (tinned 'meat and veg'), bread, rock-hard army biscuits, and tasteless plum and apple jam – all from British sources and disliked intensely by the Canadians. Strong tea was consumed in quantity, but the men missed good drinking water, which was often unavailable or so purified with chlorine as to be vile-tasting. Still, many soldiers took it as a matter of pride to live as well as they could.

The trenches, if the ground was firm and the water table low, ordinarily allowed a man to walk upright without being seen; ideally, they were wide enough that two or three men or a stretcher party could pass. Traverses broke up the straight trench line to prevent enemy soldiers from taking a few yards of trench and killing all the defenders by firing to their right and left. Sandbags protected the front (parapet) and rear (parados) of the trench, and, in good units, corrugated iron or wood made up revetments to keep the walls from collapsing under fire or rain. Firing steps in bays let soldiers shoot at the enemy, while roofed dugouts provided the crudest of living space. Officers might have a roomy dugout that provided real shelter, and sometimes they even had cots and furniture. Barbed wire lined the front of the forward trench line, and, as the war went on, the belt got thicker. Behind the front trench were the support and reserve lines, all connected by communications trenches. It was another world, where artillery shelling and sniper fire, mixed with night-time patrols, work parties to repair the wire or deepen the trenches, and stand-tos at first and last light, made up the routine.

Men lived for the end of their stints in the line, which ordinarily lasted about one week in four, although in late 1915 it was closer to one week in two. When they went to the rear areas they could sleep on straw palliasses under a roof, usually a leaky one, and get food that was freshly prepared by the Company Quartermaster Sergeant's 'cook.' Bad as this was, it was better than slop cooked over an alcohol burner in the trenches. Out of the line, they still formed labour parties for repairing the barbed wire or digging trenches, while training, drill, the cleaning of weapons and uniforms, and 'make and mend' days to put the kit into proper shape occupied the rest of their time.

Out of the line, men had the chance to attend religious services or take communion from the unit's padre, to get an issue of fresh clothing (welcome relief from the ever-present lice), and to enjoy a shower or a bath. Ordinarily, men could get something to eat and a hot drink, or could write a letter while sitting at a table and without constant preaching from the YMCA or Salvation Army canteens behind the lines. There was the probability of cheap wine or weak beer in an *estaminet* and possibly sex from a civilian, if a soldier was very lucky, or from a prostitute, perhaps in a brothel. Venereal disease could be the result, and often was. British troops had a VD rate in 1916 of 36.7 per thousand; for whatever reason, the Canadians' rate was an incredible 209.4 per thousand,[71] a military disaster, as the only partially effective and always painful treatment with Salvarsan kept men out of the line. Twelve per cent of all illnesses among the men of the CEF were from sexually transmitted diseases, which were treated by the army as a self-inflicted wound. This classification could influence postwar pensions and result in 1919 in delayed repatriation. The more conscientious soldiers probably resorted to masturbation or swabbed on the potassium permanganate that was supposed to stop transmission of disease via intercourse.*

---

* Suggestions that London prostitutes would infect reluctant soldiers with VD for a fee were possibly true. 'Men on leave ... deliberately consorted with promising women. This practice was hard to check,' the Medical Corps' official history dryly observed, 'as venereal disease is the least difficult of all self-inflicted wounds to inflict.' (Sir A. Macphail, *Official History of the Canadian Forces in the Great War: The Medical Services* [Ottawa, 1925], 279.) Self-inflicted or not, deliberate or not, VD probably saved the lives of thousands of soldiers by keeping them out of the trenches.

Time out of the line also let soldiers open up parcels from home. The cakes, cookies, cigarettes, tinned salmon, canned fruit, chocolates, candles, extra socks, and reading material they contained were all, like the letters, essential for morale. Captain Georges Vanier with the 22nd Battalion noted in one letter that his most recent parcels contained candy, cake, sardines, chicken, ham, tongue, milk, tobacco, and newspapers.[72] Parcels were always shared with brother officers or the soldiers' mates. Whatever they received from home, men worried all the time about the faithfulness of their wives and their children's health, fretted about aged parents, and hoped for leave – something that officers received four times a year, compared with the one that was allotted to other ranks. Men worried about being killed, naturally enough, but many hoped to get a wound – nothing too serious, please – that might require their transfer to hospital in England or even back to Canada. War on the Western Front was never a picnic, but in the cold and dark of winter, it was especially bleak.[73]

Winter also offered time to ruminate on the unfairness of wartime life. Why was it always hurry up and wait? Why were we here and not there? Why in the infantry and not in some safe billet in the Ordnance Corps or, better yet, on staff of a training depot well to the rear or in England? Why did the bloody staff officers have it so good in posh chateaux? Why did the people at home not understand? But then, how could they, since the war was all but beyond comprehension to those fighting it? Still, those doing the fighting knew that when, or if, they got home they could say they had had a 'good' war. Those men who stayed out of the army or those who wore a uniform, but had a safe post in Canada or Britain, would be marked for life as 'slackers.' More than sixty years after the war, an aged Toronto society matron remarked that Vincent Massey, the Canadian anglophile *par excellence* who served as a Lieutenant-Colonel only in Canada, did 'not have a good war.'[74] There were long memories about who did – and did not – do what. Sometimes this categorization was utterly unfair. The government kept men in Canada for home defence, and the coastal defence batteries on the East Coast had to be manned. The staff in Ottawa and across the country had to exist if the training and dispatch of men overseas was to proceed. But for those in the trenches, these distinctions were too fine. It was us and them, and it always would be.

In March 1916 the Canadian Corps returned to action at St Eloi, north of Messines and south of Ypres. With the French struggling to hold on at Verdun, a battle that the Germans hoped might bleed France white, everything that could be done to create a diversion of German resources could only help – or so the British high command believed. The battlefield at St Eloi was a struggle between sappers digging shafts and planting huge mines under each others' lines. Sophisticated techniques of mining and counter-mining developed, silence was the rule to defeat listening devices, and the commanders coordinated attack plans to coincide with the detonations that could wipe out whole sections of trench lines and their occupants. An officer with the 1st Canadian Tunneling Company noted: 'It is very ticklish working under ground as quickly as possible and wondering where the Huns are. You hear sounds and try to locate them. Every noise in the gallery seems like a cannon going off there.'[75] At St Eloi, six mines were placed to all but eliminate a 600-yard stretch of the German defences. The British plan called for the British Third Division to make the assault on March 27, with the Second Canadian Division taking over as soon as it took the objectives.

The mine detonations blew away two companies of enemy front-line troops, and the British assault went forward with substantial gains. But the explosions had so altered the landscape that some troops failed to recognize their objectives and seized the wrong ground. The Germans, as always, clung tenaciously to what they still held, reinforced their units, and wore down the British troops with counterattacks and artillery bombardments. The Canadian Corps moved into the line on the night of April 3–4, but Turner's Second Division found only dead bodies and smashed trenches, no workable communications trenches, and an impassable obstacle between the front and rear created by the huge craters left by the mine explosions – all of which made bringing supplies forward and the wounded back extremely difficult.[76] Efforts to strengthen the line stopped when a heavy German bombardment fell on the 27th Battalion of Brigadier-General Ketchen's 6th Brigade, causing very high numbers of casualties. On the night of April 5–6 the much-depleted battalion had to be relieved, which was itself a wearing process, given the condition of the ground. The changeover was still in process when a strong German attack caught the Canadians at the worst possible time. The Germans took back two of the craters that had once been their front line and soon had two more. The Second Division sent men forward to retake the position, but, confused, they went to craters further to the north. The men, believing they were where they were supposed to be, reported that 'fact' to brigade headquarters, and confusion reigned supreme. Bad weather made air reconnaissance impossible, so the error went unreported and uncorrected. Communications simply broke down.

For the next ten days the Canadians struggled in the morass, absorbing casualties and trying to construct a viable trench line in the mud. Not until April 16, incredibly, did headquarters realize which craters the Germans held, and preparations for further attacks finally came to an end. The Second Canadian Division lost 1373 men in this aborted operation, its first major battle. The Germans reported far fewer casualties.

Recriminations soon flew. The soldiers' view was simple enough and accurate: 'There was not much display of generalship,' wrote Private Donald Fraser in his journal. ' ... What attacks were engineered on our side were on a ridiculously small scale ... the opposing artillery held us, [but] ours could not restrain them from attacking ... casualties would have been saved by withdrawing, but the command only realized this several days later when the whole line was lost.'[77] The 27th Battalion's CO, fifty-two-year-old Lieutenant-Colonel Irvine Snider, a veteran of the North-West Rebellion and South Africa, had to be relieved because of 'nervous exhaustion.' Snider's medical file noted that he had 'no sleep for 6 days and nights and naturally felt the loss of his men personally. On retiring to billets felt naturally depressed and fatigued – but it was only when he saw his bed that he went all to pieces and broke down and cried.' There is genuine poignancy in that medical case history, and Snider is owed our understanding. He continued to serve in Britain, passing on the lessons he had learned to reinforcements.[78]

Brigadier-General Ketchen, his head properly sought by Alderson, the Army Commander, and the British GOC-in-Chief, General Sir Douglas Haig, was saved only by General Turner's flat refusal to dump him. Alderson then asked for Turner's recall, again quite rightly, but Haig, fearful that the touchy Canadians were becoming anti-English, declined to support his corps commander. 'My reasons,' Haig wrote, 'are that the conditions were abnormally difficult, under such conditions mistakes are to be expected, but that all did their best and made a gallant fight.'[79] Someone had to pay, however, and since Canadian senior officers apparently could not be bounced, Alderson got the chop instead. In May he went to England to become Inspector General of Canadian Forces there. Many believed the cause of his removal was Sam Hughes's resentment at Alderson's detestation of the Ross rifle. This rumour was untrue, though Hughes certainly had come to dislike Alderson. To replace him, Kitchener selected the fifty-three-year-old Lieutenant-General Sir Julian Byng, a very competent officer with service in France and the Dardanelles. Byng was not amused: 'Why am I sent to the Canadians? I don't know a Canadian. Why this stunt?'[80] Known as 'Bungo' to his friends, Byng was a cavalry officer with all the right connections. He ought to have been an archetypal Colonel Blimp figure, but Byng defied the stereotypes.

Before the Canadian Corps returned to action again, the Third Division, now commanded by Major-General M.S. Mercer, joined its ranks. Leading Mercer's 7th Brigade was Brigadier-General A.C. Macdonnell, the already legendary 'Batty Mac.'[81] His battalions consisted of the Princess Pats, repatriated from their service with a British division; the PF's Royal Canadian Regiment, which had arrived in France from its Bermuda exile and trained with the 2nd Brigade; and the 42nd and 49th battalions, from Montreal and Edmonton, respectively. The 8th Brigade's commander was Victor Williams, hitherto the Adjutant-General; his battalions were six Canadian Mounted Rifles units made up of men who could ride and shoot, but had been converted into four infantry battalions as the 1st, 2nd, 4th, and 5th CMRs. The 9th Brigade, commanded by Brigadier-General F.W. Hill, consisted of the 43rd, 52nd, 58th, and 60th battalions from Winnipeg, the Lakehead, the Niagara peninsula, and Montreal, respectively. The Third Division was in the line when the Canadian Corps fought its next major battle at Mount Sorrel in the first two weeks of June 1916.[82]

The Mount Sorrel battlefield was at the easternmost point of the Ypres salient's projection into the German lines, and it was the only portion of the Ypres ridge that remained in Allied hands. This position, which allowed the Canadians to see over the enemy's positions, was a constant irritant, and the Germans prepared a major push to take the high ground, force the Canadians back, and possibly push the British out of the salient. Canadian patrols had detected German activity, but there was no expectation of an immediate attack.

On the morning of June 2, Generals Mercer and Williams of the Third

Canadian Division were in the front lines held by the 4th Canadian Mounted Rifles. A huge artillery barrage fell on the 7th and 8th brigades, a barrage that, by every report, dwarfed anything previously seen on the Western Front. A German observer wrote: 'The whole enemy position was a cloud of dust and dirt, into which timber, tree trunks, weapons and equipment were continuously hurled up, and occasionally human bodies.' The 4th CMRs suffered an incredible 89 per cent casualties in this stunning blow; Mercer was wounded and subsequently killed, and his body was not recovered for two weeks. The advancing German troops found Williams, badly wounded, and took him prisoner, along with a few hundred shaken survivors.[83]

At the critical moment of the initial assault on their positions, the Third Division had lost its GOC and one of its brigade commanders. The Germans also exploded mines just short of the Canadian positions on Mount Sorrel, and they advanced with six battalions up front and an additional eleven at the ready. The Germans simply walked over the remnants of the 1st and 4th CMRs, using flamethrowers to wipe out any resistance that remained. The 8th Brigade's strength was reduced to some 700 all ranks. The PPCLI on the left lost one company in the initial crushing assault, but the remainder gave ground grudgingly, delaying the attack, but at the terrible cost of four hundred killed and wounded, including the CO; the second-in-command, Major Hamilton Gault, the regiment's founder, lost a leg above the knee.

'It is very hard to be cheerful,' wrote Major Agar Adamson, acting CO of the PPCLI, 'but the men must not be depressed.'[84] The men were depressed, of course, but most were already fatalistic about their chances of survival, though some relied on superstition – a lucky coin, different routes through the trenches, resisting every impulse to volunteer – to keep them alive a little longer. Most of their letters home left out the horror, likely because few soldiers had the words to express what they saw and experienced. Censors within their battalion and higher formations made sure no useful information reached Canada, and the press censors at home ensured that the newspapers carried little analysis or criticism of battlefield operations.[85] Ultimately, the men were alone in their thousands, alone in their terror. A few apparently felt no fear and came to like killing, feeling a fierce joy in slaughtering the Hun.[86] Most, however, clung to their friends in their platoon, joining in group raillery and trying hard not to let down their mates. That was the worst sin.

To show fear was normal; to 'funk,' to be a coward and expose your friends to greater danger by doing so, was not. Still, some soldiers recognized that all men had a breaking point, that there was a spot where the mind simply cracked under the strain of war, shelling, death, and fear. After soldiers had watched their friends being blown to pieces, a grasp on sanity was hard to maintain.[87]* Eight battalion commanders in the Canadian Corps had to be relieved because of shell shock, and another eleven lost their commands for physical breakdowns, very often with a stress component included. In all, 177 battalion commanders served more than a month in the line, long enough to make their mark, so those relieved amounted to just over 10 per cent.[88]

Most soldiers, like the high command, were not very understanding of those who cracked.† The British novelist Pat Barker, who has written most perceptively on shell shock, has one of her characters remember that 'they didn't seem to talk about [shell shock] in those days. You just had to shut up and get on with it. You know, you were alive, you had the same number of arms and legs you set off [with] so what the bloody hell were you moaning on about? ... You just had to snap back.'[89] Discipline had to be maintained at all costs, the generals believed, and men who may have served well and bravely, but had reached their limit of endurance, could be sent to brutal military prisons or even executed for cowardice or other military crimes. The ten-man firing party for executions usually came from the condemned man's unit 'pour encourager les autres.'[90] The first of the twenty-five Canadian soldiers to be executed in the Great War, Private Fortunat Auger of the 22nd Battalion, died on March 26, 1916. His battalion commander, Lieutenant-Colonel Thomas Tremblay, then paraded all his men before the corpse and told them that this was the fate of anyone found guilty of desertion.[91]

Fear of officers and NCOs, fear of punishment, kept men going when they might well have run away. But such fear could not make men fight well. Com-

---

* It is worth noting that both Lester Pearson and John Diefenbaker, Canada's only two prime ministers who had been veterans, had 'neurasthenic' episodes that kept them out of action and likely saved their lives. Pearson broke down while in flight training; Diefenbaker in training as an infantry officer in Britain. See J.L. Granatstein, 'Pearson and Diefenbaker: Similar Men?' in N. Hillmer, ed., *Pearson: The Unlikely Gladiator* (Montreal, 1999), 51ff.

† Curiously, as early as 1915–16, the federal and Ontario governments reached an agreement to use a hospital under construction at Cobourg, Ontario, 'for the treatment of mental and shock cases among returned soldiers ... The need for special facilities ... has imposed an unforeseen burden on the medical branch of the military organization of Canada.' *Canada Lancet* 49 (1915–16): 526–7.

radeship, pride in platoon, company, battalion, division, corps, country, and empire did that. So too did the slowly developing sense that many officers knew what they were doing, that not all generals wasted lives in vainglorious attacks. For the Canadians, for the British, that belief in the competence of commanders took a long time to develop, just as the competence itself had to be learned. What men hated were the privileges officers had, the additional leaves, the liquor rations, the furnished dugouts in the line. If the officer was competent and did not squander lives, these 'perks' might be forgiven. If the officer was a fool, either too brave or too cowardly, he jeopardized men's lives needlessly and could never be forgiven. As the war continued, the Canadian Corps began to promote from the ranks (which, by taking away experienced NCOs, tended to weaken leadership at the platoon level).[92] Sometimes such promotions eased tensions, but the gulf between the commissioned and the other ranks was always wide, and some soldiers complained that those rankers never learned how to be officers. Still, soldiers always complain about something, and their complaints should not be treated as gospel.

The Germans dug in after a gain of 600–700 yards at Mount Sorrel, though they could have gone much further. Canadian counterattacks went in at 2 a.m. on June 3 or, at least, they were supposed to. Mix-ups led to four battalions, three from the First Division and one from the Third, attacking in turn, rather than together, and in full daylight, rather than under cover of darkness. The Germans beat the attacks back with heavy losses, and Edmonton's 49th Battalion was all but destroyed, losing 358 men in minutes. Byng must have realized that his new command was not yet a wholly efficient and smoothly operating machine.

The British now gave Byng and Brigadier-General Burstall, commanding the Canadian Corps artillery, all the guns that could be concentrated to support the Canadian Corps. Heavy artillery pounded the German lines, but the Canadians had to delay their counterattack when air reconnaissance could not be carried out because of bad weather. At this juncture on June 6, the Germans attacked once more, again preceding the assault with the explosion of mines under the trenches of the 6th Brigade at Hooge. They hit the 28th Battalion hard and, though the Germans failed to make a major penetration because the rest of the brigade rallied, they now controlled the shattered remains of Hooge. As a Canadian Nursing Sister gloomily noted in her diary on June 8, 'It is easier to die at present than to live under conditions at the front.'[93]

Byng issued orders for the Canadians to prepare to counterattack not at Hooge but at Mount Sorrel. Currie's First Division got the job, its strongest remaining units grouped into two composite brigades The assault in the early hours of June 13 followed an intensive artillery preparation and thick smoke screen, a bombardment so carefully planned that it simultaneously pummelled and surprised the Germans. This success was an indication of the corps' increasing capabilities. So, too, was the way the Canadians followed the barrage closely and caught some Germans in their dugouts. In one hour, in the first attack in strength the Canadians had made in the war, Currie's men had pushed the Germans back to their starting point. Burstall's artillery broke up two German counterattacks on June 14. The Third Canadian Division had undergone a rough initiation in battle, but the seasoned veterans of the First restored the situation, though not before the corps had sustained almost 8500 casualties in the wasteful Mount Sorrel operations. With his careful planning and professional preparation so evident in the attack on June 13, General Byng had begun the process of turning the Canadian Corps into 'Byng's Boys.' The staff, the artillery, and the infantry had all worked on the problems involved in staging an attack, and they had produced some new approaches. At the same time, and just as important, they had made plans on how to defeat the expected German counterattack and made them pay off as well.

To replace the killed Mercer, Sam Hughes naturally wanted his son: 'Give Garnet 3rd Division,' he telegraphed the new corps commander.[94] Byng made some inquiries and decided to disobey the minister. The better-qualified Brigadier-General Louis Lipsett, promoted to Major-General, took over the Third Division. Hughes was apoplectic, in part at least because Lipsett was British, and he confronted Byng at the first opportunity in August 1916. Byng was unmoved: 'He had nothing against Garnet but there was a better man available for the post and the better man would get it. Canadians deserved the best man as a leader and they wanted that type, therefore as far as he was concerned they would get it.' The corps, Byng said privately, was 'too good to be led by politicians and dollar magnates.'[95]

Other changes followed. The Ross rifle finally went to the scrapheap (or, more precisely, to the Royal Navy and British units based in England), replaced by the trusty Lee-Enfield. The Colt machine gun joined it; its replacement was the British-made Vickers, far more reliable, and the lighter Lewis gun. Battalion and division commanders also wanted more machine guns per battalion. The Canadians acquired rifle grenades and new mortars, the reliable 3-inch Stokes; the Mills bomb, the hand grenade armed simply by pulling a pin, was omnipresent. Steel helmets began to be provided to the men. Uncomfortably heavy and awkward, they offered some protection against shrapnel, though a bullet might just as easily penetrate them as glance off. Still, head injuries declined after the use of the helmets became universal. All these changes indicated that the army had begun to learn its business.

Meanwhile the Fourth Canadian Division took form in England from battalions training there. The GOC was to be Major-General David Watson, a Quebec newspaper man and Militia officer who had gone to France as CO of the 2nd Battalion and become the commander of the 5th Brigade. His brigadiers were W. St. P. Hughes, Sam Hughes's younger brother, who had commanded a battalion successfully; British Columbian Victor Odlum, who had led the 7th Battalion with good effect and great courage; and Lord Brooke, previously a brigade commander in the Second Division. The Fourth Division crossed to France in August 1916.

On the eve of the battles on the Somme, the Canadian Corps had been in action for close to a year-and-a-half. It had gone from a raw levy of one division, formed from the Militia and men off the streets and the fields, to an experienced, well-led force of three, soon to be four, divisions and 70,000 men, with a full array of corps and specialist units that provided for it equally well as any other formation in France and in Flanders. The corps still suffered from too much of the political interference that had characterized the Militia, certainly much more than it deserved, but the soldiers' exertions had largely overcome this obstacle. The Canadians had not won every battle they fought, to be sure, but they had unfailingly given good accounts of themselves in conditions of such horror that, eighty-five years later, we can still scarcely believe they existed. Moreover, even though a large proportion of the CEF was British-born, the process of battle had begun gradually to turn the men into a Canadian national army with a sense of itself and with a special élan. The divisions stayed together in the Canadian Corps, unlike British formations, which changed places from corps to corps on a regular basis. Because they worked together for longer periods, the Canadians increasingly had come to share the same battle doctrine. This doctrine was not quite the same as the British, and it would become more unique as the war went on.

The idea that a 'citizen's army' made up of 'dedicated, part-time amateur officers' was 'the natural and most effective form of military organization for Canada'[96] was effectively dead. The corps' officers had begun to think as professionals, leaving aside their old habits as Militia officers or officers of the stunted Permanent Force. Battle forced the efficient to the fore, creating a meritocracy of its own. There was no longer a place for amateurs or amateurism in command and staff positions if men were to survive on the battlefield. The good company commanders rose to command battalions, while the able COs became brigade commanders and the proven brigadier-generals took over divisions.

Patrick Brennan, the only historian to study CEF battalion commanders, calculated that twenty-nine COs served for eighteen months or more, and another eight for at least 500 days. Seventeen were killed in action or died of wounds, and eighteen received promotions to command brigades. The average age of the first CO of fifty battalions was forty-nine, he notes, but by August 8, 1918, it had fallen to thirty-seven years, with some in their twenties.[97] E.L.M. Burns, a junior officer in the Great War and a senior officer in the Second World War, pointed out that the average brigade commander held his position for seventeen months, and seven brigadiers received divisional commands.[98] Experience mattered.

Consider Lieutenant-Colonel Louis Lipsett, who had a battalion in Arthur Currie's 1st Brigade from Valcartier onward. The day after Currie took over the First Division, he received command of his brigade. After the death of Mercer in June 1916, the proven Lipsett got the Third Division. The able survivors of battle rose, and the First Division fertilized the Second, and the First and the Second helped the Third, and they all helped the Fourth Division. Professionalism meant the possibility of victory and the chance of survival; amateurism meant inevitable defeat and the certainty of slaughter.

The defeats and victories of 1915 and 1916 belonged to the officers and the men, creating a bond of hard, shared experiences. But, unquestionably, the cost of learning how to wage war had been high, with more than 32,000 casualties to the end of June 1916, and there were already thousands of families at home mourning their losses.[99] When Corporal George Cowan, a Newfoundlander who had won the Military Medal while serving with the 13th Battalion, died in action on June 27, 1916, Sam Hughes wrote to his family to extend condolences: 'There is a consolation in knowing that he did his duty fearlessly and well, and gave his life for the cause of Liberty and the upbuilding of the Empire.'[100] Newfoundlanders and Canadians probably still believed those sentiments in 1916, but there would be many more like George Cowan before the war was over.

four

BECOMING PROFESSIONAL: ARTHUR CURRIE'S ARMY

Oh! To be killed outright,
Clean in the clash of the fight!
That is a golden death,
That is a boon, but this ...
Drawing an anguished breath
Under a hot abyss,
Under a stooping sky
Of seething, sulphurous fire,
Scorching me as I lie
Here on the wire ... the wire ...[1]

Robert Service, the Yukon poet who had immortalized 'Dangerous Dan McGrew,' served as an ambulance driver in France. His graphic, bitter, and long-forgotten war poetry was closer in tone to that of British poets such as Siegfreid Sassoon and very different from that produced by most of the other Canadian soldier-poets.

―――

If Robert Service was different, so too was Arthur Currie, who stands out prominently among the Canadian and Allied generals of the Great War. Certainly he did not look the part of a dashing commander – as the square-jawed and bristly mustached Sir Douglas Haig certainly did. Instead, Currie was pear-shaped, his smooth face and weak chin sitting atop a large expanse of chest and belly supported by pipestem legs. He was no professional soldier but merely a militiaman, who had been born in Ontario and then moved to Victoria, British Columbia. He had taught school, sold insurance, and speculated in real estate – and he found himself caught up in one of the many financial collapses that regularly troubled the prewar Canadian economy. At the risk of losing everything he had worked for, Currie had dipped into government money intended to purchase uniforms for the new 50th Regiment, Highlanders of Canada, of which he was Commanding Officer. He lived in fear that his peculations might be exposed, for he could have been sent to jail for his misappropriation of more than $10,000 – a very substantial sum in 1914 dollars. Fortunately for the Canadian Corps he was not, and he became a commander of great skill. He was also highly principled and morally courageous in military matters, so much so that he must be forgiven for his single error of judgment in his financial panic in 1914.[2]

Was he a natural soldier? He had been an effective Militia officer, and he had played his role as a brigade commander with good judgment in the chaos of Valcartier and the mud of Salisbury Plain. At Ypres he had acted unwisely in leaving his men to go to the rear to seek reinforcements, but he had returned with several hundred Canadian stragglers, and his brigade had held its position in the terrible chaos of gas and fire. In the fighting at Mount Sorrel, Currie commanded the First Canadian Division and took his objectives. He came to understand what men could do on the battlefield, learned how to prepare an attack, and discovered how to use artillery and machine-gun fire to clear the way through the barbed wire and enemy trenches for his infantrymen. His orders were invariably clear, his officers and men always well briefed, his plans sensibly based on the enemy's strengths and weaknesses, and his strategy drawn from the lessons assimilated from previous attacks and careful personal observation of the battlefield. Such an approach may sound like simple professionalism and routine common sense, but in the trenches of the Great War, common sense and professionalism were usually in short supply, and an intelligent general who could think clearly and sensibly was a great prize. That such a general valued his troops' lives and tried to minimize their casualties and suffering by using surprise and firepower to overcome the enemy greatly increased his worth.

Currie was no military genius, but he was capable of learning, personally brave, and confident in the abilities and fighting skills of his men. His one drawback was that his reserved and aloof personality separated him from his troops, while those who worked closely with him came to love and admire him. The men of the 2nd Canadian Brigade, the First Canadian Division, and the Canadian Corps all became accustomed to winning their battles while Currie was in command, and the soldiers could see that their attacks and counterattacks were professionally and carefully planned to achieve the objective with minimal loss of life. That consideration mattered greatly then, and it still does. He was no Napoleon, but Arthur Currie was the best soldier Canada ever produced. The Canadian Corps under his command became the finest, most professional formation this nation has ever put in the field.[3]

By the beginning of the summer of 1916, the war had been under way for just short of two years. For all but the naïve, and there were few of those left alive outside General Douglas Haig's headquarters, the idea of a quick victory was gone. The line of trenches in France and Flanders stretched from the Swiss border to the sea, Italy and the Austrians were struggling for control of the mountainous border between their nations, and the Russians were desperately struggling to keep an army in the field under strenuous, unremitting German pressure. There was fighting in East Africa, where German-led guerillas fought British, colonial, and South African troops to a standstill. In the deserts of the Middle East, British and dominion troops fought the Turks, and the disastrous Gallipoli campaign was now just a bad memory. It was a world war, fought at sea, in the air, and on land.

It was also a war of attrition, as both sides sought to wear the other down. The main German effort was directed at the French fortress at Verdun, a long battle that became a charnel house for both sides but almost ruined the French armies. The British contribution to the war of attrition came at the Somme, a campaign intended to ease pressure on the French and kill as many Germans as possible.

The great British attack on the Somme went in on July 1, 1916. The German lines were strongly manned and splendidly fortified, and British artillery was still too often ineffective against wire and deep entrenchments and plagued by large numbers of dud shells. Although there were some minor gains (the single French army involved took its objectives), the result was a disaster for British arms. On the first day of battle, Britain lost 57,470 men killed, wounded, and missing, as the German machine gunners fired until their barrels glowed red. The Newfoundland Regiment, part of the British 29th Division, attacked Beaumont Hamel, as a later Newfoundlander said, 'with honour and determination, bravery and fear, against impossible odds.' Altogether, 684 Newfoundlanders fell in battle, including 310 killed in action.[4]

By good luck, the Canadian Corps was not involved in the initial stages of the battle of the Somme. While others died in their thousands, Lance Corporal Archie MacKinnon of the 58th Battalion wrote to his sister on August 15: 'I only fired 5 shots in 8 days and that was only to clean the rifle.'[5] But this state of affairs would change all too soon as Haig kept up the pressure through August, achieving gains of up to 7000 yards at best, but at a cost in blood of 200,000 British and 70,000 French casualties to the end of the month. The Germans lost some 200,000 men, and the strategy of attrition could – and should – be said to have failed, but Haig kept his post. All that had been gained, though it was significant, was the cessation of the German attacks at Verdun.

As September began, the Canadian Corps prepared to enter the Somme battle at Pozières Ridge,* about 20 miles east of Amiens. Private Donald Fraser in the 31st Battalion noted: 'The Australians passed us on the way to the Ypres front with sadly depleted forces ... The platoons looked like sections while the companies resembled platoons.'[6] Now it was the Canadians' turn, and they knew it. Lieutenant Hart Leech of the 61st Battalion wrote home to Winnipeg presciently just before the attack: 'I am "going over the parapet" and the chances of a "sub[altern]" getting back alive are about nix.'[7]

Leech and his comrades had some tactical innovations at their disposal. First, the British had developed a new weapon to deal with machine guns and to crawl over barbed wire and the broken ground of the battlefield – though it did so with more difficulty than the planners had anticipated. This first tank was armed either with 6-pounder guns or machine guns, was bulky at 26 feet

---

* In January 2000 the remains of Private David Carlson of the 8th Battalion were found on the Somme battlefield by British tourists. He had been listed as missing on September 8, 1916. His remains received a military funeral in the cemetery at Pozières on May 24, 2000. *Ottawa Citizen*, May 12, 2000.

long and 14 feet wide, and carried a crew of eight. Very few of these new and mechanically unreliable machines were available and there was no time to train infantry how to work with them. Though their initial shock effect on the enemy was great, it was soon minimized by their small numbers. More important than the tanks, the Canadian Corps had put in place plans for a creeping barrage, something that could use the heavy concentration of guns amassed on the battlefield. The artillery fire would move forward in timed 100-yard increments, and the infantry would advance as close to the barrage as possible. The great advantage of this tactic was that the enemy, accustomed to waiting out British artillery fire in its dugouts, could not emerge to man the trenches. Finally, the British high command had accepted the idea of moving forward by bounds – a tactic that was intended to see the first wave stop and consolidate on its objective while fresh troops in the second, third, and sometimes fourth waves moved through them to take second and successive objectives.

The Canadian attack began at 6:20 a.m. on September 15 with General Turner's Second Division making the main effort against the defences in front of the village of Courcelette. The Third Division watched Turner's left flank. The artillery did its job superbly, and the enemy's first line of trenches fell within a quarter-hour. The 4th and 6th brigades were on their objectives by 7:30, as the startling presence of the six tanks allotted to the division terrified those Germans who confronted them. Private Fraser noted that when 'Crème de Menthe,' a saucily named tank, crawled into view, 'suddenly men from the ground looked up, rose as if from the dead, and running from the flanks to behind it, followed in the rear as if to be in on the kill.'[8] The tanks, however, broke down quickly or were put out of action by enemy artillery. Eastern Ontario's 21st Battalion of the 4th Brigade took 125 prisoners, but 'B' Company lost all its officers and ended the day commanded by the Company Sergeant-Major.

The second Canadian attack of the day, launched in broad daylight by the 5th and 7th brigades, picked up where the first had left off. The 22nd and 25th battalions moved through Courcelette and the 26th began mopping up Germans hiding in the cellars of ruined buildings or camouflaged dugouts. While the Germans were being flushed out of their holes, the other two battalions had to resist repeated counterattacks. The Van Doos' (22nd) CO, Lieutenant-Colonel T.L. Tremblay, had asked for the honour of leading the attack.

Tremblay worried that Québécois were not in the war the way Anglo-Canadians were, and he tortured himself with thoughts that English Canada and France doubted French Canadians' manhood. As a result, he intended to demonstrate that even if 'we are going to the slaughter ... morale is extraordinary, and we are determined to prove that *Canadiens* are not cowards.' The 22nd drove off seven German assaults on the first night and thirteen in all by September 17, and there was vicious hand-to-hand and bayonet fighting, as the Van Doos and the other battalions took many prisoners. His men, Tremblay wrote proudly in his diary, 'fight like lions,' but the whole struggle 'was like a bad dream: houses on fire south of the village, shells falling by the hundreds, blowing up everything, fighting with grenades, bayonet charges, battles, corpses everywhere and the constant writhing of the wounded. Man's mental and physical endurance is incredible. If hell is as horrible as what I saw there,' the tough Tremblay concluded, 'I wouldn't wish it on my worst enemy.' Over 300 of his men were killed or wounded, and Tremblay himself had to be evacuated to the rear to undergo a stomach operation.[9]

Meanwhile, the Third Division had to tackle the Fabeck Graben, a German trench system, which took time, required hard fighting, and cost many casualties, including Lance Corporal Archie MacKinnon. 'We took their front line easy,' he wrote with a mixture of bravado and delight. 'All they do is throw down their rifles and yell "mercy comrade," but we gave them mercy alright ... I went as far as I could. O, I am 100 times better off now. Just imagine – a broken leg ... Six weeks or so in bed and limp till the duration is my motto.'[10] The successful troops now fell victim to enfilade fire from Zollern Graben, yet another trench system. An attack by the 7th Brigade cleared the enemy position, aided by the extraordinary courage of Private J.C. Kerr of Edmonton's 49th Battalion, who ran along the top of the enemy trench firing down on the defenders. Kerr won the Victoria Cross. His heroism did not prevent enemy counterattacks from recapturing the Zollern redoubt on September 20. The Canadians took back most of the trench, but lost it again when the Germans attacked behind a smoke screen. Despite this setback and 7320 casualties in a week, the Courcelette operations had been a major success – at 3000 yards the largest single advance of the Somme campaign, and a further demonstration of the Canadian Corps' growing skill and confidence.

The men needed all their skill and confidence, for the next two months were terrible indeed. The next objective was a German trench line, located about a thousand yards beyond Courcelette and called Regina Trench by the Canadians. On September 26 the First and Second Canadian Divisions attacked and, in the face of fierce resistance and counterattacks, failed to reach the objective. On October 1 the Second and Third Divisions, their battalions now seriously understrength, tried again. The 5th Canadian Mounted Rifles of the Third Division went into the attack to a precise timetable: zero hour was 3:15 p.m., and from 3:15 to 3:16 an intensive shrapnel barrage was to fall 100 yards ahead of Regina Trench. For the next three minutes while the 5th Canadian Mounted Rifles advanced, the barrage was to fall directly on the objective, and for three minutes more the barrage would move forward 100 yards and for six minutes more another hundred. For the next thirty minutes the gunfire would fall 300 yards beyond Regina Trench. As so often happened, however, the barrage did not cut the wire, and the enemy artillery did great damage in the Canadian trenches. The attack went ahead nonetheless and advanced about 150 yards, before coming under heavy German fire. One company's objective was seized, but the second of two companies in the first wave was cut to pieces. That night Lieutenant George Pearkes, commanding 'C' Company, received orders to lead a bombing party down the trench for 500 yards. Rather than move down the narrow trench, Pearkes led his men along the top, beyond the parapet, dropping bombs on any enemy they saw. For eight hours Pearkes fought his *petite guerre*, going forward and being driven back, fighting with bombs and bayonets. By 4 a.m. he had taken 500 yards of trench and he held it until the battalion was relieved, thirty-four hours after going into action. Pearkes later won the Victoria Cross at Passchendaele, but he might well have received it for his gallantry at Regina Trench.[11]

Still, much of Regina Trench remained in German hands, and on October 8 the First and Third Divisions tried again, once more without success. The three divisions then left the Somme front, but the Fourth Canadian Division, recently arrived from England for its initiation into battle, took Regina Trench and Desire Trench, the next line beyond Regina, by November 18. Fighting in miserable conditions of cold and mud, Major-General David Watson's division lost 1250 men in its first battle. The butcher's bill for the Canadian Corps' seven weeks on the Somme was 24,029 officers and men; for the

British and French, more than 620,000; and for the Germans, approximately 670,000.

The battle of the Somme had been the Great War at its most futile. The losses were terrifying for meaningless gains. Men staggered into battle weighed down by equipment and mud, sometimes carrying 120 lbs. in all, and struggled to cut barbed wire that was supposed to have been destroyed by artillery but almost never was. Far too many artillery shells still failed to explode, and some blew up in the gun barrels. In January George V promoted General Haig to Field Marshal, a New Year's gift from him and the nation, as the monarch put it with dynastic blindness.[12] The dead must have been gratified.

As the Canadian Corps grew and developed, its treatment of the wounded also changed. Experienced soldiers probably came to prefer a quick death by a bullet through the head or the explosion of a German 5.9 artillery shell. What was feared was to be shot in the gut and to die an agonizing, slow death, or, worse, to be hung up on the German wire, trapped, unable to move, and to suffer a prolonged, fearful death. Gas too was feared – no one liked the idea of coughing up one's lungs from chlorine or drowning as the lungs filled with fluid from phosgene or being burned, blinded, and blistered by mustard gas.* But well-trained and properly equipped soldiers could guard against gas most of the time, and gas, at least, had the useful side-effect of killing the rats that roamed the front-line trenches living off food and the dead. Men hoped for a 'blighty,' a wound that was not life-threatening but sufficient to earn the soldier recovery time in a British hospital. What was striking, however, was that Canadian wounded received good, prompt treatment whenever battlefield conditions allowed.

The Canadian Army Medical Corps, founded in 1901, had been tiny before the war with only thirteen officers and five Nursing Sisters. The war drew half of Canada's physicians and surgeons into the service, a quarter of the country's dentists (organized into the Canadian Army Dental Corps), and 2854 nurses.[13] The medical organization these men and women created, an

---

* One particularly gruesome account was by Victor Wheeler, *The 50th Battalion in No Man's Land* (Ottawa, 2000), 108: 'The wheezing and frothing from his mouth like that of a horribly bloated bullfrog, the dilated eyeballs, the pondscum-green discolouration of face and neck, and the gurgling sound issuing from his throat.'

organization that sent hospitals to Britain, France, Egypt, and the Balkans, became very efficient. The Nursing Sisters, moreover, held commissions, the only ones in the imperial armies to do so.

For a wounded soldier, the basic front-line care came at the Regimental Aid Post, found ordinarily in every infantry battalion's support trenches. Stretcher bearers, their numbers increasing in each infantry company during the war as senior officers slowly came to realize the number of casualties and the difficulties of carrying wounded men through the awful conditions of the front, brought all but the walking wounded to the aid post. If there was a major attack with huge casualties, men sometimes waited a long time for the overworked stretcher bearers to arrive; too often, they died before help could come.[14] But if casualties were light in the lines, medical care could be given swiftly.

At the aid post, the battalion Medical Officer assessed the soldier's condition and offered the essential life-saving or stabilizing care. The casualties were then moved rearward by a field ambulance, horse-drawn or motorized (each division had three Field Ambulance units), to an Advanced Dressing Station, where dressings were put in place and morphine injected. Then ambulances or light railways (and, in the last year of the war, standard gauge trains) carried the wounded to the Casualty Clearing Station, where essential surgery took place.[15] Clearing stations employed a dozen or so Nursing Sisters and were usually located far enough to the rear that they could not be shelled by enemy artillery; German aircraft, however, occasionally bombed clearing stations and other hospitals: two notorious and apparently deliberate bombing raids in May 1918 caused 171 casualties, including seven Nursing Sisters, at the well-marked General Hospital in Étaples, and three more Nursing Sisters were killed at the equally well-identified Stationary Hospital at Doullens.* (A German U-boat also sank a well-marked hospital ship, the *Llandovery Castle*, in June 1918, drowning fourteen Nursing Sisters out of a total casualty list of 234.)

From the clearing station, casualties moved rearward by specially equipped hospital trains to one of Canada's ten Stationary Hospitals (250 beds) or one

---

* The first Nursing Sister killed in action, Maude Macdonald of Brantford, Ontario, had just written her family on May 18, 1918: 'Don't worry we are far from harm.' She died the next day. Canadian War Museum 58a/1/114.9.

of the sixteen General Hospitals (500–2200 beds), sometimes staffed from university medical and nursing schools, where further surgery took place and the wounded recovered. Additional and specialized rehabilitation of the wounded could occur at convalescent hospitals in France or in Britain, often in country homes handed over by the titled or, for those whose recovery for front-line service was very doubtful, back in Canada in military hospitals that the government created across the country.[16] Before long, there were wounded veterans all across Canada. 'Some of the returned soldiers are *terribly* crippled,' wrote a secretary in army headquarters in Military District 12 to a friend overseas, 'and it just makes your heart ache to look at them.'[17]

The standard of care offered overseas and in Canada was impressive. Despite the septic conditions in which men lived and fought in the trenches, conditions that positively encouraged gas gangrene, 876 of every thousand wounded soldiers who reached medical treatment survived. By 1916 blood transfusion had been used to stabilize the wounded, and by 1918 blood typing was routinely employed. Of the almost half a million Canadians who served overseas, moreover, only 6767 died of disease, a number that includes the terrible influenza pandemic of 1918–19.[18] (In the South African War, by contrast, twenty-two of every thousand soldiers died of disease.) The casualties and the casualty rates were very high, but the medical care provided to the troops in an age without antibiotics was remarkably effective.[19]*

One predictable dampener to this efficiency was the political infighting that marked the Medical Corps' operations. Before his political demise, Sam Hughes had totally disrupted the Canadian hospitals in Britain by dispatching Lieutenant-Colonel Herbert Bruce, a Toronto doctor to the rich and famous, to investigate conditions overseas in 1916. Bruce wrote a damning report that condemned the Medical Corps' senior officers, and Hughes soon put Bruce in command. This appointment provoked a near-revolt among the doctors – Bruce had no experience of military medical administration, after all – and, when Hughes left the government, Sir George Perley, the High Commissioner

---

* Those who died were buried in nearby military cemeteries. Next of kin often received letters, with sanitized details on the deaths, from Nursing Sisters who had cared for the men. Indeed, at an Australian Casualty Clearing Station that received Canadian wounded in November 1917 the Nursing Sister in charge, Ida O'Dwyer, used a form letter, changing only the name of the deceased and the nature of the wound. See 'What Happened to Uncle Charlie?' *Canadian Military Times* 2 (winter 2001): 3.

and Minister of Overseas Forces, promptly fired Bruce after just ten weeks in charge. Some of Bruce's suggestions, notably that wherever and whenever possible Canadian wounded should be treated by Canadian medical personnel, were good ones, but his blood feuds did far more harm than his recommendations did good.[20] Bruce spent the rest of his long life defending himself, but what was most significant was that his removal marked the end of Hughes's meddling with the Canadian Corps.

The arrangements for the wounded were only a part of the behind-the-lines operations of the Canadian Corps. The Canadian Expeditionary Force was the largest organization that Canada had ever produced, and it had to be up and running from scratch at once. That there were errors of omission and commission were completely understandable, but what is ordinarily forgotten is just how well the system operated overseas. Consider artillery shells. Produced in Canada, the United States, and Britain, shells made their way across the ocean or the English Channel to France. They were loaded on trains and moved to supply depots and then transshipped to corps, divisions, and artillery regiments. A gun in 1916 fired 3.25 tons of shells a day; a gun in 1918 fired 5.5 tons. The organizational effort, the amount of shipping and railway space needed to keep the guns firing, was immense. Artillery was the key to victory, and without adequate supplies of shells the armies ground to a halt. Canadian factories had difficulties initially in producing shells to exact specifications, but they learned. Inefficiencies in British factories caused a small percentage of dud shells, but, again, inspection techniques eventually resolved the problems.

Production was only part of the effort, albeit a critical one. The armies controlled roads and rail lines, and tens of thousands of horses and mules, carts and trucks. Arrangements had to be in place to provide grain and hay for the animals, oil and gasoline and repairs for the vehicles, and food, water, and equipment ranging from barbed wire to duckboards, grenades, and .303 ammunition for the men in the front and the rear. In periods without heavy fighting, the logistics were hard enough. If a push was on, the task became ten times harder – and the supply lines in quiet or active periods could always be subject to air attack.

The Canadian Army Service Corps' job in France was to provide for the needs of the front-line units, and its officers and men struggled through the mud to do so. By late 1915 the Service Corps operated two Reserve Parks for horses, two Railhead Supply Detachments, nine Depot Units of Supply, two Field Bakeries, and two Field Butcheries on the Lines of Communication. In the Canadian Corps area it ran a Corps Troops Supply Column, two Divisional Supply Columns, a Corps Ammunition Park, two Divisional Ammunition Sub-Parks, and two Motor Ambulance Workshops. Increasingly, wheeled transport became more critical as the war went on, and the Canadians developed the concept of 'continuous running' – using two drivers for each vehicle, one for daylight hours and the other for nighttime operations. Maintenance was carried out in the brief intervals when the trucks were being loaded and gassed. These supply arrangements expanded as new divisions joined the Canadian Corps and motor transport became more prevalent and more dependable.

The Canadians fielded three Tunnelling Companies and two Tramways Companies, the former to plant mines under enemy lines or to dig large dugouts for attacking troops to shelter in, as at Vimy; the latter to lay light railways to move men and supplies. There was also a Searchlight Company. At the same time, each division had a Salvage Company, which tried to collect equipment that might be repaired and reused. At Corps, a Labour Commandant allocated manpower for necessary works, a Laundry Officer's organization provided clean clothing to soldiers, Claims Officers dealt with damage claims filed by civilians, and Town Majors arranged billeting for troops when they were out of the line. Canteen Officers and the YMCA had responsibility for providing 'comforts' to soldiers, while the Burial Officers looked after the dead and recorded their gravesites. A Veterinary Hospital cared for the corps' horses and mules, and the Army Postal Services delivered the mail. Pay officers saw that the soldiers received their daily pittance and took care that money allocated to families at home was duly dispatched. The Corps' Military Police took care of troublemakers, stragglers, and deserters, as well as ensuring that road traffic flowed properly. A Cyclist Battalion was mainly used as messengers; Forestry Companies worked in Britain and France; and Railway Troops, at peak strength numbering 16,000, built and ran railways behind the lines.[21]

Other officers and men collected and interpreted intelligence, trained soldiers to use and survive gas, and operated a multitude of workshops and Dental Companies. Without them all, the infantry and artillery could not have fought for long. The extraordinary organization the Canadian Corps developed as the war proceeded suggested the magnitude and complexity of the operations it was involved in.[22] While no infantryman would ever express satisfaction with the work of those in the rear, the Canadian Corps ran as well administratively as it did operationally. It ought to be noted that the CEF still depended heavily on the massive British administrative 'tail' in France and, because it did, it could have a better 'teeth to tail' ratio than the Imperials.

After the Somme, the Canadian Corps moved to the area of Lens and Vimy Ridge, where it passed the winter. The soldiers had time to rest and train, time for new reinforcements to be brought forward and integrated into their platoons, companies, and battalions. There were trench raids, sometimes very large, and sometimes involving the use of gas; some succeeded, some failed, though all inflicted casualties.[23] Above all, battalion and brigade officers, as well as the division and corps staffs, had the opportunity to sort through the lessons that had been learned in battle and to seek better ways of dealing with the enemy's defences. In the Canadian Corps this process was continuous.

The attack had turned into a maelstrom of artillery. Canadian guns could lay down a creeping barrage, and men in the first wave could move behind it with minimal losses and a good chance of reaching enemy trenches alive – if the enemy positions on the flanks were neutralized, as too often they were not. But the Germans had artillery too, and their gunfire could take a terrible toll on the advancing infantry, particularly those in the second and subsequent waves. German gunners could also cause devastation in the rear areas, blocking the forward movement of supplies and reinforcements. What the Canadians needed was a more efficient way to destroy enemy guns – better and more accurate counter-battery work.

In late January 1917 Lieutenant-Colonel Andrew McNaughton, a Montreal engineer and militiaman, became the Canadian Corps' Counter-Battery Staff Officer. A scientist by training and temperament, McNaughton had the job of locating and destroying or neutralizing the enemy's batteries. He had aerial reconnaissance at his disposal, along with the information that could be gleaned by balloons tethered high above the front, flash-spotting, and sound-ranging. The aircraft and balloons could see German guns on the ground in good weather, plot their coordinates on a map, and drop the information to the gunners. Flash-spotting relied on observers to see the flash a gun made when it fired, and when two or more of them took a theodolite bearing on the flash, the position could be triangulated accurately. Again, weather could interfere with this technique. Sound-ranging was the newest technique. It relied on microphones placed in carefully surveyed locations to pick up a gun's report. From the timed intervals between the shell being fired and each microphone picking up the bang, the position of the gun could be calculated. In favourable conditions, and provided the elaborate communications systems worked properly, a gun could be located within a hundred yards in just three minutes. But a barrage rendered this system useless, and wind could also disrupt the sound waves. McNaughton took these existing tools and made them operate better, turning the corps' counter-battery work into the model on the Western Front.[24]

There were more lessons to learn in a corps that took learning seriously, encouraging constructive criticism and praising innovative tactical solutions.[25] The Somme fighting, for example, had demonstrated that the troops could not function effectively if they had to carry everything on their backs that was needed to consolidate a captured position. The necessary supplies of ammunition and barbed wire for defence had to be brought forward by men in the subsequent waves – which required that the enemy guns be neutralized. What the first wave needed above all were bombs – hand grenades – and more bombs. This was the most effective way of clearing out the enemy's dugouts and holding captured trenches. The Canadians had already established bombing sections for this task, but every infantryman had to be able to perform this role and, moreover, to know how to use any German grenades that might be captured.

Canadian attackers also learned to be ready to meet the German counterattacks that almost invariably followed on the heels of the enemy's loss of a position. The Germans used artillery, machine guns, and grenades in their counterattacks, and, since they were trying to retake their own positions, they knew the ground better than the battered men who had pushed them out. To defeat counterattacks, men needed their own machine guns and bombs, and they needed reinforcements quickly. They also needed artillery support, shrapnel being a decisive way of breaking up enemy formations. This response demanded quick communications with battalion and brigade headquarters – a difficult assignment in an era before backpacked radios. Perhaps the most reliable method was the simplest: a runner carrying a message. Aircraft could report progress, sometimes with accuracy; pigeons were sometimes used, as were other signalling devices such as lamps, flags, and Very flares; but telephone wire could not be laid by first-wave troops and, even if it could, it was vulnerable to shellfire. In general, though, communications remained an insoluble problem, given the technology in 1916.

Still, some things could be done to improve the attack. The Lewis machine guns – each battalion now had sixteen – could be brought forward in the first wave for support, and the ordinary infantrymen could carry extra ammunition for these guns. This system could work, but only if the other loads carried by the men were reduced. The Stokes mortar, a fragile weapon, had its proponents, but maintaining the ammunition supply was difficult. All that senior officers could suggest was that each infantryman carry one mortar bomb. Again, given the loads that men had to carry, this solution was all but impossible.[26]

The key step in changing and improving Canadian Corps tactics in the attack came when the GOC, General Byng, let Major-General Arthur Currie join a group of British senior officers who visited the French to study their methods of fighting. Currie was an innovator, one who, for example, interviewed officers and men from the battalions that attacked Regina Trench to find out what had worked and what had not. Currie also wanted – as many officers who disliked the French did not – to consider what might be learned from them.

The French had their problems, but they had their strengths too – particularly an emphasis on reconnaissance. It was a military adage that 'time spent on reconnaissance is never wasted,' and the French practised this strategy, putting every man who was to attack into the line so he could see the ground, the objective, and the likely enemy resistance points. The French also used air photographs extensively, distributing them to the officers of the assaulting units, who then briefed every man. When the attack went in, the objectives were geographical features, such as a hill or a wood, not a map reference or a trench. A German trench was always located to maximize Allied difficulty, not to control the battlefield the next day when the Germans counterattacked. The French also emphasized the training of the assaulting force. Currie believed that they had much to teach the Canadians: the *poilus* rehearsed major attacks on ground similar to that they faced, and they worked hard on platoon and company tactics, fire and movement, and weapons handling. Moreover, they believed attacks were much more likely to succeed if fresh troops were employed.

Above all, the French had come to the realization that the key to success was the infantry platoon. Much better armed than it had been when the war began, the platoon now included machine guns, bombs, and rifle grenades. The French divided platoons into bombers, automatic riflemen, and two sections of riflemen, and they expected their infantry to manoeuvre on the battlefield, to deal with problems as they arose, and not (as was the British and Canadian way) always to ask for more artillery support. It was up to the infantry, not the artillery, to be the master of the battlefield. Currie recommended that the Canadian Corps adopt a flexible, manoeuvrable platoon organization. At the same time, he wanted to use munitions to save his men, so artillery and its proper employment were critical to the success of attacks.

He urged as well that the Canadians adopt the French method of determining the number of waves in an attack by the requirements of the ground and the defences; the British, in contrast, had used a formulaic and rigid system. He recommended that the French system, which put the priority on forward movement, be adopted. The French infantry used rifle grenades and machine guns to keep the enemy in their trenches, so that the infantry could rush strong points. Men moved forward, expecting follow-on troops to eliminate any pockets of resistance. The attackers, Currie suggested, had to consolidate the captured position; in any case, if the attack was to move on, fresh units had to form up in the captured positions and jump off from there.[27]

Byng agreed, as did the majority of the British commanders. So did Byng's staff planners, most of them still Britons, but many by now Canadians.[28] Together they rapidly began to change the Canadian Corps into a new model army, one that was consistently ahead of all but the very best British divisions in innovative tactics. In the battle for Vimy Ridge, the corps' next major struggle, Currie's ideas played the decisive role.

Vimy has achieved a status as *the* Canadian victory, the pinnacle of Canadian military achievement. Soldiers at the time and the media at home painted it as a triumph of arms – and so it was in some ways. Part of this myth making for civilians was the sense that Canadians had scaled a cliff, struggling to the top of the great ridge in the face of enemy fire. In fact, while the ridge rose high above the great Douai plain, the sharp drop was behind the German lines and in front of the village of Vimy. Most of the enemy-controlled ground in front of the Canadians was characterized by a gentle upward slope. Courage, skill, careful planning, and perfect execution were needed to take the ridge, but no one needed pitons to scale the heights of Vimy.

More important, while Vimy was an enormously strong and well-fortified position, and while its capture by the four divisions of the Canadian Corps fighting together for the first time was a significant victory, it was a set-piece battle without any follow-up exploitation. No cavalry streamed into the gap the corps blasted in the enemy lines; no reserves moved forward to exploit the victory. Vimy was a one-off encounter, a costly battle that, while it dislodged the Germans from a key position, mattered little in terms of the overall conduct of the war. For the Canadians, it was an undoubted psychological fillip; for General Byng, it was the culmination of his highly successful command of the Canadian Corps; and for people at home it showed that 'our boys' could do great things. But its military importance, regrettably, was slight. Nonetheless, the battle was so perfectly planned and executed that it must be described.

In March 1917 the Germans had staged a strategic withdrawal along a hundred-mile front between Soissons and Arras, giving up a salient and shortening the front for secure and well-fortified positions that they dubbed the Hindenburg Line. Haig and General Robert Nivelle, the French commander, had been caught by surprise, but both persisted with their plans for offensives. Nivelle attacked on the Aisne and made small gains for heavy losses. Haig struck in the Arras area with his Third Army, his intention being to continue to wear down the enemy. The strategy, if it can be called that, remained attrition. The attack on Vimy aimed primarily to establish a strong left flank for the Third Army's attack.

The Vimy position had been in German hands since October 1914 and had resisted French and British assaults. The Germans had fortified the area superbly, their guns registered, their bunkers deep, their machine guns carefully placed in concrete nests protected by belts of barbed wire. There were three main defensive lines, separated by as many as 5 miles, with fortified positions between the lines. The entire complex was connected by communications trenches and tunnels carved in the chalky soil. The geography gave them a perfect reverse slope position for their artillery, safe from direct visibility.

Byng's plan for the attack was ready by March 5. His four objectives were each designated by a coloured line on the map. The Black Line, the first objective, called for the seizure of the Germans' forward defensive positions. The Red Line, the final objective for the left flank of the corps attack, involved taking La Folie Farm, a fortified position, and Hill 145, a high point on the ridge. On the right, Byng planned two more bounds: the Blue Line encompassed Thélus, Hill 135, and the woods overlooking the village of Vimy; the Brown Line, the last objective, covered the Germans' second line. All was planned to a strict timetable. With the four divisions lined up in numerical order from right to left, the attack would go in at 5:30 a.m., and the planners allotted thirty-five minutes for the troops to reach the Black Line. After forty minutes to regroup, they calculated that twenty minutes would allow the attackers to reach the Red Line. After a pause of two-and-a-half hours, the reserve brigades of the First and Second divisions would take the Blue Line, and after a further pause of ninety-six minutes, the same brigades were to move beyond the ridge to the final objective, the Brown Line. If everything worked, the Canadians' advance would be 4000 yards by precisely 1:18 p.m.

These particulars sounded much like the unrealistic plans that had shaped Allied offensives for two years and more, but they were not. The planners had decided to resist enemy counterattacks by bringing machine guns forward as soon as objectives were seized and by quickly digging defensive lines. More important still, the artillery planning was carefully done. McNaughton's counter-battery organization had the time and the shells it needed, and enough intelligence and scientific wizardry at its disposal to do the job thoroughly. When the Canadian attack went in, the German artillery had been thoroughly battered, if not neutralized completely: 83 per cent of the enemy artillery had been pinpointed. German counterattacks would not have heavy fire support to assist them.[29]

The Canadians had massive fire support for their attack. Eleven heavy artillery groups were in place – in all, 245 'heavies' – and the field artillery numbered 480 18-pounders and 138 howitzers. Many of the gunners were

British, and more firepower could be provided as necessary from the 1st British Corps and the First Army. There was, astonishingly, one piece of heavy artillery for each 20 yards of front, and one field gun for every 10 yards. The artillery program had been carefully devised and called for an escalating two-week bombardment on trenches, dugouts, machine-gun nests, and rear area supply dumps. Machine-gun fire was to be used to harass and hinder repair of damaged positions. The enemy wire drew special attention, and the new No. 106 fuse, which exploded on contact with wire, was used. When the attack itself began, a rolling barrage would move forward in hundred-yard increments while other guns hit defensive positions.

Byng intended the attack to commence on April 9, 1917, Easter Monday, and there was time for full preparation, training, and reconnaissance. A program of trench raids harassed the Germans, spotted defensive changes, and took prisoners. Ammunition was stockpiled for the guns, and the shells were carried by rail lines or tramway lines specially constructed by the corps' railway troops or over roads built and repaired by corps sappers. Water lines had to be laid down to supply men and horses, telephone wire was buried to provide secure communications, and tunnels were dug to let men move to their jumping-off points in safety. The subways (which still exist) had electricity, telephone cables, and water, and alcoves housed battalion and brigade headquarters. The soldiers received full briefings and rehearsed their attacks, following Currie's recommendations. 'We had been practising and rehearsing the details for several days,' wrote Lieutenant Stuart Kirkland, 'but didn't know the hour it was to start until the night before. Then the officers were informed of the zero hour.'[30] Air photos and maps came well forward, and every man knew his, his platoon's, and his battalion's tasks. Typically (if indiscreetly), Private Ronald MacKinnon of the PPCLI wrote to his father on Good Friday: 'I am a rifle grenadier and am in the "first wave." We have a good bunch of boys to go over with and good artillery support so we are bound to get our objective alright. I understand we are going up against the Prussian Guards.'[31]

The enemy knew the attack was coming, but the German high command did not know precisely when. The corps achieved a measure of tactical surprise by slackening, rather than increasing, the volume of artillery fire just before the attack and eliminating the standard heavy bombardment at the moment of the assault. When the 15,000 assault troops from twenty-one battalions, fortified with a tot of rum and a hot meal, went over the top at 5:30 a.m. on Easter Monday, they attacked in snow and sleet, the wind driving into the enemy lines.

The attack began with a bang as the guns pounded the carefully located enemy artillery with high explosives and gas, 'the most wonderful artillery barrage ever known in the history of the world,' Lieutenant Kirkland said. Behind the rolling barrage, the men moved steadily forward over the badly broken ground, most of Currie's First Division units reaching the front-line positions while the Germans still huddled in their dugouts. Parties remained behind to guard the dugout exits until mop-up troops arrived, and the leading troops moved on. At the second German line, some men again still huddled in their dugouts, but now snipers and machine guns began to inflict heavy casualties. Individual soldiers bombed the machine guns, much as Private W.J. Milne of the 16th Battalion crawled near enough to a machine-gun post to bomb it into submission. Milne survived these heroics but was killed later in the day; his Victoria Cross was posthumously awarded. The Second Division, now commanded by artilleryman Major-General H.E. Burstall, similarly moved quickly over its first objective, the Black Line, and encountered serious resistance only at its second objective. The Third Division under Major-General Louis Lipsett also had an easy time in the first phase, as the 2nd Canadian Mounted Rifles even captured 150 Saxons in a dugout.

The First Division now moved on, helped again by snow that hid its advance from the enemy. Surprised and frightened, the Germans fled or fell, and by 7 a.m. the division had seized most of its second objective. The Second Division also met further success as it moved over flattened enemy trenches, capturing large numbers of prisoners, including two battalion headquarters, and guns, though casualties were beginning to mount. Still, by 8 a.m., the two divisions were sitting on the Red Line. By 9:30 the reserve brigades from the two divisions were advancing on the Blue Line. Only Currie's 1st Battalion met heavy resistance – which it overcame – and the two brigades took their third objective, as the *British Official History* noted, 'in precisely the same manner as it had been worked out on the practice fields.' The fourth objective, the Brown Line, soon followed, though it took a downhill bayonet charge by men of the 6th Brigade to overcome enemy machine guns and artillery firing at point-blank range. Extraordinarily, the schedule laid down by Byng in March had been largely fulfilled on time on April 9. 'Hundreds of men were now walking over the open in all directions,' wrote Padre F.G. Scott. 'German prisoners were being hurried back in scores. Wounded men, stretcher-bearers and men following up the advance were seen on all sides, and on the ground lay the bodies of friends and foes.'[32] From the air, one of the thousands of Canadian pilots in the Royal Flying Corps saw what seemed to be men casually wandering across No Man's Land. The young Billy Bishop, most of his victories still to come, could see shells bursting among the Canadians and men falling, but the others continued slowly forward. It looked like something unreal, he recalled, a game, not war.[33]

Only the Fourth Division met sustained difficulties in taking Hill 145, its objective, and the point that provided the Germans with observation over the valley of the River Souchez. Here the defences were very strong, with four lines of trenches and a reverse slope with deep dugouts. Careful preparation brought the Canadians to assembly trenches just 150 yards from the first German lines, but surprise was very difficult to achieve, given the ground. The attack, launched by Brigadier-General Victor Odlum's 11th Brigade and Brigadier-General J.H. MacBrien's 12th Brigade, each reinforced with an additional battalion, partly succeeded. The 11th Brigade seized its part of the forward slope of the hill and consolidated on the summit, but enemy fire hit two battalions hard. The 54th Battalion, which had taken the summit, had to give it up;[34] the 12th Brigade's attack similarly had early success and subsequent difficulty. The men crossed the first line of trenches, but found the second strongly manned, and the brigade had to pull back under fire. The two brigades soon had to beat off counterattacks and, at nightfall, Hill 145 remained in German hands. That night two companies of the 85th Battalion, the Nova Scotia Highlanders, a battalion new to the front, took Hill 145. (One of its officers, J. Layton Ralston, was to be Minister of National Defence in the Second World War.) The next day, when the 44th and 50th battalions followed a barrage in a mad charge down the eastern slope, the Fourth Division secured the Red Line.[35]

There now remained 'the Pimple,' the northern tip of Vimy Ridge. Originally intended to be attacked by British troops, the task of taking the Pimple went to General Watson's 10th Brigade, commanded by Brigadier-General E.

Hilliam, an ex-ranker. In the early hours of April 12 in the teeth of a gale, the Canadians surprised the Guards Regiment manning the position. Heavy hand-to-hand fighting followed, many prisoners were taken, and, by 6 a.m., the Canadians had the position. The ridge was now wholly in Canadian hands, and the troops could see eastward as far as the suburbs of Lens.

Stunned by the Canadians' rapid success, the Germans soon pulled back their line far enough to eliminate the advantages of observation offered by the ridge. As they retreated, they left behind hastily planted mines and booby-traps. 'An innocent looking canteen standing on the floor,' Lieutenant-Colonel Agar Adamson, commanding the Princess Patricia's Canadian Light Infantry, wrote to his wife, 'being picked up, being connected with a wire, sends off a small mine or bomb. All the wells are poisoned.'[36] The Germans sacked their Sixth Army commander, Ludwig von Falkenhausen, for the Vimy defeat.

The Canadian Corps, having suffered 10,602 casualties in just five days of fighting, dug in on the line of the Lens-Arras railway, a gain of 4500 yards. Unfortunately, the First Army had been unable to meet Byng's request for cavalry to exploit the Easter Monday success, and the opportunity for a break-through, like others in this war of attrition, disappeared into the swirling sleet of April.

Still, it was a famous victory, hailed in Britain and France, and cheered to the echo in Canada and among the corps' soldiers. Captain Georges Vanier wrote to his mother: 'The morale of our troops is magnificent. We cannot lose – what is more we are winning quickly and the war will be over within six months.'[37] Vindicating its approach to fighting, demonstrating the worth of the new emphasis on platoon tactics, and showing conclusively how good the counter-battery work had become, the victory sent morale soaring. The Canadian Corps had captured a hitherto impregnable position and had taken 4000 prisoners and fifty-four enemy guns, many of which were turned against the enemy by Canadian gunners who had trained in their use. The corps' sterling reputation was made, and rightly so.* General Byng stood tall with Kitchener's headquarters and with his troops. The war, however, continued with scarcely a break.

---

* The *Illustrated London News* on April 21, 1917, gave Vimy huge attention, featuring Canadian War Records photographs. The American entry into the war, by contrast, had much less space.

Lieutenant-General Byng was the first beneficiary of the victory. On June 6 he received a promotion to General, and Field Marshal Sir Douglas Haig put him in command of Britain's Third Army. To replace Byng, a commander loved by the Canadian troops, Haig had selected the First Division GOC, Arthur Currie. A few days earlier the Canadian had been knighted and had escaped a direct hit on his headquarters with only a graze; now he was the first Canadian and the first militiaman to command Canada's national army in the field. He was also, at forty-one, the youngest officer to achieve lieutenant-general's rank in the British armies. No one could have deserved it more, and corps staff came to admire Currie almost as much as they had Byng.

But as was always the case, nothing was ever simple in the high political machinations of the Canadian Expeditionary Force. Haig had made the appointment without consulting the Canadian authorities in London. Sir George Perley, the Overseas Minister, had not learned of Currie's promotion until June 9, and he naturally protested to the War Office. Perley found his position uncomfortable because he dealt every day with Major-General R.E.W. Turner, the GOC Canadians in England, who was senior to Currie and who had insisted when he took his post in November 1916 that he be considered for the corps command should it become available. Turner's record in France was undistinguished by comparison with Currie's, but he had done well in England, restoring order out of the mess that Hughes's minions had created. The two generals were rivals, not at war with each other, but not destined ever to be close or to agree.

The British, who regularly forgot that the dominions could not always be treated as colonies, scrambled to rectify matters. Currie's appointment had been made 'temporarily,' they now maintained, allowing the Canadians to sort out matters themselves. From Ottawa, Prime Minister Borden told Perley that he could use his own judgment, though he should 'take advice of higher command unless you see strong reasons to the contrary.' Borden added that Garnet Hughes, commanding the Fifth Canadian Division in England, should take over Currie's First Division. That, the Prime Minister clearly hoped, might stop the flood of criticism that Sir Sam, stripped of power, nonetheless kept up.[38]

Currie and Perley met in London on June 16. They agreed, as Perley had already determined was the preferred course, that both Turner and Currie should be promoted to lieutenant-general, thus preserving Turner's seniority, and keep their positions. Turner's title was later altered to Chief of the General Staff, and Currie remained corps commander, with the 'temporarily' deleted. But Currie insisted that the 7th Brigade commander, Brigadier-General A.C. Macdonnell, a former North-West Mounted Police officer and prewar Permanent Force officer, get the First Division;[39] he refused to accept his former friend Hughes, a man he considered unfit to command in the field. Perley agreed reluctantly, knowing the hell that would erupt. Erupt it did, as the Hughes's claque exerted maximum pressure, even attempting (but failing) to get British Prime Minister David Lloyd George to intervene. Garnet Hughes himself confronted Currie in a bitter three-hour meeting that ended in threats and imprecations, but the new corps commander refused to budge. Like Byng, he would make the appointments in his corps, and they would be the best men for the job.[40] 'Batty Mac' Macdonnell it would be.

Macdonnell's appointment, like Currie's own, was hugely popular with the men at the front, and Borden and Perley accepted the result. Currie himself lived in fear that his misdemeanour with his Victoria regiment's uniforms and his debts might become public, and the distraught Perley, who knew the story and feared he might lose the Canadian Corps' most successful commander, tried to persuade Militia Minister Sir A.E. Kemp to share the cost of meeting Currie's debts with him. Kemp refused, saying that the Militia Department had paid the bill and arranged for the money to be repaid by Currie. The Prime Minister involved himself in this cover-up, presumably praying that Sam Hughes – who would have had no hesitation in using the story to blacken Currie's name – not learn of it. The General nonetheless remained vulnerable, in his own mind particularly, until two of his officers, the wealthy Major-General David Watson and Brigadier-General Victor Odlum, advanced him the money in September to meet his obligations.[41] As for Sam and Garnet Hughes, they remained the most bitter of enemies, and Currie continued to suffer from a vicious smear campaign long after Sam Hughes was dead and buried.

Now in command, Currie had to accept greater responsibilities than before. The first orders he received from Haig, through the First Army, for a major attack after assuming command directed him to capture the shattered coal-mining city of Lens. After studying the lay of the land in a personal reconnaissance, Currie decided that his orders were foolish. Lens was dominated from the north by Hill 70 and from the south by Sallaumines Hill, and the GOC decided that these two heights tactically had more importance than the city. Extraordinarily, his strong arguments persuaded the First Army commander to change priorities and make Hill 70 the corps' first objective. Once the height fell, the Germans would have to counterattack, and Currie believed his artillery could smash the Germans on a killing ground of his choosing.

Not that Hill 70 was an easy objective. The Germans defended the treeless hill in force, and the suburbs of Lens, never palatial but now smashed by artillery, lay on the southern slope. Currie's plan called for the First and Second divisions to attack, massively supported by artillery and machine-gun fire. Rehearsals stressed immediate mopping up and the rapid move forward of machine guns – forty-eight with each brigade. Each machine-gun post would then be converted into a twenty-five-man strongpoint to help fend off counterattacks. This tactic was Currie's main contribution to the Great War: putting men and weapons in place to meet and defeat the counterattacks that were the hallmark of German battle doctrine.[42]

The attack began under smoke in the morning dark of August 15 without the benefit of surprise. The Germans had detected the Canadian preparations and reinforced their positions. Their artillery also was ready, but not for long as McNaughton's counter-battery organization smothered the German guns in fire. The attack moved forward quickly, both divisions covering 600 yards in the first twenty minutes. The next phases of the assault also proceeded well except for the 2nd Brigade's 7th and 8th battalions, which moved through thinning smoke right into enemy machine-gun fire. The battalions had to retire to their initial objectives and dig in. Now Currie's artillery planning paid off as German battalions marched forward into devastating artillery fire. Fifteen battalions in all tried their hands at driving the Canadians back; fifteen were cut down by artillery and heavy machine-gun fire.[43] 'Our gunners, machine-gunners and infantry,' Currie said, 'never had such targets.'[44] At the end of the first day of battle, the Canadians' relative success had cost them 3500 casualties.

The next day the Canadians took the second objectives they had failed to seize on the 15th, but some were lost to counterattacks. This was 'the worst ever,' Private Bob Gardner of the 21st Battalion wrote. 'Old Fritz had everything barricaded and armed ... there were fights in cellars, dugouts, tunnels, and everywhere imaginable ... I was buried [by exploding shells] five times in the four days that we were holding the new line.'[45] The fighting continued for days, stroke and counterstroke repeatedly launched and repelled. The Germans used mustard gas against the Canadians. This gas was less immediately debilitating than chlorine, but the ghastly blisters it produced, the effect on the eyes, and the ability of gassed men to 'infect' others with the presence of the gas on their clothing made it no less horrible. Currie called the battle for Hill 70 'altogether the hardest battle in which the Corps has participated,' adding that, in all, twenty-one German counterattacks had been repulsed.

The GOC now determined to use the Second and Fourth divisions to attack the lower southern slope of Hill 70. Again artillery planning was careful, heavy fire raining down on the defenders in the trenches and the ruined houses, but, as before, surprise was absent. A German spoiling attack fell on the 29th Battalion just as it left its trenches and the men resorted to hand-to-hand fighting. German artillery and machine-gun fire slaughtered the attackers in droves, and there were almost no gains for heavy losses. The Fourth Division's efforts continued, its objective now a heap of mine waste, the Green Crassier, which would allow the Canadians to surround Lens on three sides. The division partly captured its objectives in the initial assault, but German resistance continued and ultimately prevailed. The 44th Battalion, its men surrounded on the Crassier, lost 257 men, including 87 taken prisoner.

The ten-day struggle at Lens had cost 9198 Canadian casualties, a horrific price for slagheaps and blasted miners' cottages. All that could be said in a positive vein was that the Germans had seen five divisions broken in the defence of Lens, and Hill 70, at least, with its commanding observation over the Douai Plain, was in Allied hands. Still, Currie's Corps had won a substantial victory by Great War standards.

By the end of the summer of 1917 the Allies' position was troubled. The Americans were now in the war, but their armies would not appear in strength for months. After a revolution in March 1917, the Russian armies were hanging on by their fingernails while more trouble brewed at home. The Italians, fighting in the mountains bordering Austria, were little better off and lacked the revolutionary fervour. The French armies, which had been in a mutinous condition a few months before, were now more resolute, but no one counted on much from the *poilus* for the next several months. The British armies, astonishingly enough, still seemed to have their hearts in the struggle, though the casualties caused Britain, Canada, France, Australia, New Zealand, and the rest to scrape with increasing desperation at the bottom of the manpower barrel. Only the German enemy still seemed in good shape, ready to defend vigorously while building up strength for major attacks against the Russians and, with Austria-Hungary, against the Italians. Both sides put their hopes on war-winning offensives in 1918, the Germans intending to knock Russia out of the war and concentrate forces on the Western Front, and the Allies waiting for the fresh American manpower. In the meantime, attrition remained the policy, a policy of limited attacks to wear the Germans down. For the Canadian Corps, this policy returned them once again to the Ypres area and to a village called Passchendaele.

Haig's armies had been fighting in the Ypres salient all summer, moving the line forward by inches for heavy casualties in appalling conditions. A high water table, heavy rains, and massive artillery concentrations had turned the entire area into a muddy bog in which men and horses could drown and every step was a struggle. By early October, objectives planned for the first day of fighting on July 31 remained in German hands. That month, Currie's Canadian Corps received orders to move into the Ypres area and to prepare plans for the capture of Passchendaele. Now it was the Canadians' turn in hell, their turn to fight for ground that had almost no strategic significance.

Currie valued intelligence about the enemy and he made the corps' intelligence staff a valued part of his team.[46] But, as usual, he conducted his own reconnaissance of the battlefield, which he had first seen in April 1915. The Germans' well-placed positions overlooked the Allied line, for a start, as they had since the Canadians first fought in the salient. Conditions were far worse now, the area littered with the debris of more than two years of fighting: unburied dead men, mules, and horses were everywhere, grotesquely swollen; mud stretched all around, with a powerful suction effect that could swallow men and machines; rain-filled shell craters and submerged heavy equipment mixed with the remains of tree trunks; and rats abounded. Timothy Findley in *The Wars* expressed it best: 'Mud must be a Flemish word. Mud was invented here. Mudland might have been its name ... the water rises at you out of the ground.'[47] 'Battlefield looks bad,' Currie noted for his part, 'no salvaging has been done, and very few of the dead buried.'

Appalled, the GOC protested that he would not send his men into this charnel house, certainly not if he had to serve under General Sir Hubert Gough's Fifth Army. Haig agreed to switch the corps to Sir Herbert Plumer's Second Army. Currie protested still, carrying his arguments to Plumer and to Haig. 'I carried my protest to the extreme limit ... which I believe would have resulted in my being sent home had I been other than the Canadian Corps Commander.' As a national commander, Currie had a somewhat special status, but he was also a dutiful subordinate in a hierarchical army and from a hierarchical society. 'I pointed out what the casualties were bound to be, and asked if a success would justify the sacrifice. I was ordered to go and make the attack.'[48] Currie estimated the cost at 16,000 casualties, but his men would take Passchendaele.[49]

The key to the attack were the guns. In the muddy battlefield, the guns had to be set on firm wooden platforms, and roads had to be built to supply them with shells and to allow them to change position. Corduroy roads, a Canadian frontier device to cope with boggy ground, began to be constructed by the corps' hard-working engineers and pioneer battalions, who laid down logs and planks, cut in the corps' own sawmill. Tramways and rail lines pushed forward to carry supplies. Currie also secured canvas breech covers for the corps' rifles and machine guns, a simple device that helped keep the gluey mud from cutting the firepower of the infantry.[50] But the enemy positions remained, higher and somewhat drier than the Canadians. Well-protected by wire, with concrete pillboxes abounding, the Germans awaited the coming attack with confidence in their arms.

By October 26 Currie was ready to begin a three-phase assault on Passchendaele. He had brought the attacking troops forward three and four days early, deliberately giving them time to recover from the hard slog to the front lines. He visited every brigade and spoke to the troops. The Canadians now fielded infantry subunits with a variety of weaponry, all supported by technical specialists; they advanced in short bounds, using manoeuvre and firepower to overcome enemy strongpoints. Ultimately, however, success depended on the determination of the infantry and the gunners.

The first attack by the Third and Fourth divisions aimed only to move the line forward by 1200 yards, a terrible enough task. Lieutenant Sherwood Lett, a signals officer with the 46th Battalion of the Fourth Division, had to help rally his signallers, stretcher bearers, and stragglers to drive off a German counterattack and retake the battalion objective, as he put it, with the men wallowing 'to their deaths in the slime and blood-soaked mud.' After twelve hours, the 600 men of the 46th who had attacked that morning had suffered 53 killed, 287 wounded, and 62 missing.[51] The Third Division's 49th Battalion had 75 per cent casualties. The Princess Patricia's Canadian Light Infantry of the same division lost 150 killed and 213 wounded or missing, and one company ended under the command of a corporal. Two Pats won VCs. 'The 160 men we have left,' Lieutenant-Colonel Adamson wrote, 'are cheerful and at this moment singing.'[52] Few others were cheerful, given the slaughter that swallowed platoons and companies whole. The struggle continued and, after three days and 2500 killed and wounded, Currie called a halt short of the objective.

On October 30, after mule trains had brought in supplies, Currie tried again, this time moving the line forward a thousand yards for a further 2300 casualties. Now it was the turn of the First and Second divisions. On November 6 the Canadians attacked so rapidly that the German artillery fire fell behind them, and they were on the enemy lines before the automatic weapons could be manned. In less than three hours, just enough time for a further 2238 casualties, the ruins of Passchendaele were in Canadian hands. Except for some fierce fighting on November 10, in what Lieutenant Andrew Wilson of the 5th Battalion called 'the awful mud' that left him and his men 'bitterly cold through the longest night I ever put in,' the battle was over except for ferocious enemy shell fire.[53] Currie's estimate of the casualties, counting those suffered before and after the main attacks, was regrettably almost spot on. Another famous victory was Canada's, another objective of no strategic importance was taken, and there were another 16,000 grieving families back home. Prime Minister Sir Robert Borden, in London for meetings of the Imperial War Cabinet in June 1918 and well briefed by Currie, told British Prime Minister Lloyd George that 'if there is ever a repetition of Passchendaele, not a Canadian soldier will leave the shore of Canada so long as the Canadian people entrust the Government of my country to my hands.'[54] If those remarks had been made in late 1916, they might have meant more.

The Canadian Expeditionary Force's casualties and need for reinforcements were the driving force behind the issue of conscription in Canada. Recruiting had slowed after mid-1916 and, by the spring of 1917, was running at only 4000 men a month – far below replacement needs. Many of the volunteers opted for any corps but the infantry, making even those low numbers deceptive. This decline was undoubtedly a reaction to the high casualties and to the gradual drying up of the pool of potential volunteers in English Canada. In French Canada, where enlistments were low and slow, there was no shortage of men, only of a willingness to serve overseas. Hume Wrong, who had served overseas in a British regiment until being invalided home to his distinguished Toronto family, wrote privately and only half-jokingly in May 1917: 'I would welcome a little military activity in Quebec. My C.O. and I have arranged a little punitive expedition ... And I should delight in catching Bourassa and Lavergne [the anti-conscriptionist leaders].'[55] Others in English Canada shared that view – and weren't joking at all.

While it was primarily Quebec's reluctance that drove the issue at home, it was also the unwillingness of fit men in English Canada to serve. The government tried every expedient to avoid an issue that even the dullest politician could see was bound to be divisive. Because many in the government had believed there was a threat from German immigrants in Canada and the United States, substantial numbers of volunteers for overseas service had been retained at home: 16,000 soldiers did guard duty against a threat that had scarcely ever existed. The government had also directed that a minimum of 50,000 CEF volunteers in training or on other duties be retained at home to guard against all eventualities.

As casualties mounted overseas, the Chief of the General Staff, General Gwatkin, looked for ways to replace the volunteers on home defence duties and get them into action. His solution, approved by the Cabinet in January and February 1917, was to recruit 50,000 men into a Canadian Defence Force for home defence. The CDF began recruiting in March. The Militia Department proposed that CDF volunteers train with CEF volunteers, be as physically fit as CEF volunteers, and serve at a slightly lower rate of pay and allowances on the same terms – up to six months after the end of the war – as CEF recruits. The department's plan called for all 50,000 to be enrolled in April and to go off to summer camp for training in May.

With the United States in the war after April 6, there was no longer even the most remote possibility of a threat from the south, though the prospect of sabotage (of which there had been almost none in Canada) remained. Potential CDF recruits could figure out this scenario, and they could also see that there was no need for 50,000 men to be retained in Canada. Most, no doubt, feared they would be converted to the CEF and dispatched overseas and, as a result, volunteers who might have been eager for service only in Canada stayed away from the CDF in droves. By April 25 fewer than two hundred had signed up. Conscriptionists in government, the military, the media, and the public viewed the CDF failure as proving that only compulsion could produce men now.[56] In the first month of recruiting for the CDF, coincidentally the month of the great victory at Vimy, casualties overseas were 23,939. Volunteers for the CEF, including Nursing Sisters, numbered 4761.[57] Conscription's time had arrived.

To the military's surprise, Borden decided to impose conscription on his return from a visit to Britain and France in May. For the next seven months, as the Military Service Bill passed through Parliament and an almost wholly English-speaking coalition government formed to fight a bitter election in December 1917, conscription dominated the public debate. Overseas, the soldiers watched and waited, most hoping that conscripts would provide the reinforcements the corps needed. General Currie had responded to Borden's congratulatory message on his appointment as corps commander in June by saying: 'It is an imperative and urgent necessity that steps be immediately taken to ensure that sufficient drafts of officers and men are sent from Canada to keep the Corps at its full strength.'[58] This message, something that Currie believed to be true, had been read in Parliament during the debate on the Military Service Bill, where it annoyed anti-conscriptionists. But when the government asked Currie (whom many Conservatives knew to be a Liberal) during the 1917 election campaign to issue a message to the troops endorsing the Union Government and conscription, he refused, seeing this request as blatant political interference with his command. By this point, Currie thought it more important to break up the 21,000-strong Fifth Canadian Division, sitting in England under Major-General Garnet Hughes, than to impose conscription, which would take months to produce results. Hughes's division was untouchable so long as his father was minister; after Sam's ouster, the government still refused to act. To Currie, it was all politics, damn politics. There were enough men in England to replace the corps' losses at Paaschendaele, add to the strength of infantry battalions, and help create new machine-gun battalions – if only the government had the courage to take on Sam Hughes's malign influence. It didn't, so Currie flatly refused the request.[59] Arthur Currie was a tough, principled man, and he eventually secured the break-up of Hughes's division in February 1918.

Whatever Currie thought and however he himself voted, his men, like English-speaking Canadians at home, overwhelmingly cast their ballots for the Union Government and conscription. Some pressure was applied to soldiers to vote the right way by a few conscriptionist Commanding Officers, and stories of political skullduggery were told. Still, it is inescapable that 92 per cent of the military vote went to the victorious Borden, enough to switch fourteen seats from the Liberals to the Union Government.[60] Acting Corporal John Saywell, a soldier from Broadview, Saskatchewan, in the 1st Canadian Mounted Rifles, wrote to his sister in December 1917 to note that some young men from their town should have joined up long before. 'Although things out here are a little tough at times still one feels satisfied that he did and is still doing right. I would not like to have been conscripted.'[61]

Conscription duly came into force in January 1918 after the election. More than nine out of every ten men called for service sought exemption, and many of those refused exemption took to the hills. Many of the exemptions that were granted, not least to farmers, were cancelled on April 19, 1918, as the great German offensive terrified the Allies. Borden told a delegation of protesting farmers that the war situation was critical and that the Canadian Corps needed reinforcements. He rejected the argument that he had broken a solemn covenant made during the election: 'Do you imagine for one moment we have not a solemn covenant and a pledge to those men?'[62] In Quebec, where evasion of the Military Service Act was greatest, there were contrary pressures to create a francophone brigade out of conscripts and volunteers, but Currie, who consulted his COs, vetoed this plan. None of his battalions would accept so much as a company of French Canadians. 'My own opinion is that they should not be kept separate,' Currie said; 'they are Canadians the same as everybody else, and the sooner it is so regarded the better it will be.'[63] The 22nd would remain the only French-speaking battalion.*

At the end of the day, Borden had hoped to generate 100,000 men by his conscription legislation and he achieved this result. Of the 401,000 men called up for service, 99,651 were on strength of the CEF on November 11, 1918, the date of the armistice. Of that number, 47,500 had already proceeded overseas, and 24,132 had been taken on strength of units in France.[64†] How many saw action was unclear, but, if the war had continued into 1919, as most expected, the conscripts likely would have been sufficient to keep the Canadian Corps' divisions up to strength. Compulsory service was politically divisive for a generation and more afterwards, but it successfully produced reinforcements when the voluntary system had broken down. Readers will have to judge for themselves if the military advantages outweighed the political costs. The certainty is that reinforcements could keep units up to strength and help minimize casualties. At the same time, however efficient they were, Canada's four divisions could not tilt the balance very much towards either Allied victory or defeat. For Canada, conscription was as much political as military in its necessity.

After almost three years in the trenches, the Canadian Corps was a veteran formation that benefited from its status as a national contingent. The corps operated its own training schools and found its own reinforcements. British formations, by comparison, had no such independence: their schools were run in common and their casualty replacements were drawn from a nationwide and ever-diminishing pool. Faced with a serious manpower shortage, British divisions each lost three battalions, and, by the beginning of 1918, their organization consisted of three brigades each of three infantry battalions. The

---

* The 60th Battalion, raised in Quebec and with a substantial proportion of francophones, was in the 9th Brigade until early 1917. Then, because it was having difficulty maintaining its strength, the 60th was dropped from the order of battle and replaced by the 116th, which had a Conservative Member of Parliament as its CO. See the official explanation in G.W.L. Nicholson, *Canadian Expeditionary Force, 1914–1919* (Ottawa, 1962), 225.

† In all, 470,224 soldiers served overseas, of whom 47 per cent were Canadian born; 194,869 never left Canada, of whom 61.1 per cent were Canadian-born – a figure that reflects the impact of conscription. Desmond Morton, *When Your Number's Up: The Canadian Soldier in the First World War* (Toronto, 1993), 278–9.

Canadians refused to conform and insisted on maintaining their divisions at a strength of almost 22,000, with three brigades each of four battalions – a benefit in the attack because the usual two up, two in reserve system meant that the follow-on or counterattack force was always strong. (The British had to employ two up, one in reserve, which weakened their second effort.) Canadian battalions also had more men than British ones, thanks to the reinforcements from the break-up of the Fifth Division in England and from conscription. The Fifth's infantry reinforced the units in France; indeed, they permitted an extra hundred men to be added to each battalion, a sufficient number to last most battalions in France until September 1918. Thereafter, a ruthless scouring of rear area units and hospitals for reinforcements had to suffice until enough conscripts from Canada arrived to keep the ranks filled.

The other arms in the corps also had more punch than in British formations. British divisions had three Engineer Field Companies and a battalion of pioneers; Canadian divisions had nine Field Companies and pontoon bridging specialists. British divisions had a Machine Gun Battalion of three companies; Canadian divisions could draw on a Machine Gun Battalion three times the size, providing one automatic weapon for every thirteen men, compared with one for every sixty-one men in British divisions. As a result, a Canadian division was vastly more potent than a British division and had 50 per cent more infantry.[65]

The Canadian Corps headquarters similarly controlled more resources: a hundred more trucks than a British corps, more and better signallers, a better maintenance organization to keep heavy equipment functioning, and, because Currie decided to keep the Fifth Division's field artillery brigades intact, the corps had an extra artillery increment. Moreover, the GOC Royal Artillery in the Canadian Corps could command all his artillery, unlike the British GOC Royal Artillery, who was more of an adviser. Canadian guns could therefore be concentrated easier, faster, and more effectively. The Canadians also had one heavy Trench Mortar Battery for each division; British corps had one battery under command.[66]

In effect, the Canadian Corps, with its four large divisions and its extra punch, was almost a small army. In early 1918, in fact, the British suggested that a two corps army might be formed, something that would have given Currie a promotion from lieutenant-general to general, and many of his officers a jump in rank. With some difficulty, Currie persuaded the new Minister of Overseas Military Forces, Sir A.E. Kemp, to decline the suggestion, leading Stephen Harris to write quite properly that 'there was no finer demonstration of the professional ethos that requires loyalty to service before self.'[67] Currie believed that the gain in real fighting strength would have been minimal because of the increased number of rear area troops necessary to maintain an army and, moreover, there was still a shortage of trained staff officers.[68] The Brigadier-General General Staff at corps headquarters, Currie's senior planner, was British, as were the two next senior staff officers, and the first Canadian GSO I, the divisional senior planner, did not take up position until November 1917.[69]

The Canadians simply believed themselves to be unbeatable, and this intangible factor was one further reason that Currie refused to agree to the creation of an army that would submerge the Canadian Corps in a larger entity. Vimy, Hill 70, and the hell of Paaschendaele, terrible in cost though they were, had persuaded the Canadian soldiers that they were special. Most might have been British-born, but the war made them Canadians, and they genuinely believed they could do what others could not – and they were right. That they had more resources was a critical bonus, an extra boost that reinforced the corps' élan. When Currie's corps began its Hundred Days on August 8, 1918, the Canadians made their greatest contribution to victory.

While the Canadian Corps made its way back from Passchendaele to the relatively calm Lens sector in November 1917, the Canadian Cavalry Brigade saw action, briefly and disastrously. On November 20 the British mounted the first mass attack of tanks of the war in front of Cambrai and utterly smashed the German line. The attack went in without an artillery bombardment, and cavalry had been put on stand-by for the breakthrough. The armour and infantry moved forward about 4 miles and the Cavalry Brigade moved on, only to be withdrawn at dusk before any units had contact with the enemy. One squadron of the Fort Garry Horse missed the recall, however, and, led by Lieutenant Harcus Strachan, overran an artillery battery and some infantry. Effectively cut off, the survivors sheltered in a sunken road. Strachan stampeded the horses and, with this diversion, led his small contingent of troopers back to Allied lines. He deservedly won the Victoria Cross, but the ineffectiveness of cavalry had been demonstrated yet again. The brigade played a role –

as infantry – on the defensive when German counterattacks took back most of the ground gained by the tanks. Canadian Railway Troops, caught up in the counterattacks, also stood and fought very well.

In March 1918, now that Lenin's Russia was effectively out of the war, the Germans began to move troops from the Eastern Front. They planned a great offensive on the Western Front, with specially trained divisions led by stormtroopers infiltrating through the Allied lines. Here the Canadian Cavalry Brigade saw action once more – again in the defence. When the German surprise attack fell on General Gough's British Fifth Army, it smashed through the British defences. In the immediate result, panicked Allied leaders agreed that a unified command was essential at last, and France's Marshal Ferdinand Foch became Supreme Commander. The Cavalry Brigade, which was in the First Army to the north, provided 800 men to cover the retirement of a British division and half of a mounted detachment to fill gaps in the line. In the confused fighting, cavalry units sometimes roamed far afield, and Lieutenant F.M.W. Harvey, VC, of the Lord Strathcona's Horse was taken prisoner by French troops in the village of Fontaine, which he and ten men had entered and cleared of a large number of Germans. But it was at Moreuil Wood, 12 miles southeast of Amiens, that the Canadian Cavalry Brigade saw its heaviest action. The attack began with three squadrons of the Royal Canadian Dragoons, followed by the Strathconas and the Garrys. The wood was cleared, not least as a result of the suicidal 'Charge of Flowerdew's Squadron' (immortalized in a superb painting by official artist Alfred Munnings) that won a posthumous VC for the Strathconas' Lieutenant G.M. Flowerdew. The troopers, now fighting as infantry, held almost all they had gained until they were relieved by three British battalions.[70] Men of the brigade participated in a further attack on April 1 that finally retook the wood.

Spared from the massive German assault of March 1918 by good luck, the Canadian Corps watched, waited, and trained. The Germans attacked to their north in Flanders in April and easily took Passchendaele, so hard won the autumn before, and attacked again to their south in Champagne in May and July. The Allied lines buckled, buckled again, and ultimately reformed and held. The Germans were making their last throw of the dice, and they came close to winning the game.

Although he was willing to see his corps used as a whole, Currie refused to lose control of his divisions – to two different armies and three different corps, he grumbled – in this crisis, though he did agree to their employment under British control as and if necessary. Part of his attitude was his awareness that he was a national commander, answerable to Ottawa, and that the country wanted Canadian troops to fight together. But he also sensed that more than a few British generals were less than competent, not least the staff surrounding General Haig.

Haig, for his part, complained bitterly about Currie's attitude, attributing it to a swelled head, and he recorded a comment in his diary after a meeting with Overseas Minister Kemp: 'I could not help feeling that some people in Canada regard themselves rather as "allies" than fellow citizens in the Empire.'[71] The British commander had remained completely oblivious to the development of Canadian nationalism in the war; Canadians, from knighted ministers and generals down to the lowliest British-born private in the rear rank, had not. The war and the Canadian Corps, its successes and its reputation as shock troops, had made them all nationalists. Added to this sense of pride was a hint of resentment that the British high command threw Canadians into attacks on the most difficult objectives to spare its own men. Given the casualties the British Army had sustained, this charge was grossly unfair, but many at the front believed it nonetheless.

Whatever the reasons for its being spared the German attack, Currie's corps was effectively out of heavy fighting for months, from Passchendaele to August 1918. The men suffered enemy bombardments, fought off raids and launched their own, but it was a period of relative quiet: in January 1918 losses were 680; in February, 737; in March, 2075; in April, 2881; in May, 1427; in June, 1043; and in July, 1233.[72] Influenza, Spanish flu, as it was called, hit the armies in June, sometimes with devastating effects. One soldier, Arthur Lapointe, noted in his diary that men suddenly began complaining of headaches, pain, and fever. Then he was affected: 'my head swims with sudden nausea, everything around me whirls, I totter, then fainting, fall to the ground.' Lapointe and most of the afflicted recovered, but many died.[73]

Out of the line, the healthy had time for rest and recuperation. Soldiers played baseball against other units or engaged in track-and-field meets.[74] Some busied themselves 'scrounging' when they needed equipment or stores. Artillery Sergeant J.R. Mutchmor, later Moderator of the United Church, wrote that 'the general view was that all property, including such movable items as tarpaulins, rubber boots and horses, were just part of the King's stores ... Canadians enjoyed this form of appropriation best,' he added, 'when gains were made at the expense of the English artillery.' Some sold the proceeds, and not a few horses ended up feeding civilians and enriching soldiers.[75] A few men went on leave, their pockets full. Many watched the Third Division's famous entertainment troupe, The Dumbells, present skits, songs, and female impersonators (the most famous of whom was 'Marjorie,' Private Ross Hamilton). All units held religious services[76] and a big celebration on July 1. There was also time for baths, which were, Major McFarland of the 4th CMR noted, 'a very important feature of the military organization.' The bath units set up near rest camps in the rear, and any building could be pressed into service. 'The equipment comprised a number of shower-baths, with plenty of hot and cold water, and a sufficient supply of soap and towels and clean under-clothing. When a battalion came out of the line the men were taken to the bath-house by platoons ... The system helped tremendously to keep down scabies and vermin.'

By the end of 1917 the Third Canadian Division also offered educational courses through the 'University of Vimy Ridge,' which taught everything from reading and writing to technical courses. Officers and men with the requisite qualifications gave the instruction. The German offensive of March 1918 disrupted the 'university,' but in England the 'Khaki University,' as it was called, flourished. Started informally early in 1917, this university took on a formal life in January 1918 and began offering a wide range of courses – from the teaching of reading and writing to graduate work. The distinguished Canadian scholar Harold Innis, in late 1917 a convalescing soldier in England, began his MA work at McMaster University through the Khaki University and wrote most of his thesis there. The University of Vimy Ridge became the basis for the extension of the Khaki University to France in the summer of 1918 and, after the Armistice, classes began in virtually every battalion of the CEF. In England a special University Camp at Ripon, staffed by academics in the CEF and others brought from Canada, offered a range of courses, and British universities also pitched in. In all, there were 50,000 course registrations, and many soldiers earned credits for university work; others became literate; and still others prepared themselves for farming or business when they were repatriated to Canada.[77]

The bulk of the corps' time was spent in training. Courses in specialist skills, some run by the British Army, saw Canadian officers and NCOs pulled out of the line for weeks at a time to learn the manifold arcane tasks of the army. At Le Havre, the first site of the Canadian Base Depot later relocated to Étaples, the corps ran a series of schools to train and retrain soldiers. One young soldier, Michael Duggan from Toronto, a reinforcement destined for the 42nd Battalion in the autumn of 1916, recorded rather bleakly his training regimen at the Canadian Base Depot:

> Early to bed and early to rise ... We have just finished our meal (dinner) which consisted of bread and butter, cheese and tea. (Tres petit) We rise generally about 5 or 4:30 in order to get breakfast over before 7 o'clock parade. The breakfast consists of tea, meat, bread and jam ... We are about 4/8 of a mile from the cookhouse and about 5 or 6,000 soldiers – some lineups all right. There are 12 men allotted to each tent ... Gas helmet practice I think for us this afternoon ... We are now taking the last instructions before leaving for the trenches laying wire entanglements, bayonet fighting, squad duty ...

Duggan continued his account by noting 'the most interesting lecture since I joined the army,' a presentation by a decorated British captain with much service who talked to the men about the German character: 'He had lost one of his own men by the man going out to give some water to a wounded German officer ... That is your Germans for you. That is why we British, as well as colonial troops, take so few prisoners. Enough said. The less taken, the less to look after.'[78]

The training at the rear was frequently a bit haphazard and devoted more to 'psyching' up the troops than useful training. Still, Currie's brigadiers and battalion commanders, by 1918 all skilled and experienced officers, ran realistic tactical exercises with and without troops, testing leaders and techniques. The senior officers of the corps learned what they could from British and French battle experience and added these lessons to what they themselves had seen. They paid special attention to mastering the infiltration tactics developed by the enemy, and the best brigade commanders, such as Brigadier-General William Griesbach of the 1st Brigade, listened to the soldiers' suggestions.[79] Training was spottier in some brigades than others, however, and stories abounded that some units worked with tanks for an hour or at best a day, scarcely time enough to learn cooperation in an advance.

The men practised the use of machine guns in the attack – there were now two teams of two sections per platoon, each with a Lewis gun – and the use of phosphorous bombs to create smoke screens.[80] The new and varied types of gas in use by the enemy, especially phosgene and mustard gas, required constant anti-gas training. One officer remembered 'one of those abominations of the flesh, a night-march with Gas-Respirators. I know of nothing more uncomfortable. One went stumbling about the country, half-stifled and almost blind, with the saliva drooling out of the valve down one's jacket.'[81]

Currie generally smiled on the work of Brigadier-General Raymond Brutinel's two Motor Machine Gun brigades, with their armoured cars, trucks carrying machine guns, motor cycles, and truck-mounted trench mortars, all of which had served well in the German advance in March and would prove useful again in the open warfare to come. His artillery staff continued to spend time calculating how best to provide fire support and turned their skill into an art. In effect, the Canadian Corps under Currie became practitioners of combined arms operations, a force able to get the maximum effect from the different weapons available to it. Technology and tactics had been married in the Canadian divisions.[82] Some imperial formations had this capacity, though only a few British generals appeared to understand either the principles or the benefits of it.[83]

Currie also refined his corps' battle doctrine, the marriage of planning and operations, and reflected this work in the way he issued orders: a detailed plan went to the divisions, which elaborated on their role and then passed the orders downward. As his biographer noted, 'In approximately three to eight hours the corps commander's order would reach the lowest private soldier and do so in an intelligible manner.' The private soldier knew his brigade and battalion objective and precisely what his platoon was to do; he knew who would be on his platoon's flanks and the support available. He learned of specific obstacles that faced his platoon, and he knew about the next meal, the location of first-aid stations, and when he could expect to be relieved. All this took place automatically, and it was replicated for the guns, the supply train, and the medical services.[84] The corps was now ready to fight again.

The Allied plan, devised by Foch, called for General Rawlinson's British Fourth Army, made up of the Australian Corps and a British Corps, to be joined by the Canadians and to strike east from Amiens with the French. The Canadians moved into position in secrecy: Currie sent medical units, two infantry battalions (the 4th CMR and the 27th Battalion), and signallers to Flanders to pass on meaningless messages while his staff even prepared plans for a fictitious operation near Arras as part of the disinformation scheme. The Canadians' reputation as elite troops meant that the enemy invariably saw their presence in the line as a signal of an attack.[85]

The emphasis on surprise extended to the entire Allied attack, scheduled for August 8. Tanks would be used *en masse* as at Cambrai, and there was to be no preliminary bombardment. Artillery registration was skilfully managed to conceal the impression of a build-up. Fortunately, the Germans who had been advancing had not had time to make their defences impregnable, and their divisions were seriously understrength.

For once, everything favoured the offence, including the good weather that firmed the ground, and, as the tanks rumbled forward and the artillery at last boomed out, the Canadian and the Australian Corps, fighting side by side, moved out in mist and smoke. The Australians, commanded by the brilliant General Sir John Monash, like Currie a pre-war militiaman, were every bit the equal of the Canadians (though perhaps more individualistic and rowdy!). For the first time the men wore 'fighting order' – light kit that consisted of weapons, ammunition, water bottle, gas mask, and shovel. And, for the first time, the Germans all but melted away before the attackers, who moved forward in extended order with skirmishers out in front. The attackers quickly crossed the River Luce, expected to be a difficult obstacle, as bridging units got pontoons across with speed. The tanks did much useful work, especially in dealing with enemy machine guns, though the Germans had developed anti-tank tactics and weapons that knocked out many tanks while mechanical breakdowns eliminated still more. Of the 342 Mark V tanks in action on August 8, only six were still operable four days later.[86]

Nonetheless, the Canadian Corps seized all its objectives, except for the Fourth Division's one of Le Quesnel, and made an advance of 8 miles – yes, miles, after battles fought for yards – at a cost of almost 4000 casualties. High as that was, the gains and the sharp shock dealt to the enemy made it all worthwhile. Georges Vanier, who won the Distinguished Service Order for his part in the August 8 battle, spoke later of 'the effect on the troops of that successful breakthrough ... We felt somehow that the Germans were beaten and ... hope stirred our hearts.'[87] The Australians, British, and French also moved well forward and more than justified General Ludendorff's description of August 8 as 'the black day of the German Army in the history of this war.'

The next two days saw the attackers pressing forward against strengthening resistance and with their supplies of ammunition, food, and water dwindling – a common problem in the last months of the war as the supply services struggled to haul ammunition and food forward in step with the advance. The artillery support on which the corps depended also could not always keep up. Le Quesnel nonetheless fell to the Third Division, and Captain Bellenden Hutcheson, a Medical Officer with the 75th Battalion, recalled that he had to move through the streets repeatedly to collect the wounded. 'As the 4th C.M.R. and tanks pushed through the village the shelling again became intense. The Germans were about 240 yds. outside the village.' A company reached the street corner a hundred feet away and 'a shell landed in their midst. About six men went down,' but, since it was attacking, it could not stop. Hutcheson and two of his medical section ran to them. 'The Company Commander lay on his face with the back of his head sheared off. I recall that he had the rank and name of "Captain Macdonald" written on some of his equipment. Three other men were killed ... One of the men who had been killed was evidently carrying phosphorous smoke bombs. These had set his clothes on fire. We tried to extinguish the fire, but his clothing and body seemed shot through with the phosphorous and it was impossible to put it out ... Later in the day ... I saw his body again. He was almost incinerated.'[88] An American citizen, Hutcheson won the Military Cross for his actions this day and the Victoria Cross on September 2.

Sherwood Lett, now adjutant of the 46th Battalion, wrote of his unit's attack on August 10: 'At 10:15 we ... started to advance. As the tanks crossed the Vrély-Rouvray road the [artillery] barrage opened up with lifts of 200 yards every five minutes. We passed through the battalions of the 1st Division ... and started on towards our objective ... As we advanced the shelling became more intense, the odd man dropping here and there as Fritz poured his artillery and machine-guns into us.' By noon, the 46th had advanced 2 miles and the enemy resistance was fierce. Lett helped consolidate the battalion position and won a Military Cross for his role.[89]

By the end of the day on August 10, after 2500 more casualties, Currie insisted that the offensive be halted until such time as preparations could be made for a set-piece assault. Astonishingly, Haig agreed and persuaded Foch of the need for a pause. The Amiens front slowed, and the Canadians moved north to the familiar area of Arras to join the First Army. Their achievement was immense, and the corps would add to its laurels in the days ahead. Using armour, indirect fire, air support, deception measures, and chemical warfare, the Canadians had begun to fight a war of movement that looked very much like a modern battlefield.[90]

The target now was the Hindenburg Line and the city of Cambrai, the centre of the enemy defences. The Germans had sited their positions in depth before the city and made use of successive defensive trenches, especially the Drocourt-Quéant Line (an extension of the Hindenburg Line, spiked with concrete fortifications) and the all-but-impassable Canal du Nord. Surprise was not a possibility here, and Currie had no choice but frontal assaults. The battle began on August 26.

The Second and Third divisions led the attack on Monchy-le-Preux, jumping off at 3 a.m. By nightfall, they had the village and had advanced a thousand yards beyond. The next day's attack called for an advance of 5 miles and the breaching of the first German line. This objective could not be won until August 30, and only after heavy casualties – 6000 men in three days of fighting. One of those wounded was Georges Vanier of the 22nd Battalion. Commanding the regiment, Major Vanier was hit in the stomach on August 28 and then, while a stretcher bearer was attending to his wound, he was wounded again by shrapnel. Doctors amputated his leg soon after at a Casualty Clearing Station. Every officer in his battalion had been killed or wounded.

Currie's task now was to crack the Drocourt-Quéant Line. British general headquarters had wanted him to attack at once, but the GOC insisted on a pause for rest and planning. As it was, his attack, quickly prepared by his now expert staff, went ahead on September 2 with the First and Fourth Divisions in front. Major Maurice Pope, a staff officer at Fourth Division headquarters, noted in a letter home that 'Vimy took months of preparation. Four days ago I knew nothing of this affair and the job is at the very least of equal magnitude.'[91] The First Division was to take the D-Q Line's support trenches and then the Buissy Switch, an extension of the line covering two small villages. The Fourth Division's objective was to pierce the five lines of trenches that made up the main D-Q position. An innovative heavy artillery barrage cut most of the German wire; tanks rolled over the rest; and the Germans, their spirit shaken as war weariness took hold, put up less than the usual resistance. The First Division took hundreds of prisoners as it moved towards the Buissy Switch, but, in the face of stiffening resistance, the division, though it cleared the D-Q trenches, could not make its final objective 3000 yards further on. The Fourth Division met its Drocourt-Quéant objectives on schedule, but an attack down the open slopes of Mont Dury halted under intense machine-gun fire. The next morning the enemy had evaporated, his forces withdrawn well to the east. With a strategic victory under their belts, the Canadians moved forward to the west bank of the Canal du Nord. Though the price was 5500 casualties, the Canadian success had forced the German withdrawal.

The canal was a formidable obstacle. The 100-foot-wide obstacle was flanked on both banks by flooded marshes, and the Germans had machine-gun nests in quantity on their side, as well as successive trench lines and a willingness to use gas against the attackers. To the south, there was a 4000-yard portion of unfinished canal, dry, and on firmer ground. Again, the Germans had fortified their bank, but Currie concluded that this approach was better than a water crossing under fire. The difficulty for the GOC was that he had to send 50,000 men through a narrow funnel and, after reaching the far bank, fan them out over a 10,000–15,000-yard front, taking out the enemy defences in the process.

This hugely complicated plan required skilled leadership and well-prepared troops. It also required surprise enough to fool the enemy: if the German artillery hit the Canadians bunched in the funnel, the result could only be disastrous. Currie's intelligence officers had advised him that the enemy's artillery was short of shells. Still, his plan required careful positioning of the guns and the ability to move them forward across the canal over bridges able to withstand their weight, as well as that of tanks and trucks – bridges to be built by the engineers, often under fire. Currie's army commander had his doubts, and so did General Byng: 'Old man, do you think you can do it?' Byng asked. 'Yes,' said Currie. 'If anybody can do it, the Canadians can,' Byng rejoined, 'but if you fail it means home for you.'[92]

Currie's plan called for the Fourth and First Divisions to cross the canal. The Fourth was then to press on to take Bourlon Wood. The First was to swing left to take villages alongside the canal. If this operation went as planned, the front would be some 10,000 yards, allowing room for the Third Division and a British division to move into the line. The four divisions would then push outwards and pinch Cambrai from the north and south.

In the early hours of September 27 the Canadian barrage began and the men moved across the dry canal. The engineers provided bridges and ladders for the troops and ramps for guns and vehicles, helping them all over the far bank. The adjoining British 17th Corps could not keep pace with the Fourth Division, and this lag exposed the Canadians to enfilade fire. The attack bogged down for a time but then progressed to clear Bourlon Wood. Even so, the final objectives were not reached. The First Division, its tasks by far the most difficult, took its objectives, and the flanking British troops also matched its success. For the next few days the struggle went on, as the Germans reinforced their troops extensively. On the night of October 1, Currie called off the attack. The last German organized defences in front of his corps had been smashed, but the casualties were huge: in six weeks of fighting, the Canadians had sustained 31,000 casualties, the majority from machine guns that the Germans deployed in such quantity and depth that the artillery could not knock them all out. Open warfare was costly: the Third Division's losses in August (4716 men) and the Fourth's in September (7352 men) were their highest of the war. Paradoxically, the superb staff work that created the plan for the Canal du Nord produced such high casualties that the effectiveness of the corps' infantry battalions began to falter.[93] The new battlefield swallowed attackers in wholesale, just as trench warfare had. The critical difference was that the gains were worthwhile and the strategic objectives were real ones.

On balance, the Canadian Corps' operations at the Canal du Nord were the best exemplar of Canadian military professionalism in the Great War. The GOC had proposed an innovative, complicated plan, his staff had drafted his orders, and his officers and men had carried them out. That sounds simple enough, but, of course, it's not. To combine artillery and infantry, to get specialist units at the right place at the right time, required great skill. Currie, his staff, and his men had mastered the Great War's demands: massive, accurate artillery support, using high explosives, shrapnel, and gas against the enemy trenches; provision of forming up areas, lines of communication, and artillery; and a tough, well-briefed infantry using fire and movement aided by their mortars, machine guns, rifles, and grenades. The Canadian Corps was not alone in being able to perform so well, and other formations – the Australians and some British corps – were as capable. But saying that takes nothing away from the Canadian Corps' achievement. The militiamen of 1914 could not have crossed the canal any more than the CEF of 1915 or 1916. Only time, study, accrued expertise, and fighting skill enabled the corps to carry out such a difficult attack. This development was in every respect a miracle, one that had been fully paid for in experience and in blood.

When Prime Minister Borden spoke to the Imperial War Cabinet in July 1918 about his dissatisfaction with British generalship and military professionalism, he used a good Canadian example to make his point:

At the outbreak of the war, Canada had a small permanent Army. What would have happened if we had laid down the principle that no man should fill a higher position than that of brigadier unless he had been a member of the standing Army? If we fail to use the brains of the nation for the best purpose, we cannot have much prospect of winning this war. Let me give an example with respect to organization. General Jack Stewart is a Scotsman. He came to Canada about thirty years ago. He is as good a railway builder as any man in North America. I understand he is now under the direction of officers who know nothing about railway construction to which he has devoted his entire life. I understand that he could carry on his present work if he were given charge with 40 per cent of the men presently employed. He was asked to build a railway for the construction of which French engineers estimated six weeks, British engineers three weeks. Stewart examined the ground and said he could build it in six days. He actually built it in four.[94]*

Borden was unquestionably correct about the British reluctance to trust warfare to amateurs. With their tiny pre-war Permanent Force, the Canadians

---

* 'Why have Canada's businessmen, serving as officers at the front, done so conspicuously well?' asked *Maclean's* in September 1916. 'Here's the reason – "Businessmen have to fight all their lives – for business is a fight. They have to match their brains against competitors ... to handle men ... They are constantly being called upon to meet emergencies."' C. Lintern Sibley, 'A Canadian Who Saved Ypres.'

could not have taken a position of leadership. Borden recognized that civilian expertise could be applied to some of the technical areas of battle, but only some. Tactics and strategy at a platoon or company level could be grasped in a relatively short time, but not at a battalion, brigade, or division level. Commanders like Currie were not available *en masse*. Borden had relied for his advice on Currie, the property speculating militiaman who had become a professional in the trenches. The Canadian militia tradition could push forward competent officers capable of learning, but that took time. There was no indication that Borden understood that this achievement was a miracle, even if Currie now did. What the Canadian Prime Minister knew after four years of war was that he was fed up with what he called the 'incompetence and blundering stupidity of the whisky and soda British H.Q. staff.'[95]

The German position all along the Western Front was now in serious difficulty. There were rumours of capitulation as Berlin and Vienna asked U.S. President Woodrow Wilson for the opening of armistice talks. The High Command was despondent, and the morale of the front-line troops, frequently short of food and weakened severely by the huge casualties sustained in their earlier 1918 offensives, sagged precipitously. All these factors had clearly aided the Canadian Corps in its advances since August, and the French and American advances to the south also made progress. The long war seemed close to its conclusion, but the pressure on the front, on Berlin, had to be sustained.

The corps did its part here. On the night of October 8–9 Currie returned to the attack with the objective of Cambrai, the Germans' key railway junction in northern France. He intended to seize bridges over the Canal de l'Escaut and cut the town off from the north. The attack went in just as the Germans were pulling out. A succession of bungles, breakdowns in command and supply, and high casualties gave clear indication that the casualties since August 8 had pushed the Canadians close to the breaking point, but Cambrai was in Canadian hands by 8:30 a.m. The Germans continued to retreat into their new Hermann Line. Liberating towns, receiving the plaudits and kisses of civilians, the Canadians moved rapidly but cautiously forward towards Valenciennes, the key point in the line.

A British attack on October 28 on Mont Houy to the south of the city failed to completely overcome stiff resistance and resulted in the cancellation of the Fourth Canadian Division's part in the assault. Currie now planned to take the objective on November 1, sending his men forward under cover of smoke and behind a huge artillery barrage – almost as heavy as that fired by both sides in the entire Boer War! One infantry brigade took Mont Houy, and the corps crossed the canal in front of Valenciennes and, by noon, had patrols into the heart of the city. Stunned by the barrage, German soldiers surrendered in large numbers, and even the official history notes that Canadians shot prisoners out of hand.[96]* (The same thing may have happened to some Canadians taken captive in action. Only 112 officers and 3715 other ranks became prisoners of war, and their treatment from capture to prison camp and work details was often rough, though ordinarily less so for officers and senior NCOs, who were frequently interned in Switzerland or the Netherlands. Repatriated at war's end, Canadian ex-POWs were not treated as heroes; on the contrary, they were often seen as cowards compared with those men who fought and, especially, those who died in action.)[97] The cost for liberating yet another part of France was 80 killed and 300 wounded, bad enough in the final days of a war but astonishingly small by Great War standards.

Now the Germans were on the run, their allies surrendering or seeking peace while the British, French, and Americans demanded complete surrender. The Canadian Corps pressed forward, its reconnaissance patrols ordinarily meeting little resistance beyond snipers and occasional rearguard machine-gun posts, usually dealt with by mortar or machine-gun fire. There were delays because of cratered roads, torn-up rail tracks, felled trees, and systematic German demolition of every bridge. The Canadians discovered that the Germans resisted in the afternoon and retreated at night, so the corps adjusted its tactics accordingly.[98] At one or two points only, German units fought hard, but their supply lines had broken down and their artillery could

---

* Robert Graves noted that the Canadians had 'the worst reputation for acts of violence against prisoners ... How far this reputation for atrocities was deserved, and how far it could be ascribed to the overseas habit of bragging and leg-pulling, we could not decide. At all events, most overseas men ... made atrocities against prisoners a boast, not a confession' (*Good-bye to All That* [New York, 1998], 184). The 4th CMR of the Third Division staged a successful raid on April 21, 1918. 'One of the sergeants was detailed to escort two prisoners back ... When he arrived at our Front Line,' the regiment's second in command noted, 'he had only one prisoner.' The explanation: 'The blighter spoke out of turn, Sir, and I shot him.' Major McFarland Memoir (unpublished manuscript, nd), chap. 2, 6.

be put into action only sporadically. By November 10 the forward elements of the corps were at Mons in Belgium, the town at which the Old Contemptibles of the British Expeditionary Force had first met the advancing German Army in August 1914. The next day, November 11, at 11 a.m., the armistice took effect, but not before one Canadian was killed and fifteen wounded in liberating Mons. The Belgians celebrated their liberation with remarkable elation.[99]

Lieutenant E.L.M. Burns, a staff captain (despite his rank) with the 9th Brigade, recalled that there was no joy among the troops, however, only 'the feeling of relief. There was no introspective analysing of personal feelings, or pondering over my uncertain future. I had survived and that was enough for the moment.'[100] Frank Cousins, a soldier recuperating in England (and John Diefenbaker's future law partner), wrote home on November 11 unenthusiastically that 'things are going as usual around this inferno.'[101] The 1st Battalion's Corporal Roy Macfie, who had earned the Military Medal and bar, recalled that the coming of the Armistice created 'a funny feelin.' All at once everything stopped. And everybody just stood around lookin' at each other ... nobody would believe it. Until night; we kind of believed it.'[102] Like so many other units whose numbers differed only in detail, the 1st Battalion had seen some 6500 men pass through its ranks, its establishment strength at the front being 900. The battalion lost 49 officers and 699 men killed, and 126 officers and 3055 wounded. Macfie was one of the very few originals of August 1914 to be with the unit in November 1918.[103] The nation lost 60,000 dead and 172,000 wounded during the war, an appalling price for a small population of just eight million to suffer – and all the more so because the toll had been borne overwhelmingly and disproportionately by fewer than five million Anglo-Canadians.*

The Canadian Corps' Hundred Days from August 8 to the Armistice had cost 45,835 casualties, almost 20 per cent of the casualties sustained by the Canadian Expeditionary Force for the entire war and 45 per cent of the corps' strength on the opening day of battle. To put these totals in perspective, the

---

* In late 1998 the town of Renfrew, Ontario, dedicated a new war memorial at a large dinner at which I was the speaker. I was struck by the very large number of Great War dead from a small town and its rural hinterland and greatly moved by the repetition of surnames. Some extended families lost three or four members and many had two dead. No one should ever doubt the terrible impact of the First World War on Canada.

casualties of the last hundred days were more than the First Canadian Army suffered in the entire campaign in Northwest Europe from June 6, 1944, to V-E Day eleven months later.[104] Open warfare had proven even more costly than the bloody trench warfare that had preceded it, and by November 11 the corps' units were almost literally on their last legs. But the Great War was over. Canada had played its full part for almost four years, but nothing distinguished the Canadian Corps' service so much as its extraordinary role in winning the victory in the final three months. Only a very professional army could have accomplished what the Canadians did.

And how had the corps accomplished its tasks so well? A key part was simply experience. Men died in huge numbers, but enough survived to pass on what they had learned about fighting the Germans to win. Good soldiers became better NCOs, and young junior officers in 1915 became still young but vastly experienced and effective company and battalion commanders by 1918. The First Division went into action at Ypres in April 1915 and had three-and-a-half years of battle experience by November 1918. The Second, Third, and Fourth Divisions went into the line at regular intervals after the First, and even the Fourth, the last to see action, had two full years of battle experience.

Moreover, after Sam Hughes's political demise, only successful commanders won promotion. The corps became a genuine meritocracy that drew on the ablest men in Canada for its officers and, in the officer ranks, the cream rose to the top. From the senior officers at corps and divisional headquarters down to the battalions, companies, and platoons, the talent was plentiful. Many able men died in action or broke down, but enough remained to ensure that the leadership of Canada's army was up to the job. So, too, were the men they led.

Moreover, Canadian infantry battalions were almost always kept at or near full strength, thanks as much to good luck as to good planning. The break-up of the Fifth Division in England provided needed men at a critical time, as did the arrival of conscripts later in 1918. Manpower matters would be very different in the Second World War.

Finally, the Canadian Corps genuinely became the embodiment of Canada, or at least of the English-Canadian nation. There was a sense among officers and men alike that they were part of something much greater than its individual components. Their achievements, their victories, said something to their Allies in the trenches, to their countrymen at home, and to themselves. They knew they had become soldiers in a special army, one that could freely adopt and adapt others' ideas and still generate and implement tactical innovations of its own. The corps performed miracles in action as a result.

For the corps and for Canada's future as a nation, however, it was a tragedy of the first order that French Canadians did not participate fully and willingly in the Canadian Expeditionary Force. Those who did helped to create the corps' mystique and shared in the pan-Canadian nationalism that developed overseas, if not in Quebec.

five

LOSING PROFESSIONALISM: THE INTERWAR YEARS

'Calgary's citizens considered the army a collection of social parasites,' wrote Tony Foster of the home station of the Permanent Force's Lord Strathcona's Horse in which his father served in 1924. 'Soldiers – particularly cavalry soldiers – were too indolent or stupid for useful employment in the "real" world. At every opportunity the men were ridiculed for their blind acceptance of the absurd military discipline that emasculated "real" men. Their childish toy-soldier uniforms, their unproductive playing at foolish war games, all of it was anathema to local citizenry.'[1]

—⁓—

The Canadian Corps had become a highly professional operation well before the end of the Great War. It would be unfair to say that it was the best corps in the Allied armies – such distinctions are all but impossible to make – but it was very good and, by everyone's assessment, one of the best. It had able commanders at corps, division, brigade, and battalion headquarters; its subalterns had learned how to lead; the NCOs and men fought with great skill and courage; and its behind-the-lines organization was a model of administrative efficiency. The Canadian Corps was the embodiment of the nation in the soldiers' minds – and in the minds of the people back home.

The interwar years, however, saw Canada's military sink back into the pre-1914 era, as Canada disarmed as much as or more than any other industrialized nation. In many ways it was as if the Great War had never happened. Yes, there were grieving families aplenty, and many returned men suffered from nervous conditions for the rest of their days while some had been completely broken by their wartime service. Others required hospital or medical care for long periods, and far too many died young as the wartime strain and the lingering effects of gas or wounds sapped their constitutions. But Canadians and their governments forgot the war as quickly as possible. The world was now safe for democracy, and professional armed forces were scarcely needed. The Militia could handle anything that might arise: Hadn't the fighting in France and Flanders demonstrated that the Canadian citizen-soldier could beat the Hun?

Why waste money on professional soldiers? governments and citizens asked. The professionals were all popinjays in toy-soldier uniforms like those worn by the Strathconas or else Colonel Blimps – fat, stupid, callous men who threw divisions onto uncut wire and squandered lives. Arthur Currie, a general who had taken care of his men's lives and used firepower to the maximum extent, actually suffered slanderous attacks from the malignant Sam Hughes and others that he had cold-bloodedly sent men to be killed on the last day of the war.[2]

One result of the public attitude was that defence budgets, tiny during the boom years of the 1920s, dried up even more in the hard times of the dirty 1930s. All the while, the army's equipment grew obsolescent, and doctrine largely calcified at the point it had reached in 1918. Canada's Permanent Force and its Militia symbolically sank into the mud of Flanders for the next two decades, with only a handful of talented men braving the public's scorn by staying in the nation's service. The professionalism of wartime, built up at such cost in lives, was allowed to disappear. The militia myth, that hardy perennial of Canadian history, once again blossomed forth without much of a militia to nurture it.

As professionalism faded into memory, so too did the nationalism of the army. The war had shown Canadians that, with time, battle experience, and study, they could do as well as or better than the British at every rank from private to general, from rifleman to General Staff Officer grade 1. But in the interwar years this nationalism and confidence disappeared. Lieutenant-General Maurice Pope recollected in 1977 that, in the interwar years, 'the Canadian military were not soldiers, although we had many experts on the King's dress regulations. The permanent force soldier learned what he learned, and got whatever higher staff training he got, in Britain. I'm sorry that I can't rate any of our men with the like of Alanbrooke or Dill [later Second World War field marshals]. I'm grateful for the things the British taught me and I admired them.'[3]

The only staff training available to Canadians was at Camberley in Britain or the British Army Staff College in Quetta, India. The only higher education for defence was at the Imperial Defence College in London, which taught much about Britain and the empire but almost nothing about Canada's particular national interests. Still, the sole place a Canadian officer could see a brigade or a division on manoeuvres was in the United Kingdom. The only modern weapons being produced in the empire were made in Britain. In a curious, deflating way, so tiny and backward did the Canadian Army become in a mere two decades that colonialism and a lack of confidence in its own abilities once again took hold of the officer corps.

When the Germans accepted an Armistice on November 11, 1918, Canada had more than 300,000 soldiers and dependants overseas and almost 75,000 more soldiers in Canada.[4] There were also the 60,000 dead, for whom arrangements for proper and solemn remembrance had to be made.

The dead were the first charge. As early as 1914 the British had begun registering grave sites. By 1916 France had agreed to cede land in perpetuity for war cemeteries, and, in 1917, the Imperial War Conference, in which Sir Robert Borden participated, agreed to establish the Imperial War Graves Commission to find the bodies of the killed, build war cemeteries, and care for them in perpetuity. The dead were not to be brought home.* Where a battalion had been slaughtered and its men buried together, such cemeteries were continued. Where graves were scattered, the commission brought the dead together and created larger cemeteries. In some parts of France such as the Somme, where fighting was heaviest, there are war cemeteries every few miles – British, Cana-

---

* At least one determined mother dug up her son's grave in France and smuggled his remains into Canada for burial in the family plot. See the extraordinary story in Virginia Cusack, 'The Family Plot,' *Toronto Life*, November 2001, 75ff.

dian, Australian, German – one after the other in an almost endless parade of the dead.

The IWGC cemeteries were and remain handsome, superbly maintained sites dominated by a Cross of Sacrifice and a Stone of Remembrance engraved 'Their Name Liveth Forevermore.'[5] Each of the Canadian war graves was eventually marked with a simple, dignified stone with a maple leaf, name, rank, unit, and often a few words from the next-of-kin. Those bodies not recovered or never identified – a huge number amounting to some 18,000 men – received commemoration in other ways. The names of the Canadian unknown dead were carved on the Menin Gate Memorial at Ypres or on the Vimy Memorial, dedicated in 1936.[6] The Vimy monument, shamefully allowed to decay such that names could not be read, was superbly restored and re-dedicated in 2007.

The living were the next charge. The task was to get the overseas men home, but how? The war had ended in mid-November 1918, a difficult season for transatlantic shipping. Transport vessels had either been sunk by U-boats or were not readily available to the Canadians for a variety of complicated Allied reasons. Canadian ports were largely ice-bound, and the country's railways, in financial trouble and strained to the breaking point by wartime pressures, could not move as many troops as they would have ordinarily: no more than 20,000–25,000 a month, they said. Moreover, the Canadian Corps was committed to providing two of its four divisions to the occupation of the German Rhineland.

If these problems could be overcome, how would the corps be demobilized? First in, first out? That method seemed fairest to the few surviving soldiers who had enlisted in 1914 or 1915. By units, so that the people in Halifax, Saint John, Montreal, Kingston, London, Winnipeg, Calgary, and Victoria could see how splendid their men looked in a final, glorious parade down the main streets? General Currie wanted this reward. Or would industry take precedence, and its demands for the orderly rehabilitation and training of the key members of the workforce carry the day?

The result, predictably enough, was a compromise. The major units of the corps would return under their officers, with just enough juggling to allow the units to be dispersed in a geographical area. The rest of the Canadian Expeditionary Force would be organized into drafts by locale and length of service, with married men having priority. Essentially, Currie got most of what he wanted.[7]

No one was happy. The First and Second Divisions complained about having to occupy the German borderlands, where the citizenry did not seem sufficiently defeated to provide a sense of triumph. The Third and Fourth Divisions grumbled in Belgium, and the CEF establishment in England bitched there. There was the Khaki University, sports days, and leave for Brussels or London, but what were the men to do tomorrow? And how soon before they could get home? The few troopships that crossed the Atlantic were filthy scows, not at all what returning heroes – or their wives and children – deserved. If better ships were needed, and they were, men had to wait for them to be found. But waiting did not suit anxious soldiers, and everyone had his resentments.

At Kinmel Park, a Canadian camp in south Wales, in January 1919, the black Sergeant-Major of 2nd (Coloured) Canadian Construction Company tried to arrest an insolent white soldier. This incident provoked a free-for-all in which knives and rocks injured soldiers. There was worse to come. When the Third Division, allegedly full of conscripts without much service, received precedence over the other divisions for repatriation, a substantial mutinous riot, fuelled by alcohol and whipped up by troublemakers, broke out at Kinmel in March. Five soldiers died and twenty-five were wounded. This event drew massive media attention, not wholly flattering to the CEF and Canada. 'In my opinion,' one officer reported to his superiors, 'the idea of the [riot] leaders was "the more demonstrations we make, the quicker we get sailings."' Smaller disturbances followed in other camps in Britain, and there was a brief mutiny also in Belgium. The CEF, Desmond Morton wrote precisely, 'had become an army of homesick civilians, cold, restless, fed up.'[8]

Miraculously, by mid to late 1919 virtually everyone was back in Canada, as shipping fortuitously appeared. The soldiers in formed units had their parades, receiving the plaudits of the grateful citizens. Men saw the wives and children they could scarcely recognize after two or more years away. Wives and mothers were frequently shocked at how Johnny had changed, at the strain his once-young features showed. Husbands and wives tried, usually with success, to pick up where they had left off.

The government endeavoured to ease the transition to civilian status. In

1917 Sir Robert Borden had addressed soldiers in France, telling them, 'as the head of the Government,' that 'no man, whether he goes back or whether he remains in Flanders, will have just cause to reproach the Government for having broken faith with the men who won and the men who died.'[9] Through its Department of Soldiers' Civil Re-establishment, Ottawa offered a variety of programs to returned men, but most of the former soldiers found these programs completely inadequate to meet their needs. The national economy failed to do its part, as waves of inflation and deflation made reintegration as difficult as it could be. Nor were matters eased by the abrupt shutdown of war plants. Even so, men received a War Service Gratuity ($420 for a single private with three years' service overseas), a $35 clothing allowance, and a year's free medical care in veterans' hospitals. Those who wanted could get long-term loans and a farmstead – even though it might be in Kapuskasing in northern Ontario. For those interested in a civil service post, the 'veterans' preference' guaranteed returned men the first crack at jobs. More than eight in ten vets had only public school education, however, so the best jobs were destined to go elsewhere, or to officers. The government offered pensions and vocational training for the wounded in body and mind, but bureaucratic, legalistic policies and procedures would frustrate almost every applicant, including the successful. Again, officers received higher pensions than those who had served in the ranks. One blind veteran received $600 a year from the government. 'I want to know how it is that the eyes of a brigadier general in Canada are worth $2700,' he told his friends in the Great War Veterans Association in 1920, 'and my eyes are worth only $600.'[10] Inevitably the Canada of the mind, the idealized nation the soldiers had created while they were overseas, failed to match up to the Canada of 1919. The soldiers had been changed by war, and the country, full of war profiteers, aliens, and slackers, or so the returned men believed, was also different and not always better. 'It is not the Canada I expected it to be,' Sir Arthur Currie wrote after his cold welcome home in 1919. 'I came back from the war feeling that all the suffering and sacrifice must have meant something. But I found ... that there was little change. Men were fighting for the dollar in the same persistent way ... and [had] very little appreciation of the world situation and its attendant problems.'[11]

The way Currie himself was treated on his return to Canada was scandalous. When he landed in Halifax in August 1919 he received a formal reception at

City Hall, nothing more. When he proceeded to Ottawa he spoke at Parliament Hill and drew as many hisses as cheers from the largely silent crowd, while Sir George Foster, the acting prime minister, spoke without much enthusiasm. This event was bad enough, but much worse was the way the government failed to respond to Sam Hughes's attacks on Currie in the House of Commons, most notably a virulent tirade on March 4, 1919, and on at least two subsequent occasions that year.[12] No longer a minister, Hughes still had his supporters, and he had lost none of his ability to denounce and bluster, which clearly frightened the government. Sir Edward Kemp, the Overseas Minister, fulsomely praised the senior officers who had worked with him in England, but, rather than get Hughes's ire going, offered only tepid praise for Currie, the consummate professional soldier. Sir Robert Borden did not speak in defence of the general until July 7, 1919. The country's greatest soldier deserved every honour the nation could offer, but he received very little; certainly, there was no gratuity such as those the British government awarded its victorious commanders. Currie did get a promotion from Lieutenant-General to General and the title of Inspector-General, making him the senior military adviser to the government. No one in Cabinet was listening to military advice, however, and in August 1920 Currie left the army to become principal of McGill University.[13] In 1927 he had to fight a libel action to clear his name of slanderous attacks made by a Port Hope, Ontario, newspaper. Currie, the *Evening Guide* had claimed in an echo of the now-dead Hughes, had wantonly wasted lives in his efforts to take Mons on the last day of the war. Currie won the case and a tiny sum for damages, but the maltreatment he suffered was indicative of the low regard in which the military was held by the people in the postwar years.[14]

Towns and cities erected their war memorials, people created a mythical version of events to try to justify and explain what had occurred and why, and most Canadians promptly did their best to forget the war.[15] 'Is it nothing to you, all ye that pass by?' Vancouver's cenotaph asked. To many, the answer seemed obvious. Soon literature reinforced the growing pacifist tendency, as best-selling, bitter, anti-war memoirs were published in Europe and the United States and a few in Canada.[16]

Canadians showed their lack of concern very quickly. As the men of the CEF fought their last battles and eventually returned home from Europe, more soldiers were proceeding overseas – to Russia of all places. The Bolshevik Revolution in November 1917 had led Lenin and his comrades to take Russia out of the war. The Reds had power in Moscow and St Petersburg, but they were opposed by the Whites, the counter-revolutionary elements who detested Communism and the Germans and who hoped to keep Russia in the war – if they could beat the Reds. The Allies had no love for the Bolsheviks, to be sure, and it was very important during the war to keep as many Germans as possible pinned down in the east. Thus, in 1918, Britain, the United States, and Japan sent troops onto Russian soil to support the Whites and to protect the huge supply caches that had been shipped to the Czarist armies. These supplies could not be allowed to fall into the hands of the Germans, with whom the Bolsheviks had made peace. Inevitably, the Allies asked Canada to contribute, and Sir Robert Borden agreed. But once in, Canada struggled as hard as it could to get out.

In October 1918 the Canadian Siberian Expeditionary Force left Vancouver for Vladivostok in Siberia. This brigade consisted of two battalions of infantry (a battalion of British troops from Hong Kong also served under the command of Major-General J.H. Elmsley), a battery of artillery, a machine-gun company, a cavalry squadron provided by the Royal North-West Mounted Police, and various supporting elements. Most of the 4000 officers and men in the force were CEF volunteers, but there were also 1653 conscripts under the Military Service Act in the ranks. Two companies of men were French Canadians, and there were 135 Canadians of Russian origin with Canadian Corps service as well; their language skills, in addition to their military experience, could be useful. The task, in cooperation with American and Japanese troops, was to train White forces and to protect supply and rail lines. All sides sought commercial advantages, though the Japanese wanted more, with their eyes fixed on annexation. There was little support in Canada for this mission and, Borden and a minister or two aside, even less in the Cabinet. The Canadians participated in one small, bloodless operation and remained in Siberia until the spring of 1919; nineteen stayed behind forever, three dead in accidents, sixteen from disease. The Canadian sigh of relief at the force's extraction from the morass was heartfelt.[17]

At the same time, more Canadians were serving in northwest Russia at Archangel and Murmansk, trying to deny these key ports and the huge quantity of supplies to the Reds. There were almost 500 men in an artillery brigade that engaged in heavy fighting against the 'Bolos,' as the Canadians called the Reds, in the Archangel region, as well as a substantial number of Canadian pilots in Royal Air Force squadrons. At Murmansk a small number of Canadians also participated in some fruitless actions. The 22 officers and 455 surviving men of the artillery and air force left Russia on June 11, 1919. Five had been killed in action and one died of illness.[18]

Again, public and government relief at the withdrawal was clear. The only result of these abortive expeditions to Russia was to earn Canada the enmity of the Leninist regime. The White leadership proved incompetent and corrupt, and the White armies showed themselves unable to resist the Red Army effectively. Although the Civil War in Russia dragged on, the Soviet Union was in the process of formation under Lenin's leadership.

The Bolsheviks had their supporters in Canada in the tiny Communist Party, and some officials in Ottawa and in the boardrooms of corporations feared that revolution was just around the corner. The Winnipeg General Strike had paralysed that city in 1919 and there had been sympathetic strikes in other centres, though nothing that constituted a workers' revolt. The government fretted, and otherwise sensible men feared that their society was vulnerable. These attitudes mattered: the questions of how the Canadian Permanent Force and the Militia were to be constituted, structured, and maintained had to be settled. Even if the public did not believe it, the government knew that the military was the bastion of the established order and the state's ultimate defence against revolution.

Some parliamentarians, soldiers, and military writers wanted to base the postwar military on conscription. The war had demonstrated, they argued, that compulsory service was both the right way to fight a war and difficult to implement in the middle of a conflict. Surely it made more sense to have a peacetime plan of conscription and national service that trained young men and, as William Hamilton Merritt of the Canadian Defence League put it, that 'will give us the stability of purpose, upbuilding of character and physique, and safety to the Dominion and Empire which comes from a virile system of national organization, based on *Universal Military Training and Service.*' This view was eagerly accepted by the Department of Militia and Defence in

Ottawa, by the Chief of the General Staff, the Minister, and a committee set up under the septuagenarian General W.D. Otter to plan for the reorganization of the Militia. It was also accepted by Major-General J.H. MacBrien, the former member of the Mounted Police who had served in South Africa, joined the Permanent Force, become a successful brigade commander, and then Chief of Staff to the Overseas Minister in late 1918. He envisaged a well-prepared military with a well-educated officer corps, a 30,000-man Permanent Force, and a large Militia based on compulsory service.[19]

The simple truth was that almost no one outside the Department of Militia and Defence wanted peacetime conscription. No politician with a grain of sense, recalling the way Quebec had reacted to compulsory service in 1917 and 1918, would touch it. No westerner or rural Ontarian, remembering the strong farm opposition to conscription, could even contemplate it. And veterans, by now organizing into associations, had little time for this sort of planning. What they demanded were bonuses for their service, pensions, and more pensions, not conscription.[20] Indeed, there seemed to be scant support even for the Militia among returned men. They had done their bit overseas, had seen too many of their friends killed, and wanted as little as possible to do with the military for the rest of their lives. 'I have asked the G.W.V.A. [Great War Veterans Association] when the men will put on the uniform,' one Permanent Force officer said in 1919, 'and they replied, on one occasion only – for the funeral of one of our comrades.'[21] Peacetime conscription was a complete non-starter, dead as a dodo by 1919.[22]

So, too, were any soldiers' hopes that the postwar Permanent Force would be a real army. The General Staff had wanted a force of 20,000–30,000, with strong garrisons on each coast and defence schemes prepared for every part of the country. This was not to be. In June 1919, on the heels of the Winnipeg General Strike, the Minister of Militia introduced a bill into Parliament to raise the establishment of the Permanent Force from 5000 to 10,000, the rationale being the need for trained soldiers to provide aid to the civil power. 'It is not the intention to increase up to that number at present,' the minister said, 'but it may be necessary in the near future.'[23] Once the Winnipeg strike collapsed, however, there was very little support for this idea from the opposition benches, and presumably very little in the Union Government caucus. The act passed, but in June 1920 the government forbade the enlistment of more than 5000 men. Even that strength was not achieved, though there was some progress in reconstituting the Permanent Force. Twelve hundred CEF officers applied to join the regular force, providing ample choice, though there were a number of pre-war PF officers who had – either by their own choice or by force of circumstances – managed to spend the war in Canada or in England. Something had to be done with them. The strong CEF opinion was that they ought to be dismissed, but that idea was put aside. The CEF view was also that only a real Permanent Force with good equipment and real soldiering would attract the best officers from the Canadian Corps. Some good officers went to the PF, but they would never get good equipment or real soldiering. The Permanent Force's officers were chosen by a selection board led by General Otter, the veteran of Ridgeway, South Africa, and Militia headquarters. Pay for the Permanent Force was increased modestly, but it was abundantly obvious to anyone with the eyes to see that Canada was not going to take defence seriously.

There was one important change: instead of a single PF infantry regiment, the Royal Canadian Regiment, there would now be three in all. The 22nd Battalion, soon renamed the Royal 22nd Régiment, and the Princess Patricia's Canadian Light Infantry joined the RCR as Canada's PF infantry. The idea that a French Canadian and French-speaking regiment should be part of the Permanent Force had the support of the Chief of the General Staff, Major-General Sir Willoughby Gwatkin, and the thirty-two-year-old artilleryman, Brigadier-General Andrew McNaughton, Sir Arthur Currie's de facto representative in Canada for postwar planning, but it ran into heavy going with the politicians. The Cabinet, McNaughton recollected, turned the recommendation down five times, arguing that the Citadel at Quebec housed the Quebec Garrison Artillery and that there was no room for an infantry battalion. Gwatkin reduced the Garrison Artillery unit to zero strength, and the Van Doos finally slipped through Cabinet in 1920.[24] In 1928 its name was officially rendered in French as Le Royal 22e Régiment. This inclusion of the 22e in the Permanent Force was a far-sighted gesture, a belated effort to suggest to Quebec and Canadians that Sam Hughes's approach to French Canada's military amour-propre had been a dreadful mistake.

The PF regiments were hardly at full strength – in 1921 the Royal 22nd numbered 12 officers and 198 men organized in two companies; the RCR 36 officers and 458 men, and the PPCLI 25 officers and 269 men. There were also two PF cavalry regiments – the Royal Canadian Dragoons and Lord Strathcona's Horse – as well as a machine-gun corps, artillery batteries, engineers, signallers, and small cadres for each of the supporting services. In Ottawa, the direction of the nation's military resided in the General Staff, which was itself tiny. The total strength of the Permanent Force at the end of March 1921 was 381 officers and 3744 other ranks.[25] These numbers were similar to those at the beginning of the Great War, and they would not change very much over the next two decades to the eve of the Second World War. The Permanent Force could be used to maintain 'peace' between workers and bosses during strikes in Cape Breton in the 1920s and Stratford, Ontario, in the 1930s, sometimes drawing the scorn of the workers – or worse. 'In the early part of the strike,' Lieutenant Guy Simonds of the Royal Canadian Horse Artillery wrote of his unit's intervention at Sydney in the mid-1920s, 'the miners and their families were very hostile to the troops ... we would get stones and bricks thrown down on us from the many rail "over passes" in the area ... and [we were] abused and insulted.' Eventually, Simonds recalled, certainly gilding his memories, the RCHA convinced the striking miners 'that we were not on anybody's "side" – we didn't represent the owners, but were there to protect lives and property.'[26] Except for this early domestic peacekeeping, Canada's regular army was completely incapable of any military action. If any officers or men joined on other expectations, they were destined to be disappointed.

Recreating the Permanent Force was the simplest part of the postwar reorganization. Thanks to Sam Hughes's extraordinary exertions in August 1914 and after, the units of the CEF had been largely cut loose from the old pre-war Militia organization. The great fighting battalions and artillery regiments of the Canadian Corps had won their battle honours the hard way, and there was scant support among interested veterans for anything that smacked of submerging the wartime traditions into the moribund Militia. 'Better that a dozen peace regiments should go to the wall,' said Major-General A.C. Macdonnell, the GOC of the First Division, 'than the CEF units be lost.'[27] But, as Desmond Morton noted shrewdly, 'the postwar reorganization of 1919–20 ... consisted essentially of grafting the country's overseas military organization onto its prewar Militia force so that a contingent identical in character, if larger in dimension, might be sent to an identical future holocaust.'[28]

Militia regiments during the war had, in some cases, contributed men to a single CEF battalion. For these the link was clear, and the wartime battle honours won by the particular battalion could be added to those of the regiment. But what of city regiments, such as Toronto's Queen's Own Rifles, which had provided drafts to a dozen CEF battalions? The reorganization committee, nominally chaired by the ubiquitous Otter, had toured the country and heard representations. The key figures were McNaughton and Gwatkin, and both men used the studies prepared by MacBrien in London. The result, after much palavering, was to work out a method of allocating battle honours to regiments and then to create enough units to satisfy almost everyone. For a time, the survival of the Queen's Own seemed in doubt, but it eventually prevailed. In Victoria the 50th Gordon Highlanders and the 88th Victoria Fusiliers combined with the 16th Battalion, CEF, to create the Canadian Scottish Regiment. In eastern Ontario the Hastings and Prince Edward Regiment perpetuated the 16th Prince Edward Regiment, the 49th Regiment Hastings Rifles, the 2nd Battalion, and other units of the CEF. A similar process was followed everywhere.

The report of the committee was ready by 1921, but the mood in the country by then had become decidedly anti-military. No public announcement was made, but the Militia was to have sufficient units to create eleven infantry and four cavalry divisions for home defence and to maintain an expeditionary force of six infantry divisions and one cavalry division. This scenario required a paper strength of more than 300,000 men, but no one thought that Canada could maintain – or the government pay for – such a Militia. The planning was based on a Militia of some 50,000, roughly the same as before 1914. This number made little sense, as even McNaughton admitted: Canada had Militia units 'without much regard to the need for them in a balanced organization or to the availability of manpower for them.'[29]

The postwar Permanent Force and Militia reflected the lack of reality that had gone into the planning for them. In the first years after the war, there was scarcely any Militia training other than that conducted at local unit headquarters, though Ottawa did assign 250 PF officers and senior NCOs to assist units in reorganization and training, and usually kept similar numbers there for the interwar period. In its annual report for 1921–2 the department noted that 'owing to the financial situation the training of the Militia ... was much restricted.' The militia vote of funds, covering the Permanent Force and the Non-Permanent Active Militia, was only $11 million, a sum destined to decline to $9.6 million by 1923–4. Not surprisingly, there were no 'appreciable strides in general efficiency,' but no one could have expected much from Militia units that were underfunded, at most at 50 per cent strength, and that received only a few days of desultory training.[30] Officers had to purchase their own uniforms, but many regularly turned their training pay over to the regiment and the money was often used to buy the boots that the Department of National Defence didn't provide for other ranks.[31] No units, except possibly for a few urban regiments, had much private money for training or mess life.

Even so, many lawyers, bank managers, and sons of industrialists, the kind of men who then constituted the officer corps, still believed that the Non-Permanent Active Militia (NPAM) was important, if largely in a social sense. The Elgin Regiment in western Ontario may not have been close to the norm. As Strome Galloway, one of its soldiers in the 1930s, recalled, 'the CO, the senior company commander, the adjutant and the Regimental-Sergeant-Major were all linotype operators in local printing offices. The Second-in-Command and my own company commander were lawyers; one company commander was an accountant and another was a coal merchant. Most of the junior officers served behind the counter in some sort of shop, the more swanky among them being bond salesmen or bank clerks. One was a farmer and another a hotel manager.' When the regiment mobilized early in the Second World War, only one officer failed to sign up.[32]

By the Great Depression, spending on Militia training had dried up completely – in 1931–2 the Militia received only $1.9 million. Militia training at summer camp virtually ceased until late in the decade, when almost 30,000 Militia trained in 1938, the largest number since the Great War. The Chief of the General Staff, in 1931 Major-General Andrew McNaughton, recognized the new reality by proposing changes to the NPAM organizational structure. Instead of the huge Militia he had joined in recommending a decade earlier, Canada now was to have a paper establishment of six infantry divisions and one cavalry division, but opposition from the regiments that were to be eliminated or amalgamated was so strong that it took five years to put these changes into effect. Still, many militiamen turned out for training one or two nights a week and, ideally, for two weeks in the summer (money permitting).

Sometimes improvisation depended on the Commanding Officer. Lieutenant-Colonel Armand Smith, a member of the E.D. Smith jam family, commanded the Wentworth Regiment (later amalgamated with the Royal Hamilton Light Infantry) and, his son recalled, established 'C' Company at the plant. He built a rifle range in the basement of the canning plant, organized the parade square in the shipping yards, and constructed the Sergeants' Mess on the second floor of the main factory. In the summer, E.D. Smith trucks carried the company to Niagara-on-the-Lake for camp.[33] Another Service Corps officer recollected that, in his horse transport company, 'we had harness. The troops were trained to take the harness apart, put it back together, and hang it up in the Quartermaster's Stores. That is about as far as it went. We never did have a horse. We never did have a wagon.'[34] The devotion of some officers and men was extraordinary.

It had to be, for the equipment brought back from the war was soon completely obsolete. Exercises too often featured 'bang, bang, you're dead' playacting, with flags representing machine guns. By the late 1930s, 'clank-clank, I'm a tank' was the refrain in cavalry regiments, which at last had rid themselves of their horses. Militia units had no tanks or armoured cars, almost no anti-aircraft guns, and weaknesses in all types of their artillery, though by 1938 most militia artillery regiments had replaced horses with trucks. They also had few specialized units, such as mobile workshops. A General Staff appraisal in 1931 stated the obvious: 'The fighting power of existing units is steadily deteriorating, through increasing obsolescence in the arms, ammunition and equipment now available.'[35]

Matters worsened as the terrible depression decade continued. Even when the Mackenzie King government relaxed its fiscal constraints and tried to take tentative steps towards rearmament, the process groaned and creaked, so long had it sat unused. When the government let a contract in 1938 for a modern light machine gun, the Bren, without first seeking tenders, the botched process became a *cause célèbre* in Parliament and the media. It led to a royal commission and the demise of the Minister of National Defence, Ian Mackenzie, in September 1939.[36] Rearmament was fraught with politics, but the army eventually got its Bren guns, an essential infantry weapon.

Many Non-Permanent Active Militia officers took their duties seriously. The Militia Staff Course, which operated after 1922, trained captains and majors for junior staff posts. Officers took lectures and participated in exercises without troops in the winter months, then spent two weeks in the summer on field exercises. The difficult courses, ordinarily directed by staff-trained PF officers, put NPAM and PF officers together, as did the month-long Advanced Militia Staff Course for majors, which began in 1935, and the examinations for Militia colonels.[37] When war came in 1939 there were hundreds of staff-trained Militia officers, a far cry from the 1914 situation. There were also, among the approximately 5000 officers of the Militia, many able men, fine leaders, and excellent administrators, although the senior NPAM commanders were all in their fifties. Few of the postwar generation of officers had any real military training, but they would be the men who would command the nation's platoons, companies, and battalions in the Second World War. Some, like Bert Hoffmeister, Holley Keefler, and Bruce Matthews, would lead divisions with great success.

The condition of the interwar Permanent Force was much the same as the blighted Militia. The booming 1920s did nothing to increase government spending on the military. Funding declined, in fact, and in 1924 the cheese-paring Liberal government of Mackenzie King slashed other ranks' pay by 50 cents a day to $1.20. Soon, only 10 per cent of other ranks could draw marriage allowances, and officers could not get permission to marry until the age of thirty on the grounds that living outside the mess was detrimental to their training.[38] For their part, PF officers had a certain social standing to maintain, expensive uniforms to buy, and dining-in nights about four times a week with mess bills to pay.[39] The mess, with its cheap drinks, ruined far too many careers – 'if a bottle was there,' C.B. Ware of the PPCLI recalled, 'you finished it.'[40] In the 1930s, pay for a lieutenant was $4.10 a day (less a dollar a day for 'extra messing,' or better food, in the mess). Captain Guy Simonds's income in 1933 was $2889.48, and the Chief of the General Staff in 1937 received $8000 a year, the equivalent of perhaps $90,000 in current dollars.

The daily routine of training in an understrength and ill-equipped army encouraged boredom for all and idleness for some. But it was also hard and discouraging, most notably because much of an officer's and NCO's time was spent in training the Militia, and very little on regimental or larger formation training. The PF cavalry regiments, despite the introduction of the tank in the

Great War, were horsed until late in the 1930s, and countless hours were passed in ensuring that officers and troopers had a proper seat and could use a lance. In almost every respect the PF – like the Militia – existed almost as if the Great War had been merely an accident, an event never to recur.[41]

There were a few glimmers of change as the interwar years rolled on. In 1930 the Department of National Defence acquired twelve Carden-Loyd machine-gun carriers for the machine-gun companies of the PF infantry battalions, and officers and NCOs trained in their use. Then, in 1938, Ottawa established the Canadian Armoured Fighting Vehicles School at Camp Borden, Ontario. With twenty-five all ranks, the school had only the Carden-Loyd carriers until, in the autumn, it received two obsolete Vickers Mark VI tanks; fourteen more arrived in August 1939.[42] That was the extent of Canadian armour before the Second World War.

The Permanent Force also had the task of operating the Northwest Territories and Yukon Radio System, a network begun in 1923 that spread throughout the southern Arctic. It provided almost the sole means of rapid communications in the north and won the Permanent Force some points with the politicians. More were earned in the depression years, when the CGS, General McNaughton, suggested to Prime Minister R.B. Bennett that the Permanent Force operate camps for unemployed men in cooperation with the Department of Labour.[43] McNaughton, who was without question the leading light of the Permanent Force in the interwar years, had two motives. First, there was a serious and growing problem of unemployment and thousands of homeless single men were riding the rods and, the government believed, falling prey to radicalism. But if the men could be housed in camps, clothed and fed, and paid a tiny wage, they might get their spirit back. Second, they could build public works and, especially, defence infrastructure across the country – military camps and buildings, airfields, and fortification repairs. To employ the Permanent Force to supervise these camps could help prevent further budget-driven reductions in personnel.

Opened in late 1932, the unemployment relief camps housed 170,000 men before a new government shut them down in 1936. They provoked scorn because the daily wage was 20 cents ('the Royal Twenty Centers,' the men called themselves) and labour unions objected to work being done by non-union members.[44] Others believed that the need for camps showed the bankruptcy of capitalism and the government's desire to militarize Canadian youth. The first might have been correct; the second was not. The officers running the camps wore civilian clothes, and there was no pretense of military discipline or training. Even so, there was enough protest that Bennett worried about the political impact on his staggering government. McNaughton was duly removed from his post as CGS in early 1935 and dispatched to the presidency of the National Research Council.[45]

Astonishingly, there were still fine officers in this miniscule, moribund Permanent Force. Many wore Great War decorations for valour and believed that Canada had to be better prepared for war than it had been in 1914. Harry Crerar, an artillery lieutenant-colonel during the war; George Pearkes, a Victoria Cross–winning battalion commander; Ken Stuart, a wartime battalion commander in the Engineers; and E.L.M. Burns, a decorated Engineers officer, to cite only the most prominent, tried to maintain professional standards and studied their profession. Crerar and Stuart, for example, cultivated young officials in the Department of External Affairs and joined the Canadian Institute of International Affairs, participating in that sometimes isolationist organization's debates. Some new junior officers, those few coming out of the Royal Military College who joined the Permanent Force or those entering from civilian universities or through recommendations, similarly worked at their new trade. Guy Simonds, who graduated from RMC with the Sword of Honour in 1925, was one young officer who could think. His Engineer classmate Chris Vokes could not, but he was burly and determined. Charles Foulkes, who had briefly attended the University of Western Ontario, was another highly intelligent, ambitious officer in the Royal Canadian Regiment.

The key to success for officers was the promotion examinations, so they had to master a mixture of theoretical and practical knowledge. The one almost certain way to future advancement was to attend the exclusive British Army Staff College, which required that an officer be a captain with at least six years' service who had passed a competitive examination open to officers throughout the British Empire. Studying for promotion and examinations was the ambitious officer's lot. The Permanent Force ran a preparatory course at the Royal Military College for those writing the Staff College examinations and insisted that these officers pass the Militia Staff Course as well. Canada usually provided four Staff College candidates a year, three for the college at Camberley and one for

Quetta. The Staff College course lasted two years: the first focused on staff work at brigade and division; the second on staff work at division, corps, and army level. Provided with a servant and a horse while at the Staff College in England, and at Quetta with a staff of six or seven, including two personal servants, two grooms, an untouchable for menial tasks, and a gardener,[46] students were expected to develop their power of command on exercises, to learn to appreciate tactical situations, and to issue orders quickly. Canadians, none of whom had collective training above company or battalion level, found the courses difficult.[47] Still, some officers, such as Simonds, loved the free-wheeling, free-thinking atmosphere of Camberley and Quetta, where they wrote papers and argued in their discussion syndicates;[48] others found it primarily a two-year-long social event and a chance to drink in the mess with Brits, Aussies, and Kiwis. Even so, attendance at Staff College let Canadians see larger formations on exercise, something they could not do in Canada. It also reinforced the imperial bond between the British and the Canadian armies that had sometimes been frayed during the war. If Canada had no army to speak of, scant capacity for realistic military planning, and almost no conception how to organize for modern war, what other country could it look to?[49] Even so, only sixty-three Canadians went to Staff College between the wars.

The Imperial Defence College in London offered a one-year course on high strategy and international politics. Usually for brigadier-generals, the course let future senior commanders see how the world looked to prime ministers and chiefs of staff. Canada sent thirteen officers to the IDC between the world wars, and that group included McNaughton and Crerar, the two men who would be Second World War army commanders; Burns, a corps commander-to-be; Pope, the chief wartime military adviser to the prime minister; and two future major-generals, Pearkes and G.R. Turner.[50]

While most PF officers were happy enough to go through these paces, able officers worried about the intellectual stagnation of the military profession in Canada. Major Ken Stuart became the editor of the six-year-old *Canadian Defence Quarterly* in 1929, a journal circulated through the Permanent Force and the Non-Permanent Active Militia with the deliberate intention of stimulating critical thinking. Until the outbreak of war in 1939, Stuart encouraged officers to write and argue, created a prize essay competition each year, had books reviewed, and stood by cheerfully as the members of the officer corps sometimes fell out with each other.[51] Burns, for example, an officer who had written a novel and published in H.L. Mencken's *American Mercury*, wrote in the *CDQ* on the uselessness of cavalry and the need to get soldiers into practical, utilitarian uniforms. His radical ideas were denounced by cavalrymen with the brains of their horses, but because he had scored the highest marks among all candidates in the British Empire for Staff College in 1927 and had developed and applied many of the techniques of aerial photography to mapping Canada, no one who was important much cared.[52]

Lieutenant-Colonel Burns also engaged in a debate with Captain Guy Simonds in the *CDQ* over the use of armour on the modern battlefield that was the high point of interwar military thinking in Canada. In 'A Division That Can Attack,' Burns wrote in April 1938 that in the recent reorganization of British divisions, the armour was grouped in tank brigades, and three brigades of infantry had been left without tanks. This configuration, he suggested, meant a return to the Great War, with tanks crawling forward at the pace of the infantry. His battlefield plan, in contrast, called for medium tanks to be used as spearheads to break the enemy line, wipe out the artillery, and smash the enemy's headquarters, followed by infantrymen to provide fire support and consolidate the ground won. A tank assault moved faster, needed less artillery support, and was immune to most of the enemy weapons. The standard division, he argued, should therefore be composed of one armoured and two infantry brigades.

Captain Guy Simonds, who had just returned to Canada after attending Staff College at Camberley and a summer attached to the British Second Division, was quick to reply in July 1938. In 'An Army That Can Attack – A Division That Can Defend,' he maintained that it was wrong to disperse the tanks among all divisions. Far better, Simonds said, to hold them in reserve to be used where the army commander determined. The division was no longer a balanced formation of all arms; rather, the army of two or more corps now filled this role. In other words, when an army had to attack, the commander could provide the artillery and the armour needed at the critical point. The role of divisions was primarily to defend, and, therefore, the permanent decentralization of artillery and armour to them was a mistake.

The debate went on in three more issues of the *Canadian Defence Quarterly*, as both officers vigorously attacked the other's ideas. Burns countered

Simonds by suggesting that once the enemy had the initiative and had launched an attack, it would be too late to use armour in the counterattack role; if the armour, infantry, and artillery didn't train together, they could not fight together well. To Simonds, this argument missed the key point: tank attacks without support would founder on the enemy's anti-tank weapons and make tank assaults of the kind Burns recommended as costly as the infantry attacks of the Great War.[53]

What was important about these exchanges was that they occurred in an army that was averse to analysis and ordinarily unwilling to question the received wisdom of British methods, tactics, and organization.[54] At a time when the Canadian Army had no formation larger than a battalion and no modern tanks, it was impressive that two PF officers could argue on an intellectual plane about the proper future employment of divisions and armies. Both had attended Staff College, both had been given the opportunity to see large formations on exercises, and both were aware of the debates in Britain, France, and Germany on armoured tactics. Both were also correct, Burns perhaps more so[55] – and in the coming war their different conceptions of organization and attack would each be tried.

Simonds and Burns both held high command in the Second World War: the former proved to be more innovative; the latter, more practical. That two such men could be found in the tiny, stunted Permanent Force was incredible. Unfortunately, they and their few peers were vastly outnumbered by drones, the over-aged, the under-qualified, and the unhealthy. It was also inevitable that, in a tiny officer corps burdened with promotion by seniority, not merit, the personal feuds that poisoned relationships across the Permanent Force were sharp and long-lasting. About all that united the force was the firm conviction that the Militia was no bloody good, a sentiment that the Militia reciprocated in spades. The lively discussions in *CDQ* had relatively little impact in changing such preconceptions.

American officers who visited their Canadian counterparts between the wars were often impressed by the Permanent Force. One noted the problems caused by tiny numbers and dispersal across a vast country, but others also saw the 'spirit of enthusiasm, interest in the work and loyalty ... [as] truly remarkable.' Another compared the Permanent Force favourably with the British Army – a 'very efficient' force, but with small combat value.[56]

Just how small became apparent when the bulk of the Permanent Force assembled in the summer of 1938 at Camp Borden for a major exercise. The results were predictably unsatisfactory. W.A.B. Anderson, an RMC graduate and then a PF lieutenant in the artillery whose uncle was CGS, remembered that the force was 'very unprofessional, play soldiering, full of old officers (but also some 1920s and 1930s duds).'[57] Nothing more could have been expected from an army that, collectively, had spent most of the last two decades training the Militia and grooming horses. The firebrand unit commanders of 1918 had become men in their early to mid-fifties when the Second World War began, and the most senior officers of the 1939 Permanent Force would be even older.

While forward-looking debates were conducted in the pages of the *Canadian Defence Quarterly*, high policy matters of genuine unreality dominated the discussion in Ottawa. In 1922 the government passed legislation abolishing the Department of Militia and Defence, the Department of the Naval Service, and the Air Board. In their place was the unified Department of National Defence under a single minister. The Chief of the General Staff's title became Chief of Staff, and the abrasive and impulsive Major-General J.H. MacBrien was named to this post to become the chief adviser to the Minister. This arrangement did not please the navy, which, with the aid of the new department's deputy minister, fought a guerilla war from within. Increasingly unhappy with the sailors' success in thwarting his plans, perhaps verging on mental instability, and desperate for more money to support his young second wife and large family, MacBrien stayed on, grumbling all the time, until 1927. He threatened resignation repeatedly and, when his departure was publicly announced, he unsuccessfully tried to persuade the Minister of National Defence to give him a house and let him carry on. Able wartime officer that he had been, MacBrien ended up playing his role badly in a farce. At least his title had remained Chief of Staff, though he had sway only over the army.[58] His successor, Major-General H.C. Thacker, gave away even the title, and the navy, in effect, had equivalent status. Not that this mattered with a tin-pot navy and a Permanent Force with a strength under 4000.[59]

Planning went on in the Directorate of Military Operations and Intelligence, which was re-formed in 1920. Its tasks were to review local defence plans in the military districts across the breadth of the country, write a general defence scheme for the nation, and think about how and what kind of expeditionary force Canada might send abroad 'if it should ever be necessary.'[60] In charge was Colonel J. Sutherland Brown, known to all as 'Buster Brown.' Unfortunately and unfairly painted by political scientist James Eayrs as barking mad, Sutherland in fact was an able, if very anti-American, officer whose plans had the support of his military superiors.

What exercised Eayrs was Sutherland Brown's work on Defence Scheme No. 1, the Canadian plan for a war between the United States and Britain in which Canada would be the subject of attack. The two superpowers had been allies during the Great War, but wartime alliance does not guarantee perpetual peace. Many, in fact, thought that Britain and the United States might clash or that Britain might be neutral, for example, in a war between the United States and Japan, a situation that could conceivably see the Americans seizing bases on the British Columbia coast. Someday soon, many feared, the Americans might also need Canadian resources and be prepared to take any and all steps necessary to secure them. Very simply, it was not mad for the Director of Military Operations and Intelligence to plan for such contingencies, and, indeed, his American counterparts were making similar plans for just such eventualities.[61]*

Sutherland Brown planned for limited spoiling attacks by Canadian forces into the United States in the event of war. The plan called for an advance 'into and [to] occupy the strategic points including Spokane, Seattle and Portland,' for forces to 'converge towards Fargo in North Dakota,' and then continue 'a general advance in the direction of Minneapolis and St Paul.'[62] Brown also ran his own intelligence-gathering operations into the northern states, collecting postcards of strategic points when he went on holiday there. Again, Canadian incursions over the border made sense if American opinion had qualms about attacking Canada, as it well might. They made sense if Britain needed time to send naval and land support to the dominion, as it most certainly would – even if Britain decided to support Canada in such a war. What was almost certainly mad was that the plans expected far too much of the Militia, which, in 1921, when the first iteration of Defence Scheme No. 1 was circulated, was already in decay. The District Officer Commanding in Montreal pointed this

---

* By the beginning of 1938, however, Canada and the United States had begun secret staff talks to assess the undefended status of Canada's coasts. The old attitudes would be altered by the force of events.

flaw out: the plan was 'drawn up for forces which are to a certain extent non-existent.' Sutherland Brown's superiors understood that the plan made sense only if the government provided equipment for the large Militia they had recommended. The fact that these plans stayed alive well into the 1920s, as the Militia continuously declined in effectiveness, suggested a lack of reality that was frightening. Sutherland Brown, however, was not alone in these views. The scheme did not begin to die until General Thacker became CGS in 1927; it was interred in 1931, and General McNaughton ordered all copies to be destroyed by fire in October 1933.[63]

Sutherland Brown had other schemes on the boil. In 1922, when the Chanak crisis threatened war between Britain and Turkey, he drew up plans for a brigade to join the British forces. Prime Minister King's declaration that 'Parliament will decide' if Canada would participate in such a war – clearly he meant it would not – scuppered any such expedition. The 1927 plan of the Directorate of Military Operations and Intelligence for a division to serve in China to protect British interests there in a Sino-Japanese war was similarly a non-starter. But such planning was never wholly useless, for it provided practice in the kind of thinking that was needed in the event of unlikely contingencies. Whether a military could plan properly or even exist with a planning staff of two or three officers was another question.

Ultimately more useful was Defence Scheme No. 3, the plan for a large expeditionary force that Sutherland Brown's successors drew up at the end of the 1920s with the explicit authority of the Minister of National Defence, Colonel J.L. Ralston. Ralston and the Chief of the General Staff, McNaughton, did not agree on very much, but they both believed that this contingency was the most likely one Canada might face, and Ralston agreed to a plan for seven divisions. Mackenzie King's Liberal government lost the election of 1930, but McNaughton pressed the case for a large expeditionary force with R.B. Bennett's Conservatives. This plan dovetailed neatly with the cutting of the hugely overblown Non-Permanent Active Militia establishment in half, and the first draft went to District Officers Commanding in 1934. Changes followed, but McNaughton, as aware as anyone of the necessity of not allowing a second Sam Hughes to usurp the army's right and duty to plan its own mobilization, even had the names of unit commanders added to the scheme to limit political interference in officer selection.[64]

There were other plans in the Directorate of Military Operations and Intelligence arsenal. Defence Scheme No. 2 was drawn up in sketchy form by Sutherland Brown to deal with the defence of the Pacific Coast in the event of an Anglo-Japanese war. McNaughton shifted the emphasis to the defence of Canadian neutrality in an American-Japanese conflict, an unrealistic plan given that most Canadians were anti-Japanese and pro-American, and the dominion almost certainly would have been drawn into any such war. This scheme, completed in 1933, won government approval only in 1936.[65] Defence Scheme No. 4 provided for minor Canadian participation in imperial wars, rather along the lines of the Boer War or Chanak, a contingency no one took very seriously. The point of these schemes, however, was to have contingency plans in place. Most of the plans were based on British defence needs, a reflection of Canada's de facto colonial status. The Statute of Westminster of 1931 may have been Canada's declaration of independence in law, but army headquarters did not believe it altered the reality very much. Neither did most Canadians, not least the media and the English-speaking elites.

The King government that returned to office in the autumn of 1935 faced a darkening global situation. Japan was enmeshed in China, Italy was attacking Abyssinia, and the Nazis were wiping out the restraints imposed on Germany by the Treaty of Versailles of 1919. All these trends disturbed Canadian public opinion, not least in Quebec, where the threat of war foreshadowed conscription in the public mind. King's electoral base of support lay in Quebec, and he was at pains to balance public opinion in English and French Canada. Plans for expeditionary forces were not plans the Liberal government wanted to hear about. The Department of External Affairs, led by the powerful isolationist Dr O.D. Skelton, also poured cold water on the military's thinking. The government soon implemented policies that aimed at the fortification of the Pacific Coast and the development of the air force in priority to the navy and of the navy in priority to the Militia. Its last priority was reorganizing and re-equipping the Militia, a term that included the Permanent Force, as soon as resources permitted – that is, never. The traditional priority of putting the army first had been completely rethought. The government also made clear in 1937 that army planning was not based on an expeditionary force, but on the defence of Canada.[66]

The military planners duly rewrote Defence Scheme No. 3 to base it on home defence. In fact, it still stipulated an expeditionary force, albeit a 'field force' of two divisions. The army had never hidden its views. One staff officer, Maurice Pope, had said in a prize essay in *Canadian Defence Quarterly* that using the Canadian Army 'to further the Imperial interest is a measure compatible with our strength and dignity as a nation.'[67] The Minister, Ian Mackenzie, understood what the planners were doing, accepted their subterfuge in rewriting Defence Scheme No. 3, and encouraged the Chief of the General Staff to plan for contingencies not specifically sanctioned by the government.[68] His planners soon exaggerated the likely scale of attack on Canada's coasts to justify a case for new equipment. After the Munich Crisis of September 1938, the military, convinced that war now was coming very soon and that Canada was sure to participate at Britain's side, dropped the pretense. The General Staff now actively planned to dispatch an eventual seven-division expeditionary force to an overseas war.[69] The government, almost wholly unaware of this shift, had certainly not given its approval. Indeed, the King government, engaged in the excruciating effort to bring a united English and French Canada into a war – should one occur – would have been furious if it had known of the General Staff planning.

When Nazi war drums were beginning to beat against Poland, the Conservative Party leader, Dr R.J. Manion, told the press on March 28, 1939, that he opposed conscription. The Prime Minister pledged in Parliament that there would be no conscription for overseas service in any war. He added as well that 'the days of great expeditionary forces of infantry crossing the oceans are not likely to recur.'[70] Nonetheless, the General Staff continued its planning. To update Defence Scheme No. 3, the plan for an expeditionary force, the CGS, Major-General T.V. Anderson, recalled Brigadier Harry Crerar to Ottawa in March from his post as commandant of the Royal Military College. A former Director of Military Operations and Intelligence, Crerar was an able staff officer, fully aware of recent British organizational changes, and he set to work with a will. There would be no cavalry division, he decided, though the units designated as such might be mechanized. The six infantry divisions were to be reorganized to British standards, which largely meant more vehicles of all kinds. The Permanent Force and the Non-Permanent Active Militia should be prepared for war in a temperate climate against a 'civilized enemy,' Crerar's paper, circulated to the District Officers Commanding, said.[71] Whether the government would agree was far from certain, but Crerar counted on public opinion to demand that Canada be represented overseas by one division and likely two, as a minimum.

This was the advice Anderson (and the Air Force and Navy Chiefs of Staff) gave the government in a memorandum of August 29, 1939: 'Active participation with other Empire forces has throughout been a secondary and incidental consideration. But it may be confidently ... anticipated that the outbreak of a major war will produce an immediate and overwhelming demand for active intervention with armed forces in direct aid of Great Britain.' For the army's part, a corps of 60,000 men should be raised and sent 'abroad as soon as arrangements can be made with the British Government, to transport it and to make good such deficiencies in its war equipment as cannot be supplied from Canadian sources.'[72]

By that date, the war that all had feared had become a virtual certainty, once Nazi Germany and Josef Stalin's Soviet Union had signed their alliance. The way now was cleared for Adolf Hitler to attack the Poles, which he did on September 1. Britain and France grudgingly fulfilled their pledges to Poland on September 3 and, after a week's delay to allow Parliament to be recalled, Canada went to war against Germany for the second time in a generation.

The Chief of the General Staff's certainty that Canadian public opinion would demand that the nation provide an expeditionary force turned out be right, but it still took some persuading to convince Mackenzie King. Now Canada's Permanent Force, with its strength of 455 officers and 3714 other ranks, had to show what its professional soldiers could do in war. The Non-Permanent Active Militia, 5272 officers and 41,249 other ranks strong, all armed with the weapons of 1918, would again have to rise to the occasion.[73*]

There was very little with which to start. The official historian of the army in the Second World War noted dispassionately that, on the outbreak of war:

Canada had no troops ready for immediate action, except for local coastal

---

* As in 1914, francophones were in very short supply. Only the Royal 22e Régiment was French-speaking, Militia administration in Quebec was still conducted in English, and in the class of 1939 at RMC there were only two francophone graduates. Serge Bernier, 'A Century of Copping Out: The Canadian Government and the Francophones in Canada's Armed Forces (1867–1967),' *The Army and the Nation* (Gagetown, NB, 1998), F4-3/5.

defence against very small raids. The tiny Permanent Force did not constitute a striking force capable either of counter-attack against a major raid or of expeditionary action. The Non-Permanent Active Militia, with its limited strength, obsolescent equipment and rudimentary training, was incapable of immediate effective action of any sort against a formidable enemy. The two forces together constituted a useful and indeed essential foundation upon which, over a period of months, an army could be built. They offered, however, no means for rapid intervention in an overseas theatre of operations.[74]

Canadian military professionalism, which had all but disappeared since 1919, now had to be recreated under the pressures of war.

six

MCNAUGHTON'S ARMY: THE LONG WAIT

'You know when I come to England?' he asked Turvey with a glower. 'December-fuckin-thirty-nine.'

'Golly, you musta seen lots of action by now. Where've you been?'

'Where've I been? Listen. First I was a whole bloody winter in Aldershot. Then they put me on a train for Norway.'

'Gee, I never met anybody who fought in Norway before!'

'Well, you ain't now. They turned us back at Dunfermline. Next month I got another train ride – to Dover. Whole First Infantry Brigade was going to France.'

'You mean you was fighting there in 1940!'

'Who, me?' He laughed sourly. 'First time we never even sailed. Then next month we got all the way to Brest. And I sat in the friggin harbour two days. Then we got the bum's rush back to Aldershot. June 1940, that was. And now it's June 1943, and I'm fightin Hitler from a Buckingham castle. What kinda shitheels runnin this army? ... Last year they didn't even send us to Dieppe – took the Second Div boys hadn't been overseas a year.'[1]

—※—

The fictional Private Turvey's friend was not a special case. The Canadian divisions that arrived in England beginning in December 1939 had critically important roles to fill, but fighting the enemy did not seem to be one of them. The Canadians waited and trained, watched the war being lost, and trained some more. It was the luck of the draw, but it was also the wish of their commander, General Andrew McNaughton, and of the government of Canada. Canadians had to fight under their own commanders, and they had to fight together. Moreover, because high casualties meant conscription, and that was a political shibboleth back home, the less battle the better. Were these not the lessons of the Great War?

So the Canadians struggled to prepare for war – somewhere. The army in Canada readied ever more men for service overseas, and the government faced division and discord at home as it mobilized the nation. The units in Britain bashed parade squares and went on long route marches. They mastered individual and platoon soldiering, and they fired their guns and learned how to operate their tanks. The Canadians did everything but fight the enemy, leading British women to jibe 'He's not a soldier, he's a Canadian.'[2] By 1942 and 1943, now organized into the First Canadian Army under the General Officer Commanding-in-Chief, General A.G.L. McNaughton, their exercises grew bigger, more complex, and much more realistic, and many of the weaknesses in leadership and training became clear. The Canadians had been very lucky to have time – though not, perhaps, as much as they got – to get ready. Competent division, corps, and army commanders did not spring up fully formed any more than did lieutenant-colonels or sergeant-majors, and the Second World War was more complex, swifter, and even more lethal than the First. Then there were the disasters of Hong Kong and of Dieppe, the army's first serious casualties in what had hitherto been a bloodless ground war. More weaknesses in professionalism, training, and planning were exposed. Finally, when the First Canadian Division was detailed for the invasions of Sicily and Italy in 1943 over the GOC-in-C's objections, the strains between McNaughton and his Defence Minister and between McNaughton and the British proved unbearable. Total war had come to the Canadians at last.

No Canadians stood in the streets and cheered the end of the twenty-year armistice when Canada went to war with Germany in September 1939. The memories of the Great War's horrors, the death, and the hardships were still too fresh. In Quebec, memories of conscription rushed to mind. Canadians watched uneasily as the German Wehrmacht cut through Poland's defences and as the Soviet Union, adhering to the bargain Stalin had made with Hitler, took over the eastern part of that country. Soon the Baltic states became Soviet republics, and Stalin launched the Red Army into a difficult war with Finland. The dictatorships of both the right and the left were on the move.

Britain and France moved their armies to the Franco-German and Franco-Belgian borders and did nothing. While Hitler was occupied with swallowing the Poles, the Allies sat back and did not even make threatening gestures in what American newspapers soon came to call the 'phoney war.' The navies patrolled, applying an economic squeeze on the Reich, and the air forces dropped leaflets on Germany. The phoney war indeed – except for Poland.

In Canada the phoney war mentality thrived as well. The Chiefs of Staff had been stunned by the reaction of the Cabinet to their initial proposals for war mobilization. There was no money, for one thing, the Cabinet said. No corps of 60,000 men would be raised for overseas service; indeed, there might not even be an expeditionary force at all. On September 4 Prime Minister Mackenzie King told the acting Finance Minister not to approve expenditures for anything other than the defence of Canada, and the next day Ian Mackenzie, the Minister of National Defence, ordered his officials not to stimulate recruiting. But on September 7, to King's surprise, the Cabinet expressed some support for the idea of an expeditionary force – three days before Canada formally declared war.[3] Indeed, on September 1, even before Britain and France had declared war, the government had authorized the implementation of Defence Scheme No. 3 and authorized the mobilization of the whole of the Mobile Force (in effect, two divisions and a corps headquarters), now to be called the Canadian Active Service Force. Militia and Permanent Force units were called up, and guards were posted at vulnerable points.[4] In this war, at least, the mobilization plans prepared beforehand were implemented. Whether the government was willing to commit men to fight remained to be decided.

Not until September 19 did the Liberal government finally make firm decisions. The army's desire for an expeditionary corps of 60,000 men, or roughly three divisions' worth of men, was simply too expensive. Instead, King directed, one division 'might be arranged for dispatch overseas when required and trained in Canada meanwhile. A second in Canada to be kept available for dispatch later if required ... It was apparent that a third division could not be thought of at this time, if we were not to occasion protest across the country itself and even more to impair the credit of Canada.'[5] Defence

Minister Ian Mackenzie told the nation in a press release on September 19 of the government's decision. (This was his last act as Defence Minister as Norman Rogers, the Labour Minister, replaced him.)

Desperately frightened of casualties that might require conscription, the King government had implicitly decided that Canada's major effort in the war, in addition to the defence of the homeland, should be in the air. There could never be enough casualties there to make compulsory service a requisite, or so the prime minister believed in September 1939. The Royal Canadian Air Force would operate the British Commonwealth Air Training Plan, a gigantic national undertaking, and enlist a quarter-million men, many of them air crew, representing the fittest and most adventurous Canadians of their day. The Royal Canadian Navy also had its role to play in defending Canada's coasts; eventually it had 100,000 men in uniform. The size of the economy, its greater complexity, and the growth in government also took away men, many of them with great leadership potential.

The implications of these manpower choices were critical for the land forces, even though events would eventually make them the major component of the national war effort. Many of the difficulties the Canadian Army would face in the war likely arose because so many men, especially so many of the best men, went to other wartime duties. In the First World War, Canada had provided some 22,000 to the Royal Flying Corps, the Royal Naval Air Service, and the Royal Air Force, and a few thousands only to the Royal Canadian Navy. That was a far cry from the 350,000 men who joined the sister services in the Second World War and the untold number who remained in the domestic economy or worked in government. At root, the 'old sweats' of 1914 had told their sons that the infantry was no place to be – better join the navy or the air force, where a recruit could learn a trade, receive quicker promotion and, with luck, not get killed. Tens of thousands followed dad's advice, and this too unquestionably weakened the effectiveness of the army.

The question for Ottawa now was how to create and staff the First Division, and which regiments would form it. The last issue was the easiest, as the planners had almost everything worked out. The three Permanent Force infantry battalions would be included, one per brigade, along with Militia units that had good records. Here the experience of the Great War mobilization would not be repeated. The Royal 22e Régiment had initially been slated for the Second Division to form part of a francophone brigade, but, presumably because of concern that there would be no French-speaking unit in the First Division, this plan was altered by headquarters planners in July 1939. Thus, the 1st Brigade was from Ontario (the Royal Canadian Regiment, the Hastings and Prince Edward Regiment, and the 48th Highlanders), the 2nd Brigade was from the West (the Princess Patricia's Canadian Light Infantry, the Edmonton Regiment, and the Seaforth Highlanders), and the 3rd Brigade was from Quebec and the Maritimes (the Van Doos, the Carleton and York Regiment, and the West Nova Scotia Regiment). The Saskatoon Light Infantry provided the machine-gun battalion for the division.

Headquarters had already filled in the staff slots, assigning good PF officers as brigade majors to assist the brigade commanders. Two of them, Chris Vokes and Charles Foulkes, would rise to command divisions, and Foulkes to corps command. PF officers also filled almost all the key division staff slots. Colonel Ernest Sansom was named as Assistant Adjutant and Quartermaster General, the senior administrative and supply staff post; Lieutenant-Colonel G.R. Turner as GSO I; while Major Guy Simonds became GSO II, the operations planner. The GSO III in charge of intelligence, John Tweedsmuir, was not from the Permanent Force but the son of the Governor General, Lord Tweedsmuir. The brigade commanders were Brigadiers Armand Smith, George Pearkes, VC, and Basil Price, for the 1st, 2nd, and 3rd brigades, respectively. Smith was a Militia brigade commander, the proprietor of E.D. Smith jams; Price was a much-decorated up-from-the-ranks officer who ran a Montreal dairy owned by his wife's family; and Pearkes was a PF officer. All three were Great War veterans with records of distinction. Clearly, consideration had been given to ensuring that the Non-Permanent Active Militia had due representation. When the GOC of the Second Division, Victor Odlum of British Columbia, was named in the spring of 1940, another nod would be given to NPAM sensibilities.

Particularly in the early months of the war, there were tensions between NPAM and PF officers and men. The militiamen resented the greater technical competence of the regulars, as well as the air of superiority they carried. The Permanent Force disliked the political connections many of the Militia officers enjoyed, and they feared that a NPAM Commanding Officer might not be competent enough to lead them into action. General Christopher

Vokes recalled that 'what was mobilized was a mob ... an organized mob, in uniform. The militia officers and sergeants had a vague notion what to do ... They could probably lead a parade down the street ... but that was about the size of it. When it came down to training soldiers for war they knew absolutely nothing.'[6] This was true, of course, but the same thing might have been said of most of the Permanent Force. A Militia officer saw it differently. Ian Johnston, an RMC graduate and Toronto militiaman, thought that 'the regulars lived much more by the book. They didn't want to make up their own minds too quickly; they were professionals ... This was their chance for promotion and all. The NPAM types were more entrepreneurial ... they were prepared to take a chance, take a fresh look at a problem.'[7] What generally did unite the Permanent Force and the NPAM, however, was a dislike for the ring-knockers from the Royal Military College, who were seen – then and now – as cliquish and snobbish.[8] As time passed, these difficulties of perception and differences in ability generally disappeared, though the professional versus entrepeneurial approach may have remained. What is certain is that, in the autumn of 1939, virtually all the Canadians – RMC, Permanent Force, or NPAM – were amateurs at war.*

Most strikingly, there was no francophone representation at First Division headquarters, the sole exception being the Chief Signals Officer, and none of the brigade commanders was *Canadien*. Recruiting in Quebec was also slow, Military District No. 4 (Montreal) having enlisted only 7803 of the 11,000 men authorized by September 30. Quebec (MD No. 5) had only 2414 men of the 3239 authorized. With the exception of Saskatchewan, the other Military Districts were over or close to their quotas, though some of the regiments of the First Division had trouble filling their ranks, including the PF regiments.[9] The perennial problem of Quebec in an army that was still English speaking and very British in orientation had clearly not yet been resolved – nor would it be during the Second World War.[10]

Who was it who enlisted in September 1939? Many of the 61,500 were militiamen who wanted to go overseas – or who felt some pressure to do so.

---

* It is also worth noting that the PF/NPAM difficulties were replicated elsewhere. In the United States, National Guard units and officers were regarded by the regulars almost exactly as the NPAM were in Canada. See Peter Mansoor, *The GI Offensive in Europe: The Triumph of American Infantry Divisions, 1941–1945* (Lawrence, Kan., 1999), 57ff.

Others were Great War veterans: more than 4200 who could pass the fairly stringent medical requirements and the age limits signed up. Almost half the First Division's men joined off the streets and farms, without even the most rudimentary military training – something true even in the PF regiments. The PPCLI's ranks were not quite full until eight weeks after the declaration of war, for example.[11] In September, unemployment remained high, and the army offered 'three squares a day' – clothing, a trip overseas, and even a cause. 'We were just coming out of the Depression, which was terrible,' one soldier's son remembered. 'Nobody had nothing. Then the war came, and the men went.'[12] As always, men joined to escape – wives, families, obligations – while others were moved by patriotism, some by imperial sentiments, and still others by the conviction that Nazism was evil and had to be stopped. In its rawness, the division was little different from Sam Hughes's first contingent – except that many more of the men were Canadian born. This factor may have been important in 1939. Without the 'old world' motivation of blood, Canadian-born recruits had to make a rational decision to sign up. That led many to the navy or the air force or to await compulsory service.

The decision to enlist was, not surprisingly, hardest for French Canadians. Years of propaganda about 'Anglos,' an absence of recent personal links to Europe, and earlier marriages and larger families tended to make enlistment a least-favoured option. One assessment of the rank and file of the Royal 22e Régiment by an officer who served with the unit put the average age of its soldiers as twenty-one, with most having a grade 7 education and perhaps 10 to 20 per cent illiterate. Very few were married, all were Roman Catholic (except the regiment's adjutant in Italy, Captain Paul Hart, who was Jewish), and most were working class. Few were physically robust. The average soldier was 5 feet 5 inches in height and weighed about 135 pounds.[13] The average anglophone recruit was not much different in terms of education or marital status, though most were taller and heavier.

The Canadian Army's young officer candidates, raised in the hard times of the 1930s, were generally better educated, most having completed high school at least. They were a few years older than their men, but they had been schooled that caution, prudence, and security were virtues. 'This,' said the leading historian of Canadian officership, 'was not an atmosphere for kindling leadership,' for creating 'the impulse of the thrust to kill.'[14]

The question of who was to command the First Division remained, and it was quickly solved. Major-General Andrew McNaughton, Chief of the General Staff until 1935, was just fifty-two years old. He had been running the National Research Council in the years since, and he had pointedly not retired from the military so he could come back if war came. Soon after the declaration of war, the Minister of National Defence told the Prime Minister that he thought McNaughton should lead. This choice pleased King. McNaughton had the reputation of being a Tory, so no one could cry patronage. As the perfector of counter-battery artillery work and a successful Great War veteran, he was a 'scientific soldier,' preferring to use guns, not men, to take the objective – a vital point to Mackenzie King, who lived in fear of casualties and conscription. But when the General met the Minister, Norman Rogers, early in October, difficulties quickly arose. McNaughton insisted that a complete division with all its units be his, which was sensible; his language, which appeared to threaten the government (in the last year of its mandate), was not. Matters were thrashed out when the Prime Minister met with McNaughton, but King's first doubts had begun to appear.[15]

The First Division was ready on paper. The Permanent Force had achieved its first war aim – ensuring that the mobilization plan was followed without ministerial interference. It had achieved its second aim as well – ensuring that PF officers had the key slots on the staff. The sole concession were the two Militia brigadiers who had, the headquarters staff believed, been prevented from doing too much harm by having able PF officers at their right hand. Harry Crerar, soon promoted to major-general so he could deal with the British from an appropriate rank, went to London to establish the Canadian Military Headquarters. His Number 2 was Lieutenant-Colonel E.L.M. Burns. Again the Permanent Force had ensured that it had the critical positions; there was to be no Sam Hughes-style croneyism in England to disrupt the fighting soldiers this time.

To get the division from paper to reality was a hard slog. With the title Inspector-General (until early December), McNaughton toured the country, visiting the units of his division and noting the problems of accommodation, equipment, and training. Some units had only Great War uniforms, complete with breeches, high puttees, and brass-buttoned uniforms. Many had no boots, most lacked the newly designed battledress, and the 1937-pattern web equipment was still in short supply; still other units had no transport. These shortages were remedied as soon as supplies could be found. When, for example, McNaughton discovered that the Royal Montreal Regiment had purchased boots from Eaton's because the army couldn't supply them and now wouldn't pay for them, he approved the purchase on the spot. The officers and men liked this approach and decided Andy would do the sensible thing.[16]

Training was slow, however. The units remained in or near their home locations this time, unlike 1914, a solution that created some problems for the division and brigade staffs and prevented anything beyond individual training. It was also evident that most of the division's heavy weapons and equipment had to be found in England from British sources, as Canada was not able to provide them. In 1939 Canada had, in all, four anti-aircraft guns, five mortars, eighty-two Vickers machine guns, and ten Bren guns. Ottawa could supply trucks, and it proposed sending them with the division, but the War Office wanted British manufacturers to get the contracts.[17] The idea of a limited liability war was not confined to Ottawa alone.

Early in December 1939 the men of the First Canadian Division entrained for Halifax and departure for Britain. As in September 1914 they were largely untrained, raw troops, without much of the proper equipment. 'We didn't know a damn thing,' one officer recalled.[18] Their spirits were high, however, even as Canada once again sent its sons overseas with nothing except uniforms and small arms.

The Canadian Division, based at Aldershot and with most of the units in much better quarters than the Canadians received in the Great War, did not get down to training until January 1940. On both the government's and McNaughton's insistence, responsibility for training lay with the Canadian authorities. Nevertheless, Canadian training, organization, and armaments always maintained uniformity with the British Army and, in operations, the Canadians functioned smoothly within the British military framework.[19] The GOC's plan was to conduct individual training in January and February, unit collective training in March, and brigade and division exercises in April – a schedule that suited the British, who hoped to use the Canadians at the front in May 1940. The quality of the training depended on the brigade commander and, even more, on the battalion Commanding Officer. Some units worked hard and trained for battle as best they could; others did almost nothing. Soldiers practised their musketry and did a tour in model trenches constructed at Pirbright, mastering the tactics of stand-tos and patrolling of the 1914–18 war. Many officers and men attended a huge variety of courses run by the British Army (although some unit commanders kept their good officers and NCOs off courses for fear that someone higher up would steal them away), while McNaughton and the division's senior officers went to France in January to see the Maginot Line and the British Army in France. The progress of training was very slow for all the predictable reasons – weather, shortage of vehicles, and the lack of equipment – and by April, when the Germans suddenly moved against Denmark and Norway, the Canadians were far from ready for action.

The German assault on Norway interrupted the Canadians' training. In mid-April, a week after the Nazi landings, the War Office sought Canadian participation in attacks planned against German positions on the Trondheim fjord. The British wanted Canadians, presumably because of their northern experience but also because their state of training was considered to be more advanced than that of other troops in the United Kingdom (a telling comment). McNaughton designated the 2nd Canadian Brigade to provide a force, under the command of Colonel Ernest Sansom. Major Guy Simonds prepared the orders for the force, working at a breakneck pace, and an impressed General McNaughton marked him for quick promotion.[20] Meanwhile, officers scrambled to find winter equipment for the 1300-man force, one junior officer going out on a limb to order sheepskin coats at a high price for the troops. The Canadians made it to Dunfermline, Scotland, but no further, when the War Office cancelled the operation because of its risky nature. Norway soon fell under the German yoke, the first disaster to British and French arms. The sheepskin coats, the story goes, ended up being worn by soldiers' girlfriends long after.*[21]

More serious was the commitment of substantial elements of the Canadian

---

* Eddie Goodman, an officer in the Fort Garry Horse, noted in his memoirs: 'My British experience and adventures were no different from those of the rest of the army overseas.' He added, tellingly, that one of his fellow officer's father with Great War experience had passed along one word of advice: 'My son, now that you are going to England, I want to tell you that in Canada fornication is in its infancy.' Eddie Goodman, *Life of the Party* (Toronto, 1988), 21.

Division to France in June 1940. The Nazi *blitzkrieg* in May blew through Holland and Belgium, knifed through the French lines in the Ardennes, and threatened to destroy the British Expeditionary Force. Winston Churchill took over as British prime minister on May 10, just as the Nazi assault began, and his first days in power were marked by a succession of defeats and his great speeches.

General McNaughton had told Mackenzie King that his division was battleworthy, though it most certainly was not.[22] It was the Canadians' good fortune that they were not yet part of the British Expeditionary Force because, as ill-trained as the division was, as ill-led by men who still thought in terms of the Great War, it could not have done well in action, if indeed it could have survived. But in June 1940, with everything collapsing before Hitler's panzers, the British thought for a brief period of using McNaughton and a brigade from the Canadian Division to protect the threatened British supply lines in the Hazebrouck and Armentières areas. By May 24, as the 1st Brigade hastened to Dover to prepare for embarkation, the situation on the ground had deteriorated further and wiser heads prevailed. The miracle of Dunkirk fortunately saved most of the BEF, minus its equipment, and for a time the British decided to try to create a second British Expeditionary Force to support those French forces still fighting in western France. There was not much that could be sent, only the 52nd Division and the Canadians, and the 1st Brigade left Aldershot on June 8, ready to set sail for Brest.

The story of this Canadian adventure is mercifully brief and almost bloodless. The brigade transport arrived in Brest on June 12 and 13 and proceeded inland, ahead of the brigade's battalions and regiments, which arrived on June 14. The British commander, General Alan Brooke, a most able officer who had served with the Canadian Corps in the earlier war, had few instructions from London that made any sense in the face of the Allied weakness and the advancing Wehrmacht. Late on June 14 he ordered the Canadians, by then scattered from Brest to Le Mans, to return to England, saving them from being swallowed whole in the unfolding catastrophe. With many adventures, they made their way back to England, leaving behind much of their transport and equipment, but not their guns. The Royal Canadian Horse Artillery's CO, Lieutenant-Colonel Hamilton Roberts, refused to destroy his unit's new 25-pounders and, after a long argument, got them (and some other equipment) loaded on a ship. Lieutenant Robert Moncel of the RCR was ordered by a British officer to destroy his platoon's scarce Bren gun carriers, but he got them loaded as ballast after ordering his platoon sergeant to shoot the officer if necessary.[23] Modern equipment was to be worth its weight in gold in England in the invasion summer of 1940. Six men of the brigade were left behind, a remarkably low number considering the panic and chaos that prevailed in France and the British Army.[24]

The collapse of France had left Canada, unarmed as it still was, as Britain's ranking ally, an extraordinary status that was to last until Hitler turned on the Soviet Union in June 1941. The Canadian task for the next three years was the defence of Britain against the anticipated German invasion. The equipment lost by the 1st Brigade in its brief foray into France was desperately needed, but, even without it, the First Canadian Division was likely the best-equipped division in Britain. Despite its relative lack of training, it may even have been the most battle-ready formation, given the mauling suffered by the divisions of the BEF in France. Joined together in late July with the British First Armoured Division under a newly promoted Lieutenant-General McNaughton, the Canadians formed the mobile reserve south of the Thames River – in effect, the main anti-invasion force. McNaughton's staff was joined by British officers to form the corps staff, and the still-green Canadian planners learned much from this experience. The Canadian brigades took up positions in Surrey, south of London, and, for a time, their training took on a new urgency as the lessons of the *blitzkrieg* began to be applied. The division acquired reconnaissance squadrons and, theoretically, anti-aircraft defences, though there were yet no guns except for completely ineffective light machine guns. By September, with the invasion seemingly set to occur at any time, the Canadians went to a high state of readiness – but the German attack did not come. A good thing too, because Britain's defences were terribly thin.

The Second Division under Major-General Victor Odlum had begun arriving in Britain, as the Canadian government at last began to exert itself in the war. The Ogdensburg Agreement of August 1940, signed by Mackenzie King and President Franklin Roosevelt, had, in effect, guaranteed the safety of the homeland,[25] freeing the dominion to send all the military assistance it could overseas. Odlum's brigades, somewhat better trained than the First Division's had been when they arrived nine months before, took up anti-invasion duties as well. By Christmas 1940, McNaughton's Canadian Corps came into existence, consisting of the First Division, now led by Major-General George Pearkes, and the Second.

In Canada the crisis of the spring and summer of 1940 led the government to put aside the tight-fisted economic policies it had been following. Ben Dunkelman, a wealthy Torontonian, recalled that the army, 'ludicrously weak though it was,' had been in no hurry to expand. 'There seemed to be a hundred volunteers for every vacancy, and the units were very choosy. As a result, enlisting took on something of the character of trying to join an exclusive club.' Edwin Goodman, another young man who would serve with distinction, recalled his interview as he tried to get into the Armoured Corps as a junior officer. His main qualification, he told a sceptical board, was that he had been the riding master at a children's camp; he added, truthfully: 'I feel I have some qualities of leadership and am a quick learner.' A month later Goodman was accepted for training, proving, he said, 'the well-known Canadian Army maxim that "Bullshit Baffles Brains."'[26] After Dunkirk the stops were pulled, volunteers began flooding into recruiting stations (almost 59,000 in June and July), and Canada was truly in the war. At last there was equipment for new recruits, and tens of thousands lined up at the Quartermaster stores to have a kitbag thrown at them containing Webb equipment, water bottle, mess tins, shirts, shorts, puttees, boots, shoes, ties, helmet, and hat. Very little fit at first try on, but NCOs demanded that all be blancoed, polished, and made to look smart.[27]

The government agreed to raise a Third Division and an army tank brigade in the summer of 1940. At roughly the same time, Canada promised to send a brigade to Iceland, which occupied a critical position in the North Atlantic near the convoy routes. In October, troops went to Newfoundland,[28] and, before long, the Canadian Army was providing battalions to garrison Bermuda, the Bahamas, British Guiana, and Jamaica. The decision to raise a Fourth Division came in May 1941. A Fifth Division followed soon after, and they all proceeded overseas in due course.

Canada had put four divisions in the field in the Great War, but the army planners wanted more in 1941. Led by the Chief of the General Staff, now Major-General Harry Crerar, they put together a plan for a large army of six infantry divisions and two armoured divisions, to be commanded in the field by an army headquarters. Crerar, who had returned to Ottawa in the summer of 1940, believed the country could sustain six divisions overseas and two at home, the overseas army to consist of two corps, each of two infantry and one armoured division. There was a long struggle to achieve this scheme, primarily because the Prime Minister feared that such a large force could only be maintained by conscription. Crerar and his successor as CGS, Ken Stuart, largely got their way, nonetheless, as Stuart assured Mackenzie King that this force could be sustained by voluntary enlistments.[29] In the end, Canada was to have an army overseas of three infantry (the First, Second, and Third Divisions) and two armoured divisions (the Fourth and Fifth Divisions), plus the 1st and 2nd Armoured Brigades. Unstated but critical, the British would have to supply some 50,000 men, including regiments of heavy artillery and rearward services, to make the First Canadian Army able to operate.[30] At home, there would be three additional divisions at the peak. Whether a nation of 11 million could maintain an army of this size in action was uncertain, especially since, for political reasons involving status and nationhood, Canada insisted on providing its own supply line home rather than relying on British sources as in 1914–18. After 1943, moreover, Canada had soldiers in two widely separated operational theatres. The price of Canadianization was high: because there were few economies of scale for Canada (compared, say, with the United States, with eighty-nine army and six marine divisions in the field), the teeth-to-tail ratio – the calculation to illustrate how many soldiers in the rear and at home were required to maintain one soldier at the front – was very heavily tilted rearwards. The army had base organizations in Canada, Britain, and in Italy after 1943; it had a large training establishment in Britain and a larger one in Canada; and there was also a substantial home defence commitment as well as conscription for Canadian service only, a policy that tied up men at home.[31]* The problem of army manpower was made more difficult still because the RCAF and the RCN were simultaneously in the throes of rapid expansion. The pressures on the manpower resources of the nation now began

---

* On December 31, 1944, the Canadian Army had 159,741 men in its fighting formations, excluding reinforcements; in the United Kingdom were 189,621; and in Canada (in March 1945 after the Sixth Division had been broken up and after 16,000 NRMA men had been sent overseas), 40,981 General Service volunteers. In other words, 230,000 men were required to support 159,000 – and many of those in the fighting formations were in the services devoted to supporting the infantry, artillery, and armour. *Report of the Department of National Defence ... 1945* (Ottawa, 1946), 36–7.

to be felt, and the seeds of the conscription crisis of 1944 can readily be traced back to the decisions made in creating the large army in 1941.

The Mackenzie King government had made repeated promises that it would never impose conscription for overseas service. The first pledge had been made in March 1939; the second during the parliamentary debate on going to war; the third during the Quebec provincial election of October 1939, which produced the defeat of Maurice Duplessis's Union Nationale government; and the fourth during the federal election of March 1940, which King won very handily. But the fortunes of war can play havoc with peacetime and phony war promises, and the Allied disasters in May and June 1940, the surrender of France, and the possibility of a calamitous British defeat led to a public clamour that forced the Canadian government to rethink its position on compulsory service.

As early as May 22, 1940, as the scale of the defeat in France became apparent, King had begun to see that a demand for conscription was soon to begin in Canada. In early June an Ontario Liberal MP called in caucus for national registration, a measure certain to be viewed in Quebec as a precursor to compulsory service. The opposition pressed for a declaration of a national emergency as well, and King buckled. On June 18 he introduced the National Resources Mobilization Bill into the House of Commons, a sweeping measure giving the government emergency power to mobilize 'all our human and material resources for the defence of Canada.' What of manpower resources? To reassure Quebec, King stated that 'it will relate solely and exclusively to the defence of Canada on our own soil and in our own territorial waters ... no measure for the conscription of men for overseas service will be introduced by the present administration.' There would, however, be a national registration, an inventory of manpower, but, King claimed, it had 'nothing whatsoever to do with the recruitment of men for overseas service.'[32]

The groundwork had been laid for conscription by the NRM Act, though initially only for the defence of Canada. The intention was to call up unmarried men for thirty days' training, a measure that stirred some unrest in Quebec, but surprisingly little, considering past history. The danger to Canada was obvious to all, and Québécois had always maintained that the defence of Canada was close to their hearts, even if Britain and France were not.

The planning for the NRMA conscripts began at Army Headquarters under the CGS, General Crerar, who had just returned from Britain. Crerar understood that the NRMA plan was 'a very superficial scheme,' but it was too late to change it. All he could do with thirty days' training was make the conscripts 'military-minded.'[33] The national registration in August 1940 demonstrated that there were 802,000 single men and childless widowers between the ages of nineteen and forty-five, so this group became the primary pool for recruitment for both the NRMA and the active forces. Over the course of a year, the plan went, eight groups of 30,000 men would be trained, as the registrars in each of thirteen administrative districts initially selected men from the twenty-one to twenty-four year olds. Allowances were also made for exemptions and deferments. Recruiting for NPAM units ceased on August 15, 1940; thereafter, only men who had had thirty days' training could join the Militia. Every NRMA conscript would automatically be deemed to be a member of the closest Militia unit (or Canadian Army Reserve unit, as the NPAM was renamed on November 19, 1940) on conclusion of training.

The first class of call-ups reported on October 9, 1940. The training focused on athletic competitions, rifle marksmanship, and the soldier's life. The army was selling the military life more than training soldiers, a reasonable enough tactic since thirty days was not enough time to turn civilians into soldiers. Still, it seemed more than slightly anomalous when the Toronto area registrar urged conscripts in the third batch, reporting January 10, 1941, 'to bring along any basketball or badminton equipment they have available.'[34]

Clearly, no one had any idea what use would be made of the thirty-day men. Although many indicated they were considering joining up, what of the others? Astonishingly, no one thought to create a way for men to volunteer for the Canadian Active Service Force (CASF) directly from NRMA training, and no one checked to see if conscripts reported to their reserve unit. The army, however, was thinking ahead. In September 1940, even before the first conscripts reported, Crerar told his Minister that what he wanted, what the army needed, was a minimum of four months' training for conscripts, a reduction in the totals to be called up, and the transfer of the trainees to the home defence formations of the CASF. The government began to bite at the cherry of conscription. On February 20, 1941, the Cabinet ordered that men twenty-one years of age were now to be liable for four months' training. Moreover, the 'R' men, those called up under the NRMA, would train with the 'A' men, those who had volunteered for active service. Ten thousand men each month were to enter the training stream, divided equally between 'R' and 'A' soldiers.

The difficulty was that 'A' recruits were starting to dwindle. Almost 200,000 men had already joined the army, ready for service anywhere, but 7000 fewer men than were needed to fill reinforcement pools had enlisted in the first quarter of 1941. No major recruiting campaign for active service had yet been launched, but Ottawa hit on the idea of keeping NRMA conscripts not for four months but for the duration of the war. This scheme would release volunteers for service anywhere. The extension was duly announced in late April 1941, a month before Colonel J. Layton Ralston, the Defence Minister since Norman Rogers's death in an air crash in June 1940, kicked off the first recruiting drive. Initially the results were slow, Ralston suggesting that the army's lack of action overseas was responsible, but, during the two-month campaign, 34,625 men joined the army, 2000 more than the quota.[35]

One reaction to the shortage of men came in late June 1941, when the army decided to create the Canadian Women's Army Corps to free volunteers for service overseas and to give women the opportunity to serve. Initially not part of the army and not subject to military law, the corps was slow to develop. But in March 1942 the CWACs became female soldiers, equal in all respects to the men, including eligibility for veterans' benefits – except that they were paid less and were not intended to serve in combat. Eventually, the 21,624 women who joined the CWACs served in Canada and overseas and took on an astonishing variety of tasks. There were clerks and cooks, radio operators and drivers, mechanics and dental assistants, all freeing men to fight.[36]

In the training camps scattered across Canada, the 'R' and 'A' men lived uncomfortably together.[37] There were differences in the uniform, an Active soldier wearing a Canada Volunteer Service Medal, a Canada flash, and the cap badge of the corps to which he was to be posted. The NRMA soldier had nothing on his chest, a maple leaf badge on his cap, and no shoulder flashes. The public, in other words, soon learned to differentiate between volunteers and conscripts. Moreover, some commanders showed favouritism to the 'A' men, giving them extra leave, for example. Others promised a three-day pass to all members of a platoon – if only the 'R' men would convert to 'A' status. The pressures were very great, and sometimes they included beatings and verbal abuse. This stigma did not cease when trainees went to home defence formations, where the 'R' men were frequently treated as pariahs and the volunteers in the units refused to accept whatever rationales were put forward to explain why the NRMA men would not volunteer.[38] Despite, or because of, these less than subtle methods, large numbers of 'R' men transferred to the navy or the air force rather than join the army. Moreover, roughly 60 per cent expressed determination to remain NRMA or 'Zombies,' as they soon came to be called, a derogatory term comparing the conscripts to the living dead of Hollywood's horror films.[39] Only 20 per cent of call-ups ordinarily joined the CASF.[40] In effect, Canada had created two armies, one of conscripts on home defence service, and one of volunteers willing to serve anywhere.

Army life was a shock to many of the civilians and had few charms, leading to a low retention rate among them. Lieutenant Harry Jolley, an officer in the Royal Canadian Dental Corps based in Peterborough, Ontario, noted in the spring of 1942: 'I get very annoyed with people who tell me how lucky I am to be in the Army – people incidentally who are not in the Army are always the ones to talk like that. If you can live for today only, have no ambition or care for the future the Army is great,' he went on. 'Maybe I'm being unfair to professional soldiers when I talk like that – but at least they don't have to readjust themselves to a new life & then worry about being able to re-adjust themselves back again. Soldiers are notoriously good relaxers. Me – that's where I fall down.'[41] Jolley, a highly qualified dentist who had abandoned a good practice in Toronto to enlist, soon asked to be posted overseas.

But traditional army training worked on 'R' and 'A' recruits alike: it broke down their individuality by housing them in drafty H-huts in which they slept, bathed, and lived together, then built them up again through training into a cohesive group with a sense of comradeship and pride. Journalist and historian Pierre Berton wrote in his memoirs that the men in his training platoon at Vernon, British Columbia, in 1942, all but three of them 'R' men, found themselves developing skills and a strong esprit de corps, much to their surprise. A platoon competition in drill, one that no one cared about initially, 'became an obsession. It is hard to believe ... that we actually gave up our precious evenings and practised at night in our own time.' The platoon won the coveted trophy, becoming the best drill platoon at Vernon. 'In just ten weeks the army had taken seventy-five strangers from all walks of life and turned them, for a little while at least, into the closest of comrades.'[42]

The issue of conscription was far from resolved, and some in the country believed that Canada's record in the war was pathetic. In November 1941 the Conservative Party chose Arthur Meighen, the draftsman of the 1917 Military Service Act and twice prime minister in the 1920s, to be its leader. Meighen remained convinced that conscription was the only way to fight a war, even though, in November 1941, no Canadian units had yet seen action. But the beginning of war in the Pacific, the loss of Hong Kong, and the new threat to the West Coast led the conscriptionists to beat the drums ever more loudly. The Prime Minister maintained as strongly as ever that conscription was a mistake. He pointed to the Pacific war as proof that the defence of Canada required more men to be retained at home.

Many in his Cabinet, especially Colonel Ralston, wanted full conscription at once, whatever political crisis it might provoke. To Ralston, to Meighen, and to many others, francophone enlistments from Quebec and other provinces still lagged far behind those in English Canada, even though they equalled perhaps three times the number in the Great War.* There were reasons for this hesitation, not least the fact that the army was still an English-speaking operation. There were now several French-speaking infantry battalions (Le Royal 22e, Le Régiment de Maisonneuve,[43] Les Fusiliers Mont-Royal, and Le Régiment de la Chaudière), an artillery unit (the 5th Medium Regiment), and other units from Quebec and New Brunswick with high numbers of francophones. Some, like the Three Rivers Regiment, an armoured unit, were effec-

---

* Throughout the entire war, army enlistments in Quebec numbered 138,269 out of a total army strength of 708,535. The English-speaking probably provided at least half of this Quebec total, and 43,823 in all were NRMA soldiers. For all three services, Quebec provided 25.69 per cent of enlistments, compared with its population of roughly one-third of the Canadian total (C.P. Stacey, *Arms, Men and Governments: The War Policies of Canada, 1939–1945* [Ottawa, 1970], 590). A more recent (and, I believe, too generous) estimate sees 161,603 francophones from all provinces in the armed forces, or 20.23 per cent of volunteers (Serge Bernier, 'Participation des Canadiens français aux combats: évaluation et tentative de quantification,' *Bulletin d'histoire politique* 3 [printemps-été 1995]: 15ff.). According to Grant Dexter of the *Winnipeg Free Press*, the army and Col. J.L. Ralston were not overly enthusiastic about large numbers of French Canadians in the army: 'Ralston protested ... [t]he army would not have masses of Quebeckers under any conditions. There is only limited room in our army for these men. They can't speak English. We have no French Canadian officers to handle them. Their fighting ability is questionable etc., etc. Ralston said that conscription was necessary to get more men from the English-speaking provinces.' Memo of December 9, 1941, in F.W. Gibson and B. Robertson, eds., *Ottawa at War: The Grant Dexter Memoranda, 1939–1945* (Winnipeg, 1994), 232. See also *Historical Atlas of Canada* 3 (Toronto, 1990), plates 47–8.

tively bilingual.[44] There was a francophone officer training school at St-Jérome, Quebec, that prepared candidates for the main officer training centre at Brockville, Ontario.[45] Even so, there was and remained a severe shortage of francophone officers, especially of senior officers who, like the English-speaking, could not be created out of nothing. Moreover, the number of PF and NPAM French-speaking officers was tiny.[46] In the Permanent Force, for example, in September 1939, there were only fifty-two francophone officers.[47] Ultimately, however, the difference in numbers was caused by precisely the same situation as in the Great War: in Quebec, the pressure was to not enlist; in English Canada, it was the opposite. A highly intelligent young man like Pierre Elliott Trudeau could write in his memoirs as though the war was merely noise offstage of interest only to Anglos. To him and his compatriots, Europe was not Canada's concern, and the drumbeating for volunteers and the pressures for compulsory service were nothing more than the age-old struggle for domination over French Canada.[48]

They were wrong. The Second World War was a war for survival – for the survival of freedom and democracy, for Canadian survival, for the defeat of an unparalleled evil. If the Allies lost the war – and at the end of 1941 there was a better than fifty/fifty chance they would – the Canadian nation would have died along with the other democracies. That threat justified Canada's total war, a war that involved every man, woman, and child and that imposed the heavy hand of government on every citizen and business in the land. The extent of mobilization in the Second World War made that of the Great War look like child's play.

But Québécois did not see the war this way, and they viewed the government's efforts to persuade them of the dangers as so much propaganda. English Canadians did believe in the danger, although most of them still filtered it through a lens that made them see a danger to England as a global threat. The English Canadian pressures for conscription were present, nonetheless, and the result, in January 1942, was King's decision to ask the country – the whole country and not just Quebec – to release him from his pledges against compulsory overseas service. Quebec professed outrage, seeing his request as a violation of a promise made to French Canada alone. English Canada was not much happier, viewing King's action as verging on cowardice and pandering to Quebec. The result of the plebiscite (a plebiscite, unlike a referendum, was not binding) on April 27, 1942, was a victory of sorts for the government: 2.945 million voted Yes and 1.643 million, No. The difficulty was that 72.9 per cent of the vote in Quebec, or virtually the entire franco-phone vote, was *Non*.[49]

Conscription was not to be imposed, at least not yet. Through deft manoeuvring and the elimination of the NRMA clause restricting conscripts to service only in Canada, the Prime Minister kept his English-speaking ministers on side and lost only one Québécois. The clause might have been removed, but no men were yet being forced to go overseas. 'Not necessarily conscription,' King told the House of Commons in his most famous phrase, one that exactly defined his policy, 'but conscription if necessary.' How necessity was to be defined was unclear and remained so for another two years, but, for now, the volunteer and home defence conscript systems continued to co-exist uneasily.[50]

The first action for the Canadian Army in the Second World War came not in Europe but in Hong Kong, the British Crown Colony near Canton, China. In 1941 Hong Kong was a large, squalid port city, an imperial foothold extracted from the Chinese a half-century before and now a major source of supply for Chiang Kai-shek's Nationalist armies. The Japanese, who had been fighting their war with China vigorously since 1937, occupied the countryside nearby. Though the colony's territory was very hilly, making it ideal terrain for an outnumbered defence, no one believed it could be held successfully for long against a determined attack. Certainly this was the War Office view.

In August 1941 the retiring commander of British forces in Hong Kong, Major-General A.E. Grasett, stopped in Ottawa to visit with Major-General Harry Crerar, the CGS. Grasett and Crerar had attended the Royal Military College together, and this time the old boy net put Canadians into trouble. In Grasett's view, the Japanese could not fight successfully against white troops, however well they had performed against the Chinese. A small reinforcement of Hong Kong would have real military value and would send a message to Tokyo that Britain was prepared to fight to retain its possessions in Asia. After Grasett returned to London, a request arrived on September 19 from the War Office for Canada to send troops to defend Hong Kong.[51]

This request posed political problems for the government. There was no desire to dispatch soldiers to Asia, *terra incognita* for a people and a military that believed Canada's frontiers began and ended in Europe. Army headquarters had no independent sources of intelligence on Japanese intentions, and no one thought to do an appreciation to consider the garrison's chances in the event of war. The opposition Conservatives, however, were clamouring for Canada to do more in the war, charging that Mackenzie King's nationalism was shortchanging the imperial war effort, and claiming that recruits were in such short supply that conscription was needed. If word got out, as it inevitably would, that Ottawa had refused a British request for troops for Hong Kong, the political costs could be serious. If Ottawa had turned down the request because war was imminent (which in September few believed), it would certainly have been charged with cowardice. Snookered and operating in ignorance of the situation beyond what London had told them, the Cabinet War Committee's ministers told General Crerar to proceed.

The orders passed down the line at army headquarters, ending on the desk of Captain H.A. Sparling, a PF artilleryman, who was serving in the Directorate of Military Training. Find two battalions for a tropical post on garrison duty, he was told. Sparling prepared a three-part list of units: fully trained battalions from which selection could be made at once; battalions that required more training before selection; and battalions that should not be selected. [52] The list moved up the chain to Crerar's desk and he selected two units from the third category, battalions that had had a stint of garrison duty. The Royal Rifles of Canada, a Quebec City regiment with a good representation of French Canadians, had served in Newfoundland, and the Winnipeg Grenadiers had provided Jamaica's defence. Garrison duty in Jamaica and Newfoundland, army headquarters hoped, would not be much different from garrison duty in Hong Kong. Crerar believed that any training deficiencies, and there were many, could be made up after the regiments reached Hong Kong. The War Office soon asked for a brigade headquarters and additional units, and for maximum haste in getting the troops to Hong Kong. Again, Ottawa agreed.

Under the command of Brigadier J.K. Lawson, an able PF officer, the Canadian force of ninety-six officers, two Nursing Sisters, and 1877 men left Vancouver on October 27 aboard the British merchant vessel *Awatea* and the armed merchant cruiser HMCS *Prince Robert* and arrived in Hong Kong on

November 16. Thanks to a variety of bungles, none of the force's 212 vehicles and other heavy equipment reached the Pacific coast in time to be loaded on the transport with the men. They followed, instead, on an American transport ship that departed on November 4, with stops at Honolulu and Manila. The U.S. ship arrived in the Philippines on December 12, after the Japanese had launched their surprise attacks that plunged the Pacific into war. The American forces took the vehicles for their own purposes, and not one arrived to help the Grenadiers and Royal Rifles.

The Canadian soldiers in Hong Kong knew nothing of this catastrophe. Settling into their barracks and forming part of a largely British and Indian garrison of 14,000, they listened to briefings on the Japanese – only 5000 troops in the area, ill-equipped and lacking artillery, unused to night fighting, and supported by myopic pilots in obsolete aircraft, or so they were told.[53] In fact, orders to seize Hong Kong had gone out from Tokyo on November 6, 1941, and the experienced, well-led 38th Division received the task.

The Japanese attacked on December 8, a few hours after their forces fell on Pearl Harbor and Malaya. They quickly breached the British defences on the mainland, the Gin Drinkers' Line; on the first day eliminated the five aircraft allocated for the defence of the territory; and devastated the morale of the colony's defenders. The Canadian units were in their assigned positions on Hong Kong island and the Japanese, having cleared the mainland defences, launched an amphibious assault on December 18. The defenders (and the civil population) were already suffering from shortages of water, food, and medicines, and matters worsened over the next week.

Though they had their own brigade staff, the improvised British plan for the defence of the island split the Canadian battalions, leaving only the Grenadiers under Lawson. The War Diary of the Royal Rifles euphemistically noted that the British brigade staff under whom they were serving on December 11, even before the water-borne assault, 'were in a highly nervous state and apparently very tired.' The Rifles defended their area tenaciously, but the Japanese soon drove them back. The confusion became more obvious as the battle spread and command and control disintegrated. General C.M. Maltby, the British commander, had curiously chosen to man the gaps and the valleys, leaving the high ground to the Japanese – who time and again made good use of it. On December 19 they overran Brigadier Lawson's headquarters, located at the critical Wong Nei Chong gap in the centre of the island. Lawson had radioed Maltby that he and his staff were 'going outside to fight it out,' a pistol in each hand. Lawson died almost at once, along with many of the Winnipeg Grenadiers, though they inflicted heavy casualties on the attackers. Shortly before, Company Sergeant Major John Osborn led a successful counterattack on the Japanese on Mount Butler, but, after picking up and throwing back enemy grenades, he pushed a sergeant aside and fell on one, saving at least seven men. Osborn won a posthumous Victoria Cross, the first awarded a Canadian in the Second World War. His company was virtually wiped out. At roughly the same time that Osborn died, the Royal Rifles' mascot, a Newfoundland dog named Gander, saved seven men on the other brigade front by seizing a hand grenade that had landed in their midst at Lye Mun and running off with it. The dog died, but the men lived. Almost sixty years later, Gander received the Dickin Medal for animal heroism.[54]

The battle for Hong Kong now degenerated into a series of Japanese attacks and increasingly ill-coordinated British and Canadian counterattacks, usually launched without support and into the teeth of Japanese resistance.[55] There was no hope of relief and no tactics or strategy, only desperate struggles against a better-prepared, better-led enemy that met none of the stereotypes. In the opinion of the senior Canadian officers who survived, the British commander lost touch with the reality of the situation,[56] and the only question that remained was when the fighting would cease. On the evening of Christmas Day, finally, the British ordered their troops to surrender, but not before the remnants of 'D' Company of the Royal Rifles staged a 'last glorious charge' to drive the enemy out of Stanley Village. The sergeant in command of one platoon, George MacDonell, gave his men their orders, which they 'received in complete silence. Not one of them could believe such a preposterous order.' Macdonell gave his troops a pep talk and told them 'at least this was better than waiting ... for the inevitable.' The sergeant put his men in position, ordered them to fix bayonets, and charged, a manoeuvre that took the Japanese by surprise. Incredibly, the Rifles took their objective, but at a cost of twenty-six killed and seventy-five wounded.[57] The surviving Canadians laid down their arms that evening.

As had been their practice in China, the victorious Japanese promptly began an orgy of killings, rape, and looting. 'The Japanese troops went wild,' said one of the Canadian Nursing Sisters who had accompanied the force. At St Stephen's College at Stanley (where the enemy might have found weapons),[58] the Japanese soldiers 'bayonetted patients in their beds. Sisters and 4 [volunteer aides] were raped and then they killed three.' Captured soldiers were killed while others were mutilated, one at least having his tongue cut off.[59] 'They took us,' one private later wrote, 'ripped off our insignia, took our shoes, belts, pictures, and wristwatches. We walked with our hands up and they nicked us in the back with bayonets. They took out DeLaurier and two or three others and used them for bayonet practice all night long. We could hear them.'[60]

The last telegram to reach Ottawa arrived after the surrender on Christmas Day. 'Situation critical,' it read. 'Canadian troops part prisoners residue engaged casualties heavy ... Troops have done magnificent work spirit excellent.' For under-trained troops lacking vehicles and serving in a wholly different subtropical environment to which they were not yet acclimatized, the Canadians had fought very well. They inflicted heavy losses on the enemy in the Wong Nei Chong battle and other engagements, and their counterattacks delayed the enemy repeatedly. The Japanese killed 290 Canadians in the fighting and wounded 493, an extraordinary casualty rate of 40 per cent of the force in a week's battle. That was testimony to the ferocity of the fighting.

The survivors faced almost four years as prisoners of war in the hands of a nation that rejected the terms of the Geneva Convention and viewed soldiers who surrendered as cowards. Some of the POWs received the special attentions of 'the Kamloops Kid,' a Japanese Canadian serving in the Japanese army who despised his former countrymen and took out his resentment on them with the utmost brutality. A total of 128 Canadian POWs died in their Hong Kong cages of disease, starvation, and maltreatment; a further 136 died in Japan, where they had been taken in 1943 to work as slave labour in mines and shipyards.[61] Of the 1975 Canadians who sailed from Vancouver in October 1941, just over 1400 would return home.[62] The survivors, never compensated by Japan for their suffering, never the recipients even of an apology, remain exceedingly bitter at Tokyo. More than half a century after their capture, those still alive received a small monetary compensation from the Canadian government, but, in general, they feel forgotten, neglected, and frustrated. They deserved better from their country – and Japan.

The defeat at Hong Kong had major consequences in Canada and for the army. First, it helped propel the public on the West Coast to demand that the government act against Japanese Canadians living in British Columbia. In all, 22,000 men, women, and children would be moved inland, their property largely confiscated. For the government, the disaster led to a major press and political campaign, to renewed and strengthened calls for conscription, and to a royal commission under the Chief Justice of Canada, Sir Lyman Duff. Seen by many then and since as a whitewash, Duff's report, released after long hearings that pored over all the records and took testimony from almost all the army planners responsible for the expedition, concluded that the Hong Kong force had been neither ill-conceived nor ill-managed. But many of the men had not been adequately trained, particularly 120 soldiers added to the force as reinforcements in the last days before it departed from Canada. Few units in Canada (or overseas) were well trained in the autumn of 1941, and there was nothing surprising in the fact that the two regiments dispatched to Hong Kong were not ready for battle or that reinforcements were ill-prepared. Had the units had time to train in Hong Kong, as expected, this inexperience would not have mattered; in the circumstances of December 1941, regrettably it did. More seriously, as the Chief Justice wrote, inefficiency at army headquarters had led to the force being separated from its transport. Colonel Ralston frankly told Parliament in late July that there had been confusion in the various branches of army headquarters, and he put most of the blame on the Quartermaster General, Major-General E.J.C. Schmidlin, who had been relieved of his post in January 1942. There had also been 'a very complete reorganization in the quartermaster-general's branch,' he said, and up to twenty changes in 'the senior staff appointments' since the Hong Kong expedition.[63]*

The lessons of Hong Kong were many and various. The Japanese enemy was a fierce and efficient force, now viewed almost as supermen after its sweeping victories in 1941–2. The Canadian Army was not yet as effective in administration and planning as it needed to be, nor were its training methods and

---

* Colonel Ralston himself was the subject of criticism, not least from General McNaughton. On a visit to Canada in February–March 1942, McNaughton spoke off-record to journalists and others of his dissatisfaction with Ralston as 'completely unfitted for his job ... unable to distinguish between policy and detail' (Gibson and Robertson, eds., *Ottawa at War*, 284ff.). There was much truth in this criticism, but McNaughton was deliberately stirring the pot and showing marked disloyalty.

results yet at the standard required. Just as important, Canada needed its own intelligence apparatus, its own ability to determine if troops should be committed to operations. In effect, Canada needed to act like a nation, not a colony.

The joint American-Canadian attack in August 1943 on Kiska, an island in the Aleutians that the Japanese had occupied in June 1942, had been preceded by planning and thinking, even though the attackers found that the enemy had withdrawn.[64] Such preparation remained essential to all military operations. The Kiska operation, along with the United States Army's wartime presence in Canada along the Alaska Highway, indicated, however, that Canada was beginning to move into the American orbit.

Meanwhile, the Canadian Corps in Britain continued to train – and train some more. As the invasion threat receded in 1941, the Canadians moved inland off the beaches. General Odlum's Second Canadian Division, like the First, had arrived in Britain with only rudimentary training, but the GOC (known to his men as 'Hoodlum') seemed more interested in keeping the vehicles shiny than in any serious work, in creating regimental bands and a distinctive shoulder flash, and in preparing his men to fight the Hun in 1918 style. In this war, with far more vehicles than in the First, movement control was critical. Similarly, landmines had largely replaced barbed wire, mortars were the key infantry weapon, infantry had to cooperate with armour far more than previously, and speed of movement and decision-making was essential. Odlum, proudly wearing his Boer War and Great War ribbons, was second to McNaughton and a potential corps commander – a prospect that worried Canadian and British officers alike. He was duly shuffled off to Australia as High Commissioner in the autumn of 1941, though he complained all the way that he was the victim of a PF conspiracy.[65]

The British were deeply concerned about the Canadian senior commanders generally, but there were few options to those at the top, given the tiny size of the Permanent Force, the weak state of the Non-Permanent Active Militia, and the simple fact that only time and experience could create military leaders. McNaughton recognized this progression, for he told an American reporter in 1944 that the first senior officers were 'a cover crop, to help the younger men through the wilting strains of the first responsibilities, in the same way that older trees are used to shelter saplings through the heat of the day.'[66] The younger men, the commanders of 1943, 1944, and 1945, had some time to learn their trades, and McNaughton, to his credit, spotted officers like Guy Simonds, Chris Vokes, Tommy Burns, and Charles Foulkes. To many, however, McNaughton in 1940, 1941, and 1942 was part of the problem. He dabbled in weapons development, crawled under trucks to check the numbers of welds, and ran the political interface between army headquarters in Ottawa, Canadian Military Headquarters in London, and the War Office. There was no time in McNaughton's world for training – and effective, programmed training that built on what had been learned last week and last year was what the Canadian divisions desperately needed.

The man who really began the process of change in the Canadian Corps was Lieutenant-General Bernard Montgomery, the commander of South Eastern Command in which the Canadians served. Montgomery was one of the few British senior officers to emerge with credit from the shambles of France in 1940, and he took his job of training soldiers and picking their leaders seriously, much more so than McNaughton and his cover crop of senior commanders. Montgomery inspected Canadian units carefully, ran tough exercises, and interviewed battalion and regiment commanders.[67] He told the Canadian commanders bluntly what he liked and what he didn't, and, infuriating as he was, Montgomery was almost always right. A succession of older generals of whom he disapproved found themselves on the way home: 'I hope to be sending you Pearkes, Potts, and Ganong back to Canada shortly,' he wrote to Trumball Warren, his Canadian aide-de-camp in Canada for a staff course. '[Y]ou will find them useful your side, I hope, you need some really good officers back in Canada.' Pearkes had commanded the First Division, and Potts and Ganong, both Militia veterans, were brigade commanders. Major-General Basil Price, GOC of the Third Division, followed his friends out of senior command: 'He will be of great value in Canada where his knowledge of the milk industry will help on the national war effort.' Unit commanders, company commanders, regimental sergeant majors, and many others followed their seniors back home. They deserved the nation's thanks for giving up their jobs and leaving their families at home so the army and the nation could have the time they needed to ready themselves to fight. Soon the younger, capable officers rose to fill the key positions, and, by 1943, selection and appraisal boards were finding junior officers from the ranks.[68]

Snotty as his comments were, Montgomery (known with good reason as 'the little shit' in the British Army) was correct. He understood that the Canadians, while first-class material, were not well led or well trained because their commanders were not competent 'in the stage management of battle operations, and in the technique of battle fighting generally.'[69] The GOCs were not prepared to train their brigadiers, he said, and the brigadiers were unable to train their battalion COs. The nub of the problem was that the senior officers were not as good as their troops. Generals send their men into battles where men were certain to be killed, so only the competent could be allowed to lead. In effect, this criticism was directed at General McNaughton and his supervision of training for his divisions, and Montgomery told the Chief of the Imperial General Staff, General Sir Alan Brooke, that McNaughton was unfit to command an army in the field.[70] In the autumn of 1941, his admiring biographer noted, McNaughton believed that his corps was 'thoroughly prepared for battle.'[71] Montgomery profoundly disagreed and he was right, and good Canadian officers knew it. Major Bert Hoffmeister of the Seaforth Highlanders in the First Division, for example, worried himself into a nervous collapse in January 1941 because he believed himself unprepared to lead his men into action against a first-class enemy, and his regimental CO refused to allow him to take the courses that might better prepare him. Hoffmeister, intelligent and able, understood the problem exactly as Montgomery did.[72]

The Canadians also had to be made fit and ready to fight, something they were not. Most had become part of a garrison army, preoccupied with leave and casual relationships with the locals. Their officers looked for things for them to do, for educational classes to fit them for life after the war, and for ceremonial and guard duties.[73]* Such inactivity did not please Montgomery, who demanded that every soldier be able to cover 10 miles in two hours with full battle order on his back and that officers – all officers – do thirty minutes physical training each day, and he got what he wanted.

The average recruit joining the army, a study in 1944 found, was a Depression kid, about nineteen-and-a-half years old, and many of the older soldiers –

---

* One officer recalled that Major General George Pearkes, a fox hunter, encouraged his officers to join in by giving them two afternoons off a week if they participated in the hunt. Granatstein interview with Brig. Frank Lace, May 17, 1991.

only 14 per cent were over thirty years old – had been unemployed, often for years. Almost three-quarters were unmarried. Soldiers' physiques generally were slightly stunted, a product of the hard times in which they had grown up, and most were eating better in the army than ever before. Education was limited: only 2 per cent held university degrees, and 16 per cent had completed grade 6 or less. The men came almost equally from farms, small towns, and small and large cities.[74] They were adaptable, easy to train, and more than tough enough to cope with Monty's demands. They yearned for mail from home,[75] but they liked the English girls (who liked them in turn because they were better-dressed and had more money than British troops and also had an air of the exotic about them), the pubs, Vera Lynn's 'The White Cliffs of Dover,' and the *Daily Mail* comic strip about Jane, a girl 'who is endlessly concerned with her undergarments and often appears nearly naked,' wrote Lieutenant Alexander Ross. 'She's supposed to be good for troop morale.'[76]* Jane undoubtedly was good for morale, but what the Canadians really needed was to be trained effectively and led by officers who knew what they were doing.

Beginning in the fall of 1941, all the Canadian divisions ran their units through Battle Drill Training, a rigorous course that aimed to harden the soldiers physically and mentally and teach them the minor tactics they needed in action – tactics that should become instinctive reactions. Trainers used animal offal and blood to shock the men, thunderflashes simulated artillery, and Battle Drill staff fired live ammunition close overhead in exercises. Men learned how to respond in ambushes, and how not to stop, analyse, and decide before reacting. Such training could save lives – or it could cost them. Whatever its ultimate value, Battle Drill added some interest to army life that had become stultified by lack of action.[77]

Montgomery put the Canadian divisions through extensive and large exercises to test their capabilities. Before his appearance, the Canadians had taken part in a succession of exercises – Fox, Dog, Waterloo, Bumper – which tested the divisions in road movement and anti-invasion operations.[78] Many flaws

---

* Canadian soldiers wanted Canadian entertainment too, but 'The Canadian Army Show,' featuring Johnny Wayne and Frank Schuster, did not get overseas until late 1943. One private wrote that 'it sure was good. Our sense of humour is quite a lot different from the English people's and it being the first Canadian show we have seen since we came over here it sure was appreciated.' Quoted in Bill Twatio, 'The Entertainers,' *Air Force* (winter 2000): 10.

were uncovered in the prevailing confusion. Monty's exercises Beaver III and Beaver IV began to test the formations in offensive operations. His major exercise, Tiger, staged in May 1942, pressed men and commanders to their limits physically and mentally, so much so that its rigours are remembered more than a half-century on.[79] Some units covered 250 miles on foot, all lived rough in the field, and reputations were made and dashed. Harry Crerar, commanding I Canadian Corps, for example, did well and won Monty's praise; so did his Brigadier General Staff, Guy Simonds.[80] Montgomery's critiques were tough and unsparing, and he insisted on systematic training to remedy the errors he found. But the difficulty remained: How could the commanders put the men 'into battle properly and with a good chance of success'? The Canadian soldiers were first-rate material; the problem lay with their officers.[81]

Montgomery began the process of turning the First Canadian Army into a real army. He weeded out many of the elderly and unfit, spotted the 'teachable' and the young comers, and began the task of impressing his personality on the officers and men. Many historians dislike Montgomery (as did many of his contemporaries), but he was a great trainer of soldiers. He, and not Andy McNaughton, their commander, made the Canadians into soldiers. By the time he left South Eastern Command in the summer of 1942 to go to the Western Desert to fight Rommel's Afrika Korps, Montgomery had pushed, pulled, and kicked the Canadian commanders into professionalizing the First Canadian Army's training.

The genesis of the Canadian involvement in the raid on Dieppe, like Hong Kong, came from Harry Crerar. In October 1941 he was Chief of the General Staff in Ottawa; in the winter of 1942, in the temporary absence of General McNaughton on sick leave in Canada, he was acting commander of the Canadian Corps in Britain. Now a Lieutenant-General, Crerar had heard rumours that Combined Operations Headquarters, run by Admiral Lord Louis Mountbatten, was planning a major raid, one of a series designed to test combined operations procedures. Raids kept the enemy uneasy, the thinking went, and they were good for British morale. As a national commander, as someone who, since his arrival in England in December 1941, had been convinced that the soldiers' morale was bad and that Canadians at home wanted their army to see some action, Crerar had demanded of the British Chiefs of Staff that his men be picked for the raid. By the time McNaughton returned in April 1942 to be GOC-in-C of the First Canadian Army, the War Office had made the decision: the Second Canadian Infantry Division would stage the raid on Dieppe. General Montgomery believed the division was the best trained of the Canadian divisions, and he thought the GOC, Major-General Hamilton Roberts, a Lieutenant-Colonel of artillery just two years before, to be the ablest of the Canadian division commanders.[82] Moreover, Crerar's assessment of morale and public opinion in Canada was certainly correct, and he had acted properly in pressing for Canadian participation. He was right about soldier morale, too. Corporal Robert Prouse of the Canadian Provost Corps remembered that 'like every other Canadian soldier, I was bored to tears with the long inaction and was itching for battle.'[83] There were also larger political imperatives – namely, the American desire for a Second Front in 1942 and the demands of the Soviet Union, reeling under the weight of the huge Nazi invasion, for relief. A big raid across the Channel might satisfy these demands; it might also test the theory and practice of amphibious operations and help determine whether a defended port could be taken.

From the decision to make Dieppe a largely Canadian 'show,' Canadian officers, including General Roberts and his GSO I, Lieutenant-Colonel Churchill Mann, became involved in the planning. Some of the controversial decisions that affected the raid, notably the decision not to bomb the town before the attack, were made either by or with Canadian concurrence.[84] Combined Operations Headquarters had its finger in the pie, of course, and so too did Montgomery. He had the 'go/no go' responsibility, and, when Operation Rutter, the original attack scheduled for the first week in July 1942, was cancelled because of bad weather, Montgomery made the decision. In the interim between the cancellation and the remounting of the operation, now called Jubilee, Montgomery went to the Middle East. The decision to attack Dieppe on August 19, 1942, thus was made by Mountbatten, Crerar, and Roberts.[85] As General Guy Simonds later recollected, 'There has never been any doubt in my own mind that Crerar was primarily responsible for the revival of Dieppe as a Canadian operation.' Simonds also remembered Crerar saying to him: 'It will be a tragic humiliation if American troops get into action on this side of the Atlantic, before Canadians, who have been waiting in England for three years.'[86] Again, Crerar's assessment of the likely Canadian government and public response was absolutely correct. Whether he should have supported the revival of a once-cancelled attack with the same troops on the same objective was another question entirely, for some soldiers must have gossiped in pubs and to friends about Rutter. Even so, there is no evidence that the enemy knew the raid was coming.

The Dieppe plan called for a brigade's worth of Canadians – 4963 officers and men drawn from all three brigades of the Second Division and an armoured regiment from the 1st Canadian Armoured Brigade – 1075 British commandos, and some 50 American Rangers to assault the town and the surrounding area from the sea. Covered by six squadrons of fighter-bombers overhead (in fact, seventy-four squadrons eventually took part in what became the largest air battle of the war to that time) and eight destroyers, a gunboat, and a sloop offshore, infantry from Ontario's Essex Scottish and Royal Hamilton Light Infantry, as well as tanks from the Calgary Regiment, were to assault the beach in front of Dieppe. To the east at Puys, the Royal Regiment of Canada from Toronto and three platoons of the Black Watch (Royal Highland Regiment) of Canada from Montreal were to disembark. To the west, the South Saskatchewan Regiment and the Queen's Own Cameron Highlanders were to hit Pourville. The Fusiliers Mont-Royal formed a floating reserve. The British commandos were to eliminate the German coastal batteries east and west of the main landing areas. The objective was to take Dieppe, establish a defence perimeter, and hold it long enough to allow the destruction of the harbour facilities. The force would then withdraw by sea. No heavy bombers were assigned to soften up the enemy defences, and the Royal Navy refused to assign battleships to support the attack. The Channel was too risky with the Luftwaffe nearby. For their part, the Germans had the 302nd Infantry Division in the Dieppe area, with substantial reserves nearby.

The men of the attack force boarded their landing craft on August 18 and set sail before dark. Soon after, the plan began unravelling when a German coastal convoy ran into the attack flotilla; the firing that resulted was enough to alert the German coastal defences. The Germans did not necessarily know that the raid was coming, as some have claimed, but the encounter was very bad luck. Very quickly, everything fell apart.

The Royal Regiment and the Black Watch touched down thirty-five minutes late at 5:10 a.m. on Puy's Blue Beach, and so were easily visible to the enemy. They instantly came under withering fire from the two platoons of German troops manning a fortified house on the beach and atop a cliff over-looking it. The fifteen or so survivors of the first wave made it from their landing craft to the seawall, or to what shelter there was under the cliff; the second and third waves landed, only to be shot to pieces by enfilade fire from a machine gun in a tank turret beside a house. Some twenty Canadians, including Lieutenant-Colonel D.E. Catto of the Royals, managed to reach the top of the cliff and moved westward, with the object of joining up with men of the Essex Scottish who, the plan said, would be there. But the men of the Essex had died on the beach, and Catto's small party surrendered about 4 o'clock. The remaining men of his battalion and the Black Watch surrendered before 8:30 a.m. A few made it off the beach to a landing craft, but the Germans fired their machine guns at most of the Royals who tried to escape.

The situation proved only marginally better at Pourville's Green Beach. The landing beach was dominated by cliffs at both sides and by the ridge of the Scie Valley, but because the South Saskatchewans landed on time and under darkness, they achieved surprise. The navy landed part of the battalion on the wrong side of the Scie, however, and part of the South Sasks had to enter Pourville and cross a bridge. The one company whose objectives were west of the river took them successfully. The remainder could not cross the bridge and get to their objectives (a radar station and anti-aircraft guns) because of enemy gunfire from the heights. At this point, the battalion commander, Lieutenant-Colonel C.C.I. Merritt, took charge and, walking calmly across the bridge under a hail of fire, led his men across by sheer force of will. 'Come on over, there's nothing to it,' the South Sasks' CO called out, swinging his helmet in his hand and standing upright. Merritt led attacks up the hill, clearing several concrete emplacements with his own men and men of the Queen's Own Cameron Highlanders. The Camerons had landed late and astride the Scie, their pipers playing, but their CO had been killed in the first moments; still, half the regiment aided the South Sasks. George Gouk, the Camerons' Company Sergeant Major, recollected the heavy casualties from enemy mortar fire: 'They sure could place their shots. Well, there was no stopping the boys then. They were seeing their pals for the first time being killed and wounded ... and the only thought ... was to have revenge. It sure was great to see the boys with blood all over their faces and running from wounds in their arms and legs not worrying about getting first aid but carrying on in a systematic manner, clearing out the "Nazis" from the houses.'[87]

The remainder moved inland up to 2000 yards, until the Canadians ran into heavy German fire they could not counter. Once the order to withdraw was given, the men returned to the beach, hoping they might be taken off. The landing craft were there at 11 a.m., as intended, but a hail of machine-gun fire met the Canadians as they attempted to board. Colonel Merritt commanded the rearguard that let the surviving South Sasks and Camerons escape, but he was captured. Merritt – whose father had been killed during the Great War and who went overseas in 1939 wearing his father's Seaforth Highlanders kilt and Glengarry[88] – won the Victoria Cross for his extraordinary courage and leadership. 'When last seen,' the VC citation read, 'he was collecting Bren and Tommy Guns and preparing a defensive position which successfully covered the withdrawal from the beach.'[89]

The landings on Red and White beaches, directly in front of Dieppe, saw the Royal Hamilton Light Infantry come in on the right and the Essex Scottish on the left, with the Calgary tanks offering support. There was no surprise, as the landing craft touched down after the assault at Pourville had brought the Germans to full readiness, but the air force attacked the eastern cliffs and laid down smoke while Hurricanes effectively strafed the beach defences. The Rileys and the Essex debarked while the enemy was still stunned, but, unfortunately, the tank landing craft were late. The interval without fire support proved fatal to the attackers as the enemy, holding the heights and the casino at the west end of the beach, reacted fiercely. Most men went to ground and either could not or would not get up again, whatever Battle Drill Training had taught them. Captain Denis Whitaker recalled: 'The ramp dropped. I led the thirty odd men of my platoon in a charge about twenty-five yards up the stony beach. We fanned out and flopped down just short of a huge wire obstacle. Bullets flew everywhere. Enemy mortar bombs started to crash down. Around me, men were being hit and bodies were piling up, one on top of the other. It was terrifying.'[90] Nonetheless, Whitaker led his men through the wire and the RHLI cleared the casino in a hard fight, while a few handfuls of men got into the town. Most, however, remained pinned on the Promenade, seeking shelter where they could, and where their padre, Captain John Foote, earned the Victoria Cross for his extraordinary courage in seeing to the needs of the wounded and the dying – and deliberately refusing evacuation so he could continue to serve his parish. The Essex Scottish did not get more than a dozen men off the beach, as the regiment's landing was exposed to heavy fire from the east and the west headlands that dominated the waterfront. The sole Essex Scottish officer to return to England estimated that up to 40 per cent of the men were killed or wounded by 5:45 a.m., a half-hour after landing.

The debacle was compounded when General Roberts, offshore and with only fragmentary information on the course of events, decided to send in the reserve. The Fusiliers Mont-Royal landed at 7 a.m., but their craft was shelled by German artillery as it approached the beach and the men were slaughtered when they tried to get ashore. Only a few made it into the town. Their CO, twenty-nine-year-old Lieutenant-Colonel Dollard Ménard, who had urged his men to 'show 'em what French-Canadian boys can do,'[91] was wounded many times, then dragged onto a landing craft and returned to England. He was the only CO of the regiments involved to do so.

The Calgary Regiment's brand-new Churchill tanks had little impact on the battle. Half of them never managed to get over the seawall; some could not move on the baseball-sized stones and steep grade of the shingle beach; others were unable to land or were knocked out by German guns; and those that did get onto the Promenade found the way blocked by heavy concrete barriers. The Commanding Officer, Lieutenant-Colonel J.G. Andrews, drowned his tank and died at the shoreline, but three tanks made it onto the Esplanade and, Lieutenant Ed Bennett remembered, 'the Germans started to run out of the trenches and we had a field day.'[92] The Calgarys' tanks, stuck on the beach or not, carried on fighting, providing the gunfire that let some of the men be evacuated.[93]

The Dieppe raid had turned into a disaster, a jubilee of death and destruction. As at Hong Kong, there were neither tactics nor strategy for those on the beach. The errors of those responsible for the planning were staggering, and there was only terror and futility for the troops. Many of the men demonstrated great courage, and some great cowardice, but all suffered the same fate. The casualties were horrific: the Royal Regiment lost 524 and managed to get only 65 men back to England; the RHLI, 480 and 217; the Essex, 530 and 52; the Fusiliers Mont-Royal, 513 and 125; the Queen's Own Cameron Highlanders, 346 and 268; the South Sasks, 339 and 353; and the Calgary Tanks, somewhat protected by the steel of their tanks, 174 and 247. Many of those who survived never even landed. In all, 56 officers and 851 men died on the beach or later of wounds, 586 were wounded, and 1946 were taken prisoner, more than in the entire campaign in Northwest Europe. Only 2200 in all returned to England, including some 600 wounded, some of whom arrived at Canadian military hospitals right off the landing craft and wearing 'their complete battle equipment, and with live grenades in their pouches.'[94]

The almost two thousand men left on the beach, and especially the wounded if they survived, had to endure a long captivity. The unit medical officers gave what care they could, and the Germans generally behaved correctly in giving first aid. There were unconfirmed reports of wounded men being killed by the enemy, but what is known is that the Germans gathered the wounded at a military hospital and gave first aid there; others received treatment at Dieppe's main hospital and, through a process of triage, the enemy sorted and categorized the POWs and sent them on to other hospitals. Later, the Germans moved many casualties in boxcars in dreadful conditions to POW camps. They shipped the unwounded POWs to camps to the east. Most had to endure a lengthy period of shackling, in reprisal for orders captured on the beach that called for German prisoners to have their hands tied wherever possible.[95] Of the men taken prisoner, 1874 returned to Canada at the end of the war, a far higher survival rate than the men taken prisoner at Hong Kong.[96]

The appalling waste of life at Dieppe had long-lasting effects. The nation, cheered by wildly optimistic press reports immediately after the raid, reeled under the impact of the casualty lists that followed soon after. The young manhood of Montreal, Toronto, Hamilton, Ottawa, Windsor, Calgary, and, in Saskatchewan, from Estevan, Weyburn, and Bienfait, seemed to have been eliminated at a stroke. The RHLI company originally based at the Winona, Ontario, plant of E.D. Smith jams, for example, lost every man of fighting age, killed, wounded, or captured – a devastating blow to a tiny town.*[97]

---

* 'The Dieppe raid got me down,' Norah Egener wrote to her husband overseas on August 27, 'and I wondered how brave I would have been if ... you were in it and if I had lost you' (Joan Barfoot, ed., *A Time Apart: Letters of Love and War* [Owen Sound, Ont., 1995], 80). Thousands of similar letters must have been written after news of the disaster reached Canada.

Overseas, the traumatized Second Division took a long time to rebuild. General Roberts, who deserved only a small part of the blame, was sacked in March 1943. General Crerar, shocked by the casualties, went to visit the RHLI wounded in hospital – Hamilton was his home town[98] – but, with his apparently charmed military life, his career continued to rise and prosper. So too did Montgomery's and Lord Mountbatten's.

At least the Allies dropped the idea of attacking a defended port, and many lessons were said to be learned.[99] Better intelligence was obviously necessary on the condition of beaches and on German defences. Ship-to-shore communications had to be improved, heavier naval gunfire and bombers had to be present in quantity, artillery had to be on landing craft to fire as the assault went in, and more, better, and specialized landing craft were necessary. Tanks also had to be developed to get over obstacles or to blow them up if they could not be circumvented. These lessons ought to have been self-evident, however, and there was absolutely no excuse for the planners not knowing about the Dieppe shingle or discounting the cliffs that dominated them. Where else would the Germans have put their main defences? Dieppe was a Channel port, after all, a day-trip excursion for countless British families for generations. It was not thousands of miles away. No one who had ever stood on the beach and looked at the cliffs on each side could have assumed that a frontal assault would succeed. About all one could say was that Dieppe had been a hard lesson on how not to mount an invasion.

Appalling as it was, Dieppe was only part of the vastly larger atrocity that was the Second World War. Defeats in war had to be expected, however, and, in 1942, defeat was the Allies' portion. Although there was much ignorant stupidity in the raid's planning, much of what historian W.J. McAndrew called 'another gross lapse in command sense and leadership,'[100] there was no conspiracy to waste Canadian lives (as some still believe), no German foreknowledge,* and even some strategic utility to it. The raid helped dissuade the Americans from pressing for an invasion at once, something that certainly saved lives; it led to reinforcement of the German garrison in France, which

---

* 'Today I feel that we were sacrificed,' a Fusiliers Mont-Royal veteran said in August 1999. 'The Germans were waiting for us' (*National Post*, August 14, 1999). John P. Campbell, *Dieppe Revisited: A Documentary Investigation* (London, 1993), convincingly argues against enemy foreknowledge.

may have helped the Soviet Union hang on; and it demonstrated that Canadian troops needed better training before they could take on the Wehrmacht. Still, the limited salutary results of Dieppe were much overshadowed by the casualties, the suffering, and the horror. Even so, Lieutenant-Colonel Cecil Merritt said of the raid after the war: 'We were very glad to go, we were delighted. We were up against a very difficult situation and we didn't win; but to hell with this business of saying the generals did us dirt.'[101] The unhealthy Canadian penchant for wallowing in disaster was not one Merritt could share.

Two years later, when the Second Canadian Division liberated Dieppe for good, war correspondent Ross Munro walked along the Esplanade on the main beach in front of the town with Lieutenant-Colonel Eric Bell of Regina, an officer who had been on the raid. 'He had gone through the hell of that main beach and could not keep his eyes off it,' Munro wrote. 'The sight of that beach and that Esplanade nearly mesmerized us. Eric's jaw just tightened ... He turned and walked silently back into the town.'[102]

General Crerar's concern that the Canadians had to see action was widely shared in Canada and overseas, and the disaster of Dieppe did not change it. The difficulty in getting the First Canadian Army into action was its GOC-in-C, General McNaughton. A prickly nationalist who had a succession of battles with the War Office and British senior commanders,* McNaughton insisted that the Canadians must fight together and fight under Canadian command. Canadians had the responsibility to command their troops, to train them, and to supply them. These responsibilities were all signs of nationhood, and McNaughton was correct in this belief. The problem by mid-1942 was that the First Canadian Army, its divisions, its officers, and men were untested in battle, and an army was a huge formation to throw unblooded into action. Moreover, in the autumn of 1942, it was subjected to another major reorganization of its battalions, which added a Support Company with 3-inch mortars, 6-pounder anti-tank guns, and pioneers to its strength.[103]

---

* The Chief of the Imperial General Staff, General Sir Alan Brooke, noted in July 1943 McNaughton's 'ultra political outlook to look always for some slight.' He added that the Canadian was 'devoid of any form of strategic outlook, and would sooner have risked losing the war than agreed to splitting the Canadian forces.' Public Record Office, London, War Office Records, Viscount Alexander Papers, Alexander-Brooke telegrams, July 18, 19, 22, 1943; Liddell Hart Centre, King's College, London, Viscount Alanbrooke Papers, file 3/A/IX, Notes on My Life, July 21, 1943.

The British raised various ideas for employment (North Africa? Norway?), and the Canadian commander usually rejected them, though in early 1943 McNaughton did agree to dispatch some 350 Canadian officers and NCOs to serve with British units in North Africa for three-month periods.[104] It was a small step forward, but far from sufficient for the Minister of National Defence, J.L. Ralston, who pressed McNaughton hard as well, but with no more success. Finally, in April 1943, Ralston and Lieutenant-General Kenneth Stuart, the Chief of the General Staff, prevailed upon the British to include the First Canadian Division and the 1st Armoured Brigade in the invasion of Sicily, set for July. McNaughton objected strongly, but agreed in the end, so long as the division returned to England after the island's liberation. The First Division did not return to Britain after Sicily was liberated, as McNaughton had wanted. Indeed Ottawa then lobbied the War Office to send the Fifth Armoured Division and I Canadian Corps headquarters, creating a corps to participate in the Italian campaign. This decision, taken because it would let senior Canadian officers get experience and because the war could conceivably come to an end before most Canadian soldiers saw sustained action, left the existence of the First Canadian Army, now with only II Canadian Corps in England, in doubt. Certainly it reduced the army to a follow-on formation in the invasion of Europe. McNaughton furiously threatened to resign.

At the same time, McNaughton's own position was in doubt. Colonel Ralston was not an admirer, for one, and he had serious doubts about the general's ability to withstand the stress of battle. Harry Crerar, one of McNaughton's old friends and one of his corps commanders, intrigued against him almost continuously, most notably with his Great War friend General Sir Alan Brooke, the Chief of the Imperial General Staff.[105] Brooke had his own doubts, as did other senior British commanders. McNaughton, in their view, was not a good trainer, not a good judge of men, and not a good field commander. That view had hardened into certainty after Exercise Spartan in March 1943, when McNaughton's handling of his army had been clumsy in the extreme. Spartan was a huge exercise designed to test a breakout from a bridgehead – in effect, a preview of the invasion of the Continent – and McNaughton, in Brooke's judgment, created an 'awful muddle! ... I felt that I could not accept the responsibility of allowing the Canadian Army to go into action under his orders.'[106] General Sir Bernard Paget, the Commander-in-

Chief Home Forces, was equally critical, censuring the Canadian for dilatory tactics, missed opportunities, changes of orders, and frequent and conflicting shifting of units.[107] The Second Canadian Division was all but 'wiped out' in the exercise, for example.[108] When II Canadian Corps vehicles were caught in a giant traffic jam, one officer swore that he saw the army commander at a crossroads directing traffic.[109] Whether this was true or not, McNaughton tried to pass one corps through another in full darkness, an absolute impossibility. There were some reasons for the Spartan fiasco – Lieutenant-General Ernest Sansom's II Canadian Corps had been formed only in mid-January 1943 and was very raw – but not enough to provide exculpatory evidence.[110] The commanders who had failed, after all, were all McNaughton's appointees. McNaughton refused to sack Sansom, as the British desired. Worse even than the British unhappiness,* Canadian junior and middle-rank officers realized that Spartan had been a cock-up and blamed McNaughton.[111]

The fight over the Canadian commitment to the Sicilian and Italian campaigns combined with McNaughton's Spartan failure to force the issue. Ralston and Stuart came to England in November 1943 determined to oust McNaughton and had heated discussions with the GOC-in-C. For the first time, the general heard of the British doubts about his abilities, and he had more acrimonious discussions with them. Convinced that he had been railroaded out of his command by the British, who resented his Canadianism, and by the backstabbing of Stuart and Ralston, McNaughton raged and stormed and made himself ill. In the end, he returned to Canada, and the Canadian people were told only that ill-health had made his retirement necessary.[112] Astonishingly, the one key player in whom McNaughton retained confidence was Harry Crerar, the man destined to be his successor.

McNaughton was a doughty Canadian, a nationalist leader in a time when the Canadian military – and politicians, too, who accepted British and then Anglo-American strategy without a whimper – tended to go along to get along. Currie's Canadian Corps, where McNaughton had cut his teeth, might

---

* During Spartan, Medical Officer Jack Leddy noted, 'officers and men had to line up together for each meal instead of having separate messes. This upset some of the British officers, who were definitely snobs and did not like eating with the men. The Canadian officers got a kick out of this and would take great glee in telling a British officer to get in line with the rest of us and wait his turn.' Mary Jo Leddy, *Memories of War, Promises of Peace* (Toronto, 1989), 82.

have been half British-born, but it had a confidence in itself, in its tactics, and in the Canadian methods of fighting a war. They were superior, they claimed, and the corps was the best on the Western Front. The First Canadian Army of the Second World War, by contrast, at least until it had been in action for some months, had somehow lost that sense. The British ways may have failed against the Wehrmacht, but they were still the methods the Canadians used. How could they be argued against, when the British had trained the staff officers and commanders before the war and when the Canadians had no battle experience to create their own doctrine? How could they be resisted, when the Canadians had spent three-and-a-half years in Britain imbibing British doctrine and training methods? The innovations that came out of fighting the enemy and the conditions of the Western Front from 1915 to 1918 had to be relearned again. McNaughton was an innovator, to be sure, but his nationalism, sometimes obstructionist and self-serving, was out of sync with the times and circumstances of 1939 to 1943.

By the spring of 1943 the Second World War, while its outcome was still in doubt, had seen the end of disastrous Allied defeats. The Russians had defeated the Nazis in the epic struggle at Stalingrad, and Montgomery had bested Rommel at El Alamein. The Anglo-American allies had followed El Alamein by driving the enemy out of North Africa. In the Pacific, the Americans and British had begun their long way back. Canada, however, had yet to devote the full force of its carefully constructed and husbanded army in Canada and in Britain to battle. Dieppe, like the debacle of Hong Kong, was not a good omen. Nor was the acrimony between the politicians and the generals. The coming months of fighting were to put the Canadian Army to the test.

seven

INTO BATTLE: SICILY AND ITALY
July 1943–June 1944

We are the D-Day Dodgers, out in Italy,
Always on the vino, always on the spree.
Eighth Army skivers and their tanks,
We go to war, in ties and slacks,
We are the D-Day Dodgers, in sunny Italy ...

The Moro and Ortona were taken in our stride,
We didn't really fight there, we went there for the ride,
Sleeping 'til noon and playing games,
We live in Rome with lots of dames,
We are the D-Day Dodgers in sunny Italy ...[1]

With the 1st Canadian Army Tank Brigade, the First Canadian Division formed part of the Allied force that invaded Sicily on July 10, 1943. The successful conclusion of the North African campaign in early 1943 had marked the first Anglo-American victory of the war – an especially satisfying one because it encompassed the destruction of Rommel's fabled Afrika Korps. Now President Franklin Roosevelt and Prime Minister Winston Churchill had decided that Sicily and, likely, Italy were next. An invasion could topple the Mussolini regime and, ideally, it would force the Germans to deploy large numbers of troops in Italy, troops that could be used to more effect elsewhere.

The Canadian government, much more eager than the General Officer Commanding-in-Chief of the First Canadian Army, General Andrew McNaughton, to see its men in action, won agreement to have the division and the tank brigade included in the assaulting force. There they would join General Bernard Montgomery's Eighth Army, a legendary formation after Monty's North African victories. McNaughton accepted this arrangement, so long as the troops returned to England after the conquest of Sicily.

But the Italian campaign turned out to be long, wearing, and costly. The Germans used the ground with great skill, creating defensive lines that took a terrible toll on attacking troops. A holding action designed to tie down German divisions, Italy turned, instead, into a struggle that wore down the Allies. Worse, for the men doing the fighting, the Italian campaign became a backwater after the Allies invaded France in June 1944, forgotten, ill-supplied, and all but scorned. D-Day Dodgers, indeed.

For the Canadians, soon to include the Fifth Canadian Armoured Division and I Canadian Corps headquarters, Italy was a killing ground. In just over a year and a half, the Canadians lost one-quarter of the men sent to the Mediterranean, a very high casualty rate considering that many soldiers' duties never took them close to the front line. But Sicily and Italy gave the Canadians and their commanders the experience they needed, the chance to test in action the theories and the tactics they had studied on sand tables, in Staff College, and in exercises in Britain. Fighting the Germans was never easy, but the Canadians in Italy showed they could fight against the best the enemy had to offer and prevail.

The First Canadian Division had been in Britain since the end of 1939 and it had seen no action, except for the abortive excursion to France in June 1940 and a small raid on Spitzbergen. Moreover, the division had had four commanders, the penultimate being Major-General H.L.N. Salmon, who died in an air crash on April 29, 1943, on his way to North Africa to discuss the planning of the Sicilian invasion. A Royal Canadian Regiment Permanent Force officer with Staff College training, Salmon had been a tough, demanding trainer and an able officer, probably destined for higher command.[2] In his place, General McNaughton quickly appointed Major-General Guy Simonds, who had been in command of Second Division for just two weeks. Simonds was clearly the rising star of the army. A Royal Military College graduate and a PF artilleryman, he had gone overseas as General Staff Officer II of the First Division, commanded an artillery regiment successfully, organized the Canadian Staff College in Britain, attracted Monty's sharp eye on exercises, and moved rapidly up through the ranks thanks to his brilliant staff work. Now he was to command the first Canadian division to fight as such in the war.

The First Division was generally thought to be adequately trained and a good division. The infantry units had had the Battle Drill training designed to develop standard routines and instinctive reactions, as well as substantial combined operations training and a gruelling assault-landing course. The division included the three PF infantry battalions, which ought to have provided a leavening of discipline and professionalism, though they did not always do so. The 2nd Brigade included the Princess Patricia's Canadian Light Infantry, which, some claimed, was not yet well led by its PF officers; Vancouver's Seaforth Highlanders, led by Lieutenant-Colonel Bert Hoffmeister, a regiment considered to have the best officers in the division; and the Loyal Edmonton Regiment, which was recognized for the quality of its rank and file. The brigade commander was the tough-talking but not always tough Chris Vokes, Simonds's RMC classmate. The 3rd Brigade, led by a portly, slow-moving regular force officer, Brigadier M.H.S. Penhale, consisted of the Royal 22e Régiment, the Carleton and York Regiment from New Brunswick, and the West Nova Scotia Regiment, and was thought to have been less well trained than the other brigades. This fault was not due to Penhale but to the previous brigade commander, Brigadier Charles Foulkes, or so General Vokes claimed in his memoirs.[3] In the 1st Brigade were the Royal Canadian Regiment, the Hastings and Prince Edward Regiment from eastern Ontario, and Toronto's 48th Highlanders under Brigadier Howard Graham, a lawyer, Militia stalwart, and former Hasty Ps' officer. In the division, the battalions' commanding officers had all been changed frequently in the years since mobilization, and there had also been much moving around of non-commissioned officers and men, with older men returning home, reinforcements coming aboard, and promotions and cross-postings changing the mix.

The division staff was again good, but untried. The GSO I, Lieutenant-Colonel George Kitching, was British, an officer who had joined the RCR at the outbreak of war after British Army service. The Commander Royal Artillery, Brigadier Bruce Matthews, was a Militia gunner of great ability. The administrative side fell under Lieutenant-Colonel Preston Gilbride, the wonderfully titled Assistant Adjutant and Quartermaster-General (AA&QMG), another able man and 'great operator.' And the Commander Royal Engineers, Lieutenant-Colonel Geoffrey Walsh, was a PF officer, a tough, forceful man. All would rise in Simonds's wake.[4]

The 1st Canadian Army Tank Brigade (in August redesignated as the 1st Canadian Armoured Brigade), commanded by Brigadier R.A. Wyman, deployed three regiments: the Ontario Regiment, the Three Rivers Regiment (which had many francophones in its ranks), and the Calgary Regiment. In England the brigade had initially used Matilda tanks and had then converted to Rams, the one Canadian-designed tank of the war.[5] For the Sicilian operation, the brigade switched to the Allied standard tank, the American-made 29-ton Sherman with its low-velocity 75 mm gun, relatively thin armour, and less than 30 miles per hour maximum speed. The brigade had little time to train on its new tanks before embarkation, but British officers, sent from the Mediterranean to assist the units, sped up the process.

The convoys carrying the Canadian division sailed from Great Britain, the last departing on July 1. The men, including some 120 reinforcements for each battalion, received complete briefings on board their ships, where they continued their physical training to keep in fighting trim. The fast convoy of ships arrived off Sicily untouched; the slow convoy lost three ships to U-boats, and fifty-eight of the nine hundred Canadians aboard were drowned. More than five hundred vehicles and forty guns went to the bottom as well, depriving General Simonds's headquarters of most of its vehicles and signals equipment. British and American convoys simultaneously converged on Sicily, and on July 10 the great enterprise began.

Defended by the Italian Sixth Army, a truly weak formation, along with the newly reconstituted 15th Panzer Grenadier Division and the Hermann Goering Panzer Division of the Wehrmacht, Sicily was a tough nut. The steep hills and winding roads made it relatively easy to defend, and the heat, dust, and dryness were bound to take their toll on attacking troops.

The Allied plan saw the Canadians and British forces concentrating on the eastern half of the island, and the Americans on the west. The First Division came ashore successfully in very rough water near Pachino, met light resistance from Italian forces, and moved inland. Losses on the first day were seven killed and twenty-five wounded. British and American landings went equally well, though U.S. paratroops were blown far from their drop zones. Still, it seemed a textbook assault, a masterpiece of planning and execution, especially when compared with Dieppe, the last Canadian assault landing. The next few days were for marching, as the Germans fell back and the units of the division moved rapidly inland, collecting Italian prisoners. On July 13 General Montgomery, recognizing that the division was not accustomed to Mediterranean heat, unlike all his other divisions, called a halt to let the men rest and allow supplies to come forward – by mule trains!

At last, the Canadians had the chance to eat their fabled 'compo' rations. Lieutenant Farley Mowat of the Hastings and Prince Edward Regiment recalled that the compo pack was a wooden crate with everything fourteen men needed to eat for twenty-four hours: 'hard-tack biscuits in lieu of bread; canned yellow wax, misleadingly labelled margarine; tins of M&V (unidentifiable scraps of fat and gristle mushed up with equally unidentifiable vegetables); canned processed cheese which tasted like ... casein glue; powdered tea, milk and sugar, already mixed; turnip jam (laughingly labelled strawberry or raspberry); eight ... tiny hard candies for each man; seven India-made Victory cigarettes ...; six squares of toilet paper per man ... and ... a twelve-ounce can of treacle pudding that was an irresistible object of desire to every one of us.'[6] The only virtue of army rations was that they provided calories in large quantities: a soldier needed some 3000 a day to be able to function in action. Frequently, local vino could be found to wash away the dust and the foul taste of the rations. 'After a glass of that stuff,' Brigadier Vokes noted, 'one would consider cutting one's own mother's throat.'[7]

The soldiers were, as always, heavily laden. Each private had a rifle and one or usually two 50-round bandoliers to carry his own ammunition. He carried four 30-round magazines for his section's Bren gun, at least two hand grenades, and likely a 2-inch mortar bomb or anti-tank projectile for the Projector Infantry Anti-Tank (PIAT). On his belt or backpack hung a water bottle, an entrenching tool (which quickly became his best friend in the all-too-frequent ritual of digging-in), and a bayonet. In his pack he had a groundsheet, a few tins of food, hard tack, cigarettes, mess tins, and probably mail and photos from home. Bren gunners and wireless operators had even more to carry, and the normal load was never less than 60 pounds.[8] The omnipresent Sicilian mules took the load off many soldiers.

Now the Germans came into the picture. On July 15 at Grammichelle, troops of the Hermann Goering Division fought a delaying action that obliged the Canadians, mainly Hasty Ps supported by tanks of the Three Rivers Regiment, to deploy in order to take the town. Their first time under fire, their first experience of the Germans' awesome 88 mm gun that had such high velocity that its shell arrived almost without warning, the Canadian troops suffered twenty-five casualties. The pattern of the campaign was set: small enemy blocking forces would try to delay the advance, inflict casualties, and then retire to the next position. This sequence happened the next day at Piazza Armerina, a town best known for its fine Roman mosaics, where Panzer Grenadiers delayed the advance for a day until the Loyal Eddies took the town at a cost of twenty-seven casualties. The Sicilians cheered the entry of the Canadians into the 'squalid city,' but a Seaforths company commander observed dryly that 'they huzza by day and snipe by night.'[9] Again on the 17th, the Panzer Grenadiers, this time in battalion strength, fought a stubborn action at Valguarnera, where the topography, as always in Sicily, favoured them. With the 3rd Brigade in reserve, Simonds, a gunner by trade, ordered a two-brigade attack, with the heavy artillery support that was to become his trademark.[10]

The resulting fighting was the first major action by the First Canadian Division. On the left, the 2nd Brigade secured the high ground quickly. On the right, the 1st Brigade met stiffer resistance, its troops hampered by the steep hills, winding tracks, and, as a result, frequent inability of the carrier-borne mortars, tanks, and artillery to give support. The RCR faced the most difficult fight south of Valguarnera, when German fire inflicted heavy losses and killed the regiment's second-in-command as he attacked a tank single-handedly.[11] Amid the mix of terror and fatigue, the Canadians discovered that the enemy had more machine guns than they did and weapons with a higher rate of fire. The German also employed their mortars with great and lethal skill. The only protection was to dig in – and deeply – but, for the advancing troops, that was scarcely possible. Not until after midnight did the Canadians take the town, and by then the enemy had pulled back successfully. The day's fighting had cost 145 casualties.

A fundamentally shy man with an icy exterior, an abrupt style, and no tolerance for failure, Simonds had been unhappy with the performance of Brigadier Graham's units at Grammichele. In fact, the GOC had proposed to sack him then and there, but was dissuaded from doing so by Lieutenant-General Oliver Leese, the corps commander under whom the First Division served. General Montgomery, the Eighth Army commander, also became involved and obviously spoke to Simonds about the proper way to treat his subordinates. Everyone, from Simonds down to Private Jones in the rear rank, had much to learn about how to fight a war. The result, after Valguarnera, was that Simonds congratulated Graham, who had done well, and told him he had been recommended for the Distinguished Service Order. Simonds, noted his GSO 1, 'could be human after all.'[12]

For the next seventeen days the Canadians fought their way up the hills and down the ravines of central Sicily. Each winding turn in the road constituted a potential enemy position, each blown bridge a major obstacle, each town a delaying party – and most did. So steep were the goat paths that 'liberated' mules became essential to haul food, water, and ammunition to forward units. Some fruit could also be plucked from small orchards – 'we can get all the fruit we want,' Sergeant Amos Chadwick wrote to his parents in Napanee, Ontario. 'Figs are delicious when we pick them off the trees'[13] – but dysentry and diarrhoea were a constant threat, and so too was malaria in a fly-ridden, mosquito-rich region.

At Assoro the 1st Brigade faced strong German positions on a high mountain that dominated most of the surrounding area, but the Hastings and Prince Edward Regiment, having just lost its CO and Intelligence Officer to an 88 mm gun, went wide and to the right and scaled an adjoining and higher peak that topped Assoro. Led by the acting CO, the thirty-year-old Major John Buchan, Lord Tweedsmuir (the son of the late Governor General), the eastern Ontario regiment followed goat paths down into the valley at nightfall and scaled the mountain in the dark, all the while trying to keep silent so as not to alert the enemy. At one point a Sicilian boy herding goats blundered into the Canadian column but, stunned, passed by without a word. Mowat recorded that the boy came 'face to face with me, gaping incredulously as he took in the motionless shapes of armed men on every side. He said not a word but passed slowly on as in a dream.' A German observation post was startled into surrender, though the Wehrmacht sergeant in command had to be killed. 'The crazy bastard ... went for his damn gun,' said the soldier who shot him.[14] At last at daybreak the exhausted Hasty Ps stood at the crest and completely surprised the enemy, walking about in full view below. The heights commanded a view of some 50 miles. The battalion had not lost a man in scaling the mountain, and it poured fire onto enemy troops and convoys. The Germans, seasoned professionals, reacted quickly, and even the cooks fought back. The Canadians had begun to discover that the enemy, with more automatic weapons and mortars in each platoon than they had, was always quick to recover. Enemy artillery began pounding the crest, but counter-battery fire, directed by Tweedsmuir himself, silenced the guns. A hundred volunteers from the RCR lugged supplies up the cliff to let the eastern Ontario regiment hang on. The rest of Graham's brigade – 'mountain boys,' the Germans called them – had, by July 22, consolidated the victory and completely disrupted the German defence plan.[15]

Meanwhile, the 2nd Brigade was cracking the hard core of Leonforte's defences. A good-sized town of 20,000, well protected by hills, ridges, and German armour and infantry, Leonforte was initially to be tackled by Lieutenant-Colonel Bert Hoffmeister's Seaforth Highlanders. Unfortunately, four 'shorts' from the supporting artillery barrage hit the battalion's headquarters and disrupted the planning. Brigadier Vokes, driving around in his four-wheel-drive Jeep flying a 'bear' pennant and seeing that Hoffmeister was badly dazed and several of his key staff killed or wounded, sent the Loyal Edmonton Regiment into the delayed assault instead. Climbing a steep ravine, the Eddies made their way into the town, but the Germans counterattacked strongly, cut the regiment off from the rest of the brigade, and trapped it in a vicious cycle of hand-to-hand fighting. Canadian engineers, meanwhile, worked overnight to get a bridge over the ravine and, furthermore, sent a fighting patrol of their own into the town. Gambling, Vokes decided to create a strong flying column of four tanks, anti-tank guns, and a company of PPCLI to rush the bridge and get into Leonforte. The tactic worked, the column freed the Edmontons from their trap, and, though there was heavy fighting, liberated the town. The hills to the east and west of the town duly fell to the PPCLI. Two days of hard fighting had cost the First Canadian Division 275 casualties, including thirty Seaforths killed and wounded in the errant shelling. Hoffmeister, destined to be one of the greatest Canadian fighting generals of all time, had narrowly escaped death.

General Simonds's soldiers pressed on with all haste, their next objective the town of Agira.[16] The GOC's plan called for infantry to attack behind a 'timed program of artillery concentrations on successive targets,' a rigid plan that led Brigadier Graham to complain to himself 'My God! The man must be crazy.' Graham's concerns were correct, as the RCR discovered when they tried to pass beyond Nissoria, 4 miles west of Agira. Panzer Grenadiers, missed by the artillery concentrations that largely fell on empty fields, raked the Canadian attackers with mortar and machine-gun fire, driving off a two-company attack in the midst of the chaos caused by the breakdown of radio communication – an all-too-frequent occurrence in Sicily. The CO, Lieutenant-Colonel R.M. Crowe, tried to go forward to assist his hard-pressed men, but he and his signaller died from machine-gun fire. The surviving RCR consolidated their position in the dark and waited for relief. Tanks of the Three Rivers Regiment tried to help, but they, too, came under heavy fire. They lost ten of their Shermans, which, with their high silhouette and thin armour, proved alarmingly vulnerable to anti-tank fire and less than equal to German tanks. The Nazis' Panzer IV, in contrast, had a low silhouette and a high-velocity 75 mm gun with good armour penetration. Its road speed was slower than that of the Sherman, but its better gun and skirts, which enabled it to survive against infantry anti-tank weapons, made it an all-round better tank. That the Canadian infantry and the troopers had not yet mastered the techniques of cooperation needed to assist both survive did not help. Nor did Simonds's reliance on precisely planned artillery concentrations to which the infantry had to conform without any flexibility.

Simonds's orders next sent the Hastings and Prince Edward Regiment at the German defences. This attack also failed, and the regimental CO was wounded, one of the eighty casualties suffered against the well-situated and tough Panzer Grenadiers. Brigadier Graham's only remaining battalion, the 48th Highlanders, was the next to try, but it, too, had no success in dislodging the enemy. Clearly, one battalion at a time could not do the trick. The 2nd Brigade took up the task on the evening of July 26, following a two-phase plan devised by the division's GOC that, this time, coordinated the attack properly.[17] Under a devastatingly heavy barrage and supported by tanks and anti-tank guns, the PPCLI quickly took their first objective, a ridge west of Agira. Nothing more was easy. The enemy, recovering composure rapidly, drove off the attack on the next ridge objective and savaged a follow-up attack by a company of Seaforths. In the end, though, it had to cede the ground. Another Seaforth company scaled a sheer 300-foot cliff to reach the top of Mount Fronte, where it drove off the German defenders. The Loyal Edmontons then attacked the remainder of the ridge line to the west of Agira and took it after a stiff fight. With the heights in their hands now, the 2nd Brigade completed the capture of Agira, the PPCLI gaining the honours. This fighting was the heaviest the Canadians faced in Sicily, and they defeated the Germans, who invariably had the high ground for their emplacements. It was no mean feat, as the 438 Canadian casualties demonstrated.

The 3rd Brigade, fighting some distance away, was part of a large British operation to take Catenanuova. The West Nova Scotia Regiment and the Carleton and Yorks took the town with ease.[18] The 1st Brigade similarly worked with British infantry to clear Regalbuto.

The Sicilian campaign was not yet over, but the end was near. The Americans had swept through the western part of the island, taken Palermo, and were roaring east. The British had moved north on a parallel track to the Canadians. All that remained now was the liberation of northeastern Sicily. In Rome, meanwhile, the Duce, Benito Mussolini, fell from power, the first Axis leader to be deposed.

The final act for the Canadian Division and its attached armoured brigade came in the relatively level valley of the River Simeto. Having studied the terrain from one of the commanding hills, Simonds conjured up a plan to create a striking force out of an armoured regiment, a reconnaissance squadron, an infantry battalion, a self-propelled artillery battery, and anti-tank guns. He intended to create 'a good mix-up in open country.' The attack, set for August 5, went to Vokes's 2nd Brigade, and Booth Force, consisting of the Three Rivers Regiment and the Seaforth Highlanders as its main components, took form. The two COs jointly drafted the plan, and Lieutenant-Colonels Hoffmeister and Booth rode together in the same tank. The tanks would carry the infantry as close to the objective as possible, and speed was everything. The attack, declared by all involved to be a model infantry and armour assault, surprised the defending 3rd Parachute Regiment which, though it had the advantage of position, for once lacked anti-tank weapons. When Booth Force came under fire, the infantry dismounted and the Shermans provided them with close support, blasting the defenders with their cannon and machine guns, and sometimes deliberately setting the grass on fire with tracer bullets to force the Nazis from their trenches. The enemy resisted to the last man, but the attack succeeded completely. The Seaforths suffered forty-three casualties.

Hoffmeister recollected that he had been suffering from 'tummy-bug' and was exhausted, but noted that the infantry and armour 'married up company for company.' The Seaforths CO left Booth's tank whenever 'it was obvious we were going to be stationary for a while and [would] go to my own HQ to satisfy myself everything was all right there ... I had a No. 18 [radio] set in Booth's tank netted to my companies. The whole thing,' Hoffmeister said rightly, 'was tied in extremely well.'[19] Infantry and armour cooperation could be mastered.

This operation was the last major task for the First Canadian Division in Sicily. By August 10 the Germans accepted that the game had ended and began a brilliant withdrawal to the Italian mainland. When the Americans entered Messina on August 17, they found it deserted of enemy defenders, all of whom had escaped. The Germans had put four divisions into the defence of the island and had sustained losses of some 11,600 men. The Allies, in comparison, suffered 19,000 casualties among the dozen divisions involved. In the thirty-eight-day campaign, the Canadians had lost 2310 casualties – 562 killed, 1664 wounded, and 84 prisoners of war – but by every account, including General Montgomery's, they had acquitted themselves well in their first actions. Italy was next on the Allied agenda. It would soon surrender to the Allies and change sides, but it was still occupied by the Germans.

Although the decision that the First Canadian Division would join in the attack on the Italian mainland did not reach General Simonds until close to D-Day, no one in Sicily had any doubt that the Canadians would fight on the mainland. Whatever General McNaughton had wanted, it made no military sense to send the division back to England after just five weeks in action. On September 3, therefore, units of Simonds's division, the 3rd Brigade in the lead, landed on the toe of the Italian boot. Under heavy supporting naval gunfire, the men stormed ashore to find – nothing. Other than a few demoralized Italian troops, there were no manned defences, no wire, no mines, nothing. The Germans in the area had retreated inland two days before, and the pursuing Canadians moved on, almost the only difficulties coming from well-executed demolitions that slowed the advance. A group of one hundred Italian paratroops fought a stiff action against Loyal Edmonton and West Nova Scotia Regiment infantry on September 6 and 7, but Italy's capitulation, announced on the 7th, put an end to that. On the 8th the Allies landed to the north at Salerno, and the Germans, under heavy pressure, rushed troops from the south to counter the seaborne attack. The Canadian advance, operating under Montgomery's Eighth Army, proceeded without opposition and soon posed a potential threat to the rear of the German position at Salerno.

Aside from encounters with German demolition parties that systematically destroyed bridges, laid mines, and cratered the roads, the Canadians advanced as fast as their vehicles could roll. The difficulty was getting supplies of petrol and food forward, the same problem that all units faced. Meanwhile, as the Eighth Army moved up the boot of Italy, the enemy pressure on the bridgehead at Salerno eased, and the British and American troops of the Fifth Army also began to move north. By October 1 Naples had been liberated, a few days after the Foggia airfields. The first month of this rapid war of movement was over, and the First Canadian Division had covered almost 300 gruelling miles. Extraordinarily, this advance had been accomplished with very few battle casualties. One of the sick, however, was Simonds, who came down with jaundice and had to be evacuated to hospital. Brigadier Vokes, a very different personality to the cold Simonds, replaced him temporarily, and Hoffmeister took command of the 2nd Brigade.

The advance northward soon continued, with Campobasso the ultimate objective, about 50 miles north of Naples in the centre of the Italian peninsula. The enemy now was present in strength, but the German tactic was still to put up stiff resistance, force the Canadians to halt, bring up artillery and armour, and prepare to attack. The Germans then resisted for a time, only to withdraw, and to repeat the cycle at the next suitable point to the north. Some engagements were costly – at Motta Montecorvino on October 1 German paratroops knocked out six tanks and inflicted casualties on the RCR; at the Castelnuovo road a few days later, two days of hand-to-hand fighting cost the

RCR, the Hasty Ps, and the Calgary Tanks seventy-eight casualties. It was now becoming clear, thanks to intelligence reports, that the Germans intended to establish a winter line 50 miles to the north and wanted to delay the Allied advance until the line was completed at the beginning of November.

The routine of bitter fighting continued through early October. The weather was frequently wet, the winding roads almost as steep and twisting as in Sicily, and the rivers, running from the centre of Italy to the sea, formed natural defensive barriers. The Germans, moreover, continued their demolitions, which, though they did not stop the infantry from advancing, delayed artillery and armour and choked supply columns. Meanwhile, the German artillery could hammer the advancing Canadians without retaliatory fire – until the guns caught up with the infantry, by which time the Germans were pulling out for their next defensive position.

The Canadians took undamaged Campobasso on October 14 almost without opposition, the large town centred around a 650-year-old citadel perched on a 350-foot-high rock. One suburb was located on a 600-foot-high spike. Painter Charles Comfort, one of the army's official war artists, captured the extraordinary scene in an oil that could have been painted during the Renaissance – except for the column of Canadian troops and armour at the base of the citadel. Campobasso would become 'Maple Leaf City,' a major Canadian administrative and recreational centre. Units set up shuttles to carry troops into town to see a movie or visit a canteen, and regiments took turns mounting ceremonial guards in the town square.

The Canadian advance continued after a few days of rest and recreation, following much the same pattern. In command again after October 15, General Simonds ordered an attack across the River Biferno, and the Loyal Eddies had the task of capturing Colle d'Anchise, a town atop a 700-foot hill. Wading the river, the infantry scaled an escarpment that took them to their objective. They found the soldiers of the 67th Panzer Grenadiers asleep, but the fight was no walkover as the Germans recovered quickly. Bitter close-quarter fighting followed, Canadian tanks failed to reach the Eddies, and a strong German counterattack supported by tanks almost drove the Canadians, by now short of ammunition, out of the hard-won town. But the Germans surprisingly pulled back, having lost a hundred men. The Loyal Edmonton Regiment had thirty casualties.

In a platoon-strength patrol on October 26, 1943, a typical action at this point in the campaign, Lieutenant Sydney Frost of the PPCLI was badly wounded in the face, but managed to bring all his men back to his unit's lines. The medical attention he received was indicative of the arrangements in the field and behind the lines. Still conscious, Frost received immediate treatment from the regiment's medical officer. Then he went by a Field Ambulance jeep to a Canadian Casualty Clearing Station in Campobasso, a terrible journey through the rain and mud. Unconscious by the time he reached Campobasso, Frost next went by ambulance to another Casualty Clearing Station at Foggia, where surgeons from No. 1 Maxillo Facial Team tried to restore his shattered jaw and mouth. All this had taken only four hours since he had reached his Regimental Aid Post. Frost spent a week recuperating, moved again to the 98th General Hospital in Bari for two weeks, and then to yet another General Hospital in Algiers, where he passed six weeks. A hospital ship took him back to England, where for two months he had more operations to restore his face and jaw in Basingstoke Neurological and Plastic Surgery Hospital.[20] Later in the war other specialized units were in place, able to do surgery closer to the front.

Routinely, sulfa and, by 1944, penicillin were available for the wounded, a huge improvement in treatment against infection since the Great War. Blood transfusion similarly had been perfected, and again its use was routine. The result of the speedier care and of better drugs and blood use was that only 66 of every 1000 wounded men died, compared with 114 per 1000 in the First World War. Deaths from disease also declined dramatically to 0.9 per 1000 in the 1939–45 war. The extraordinary care Frost received, and the speed of treatment (air transport from Northwest Europe to hospitals in Britain was also routine by 1945), were entirely typical for Canadian wounded in the Second World War.[21] Altogether, 35,000 men and women served in the Royal Canadian Army Medical Corps, providing this care, and Nursing Sisters raised morale by their presence alone. In December 1943, while the First Canadian Division was mired in the Moro and Ortona fighting, Brigadier Hoffmeister asked Canadian Nursing Sisters at base hospitals well back of the lines to volunteer to serve in the Casualty Clearing Station at San Vito, where the wounded, dirty and demoralized, were coming in faster than they could be treated. Army policy declared that nurses could not be sent into a battle zone – San Vito was regularly shelled – but the Sisters volunteered en masse. The wounded saw a smiling face and received the care they needed, and their sagging morale soared.[22]

On November 1 Simonds left the division to take command of the 5th Canadian Armoured Division, expected to arrive shortly in Italy along with the 8500 men of I Canadian Corps headquarters. Neither the armoured division nor a corps headquarters was needed by the Eighth Army. General Sir Harold Alexander, commanding the 15th Army Group in Italy, testily complained to London that he had not even been consulted about their dispatch. The leadership of a Canadian corps might be so inexperienced, he fretted, that other divisions could not be attached to it, leaving it rigid and ill-balanced. For Canadian military and domestic purposes, however, the additional troops were essential.[23] Vokes was confirmed as GOC of the First Canadian Division, and Hoffmeister was placed in command of the 2nd Brigade. Brigadier Penhale returned to England to take up a post at Canadian Military Headquarters, and Brigadier T.G. Gibson came from the Third Division in England to replace him. Lieutenant-General Harry Crerar also arrived from England in October to prepare to take command of the corps and, it was hoped, to acquire the battle experience he needed. It was already clear that Crerar would have command of the First Canadian Army when the Allied invasion of France took place. Andy McNaughton, fired from his post and returned to Canada in ill health, was now out of the military picture. The additions to Canadian strength, soon to number more than 75,000 men in Italy, and the command changes took time to come into effect. After a brief respite in November, the First Canadian Division and the 1st Canadian Armoured Brigade were about to face the army's most severe test in the war to that point.

The Germans' winter line was strongly held, and the enemy had pursued a ruthless scorched-earth policy on the approaches to the line. Houses and farms were burned, wells poisoned, bridges blown, mines laid, and booby-traps placed. The enemy's blown bridges tested the Royal Canadian Engineers' field companies. On one occasion that November the sappers of No. 2 Platoon of the 1st Field Company built one bridge near to completion, sent No. 3 Platoon across with its equipment to build the next bridge, and then dispatched No. 1 Platoon over that barely finished bridge to build yet a third – a game of leapfrog that extended when orders came down to build two more. All five bridges were completed within twenty-four hours.[24]

In the last two weeks of November, units of the First Canadian Division operating in cold, wet weather worked their way towards the Sangro River. They were sometimes in difficulty as enemy paratroopers staged their usual skilful delaying actions. At Point 1009 on the near bank of the Sangro, the enemy lured a platoon of the West Nova Scotia Regiment of the 3rd Brigade into a carefully laid trap and wiped it out, killing and wounding fifteen men and capturing sixteen.

But the Sangro had been reached, and soon British troops had crossed it at heavy cost. On December 1 the Canadians crossed the river in the midst of a giant traffic tie-up. Had the Luftwaffe in Italy had more than 300 aircraft or even local air superiority, this advance could have been disastrous.[25] General Montgomery had determined to 'hit the Germans a colossal crack,' and the Canadians' role in the Eighth Army's effort to drive up the Adriatic coast obliged them to fight in the heavily ridged coastal plateau, an area cut by rivers. On the Moro River, just 9 miles north of the Sangro, and at Ortona behind it, the Germans would make their stand.

The Canadian attack began on December 6, when the Princess Patricia's Canadian Light Infantry of Brigadier Hoffmeister's 2nd Brigade stormed Villa Rogati, a town atop the north bank of the Moro. The PPCLI forded the river in silence and surprised the defending Panzer Grenadiers. After a heavy firefight and difficult house clearing, the PPCLI had the town. The Seaforths tackled San Leonardo, where the British Columbians faced a strong defence. One company on the right was hammered by at least fifteen machine guns, and the battalion could do little more than hold a small bridgehead on the far bank of the Moro.

The next morning, in the midst of an icy squall, the PPCLI in Villa Rogati came under heavy shelling and attack by strong parties of enemy infantry. Fortunately for the Canadians, tanks and more ammunition arrived in the nick of time, helping them to drive off the first attack. The second began in mid-afternoon, and this time the Germans used tanks of their own. The struggle was fierce, as the Germans regrouped and renewed their assault five times. In the end, the enemy withdrew, leaving behind forty POWs and an estimated one hundred dead. The PPCLI's own casualties were sixty-eight, including eight killed and eight taken prisoner. That was the only success of the day, however, for the Germans, reinforced at San Leonardo, obliged Hoffmeister to order the Seaforths to retreat back across the Moro.

On the division's right flank, the 1st Brigade also tried to get across the river. The Hastings and Prince Edward Regiment, which had staged a diversion to help the 2nd Brigade on December 6, now attempted to cross the river in earnest. The Hasty Ps came under heavy fire, and two of the companies were checked and ordered to withdraw. 'We were appalled by the ferocity of the German reaction,' Farley Mowat said, and 'realized we had never before seen war in its full and dreadful magnitude.'[26] But a third company, its communications down, did not get the withdrawal order and, persisting, took its objective on high ground. The Commanding Officer then led his companies back across the Moro to exploit this success, but, without tanks or anti-tank guns, the battalion had to dig in and engage the enemy. Meanwhile, General Vokes, told by his engineers that it was all but impossible to build a bridge across the Moro to allow the Villa Rogati position to be used as the jump-off point for the bigger attack he had planned, believed he had no choice except to look again at San Leonardo. (Indian troops promptly built a bridge across the 'impossible' Moro, in one of the great engineering feats of the campaign.) So the First Canadian Division prepared to hit San Leonardo once more. The change of direction forced the Canadians into a series of frontal assaults that proved terribly costly.

Vokes's plan called for the 1st Brigade to lead and the 2nd Brigade to exploit. The RCR were to move southwest from the Hasty Ps' position while the 48th Highlanders staged a frontal attack across the river. After a firm base was gained on the San Leonardo escarpment, the 2nd Brigade would head for the critical road junction south of Ortona, assisted by the tanks of the 1st Armoured Brigade, which had once again joined up with its compatriots.

The key element in the plan was the RCR attack, which forced the regiment to move laterally across the enemy's front. This advance was dangerous at any time, even with the plentiful air and artillery support the RCR received. But there was no luck that day for the regiment. An entirely coincidental enemy attack caught the lead company in a hail of mortar and machine-gun fire just as it jumped off. Even though the Germans were beaten back, the RCR timetable fell to pieces. The advancing companies next came under heavy fire and went to ground halfway to San Leonardo, an area sown with deadly *schuminen*, wooden mines packed with just enough explosives to blow a man's foot off or pepper his testicles with metal pellets. The enemy then sent tanks at the RCR, and the CO, Lieutenant-Colonel Dan Spry, called for artillery fire on his own positions. This tactic worked, but Spry pulled back to a reverse slope, leaving one platoon in a small farmhouse. Meanwhile, the frontal assault by the 48th succeeded and, with all its companies across the river, the Toronto regiment dug in.

Vokes now ordered the 2nd Brigade to take San Leonardo itself, and Brigadier Hoffmeister sent a squadron of Calgary Tanks and a company of Seaforths to do the job. The tanks, commanded by Major Ned Amy, had great difficulty negotiating the twisting roads and the enemy mines, and the infantry suffered heavily from mortar fire. But Amy and the Seaforths got into the town, and the Seaforths silenced the enemy machine guns. Amy and his much-reduced squadron of five tanks somehow drove off a German counterattack with twelve tanks. By nightfall on December 9, San Leonardo was firmly in Canadian hands.

For their part, the Germans now directed their main effort at the RCR and Hasty Ps' positions closer to the Adriatic coast. An intense attack with armour, mortars, and machine-gun fire on the RCR positions forced Spry to withdraw his companies. One platoon, however, tucked into a farmhouse, which subsequently became known as Sterlin's Castle, when the platoon commander, Lieutenant Mitchell Sterlin, did not receive the withdrawal order. The full force of the enemy attack fell on the castle, and, when the platoon's Bren guns, dug in outside, had fired off all their ammunition, most of the men retreated across the river, leaving Sterlin and ten others in the farmhouse. As the Germans attacked repeatedly, these men defended their castle, killing the enemy right against the windows. After an artillery concentration broke up the last attack, Sterlin and his surviving men managed to get to the Hasty Ps' lines.[27] But they were leaping from the frying pan into the flames, for the eastern Ontario regiment became the target of eleven enemy attacks in the next thirty-six hours. Fortunately, the Hastings had dug in well, their weapons carefully sited and their mortars registered. Two companies of Panzer Grenadiers and tanks smashed repeatedly and ineffectually against the defences, losing 200 men in the process. As General Vokes recollected correctly but with rather more braggadocio than necessary, the 90th Panzer Grenadiers 'kept making one great tactical mistake: every time we attacked or indicated that we would attack, he would counterattack. My troops killed many Germans in that way.'[28] Even so, a third of the 400 eastern Ontario men in the line were killed or wounded. The Nazis abandoned the San Leonardo feature and began the process of fortifying Ortona.

The battle for San Leonardo, the first action that pitted Vokes's entire division against the enemy, had been a success – but a costly one for a formation and a commander still discovering what worked and what did not. The RCR alone had lost twenty-one killed and fifty-three wounded or missing. Strome Galloway, the acting CO on December 21, the regiment's birthday, asked the acting 1st Brigade commander, Lieutenant-Colonel Spry, to return to the regiment to drink its health. (Brigadier Graham had to be evacuated for medical reasons on December 16.) Crawling through a ditch, Spry did so, and, in the midst of this little ceremony, the regiment's padre arrived with a dozen crosses under his arm. There were, Galloway recalled, 'about thirty stiffened corpses' awaiting burial.[29]

The Moro crossings now secure, the Canadians moved north again to their objective – the road that ran inland from Ortona to Orsogna. It was hard slogging, for the Germans had based their defences on the feature known as the Gully, a deep cut that ran inland from the sea and formed a natural barrier to tanks. The Gully's banks also provided virtually impregnable shelter for the enemy's troops – who had, moreover, thoroughly mined the southern edge and registered their guns on forming-up areas and crossing points. It was against this feature that the Canadians were destined to batter.

Bulling forward in his customary manner, Vokes chose to attack the Gully head on and gave Hoffmeister's 2nd Brigade the task of securing a crossroads called Cider. On December 10 and 11 all three of his battalions went nowhere, despite strong efforts by the men to struggle up the enemy bank in thick mud and under fire. Vokes now decided to throw his 3rd Brigade into the attack, but the West Novas, who lost their CO, Lieutenant-Colonel Pat Bogert, and many others, could only hold on to the small gains they had made. Vokes then sent the Carlton and Yorks into the attack under a heavy barrage. The New Brunswickers did eliminate three machine guns on their side of the Gully, but they were cut down by fire from the German positions on the far side. Worse, the enemy captured twenty-eight Canadians when they surrounded one of the C&Y company headquarters.

The only bright spots on a day full of woe came from two independent armoured-infantry teams. In the first, a West Novas platoon and a squadron of the Ontario Regiment's tanks stormed into a German tank laager guarding the approach to the Ortona road. Four panzers were put out of action, but, unfortunately, the Canadian commanders failed to seize the opportunity to exploit this success. In the second, a Seaforth company (down to forty men) and four tanks from the Ontarios swept around the head of the Gully and rolled into the rear of the enemy positions. Taking prisoners, shooting up a battalion headquarters, and destroying two tanks, the raiders eventually had to withdraw. The two teams had hit upon a seam in the defences, but the follow-up did not materialize.

General Vokes now determined to send the Royal 22e Régiment, the sole Canadian unit still uncommitted, into action. Unknown to Vokes, the battered Panzer Grenadiers holding the line had been augmented by fresh battalions of paratroopers. The Van Doos had the task of outflanking the German positions by moving to Cider crossroads on December 13. Heavily supported by tanks from the Ontario Regiment and artillery, the Royal 22e's move was coordinated with a PPCLI strike across the Gully. Once again a German attack coincidentally occurred just as the Van Doos started off, but they forced the enemy back. The Germans had more tricks up their sleeve, however, and a well-camouflaged panzer caught the infantry in the open while the Shermans were still well back. Still, a platoon using a PIAT, awkward to fire and giving a powerful kick to the operator, destroyed the enemy tank. The Shermans caught another tank and destroyed it, and a Van Doos' company, led by Captain Paul Triquet, moved on. Triquet had a gift for the grandiloquent phrase and he told the Van Doos' second-in-command, Major J.V. Allard: 'On va les avoir les Boches' ['We're going to get the Jerries'].[30] But he soon faced fierce resistance when the Germans assessed the danger from the flank.

Triquet's men and the tanks worked together well, supporting each other. Then an artillery barrage caught the Van Doos and inflicted casualties, leaving Triquet as the sole officer alive. 'There are enemy in front of us,' he told his men, enemy 'behind us and on our flanks. There is only one safe place – that is on the objective.' The ever-dwindling band made it to Casa Berardi, a farmhouse, and almost to Cider before the men had to retreat back to the farm. Triquet organized the defences: he had four tanks, five Thompson submachine guns, five Brens, and eleven Van Doos. The remainder had been killed, wounded, captured, or were straggling behind.* The infantry dug in around the tanks overnight to protect them from German infiltrators and, with daybreak, the tanks revved up their engines and moved around to confuse the enemy. Triquet beat off the Germans – 'Ils ne passeront pas,' he said – until his acting CO, Major Allard, could reinforce the Casa Berardi position in strength. The leadership and courage of Triquet, who won the first Canadian Victoria Cross of the Italian campaign, had turned the enemy flank successfully.[31]

In the fighting on December 15, Private Alton Kjosness of the First Division's machine-gun battalion, the Saskatoon Light Infantry, died when the tank he was riding struck a mine. His mother, duly informed, wrote to the regiment to say she had seen her son in her dreams at the time he died. 'He was standing in the entry with a smile on his face' and he said, 'I'm home to stay.' The padre who buried Private Kjosness in an olive orchard overlooking the sea wrote to Mrs Kjosness to say, 'There are about fifty Canadian lads buried there. No one ever dies in vain, least of all a soldier of Canada.' Kjosness's remains were later reburied in the large Moro River war cemetery. His mother chose the inscription 'Alton was a poet' to be carved into her son's headstone.[32]

Now the 1st Brigade had to take Cider, a task it undertook on December 18. Described by the official army historian as setting 'a standard of almost faultless co-operation between artillery, infantry, and armour,'[33] Operation Morning Glory aimed to drive a deep salient into the enemy defences south and west of Ortona, creating the base from which the city with 17,000 inhabitants itself could be seized. Supported by an extraordinary artillery barrage, the heaviest yet for the First Division, and using the Three Rivers Regiment's Shermans, the attack began at 8 a.m. with the 48th Highlanders in the vanguard. The first objective quickly fell; the attack on the second began at 11:45 a.m. with the RCR in the lead. The 48th (known as the 'Glamour Boys' to

---

* One experienced front-line soldier defined stragglers as 'soldiers ... who having gone to ground (quite properly and usually as a result of enemy fire) did not get up and go forward when the time came to do so.' The writer suggested that, before Ortona, a whole battalion of 500 officers and men were stragglers by his definition. Memo by LGen Henri Tellier, 'Courts Martial (FGCM) 1940–1945,' March 29, 1990. Gen Tellier gave me a copy of this memo.

their friends, presumably because they were a well-off kilted Militia regiment from Toronto) had met little resistance, but the RCR (the 'Shinola Boys,' because of their PF emphasis on having a good turnout at all times) were not so fortunate, for the 'almost faultless' barrage fell in part on the Carlton and Yorks positions and had to be shifted 400 yards further ahead. This move left the attacking infantry fully exposed to fire from German paratroops, who smashed two companies. The surviving RCR clung to the ground a hundred yards ahead of their start line. The regiment, reinforced with every available man from the 'LOBs' (men left out of battle to preserve a nucleus for rebuilding a battalion in the event of disaster), returned to the charge the next afternoon. The barrage was effective this time, as the tanks cooperated closely. The RCR established itself at Cider and lost only three men in this second attempt.

With the crossroads now secure, Ortona was the next objective – a task given to the 2nd Brigade.[34] Initially the attack went well, the Loyal Edmonton Regiment moving forward 3000 yards to the outer limits of Ortona. The Eddies were reinforced by the Seaforths, anti-tank guns, and medium machine guns that night. The next day, however, the Germans' determination to hold Ortona became clear. The Eddies ran into carefully sited enemy positions in the town, where shrewdly placed demolitions made killing grounds of the streets. The only way to avoid those death traps was to stick to the houses, but the row houses too had been booby-trapped, and a toilet flush could easily kill civilians as well as Canadians. The Eddies and the Seaforths took an entire day to clear a score of houses, and it became clear that only strenuous house-to-house fighting could dislodge the defenders from the 1st Parachute Division. Developing techniques of mouseholing – blowing holes through the wall of one row house to gain entry to the next – the Canadians systematically worked their way forward. A Seaforths officer recalled the process years later:

> Streets of houses were to be taken, both sides ... A section would perhaps storm its way into a house at the head of a block, clear it to the top, then blow a way through at roof-level into the adjoining house, where it would clear to the bottom. Then back it would go to the top ... the Germans withdrawing on the other side of the street as the houses opposite were taken. Others under different circumstances developed a preference for criss-crossing the street, entering buildings always from the ground level. First, smoke grenades would

be thrown up the street and the door opposite smashed with bullets; then, one group giving covering fire, a second group would race across, burst into the house and clear it from the ground up ... And always, of course, there was the resourcefulness and determination of the paratroopers to be reckoned with: houses taken by the Seaforths during the day re-occupied by the Germans at night; snipers infiltrating positions ... doors booby-trapped, buildings mined with delayed charges.[35]

The Canadian infantrymen found themselves in deadly battle. The Germans would let a platoon get into a house, then blow it up. On one occasion they caught twenty-four Eddies together and killed nineteen; rescuers pulled one of the Edmonton soldiers from under the rubble after three days. At Brigadier Hoffmeister's urging, the Canadians quickly retaliated and destroyed two houses with an estimated two platoons of paratroopers inside.[36] Still, the Germans fought on from the upper storeys. Canadian tanks were of limited utility in such close quarters, but the Shermans of the Three Rivers Regiment did what they could.[37] The 6-pounder anti-tank guns, however, were mobile enough to provide close support, firing an anti-tank projectile through a wall, then putting high explosive shells into the hole. Medium artillery south of the town picked off enemy strongpoints one by one. Nonetheless, it took the Loyal Edmonton Regiment the whole of December 23 to progress 200 yards, and the battalion paid for every yard in casualties. The Seaforths, with half the town to clear, made similarly slow progress, despite a sweeping left hook around Ortona by the 1st Brigade that aimed to force the enemy to pull back.

Civilians huddled in basements or in tunnels, but inevitably suffered heavy casualties as their city was blasted to pieces.[38] On Christmas Day 1943, the fifth away from home for the dwindling numbers of old sweats of the First Canadian Division, companies of Seaforths and troopers from the Three Rivers Regiment pulled out of the line one by one for a sumptuous roast pork dinner in the ruined Church of Santa Maria di Constantinopoli. A Seaforths officer played the church organ and the padre, Captain Roy Durnford, rose to the occasion, telling the shattered men that 'at last I've got you all in church.'[39] For some of those who celebrated the feast that day it was their last, for the soldiers shuttled back to the battle after their meal.

Ortona had turned into a battle of wills, a terrible struggle for prestige.

The town itself had no particular military importance, and the Arielli, a stream just to the north, was a natural defensive position. But German and Allied media turned the battle into a little Stalingrad, and neither side could afford to yield. Matthew Halton, the CBC reporter in Italy, cast the struggle in epic terms: 'The action is as fierce as perhaps modern man has ever fought.'[40] The Canadian public, anxious to see the army's reputation begin to match that of the Great War, at last had a battle they could visualize. The soldiers, exhausted as they were, picked up this sense too. Brigadier Hoffmeister, asked by Vokes if he wanted to pull his men out, replied 'absolutely not.'[41] In fact, he committed the PPCLI to the struggle to increase the pressure. Hoffmeister was no bloodthirsty commander, but he knew a defeat would shatter his brigade's morale completely. Perhaps he was right to persist, for the enemy finally did concede, pulling out of Ortona on December 27. The front stabilized, though not before the division drove the Germans north to the River Riccio. On Ortona's outskirts after the battle, Hoffmeister's brigade erected a sign: 'This is Ortona, a West Canadian town.'[42]

The cost of moving the First Canadian Division and the 1st Armoured Brigade the 5 miles from the Moro to the northern outskirts of Ortona was 176 officers and 2163 men killed, wounded, and missing. Illness and battle exhaustion – approximately one in five of the men evacuated for illness had cracked under the strain of heavy fighting – added another 1617 casualties.[43] Time and again, exhausted men had been thrown at German positions in foul weather. Their companies dwindled in strength, their platoons shrank to fifteen or sixteen men, their sections to three or four. These high casualties amounted to half the division's fighting strength at the opening of the final phase of the battle in mid-December. While the division received some 2400 reinforcements from Britain in this period and committed many of these green men to battle in the Ortona streets at once, it remained seriously understrength. The infantry battalions especially had suffered 50 per cent casualties in rifle strength, the armoured regiments had absorbed their heaviest losses thus far in the campaign, and the First Canadian Division and the 1st Armoured Brigade had effectively shot their bolts. 'I am compelled to bring to your attention,' General Vokes told his British corps commander, General Allfrey, 'that in my opinion the infantry units of this division will not be in a fit condition to undertake further offensive operations until they have had a period of rest ... [and] intensive training.'[44] The only compensation, according to Halton, was that the Canadians had mauled 'two of the finest divisions that ever marched, killing them, man by man, in a long-drawn-out fury of fire and death.'[45]

Was the battle necessary? Did Ortona have to be taken street by street and house by house or could it have been bypassed? First, the Germans chose to defend the city in defiance of the logic that ought to have pulled them back to the next river line.[46] Second, Major-General Vokes was not an independent actor but had to follow his superiors' orders – and Montgomery had called for a 'colossal' crack at the Hun. British (and hence Canadian) Army doctrine called for rigid, top-down control, the use of artillery to 'soften-up' the enemy, and time to plan and prepare. Third, the Moro and Ortona struggle was Vokes's first action where he had to direct his entire formation in battle; the war on the Italian mainland up to that point had been one of pursuit and smaller-scale brigade or battalion actions. Like his men, the GOC was still new at the big jobs. Finally, the ground was such that once he had been told that the Moro could not be bridged at Villa Rogati, Vokes was probably limited to frontal attacks across the Gully.

Still, after his men took the Cider crossroads and Ortona could have been bypassed, the GOC may well have erred in putting single battalions into the attack on the town, then following them with another, and yet another. Certainly his corps commander thought so: he wrote in his diary of 'half-baked' attacks that were 'tiring out' the division and producing 'nothing because of the lack of co-ordination.'[47] Vokes's persistence was admirable, but his tactical solutions were much less so.

A battalion ordinarily put one or two companies forward, and each company placed one or two platoons in the lead; each platoon then had one or two sections of ten men (and usually five or six if casualties had not been replaced) out in front. A battalion attack, therefore, might have only ten to thirty or forty men up front, a small number to throw at prepared and determined defenders. The better Canadian artillery, the abundance of armour, and Allied air superiority were compensatory advantages, but all too often it was a few Canadians with rifles and Brens against an enemy in prepared positions behind machine guns. Still, sometimes battles must be fought. Vokes was on the ground, in command, and obliged to follow his orders. His armchair general critics, viewing everything with twenty-twenty hindsight a half-century later, were not.[48]

Trooper M.H. Rimer of the Strathconas wrote to his parents in mid-December that 'after what I've seen over here, I'm only too glad to do my share so as that you back home won't have to live like the people of this country do.' Such sentiments were common among the men. So too were those of Captain Harry Jolley, a dental officer in No. 1 Company, Canadian Dental Corps, in Italy. Jolley had been bored in Canada, frustrated by the military. In Italy, he found himself caught up in the struggle, writing to his sister that 'I am on a front of which Canadian veterans of this war will speak in the future in awesome tones.' That was absolutely true, as was his next comment: 'I imagine this is about as tough a go as anything we have yet encountered. If any Canadian soldier ever had any doubts about the German abilities as a soldier his experience here has undoubtedly set them at rest.'[49]

While the First Division bound up its wounds and recuperated from the Moro and Ortona, the Fifth Canadian Armoured Division and I Canadian Corps established themselves on the ground. The division had been subject to successive reorganizations in its lifetime as army doctrine on the use of tanks in operations changed.[50] By the time it reached Italy in early November, the Armoured Division consisted of two brigades, the 5th Armoured Brigade under Brigadier G.R. Bradbrooke and the 11th Infantry Brigade under Brigadier George Kitching. A second infantry brigade, the 12th, would be added to the division in July 1944, primarily because a two-brigade division was deemed unbalanced for conditions in Italy. When the additional brigade could not be sent from Britain – the Normandy campaign was absorbing all resources – I Canadian Corps cobbled the 12th together by re-roling units, turning unneeded anti-aircraft units and a reconnaissance regiment into infantry. There were hard feelings all round, especially from ack-ack gunners converted to the much more dangerous role of infantry.[51]

The Fifth Canadian Armoured Division regrettably arrived without heavy equipment. Its guns and vehicles were to be secured from the British 7th Armoured Division that had nursed its clunkers through the desert war and up the Italian boot. Every piece of mechanized junk in the Eighth Army found its way to the Canadian division. Worse still, General Crerar appropriated the new Canadian-made vehicles en route from Britain and intended to be shared between the division and I Canadian Corps headquarters units.[52] Simonds argued that new Sherman tanks were required for his division and he got his way, but the first tanks did not begin arriving until just before Christmas.

After two dispiriting weeks in sodden tents, the brigades moved to Altamura to train under General Simonds. The routine was tough, Simonds telling everyone, officers and men alike, that Canadian soldiers were 'the best in the world *bar none* – if they had good leadership.' He ran divisional TEWTs – tactical exercises without troops – for the officers, and changes followed as the GOC promptly disposed of commanders in whom he did not have confidence. He fired Brigadier Bradbrooke because he disagreed with him about the utility of using tanks as mobile artillery, an action that showed Simonds at his know-it-all worst.[53] But the one officer Simonds could not replace was his superior, Harry Crerar. The corps commander and Simonds were both PF artillerymen, and Simonds had served under Crerar when he was commandant of the Royal Military College. They did not like each other, Simonds resenting Crerar's fusspot mannerisms and the older man disliking what he believed was Simonds's cocksuredness and arrogance. Inevitably they clashed soon after Crerar arrived in Italy, fighting over trivial matters in correspondence. The dispute soon escalated to the point where Crerar began to doubt Simonds's 'stability' – as he told Montgomery and senior Canadian officers.[54] It was probably with short-term relief, therefore, that Crerar recommended the younger general to command II Canadian Corps in Britain in January 1944, an appointment that quickly followed. To replace Simonds as GOC of the armoured division, Crerar secured Major-General E.L.M. Burns, a protégé who had been a staff officer and the developer of the Ram tank. Like Crerar and Simonds, Burns was a cold fish who soon won the name 'Smiler' from his troops because of his perpetual grim countenance.[55]

Crerar himself did not have much opportunity to gain the battle experience he wanted in Italy. While the Fifth Armoured readied itself for battle, the First Division was recuperating, effectively out of action. Crerar based himself in Sicily until early in January, when his new headquarters opened near Altamura, where his corps troops, consisting of everything from Mobile Bath and Laundry Units to medium artillery, began intensive training. Crerar's role was strictly limited, and he became GOC-in-C of the First Canadian Army in

March, once more having Simonds under his command. His successor as corps commander was Burns, while command of the Fifth Armoured Division went to Bert Hoffmeister. In July 1943 Hoffmeister had been a lieutenant-colonel, and in March 1944 he was a division commander. He had been promoted with extraordinary rapidity on sheer merit, and he told his armoured brigade commander frankly that he knew 'sweet bugger all' of tank warfare.[56] His impressive personal qualities aside, his meteoric ascension was likely a benefit to his soldiers. Unlike most Canadian GOCs who had not commanded a battalion in action, Hoffmeister knew what men could and could not do, and he understood – as Simonds, Burns, and Crerar certainly did not – that inspirational leadership could make men do more than they believed possible.[57] 'During a sticky battle,' one of Hoffmeister's successors as CO of the Seaforths said, 'morale is as important, if not more important than good tactics.' Hoffmeister understood that morale soared 'just by the appearance of a senior commander in the line when and where the bullets are flying.'[58]

The 11th Infantry Brigade meanwhile moved north at the beginning of the New Year. Attached to the First Division, it was to take up some of the burden while the First continued to integrate its replacements and recovered its élan. Brigadier Kitching's men replaced the 3rd Brigade in the line on January 13, and the battalions began active patrolling. To Kitching's surprise, he learned that his unblooded brigade, instead of holding the line and gaining battle experience, was to play the lead role in a major attack on the 1st Parachute Division's positions designed to stop the Germans from thinning out their defences on the Adriatic. The Allies planned to land at Anzio and take a crack at Cassino, the high mountain topped by a monastery that blocked the road to Rome, and pressure had to be maintained. Even so, the 11th Brigade was far from ready. As Kitching reflected, how his brigade, 'which was going into its first action,' was expected 'to take on two battalions' of well-trained and experienced paratroopers without heavy casualties was beyond his ken. Kitching did get heavy artillery and armoured support for the attack across the Riccio and towards the River Arielli on January 17, but the plan that put the Perth Regiment and the Cape Breton Highlanders successively into the attack was fatally flawed.[59]

First, the barrage ran ahead of the infantry, and the tanks of the Three Rivers Regiment were slow in crossing the Riccio and, Kitching believed, hesitant in lending the infantry support.[60] The Perths were left to move ahead on their own against fierce resistance, and some men broke and ran. The Highlanders, their attack launched with the Germans fully alert, quickly found themselves pinned down. Kitching ordered both battalions to extricate themselves as soon as it was dark, but 137 men from the Perths and 46 from the Highlanders were killed or wounded. 'It was a fiasco,' wrote Private Fred Cederberg of the Cape Breton Highlanders, made even worse when the Irish Regiment, mistaking retreating Canadians for the enemy, shot some of the Highlanders.[61] One man from the Irish Regiment was killed, and the padre, Captain Barry Rowland, as green as his unit, noted how hard it was to write the next-of-kin.[62] Fortunately for the Irish, Kitching's plan to send the battalion into the attack the next day was cancelled or there would have been more dead and more letters for the padre to write. Kitching himself returned to Britain in February to take command of the Fourth Canadian Armoured Division. His successor as commander of the 11th was Brigadier T.E.D'O. Snow.

The task of rebuilding the brigade's spirit and inspiring confidence in the Fifth Armoured fell to Hoffmeister when he took over as GOC from Burns in March. Men of the First Division had jeeringly labelled the Fifth, with its maroon shoulder patch, 'the Mighty Maroon Machine' after the disaster on the Riccio. Hoffmeister visited the units, inspected their quarters and their weapons, and talked frankly to the men. He probed for problems and searched out the weak leaders and replaced them. He ran large training exercises for each battalion and was right in front, teaching the infantry how to 'lean into' a barrage.[63] Morale quickly began to rise after that, and the Fifth Armoured was soon on its way to becoming one of the great professional fighting formations in Canadian history, 'Hoffy's Mighty Maroon Machine.'

For the I Canadian Corps, the war in Italy, small-scale actions aside, settled down into a period of stasis for several months after Ortona. The weather was miserable, a winter of snow, cold, trench foot, frostbite, and mud. So I Canadian Corps Headquarters stepped up a paper blizzard and tried to impose stiffer discipline, as the senior officers and privates alike complained about the new and stuffy formality that was in stark contrast to the easy informality of the Eighth Army.[64] The units absorbed their new replacements, the men trained, and the wounded in body and mind recovered. Some went to Britain or home to Canada, but most who had broken down in battle went to base hospitals for intensive treatment or served time in non-combat labour units and then returned warily to duty.

The war was entering a new phase. In Russia the Red Army sent the Wehrmacht reeling westward in a series of titanic battles. In Britain, General Dwight Eisenhower and General Sir Bernard Montgomery made their final preparations for the invasion of France. And in Italy, General Sir Harold Alexander's Allied armies now understood that the plan to tie down enemy forces had not worked as intended. In January 1944, for example, the enemy had twenty-one divisions in Italy compared with nineteen Allied divisions. But the German divisions were at two-thirds strength, six battalions instead of nine, and its air force was tiny. The Allies had air superiority and far more guns, tanks, and supplies. The Wehrmacht, in other words, had succeeded in pinning superior forces on perfect defensive terrain to fight a delaying action.[65] Alexander's armies nonetheless readied themselves to drive the Germans out of their prepared defences and to liberate Rome. In this struggle, the Canadians were to play their full part.

The Allied intention was to drive up the Liri valley, breaking through the Gustav and Hitler Line defences. I Canadian Corps, moved from the Adriatic to central Italy, had a key role in the Eighth Army's attack, though efforts by Allied 'spooks' tried to convince the enemy that the Canadians were training at Salerno for an amphibious assault. In fact, the two Canadian divisions and the corps staff were training hard for the coming attack, the first action by a Canadian corps since November 1918. And well they might prepare. The formidable German defences, fortunately not yet complete after five months of work, made use of the geographical advantages the enemy had, supplemented by mine belts a hundred yards deep, concrete and steel machine-gun emplacements, pillboxes, the turrets of huge Panther tanks embedded in concrete as anti-tank weapons, as well as anti-tank ditches and barriers.[66] Moreover, the enemy planned for a defence in depth. The weak point for the enemy was the Anzio beachhead to its rear that, if the Allies could break out, threatened either to force a withdrawal or to cut off the enemy completely. The Anzio forces included the 1st Special Service Force, a joint American and Canadian unit that fought with great distinction.

Alexander's plan called for the British Eighth and the American Fifth armies to open their attack on the Gustav Line on May 11, coordinated with a breakout from Anzio a few days later, the whole carefully timed to allow for the concentration of Allied air power. The Eighth Army's commander, Lieutenant-General Sir Oliver Leese, planned to use I Canadian Corps as his reserve, his intention being to commit it on May 14. The 1st Canadian Armoured Brigade, supporting Indian Army units, was to be in action from the outset.

The first day of battle went badly. The rushing River Gari swept away boats and men, and the enemy defences recovered from their surprise quickly. Leese's attack gained only a small bridgehead and, over the next two days it slowly expanded, though at high cost. Other Allied troops made better progress, notably the French General Juin's Algerian and Moroccan divisions. As a result, the enemy began to withdraw from the Gustav Line back to the Hitler Line on May 16. At this juncture, Leese ordered the First Canadian Division into battle.[67]

Though the main German force was pulling back, the customary rearguards resisted the Canadian advance strongly. On May 16 the 1st Brigade met great difficulty in overcoming German resistance at Pignataro, earning Leese's displeasure. Vokes called for a determined push forward to the Hitler Line, and the next day and night the 3rd Brigade, now commanded by Brigadier 'Paolo' Bernatchez, who had replaced Gibson the month before, moved well forward; the Van Doos, in particular, made good gains.[68] Spry's 1st Brigade again faced heavy fighting, and the Hastings and Prince Edward Regiment took the entire day to overcome Panzer Grenadiers holding a gully at Spalla Bassa. The 48th Highlanders, their supporting British tanks largely wiped out, pushed on, and one platoon led by Lieutenant N.A. Ballard stormed a key hill. Ballard himself subdued a German officer with his fists, while his men killed or captured twenty of the enemy and their vehicles. A 75 mm gun on the hill was put out of action, and Ballard won the Distinguished Service Order, a rare award to a junior officer and very close to the Victoria Cross.

The Canadians were now within 3 miles of the main enemy defences on the Hitler Line, and their task was to maintain pressure on the enemy. On May 20 Leese ordered the corps to stage a set-piece attack to crack the line near Pontecorvo. The carefully planned attack, launched on May 23 by the 2nd and 3rd brigades supported by British armour, followed after strong probing attacks. The 48th Highlanders, for example, hit hard at an ersatz battalion, a composite German formation, and almost made it through the Hitler Line and into Pontecorvo.[69] Estimates of German strength in front of the division were only 800 men, but the fixed defences remained very strong, and the Canadians had the task of getting through them.

After a 4 a.m. reveille and a cold breakfast, the attackers moved up to the start line. As they approached German paratroops from behind the fire of 810 guns, the heaviest artillery barrage yet employed by the Allies in the war, the Seaforth Highlanders and the PPCLI on the right of the Canadian advance encountered immediate and heavy fire from six-barrelled, rocket-projecting *Nebelwerfers*, artillery, and machine guns. It was 'more intense than anything the battalion had known,' Seaforths officer Robert McDougall wrote later, 'worse by far than the fire in front of Ortona'[70] The Princess Pats nonetheless made good progress, but their supporting British tanks had difficulty crossing a minefield and fell victim to the Panther turrets sunk in 3 feet of concrete with a 360 degree field of fire, and with the ground cleared to maximize the killing zone. The PPCLI casualties mounted, and the advance stalled in the Germans' barbed wire under a rain of mortar shells and attacks by German tanks. The 'slaughter was indescribable,' the regiment's historian noted, and one soldier recalled that this battle 'was the first time I really saw our own Canadian boys really massacred, especially PPCLI.'[71] The Princess Pats had a fighting strength of seventy-seven at day's end. The Seaforths, their supporting armour stopped by mines and anti-tank guns, pressed on, and the remnants of four companies, just a hundred men, consolidated on the objective. Their PIATs without ammunition, the powerless Seaforths could do little when three panzers rolled forward, shooting up everything with their machine guns. The remnants of the battalion were simply overwhelmed.[72] The Loyal Edmonton Regiment moved out at 8 p.m. in an attempt to exploit the gains of the day, but the Germans cut the attackers to pieces on their wire. The 2nd Brigade had made some progress, but its attack had petered out in the face of enemy strength; it was now under attack by German tanks, and anti-tank guns had not yet been moved forward.

The 1st Brigade on the left followed up on the 48th's probing attack and, with the Hasty Ps, the two Ontario regiments secured Point 106, a mile from Pontecorvo. The fighting was 'not too tough. Not for the 1st Brigade anyway,' RCR company commander Strome Galloway recalled, the costs light only in comparison with those borne by the 2nd Brigade.[73] The RCR took the town the next morning.

The 3rd Brigade, however, had even more success in the centre. The Carlton and Yorks reached their first objective on schedule, their supporting tanks overcoming anti-tank guns and panzers. Vokes delayed the advance of the West Novas, intended for the second phase of the attack, because the GOC continued to hope that the 2nd Brigade could move forward at the same time. At midday, finally, Vokes won General Burns's agreement to throw everything he had into support of the 3rd Brigade. Tanks of the Three Rivers Regiment and the Van Doos moved forward to support the West Nova Scotia Regiment in a renewed assault. The infantry moved rapidly forward behind the artillery barrage, progressing so quickly that enemy shells passed harmlessly overhead. A German counterattack appeared to succeed, but the Panzer Grenadiers themselves soon became POWs of the West Novas. The Royal 22e moved through the Hitler Line, proceeding 1200 yards north of the West Novas, and firmly established itself. The 3rd Brigade had suffered 165 killed and wounded in cracking the Hitler Line.

The battered Seaforths, however, faced repeated attacks by enemy tanks in their hardest day of fighting thus far – a terrible commentary for a battalion that had cleared half of Ortona – and, without anti-tank weapons, was all but destroyed. Fifty-four of their men became prisoners. The Loyal Eddies had only 161 men left. The 2nd Brigade had 543 casualties, the highest toll for a Canadian brigade in the Italian campaign. Nonetheless, the Hitler Line had been breached, and the 5th Canadian Armoured Division now moved in to exploit the gains of May 23.

The division's task was to advance to the River Melfa, 5 miles beyond Pontecorvo, and then to the village of Ceprano, a further 5 miles on. General Hoffmeister gave the first objective to his 5th Armoured Brigade and the second to the 11th Infantry Brigade, though there was much regrouping to achieve the proper balance for the attack. After heavy fighting and many casualties, the division did the job. The chief problems were two. First, operating from his own tank or a jeep, the GOC had a tendency to go far forward, leaving his headquarters and its communications behind and his staff to direct the battle. The troopers loved to see the boss and took encouragement from his fearless presence at the front, but it was a problem nonetheless.[74] Second,

Hoffmeister's staff was not yet as smoothly functioning as it would later be. This deficiency showed up at once when the Fifth Armoured Division took to the roads in the Liri valley, or rather, the one main road for which it was in competition with the other four divisions from the Eighth Army. (One Canadian battalion CO recalled one traffic jam being caused by a British truck with a piano on board that blocked a road!)[75] The resulting traffic jams slowed the pursuit of the enemy, infuriated Leese, and put Burns into difficulties. After all, it took 1000 gallons of gas to move an armoured division 1 mile and, if oil tankers could not get through, every attack ground to a halt.

Still, everyone from Alexander and Leese on down cheered how well Vokes's and Hoffmeister's divisions had fought. 'The troops fought magnificently,' Leese said of I Canadian Corps, 'but were hampered by the lack of co-ordination and control from above.'[76] The first part of the comment was surely accurate, but it was Leese's own plan that called for five divisions and their 13,000 vehicles, tanks, self-propelled guns, scout cars, and armoured cars to use the single highway up the Liri valley.[77]

The recriminations were all in the future when Hoffmeister's division set off to its first divisional attack in the morning of May 24. The GOC had directed Brigadier Des Smith of the 5th Armoured Brigade to cobble together two battle groups of tanks, anti-tank weapons, engineers, and infantry, the latter in either carriers or trucks. Their attacks went well, though the extensive vineyards slowed the tanks by tangling them in the wire used to hold up the vines. Shermans of the British Columbia Dragoons came out roughly even in the first battle with what one BCD officer called 'the most enormous tank I had ever seen.'[78] The Nazis' Panther tanks, used for the first time on the Italian front, destroyed four Shermans for a loss of three of the behemoths.

The Lord Strathcona's Horse reconnaissance troop of the second battle group, led by Lieutenant Edward Perkins, reached the Melfa in mid-afternoon and, with great skill and initiative, established a precarious bridgehead across it with three tiny Honey tanks and fifteen men. Other squadrons of the regiment fared less well. In a battle with Panthers, they discovered that the Sherman's 75 mm gun could not ordinarily penetrate the beautifully designed Panther's sloping armour on the turret and the tank's front. As a result, the Straths lost seventeen of their under-gunned tanks while knocking out five, not all Panthers.[79] Even so, they and the Governor General's Horse Guards still swept over and through most of the opposition they encountered. One LSH troop commander took seventy prisoners in a house and captured the Germans' code books to boot.

The crux of the action now passed to the mechanized infantry of the Westminster Regiment, which went into battle on its vehicles but dismounted at the Melfa and crossed it in company strength, providing desperately needed assistance to Perkins and the Strathconas' reconnaissance troops, who were hanging on by their fingernails. Digging in quickly, Major J.K. Mahony's men prepared for the worst. They had only PIATs and no anti-tank guns, but they drove off an attack by four tanks and fifty infantry. A second enemy attack failed when Private J.W. Culling destroyed a tank and killed its crew single-handedly. Heavily shelled by 88 mm guns, losing men rapidly, Mahony ordered his platoons in closer to his farmhouse headquarters as night fell. Brigade headquarters struggled to get reinforcements forward, but men began to cross the river only about 9 p.m., as did eight anti-tank guns that were man-handled across the Melfa.

The Westminster's company had saved the day, and Mahony, wounded three times, earned the second Victoria Cross of the Italian campaign. A part-time correspondent for the Vancouver *Province* in New Westminster before the war, Jack Mahony was 'a nice guy, mild mannered, soft-spoken, who would never hurt anyone,' Peter Stursberg of the CBC recalled. 'I could not have imagined him as a fighting officer and leader in battle, which just shows how mistaken one can be from appearances.'[80] The Strathcona reconnaissance troop commander, Lieutenant Perkins, was also recommended for a VC, but had to settle for the Distinguished Service Order.

The next day the 11th Brigade entered the battle and greatly expanded the bridgehead, but the pursuit, for so it was now, was hampered by Brigadier Snow's apparent inability to keep control of his battalions and get them moving forward.[81] Tanks ran out of gas and the infantry stopped moving, but Ceprano fell on May 27 and the troops soon cleared the first enemy delaying positions beyond the town, some fighting furiously, others eager to surrender. The Liri River was the next major obstacle, and the Fifth Armoured's engineers, not yet as skilled at throwing Bailey bridges over obstacles as were the First Division's engineers, experienced delays. This and the traffic congestion delayed the pursuit, but now the way to Rome had opened up. The U.S. Fifth

Army had been ordered to take the city, which it did on June 4. The Canadians had played a major role in breaking the Hitler Line, but in the recriminations that followed, some of the lustre disappeared.

The casualties had been very heavy: I Canadian Corps had lost close to 3300 killed and wounded and some 4000 sick and injured in three weeks of fighting. The Irish Regiment's padre wrote that he had a service for the fifty-six men from the unit killed in the Hitler Line struggle: 'It is not too high they say for the work done, but to me just one is too many.'[82] One wounded Irish, however, had been spared when Sergeant Pearce Reutz of the 24th Field Ambulance carried him on his back for 2 miles to the Irish Regiment lines.[83]

Fear in battle infected many soldiers, the 'stomach in knots, bowels loosened, bladder emptying, legs gelatinous, the sheer fetal-position, mind-unstabling terror of being under artillery or mortar fire,' or so American writer John Gregory Dunne brilliantly put it.[84] Even worse for most soldiers was the thought that their fear might endanger their friends, their brothers-in-arms. Despite their best efforts, many simply could not overcome their panic and froze or broke and ran. The numbers so affected were huge. Neuropsychiatric, or battle exhaustion, cases amounted to just under a quarter of all battle casualties in the infantry units of I Canadian Corps during the battle. This number badly frightened Canadian commanders, who worried about demoralized soldiers infecting their comrades with fear.[85] The difficulty was that for all soldiers, as Wilfrid Owen put it so well in the Great War, 'Courage leaked, as sand / From the best sand-bags after years of rain.'[86]

Perhaps better leaders could deal with the problem, and changes followed. Sharply criticized by his Eighth Army superiors and not admired by his subordinates, Burns was saved only by direct intervention from Canadian Military Headquarters, London, and he had to replace some of his key staff officers.[87] Hoffmeister's two brigade commanders also changed: Snow was sacked, Smith made Brigadier General Staff at corps headquarters, and the addition of a second infantry brigade soon followed to give the Fifth Division a better balance.

Rome was the first Axis capital to be liberated, but the victory, important though it be, was immediately overshadowed by the invasion of France. D-Day was June 6, and the world's attention thereafter focused totally on Normandy. Italy almost instantly became a sideshow, the Mediterranean theatre ever after shortchanged in reinforcements, equipment, and supplies.

British Member of Parliament Lady Astor stupidly called the men of the Eighth Army 'D-Day Dodgers,' literally implying that they were slackers, almost deliberately avoiding the real war in France. That stung – as the bitter lyrics of 'We Are the D-Day Dodgers' suggest – and, ever after, veterans of the Italian campaign sought in vain for the recognition their achievements merited.

For the Canadians of the First and Fifth divisions and the 1st Armoured Brigade, Italy remained their area of operations for another eight months. They had learned to fight and beat the Germans at a cost of 13,000 casualties to early June 1944, and in Italy they and their commanders, not without difficulty, became a truly professional and proficient force. After Ortona, after the Hitler Line, both divisions were veteran formations. Farley Mowat's father, a Great War infantry officer, responded to a letter from his son in the Hasty Ps praising the extraordinary Canadian achievement in cracking the Hitler Line with some elegaic thoughts of his own: 'The moment of elation, which goes deeper than any man could express, and that feeling of oneness with the finest of mankind will live with you forever ... nothing can ever take that moment of insight and understanding from you. And this is a gift reserved in its fullness for the infantrymen ... from total unity with one's fellow men (not just with individuals) – at their absolute best.'[88]

eight

INTO BATTLE:
NORTHWEST EUROPE AND ITALY
June 1944–May 1945

'Drove through Deventer,' wrote Lieutenant Donald Pearce of the North Nova Scotia Highlanders on April 4, 1945, 'a good-sized modern city in the heart of the Netherlands, an hour after it was liberated. A freshly liberated city feels and gives off a strong emotion. There is absolutely nothing like it, nothing to which it can be compared, for it is something coming from the hearts of 30,000 people who are all touched by an irrational joy, animal and human. You can feel freedom. It exists. The smells and sounds of battle were still in the streets ...' he said. 'But the people knew it was really over, and poured into the streets in throngs, surging this way and that, demonstrating their freedom by a happy aimlessness.' By night, 'nearly all the soldiers had found girls, or were found by them; and Deventer spent its first day and night of liberation in a kind of mad Elysium.'[1]

—◦◦◦—

The fight for freedom was what the Second World War was about, and the struggle was vicious in its intensity. The fighting in Italy was matched – and exceeded – in fury by the invasion of France, the liberation of the Low Countries, and the attack across the Rhine into Germany itself. Hitler's armies had some three-quarters of their strength on the Eastern Front, but the Russians relentlessly pushed them westward in huge, costly struggles. At the same time,

Allied bombers methodically destroyed the Reich from the air. All the while the Nazis continued to resist, until their hateful regime was ultimately erased, but only after millions more died.

Canadians at home, and many British, American, and some Canadian historians since, have often asked the question: Why did the First Canadian Army not instantly operate in action in Northwest Europe with the efficiency and effect of the 1914–18 Canadian Corps? The Canadians were slow at Falaise, we are told, allowing substantial numbers of German troops to escape the pocket. They were not as fierce as they might have been at the Scheldt, so some say, or in the Rhineland. What, if anything, went wrong?

The first and easiest answer is that General Harry Crerar, the commander of First Canadian Army in Northwest Europe, was not Sir Arthur Currie. Crerar was competent enough, a superb staff officer who did not make serious mistakes, but there was absolutely no spark of genius there. Guy Simonds, commander of the II Canadian Corps in Northwest Europe and, when Crerar was ill, acting army commander, had that genius, but his rigid, complex plans sometimes went beyond the abilities of mere mortals and still-untried units.

The real answer to the differences between the Canadian Corps and the First Canadian Army lies in the combination of time with accrued experience and expertise. In the Great War the First Canadian Division was in action from early 1915, and the Second, Third, and Fourth Divisions arrived at regular intervals, the last going into the line in late 1916. In other words, all the divisions in the corps had at least two years' experience – two years to master trench warfare, and, in the Hundred Days, open warfare too. The First Division provided a cadre of experienced men to the Second, the Second to the Third, and the Third to the Fourth. The experience learned was shared, easing the transition from training to action.

How different it was in the Second World War! Apart from Hong Kong and Dieppe – where in Hong Kong all were killed or captured and in Dieppe there were few tactical lessons other than courage to be learned – no Canadian formation saw action until July 1943, three-and-a-half years after the First Canadian Division arrived in Britain. The Fifth Canadian Armoured Division did not go into the line in Italy until early 1944. In other words, neither of the divisions to fight in the Mediterranean saw even two years of action in all. Although some effort was made to bring small numbers of officers and non-commissioned officers from Italy to the divisions readying themselves in Britain for Northwest Europe, this was only a minor increment of experience. The Third Division that participated in the Normandy campaign had eleven months of battle experience (from June 6, 1944, to May 8, 1945); the Second Division and the Fourth Canadian Armoured Division had a month or two less in action.

Compared with the Great War, the Canadians in the 1939–45 campaigns had comparatively little battle experience. The Second World War, moreover, was more complex, more fluid, and even more lethal than the earlier war, and the skills required of soldiers were more demanding. These factors, more than anything else, account for the difficulties the officers and men of the First Canadian Army experienced in battle.

The Canadians, in fact, performed well in action, certainly as well as or better than British or American troops with similar battle experience. The Canadians fought with great skill and courage in France from D-Day to the closing of the Falaise Gap; they liberated the Channel ports and cleared the Scheldt, a critical step to victory; they crossed the Rhine; and they gave the Netherlands back its freedom, winning the eternal gratitude of the Dutch. They learned in action what their training in Canada and Britain had not taught them: how to fight against what was likely the most skilled army of modern times and how to defeat it. They earned the respect of their countrymen, their Allies, and their enemies.[2] They deserve the respect of historians.

The long-awaited invasion of France on June 6, 1944, was a massive undertaking that had been in planning since the Anglo-French debacle of 1940. Dieppe had been one step in that process, a disastrous one that helped to persuade the Americans, who were eager to invade, that more time was needed to prepare. One key to a successful attack was more and better landing craft, but first they had to be built. Another was more divisions and better training in assault landings, as well as more naval and air support for any invasion. The successful invasions of North Africa in November 1942 and of Sicily in July 1943 were useful tests of doctrine, and the LSTs – the Landing Ships Tank that could put up to twenty tanks onto a beach – moved off the ways in increasing numbers, along with other specialized craft.

Many questions had to be determined. Where should the attack occur? At the Pas de Calais, closest to Britain? or in Normandy, further afield but with somewhat lesser defences? Normandy ended up as the choice. Who should lead the attack? And how much strength had to be devoted to it? General McNaughton had wanted the First Canadian Army to be in the vanguard, but this was politically impossible. The British and the Americans, with thirty-four divisions in all in Britain, were going to be present in force, and Canada had to settle for as much representation as it could get in the assault. Certainly the Canadian generals had no input into the planning of D-Day or, indeed, into any wartime strategy.[3] Initially the planners of Overlord, as the D-Day operation was code-named, thought in terms of a three-division front, but Generals Dwight Eisenhower and Bernard Montgomery insisted that at least five seaborne and three airborne divisions had to constitute the first wave if the Nazi defences, directed by Field Marshal Erwin Rommel, were to be over-come. In early May 1944 Eisenhower, the Supreme Commander, fixed June 5 as the invasion date, the time when the tides would be right.

By this date the Third Canadian Division and the 2nd Canadian Armoured Brigade had been chosen for the seaborne attack, and the II Canadian Corps and the First Canadian Army labelled as follow-on forces to build up Montgomery's 21st Army Group. The army, commanded by Lieutenant-General Harry Crerar, consisted of the three divisions in England; other formations from other nations would be attached to it as necessary, at least until the I Canadian Corps in Italy reunited with the II Canadian Corps. Lieutenant-General Guy Simonds commanded the corps, consisting of Second, Third, and Fourth divisions, and he had swept in from Italy with a new broom, changing senior officers freely and putting in command those in whom he had confidence. His changes were necessary, not least because they conveyed a sense of urgency as the invasion drew near.[4]

The Third Canadian Division, commanded by Major-General Rod Keller, had spent months on its special invasion training regimen. Keller's staff began working with I British Corps, under which it would initially serve, in November 1943; the infantry battalions practised and repractised, their exercises growing in size and complexity. The 7th Brigade, commanded by Brigadier Harry Foster, the Permanent Force officer who had led the 13th Brigade in its assault on unoccupied Kiska, consisted of the Royal Winnipeg Rifles, the Regina Rifles, and British Columbia's Canadian Scottish. The 8th Brigade, led by Brigadier K.G. Blackader, encompassed Toronto's Queen's Own Rifles, Le Régiment de la Chaudière, and New Brunswick's North Shore Regiment. The 9th Brigade, under Brigadier D.G. Cunningham, had the Highland Light Infantry and the Stormont, Dundas, and Glengarry Highlanders, both from Ontario, and the North Nova Scotia Highlanders. The 2nd Armoured Brigade, which comprised the Fort Garry Horse, the Sherbrooke Fusiliers, and the 1st Hussars, had Brigadier R.A. Wyman as its commander. Wyman had led the 1st Armoured Brigade in Sicily and into Italy, and he supervised the training of his two assault regiments as they practised with Duplex Drive tanks, the ingenious flotation device that let tanks leave their landing craft and paddle to shore (thus preventing the landing craft becoming sitting ducks close inshore), and also waterproofed every one of their vehicles.

The Canadian plan called for a two-brigade assault, the 7th and 8th brigades with the Shermans of the 1st Hussars and the Fort Garry Horse landing on Juno Beach with its villages of Courseulles-sur-Mer, Bernières-sur-Mer, and St Aubin-sur-Mer. The 9th Brigade and the Sherbrooke Fusiliers would follow once the initial lodgement had been made. The beaches were gently sloping, with no natural obstacles that might prevent the invaders from moving inland. The plan for the first day called for the Third Division to seize an area that extended 10 miles inland, including the high ground just to the west of Caën.

Everything that could be done had been done, and the invading forces moved towards the British coast at the end of May. On June 1 the first Canadians began to board their ships, and by June 4 everything was ready – except the weather. A large storm blew into the English Channel and an anguished Eisenhower ordered a twenty-four-hour delay. The next day the weather remained bad, though there were signs of clearing. If the assault had to be postponed again, there was a month's delay before the tides again would be right. Eisenhower gave the order to proceed, and seasick Canadian, British, and American soldiers set off to liberate Europe.

'We attack in the morning,' Lieutenant Tony Ladas of Ottawa told his platoon from Le Régiment de la Chaudière on board HMCS *Prince David*. 'There was a spontaneous cheer,' recorded journalist Gerald Clark in his memoirs, 'and a common expression swept everyone's face: joy. But was it really joy? Or was it protective coating camouflaging another emotion? Who could be certain? Who could know that Tony Ladas was soon to die?'[5]

The Allies landed in the early morning hours of June 6. Paratroopers, including the 1st Canadian Parachute Battalion, which had critical bridges to take and hold, landed on the flanks of the seaborne force and cleared the way,[6] while a massive air and naval armada tried to bomb, strafe, and shell every known position on the beach and inland. So heavy did the bombardment seem from the landing craft that soldiers approaching shore wondered how anyone could have survived. They did not have long to discover that the bombing and shelling had had little effect on the enemy's concrete defences and that Typhoons, assigned to hit the beach, had their missions almost completely disrupted by the heavy cloud. A later air force study amazingly concluded that no enemy positions had been hit by bombs. The naval gunfire was not much more effective against the German emplacements.[7] The success of the landings entirely depended on the courage of the attackers.

The Queen's Own touched down on Juno Beach at 8:12 a.m., twenty-seven minutes late, the sea so rough that the supporting Shermans had to be landed directly on the beach rather than floated to shore. The infantrymen were in five assault boats per company, with two companies in the first wave, and had to attack a 1500-yard frontage of beach. 'Ten boats stretched out over fifteen hundred yards is not really a whole lot of assault force,' wrote Company Sergeant Major Charles Martin of the QOR. 'None of us really grasped at that point, spread across such a large beach front, just how thin on the ground we were. Each of the ten boatloads had become an independent fighting unit. None had communication with the other.'[8] The enemy was at the alert, the landing occurring in full daylight, and the infantry came under heavy fire from positions that had either been successfully hidden from air observation or, more likely, escaped the shelling completely. An 88 mm gun, the German weapon that had already killed so many Canadians in Italy, did its work of death once more and almost eliminated a platoon from 'A' Company, commanded by Major Elliot Dalton, before it was put out of action. 'B' Company, commanded by Dalton's brother Charles, ran into even heavier resistance from a large concrete bunker, losing almost half its complement in the race for the cover of the seawall. Dalton, hit in the head and bleeding profusely, knocked out a pillbox and led his riflemen across the beach. The North Shore Regiment faced a similar situation – a hundred-man concrete bunker, 4 to 6 feet thick, completely untouched by the supporting gunfire and air bombing – but they overcame it with the help of Fort Garry tanks.[9] The reserve battalion, the Chaudières, ran into mines offshore, and men had to swim for it. They regrouped and cleared Beny-sur-Mer, hailed by the few Frenchman who emerged from cover as compatriots. Just behind the infantry came the guns, the 14th Field Regiment, which had begun firing from 5 miles out. The regiment was using 105 mm guns mounted on tank chassis, instead of its usual 25-pounders (and did so until August), because the artillery could not be waterproofed enough to make it to shore. The gunners carried extra ammunition for the infantry, as well as mortar bombs and land mines on their self-propelled vehicles, making them very dangerous for the crews if they were hit. Three of the four 'artillery tanks' in a single troop, hit by 88 mm shells from a dug-in and well-camouflaged gun, blew up just beyond Beny.[10]

The Regina Rifles and the 1st Hussars, its tanks swimming and frequently sinking on the run to the shore, landed, only to be faced by an enemy strong-point – 35 feet across, with concrete 4 feet thick. Inside were three machine-gun posts, a swivelling anti-tank gun, and concrete shelters for the defenders. The Rifles used the Hussars' Shermans to knock out the enemy guns one by one, and the men moved off the beach and into Courseulles. One of the Reginas' reserve companies ran into mines in the water, and only forty-nine survivors made it to shore. 'C' Company's Officer Commanding, Major C.S.T. Tubb, remembered standing beside a Hussars tank and planning the next move, when two Germans riding a motorcycle and sidecar suddenly appeared on the road in front. The driver tried a quick U-turn. 'But he was too late. The tank turret swung slowly and deliberately around, its fixed automatic gun came to bear, opened fire and the motorcycle crashed into the ditch. Both occupants were killed.' The whole affair took just seconds, but somehow, Tubb remembered, it seemed to have 'the strange quality of a slow motion film.'[11]

The company of the Canadian Scottish touching down on the 'Mike' sector of Juno Beach had an easy time, as naval gunfire had destroyed the German gun there. But the Royal Winnipeg Rifles, landing to the west of Courseulles, found that the preliminary bombardment had 'failed to kill a single German soldier or silence one weapon.'[12] The 'Little Black Devils,' as they were called, were shelled in the water and then had to fight their way through minefields and the town, losing heavily in the process. The reserve battalion, the Canadian Scottish, landed without much difficulty and moved inland.

The Third Division had done extraordinarily well, despite the failure of the preliminary bombardment to knock the Wehrmacht defenders out of action.

For the Canadians, D-Day, though costly, was less so than planners had feared: 340 killed and 574 wounded, or about half the predicted ghastly toll. Most important, the brigades were ashore and moving towards their objectives. One troop of tanks actually reached its goal, the only Allied unit to do so on D-Day. The British and Americans had also successfully secured their lodgements, and the effort now was to link the beachheads and prepare for the inevitable enemy counterattacks.

The Germans, delayed by air attacks and the conviction that Normandy was a feint to mask the real objective of the Pas de Calais, were slow to attack. Postwar analysis of the effects of the air attacks on the enemy army minimized the losses; contemporary evidence, however, indicated that the Germans believed that Allied air superiority, and especially Typhoon attacks in Normandy, were devastatingly effective.[13] Whatever the reasons, the Allies had put more than 150,000 men and a vast array of equipment into France on the first day. The slow enemy response allowed a crucial period of hours to establish firm positions and then to move inland. And there the Allies found the Germans. The first Canadian troops to bump into the enemy behind the beaches were men of the North Novas and the Chaudières. That night they faced attack by mechanized infantry and suffered some losses. The next morning the Canadians began to advance towards Carpiquet airfield near Caën. At Buron, a company of North Novas and a squadron of Sherbrooke tanks destroyed two 88 mm guns. At Authie, a few hundred yards away, the town fell easily, but the enemy, teenagers from the 12th SS Panzer Division with good military skills, imbued with Nazi doctrine, and well led by experienced officers and NCOs, soon appeared in strength.* The North Novas, their flanks open and with neither artillery support nor reinforcement from their brigade, began to pull back to regroup, and the Germans caught them in Authie and Buron. The young SS soldiers overran a company of North Novas, and their Panther and Tiger tanks did terrible damage to the Shermans. The Canadian armour now hur-

---

* General Bernard Montgomery had told the Allied war correspondents on May 16 that the German 'technically ... knows how to use his weapons superbly. Technically, he is admirably trained, perhaps better than our own men.' Gerald Clark, *No Mud on the Back Seat: Memoirs of a Reporter* (Montreal, 1995), 58.

ried back to the 9th Brigade 'fortress,' losing more than 300 men and 28 tanks destroyed or damaged. The Sherman tanks, 10 feet high and lightly armoured, burst into flame all too easily, earning the bitter nickname of 'Ronsons,' after the popular brand of cigarette lighter. (The enemy called the tanks 'Tommy cookers,' not without reason, and Allied tank crews lived in constant fear of being burnt to death.) The Sherman Firefly, armed with a high-velocity 17-pounder gun, could knock out the best enemy tanks, but, with its distinctive gun, it was an obvious target for enemy gunners. Moreover, there was only one Firefly to each troop of men, too few to give the armoured regiments a fighting chance against Tigers or Panthers.[14]

Many North Novas and Sherbrookes had to surrender, and that night the thirty-four-year-old SS regimental commander, Standartenführer Kurt Meyer, either ordered or acquiesced in the murder of twenty-three prisoners of war at the Abbaye d'Ardenne, his field headquarters. The same SS division and the same and other senior officers committed similar atrocities in the days following, most at the Château d'Audrieu and notably against soldiers of the Stormont, Dundas, and Glengarry Highlanders and the Royal Winnipeg Rifles.[15] Some 106 prisoners of war, mostly Canadians and a few British, had been murdered. The Waffen SS leaders had been schooled in brutality on the Eastern Front.

Canadian soldiers undoubtedly committed atrocities of their own in Normandy, and after. A Fort Garry Horse officer recalled that one of his tanks fired on a group of Germans under a white flag a few days after D-Day: 'It was a cruel, senseless, and stupid act. Not only because the Germans were surrendering, but also because the survivors immediately went to ground, forcing us to spend another hour clearing them out of the wood.'[16] There is a clear difference, however, between this story and the 12th SS murders. Those killings were almost certainly ordered by a senior officer and carried out at his headquarters. There is only hearsay evidence that any such order was ever uttered by a Canadian senior officer,* and killings of German POWs were almost cer-

---

* In late May, 1940, as the First Canadian Division prepared to go to France, General McNaughton apparently told some officers that 'it's going to be a sticky business, you must be absolutely ruthless ... tell the men we are not particularly interested in prisoners' (Gen Harry Foster Papers, Halifax, Diary, May 23, 1940). How much weight should be placed on this comment is uncertain; in the event, nothing came of it because the one Canadian brigade that reached France did not come into contact with the enemy.

tainly random, senseless acts or else committed in the frenzy of battle. A soldier who shoots at attacking troops and, outflanked, puts up his hands after killing two or three is not always likely to receive the benefit of the laws of war. Another soldier recalled saying to a friend whose brother had been killed in action, 'I will never take a German prisoner.'[17] Such reactions are understandable. The 12th SS's calculated acts were qualitatively different.[18]*

The first encounter after D-Day had gone to the Germans, and Carpiquet airfield, almost within view on June 7, would not fall to the Canadians for a month. That was the way the battle went for the next few days. The 12th SS hit the Royal Winnipeg Rifles and the Regina Rifles hard on June 8, as up to twenty-two Panther tanks penetrated right into the Reginas' headquarters defences. A counterattack by the Canadian Scottish, while successful, was costly. After only three days, the men of the Third Division knew what the First Division had already learned in Sicily: the Germans were excellent, ruthless soldiers. Still, the division had held its ground in the face of heavy attacks, and the 12th SS's aim of driving it into the sea had failed. The SS had lost heavily, too, in a succession of piecemeal and small-scale attacks that Brigadier Foster described as 'launched without any semblance of tactical sense.' The enemy, he added, 'flung himself straight against the strongest points and utterly to exploit the undoubted weakness of his opponent's position. All his attacks were beaten off.'[19] The SS, excellent and effective soldiers as they were, made mistakes.

So did the Canadians. Hastily prepared attacks at Rots and Le Mesnil-Patry on June 11 were costly failures, as the SS pounded the tanks with 88 mm gunfire and struck the infantry hard with mortar and machine-gun fire, inflicting heavy casualties. The armoured regiment engaged at Le Mesnil, the 1st Hussars, had thirty-seven tanks destroyed; this regiment lost eighty killed and wounded, while the Queen's Own Rifles, who had gone into battle riding the tanks, lost fifty-five. Again, the 12th SS murdered many of the Canadians they captured.[20]

---

* POWs felt a certain guilt at their situation: Should and could they have resisted more? Strikingly, the numbers of POWs from different Canadian regiments varied widely, from 0.2 per cent of total casualties to 21.4 per cent, a product of circumstances certainly, but also possibly of cohesion and training. Reinforcements, new to a unit and without the links of acquaintance and community, might have been more susceptible to surrender. See Jonathan Vance, 'Captured in the Victory Campaign: Surrenders of Canadian Troops in North-West Europe, 1944–1945,' in T.O. Kelly, ed., *World War II: Variants and Visions* (Collingdale, Penn., 1999), 125ff.

Le Mesnil was the last Canadian battle until July, for newly landed British divisions took over from the Third Canadian. In just six days of fighting, the division and its attached armour lost 1017 men killed in action and more than 1700 wounded. Still, the bridgeheads were secure and formed a continuous line, though the advance inland on all fronts was much slower than planners had hoped. Altogether, the Canadians had played a major part in this desperate struggle.

The headquarters of the First Canadian Army and the II Canadian Corps now crossed to France, but did not immediately become operational. The crowded beachhead meant that they had to wait their chance. The arrival of the Second Canadian Infantry Division in early July let Simonds's corps get to work.[21]

Montgomery's plan, far clearer in his recollection than it seemed at the time, was to hold the Germans on his front with most of their armour, making it somewhat easier for the Americans, stuck in the *bocage* to the west, to break out. A series of British and Canadian attacks aimed to fix the Germans in place and to threaten Caën, a good-sized city on the River Orne. A British attack on June 26 ran into heavy opposition, though rocket-firing Typhoons of the Royal Air Force devastated the defending panzers. Then it was the turn of the 8th Brigade of the Third Division: its task was to take Carpiquet airfield.

The airfield, reportedly held by only 150 men of the 12th SS in well-prepared and camouflaged bunkers, was to be assaulted by four battalions – the entire brigade plus the Royal Winnipeg Rifles and the Fort Garry Horse. Advancing through a wheat field behind a barrage, the Canadians ran into machine-gun fire from large concrete bunkers and heavy artillery. Men struggled to kill each other in the airfield's ruins, and the North Novas had their heaviest casualties of the war, 132 killed or wounded in little more than an hour. As an infantry battalion ordinarily put no more than 500 infantrymen into battle, the extent of the disaster and the fierceness of the fighting were evident. Meanwhile, the enemy fire cut down the Winnipegs and the Garrys at the southern edge of the field. The 12th SS counterattacks by 'little boys,' in journalist Ralph Allen's memorable phrase, 'who never had the chance to become the little boys they might have been,'[22] were fierce. They overran an entire Chaudières company, and more murders of POWs followed. But the airfield was Canadian – at a cost of 371 casualties out of some 2000 engaged.

Caën was next. A huge attack by bombers on the city boosted Canadian morale, but it harmed mainly civilians, for the Germans' positions were sensibly located away from the town centre. Then the advance began. At Buron the Highland Light Infantry had massive fire support, but, as so often happened, the enemy positions remained largely unharmed, and the supporting armour could not cross an anti-tank ditch protecting the town. As a result, the HLI lost its commanding officer and 261 men, two-thirds of the attackers' strength, in a day-long struggle on July 8, when most of the killed and wounded were hit as they lay in the fields by the enemy's skilful use of mortars. The battalion's pipe band, acting as stretcher-bearers, suffered 100 per cent casualties (and, later, the Regimental Sergeant Major complained, 'We need pipers,' and stopped their use in this role). The HLI took the village nonetheless and held it against a counterattack of panzers, thanks to British self-propelled 17-pounder anti-tank guns, which knocked out thirteen of the enemy tanks.[23] The Regina Rifles liberated Kurt Meyer's headquarters at the Abbaye d'Ardenne, but only after Meyer himself led a stubborn defence and managed to pull his men out successfully. Authie fell to the North Novas again, and the costly advance moved on. By July 9, thirty-three days after it was supposed to be seized, the Canadians had the ruins of Caën, but another 330 men had been killed and 864 wounded. Fighting the Germans was always costly; moving south from Caën would be costlier still.

A major British attack, Goodwood, began on July 18 behind the heaviest bombing attack of the campaign. Its objective was to keep the enemy pinned around Caën and to wear down the defenders. Perhaps there was too much strength there, for the Germans were unmoved, as their 88s and rocket-firing *Nebelwerfers*, the dreaded 'Moaning Minnies,' hammered the Guards Armoured Division and the British 11th Armoured. The one advantage the Allies had was that their Shermans could be replaced. With the German factories bombed into rubble, the Panthers and Tigers could not be so readily reinforced.

On the left flank of Goodwood, the II Canadian Corps fought its first battle, code-named Operation Atlantic. Effectively using tank-infantry cooperation, the Third Division crossed the Orne to the ruins of a steel mill at Colombelles, which provided the enemy with good defensive positions, and took it, along with the suburbs of Cormelles and Faubourg de Vaucelles. The

Second Division, under Major-General Charles Foulkes, had a relatively easy initiation into battle on July 18 and 19, with the Régiment de Maisonneuve taking Fleury-sur-Orne and the Black Watch seizing Ifs.[24]

Blocking the road south from Caën was Verrières Ridge, a gentle 250-foot-high ridge that gave the German defenders ideal positions into which their tanks, guns, and infantry could be placed with good visibility and fields of fire. The Germans held their forward positions lightly and kept a strong reserve with tanks and self-propelled assault guns for counterattacks. Their interlocking defences typically were some thousand yards deep and had support from artillery, *Nebelwerfer*, and mortar positions hidden further back on reverse slopes.[25] Guy Simonds's plan for Operation Atlantic ordered the Second Canadian Division and the British Seventh Armoured to drive the enemy off the ridge.

Brigadier Hugh Young's 6th Brigade moved across the Orne on July 20 without armoured support. The Queen's Own Cameron Highlanders captured St André-sur-Orne and held it against fierce counterattack. Les Fusiliers Mont-Royal took Troteval and Beauvoir farms, and stayed put. The South Saskatchewan Regiment, its objective Verrières village, ran into heavy rain and the panzers of two battle groups from the 1st SS Leibstandarte and the 2nd Panzer divisions. The regiment called up every available anti-tank gun and fought desperately, but the Germans overwhelmed it. As the retreating infantry passed through the lines of the Essex Scottish, they sowed panic. Two companies fled, but the rear companies remained and held off the Germans. An enemy attack the next morning, again under the heavy rains that grounded the Allies' Typhoons, shattered the luckless Essex Scottish and two companies of the Fusiliers Mont-Royal. The timely arrival of the Black Watch stabilized the line, but Verrières Ridge remained in German hands.

Almost 2000 Canadians had been killed, wounded, or captured in the bloody struggle, and many other men collapsed with battle exhaustion. Jack Leddy, a Medical Officer in a Canadian Casualty Clearing Station, saw many such men: 'Some of them had seen their buddies blown to smithereens. They would be picked up wandering around on a road or huddled by some tree. They were brought into the station, where we had set up a special ward for them. They would be crying hysterically or just sitting and staring into space. There were those who trembled and shook uncontrollably. They were in shock but with no visible wounds. The doctor in charge of them would give them sedatives and get them to sleep.'[26] The psychiatrists evacuated the worst cases back to England.

The failures of Goodwood and Atlantic focused the critics on Montgomery. Generals and historians have argued endlessly about his plans for the Normandy battle. After the failure to take Caën in the first rush after D-Day, the battle had turned into one of attrition, and, by July, the situation for both sides verged on the impossible. The Allies had to break out but were worried they might not have the strength to do so. The Germans had to hold the Allies but knew that their own casualties increased daily. For the Canadians, completely divorced from the strategic discussions, the question of whether Montgomery was right in insisting that he fought the battle to his pre-D-Day plan was essentially immaterial. What they knew was that there were fourteen divisions and 600 tanks in front of the II Canadian Corps and the British, and only nine divisions facing the Yanks – but the Americans' breakout, Operation Cobra, had to be delayed to July 25. This wait meant another holding attack, Operation Spring, by the II Canadian Corps to keep the enemy armour glued to the eastern flank of the Normandy bridgehead.[27]

Simonds's detailed plan assigned roles to each unit and called for the two Canadian infantry divisions, the badly battered Third and the green but shattered Second, as well as the British 7th Armoured, to stage a deliberate attack on Verrières Ridge. This attack was easier ordered than done. The Third Division had the job of driving the 1st SS out of Tilly-la-Campagne, a dot on the map held by a battalion of Panzer Grenadiers and a company of panzers, so the 7th Armoured could move through to take the high ground. On the right flank, the Second Division had to clear its own start line at St André-sur-Orne, then seize Verrières and May-sur-Orne, followed by Rocquancourt. As so often, the Canadians had the task of hitting the enemy in his prepared positions, where the Shermans and the infantry operated at a terrible disadvantage. The enemy, in addition to the 1st SS, was the 272nd Division, a good Wehrmacht division, and tanks, panzer grenadiers, and soldiers from four veteran divisions, all led by the very able SS General Sepp Dietrich. Crucially, the Verrières Ridge position gave the enemy ideal positions from which to fight, and the Germans had fortified the towns strongly. Most important, they had large numbers of their 75 mm and 88 mm guns well sited, and they employed their artillery and mortars with deadly effect.

Preceded by the clearing of the Second Division's jump-off point, the attack began at 3:30 a.m., the men finding direction with the aid of artificial moonlight, searchlights bouncing off the clouds to create a ghostly half-light. A good idea, but one poor in execution, for the Third Division's North Nova Scotia Regiment, moving forward towards Tilly in pitch black at the intended time, found itself silhouetted when the artificial moonlight lit up the ground. Enemy machine-gun fire ripped into the four companies of men, who had to struggle to reach the outskirts of their objectives. Fort Garry tanks came to assist, but eleven of fifteen Shermans were soon burning, along with self-propelled artillery and carriers. The Third Division attack had stalled in confusion with heavy losses. Two battalion commanders, Lieutenant-Colonels C. Petch of the North Novas and G.H. Christianson of the Stormont, Dundas, and Glengarry Regiment, refused to make a daylight attack on the German positions at Tilly, an assault they both believed to be hopeless. The 9th Brigade commander, D.G. Cunningham, reported this refusal to his GOC, General Keller, indicating that he agreed with his COs. The attack did not proceed.

On the Second Division's front, the shambles compounded. The division had had little training in night attacks, and the chaos of battle compounded the difficulties. The Calgary Highlanders ran into heavy opposition at St André, St Martin, and May-sur-Orne and lost heavily. The Royal Hamilton Light Infantry, led by one of the great fighting officers of the war, Lieutenant-Colonel John Rockingham, took Verrières early in the morning of July 26, giving the Royal Regiment of Canada a firm base to hit at Rocquancourt. Their attack ground to a halt in the face of a reported thirty enemy tanks pouring fire at them.

Montreal's Black Watch had been ordered to move past May-sur-Orne, still held by the Germans, towards the summit of the ridge. But the regiment came under fire at St Martin about 5 a.m. and the CO, Lieutenant-Colonel S.S.T. Cantlie, was mortally wounded. The acting CO, twenty-four-year-old Major F.P. Griffin, took over and, after consulting his brigade commander and Major Walter Harris, OC of the 1st Hussars squadron supporting his unit, he led his remaining men up the ridge in the face of heavy enemy fire from a battalion of the 272nd Division and a battle group of tanks from the 2nd Panzer Division. Of the three hundred Black Watch who started, perhaps sixty made it to the top – only to find themselves surrounded by dug-in Tiger and Panther tanks. Griffin, a scholar with an almost complete PhD, ordered the survivors back, but only fifteen made it. Montreal had lost 324 of its sons, including Major Griffin, in a single bloody day. The Hussars squadron lost six tanks. Harris survived to become the able Finance Minister in the government of Louis St Laurent.

Of all the infantry assaults that day, only the RHLI's had taken and held its objective. The Germans now turned on the well dug-in Rileys, two battle groups of infantry and armour attacking them relentlessly. The enemy destroyed three of the four 17-pounder anti-tank guns attached to Rockingham's unit, and at one point eight panzers rolled over and through the regiment's positions. Rockingham galvanized the defence, even sending out patrols to eliminate enemy machine guns. The Hamilton men held on by the barest of margins.

Operation Spring had failed in the bloodiest day of the war for the Canadian Army, Dieppe excepted. At least 450 men had died and another 1100 were wounded. The RHLI alone had 200 casualties. Morale in some Canadian units plummeted. Unlike Major General Bert Hoffmeister, whose concern for those under his command was legendary, General Simonds was not a commander who thought much about the subordinates whose job it was to carry out his orders.[28] To him, Spring had failed because of 'a deterioration of ... fighting efficiency,' and he sacked a number of commanders who had not pressed their men forward.[29] He replaced Colonels Petch and Christianson, along with Brigadier Cunningham. Rockingham of the RHLI succeeded Cunningham.

Simonds's own job was in no danger, for he was a Montgomery favourite. Simonds was the only Canadian for whom the British commander had any regard, and Montgomery was right: despite his personality flaws, Simonds unquestionably was the ablest Canadian general in Northwest Europe and, with the possible exception of Bert Hoffmeister, of the entire war. After July 23, however, as in Italy, Simonds again had a Canadian superior officer. The First Canadian Army became operational, the largest Canadian-led force in history, with the II Canadian Corps and I British Corps under the command of General Harry Crerar. The Canadian Corps had also added the Fourth Canadian Armoured Division, commanded by Major-General George Kitching, which arrived in late July. This division had relatively little recent field training in England; indeed, since Kitching took command after being brought back from Italy, it had not been able to hold any major exercises at all.

Now, at last, the Americans were on the move and Operation Cobra was finally under way. After five days of bitter fighting, they reached the Atlantic coast at Avranches, and General George Patton's Third Army turned eastward. The Germans, seeing their front fractured, wanted to dispatch men from the British-Canadian front, but Montgomery kept the pressure on them there with another British attack. Military good sense demanded that the enemy withdraw, pulling his formations behind the River Seine to save what he could, but Hitler ordered a counter-stroke at the Americans: mass the panzers and throw them at Mortain and Avranches, the Führer said, and the U.S. armies were certain to crumble. Intelligence told the Americans what was coming and where, and General Omar Bradley braced his men. Moreover, Montgomery and Eisenhower could see a huge opportunity taking shape: if the Germans drove west, they might be caught in a pocket between the British and the Canadians driving south from Caën and the Americans moving east and north.[30]

To get south from Caën was the challenge. A series of battalion-sized attacks on the unsecured objectives of Operation Spring demonstrated that the Germans remained present in force. The Calgary Highlanders, the Lincoln and Welland Regiment from the Niagara peninsula, and Montreal's reconstituted Black Watch all lost heavily in fruitless attacks. But now Simonds had a new, big plan, Operation Totalize. As was his usual practice, the corps commander devised the plan himself, consulting his staff, if at all, after the fact. Their task was to make his plan work.[31]

Simonds realized that previous preparations for major attacks had done great damage to the Germans' forward defences, but usually left their main positions unscathed. His plan this time coordinated massive firepower from artillery, bombers, and fighter-bombers to neutralize the forward *and* main enemy positions.[32] Totalize directed the II Canadian Corps, the British 51st Highland Division, a British armoured brigade, and the newly arrived 1st Polish Armoured Division to crack the German anti-tank defences that blocked the way. How to smash them? Here, Simonds called for the first tactical support operation at night by heavy bombers, a night attack by his divisions, and, his fertile tactical mind working, the conversion of seventy-six 'Priests,' self-propelled 105 mm guns, into the first genuine armoured personnel carriers. The idea had been around for some time, but Simonds was the first to put it into practice. The vulnerable infantry, or some of them, could now be carried in relative security in armed personnel carriers towards their objectives.

That was Simonds at his best.[33] But Totalize was hugely complex, not to say ponderous, calling as it did for the Second Canadian and 51st Divisions, led by two armoured brigades, engineers, and anti-tank guns, to roll forward at night in separate regiment-sized columns, each with one infantry battalion in Kangaroos, as the new armoured carriers were dubbed.* Drivers would keep direction by following radio beams, artificial moonlight would provide some visibility, and tracers from anti-aircraft guns on the flanks would point the way. While the armoured columns blasted through, follow-on infantry would hit other objectives that ideally had been levelled by the bombing. Once the Second Division had broken through, the Third and Fourth Divisions would push through the gap. Finally, the Fourth and Polish Divisions were to drive on to Falaise, putting the cork in the bottle in which the Germans were to be trapped. Altogether, it was one hugely ambitious plan.

To make Totalize work, great quantities of supplies had to be brought forward. The Army Service Corps' trucks ran an ammunition dumping program that brought 200,000 rounds of ammunition forward, up to 650 shells for each of the 700 guns supporting the attack. Then the gasoline for the thousands of vehicles in the attack had to be brought to the tanks and half-tracks – in all, some 150,000 gallons.[34] Food and supplies of all kinds moved to the front and, at the same time, signallers strung telephone wire to tie together the fighting units and their headquarters, while the field ambulances and hospitals behind the lines readied themselves to receive the wounded. Simonds's staff had to work with the jealously independent Royal and United States Army Air Forces to arrange the bombing plan and to ensure that the right ordnance would be dropped on the right targets at the right time. All this planning was taking place as the Germans shifted their divisions around, trying to reinforce

---

* The Totalize columns consisted of four vehicles abreast on a 16-yard frontage, the width that could be cleared by four anti-mine flail tanks. Every 10 feet there were four more vehicles. Each column was headed by two tank troops, followed by two flail troops and a lane-marking AVRE (Armoured Vehicle Royal Engineers) troop. Infantry followed on Kangaroos or half-tracks. Further back came the rest of a tank squadron, two anti-tank troops, a machine-gun platoon, and an engineer section. The rear was covered by an armoured regiment less one squadron. One collision, very easy in the dust churned up, and chaos resulted. John A. English, *The Canadian Army and the Normandy Campaign: A Study of Failure in High Command* (New York, 1991), 273.

the army struggling to contain the Americans to the west. Simonds's intelligence officers endeavoured to make sense of it all, at once overwhelmed by a flood of information and in difficulty because so little of what they knew was firm.[35] A major attack was an extraordinarily complicated exercise, involving men and machines in their tens of thousands.

Simonds's plan was brilliant, one that experienced, rested troops might possibly have accomplished. But the Fourth and the Polish Divisions were new to battle, the Third Division had been severely beaten up in its long fight from the D-Day beaches, and the Second still ached from Operation Spring. Nonetheless, on August 7 the formations moved into position for the attack the next day. General Crerar reminded his officers and, later, the war correspondents that on August 8, 1918, the Canadian Corps had smashed the Germans. Now, twenty-six years later, he foresaw an even blacker day for the enemy, one that could shorten the war.

It was not to be. The RAF and the RCAF bombers, over a thousand of them, arrived on schedule at 11:15 p.m. and plastered the enemy positions, throwing up a terrific cloud of dust. The first columns moved off at 11:30 p.m., almost instantly foundering in the dark and the dust storm. Two of the three columns lost their way, and the Germans, as always recovering quickly, poured gunfire into them. Nonetheless, despite the chaos, by noon on August 8 the attackers were on or near their objectives. Behind the armoured columns (whose Kangaroo-borne infantry had very light losses) the 6th Brigade cleaned out the little villages that had delayed the Canadians so long, sometimes at heavy cost and in the face of counterattacks from German troops who had escaped the bombing. Now Phase 2 began eight hours after the end of the successful first phase, and instantly the Fourth Armoured and Polish divisions became stuck in a traffic jam. Matters worsened just after 1 p.m. when another huge bombing force, this time from the U.S. 8th Air Force, dumped part of its load on the Canadians and Poles beneath. One of the wounded was the Third Division's General Keller,* and the bombing hit two companies of the North Shores and the 4th Medium Regiment hard. The casualties disrupted the

---

* When Keller was wounded in the bombing, he was said to have called his batman: 'Roberts, give me my revolver. I'm going to shoot the first goddam American I see' (Tony Foster interview with Brigadier J.W. Proctor, December 6, 1985). 'Friendly fire,' from bombers dropping their loads off target, artillery 'shorts,' or badly aimed small arms, undoubtedly killed hundreds of Canadians.

attack. So too did the loss of senior officers, and the time needed for their successors to arrive and take command. Brigadier Wyman, commanding the 2nd Armoured Brigade, was wounded in action that day. Keller's replacement, Major-General D.C. Spry, a far better commander by every account than his predecessor,[36] had to fly in from Italy and did not arrive until August 18; Wyman's successor, Brigadier J.F. Bingham, was on the scene and took over at once. Very little damage was done to the enemy by the 1500 tons of high explosives dropped by the USAAF bombers.[37]

The real Canadian nemesis now arrived. Kurt Meyer's much-depleted but still effective 12th SS Division had been moving west when Totalize started, and he swung back to help. The galvanizing energy of 'Panzer' Meyer, personally siting his 88 mm guns astride the Caën-Falaise road, and the hesitant drive south of the two armoured divisions, began to slow the attack. At dusk on August 8 most of the armoured regiments stopped for the night, following the British practice in the desert war and the way they had been trained, but Simonds was furious. The 4th Armoured Brigade put together Halpenny Force out of the Canadian Grenadier Guards and the Lake Superior Regiment and sent it towards Bretteville-le-Rabet. The British Columbia Regiment and infantry from Northern Ontario's Algonquin Regiment were to take high ground southwest of Quesnay Wood, crossing the highway to Falaise. The BCRs became lost in the black of night and halted on what they supposed was the objective. As day broke, however, the tanks and infantry found themselves in an open field – 3 miles northeast of their real objective – and almost under the guns of a battle group of the 12th SS with five Tiger and fifteen Panther tanks. A hopeless daylong fight followed and, because no one knew where B.C. Regiment was, no help came, though units of the Polish Division were just a mile away. The armoured regiment lost forty-seven tanks and 112 men, the infantry 128 men, and both regiments their COs. Meyer's youngsters, now as experienced as grey-bearded veterans, drove off another attack on Quesnay Wood by the North Shores and the Queen's Own of the 8th Brigade with heavy casualties.

That was enough for Simonds, who called off Totalize. Pressed hard by Montgomery, however, who desperately wanted to catch the enemy in the pocket at Falaise, Simonds immediately began planning Operation Tractable. The German attack at Mortain had failed by August 8, and the panzers and infantry now were trying to escape eastward. The Falaise pocket, a narrow passage between the Americans to the south and the Canadians to the north, was still open but much of it was subjected to continuous shelling and air attack. Tractable, Monty told Simonds, had to close it tight.

The II Canadian Corps GOC's plan again was daring and imaginative: in full daylight, he proposed to form his armour into two huge 150-tank squares, one based on the Fourth Armoured Division, the other on the 2nd Armoured Brigade and the Third Division, and send them hell-for-leather at the Germans, their flanks covered by heavy bombing and huge smokescreens. Every available gun was to provide support, and, to ensure surprise, there were no written orders. But a Canadian officer returning from the meeting with his marked maps fell into German hands, so the enemy, two relatively fresh divisions, knew what to expect.

The attack began at 11:42 a.m. on August 14. The RAF bombers hit at Quesnay Wood, but again bombs fell into the Canadians and Poles below, killing 65.[38] The Germans killed more, pumping 88 mm and 75 mm shells into the closely packed armour and Kangaroos. The commander of the 4th Armoured Brigade of the Fourth Armoured Division, Brigadier E.L. Booth, was one of those killed. In the command confusion that followed at various headquarters, it was August 19 before Lieutenant-Colonel Robert Moncel could be promoted to command the brigade. Then the Laison River, just a trickle on the maps, came into view and tanks became mired on its wooded banks and muddy bottom. Desperate troopers chopped trees and tried to get the Shermans across, while infantry disembarked from the Kangaroos and stormed defended villages. At last, under the sheer weight of numbers, the German defences began to yield. The occupation divisions were nothing like the 12th SS.

But the 12th SS were still around, and on August 15 Meyer's fifteen remaining tanks struck at the 1st Hussars' Shermans. The regiments of the 4th Armoured Brigade came under fire, and the Nazis inflicted heavy casualties on the infantry. General Patton's armoured spearheads had reached Argentan but inexplicably stopped there – to avoid colliding with the Canadians, Patton said. It was now up to the II Canadian Corps to push the few remaining miles south to seal the escape route.

Simonds issued new orders, sending the Fourth and Polish Armoured divisions to bar the German retreat and the 2nd Division to take Falaise from the west.[39] The long German columns of armour, trucks, and horse-drawn carts (the Wehrmacht, unlike the Allied armies was not fully mechanized) faced constant air attack – the pilots who brought death to the fleeing enemy columns soon reported that they could smell the scent of putrefying flesh in the air – and the Allied armies kept closing in. The confusion of battle, the mixing up of units, was total. Lieutenant-Colonel Peter Bennett, CO of the Essex Scottish, recalled his regiment being held up by trucks on the road in front of him. Bennett went forward, whipped back the tarpaulin – and found German soldiers trying to flee the pocket.[40]

On August 17 the 2nd Division captured Falaise – except for a school defended by fifty SS men that took the Fusiliers Mont-Royal another day to clear – and its key road junctions. On August 18 the Americans began moving north towards Chambois in the face of desperate resistance. Meanwhile, the Poles raced into position to hold off a developing German assault from the east, which aimed to pry open the escape route through the gap, and the remnants of twenty fleeing Nazi divisions pouring out of the west. Their key defensive position was a hill dubbed 'Maczuga' (or Mace, because of its shape), on which two armoured regiments and three infantry battalions dug in. The Canadians meanwhile drove a corridor down the road from Falaise to Trun, and infantry from the 9th and 10th brigades dug in along the River Dives and shot down the Germans in their hundreds. From the Fourth Armoured Division a squadron of the South Alberta Regiment, led by Major David Currie, and a company of the Argyll and Sutherland Highlanders from the Hamilton, Ontario, area, commanded by Acting Major Ivan Martin, moved to St Lambert, astride the only remaining escape route with a bridge capable of carrying tanks across the Dives. Trying to keep the road open, the Germans fought hard, but the Canadians had half the town after a six-hour struggle, and, in the afternoon, more infantry joined them.[41]

The Falaise Gap struggle was now at its terrible climax. The Poles on Maczuga had eighty tanks and 1600 men. Currie and Martin had a handful of tanks and 200 men. The Shermans fought unequally against the Tigers, and Currie called in artillery fire to slow down the enemy. The enemy killed Major

Martin,* along with most of the other officers, and Currie, a sad-eyed man who destroyed a Tiger singlehandedly, killed snipers, and cleared a house by himself and took six prisoners, was everywhere at once, bolstering the defences here and directing fire there. A German convoy, preceded by a motorcyclist in whose sidecar sat a German captain 'with a peaked cap and goggles similar to those favoured by Rommel,' stopped when confronted by Currie's men. The officer came forward with hands up, recorded army photographer Lieutenant Don Grant, 'looking at his map and hoping that what was happening to him, wasn't happening.'[42] In the midst of the terrific confusion of battle, the noise of gunfire, artillery, and aircraft, the panic, and the death, Currie kept his head and galvanized his men. Currie's tiny command destroyed seven tanks, a dozen 88 mm guns, forty vehicles, and killed, wounded, or captured some 3000 Germans. Low on gasoline and ammunition, the Poles too did their very large share: under heavy German fire, they held off repeated German attacks by armour and infantry. The Poles took 6000 POWs, destroyed 70 tanks and 500 vehicles, and lost 1400 killed and wounded of their own. At last on August 21, tanks from the Canadian Grenadier Guards reached the Poles and, mopping up aside, firmly sealed the Falaise Gap.

The costs were enormous. Twenty thousand French civilians died in the struggle for their liberation, and the fighting turned village after village into rubble. The Germans had perhaps a hundred thousand men in the pocket and lost at least half, 40,000 to 45,000 becoming POWs and 10,000 to 20,000 being killed. Meyer's 12th SS, 20,000 soldiers and 159 tanks on D-Day, had just 100 men and 10 tanks remaining. The Canadians, for their part, paid dearly: from August 8 to 21, casualties were 1470 dead, 4023 wounded, and 177 POWs. The Second and Third Divisions had suffered most – the Third the most of any division in Montgomery's British-Canadian 21st Army Group. Men died and were wounded in higher numbers for each thousand

---

* Major Martin was a courageous man. A German machine gunner was firing at the Argylls in St Lambert when Martin decided to act. 'He went over to a slit trench and asked an Argylls private to 'help me get that machine gunner.' The private looked up at him from the security of his trench and replied, 'You're kidding, of course.' Undeterred, Captain Martin took off alone with a Sten gun; a few minutes later we heard a burst of gunfire and back he came with an MG-42 machine gun over his shoulder.' Arthur Bridge, '"In the Eye of the Storm": A Recollection of Three Days in the Falaise Gap, 19–21 August 1944,' *Canadian Military History* 9 (summer 2000): 66. Martin was awarded a posthumous Distinguished Service Cross by the United States.

soldiers employed than had been the case at Passchendaele. The casualties of June, July, and August, some 75 per cent caused by the Germans' extraordinarily effective use of mortars and *Nebelwerfers*, together with those suffered in Italy, led to the great conscription crisis of the Second World War in October and November 1944. The men killed and wounded, the corporals, sergeants, lieutenants, and majors who were the regiments' junior leaders, could never be replaced.

In Guy Simonds's view, poor leadership – not his, but that of his subordinates – had been one of the reasons his plans in Tractable had not unfolded as he intended. He sacked his friend George Kitching, who had commanded 4th Canadian Armoured Division in action only from August 7 to 21,[43] and replaced him with Harry Foster, the commander of 7th Infantry Brigade. The lack of information in the chaos of battle, along with the rawness of his division, had done in Kitching. Brigadier Hugh Young of the Second Division's 6th Brigade was also replaced, as was Brigadier J.E. Ganong of the 4th Brigade. Simonds considered that Major-General Charles Foulkes, the division GOC, had not done well, but Foulkes had strong support from Crerar; he could not be touched. After the major battles he had directed in July and August, Simonds in all sacked a division commander, six of nine brigadiers, and fourteen of twenty-four battalion commanders.

Had the Canadians been slow in closing the gap? Could the exit door have been slammed shut faster? The answer to both questions must be a qualified yes. Simonds's plans, complex though they may have been, might have worked with experienced divisions, but the Fourth and the Polish Armoured divisions were new to action, and Simonds ought to have factored this consideration more fully into the equation. The Germans' resistance, as always, was fierce, and their tactically proficient use of 88 mm anti-tank guns and superior armour proved deadly to the Shermans. The terrain greatly favoured the enemy, and the fury of the SS divisions, especially the 12th SS, and the astonishingly ruthless galvanizing energy of Sepp Dietrich and Kurt Meyer, could not be equalled in the Canadian ranks. The Canadians also suffered from bad luck, the wounding or death of key commanders, the wrong turns that led to disastrous losses, and the dozen mischances that prevented a quick, clean victory. Moreover, as the fine American scholars Williamson Murray and Allan Millett say with brutal frankness: 'The Canadians still displayed all too much of the cautious, unimaginative training they had received at British hands from 1940 through 1944.'[44]

Simonds's battle plans were neither cautious nor unimaginative, but were shaped by the terrain on which he had to fight. His subordinate commanders, however, shocked by the casualties their divisions and brigades suffered and not as ruthless as their boss, sometimes *were* too hesitant. Nor was there much indication that many Canadian and British commanders thought beyond a frontal assault as the answer to every tactical situation. Simonds, the only senior Canadian general well regarded by the British and the Americans, used the pieces available to him far better than others, yet for the most part he sent men and machines straight at the Germans. Casualties suffered today to take an objective could save higher casualties tomorrow, he believed, and few doubted his high intelligence and great competence.[45]

Yes, Falaise should have been reached more quickly. To say that does not take anything away from the courage of the Canadian soldier, though it implies that a long period of training can never be a substitute for battle experience. The chaos, the death, and the terror that impelled any normal man to flee all preclude anyone who has not fought from condemning those who were thrown into battle without the requisite experience. After Normandy and Falaise, the Canadian divisions had that experience. Historians who have not walked the ground to see the strength of the enemy positions might be more forgiving in their assessments.[46]

Of course, the delays might also be a commentary on the Canadian way of war. Canadian battles were a top-down experience, with detailed plans emanating from corps headquarters and laying out the actions of divisions, brigades, and battalions. 'Doctrine relied on centralized planning,' historian Bill McAndrew noted, with 'highest level control; staff management of the battlefield; reliance on indirect fire support; scant manoeuvre; cautious exploitation.' Ordinarily Private Jones would know little of the overall objective other than his platoon's task, and too often his platoon was doomed to strike head first at an enemy strongpoint. The Wehrmacht and the SS, curiously for the army of a monstrous dictatorship, put more trust in their soldiers, treating them as partners in a common enterprise. The Canadians, by contrast, were the never-consulted factory workers doing what they were told on an army production line. In an army where the key commanders – McNaughton,

Crerar, Simonds – were gunners, artillery was always the key, with everything tied to the range of the guns. In McAndrew's memorable phrase, the Canadians practised the slinky-toy method, the attack at best moving forward just enough to keep the guns in range, then halting until the guns advanced before another bound could follow – providing the enemy had not already moved to counter it. Initiative was not usually encouraged in the Canadian Army: the officers did not feel certain enough of their men, and the men, in turn, were not all that sure of their officers.[47]

Yet for Canadians, the artillery *was* the key to the battle. The 25-pounders and the medium and heavy artillery could lay down massive concentrations of fire with incredible rapidity. The artillery made up for the flaws of the Canadian Shermans and the (usually) better training and tactical skills of the enemy, and provided the Canadian edge. Even so, it is extraordinary that a nation of car owners and hockey players, innately skilled at quick movement and seizing the opportunity, should have formed such a slow and ponderous army, centrally driven and directed and with initiative all but discouraged. Perhaps it was British tactical doctrines and British hierarchical values that crimped the Canadian style. Perhaps it was the dead hand of Permanent Force officers at the top who feared losing their control to the Militia officers. Perhaps it was the enemy's deadly effectiveness. Whatever the cause, the Canadians too often seemed overly cautious. True, individual leaders and soldiers demonstrated initiative, and men overcame obstacles and death, but these acts were triumphs of the spirit more than tributes to the style of Canadian command or the quality of Canadian training.

At the same time, whatever the flaws in executing plans, the entire Normandy campaign was an undoubted Canadian and Allied victory. From June 6 to August 21 the Canadians had fought and destroyed a succession of German divisions. The 12th SS, fierce as it had been, existed only in memory after August 21, and the outgunned Shermans put paid to the German tanks. The cost was high, but the enemy defeat was complete. After their debacle in Normandy, there was no longer any possibility that Hitler could win the war. The Nazis suffered a half-million casualties, twenty-seven enemy divisions ceased to exist, and twelve panzer divisions altogether now had only 120 tanks. The Allies had sustained 206,700 casualties since June 6, a dreadful price but still less than half of the German losses. The First Canadian Army, like the British, Americans, Poles, and French, now turned to the east, certain that the end of the war in Europe must have been hastened by the Nazi disaster in Normandy.

Soon after the bloody victory in Normandy had been won, the forgotten I Canadian Corps achieved the single greatest Canadian feat of arms of the Second World War. The victory at the Hitler Line in Italy had driven the Germans back beyond Rome and Florence. The Germans fought skilful delaying actions and used demolitions much as they had done in the first months of the Italian campaign. By mid-August they were occupying their new defensive works in the Apennines, the so-called Gothic Line. After two months of rest and training, the I Canadian Corps had the task of cracking the Adriatic end of the line and opening the way to Rimini and the Po Valley.

The Canadians alone moved almost 11,000 wheeled vehicles, 280 carriers, 650 tanks, a million shells, and 12.5 million gallons of gasoline over the mountains, a testimony to the huge organizational effort required to move armies in the Second World War.[48] The Canadians' overall teeth-to-tail ratio – the number of front-line soldiers divided by the number of troops required to support them – was the worst in the Allied armies, but in Italy they benefited from British supply lines as much as possible, and the Canadian rear area organization was compact. The Royal Canadian Army Service Corps provided the transport companies that moved the fuel, food, and ammunition forward, and the Ordnance Corps, the Royal Canadian Electrical and Mechanical Engineers, postal units, military police, and the panoply of necessary but unsung units kept the organization functioning.

A stiff fight put the Canadians across the Metauro River and brought them to the Gothic Line defences by August 27. Major-General Bert Hoffmeister, GOC of the Fifth Canadian Armoured Division, went forward to study the enemy defences before the attack on the night of September 1–2. Examining the ground, looking for the enemy, he was startled to discover that there was little sign of the Germans, almost as though they had not yet moved into their positions. 'We could look down on the anti-tank ditch ... [and] pick out the odd concrete gun emplacement,' he said, but 'the whole thing looked terribly quiet ... there's something wrong with this whole situation,' Hoffmeister said, 'it just does not sit right with me.'[49] In fact, disinformation had persuaded the

Germans that the attack was likely to fall further west, and they were in the midst of moving units in and out of the line.

The corps commander, Lieutenant-General E.L.M. Burns, had already planned the attack for the night of September 1–2, but after hearing from Hoffmeister and from patrols, Burns ordered his divisions to 'endeavour to effect a lodgement in the line while it was still unmanned.'[50] The attack went in early, with the First Division on the right and the Fifth's two brigades of infantry blasting open the hole through which, while the struggle was still ongoing, Hoffmeister daringly sent his armoured brigade, the British Columbia Dragoons and Lord Strathcona's Horse in the lead. The Perth Regiment played a key role in the attack, seizing Point 111, a key feature, and winning the right to claim to have been the first unit to crack the line.[51] This success gave Hoffmeister special pleasure: in January 1944 the Perths had been shattered on the Arielli and the GOC had devoted much time to rebuilding the unit's confidence.

The battle was difficult for the two Canadian divisions, and some regiments took fearful casualties. The West Nova Scotia Regiment, for example, lost seventy-six men when it was caught in a minefield killing zone and raked with fire. On August 31 the British Columbia Dragoons fought their way to Point 204, behind the main defences, but enemy paratroopers, anti-tank guns, and the open, treeless countryside did them in. One of those who died was the CO, Lieutenant-Colonel Fred Vokes, brother of the First Division's GOC, along with twenty-one of his men. A troop sergeant recalled getting onto the objective and watching forty Germans marching down the road towards him in platoon formation. 'They didn't even know we were in the area,' he said. 'I don't think we missed three of the 40.'[52] The BCDs, eventually relieved by the Strathconas, ended the day with just eighteen tanks. The Strathconas and some men from the Perth Regiment, stuck into the Gothic Line like an arrow embedded in flesh, faced heavy counterattacks but drove them off with help from the artillery. The battle demonstrated that the Germans had been surprised, out-thought, and outfought, and they began to pull back on September 1 in conditions that sometimes suggested a rout. The Mighty Maroon Machine had amply lived up to its name, and the Eighth Army's commander paid special tribute to Hoffmeister and his men: 'A great deal of our success was due to the energy and daring of the Commander and his Division.' Historian Lieutenant-Colonel John English later noted that 'the performance of the 5th Canadian Armoured Division on the Gothic Line may have been the finest by any Canadian formation in the Second World War.'[53]

The optimism of September 1 faded quickly as the enemy rushed reinforcements into the area. Then the rains came, turning nearly dry river beds into torrents once more and churning up the mud. As so often in Italy, the pursuit turned into a slogging match with each river, each height of land a well-defended position that had to be cracked in set-piece attack after set-piece attack.* Not until September 21, after crossing six river lines and incurring very heavy casualties, did I Canadian Corps reach Rimini, and the city fell to the Greek Brigade that had been operating under the corps' command. In the almost four weeks since the attack across the Metauro, the Canadians had busted the Gothic Line and taken Rimini, advancing a distance of some 30 miles. Equally important, they had forced the Germans to pull strength from the centre of the Gothic Line, easing the way for the Americans attacking there. But the losses were the heaviest for any equivalent period in Italy: the First Division lost 626 killed out of a total of 2511 casualties and had another thousand men evacuated for battle exhaustion and illness; the Fifth Armoured lost 390 men killed and 995 wounded.

The breakthrough on the Gothic Line was a great victory for General Burns, who received an immediate Distinguished Service Order from the Eighth Army. But Burns's senior Canadian officers had become increasingly unhappy under their dour commander's direction, and both Vokes and Hoffmeister, along with the key staff officers at corps headquarters, were almost literally on the verge of mutiny. Vokes wrote privately that they were 'prepared to adopt the only course possible' – to resign. 'In spite of no able direction we have continued to bear the cross for an individual who lacks one iota of personality, appreciation of effort or the first goddamn thing in the application of book learning to what is practical in war & what isn't,' he

---

* On September 15, 1944, the First Canadian Division took the Palazzo des Vergers, owned by the Ruspoli family, near Rimini. The palazzo was a huge house full of art and treasures, with signs warning German troops against looting, and the Canadians clearly viewed the contents as spoils of war from a Fascist family. Individuals and, quite possibly, units helped themselves. Investigations spurred by the Ruspolis, who had good anti-Fascist connections, went nowhere. See the lengthy articles on what was apparently the largest case of looting by Canadians in the war by Ian MacLeod in the *Ottawa Citizen*, March 17–18, 2001, and in a shortened version in the *National Post*, March 17, 19, 2001.

explained. 'I've done my best to be loyal but goddammit the strain has been too bloody great.'[54] General Crerar tried once more to save Burns, but this time he failed. Instead, Major-General Charles Foulkes was taken from the Second Canadian Division in Northwest Europe, promoted, and given command of the corps. By every report, Foulkes had been an undistinguished division GOC; surprisingly, perhaps, he apparently did better as a corps commander.

The Canadians' struggle in Italy continued, a fight against the enemy, the terrain, and the weather. The Canadians attacked across the Savio River, the First Division attack pressed by the Seaforth Highlanders and the Loyal Edmonton Regiment on the evening of October 21. The Seaforths' anti-tank platoon, a new organization that had been created around four two-man PIAT teams after units persuaded themselves that their anti-tank weapon could kill a Panther or a Tiger tank, faced a strong German counterattack of three Panthers, two self-propelled guns, and some thirty infantry. His cigarettes wrapped in a condom, thirty-year-old Private Ernest Smith had led his six-man section across the swift waist-deep river and into a ditch when they came face to face with a Panther. From a distance of 30 feet, Smith fired his PIAT and hit the tank, blowing it off its tracks, but the ten soldiers riding on the back jumped off and came for Smith. Moving into the centre of the road, he killed four with his Tommy gun and scattered the rest. A second tank now opened fire and more Panzer Grenadiers started closing in. Getting ammunition from a wounded soldier in the ditch, Smith continued to fight off the Germans until they pulled back. Smokey Smith won the Victoria Cross. The remainder of his anti-tank platoon killed a second Panther, added a half-track, a scout car, and two self-propelled guns, and the platoon commander, Sergeant K.P. Thompson, received the Distinguished Conduct Medal. A few brave and determined Seaforths had beaten off a small army.

Fighting in thick mud and cold on December 4, the 1st Brigade of the First Division launched a hastily prepared, ill-coordinated attack across the swift and 25-foot-wide Lamone River in assault boats and over temporary bridges. After great difficulty in getting across the river, the Royal Canadian Regiment met very rough treatment from the enemy. One platoon was virtually wiped out by enemy mortar fire, and a strong German counterattack with tanks and infantry almost totally eliminated two companies. The RCR lost

96 of the 205 men who had crossed the river; the Hasty Ps, who had crossed beside the RCR, lost 58. Both regiments were shaken and, for a time, their morale was shattered.

The continuing high casualties combined with the overall shortage of infantry reinforcements to create serious problems in I Canadian Corps. General Foulkes reported that he personally had visited a soldier in hospital who had been wounded, evacuated, returned to his unit, and wounded once more – all in a twenty-five-day period. The corps commander also learned from one of his COs that reinforcements were coming forward with 'open wounds, limitation of movement and unfit for duty.'[55] The Canadian Army, like all the Allied and enemy forces, had serious manpower problems as the war dragged on.

And the war continued on. The Canadian Corps took Ravenna, and several days later a two-division attack crossed the Lamone, though not without heavy losses that many soldiers thought unnecessary and for which they blamed General Foulkes. The Canadians reached the Senio River by Christmas.

Patrolling and occasional probes aside, that was it for I Canadian Corps in Italy, though casualties and dreadful conditions continued to sap morale. In February 1945, after pressure from Ottawa, where General Andrew McNaughton had become Minister of National Defence at the beginning of November 1944, the corps received orders to join the First Canadian Army in the Low Countries. It arrived there in March, leaving behind forever the 5399 officers and men who had been killed in the Italian campaign. Just under 20,000 Canadians had been wounded in action and almost 1000 had been taken prisoner. In all, I Canadian Corps suffered 26,254 casualties, well over 25 per cent of the 92,757 Canadians who served in Italy. The D-Day Dodgers in sunny Italy had paid a heavy price.

What had the campaign been all about? The Allies had hoped to tie down German forces in Italy, but, thanks to the terrain that favoured the defence, more Allied troops than Germans had been deployed in a campaign that lasted two years. There were no breakthroughs, only a tough, brutal slogging march up the Italian boot. The campaign was a mixed blessing for Canada. It was essential that the army get into action in 1943 (just as it was essential for the Allies to get into Europe then), and the Canadians learned to fight in Italy. But the need to run and maintain supply lines to Italy, as well as to Britain and, after June 1944, to France, was beyond the capacity of a nation of 11 million. Canadians thought too big with resources that were too small – a trait that is perhaps not unknown in the present-day Canadian Forces. Moreover, splitting the army meant that Canada could not exercise true control over its forces. 'Not quite colonials in Italy,' McAndrew observed, 'neither were the Canadians full allies. Having no say in policy, they could merely implement the decisions of others.'[56] But that had always been the case in the past – and remains so today.

For the soldiers, if not for staff officers and politicians, the war was not yet over when they smashed the Germans in Normandy. The Canadians, Americans, and British now raced forward to complete their task, and for a time in August it seemed they had only to march eastward. The French army, reconstituted after the debacle of 1940, liberated Paris, and the Canadians moved along the French coast, besieging fortress cities still occupied by the Nazis, and into Belgium. But it was no cakewalk. When they crossed the Seine in the last week of August, the Second Canadian Division had a difficult time driving the Germans out of the Forêt de la Londe. With their determination to allow their armies to retreat, the enemy soldiers could inflict a bloody nose on the incautious at any time. The COs of the Royal Regiment and the RHLI argued against an attack on the grounds 'that this task was beyond the powers of a battalion composed largely of reinforcement personnel with little training,' but General Charles Foulkes, still the Second Division GOC in August 1944, ordered them in. Both battalions suffered severely and had to pull back. The Calgary Highlanders, holding a firm base, took constant enemy fire and lost forty-six casualties, noted historian Terry Copp, 'without firing a single round or seeing a German soldier.'[57] The Third and Fourth Divisions also had problems in the region above Elbeuf, but the First Canadian Army made its way over the Seine and freed Rouen.

On September 1 Dieppe fell to the Second Division, a bittersweet day. The division held a parade to honour its dead from August 1942, and the GOC-in-C, General Crerar, attended, standing up the newly promoted Field Marshal Montgomery to do so. This incident provoked a bitter argument between the two, Montgomery simply failing to understand the symbolic importance of the day to Canada and Canadians,[58] and Crerar standing firm on his right as a national commander to preside at an important Canadian event. Montgomery soon backed down, but relations between the generals, not the best since Italy, were never the same again.

Dieppe had some port capacity, as did a few of the other coastal towns liberated by the Canadians. Boulogne, Calais, and Dunkirk were also important enough for Hitler to order them to be defended to the last. The First Canadian Army set about taking them in September, meeting some criticism at the time, and since, for the deliberate pace it followed. It had them all by October 1 except for Dunkirk, which was still besieged by the Czech Brigade, and had thoroughly destroyed the port facilities.[59] The Nazi commander at Calais, one junior officer recalled, 'was content enough about the defeat; it was an objective fact, no tears shed over it at all. But he was burningly interested in knowing the details of the Allied tactics: '"Now why did you come in from the precise direction you did?" What he was interested in was the tactical lessons ... he wanted to file them away in the Berlin Military College for the meditation of future tacticians.' The Third Division GOC, Major-General Dan Spry, a PF lieutenant in September 1939, refused to play the game, called it 'damned nonsense,' and sent the German to a POW camp.[60]

Regrettably, the ruined Channel ports could do little to supply the Allies' enormous needs for food, fuel, ammunition, and equipment; only Antwerp, the largest port in Europe, could do that, and Antwerp had been captured undamaged. The difficulty was that the usually hypercautious Montgomery had seen what he thought was the chance to end the war quickly. Sending parachute divisions across the River Maas to secure a lodgement there and racing armoured troops towards them, Montgomery gambled for a quick entry into Hitler's Germany – and lost. The German resistance proved too much for the lightly armed airborne soldiers, and suddenly Antwerp became absolutely critical.[61]

The problem was that the great port was 50 miles inland and the water route to the city was the River Scheldt, which passed by the South Beveland peninsula and Walcheren Island. At the beginning of September 1944 these places might possibly have been cleared of a shaken enemy with relatively little cost.[62] In late September, when the First Canadian Army received orders to clear the Scheldt estuary, the Germans were well entrenched, fortified by the Führer's order to hold to the last. The hardest struggle of the war for the army, now under the acting command of Guy Simonds while Crerar recovered from a serious case of dysentery, was about to begin.

The challenge of clearing the Scheldt was horrendous. The weather was cold and wet, the battlefield a sea of mud. Virtually all the area was below sea-level, the North Sea held back by dikes and much of the land reclaimed *polders*. The dikes, as much as 15 feet high, and two canals offered natural defensive positions for the well-supplied and well-equipped enemy. And the Germans understood that if the water route to Antwerp opened, their chances of holding back the Allies were all but gone.[63] Crerar had seemed stymied by the problems facing him, but Simonds took over, collected the facts, and retired to his caravan to think. When he emerged, he called a conference and announced what the army was to do. Under Simonds, but not under Crerar, the First Canadian Army headquarters controlled events.[64] Simonds's plan of attack was simple: the Third Division, assisted by the Fourth Armoured and the 52nd British Division, would clear the south bank of the Scheldt, the so-called Breskens Pocket; then the Second Division would free South Beveland; finally Walcheren Island, controlling the entrance to the estuary, would be attacked over the causeway joining it to South Beveland and by assault from the sea.[65]

South of the Scheldt, the Third Division, led by General Spry, struggled in miserable conditions to accomplish its objectives. The Germans' 64th Division, a first-class formation, occupied the Breskens Pocket, protected by the Leopold Canal. With the aid of twenty-seven Wasp flamethrowers each with 80 gallons of jellied fuel on their side of the bank, the Canadian Scottish and Regina Rifles got across the water obstacle on boats on October 6 and overcame the temporarily demoralized enemy on the far bank, though not without difficulty. Two small bridgeheads had been created, but the men could not dig for shelter against the enemy's heavy fire because of the mud and the high water table. The Germans fought fiercely, sending in repeated heavy counterattacks, including one at the Canadian Scottish on October 7 that overran an entire company.[66] Not until October 14 did the Germans begin to pull back.

Meanwhile, Brigadier Rockingham's 9th Brigade used Buffaloes – tracked, water-going troop carriers that could lift thirty men over any water obstacle – to launch a surprise amphibious assault on October 9, crossing the Terneuzen Canal. The Highland Light Infantry and the North Nova Scotia Highlanders landed almost without opposition, but the HLI came under a heavy counter-attack from 'soldiers of a highly trained field division.' The attack was beaten off and reinforcements, Eastern Ontario's Stormont, Dundas, and Glengarry Highlanders and the machine-gun and mortar platoons of Ottawa's Cameron Highlanders, soon arrived. Using artillery as much as possible in a continuing effort to save men's lives, the Third Division gradually cleaned out the pocket, though some battalions incurred heavy casualties. The SDGs suffered seventy killed and wounded in liberating Hoofdplaat, and the Chaudières lost all but fifteen men of a company at Oostburg. The Chaudières showed great ingenuity in crossing the water obstacle in front of Sluis: the regiment drove a Bren gun carrier into the canal and piled logs and dirt on top, creating a bridge strong enough to support tanks. The Queen's Own used that link the next morning to carry the attack onward on November 2. They discovered that the Germans had cut down trees and put them into a crisscross, herring-bone pattern that could only be sawed apart one by one. The enemy methodically fired mortars at the soldiers doing the sawing, 'a fiendishly clever piece of work,' the new 8th Brigade commander, Brigadier James Roberts, recalled.[67] Worse yet, the enemy booby-trapped the bodies of their own dead, inspiring absolute loathing in the Canadians, who thereafter left German corpses where they fell to bloat and rot.

As the Third Division liberated the Breskens Pocket, the Second Division, commanded temporarily by Brigadier Holley Keefler, had the task of taking Woensdrecht, which controlled the German land route from Beveland. The enemy's main position was on the reverse slope of the only high ground behind breached dikes and flooded *polders*. This location preserved movement for themselves but largely denied it to the attackers. The attacking troops, men of the Royal Regiment, the Royal Hamilton Light Infantry, the Calgary Highlanders, and the Black Watch, either moved along the top of the dikes, exposed to zeroed-in enemy fire, or struggled through waist-deep water and mud from October 6 to 24, trying to cut the isthmus and isolate Beveland. The standard tactics of fire and movement, one section supporting another while it moved, did not appear to work well under water. The conditions were impossible and the casualties high. The Calgary Highlanders fought what the German commander described as 'fanatical and eager' young paratroops[68] for three days and nights, made little headway, and the division had to drive off enemy counterattacks.

The Fenian Raids of 1866 tested the Canadian Militia. This decorated railway engine transported volunteers to the Niagara frontier and the battle at Ridgeway.

When Fenians attacked targets in Canada East, crowds hailed the Militia volunteers on Montreal's Champs de Mars.

Getting British regulars and Canadian Militia to the Red River in 1870 was three-quarters of the battle against Métis rebels. This watercolour by William Armstrong shows Colonel Wolseley's camp at Prince Arthur Landing.

In the 1885 North-West Rebellion, the railway went only part way. Militiamen pressed ferries into service.

Largely untrained but fit and adventurous, General Middleton's troops in 1885 were a good cross-section of Canadian manhood.

War art of 1885 could turn humiliating defeat into gallant victory. This wholly imaginary representation of the Battle of Duck Lake was good for morale.

General Frederick Middleton, the portly figure in the foreground visiting wounded soldiers after Batoche, was caution personified. With his untrained force, he had to be.

The South African War was Canada's 'splendid little war,' and Winnipeg cheered the departure of its first contingent.

Paardeberg was Canada's first great victory overseas. The Royal Canadian Regiment's role was celebrated, as in this contemporary illustration.

The reality of Paardeberg was much messier. Wounded men of the Royal Canadian Regiment lie on the ground waiting treatment.

The Boers were better marksmen than their opponents, and the arid, stony terrain
sometimes gave scant cover to the Royal Canadian Regiment.

By imperial standards, the Boers were a motley lot of bearded old men and youngsters, though they fought with great skill. These prisoners were taken at Paardeberg.

Men of the 5th Canadian Mounted Rifles, en route to South Africa in 1902, engage in 'mounted combat' at sea.

Major-General Sir Sam Hughes, Canada's Great War Minister of Militia and Defence.

The response to war was instant and enthusiastic in the West. This parade of volunteers, part Militia, part new recruits, took place in Rosetown, Saskatchewan, in August 1914.

Getting the First Contingent and its equipment, including this 18-pounder gun, loaded aboard ship in September 1914 was a major task.

The most terrifying, if not always the most effective, weapon of the Great War was gas. This striking photo shows a gas attack on the Somme.

Some Canadians showed extraordinary courage in battle. Major George Pearkes, wearing the ribbon of the Military Cross, soon had a Victoria Cross and a chestful of other awards for gallantry.

The Canadian Corps developed its techniques through trial and error. Here Canadians put together a bridge over the Yser, near Ypres, in 1916.

THE CANADIAN CONVALESCENT HOSPITAL AT BEAR WOOD, WOKINGHAM
(1) Dinner-time. (2) At dinner. (3) Nothing is wasted. (4) Getting into khaki again. (5) The blue suit. (6) Repairs.
(7) A game under difficulties. (8) Writing home.

The medical services overseas were remarkably efficient, despite difficult conditions.
The soldiers' goal was a 'blighty,' a wound requiring treatment in a convalescent
hospital in Britain.

Life in the trenches was bleak at best. Two soldiers cook their rations over an improvised stove in 1915–16.

The home front, harangued to scrimp and save, believed it was doing its part.

The attack on Hill 70 in August 1917 was bloody. Here, a 'walking wounded' (foreground) pauses for a hot drink at a field kitchen on his way to the rear.

The CEF liberated Mons, Belgium, on the last day of war. For these men
the war was over at last.

The cost of war was horrific. Here amputees and other wounded sit in the sun at Yonge and Carlton streets in Toronto in 1916.

The war provided a strong bond for those who fought and survived.

The beginning of the Second World War found Canada's Militia fully prepared –
to fight the Great War. This Montreal scene was not typical, because few
artillery regiments had trucks.

These toy tanks at the Canadian Armoured Fighting Vehicle School at Camp Borden, Ontario, were all the armour Canada possessed in 1939.

The disaster at Dieppe in August 1942 sits like a scar on the Canadian conscience. It was also a boon for enemy propagandists, who released this photo around the world.

Canadian women wanted to serve. These Canadian Women's Army Corps recruits head off for training at Vermilion, Alberta, in 1943.

The army's first sustained action came in Italy. This superb photo, showing a Canadian Sherman tank, illustrates the terrain I Canadian Corps fought over – at such great cost.

The battle for Ortona, while ultimately victorious, nearly finished the First Canadian Division. Here Seaforth Highlanders, pulled away from house-clearing for a few hours, enjoy their 1943 Christmas dinner.

The D-Day invasion was the greatest amphibious operation in history, and these men of the
Third Canadian Division, awaiting the order to go on June 5, 1944, were part of it.

Generals Rod Keller of the Third Canadian Division (left) and Harry Crerar
(First Canadian Army) on July 1, 1944.

General Guy Simonds, II Canadian Corps, and Defence Minister J.L. Ralston worry about the reinforcement situation in October 1944.

The Scheldt campaign was a battle fought in appalling conditions of cold and mud. Here tanks of the Fort Garry Horse operate near Beveland on October 30, 1944.

Conditions in the Hochwald forest inside Germany were little better, as trucks, half-tracks, and jeeps all struggled to proceed over muddy, narrow forest roads.

"NO! I CERTAINLY WOULD NOT ADVISE MAKIN' A NOISE LIKE A DUCK!"

The army's great cartoonist Bing Coughlin created 'Herbie,' the archetypal Canadian soldier.

Action photographs are rare. This photo, taken near Groningen, The Netherlands,
in the last weeks of the war, shows men of the South Saskatchewan Regiment
responding with fire to the enemy.

The 1st Canadian Parachute Battalion moved further into Germany than any other Canadian unit and, on May 4, 1945, linked up with the Russian army at Wismar.

Victory meant repatriation and, for this shipload of soldiers, home.

Oshawa, Ontario, greets the Ontario Regiment on November 29, 1945.

The Korean War found Canada fighting for the United Nations. Here Brigadier John Rockingham (fourth from left) briefs some of his officers.

The Canadians fought the Korean War with Second World War weapons like this mortar.

Soldiers of the 2 Princess Patricia's Canadian Light Infantry, here trudging across a valley in March 1951, were the first Canadians to see action in Korea.

A weary soldier loads a Bren gun magazine while KATCOMs behind look on.

As the Korean War dragged on in stalemate, bunkers, such as this mortar position, became ever more elaborate.

The 1953 armistice finally brought the Korean War to a close. Soldiers of the 3 Royal 22e Régiment muster a cheer at the news.

Peacekeeping was the only area of growth for the Canadian Army. Here, soldiers from a reconnaissance unit in the Sinai pause to let a flute-playing shepherd pass by.

Peacekeeping duty in Cyprus stretched out for almost three decades. This patrolling soldier, his weapon at the ready, faced great boredom and occasional terror.

These Canadians, under fire in an armoured personnel carrier during the Turkish invasion of Cyprus, show entirely normal reactions of fear and concern.

Not all peacekeeping was done for the United Nations. This soldier in Vietnam was serving
with the Canadian contingent in the International Control Commission.

Defence Minister Paul Hellyer's plan for integration and unification of the Canadian Forces stirred huge controversy in the 1960s, as this brilliant Macpherson cartoon shows.

The army's struggle with Mohawk 'Warriors' at Oka, Quebec, in 1990 was a propaganda battle. Here the Van Doos' Commanding Officer, Lieutenant-Colonel Pierre Daigle, catches up on the progress of the newspaper war.

Post–Cold War peacekeeping took Canadians into the Former Yugoslavia. This Cougar, driving in the rain in Bosnia in 1998, was part of the large Canadian contingent there.

From the autumn of 1999, Canadian troops, numbering 650 at peak, served in East Timor, a small territory struggling to win independence from Indonesia. This reconnaissance platoon of the Royal 22e Régiment, part of a reinforced company of Van Doos, left for home in 2000.

The first Canadian infantry to arrive in Afghanistan were 3 PPCLI. In February 2002, this company commander briefed his soldiers before one of their first patrols. Note that the soldiers were wearing green CADPAT uniforms, not the more appropriate desert camouflage.

The militia provided up to 25 per cent of the soldiers for Afghanistan. In November 2005 an infantryman from Toronto's 48th Highlanders provided security while soldiers from the Provincial Reconstruction Team talked to Afghans in Kandahar.

LCol Ian Hope, the commander of Task Force Orion, shown as he arrived at Kandahar Airfield in January 2006, led his battle group through some of the toughest fighting Canadians faced in Afghanistan.

In May 2006, a company commander from Task Force Orion's 1 PPCLI held an 'O' Group in the desert in Helmand province, west of Kandahar. In the next three months, this company would defeat formed Taliban units, inflicting and suffering casualties.

The Second Division returned to the offensive on October 13 – Black Friday ever after to the Black Watch. The Montrealers launched a mad daylight attack over 1200 yards of beet fields, and the Germans literally destroyed the battalion. They killed or wounded all the company commanders, and one company had four men left out of the ninety who had begun the attack. 'The battalion seems to have horrible shows periodically,' one wounded officer wrote home, 'and this was one of them.'[69]

On October 16 the RHLI launched a well-prepared and heavily supported night attack and made substantial headway. But the Nazis counterattacked and overran one company. The Canadians had long since perfected the use of artillery concentrations: one call could get the fire of one or many regiments on a particular map reference in a moment. The company commander, Major Joe Pigott, called in a massive artillery barrage on his own positions, and the 4000 (!) shells killed or wounded most of the enemy and spared almost all the dug-in Canadians. 'The fire caught the enemy in the open,' the Rileys reported, 'whereas our men were deep in slit trenches having been warned. Our troops cheered; the slaughter was terrific.'[70] Even so, the Rileys had only 6 officers and 157 men left after twelve hours of fighting. Not until October 24 was the isthmus cut by units of the 5th and 6th brigades, notably the Fusiliers Mont-Royal led by their acting CO, Major Jacques Dextraze, another of the extraordinary young leaders in the army. Thereafter, the 4th and 6th brigades achieved a better pace, assisted by a seaborne assault by British troops across the West Scheldt. Beveland had been cleared.

On October 31 Lieutenant Ted Sills, an RMC graduate of 1942 serving in the artillery, suffered a wound in his knee while he was acting as a Forward Observation Officer in the Scheldt battle. Hit by a German mortar in a house being used as an infantry company's headquarters, Sills wrote to his mother:

> I started down the lines of communication of the medical services, which are superb. First, to the Regimental Aid Post of the Armoured Regiment to which I am attached, where the Medical Officer dressed the wound and told me to go to my regiment. So I got my tank and went off another mile to the regiment where our own M.O. had a look at the leg and thought there might be shrapnel in it. So he re-dressed it with sulphanilimyde and gave me four pills and filled out more papers which started accumulating from the first

R.A.P. Then I went by a large ambulance, feeling perfectly O.K. back to the casualty clearing station, where I was given food – the first that day, and it was now 9 p.m. – and filled out more papers and was shipped back to this General Hospital. Here, after more questions had been answered, and more papers made out, I was given a bed with sheets, and hot water for a bath – (you see, the five of us in the tank crew had had to sleep in the tank every night ... and we never had our clothes off for two weeks ...) So the whole thing seemed like heaven ... every three hours I had a needle of penicillin. Then, this morning, I was X-rayed and visited by a major doctor – then ... to the operating room ... I am feeling fine and having a great rest.[71]

Just as in Italy, the wounded received exemplary care.

The Scheldt struggle went on. Simonds's fertile brain had earlier produced a plan to liberate Walcheren. Use the Royal Air Force to bomb the dikes on Walcheren, sink the island, isolate the enemy on patches of high ground, and then attack from the sea under a heavy artillery bombardment. The opposition of the Netherlands government-in-exile first had to be overcome – the flooding would ruin good farmland for years to come. The Royal Air Force was lukewarm to the idea, but Simonds, meeting Bomber Command officers in the caddy shack on the golf course at Ghent, fixed them with his eyes, said he could not argue with their opinions, but warned them their opposition would cost lives. The RAF men left the room and returned to say that, while they could not guarantee success, they would try. According to G.E. Beament, the Brigadier General Staff at the First Canadian Army who was present, Simonds had demonstrated real leadership.[72] Beginning on October 3, the bombing destroyed the dykes and flooded Walcheren. British commandos and soldiers, serving under the First Canadian Army, finished the job in two seaborne assaults by November 8.

The Canadian attack on Walcheren still had to proceed to divert enemy attention away from the seaborne commando assault. Joined to Beveland by a 1200-yard-long and 40-yard-wide heavily cratered causeway, protected on both sides by mud flats, the Walcheren causeway was a death trap. Impassable to tanks and trucks, good German soldiers with artillery, machine guns, and mortars covered the causeway, but the Canadians' orders were to assault across it. The reconstituted Black Watch, Canada's hard-luck regiment, suffered heavily in the first attempt to cross on the afternoon of October 31. So too did the Calgary Highlanders, who tried and failed that night, and tried again the next morning. Behind a fierce artillery barrage from two field regiments and air support, they made it across this time, clinging by their fingernails to a narrow bridgehead. One Calgary company was rallied by the Brigade Major of 5th Brigade, George Hees, who happened to be on the scene and took command when the men were stuck in the middle of the causeway and all officers had been killed or wounded. He led the company as long as the regiment remained there, despite being wounded in the arm. A fierce counterattack with flamethrowers ultimately drove the Highlanders back.[73]

The Régiment de Maisonneuve was next to try on the night of November 1–2, but never made it to Walcheren, its attack held up by errant British artillery fire. One company, however, did not halt and fought a bitter, lonely struggle with the defenders. The 52nd British Division's GOC sensibly refused to make the next direct assault, and his men found a place where the Scots could walk across the mud flats and outflank the causeway's defenders. The addition of these men, along with the landings from the sea, the first on November 1, finally ended the struggle on November 8. The attacks over the causeway had to be pressed forward to keep the enemy's attention divided after the first seaborne landings, and the Highlanders and Maisies paid the price in full.

Almost three weeks later, as soon as the mines had been cleared, the Scheldt was at last a safe route for supply vessels. The battle had been gruelling, a horrid experience. Preoccupied with Market Garden, his great but failed airborne and ground assault to end the war by seizing the river crossings leading to the Reich, Montgomery had assigned the First Canadian Army an all but impossible task. Worse, he had failed to give it the resources it needed to do the job, even though the Allied armies were faltering for want of the supplies that could have come through Antwerp. The Canadians succeeded, but at a cost of 6367 Canadian casualties, and an equal number of British killed and wounded as well. More than 24,000 of the enemy surrendered to the Second and Third Divisions and their British compatriots.

The casualties in Italy, added to those suffered in Normandy and on the Scheldt, had left Canadian infantry regiments desperately shorthanded. The French-speaking units – the Maisonneuves, the Chaudières, the Van Doos, and the Fusiliers Mont Royal – were especially hard hit, and unilingual

English-speaking officers had to be posted to these battalions for a time. The root of the problem was simple: the Canadian Army planners had slavishly based their replacement estimates on earlier British studies made in North Africa when the Germans still had an air force. Men in arms other than infantry and in the rear areas had been expected to sustain some 52 per cent of all casualties. But the Luftwaffe had been driven from the skies, and riflemen suffered a very high percentage of casualties – up to 77 per cent. The War Office had also calculated that half of the wounded men could return to their units, but recovered men often could not withstand the strain of infantry service. These discrepancies were huge, and no reinforcement scheme could cope with such wildly errant calculations.[74] If there was blame to be affixed, the army staff could be faulted for blindly accepting British data. Certainly Mackenzie King had his doubts: 'Really the more I see it all, the more I am convinced that the Department of Defence has made a terrible mess of our whole war effort. The army has been far too large; the planning has been anything but sound. The judgment, far from good.'[75]

King's view may have been correct, even if it was his regular practice to shift blame to others. In August 1944 Lieutenant-General Ken Stuart, the Chief of Staff at the Canadian Military Headquarters in London, had told the government that he had enough infantry reinforcements on hand and in the training pipeline to meet all foreseeable needs.[76] By September, CMHQ realized that it had an overall reinforcement surplus of 13,000, but an infantry reinforcement deficit of 2000. Based on casualty estimates to the end of 1944, the First Canadian Army faced a shortage of 15,000 infantry before 1944 was over. Like almost every Allied commander, Stuart had gambled on a German collapse after the Normandy battles. He was wrong.[77]

The implications of an infantry replacement shortage were serious: understrength infantry regiments went into action with fewer riflemen, and every man was in greater jeopardy. Battalions could be reduced to 400 men, companies to 80, platoons to 15, and sections from 10 men to 5. Senior officers all too often threw a battalion at an objective, forgetting that 400 men could never be as effective as 800. The result was usually higher casualties and more stalled attacks. Reinforcements came forward from training regiments in Britain, but such men too frequently received little training there and sometimes had received precious little in Canada. Many of the reinforcements coming into the line had been remustered from other trades and had received only the most rudimentary infantry training – many had never thrown a grenade or fired a Bren gun.* Green men took time to adapt to the front line and, while they did, they were a burden on their mates; moreover, they were a risk to themselves, for the ill-trained and inexperienced always seemed to die sooner than the old sweats.[78] Moreover, the new men, without the complex support system the originals had built up, were and knew they were alone, their group loyalty simply non-existent on their arrival.[79] Historian Bill McAndrew noted that the Royal Winnipeg Rifles lost a company's worth of men on D-Day, the equivalent of two more on June 8, and as many a month later. Reinforcements, in effect, made up the whole unit and, sent forward as individuals, 'too often lacked an opportunity to form the self-supporting groups that were the key to combat effectiveness.'[80]

When Colonel J.L. Ralston, the Defence Minister, visited the troops in Italy and France in September and October, officers and senior NCOs bent his ear on their understrength condition, and the doughty minister went home to Ottawa determined to force the issue with Prime Minister Mackenzie King. The details of the struggle in the Cabinet War Committee have been treated elsewhere.[81] What is relevant here is that papers produced for the Cabinet demonstrated that there were 120,000 General Service volunteers in Canada and a further 90,000 in Britain, but only a maximum of 15,000 were considered fit enough for front-line service. For the best of reasons and with all good intentions, the army brass had listened to doctors and psychologists and created a system of medical categories and age restrictions that hampered their ability to adapt in crisis. This approach had made it all but impossible to find reinforcements for the fighting battalions, despite repeated efforts to comb out fit men from the General Service pool. In the circumstances, there seemed to be only one place left to get the infantry reinforcements: the home defence conscripts raised under the National Resources Mobilization Act. There were 60,000 of these men in Canada, 42,000 of whom could be used to meet the infantry reinforcement needs. The political costs of sending them

---

* Reinforcements' records suggest adequate training, but records, as some have noted, lie and cannot measure the quality of training received. See the important analysis in Bill McAndrew et al., *Liberation: The Canadians in Europe* (Montreal, 1995), 61–3.

overseas had to be balanced against the military necessity in Northwest Europe and Italy. This had to be calculated against the likelihood of Canadian divisions facing heavy fighting and high casualties in what everyone agreed was a war that could not last much longer.

Mackenzie King's every instinct was to put political considerations first. He forced Ralston's resignation on November 1 and replaced him with General Andrew McNaughton,* who hated Ralston and believed that he could persuade the home defence conscripts to volunteer. In a series of speeches, McNaughton tried, but after being booed by Great War veterans, convinced that the government was pandering to Quebec, at a Canadian Legion gathering, the General lost his confidence.[82] In fact, the 42,000 NRMA men being considered as reinforcements were roughly representative of the Canadian population, with 10,250 from Ontario, 10,000 from the Prairies, 16,300 from Quebec, 2600 from the Maritimes, and 2850 from British Columbia. No more than 37 per cent were francophones, just above the French Canadian percentage in the population as a whole.[83] The English Canadian public, then and since, did not want to believe this breakdown.

Despite the new Minister's efforts and those of his commanders, the NRMA soldiers overwhelmingly remained unmoved and refused to volunteer for overseas service. If they want to order us to go, the refrain went, we'll go, but don't expect us to volunteer to get the King government off the hook. Faced with this stone wall, restive senior officers, notably Major-General George Pearkes, commanding in British Columbia, began to break ranks. Pearkes authorized his officers to speak to the media and one District Officer Commanding resigned; others threatened to do so. On November 22, finally, the senior officers at army headquarters told McNaughton in a memorandum of their 'considered opinion [that] the Voluntary system of recruiting through Army channels cannot meet the immediate problem.'[84] The senior staff acted properly in giving the Minister their advice; the DOC who resigned acted

---

* General Harry Crerar told Canadian High Commissioner Vincent Massey in London of his concerns about 'McNaughton's astonishing appointment' and worried that the new Minister might demand I Canadian Corps be moved from Italy to Northwest Europe. 'If this were resisted ... on the valid grounds of operational and administrative difficulty, McN. he thought might well seize upon this and make an anti-British issue out of it.' University of Toronto Archives, Massey Papers, box 312, Diary, November 6, 1944.

properly; but Pearkes did not. Within a few moments of hearing of the memo to McNaughton, the Prime Minister switched his position and decided to send 16,000 NRMA men overseas. McNaughton gulped and agreed; so did all the ministers, except for Air Minister C.G. Power, who resigned. Some ministers were undoubtedly swayed by King's ludicrous claim of a generals' revolt.[85] There was substantial unhappiness in Quebec, but Québécois could see that King had resisted conscription as long as he could.

King's *volte-face* effectively ended the political crisis. The military crisis had a few more days to run. There was trouble amounting to mutiny in some British Columbia camps housing the 6th Division, where its units were stuffed with NRMA men.[86] Some conscripts deserted, and others threw away their rifles when they boarded ship for overseas.* Overall, however, the NRMA men did what many had always said they would: when ordered to go overseas, they went. In all, 12,908 conscripts proceeded to Britain and 2463 went to units of the First Canadian Army. By all reports, the conscripts did well. 'I have some N.R.M.A. men in the platoon now,' Lieutenant Donald Pearce of the North Novas wrote on March 20, 1945. 'There is, of course, a considerable prejudice against them ... But for some reason they have made excellent soldiers, so far; very scrupulous in the care of their weapons and equipment, certainly, and quite well versed in various military skills.'[87] In all, 69 conscripts were killed, 232 were wounded, and 13 became POWs.

Curiously, happily, the casualty estimates that had provoked the crisis proved worse than the reality. If the training stream had been allowed to do its work by April 27, 1945, the reinforcement pool overseas would have had a surplus of 8500 men. Armies live and die on estimates of wastage, the military's terrible word for casualties. The Canadian Army's conscription crisis of 1944 ultimately arose because the estimates of infantry casualties were too low, and it ended with estimates that were too high.

One reason casualties were lower was that, after the gruelling struggle in the Scheldt estuary, the battered First Canadian Army had three months of rela-

---

* These actions infuriated many soldiers overseas. Lieutenant J.E. Boulet wrote to his wife in his last letter, on February 15, 1945: 'It made mighty poor reading over here and certainly could be a propaganda tool for Jerry.' Boulet was killed on February 26 on the Goch-Calcar road (letter available at www.collections.gc.ic/courage/j.e.boulet).

tive quiet. The strain of combat, the constant dirt and mud that could never be washed completely away, the poor food (often eaten cold), the filthy clothing, the hurry up and wait routines of the army, and the utter weariness of hauling heavy equipment wore down the men, even those who were young and fit. Alex Colville's superb painting *Infantry, Near Nijmegen* shows a column of Canadians moving on a dike through flooded fields, and the weariness etched on the faces is unforgettable.

There were long periods of rest that helped in recuperation and brief periods in the line with patrols and small engagements. Some, as at Kapelsche Veer in the Netherlands at the end of January 1945,[88] were very costly. For the most part, the soldiers had short periods of leave, longer spells of training, and their units received the chance to absorb new reinforcements and train them to the unit standard. Almost no one received leave to Canada, making the Canadians very different from the Americans, who had a generous scheme, or the British, who had a much shorter distance to go.* As a result, men were away from home for years. Soldiers waited in fear for a 'Dear John' letter, worried about their children, and grew distant from their parents. Major-General Bruce Matthews, whose wife had twins in 1940, did not see his children until he returned home at the end of the war. 'Mommy, who is that man?' his four-year-olds asked.[89]

There was time to change senior officers too. In November, Matthews replaced Charles Foulkes at Second Division, Foulkes taking command of I Canadian Corps in Italy. There was much enthusiasm for this exchange in the division, especially when it was learned that Matthews, unlike Foulkes, listened and took advice.[90] In December, Chris Vokes took over the Fourth Canadian Armoured Division, while Major-General Harry Foster replaced him with the First Division in Italy. At Matthews's 6th Brigade, when Brigadier J.G. Gauvreau, a very competent francophone officer, was wounded by a mine, Brigadier Holley Keefler succeeded him. The shifts of senior officers, under way since the war's early days, almost always replaced the older officers with the younger and, once all the First Canadian Army was in action, the failures and the less successful commanders with those who led effectively. There was polit-

---

* Leave to Canada for men with 'five years' satisfactory continuous service overseas' did not begin until November 1944 and was limited to 450 men per month. Stacey and Wilson, *The Half-Million*, 154.

ical infighting for promotion, of course, and senior commanders had their favourites. But effectiveness was ordinarily the key. A private in 1940 with no military experience at all, Jacques Dextraze was a much-decorated lieutenant-colonel and the CO of the Fusiliers Mont-Royal by late 1944 at the age of twenty-four. Battle was stressful, a young man's trade, and most older officers understandably seemed unable to withstand the strain. Experience, the ongoing process of learning how best to organize, lead, and motivate men, gradually accrued, and senior officers like Matthews and Keefler, militiamen before the war and intelligent, adaptable wartime officers, passed and surpassed many of their Permanent Force colleagues. In effect, during a half-dozen years of active service, they became professional soldiers, whatever their pre-war occupations.

The older officers moved into staff and training positions at home or in Britain. George Pearkes, for example, went from commanding formations in the United Kingdom to commanding troops on the West Coast. Major-Generals A.E. Potts, H.N. Ganong, and P.E. Leclerc had similar experiences. The Chiefs and Vice-Chiefs of the General Staff were almost all older PF officers, as were many of the District Officers Commanding. Some of these men were more efficient, more powerful than others, naturally enough, but there could be little doubt that their contribution was huge. They kept the wheels turning in Canada, raising and training the officers and men who went overseas over six years of war.

In December, with the Canadians posted on the Rivers Waal and Maas and in the area of Nijmegen in the Netherlands, the Germans launched their last offensive gambit. The Ardennes offensive, the Battle of the Bulge, was a massive attack that aimed to reach Antwerp, a kill-shot at the Allies. The scheme failed because the American troops at Bastogne resisted fiercely and because General George Patton's Third Army was able to relieve the defenders. The 1st Canadian Parachute Battalion, part of the British 6th Airborne Division, played a part in the final stages of the battle.[91] Had Hitler's strike succeeded, had he had more airpower at his disposal and more gasoline for his panzers, the First Canadian Army (and the Second British and Ninth U.S. Armies) might have been caught in the pocket. Luck, for once, favoured the Canadians. What the German offensive did was to delay the next major operation of the First Canadian Army for six weeks.

This operation, beginning on February 8, 1945, saw the First Canadian Army crossing into Germany for the first time.[92] For the battle in the Rhineland, Operation Veritable, Harry Crerar led the largest Canadian-commanded force ever – thirteen divisions, including nine British, and smaller formations of Belgians, Dutch, Poles, and Americans. In fact, the two corps involved, II Canadian, commanded by Simonds, and XXX British, commanded by Lieutenant-General Brian Horrocks, were directed in the battle by Horrocks, a charismatic and able leader. The aim of Veritable was to clear the ground between the Maas and the Rhine rivers, a necessity before the Rhine itself could be crossed. For their part, the Canadian divisions confronted three lines of fortifications: an outpost line of trenches, anti-tank ditches, minefields, and fortified strongpoints; the Siegfried Line of dugouts and concrete bunkers that ran through the heavily treed Reichswald; and the fortified and forested Hochwald area, which, on high ground, controlled the Rhine crossings.

Brigadier James Roberts, who commanded the 8th Brigade of the Third Division, later recalled an Orders Group of his brigade staff before Veritable. He had looked around the room and 'realized that those officers present, in addition to my own brigade staff, included three battalion commanders, the commanding officer of our own field artillery regiment, and others representing machine guns, anti-tank and anti-aircraft guns, signals, transportation, smoke ... assault landing craft, searchlights and military police ... We looked at wall maps and aerial photos and used slide rules to estimate the timing of various phases of the operation.' How different it had been for Roberts's father, who had served in the Boer War. His commanding officer there would have pointed at the hill and said '"There they are, gentlemen, charge!" So had the conduct of war changed in one generation.'[93]

Operation Veritable began at 10:30 a.m. on February 8 behind an incredible artillery and rocket barrage and heavy bombing from more than 850 aircraft of the RAF Bomber Command that obliterated Cleve and most of Goch. Then the tanks, churning up the mud, tried to clear the way for the infantry, who struggled through the badly flooded terrain – the enemy had breached the Rhine dikes – and the Chaudières actually used skiffs to move their men while the North Shores moved on Buffaloes. The outpost line, much of it manned by the slapdash 84th Division and *Volkssturm* units, made up of elderly civilians who had been pressed into service, fell quickly. Not all German units were effective in combat, and scratch units like these cannon fodder were in place simply to provide a screen behind which the still capable enemy units could manoeuvre. The Calgary Highlanders and the Maisonneuves took their objectives but suffered heavy casualties from cunningly planted *Schu* mines.

The Siegfried Line and the Reichswald were tougher nuts to crack. The Wehrmacht, fighting on German soil and with the SS and Gestapo just behind the line to ensure that men did their full measure of duty to the Führer, resisted with extraordinary determination. The enemy flooding had created a Scheldt-like quagmire, and attacking infantry had to wade under fire through chest-high water in the February cold. Trucks and armour could find the roads only by following lines of trees. The Third Canadian Division bore the brunt of the fighting, some of its units reaching their flooded objectives and effectively being cut off by high water. Buffaloes had to be called in to 'rescue' some 7th and 8th Brigade battalions. By February 10 the Third Division and British troops had broken through the Siegfried Line, and, three days later, the Canadians had cleared the Reichswald.

The next task was to clear the route to the Hochwald, and the Third Division got the job. First, strong enemy forces in Moyland Wood and along the road from Goch to Calcar had to be eliminated. The Canadian Scottish ran into enemy paratroopers at Moyland Wood and suffered heavily, losing fifty-three POWs to a German counterattack. The Regina Rifles on February 18 used Wasp flamethrowers to force the enemy back, but came under heavy artillery fire from across the Rhine and had to repel repeated counterattacks by fresh, first-class troops of the 6th Parachute Division. The Royal Winnipeg Rifles also took a battering but drove the enemy from the wood by February 21.

The 4th Brigade's job was to open the road from Goch to Calcar in the face of bitter resistance. A two-battalion attack by the RHLI and the Essex Scottish on February 19, using Kangaroos and supported by Shermans of the Fort Garry Horse, was brutal. German 88s smashed some of the carriers, and a panzer assault caught the Canadians without armoured support. The situation was desperate overnight, as both the Essex and a company of the Rileys were overrun at times and barely hung on, though anti-tank guns of the 18th Battery knocked out seven panzers. Casualties were heavy – the Essex lost 204 men, the RHLI 125, and the Royal Regiment, rushed in to bolster the line, 64. For his leadership and courage, Company Sergeant Major F.L. Dixon of the Essex Scottish won a second bar to his Military Medal, making him the only Canadian to win this award three times in the war. The enemy lost heavily too, and the Canadians duly cleared the road, though all the Canadian infantry – wet, chilled, and exhausted – were near their breaking point. 'These personnel, logistic, geographic, and weather problems,' said Major-General Dan Spry, 'were being partially ignored by the higher commanders. They really didn't understand the sharp end of battle. They had a mental block; they'd never been there.'[94]

In the early morning of February 26 Operation Blockbuster targeted the Hochwald itself, the Second and Third divisions leading the way. German paratroops struck at the Second Division's jumping-off point just before the planned attack, but the Royal Hamilton Light Infantry and Shermans of the Fort Garry Horse drove them off. The attack then began on schedule at 3:45 a.m., as men found their way by aid of artificial moonlight and tracer fire, and the carrier-borne troops and tanks moved as fast as the ground permitted. The Queen's Own Rifles of the Third Division discovered that the hamlet of Mooshof was strongly defended, and the sodden ground slowed the tanks. 'D' company was hit especially hard, the losses heavy. Sergeant Aubrey Cosens, his platoon commander and most of his men killed or wounded, braved the hail of enemy fire to bring up a 1st Hussars tank. Sitting in front of the turret, he directed the Sherman's fire at enemy positions and led the tank directly into the midst of counterattacking paratroops. Then, with the four remaining men of his No. 16 Platoon, he directed the Sherman to ram one of the fortified farm buildings and, covered by his men, entered and cleared it. The second building was empty, and Cosens singlehandedly cleared the third building of several Germans. After consolidating his position, he went to report to his company commander, but a sniper's bullet killed him. He won a posthumous Victoria Cross. The Queen's Own took its objectives but lost 101 killed and wounded.

The Germans held on in carefully sited and concealed trenches until they had to pull back to the next prepared position. As soon as the Canadians reached the first enemy positions, mortar and artillery fire, pre-planned and registered, fell on them. Frequently counterattacks, coordinated with the mortars and *Nebelwerfers*, took back the ground just vacated. The Canadian drive went on, backed by massive firepower and endless armour, and the Germans, however skilled their tactics, found themselves relentlessly pressed back. The Régiment de la Chaudière, facing the heaviest fighting it had thus far seen, took Hollen and eighty-four prisoners and then, behind artillery and with tank support, the rest of their day's objectives. In all, the Chauds captured 224 paratroops and killed many more. Their losses on February 25 were sixteen killed and forty-six wounded.

The Fourth Armoured Division's task was to secure the northern part of the Calcar-Udem ridge. Brigadier Robert Moncel's 'Tiger Group' consisted of three armoured regiments, a motor battalion, and two battalions from the 11th Brigade. Each flank of the attack had an armoured regiment, mine-clearing Flail tanks, and two companies of carrier-borne infantry to press ahead while follow-on forces, including flamethrowers and self-propelled anti-tank guns, mopped up. The Nazis resisted strongly, troops using rocket-launching *panzerfausts* to knock out tanks, but the sheer weight and force of the attack overwhelmed them. Moncel's Tigers took their objectives with relatively light casualties in a model armoured and infantry battle, though the Argyll and Sutherland Highlanders suffered the most losses with fifty-three killed and wounded. Moncel ever after argued that well-planned assaults could do the job without heavy losses.

The Canadians were closing in on the Hochwald, the enemy's last line of defence on the western side of the Rhine. On February 27 the South Alberta and Algonquin Regiments formed 'Lion Group,' a force that would be complete when two battalions of the 10th Brigade returned from 'Tiger Group.' The Algonquin objective was a hill between the Hochwald and the Balberger Wald. With Sherman support, two companies had to crack the enemy line and two others occupy the crest, all moving behind heavy artillery support. The attack, a nightmare march through thick mud, went in at 6:00 a.m., surprising the defenders, and seized the crest. It was, one South Alberta trooper recalled, a scene 'more dramatic than anything from Wagner: flashes from German guns lit up the horizon ahead, and our own artillery made the one behind even brighter.'[95] But the Germans reacted promptly, deluging the Algonquins with artillery and mortar fire that lasted all day and inflicted heavy casualties. Attacks to widen the breach ground to a halt, and General Vokes, the GOC of the Fourth Armoured, ordered a new attack in the early morning of February 28. This substantial effort, led by the Argylls and the Lincoln and Welland Regiment, two Ontario units, ran into a fresh parachute battalion and tanks from the 116th Panzer Division. The Argylls suffered heavy losses, one company being reduced to fifteen men, and the supporting South Alberta Regiment's war diarist called the enemy shelling 'the most concentrated that this regiment ever sat under,' including at Falaise. The Germans sent in more paratroopers, concentrated their artillery, and held off the Canadians for three days.

On March 1 the Second Division's 6th Brigade moved into the line, led by Major Fred Tilston's company of the Essex Scottish. The Windsor, Ontario, regiment had 500 yards of open ground to cross and a massive barbed wire entanglement facing it. Though shot in the head, Tilston was the first into the enemy trenches, where he destroyed a machine-gun post with a hand grenade. Wounded a second time, he led the attackers to the next enemy line and cleared it. A German counterattack hit the company, and Tilston organized his few remaining men to drive it off. Six times he went back for grenades and ammunition for his men. Hit a third time and near death from loss of blood, Tilston passed his orders to his one surviving officer, who, with the men, stubbornly held the position. A pharmacist in civilian life, a quiet man whose actions that day astonished his soldiers, Tilston survived but lost both legs. He won the Victoria Cross for his inspiring leadership and raw courage.

On March 2, with enemy resistance finally beginning to falter, or so he thought, Brigadier Moncel's 4th Armoured Brigade had the Algonquin Regiment, his Lake Superior Regiment of motorized infantry, and his armoured regiments ready to drive to the Rhine. The infantry were understrength and tired, the men so weary that nothing in their civilian experience could have compared. Heavy mud slowed the attack, but it made excellent progress until accurate and heavy anti-tank fire stopped it cold. The tanks had to pull back, leaving the infantry to drive off the enemy attacks alone. They tried, but both battalions lost heavily, and two companies were all but obliterated. The Hochwald was not cleared, and the ancient town of Xanten beyond was not taken until March 8, when Operation Veritable came to its end. The Nazis had put elements of ten divisions into the line and had lost 22,000 prisoners and perhaps 22,000 more killed and wounded; the Canadians had suffered 5304 killed, wounded, and captured. The First Canadian Army, and the British and American armies, were on the Rhine at last, and the end of the war finally seemed in sight.

Between the end of February and the beginning of April, I Canadian Corps left Italy by ship, arrived in Marseilles, and drove through France to join the First Canadian Army in Northwest Europe. The corps' two months out of action had helped greatly in easing the pressure for reinforcements that had been so acute in the autumn and early winter. Moreover, it was good for Canadian nationalism to have its two corps reunited. For largely political reasons, Canada had not sought to exercise much, if any, strategic control over the disposition of its forces, an act of self-abnegation that was surely extraordinary. Defence minister Andrew McNaughton's insistence on bringing I Canadian Corps from Italy was a belated but necessary exercise of national will.

The privates and generals alike of I Canadian Corps were literally astonished at what they saw in Northwest Europe. In Italy, they now realized, the war had been fought on the cheap, without much air cover, and with too little equipment and too few supplies. In Northwest Europe the big battalions of modern warfare were in place and, comparatively speaking, the flood of tanks, trucks, and supplies of all kinds seemed endless. So too were the specialist units such as the 1st Radar Battery, the 1st Field (Air) Survey Company, the 1st Air Support Signals Unit, the vast array of workshops, repair depots, salvage units, specialized transport companies, and even the No. 3 Non-Effective Transit Depot – whatever that was.

The armoured regiments of the Fifth Division and the 1st Armoured Brigade received new tanks for the Northwest Europe campaign, usually upgraded Sherman Fireflys with 17-pounder guns that could penetrate German armour and Stuart reconnaissance tanks – far better than the obsolete Honeys they had used in Italy. The one area that seemed more difficult to work with was air support: in Italy the Desert Air Force was always on call, but in Northwest Europe, formations seemingly had to queue for support.[96] The enemy, however, was still the same, and on March 23 the Allies crossed the Rhine in Operation Plunder.

The Canadian involvement in Plunder was comparatively light. The 1st Canadian Parachute Battalion took part in the huge air drop that preceded the water crossing. This elite unit, despite being widely scattered in the drop, took its objectives, captured 500 of the enemy, and killed another hundred. Corporal George Topham, a medical orderly with the battalion, won the Victoria Cross for carrying a wounded man to safety, despite being shot in the face; later, he risked his life once more by pulling wounded from a blazing carrier and getting them to safety. The Paras' CO, Lieutenant-Colonel Jeff Nicklin, a well-known football player before the war, died in the drop, along with twenty-five of his men; almost fifty were wounded and twenty were missing, a 20 per cent casualty rate out of the 475 men dropped. The 9th Brigade of the Third Division joined in the assault, crossing the Rhine on Buffaloes in the early morning of March 24. The Highland Light Infantry was the first Canadian infantry battalion across the river. The HLI faced heavy resistance from German paratroops, but, supported by massive artillery concentrations and flamethrowers, and clearing houses one by one, they took their objectives northwest of Rees. The remainder of the brigade, the North Novas and the SDGs, similarly faced first-class troops from the 15th Panzer Grenadier Division, and the enemy fought to the last man. By March 27 the whole of Third Division was east of the Rhine and, in heavy fighting, took the large town of Emmerich and the prominent feature of Hoch Elten, 3 miles to the northwest. Once the Hoch Elten was in Canadian hands, the Royal Canadian Engineers built a 1373-foot-long bridge over the Rhine. Two more bridges soon followed.

On April 1 the First Canadian Army took control of both Canadian corps and prepared to liberate the northern Netherlands. The forecast of operations General Crerar issued called for II Canadian Corps to cross the Ijssel River south of Deventer and take the Appeldoorn–Otterloo line and then liberate the northeastern part of Holland. General Foulkes's I Canadian Corps was to clean up the Neder Rijn, cross the river west of Arnhem and take that city, and then liberate the western Netherlands. With every man aware that the war was drawing to a close, with most also understanding that the Nazis would fight desperately and that the Dutch were starving, there was a complicated series of personal equations to work out. No man wanted to be killed in the last days of a long war, but if the enemy resisted strenuously, what then?

The advance into northern Holland and northwestern Germany proceeded rapidly. Deventer, Zwolle, Emden, and Wilhelmshaven fell quickly, as did Arnhem and Appeldoorn. At Groningen on April 15, where a Dutch SS battalion had nothing to lose, a fierce hand-to-hand fight cost 209 casualties in the Second Division. There, Calgary Highlanders took a German naval base. A private, John Shaw, had climbed a fence, leaving his weapon and webbing with his comrades. 'When I straightened up and looked about I saw standing before me a smartly dressed naval officer of high rank with his staff milling about him ... The [German officer] said to me "I wish to surrender but not to a private." ... The sergeant heard and, as he and the rest of the platoon entered the building, he snapped back ... "he is surrendered and if he gives you any trouble shove your bayonet up his you know what."'[97]

In the middle of the night of April 17 German troops tried to break out of the Canadian net, running over elements of the Fifth Canadian Armoured Division at Otterloo. The 17th Field Artillery Regiment, unfortunately and inexplicably sited ahead of the infantry and armour, bore the brunt of the enemy attack and a confused, deadly, six-hour struggle took place, the enemy burning a battery command post and moving through the units' areas, including the vehicle lines. With the help of tanks and flamethrowers in the morning, the enemy – 'all facing the same way and nicely spaced' – was dispatched. Alexander Ross, a battery commander, had three of his four guns destroyed, and his battery had seventeen casualties. His gunners killed or captured at least thirty of the enemy.[98] The story had it that the division GOC, General Hoffmeister, led one part of the battle in his 'very colourful' pyjamas.[99]

Otterloo was almost an aberration. 'We marched through Friesland,' Brigadier Roberts wrote later of the liberation of Holland, 'like Napoleon's troops through Austria in 1805.'[100] But his 8th Brigade had hand-to-hand fighting against young Nazi soldiers on April 8 at Zutphen and won its way forward behind flamethrowing Crocodile vehicles. The flames could shoot out more than a hundred feet, and the terrifyingly effective chemical mixture stuck to whatever it hit. Later, at Utrecht, the Germans again had prepared a strong defence, and the Canadians were readying themselves for a major attack. The Nazi Reichskommissar in the Netherlands, Seyss-Inquart, desperately currying favour for the postwar reckoning (he was hanged nonetheless), offered a truce to let the Canadians provide food for the Dutch, who were wasting away on 320 calories a day. General Eisenhower and Field Marshal Montgomery agreed, and fighting ceased on April 28. Meanwhile, starting on May 3, convoys rolled every thirty minutes on safe corridors through the lines with food, and RCAF bombers dropped parachute loads of foodstuffs. The Dutch rejoiced, as did the Canadians who were delivering the rations. But it was not until May 6 that the First Division moved into Amsterdam and Rotterdam, liberating Holland's largest cities.

The war was drawing to its close very rapidly now. American and Soviet soldiers met at Torgau, Germany, cutting Hitler's Reich in two. Men of the 1st Canadian Parachute Battalion, far to the east after some stiff actions at Minden, met Russian troops at Wismar on the Baltic Sea in the afternoon of May 2, part of a successful Allied effort to prevent the USSR's troops from 'liberating' Denmark. The Soviet commanders, men who had led the armies that inflicted almost 90 per cent of the casualties the Germans had suffered in the war, were not pleased to see Allied troops so far to the east. Already the beginnings of the Cold War were affecting the armies, but with prisoners of war being taken in the tens of thousands, and the concentration camps being liberated at last, few noticed the growing tension in the mixed horror and euphoria of the moment.

Still some Nazis resisted to the end. On May 1, after ten days while the Fifth Canadian Armoured Division squeezed the town, the Cape Breton Highlanders and other units of 11th Brigade of the Fifth Canadian Armoured Division attacked the heavily defended Dutch port of Delfzijl, across from Emden, and had their hardest battle of the war, or so soldiers recalled. Twenty Capes died in freeing the town[101] – on the same day that Hitler committed suicide in his Berlin bunker. Many thousands of Nazis surrendered, but enough fanatics wanted to die in the ruins of the Reich to make the Canadians suffer in the last hours of the Second World War in Europe. Late on May 4 the German armies in Holland surrendered, but not before an officer and the padre of the Canadian Grenadier Guards died while trying to help enemy wounded. Remembering the travails Sir Arthur Currie had suffered for taking casualties in the liberation of Mons on the very last day of the Great War, General Crerar called off all operations the moment surrender talks began, but it was too late for the two Guards, who were among a dozen Canadians to die in action on the last day of battle. All the Nazi armies capitulated on May 7, and the next day was declared V-E Day. The war in Europe was over.

John Gray, an intelligence officer with First Canadian Army, was one of the first Canadians into newly freed Rotterdam. He recalled that, as he came out of the Stadthuis, there were ten or fifteen men around his jeep, and he passed to them the remains of his lunch. The men ate the sandwiches slowly, savouring every crumb, smacking their lips. 'Many soldiers had a similar experience that first day and in the days that followed; and to many Dutch people the very taste of liberty remained for a long time a mouthful of good bread or pastry such as they had almost forgotten.'[102] The staid Dutch went giddy with gratitude in May 1945, and ordinary Canadian soldiers found themselves treated like the conquering heroes they were. 'Here comes liberation,' one teenager in The Hague thought in almost biblical cadences when she saw the first Sherman. 'The soldier stood up and he was like a saint ... And the people climbed on the tank, and took the soldier out, and they were crying. And we were running with the tanks and the jeeps, all the way into the city.'[103] Too many Canadians today have either forgotten the war or never been taught anything of it. Not the Dutch – nor have they forgotten those who liberated them and the price Canadians paid to do so.[104]

Brigadier Roberts played the critical role in negotiating the Nazi surrender on the Third Canadian Division's front, and he shuttled back and forth between the lines. After the signing of the capitulation document, as he escorted the German general back to his quarters, the general asked if he was a professional soldier. The question startled Roberts, an ice cream salesman and Militia lieutenant before the war, and he realized that for six years he had not thought of anything but his military duties. As he recalled, 'I replied, simply, that I was never a professional soldier but that, like most Canadian soldiers, I was a civilian volunteer and that, in my former pre-war life, I had been an ice cream manufacturer.' The German was more than slightly affronted that he had been obliged to surrender to 'a common civilian.'[105] In fact, Roberts had become a professional soldier, a man who rose from lieutenant to a very competent brigade commander in almost six years of war. Like 75 per cent of brigade commanders and 90 per cent of unit commanding officers, he had been a militiaman before the war. But like all those who fought with the First Canadian Army, he had learned on the job, in training, and in action how to fight and defeat the enemy. As one Canadian senior officer put it, 'by the end of the war' the First Canadian Army 'was superb. It could move instantly, it was magnificent, and it had taken five years to build it.'[106] The First Canadian Army, like the Canadian Corps of 1918, had become the most professional fighting force Canada ever had. 'The best little army in the world,' Lieutenant-Colonel Jack English called it.[107]

In Canada, the German surrender was hailed jubilantly across the land. 'Everyone has been wildly excited about VE day,' wrote Farley Mowat's father from Toronto.[108] At the front, however, the news of the surrender stirred little exuberance in the soldiers. The South Alberta Regiment's adjutant noted in the unit war diary the feeling of every member of his regiment: 'I wish the hell we were out of this mud hole and in London – but much better Canada at home.'[109] Captain Harry Jolley, the dental officer with 12 Field Ambulance, noted the calm with which the news was received. 'I saw a few men gathered about our Signals wagon,' Jolley wrote, and went over to hear the announcement of V-E Day. 'None of us shouted, threw hats in the air, nor anything of that sort.' Jolley passed the news to a friend, who 'barely acknowledged having heard what I said & continued talking to the others in the group he was with. I felt – I don't know practically nothing. If anything what I felt most was surprise, maybe an important vexation with myself for failing to react in a manner more in keeping with the moment.' No one did, Jolley said. 'It was amazing.' But then, when he thought more about it, he realized that the last few weeks of expectation and steady advances had made it all a bit anticlimactic. Most important, 'we're tired – physically & emotionally. I wonder whether we'll ever recapture great depths of feeling about important events ... It's just that our sense of balance is a little out of kilter. Death, dirt, destruction – human & material – have become so commonplace.'[110] Jolley, promoted to major shortly after and awarded both a Mention in Dispatches for his role in driving off a German counterattack and Membership in the Order of the British Empire for his service, would recover his balance, as would almost all his comrades. But, first, lives had to be restored and the world rebuilt, and the numbed, low-key response, the lack of exultation at the front, was completely understandable.

The day after V-E Day, many units held parades to honour their dead. The 4th Medium Regiment, Royal Canadian Artillery, was one and, as Gunner J.P. Brady recorded: 'The Colonel begins to read the 36 names of our fallen. Tears are in his eyes. He falters and hands the paper to the Adjutant who calmly folds the paper and puts it in his pocket and quietly says: "It is not necessary. They were comrades. We remember."'[111]

As the years passed, the men who fought gained perspective on what they had been through. The survivors never ceased to mourn their friends and comrades, 'those beautiful young men,' as postwar Defence Minister and wounded veteran of the Queen's Own Rifles, Barney Danson, always calls them. All recognized their own good fortune. Lawyer and political organizer Eddie Goodman, who fought with the Fort Garry Horse, wrote that the war gave those who survived the opportunity 'to judge yourself and know your worth. Much of my own confidence has come from knowing I have been tried in battle and not found wanting.'[112]

nine

THE PROFESSIONAL ARMY, 1945–1968

'I have found a certain atmosphere of the mercenary in Canadian battle units,' wrote Lieutenant-Colonel Herbert Fairlie Wood in his novel of Korea, *The Private War of Jacket Coates*. 'Our units just hunker down in the country of operations, look around for a source of the local screech, get chummy with the village maidens, and enjoy the country.' Of course, Wood added in the voice of his anti-hero, Jacket Coates, 'We were all eager to get overseas ... the reasons ... rested entirely on the rumours generated by the letters we got from friends who were already there. A Korean girl charged one pound of sugar for her favours, we were told, and as for drink, beer was free. You could buy a jeep from a Yank for a bottle of rye ... It was no wonder that soldiers were turning down promotion in order to get on the next draft [for Korea].'[1]

Crude as this comment was, Jacket Coates almost certainly caught the attitudes with which many Canadian soldiers went off to Korea. There was some idealism in the men of the Special Force, but for most that probably took second place to baser concerns, to a desire for adventure, and a love of soldiering. Many of the men who enlisted for Korea went on to serve in Canada's brigade in NATO and, there and in Canada, they laid the basis for the nation's Cold War military professionalism.

The Canadian Army that emerged from the Second World War disappeared with amazing rapidity, exactly as the Canadian Corps had in 1919. The professionals of 1945, whether Permanent Force, Militia, or civilians who served, got on with their lives as quickly as they could. The new Active and Reserve forces were small, underfunded, and ill-equipped in the early years of the Cold War between the democracies and the Soviet Union and its satellites. But the signing of the North Atlantic Treaty in April 1949 and the beginning of the limited war in Korea in June 1950 began a period of rapid expansion and rearmament. Peacetime army strength rose to unprecedented heights, and the brigade groups in Korea, in West Germany, and in Canada became highly professional forces – well equipped, well led, and carrying a military punch far beyond their weight. For the first and only time in its peacetime history, Canada mattered militarily.[2]

This heyday of Canadian military professionalism did not last long. The election of John Diefenbaker's Progressive Conservative government in 1957 coincided with the end of the postwar economic boom, and budgets and numbers soon began to decline. The Suez Crisis of 1956 started the process of making peacekeeping a major Canadian defence priority and also signalled the end of Canada's automatic deference to British military professionalism. The debate over nuclear weapons a few years later symbolized the ultimate Americanization of the Canadian military; it finished Diefenbaker's administration, and it also dealt a psychological blow to the armed forces. So too did the integration and unification of the three services in the mid-1960s, pressed by Prime Minister Lester Pearson's Defence Minister, Paul Hellyer. Any one of these hammer blows might have shaken the Regular Army; the combination of them all created a storm from which it could not recover. The arrival of Pierre Trudeau's government in 1968, a government that did not much like either the military or Canada's alliance commitments, indicated that, however bleak the preceding half-dozen years had been, the future of the professional army was destined to be far worse.

The cost of the Second World War for Canadian soldiers was very high. Those killed in action or dead of wounds numbered 17,682. Another 5235 died in training, in accidents, or from disease. The wounded numbered 52,679, and 6433 were taken prisoner. In other words, more than 80,000 soldiers became casualties out of the 730,159 who enlisted or were conscripted. Considering that many were enlisted and discharged in short order, that many never left Canada, and that the greatest strength of the army was 495,804 at March 31, 1944, the casualty rate of those who served in action was much higher than the roughly 11 per cent of all those who enlisted that the figures suggest. The totals were blessedly far less than those from the Great War, but, considering that the army was in sustained action for a much shorter period in the 1939–45 conflict, they were roughly proportionate.

The casualties might have been much worse had the Canadian government's plans for the Pacific War come to fruition. In September 1944 Canada agreed to provide ground forces for the war against Japan, and two months later the Cabinet agreed to contribute an infantry division, organized, equipped, and trained on American lines.[3] The Sixth Canadian Infantry Division, with a maximum of 30,000 men in its ranks, including an armoured regiment and reinforcements, was to be manned by volunteers initially from the First Canadian Army in Northwest Europe and, secondarily, from General Service volunteers in Canada. Army Headquarters named Major-General Bert Hoffmeister, the General Officer Commanding of the Fifth Canadian Armoured Division, to be the commander of the Canadian Army Pacific Force, of which the Sixth Division was the heart. There was no shortage of volunteers for the CAPF, which many men saw as a way of getting home to Canada faster than waiting for demobilization. The Sixth's regiments took the names of the units that had made up the First Canadian Division of 1939, and Hoffmeister won General Harry Crerar's permission to have his pick of staff officers and unit commanding officers from Europe.[4] Training was only just under way[5] when the atomic bombs dropped on Hiroshima and Nagasaki in August 1945 forced Japan to sue for peace. Had the war continued, the invasion of the Japanese home islands would have been very costly both for the attackers and for the defence.

While the CAPF was taking shape, the 281,757 men and women of the First Canadian Army faced reorganization and repatriation. Service personnel, the fighting over, wanted to return to Canada as quickly as they could, and staff officers drafted and redrafted many plans for an orderly demobilization. The key player in the planning was the General Officer Commanding-in-Chief of the First Canadian Army. Like Sir Arthur Currie before him, Harry

Crerar wanted to return units to Canada as units, but the pressure for a system of 'first in, first out,' so that those men with the longest service overseas could get back to Canada at the head of the queue, was almost irresistible. The result was a delicate compromise between individual and unit repatriation: long-service personnel could be withdrawn from their units if they could be spared, and only then would major units return to Canada in the order they arrived overseas. When men waiting for shipping to become available at Aldershot in England in early July 1945 rioted and tore apart their camp and the town, General Crerar quickly seized on this unfortunate event to accelerate the repatriation process in the direction he wished it to go. He announced his decision to the army on July 10, but almost no long-service men had yet sailed for home, thanks to shipping delays and the absolute priority given to volunteers for the Pacific Force. Lieutenant-General Guy Simonds, taking command of the Canadian Forces in the Netherlands after Crerar's departure for Canada on July 30, had to deal with a major morale problem. Simonds made the system work, and Canada's army, which had taken six years to get overseas, 'returned in the thousands in one-sixth the time, 60,000 new wives and children in tow.'[6] All told, 184,054 army personnel had returned by December 31, 1945, and most of the remainder got home in the next few months. Units had their parades through cheering crowds, but most soldiers simply disappeared into the population, eager to restart their lives.

Each soldier and each member of the Canadian Women's Army Corps went onto 'civvy street' with an array of benefits that was likely the best in the world. Pre-enlistment jobs were guaranteed and schooling was there for those who wanted it: doctors, engineers, professors, mechanics, watchmakers, and skilled machinists all had their education and training funded through their vets' benefits. They had money to start a business, land to farm, medical care as long as they needed it, a generous gratuity based on months in service, and even a new suit of clothes. Canada's Veterans Charter was a model of how service personnel could be reintegrated into civil life with the country's tangible thanks for their efforts.[7]

The army overseas had some occupation duties to fulfil as well. Some 10,000 volunteers and another 8000 men with low priority for repatriation were constituted as the Third Canadian Division under Major-General Chris Vokes and posted on German soil as the Canadian Army Occupation Force.

Aside from a battalion of Canadians who took part in the formal Allied entry into Berlin,[8] the CAOF was stationed in the Emden-Wilhemshaven area of northwest Germany, where it lived amid the devastation that was postwar Germany. 'No fraternization' rules only lightly hampered the soldiers' efforts to find female companionship, and friendly Denmark and Holland were near-by. Many drank well, if not wisely, on 'liberated' stocks and, perhaps as a result, the complaints began to be heard in Vokes's headquarters and in Ottawa. Very soon, the government began pressing for an early end to the commitment: it was difficult to maintain a small force overseas, Ottawa said. Despite strong British protests at Canada's early departure, the government pulled its men out of the occupation of Germany in the spring of 1946.[9]

In the Netherlands, the joy of liberation began to go sour. The Dutch, occupied by the Germans for five years, began to chafe under the burden of the friendly Canadian occupation. Factories, schools, houses, and recreation areas had been commandeered by the Canadians, and the Dutch came to resent this use at a time when many buildings were in ruins. Men bristled at the money, cigarettes, and chocolate soldiers used to attract their girlfriends, and large numbers of women became pregnant. (To this day there is an orga-nization in the Netherlands of half-Dutch, half-Canadians who seek their fathers in Canada.) 'Let's face it,' one war bride recalled with startling honesty, 'after what we had been through the Canadians looked delicious.' A Dutch journalist put it more brutally: 'Dutch men were beaten militarily in 1940, sexually in 1945.'[10]

Some soldiers, including some senior officers, quickly turned to the black market to profiteer. One senior officer became known as 'Diamond Jim' because of his wheeling and dealing in the Amsterdam diamond market. Urged by Ottawa,[11] General Simonds dealt ruthlessly with the corrupt, but the stories spread. By early 1946 almost everyone, Canadian and Dutch, agreed it was time for the friendly occupation to end. A newspaper in Nijmegen put it bluntly: 'Let them go home. We are grateful to them, but let them go home. We won't forget these nice smiling boys, and they will always have our good wishes and our gratitude, but let them go home.'[12] By March 31, 1946, only 750 Canadians remained. The Headquarters of the Canadian Forces in the Netherlands closed on May 31. The Second World War was finally over.

Wartime military thinking had not disappeared from Army Headquarters in Ottawa, however. Exactly as after the Great War and its conscription crisis, army planners in 1945 had put together plans for peacetime conscription. As the United Nations formulated schemes for collective security to be enforced by member states of the global organization, army planners believed that Canada, as a middle power, needed an army to match. In June 1945 they presented the Minister of National Defence with their plan: the Canadian Army, the official designation that now replaced the historic Militia of Canada, should have a peacetime Active Force of 55,788 men organized into a self-contained brigade group, with additional units for coast defence, research and development, and administration and training. To find the necessary manpower, the planners argued, Canada needed a form of universal military training. Young men between eighteen and nineteen years of age would be inducted at four-month intervals for one year of military training, and 48,500 conscripts would be in training at any one time. The trained soldiers would then be obliged to serve in the Reserve Force for a fixed period. The Reserve's strength of 177,396 was to be organized into two corps of six divisions and four armoured brigades.[13]

This carefully worked out scheme made military sense, perhaps, but absolutely no political sense. After the conscription crises of 1942 and 1944, after ministerial firings and resignations because of manpower issues, and after the hard feelings between French and English Canada over compulsory service, no government led by Mackenzie King was going to consider peacetime conscription. When King learned of the army plan in August, he called it 'perfectly outrageous,' indicating his resentment at 'the postwar proposals based on the needs of another major war and the necessity of being in readiness for it.' King was wrong on the question of readiness, but certainly correct on the political impossibility of compulsory service in postwar Canada. The Cabinet agreed on August 3 and 'decided strongly against beginning any compulsory training.'[14] No one at Army Headquarters with one iota of political sense should have been surprised.

The impact of this abortive effort on the overall postwar plans for the army was likely severe. The Cabinet Defence Committee (which had replaced the Cabinet War Committee) decided in late September 1945 that it was not yet possible to assess Canada's defence needs and recommended that no final decisions on force strength be made. The government told the army that it could begin planning for a professional force of 20,000 to 25,000 in a peacetime armed forces of approximately 50,000 to 55,000. By the end of 1945, the army's strength had been fixed at 27,000 and the total defence budget at $172 million.[15] Although these numbers were much less than the army had wanted, the plan envisaged the largest peacetime regular force in Canada's history. But those totals would not be achieved. Brooke Claxton, the Defence Minister appointed in December 1946 with responsibility for all three services and a mandate to encourage coordination between the army, navy, and air force, told the country in January 1947 that the services could recruit up to 75 per cent of their authorized strength. Even that was not to be realized. By July 1947 the army's strength was 13,985, in a military force of 32,610 all told.[16]

The primary role of the Active Force was the defence of Canada. The army had three infantry battalions, each with a single company of paratroops, grouped into a Mobile Striking Force, two armoured regiments, and a regiment of field artillery. This rough equivalent of a brigade of troops was intended to satisfy the Canadian commitment, made under the Canada/US Basic Security Plan of 1946, to provide an airborne/air transportable force as the Canadian share of continental defence.[17] The infantry, supposedly trained to defeat any Soviet lodgements in the north if war should occur, consisted of the Royal 22e Régiment at Valcartier, Quebec, the Royal Canadian Regiment at Petawawa, Ontario, and the Princess Patricia's Canadian Light Infantry in Calgary, Alberta. The Royal Canadian Dragoons were posted to Petawawa, and the Lord Strathcona's Horse to Currie Barracks in Calgary. The Royal Canadian Horse Artillery was stationed at Camp Shilo, Manitoba. There were administrative and training establishments and the headquarters for five regional commands in Halifax, Montreal, Oakville in Ontario, Winnipeg, and Edmonton. Each command had responsibility for the militia,[18] but the Reserve Force, numbering only 33,704 in July 1947, was left to wither. The government actively discouraged recruiting, and summer camps trained only officers, non-commissioned officers, and specialists. Pay ceilings restricted numbers, and some regiments fell to a hundred or so die-hards. The army converted a number of infantry battalions and armoured regiments to anti-aircraft units, rubbing more salt in the Reserve's wounds. Not until 1948, with the Cold War beginning to heat up, did Ottawa give the Reserve Force the go-ahead to begin recruiting once more. After Moscow tested a nuclear weapon, the Mobile Striking Force began to evolve into a conventional brigade group designed to defend the country against Soviet diversionary attacks. No one any longer believed that the Soviet Union would attack the Arctic with airborne troops: Why fight for what Lester Pearson called 'scorched ice' in the Arctic when the Russians could hit New York or Montreal with an A-bomb?[19]

The Department of National Defence made some progress in officer training. In 1948 the Royal Military College, operated during the war as a staff college, reopened to educate cadets for a four-year course on a tri-service basis. Royal Roads, a naval cadet college in Victoria, British Columbia, began in 1947 to take in RCAF and RCN cadets for a two-year course, and in 1950, tri-service since 1948, started sending cadets to RMC for the third and fourth years of their education. The department created the Regular Officer Training Plan, a scheme that paid all education costs in what were now called the Canadian Services Colleges or at a university in return for a commitment of three years' military service after graduation.[20] The department also opened the Collège Militaire Royal de St-Jean, a third military college in St-Jean, Quebec, to encourage francophones to join the forces and to produce bilingual officers for the three services. Opened in 1952, CMR drew cadets from across the country and, each month, functioned two weeks in French and two weeks in English. Its cadets went to RMC for the final two years of education and training. In 1959 RMC secured the right to award degrees; Desmond Morton, later a distinguished historian, received the first Bachelor of Arts degree.

This standard of education was a change for the Canadian forces. General Charles Foulkes, the first postwar Chief of the General Staff, wanted every army officer to have a university degree, but this idea was too radical in the immediate postwar years – and for a long time thereafter. A degreed officer corps might not summon the courage to go over the top, or so some appeared to fear. As a result, the army leadership – except for RMC graduates and the officers produced by the ROTP from civilian universities – remained resolutely ill-educated; as late as the 1960s just one-third of army officers had degrees. Other ranks ordinarily had incomplete high school education, and disproportionate numbers came from the West and, increasingly, from the country's area of persistent high unemployment, Atlantic Canada.[21] The Second World War had raised battlefield technology to new peaks; the battlefield of the future almost certainly demanded a better-educated army. Foulkes had seen the coming requirements, but almost no one else did.

One area in which the Department of National Defence did encourage military and strategic thinking was in its training of senior officers. In 1948 DND established the National Defence College in Kingston, Ontario, to give civil servants and senior officers of all three services a broad perspective on national policy and international relations. The existence of NDC, with its neighbour, the Canadian Army Staff College, meant that army officers did not have to attend British establishments to receive training for higher rank. A few officers each year did attend British or American staff colleges, and, as NDC and the Staff College developed, British, American, NATO, and Commonwealth students in small numbers attended the Canadian institutions. For Canada to have its own officer educational system marked a change of substantial import. In 1926 Lieutenant-Colonel Harry Crerar had written that he could 'imagine no worse blow to the practical assimilation of the Military Forces of the Empire than that each Dominion should have its own Staff College.' The dominions had to 'march in step' and 'must absorb the same doctrine – the same learning.'[22] Canada was at last out of step with London and, though the imperial link lingered on for ten or more years in the minds of some Canadians and some soldiers, it was all but dead as a matter of government policy.

At the top of the postwar army was the Chief of the General Staff, Lieutenant-General Charles Foulkes. Just after V-E Day in 1945 the then CGS, Lieutenant-General J.C. Murchie, had asked Harry Crerar for advice on the future employment of Lieutenant-Generals Guy Simonds and Charles Foulkes, the army's two corps commanders at war's end. Crerar, who understood that he was being asked to recommend the next Chief of the General Staff, described Simonds as an 'outstanding officer ... [f]ully qualified for any appointment of high military responsibility.' Foulkes he pronounced 'a very able intelligent and thoughtful officer' whose 'particular qualities make him specially suitable for very senior staff appointment.'[23] His carefully honed recommendation likely led to the forty-two-year-old Foulkes becoming CGS on August 21, 1945. Dour, short, cold, but very shrewd (reading the wind from the south, for example, he already favoured closer military links with the United States), Foulkes was a far better military politician than he was a field commander. He would never have made the mistake of asking Mackenzie King's government for peace-time conscription.[24] Foulkes remained at the top of the military hierarchy for fifteen years, the only senior officer in postwar Canada with the ability and clout to deal on even terms with the public service mandarins. Simonds, the great battlefield tactician, remained in command of the Canadian forces in the Netherlands. He later attended the Imperial Defence College in London, first as a student and then as an instructor. Unlike Foulkes, he probably would have called for compulsory service in 1945, as he later did in the 1950s.

Because the government and Foulkes had to find something for Simonds to do, they made a place for him as commandant of the new National Defence College in Kingston. 'A little headstrong,' Field Marshal Montgomery had called him, rightly enough.[25] Ruthless, others said. Simonds finally had his opportunity to be CGS on February 1, 1951, when Foulkes became the first Chairman of the Chiefs of Staff Committee, a separate body advising the Minister and one equipped with its own secretariat. Foulkes was the Minister's principal adviser.[26] No admirer of Foulkes (and vice versa), Simonds now had to report to him. Simonds, nonetheless, became arguably the best CGS the army ever had, the man who shaped the Canadian contribution to Korea and the North Atlantic Treaty Organization.[27]

By mid-1948 the Soviet Union's expansionist policies had begun to thoroughly frighten the democracies. Defence Minister Brooke Claxton told the House of Commons on June 24 that since 1945 'the Soviet Union has flouted these war-won friendships, obstinately obstructed every move to arrive at understanding, and promoted chaos and disorder and the darkness of the iron curtain as the only conditions in which communism can exist and spread.'[28] This allegation was baldly stated, but truthful too. In light of the difficult relationship with Moscow, which was well along in swallowing Eastern Europe, Canada and the United States in 1947 agreed to continue and enhance their wartime military partnership.[29] Nonetheless, Canada made few efforts to increase its armed forces.

Even the secret negotiations between Canada, Britain, and the United States for a North Atlantic military alliance, soon expanded to include other Western European nations, did not change Canadian defence policy. On April 1, 1949, Canada and eleven nations signed the North Atlantic Treaty, and NATO, the North Atlantic Treaty Organization, very slowly began to take form in Western Europe. Committed to its first peacetime international military alliance, Canada still did nothing significant to increase its forces, to begin preparations to send forces overseas, or even to train the army in a serious way. The defence budget in 1949–50 was only $375 million, and the army portion just $124 million of that. The army's Active Force strength was still under 20,000 and the Reserve Force, 38,500. Equipment was all of Second World War vintage, but, because the government, urged on by Foulkes, had decided to begin using American weaponry, Italy, the Netherlands, and Belgium were given the equivalent of a division's worth of British-pattern equipment.[30]

The world changed on June 25, 1950, when communist North Korea invaded South Korea. The Truman Administration in the United States, convinced that this invasion was a Moscow-inspired attack, believed it to be a dangerous escalation in Soviet aggressiveness. Because the Soviet Union was boycotting proceedings at the United Nations Security Council, Washington won agreement for a United Nations force to fight in Korea. The pressure on Canada to commit troops to the war began and quickly increased. The government dispatched three destroyers and an air force transport squadron, but it initially resisted any commitment of ground troops. The Active Force was small, its task the defence of Canada. The government announced on July 19 that it intended to increase the regular forces to their authorized strengths. The American pressure continued[31] and, while Prime Minister Louis St Laurent and his Cabinet were returning to Ottawa by train from the funeral of Mackenzie King in Toronto at the end of July, the Ministers made the decision to raise a brigade group for Korea.

Because the United States believed that Korea was a Russian diversion and that the real threat was to Western Europe, Canada also began to consider a major commitment of forces to NATO. In his announcement that a Canadian Army Special Force brigade group would be raised, St Laurent put it clearly: the brigade was to be 'specially trained and equipped to be available for use in carrying out Canada's obligations under the United Nations Charter or the North Atlantic Pact. Naturally, this brigade will ... be available for service in Korea as part of United Nations forces, if it can be most effectively used in that way when it is ready for service.'[32]

By November 1950, when Communist Chinese troops in massive strength first engaged UN forces in Korea, the threat of a third world war seemed very real in Ottawa and other Western capitals. Korea was important, but Europe was much more important for historical and commercial reasons and, the Defence and External Affairs Ministers told their colleagues, 'the period of greatest danger has already begun.' Pressure on Canada from NATO for a major military contribution to the defence of Western Europe had already begun to increase and, on December 29, 1950, the Liberal Cabinet decided that the defence budget had to triple, from $403 million in 1950–1 to just below $1.45 billion in 1951–2. The government also created a new Department of Defence Production under C.D. Howe. The country would commit eleven Royal Canadian Air Force fighter squadrons, significant naval forces, and earmark a division of troops for NATO. The size of the military was to rise to 105,000, and the Active Force's strength was to be more than doubled.[33] The government presented these decisions to the Canadian public the next month.

With the outcome of the Korean War still very much in question, on February 5, 1951, the Minister of National Defence informed Parliament that the brigade group was to be sent to Korea. In May the government announced that, by the end of the year, it would send an additional brigade group to Europe. In a few months the postwar shape of Canadian defence had altered in the most dramatic way conceivable.

Divided by the United States and the Soviet Union at the end of the war with Japan, Korea's northern half had been handed over to local Communists by Moscow, and the United States had given South Korea to Syngman Rhee, a 'democratic' leader. The country was supposed to be unified eventually, but the Cold War put paid to that notion, and the hostility between the two Korean regimes was marked by repeated armed raids across the border by each side. The war began on June 25 when strong North Korean infantry and armoured forces rolled over the Republic of Korea's ill-trained, ill-led forces. Within two days the invaders had captured Seoul, the capital, and continued to move south. On June 27, following a resolution of the United Nations Security Council, President Harry Truman ordered American forces in Japan into a 'police action,' not a war. The Americans had their first units in South

Korea by July 1, and they went into action on the 5th. The initial engagements between North Korean and American troops were short and sharp; the Second World War–vintage Soviet T-34 tanks used by the North proved very effective in resisting American hand-held anti-tank weapons. The North Koreans were also better trained and equipped than the Americans' garrison troops and outnumbered the American and South Korean forces substantially. By August the outgunned UN forces, since July directed by a unified UN command led by U.S. General Douglas MacArthur, were penned into a small perimeter around the southeastern port of Pusan. They faced imminent defeat.

This was the military situation on the ground when the St Laurent Cabinet decided to raise a brigade for Korean service.[34] The Canadian Army Special Force was to be part of the Active Force, and the men enlisted for eighteen months, or for a further period if required 'in consequence of any action undertaken by Canada pursuant to an international agreement or where the term of service expires during an emergency or one year of the expiration thereof.'[35] The units of the brigade became new units of the existing regiments, and the authorized strength of the brigade, soon to be called the 25th Canadian Infantry Brigade Group, was set at 4960, with a reinforcement increment of 2105.[36] On August 18 the Cabinet further agreed to recruit up to 9979 men, to provide reinforcements for a full year of action.

The brigade's recruitment was chaotic. The existing recruiting system, based on Personnel Depots scattered across the country, was understaffed and organized to deal with recruits in ones and twos. On August 8 hundreds of men lined up. Within a few days Claxton ordered the attestation process accelerated. 'Damn the regulations!' Colonel Wood had the Defence Minister say in *The Private War of Jacket Coates*. 'These fine lads have come here to enlist in Canada's Army to fight Communism. Enlist them, sir – at once! If the odd lemon gets in, there will be time to do something about it later.'[37] Substantial numbers who ought to have been turned away were enlisted instead, including 'a man with an artificial leg and one who was 72 years old.' So lax was the process that one man boarded a troop train in Ottawa to be with a friend and was noticed four weeks later drilling with the PPCLI in Calgary.[38] The wastage rate was abnormally high: as of March 31, 1951, of the 10,208 who had enlisted, 2230 had been discharged and 1521 had deserted.

A large proportion of the initial volunteers were Second World War veterans. So too were the officers chosen to lead the brigade. To command it, the army secured Brigadier John Rockingham from his business in British Columbia. Rockingham had been a highly successful battalion and brigade commander in Northwest Europe, and he picked his unit commanding officers from decorated volunteers and the Active Force. War-time experience was the key criterion, and most of the officers, except for the brigade staff and commanding officers, were Special Force volunteers.

The units of the brigade were soon designated as second battalions or regiments of the Active Force regiments. The intention initially had been to equip the brigade with American weapons, but in mid-August General Foulkes decided that this plan would not work. Some American weapons required different tactics, so would demand extra training for the veteran volunteers; in the interests of speed, the brigade would use existing stocks of equipment, but arrangements were made to draw on American sources in Korea for vehicle maintenance, wireless sets, and support weapons such as mortars and rocket launchers. The 25th Brigade would be transported to Korea on American vessels. Even so, total Americanization of the army would be delayed – an unfortunate decision. Most U.S. weaponry and personal kit, such as helmets and winter clothing, were infinitely superior to the British patterns Canadians used. The troops in Korea, nevertheless, ate American rations and their commanders resisted every suggestion that they draw on British or Australian supply lines.[39] The 25th Brigade eventually served in Korea as part of the Commonwealth Division for practical and traditional reasons, but tradition could be pushed only so far. The Canadian soldiers simply wanted the much more appetizing American rations. How much mutton could a man eat?

While the volunteers underwent individual training in Calgary, Petawawa, Camp Borden, and Shilo, General MacArthur's UN forces staged a daring and wholly successful landing at Inchon, well to the north of the Pusan perimeter and on the peninsula's west coast. The North Koreans collapsed immediately. By late September Seoul had been recaptured. MacArthur's forces soon crossed the 38th parallel, the old boundary between the two Koreas, and by November were drawing close to the Yalu River and the Chinese border. The war seemed won. Were the Canadians to be needed at all? And if so, where should they train over the winter? By the last week in October the United States Joint Chiefs of Staff had told Foulkes that they required only a single battalion, expected to be used for occupation duties; the rest of the brigade could complete its training at Fort Lewis, Washington. The battalion selected for Korea, 2 PPCLI, commanded by Lieutenant-Colonel Jim Stone, spent only four days at Fort Lewis and left for Korea on November 25, still largely untrained in company or battalion operations. The rest of the brigade, its future uncertain, settled down to serious training.

By the time Stone's battalion arrived at Pusan on December 18, the situation had altered again. Chinese Communist 'volunteers' had streamed over the border in late October and, in late November, had fallen in force on American and other UN troops. The advance northward rapidly turned into a headlong retreat. By December 16 the UN's main defence line had been located on the Imjin River north of Seoul. As soon as it landed, the hard-pressed UN Command sought to put 2 PPCLI into action immediately, but Stone's instructions from Army Headquarters were clear: he flatly refused to go into action until his men had had at least eight weeks' training. The war went on, the Chinese driving the UN armies even further south and again capturing the almost completely ruined capital of Seoul.

The future of the remainder of the 25th Brigade, still training at Fort Lewis, remained undecided. At the beginning of February Ottawa seemed poised to ship it to Western Europe for NATO service, but on February 21 the Minister made the decision: Korea. The brigade departed from North America on April 19–21, 1951.

Meanwhile, 2 PPCLI, finally deemed fit for action by Colonel Stone, went into the line some 45 miles southeast of Seoul as part of the 27th British Infantry Brigade Group on February 17. Though it was a quickly mobilized unit, 2 PPCLI had already begun to take on the aspect of a regimental family. The men had convinced themselves of their uniqueness, invincibility, and worthiness to carry the PPCLI badges on their uniforms. Such things mattered, as they always had.

The PPCLI's training in Korea had emphasized physical fitness, the conduct of all-round defence on widely separated hilltops, and fighting on high ridge lines. They also had a few days of fighting Communist guerillas. They would soon have more action, for the UN armies had been rejuvenated by their new field commander, U.S. Lieutenant-General Matthew Ridgway, and the retreat was over.

The Canadians began their first attack on February 19. The PPCLI received a sobering lesson as it passed sixty-five dead American soldiers, all killed in their sleeping bags by Chinese troops. The first Canadian objective, Hill 404, fell without opposition. The next day the 27th British Brigade's advance proceeded with equal ease, though the weather and the icy hills posed severe problems. On February 22 the PPCLI suffered its first casualties, four killed and one wounded, in an unsuccessful two-platoon assault on Hill 444. A further advance on Hill 419 had more success, as two platoons overran the Chinese outposts, but the Chinese beat back a second attempt at Hill 444 on February 23, killing six and wounding eight of the PPCLI. The Canadians employed the minor tactics they had used in the Second World War – fire and movement covered by concentrations of artillery fire. The tactics still worked, but a strong and well-led defence could often prevail.

An attack by the Royal Australian Regiment outflanked the Chinese position on Hill 444 and, after the Chinese withdrew, the Canadians secured the position. These first actions confirmed that the Chinese, in action continuously for more than fifteen years in their war with Japan and in civil war, could fight tenaciously. Even the UN superiority in artillery and air support had little effect against the well-dug-in enemy. The days in the line also demonstrated that Canadian cold-weather clothing was simply inadequate, the boots shoddy and the noisy nylon parkas neither wind- nor water-resistant. 'It seems unbelievable,' noted a later report, 'that Canada is far behind the United States and the U.K. in the design of winter clothing.'[40]

The tempo of the UN advance continued, and the Canadians again set off on March 7. An attack that day against camouflaged and dug-in troops proceeded with great difficulty in snow, and the Princess Pats lost six killed and twenty-eight wounded for little gain. Private L. Barton, the batman to a platoon commander in 'D' Company, took over the leadership of the attack and drove it forward. Wounded three times, Barton won the Military Medal, the first decoration awarded to a Canadian in Korea. The next morning, after being subjected to grenade attacks all night, the PPCLI charged the previous day's objective and found it deserted. The Chinese had retreated north, leaving forty-seven dead behind. For the PPCLI, the first three weeks of action had cost fifty-seven casualties, a high price to pay for nameless hills in a UN police action.

Stone, the battalion CO, was generally pleased with the aggressiveness his officers had shown. But he was very unhappy with the soldiers' lack of basic training and the presence of what he termed 'scruff' – 'hastily recruited' men whom he returned to Canada as quickly as he could. These rejects numbered up to 146, more than 15 per cent of the single battalion's complement. Stone also set up his own field punishment camp, Stone's Stockade, 'to teach a few guys a lesson ... I decided it would be the toughest field punishment camp since Admiral Nelson.' Soldiers who got into trouble had their heads shaved, ate while running on the spot, and doubled everywhere, even 'having a leak,' one soldier groaned. He'd thought that was impossible, 'but I found out it wasn't.' Those PPCLI put through field punishment straightened up, or so Stone said.[41] Disease was also a threat, and Stone himself contracted smallpox, endemic in Korea, and had to be evacuated.

Ridgway's UN forces continued to move north. Seoul fell to the South Koreans once again, and the Chinese established a new line above the 38th parallel. The Canadians joined in a general UN advance that saw them move forward 50 miles by truck on March 25. For the next two weeks and more the Canadians marched northwards without much opposition. By April 18 the PPCLI were in positions at Kap'yong, just north of the pre-war dividing line. The Communists' withdrawal had been calculated, designed to lure the UN troops into positions where maximum casualties could be inflicted on them.

The Chinese counteroffensive began on Easter Sunday, April 22, first smashing two Republic of Korea regiments. The ROK troops reeled back 10 miles and then broke, streaming down the Kap'yong valley. The Australian regiment and the PPCLI, carefully placed by the 27th British Brigade, held the key hills overlooking the valley. Lieutenant-Colonel Stone, back in command, sited his companies on scrub-covered Hill 677 and watched as the Australians came under repeated and heavy Chinese attacks from what was later estimated to be 6000 men. His men dug in, put up more barbed wire, registered their mortars, and cleared away brush and trees to create good fields of fire.

On the 24th, brigade headquarters ordered the outnumbered Aussies to pull back. The enemy attack by perhaps 400 soldiers then fell on a single company of Canadians, preceded by mortar and machine-gun fire. 'There's a whistle,' one sergeant said, 'they get up with a shout about 10 feet from our position and come in. The first wave throws its grenades, fires its weapons and goes to ground. It is followed by a second ... and then a third comes up ... they just keep coming.'[42] The attackers broke into the company position, but a counterattack drove them off. A Bren gunner, Private Wayne Mitchell, won the Distinguished Conduct Medal for his courage in that engagement. Wounded, Mitchell was evacuated by helicopter for treatment at the end of the battle, a routine state of affairs in Korea. In the few years since the Second World War, battlefield medical care had improved significantly: only 34 of every 1000 casualties died, compared with 66 of every 1000 between 1939 and 1945.

At night, another enemy party struck at the battalion headquarters' position, but the Pats' automatic weapons, mortars, and half-tracks with .50- and .30-calibre machine guns broke up the attack. The Chinese troops fought very well in the dark, Stone observed. 'They lived in the dark. We lived in the light.'[43] Artillery broke up another enemy thrust, but at 2:00 a.m. on April 25 a large Chinese force fell on 'D' Company, its defence led by Lieut. M.G. Levy. Waves of attackers hit the company's forward weapons pits and, though every weapon in the battalion was firing, the Chinese skilfully infiltrated men into the company position. The attackers used their machine guns and mortars well and simply overran the company by force of numbers. 'Will you fire artillery right on top of my position?' the company commander, Captain J.G.W. Mills, asked his Commanding Officer. 'Are your men dug in?' Stone asked, and, assured they were, ordered the New Zealand artillery to fire directly onto the 'D' Company trenches.[44] The shrapnel bursts, timed to explode about 15 feet in the air, literally cut the Chinese to pieces. They attacked repeatedly, their assaults heralded by bugles, but each time artillery fire from the Kiwi 25-pounders supporting the PPCLI drove them off.

During the fierce battle, one private soldier, the 6-foot 4-inch Kenneth Barwise singlehandedly recaptured the Vickers machine-gun position in 'D' Company, picked up the gun, and carried it back to his platoon position. He also killed six Chinese in an attack on his company: 'They kept coming in waves,' he said. He was awarded the Military Medal – and ever after was known in the army as 'Barwise, MM.' At one point, with the battalion headquarters under assault, Colonel Stone ordered the half-tracks carrying his mortars and two machine guns each to hold their fire until the Chinese emerged from the trees some 300 yards away. 'Eight machine guns cut loose together,' and the attack collapsed. The PPCLI suffered thirty-three casualties, including ten killed in action, but the regiment and the 27th British Brigade had plugged the hole in the UN line left by the precipitate retreat of the ROK troops.[45]

The Chinese continued to shell the PPCLI when day broke, but there were no further attacks. The battalion, cut off by the enemy, had to call for an air drop to get ammunition and food. The regiment's supply problems disappeared when four C-119 Flying Boxcars dropped food and ammunition with almost perfect accuracy. That afternoon, patrols found the way to the brigade clear, and supplies began to arrive by road. The PPCLI and the regiments of 27th British Brigade had held off 6000 Chinese and stopped the enemy advance. The 2 PPCLI won a U.S. Distinguished Unit Citation, the only Canadian unit ever awarded this recognition (members of 2 PPCLI wear the distinction to this day), and Colonel Stone added a second bar to his Distinguished Service Order.

The 25th Canadian Infantry Brigade Group began to arrive at Pusan on May 4, 1951. Brigadier Rockingham had earlier paid a flying visit to the PPCLI to get a sense of the war, and his brigade, after some field exercises to get the men in shape, moved north in the middle of May. The brigade's tank squadron needed to find tanks and, in the end, it got twenty M4A3 Shermans from the United States Marine Corps. On May 20 the armour and the infantry found themselves involved in a UN advance and, five days later, they went into action. The 2nd Battalion of the Royal Canadian Regiment was the first to face enemy fire, followed soon after by the 2 Royal 22e Régiment, and the advance went ahead without difficulty. The Laundry and Bath Platoon of the brigade's Ordnance Company took the first prisoners, rounding up five stragglers bypassed by the advancing infantry.

To celebrate Dominion Day, the men of the 25th Brigade received a beer ration provided by Labatt's Brewing Co. The company sent a gift of 3440 cases of Labatt's 50 in tins – then never seen in Canada – and the RCAF's Dakota aircraft carried the beer to Seoul. The movement control section at the airbase took over, off-loaded the transports of their cargo, and loaded the beer on Service Corps trucks. The drivers delivered the precious cargo to units and, by July 1, each man had two tins of ale, and there was enough beer on hand for a few more issues. 'That's the first beer you can say is beer we've had since leaving Canada,' one soldier said.[46]

Late in July the Commonwealth Division took form, composed of the Canadian brigade and two British brigades, the latter including Australian and New Zealand troops. Under British Major-General J.H. Cassels (a brigade commander with whom Rockingham's 9th Canadian Brigade had worked in the Rhine crossing in March 1945), the division was part of the U.S. I Corps and the U.S. Eighth Army. For the Canadians, having a British division commander between 25th Canadian Brigade and the Yanks did not displease anyone. 'From this time on,' PPCLI Lieutenant-Colonel N.G. Wilson-Smith noted, 'the direct effects of serving under U.S. command were fairly well filtered out.' For example, the American practice was for senior commands to issue detailed instructions to subordinate commanders. The British practice was to permit junior commanders substantial discretion in carrying out assigned tasks. The Canadians claimed to follow the British approach, though in the Second World War this claim was more honoured in the breach than the observance. In Korea, nonetheless, the British and the Canadians sometimes chafed under their ally's direction.[47]

At the same time as the Commonwealth Division came together, the front line was stabilized, essentially in the position it maintained for the rest of the war. There were sharp skirmishes, many larger operations, and frequent casualties, but the war settled down into a stalemate. The UN forces had liberated South Korea, and none of the countries providing troops wanted unnecessary casualties. The Chinese, for their part, had driven the Americans and South Koreans away from the Manchurian border and shown their mettle.

Both the UN and the Chinese forces continued to strengthen their defences, the trenches getting deeper, the dugouts more elaborate, the wire thicker, and the mines increasing in number. The firepower of the Canadians increased as well. The Shermans provided direct fire support, their primary role, and the gunners were superb in bringing fire on any target on demand. The infantry too had 'up-gunned' for the Korean War version of trench warfare. By 1952 PPCLI platoons had three .30-calibre Browning medium machine guns, seven Bren guns, a .50-calibre heavy machine gun, a 3.5-inch rocket launcher, and a 2-inch mortar. 'A section,' wrote platoon commander Robert Peacock, 'had more automatic firepower than an infantry battalion of a thousand men had at the outbreak of World War I.' The platoons organized themselves into weapons teams, each covering the next with their fire zones interlocking.[48] By late 1951 some men also wore heavy armoured vests, increasing their chances of survival, though the vests were so bulky and covered with such a noisy fabric that many soldiers thought them more trouble than they were worth.

Canadian soldiers were not bitterly anti-Communist. They knew the Chinese posed no threat to Canada, and they understood that there were no national war aims at stake and scarcely any agreement on what the United Nations wanted from the war. The soldier 'was being paid to carry out his government's policy,' whatever that was, the army official historian wrote. 'He was a technician, trained for this kind of work, and he was being pitted against the technicians of an adversary with which his country was not at war.'[49] Perhaps that detachment explained why the Canadians developed a high regard for the enemy as tough, efficient soldiers. Comfortably clothed, shod in rubber footwear that let them move silently, the Chinese soldier could live on slim rations and work hard. The enemy's capacity to dig trench lines with great speed was impressive, and the Chinese soldiers' burp guns were effective weapons, far better than the inaccurate, dangerous Sten guns still used by the Canadians. The Chinese planned their attacks carefully, but initiative took second place to set-piece tactics. Enemy patrols were highly skilled, and the men followed effective drills.[50] In a stalemated war, patrolling was important, and the Canadians were not as good as the enemy. In 1953 Major Harry Pope of the Van Doos organized a brigade patrolling school to improve matters.[51] The main Canadian advantage was in artillery fire support. As in the Great War and the Second World War, concentrations of artillery fire could be called for in a few minutes. The Chinese artillery, effective enough but inflexible, was no match for the Canadians' sophisticated counter-battery work.[52] Another unlikely advantage, Brigadier Rockingham recalled, was that at least one soldier in the 2 Royal 22e Régiment spoke Chinese. The soldier had lived next to a Chinese laundry in Quebec City and learned some Chinese. In a forward outpost one night he overheard a Chinese radio transmission that gave the location of an ammunition dump, and he passed the information up the chain of command. The brigadier was understandably dubious, but he agreed that the RCHA's 25-pounders could fire a few rounds. 'There was a most wonderful display of fireworks and we knew they had destroyed the dump. The guy in the forward outpost,' Rockingham said, amazed, 'had been right after all.'[53]

Administrative questions soon troubled the Canadians. Were the units serving in Korea to be replaced by new units? More than two-thirds of the Canadians in Korea had enlisted in the Special Force for eighteen months, a term that expired in February 1952. The 2 PPCLI had a year of Korean service in December 1951. The Chief of the General Staff, now General Simonds, resolved matters by directing that 1 PPCLI replace the battalion in Korea. This soon became the norm, regiments or subunits rotating after a year (plus or minus one month). The army formed third battalions of the infantry regiments in November 1950 and January 1951 and created the 25th Canadian Infantry Brigade Replacement Group. In the summer of 1951 the replacement brigade concentrated at Wainwright, Alberta, and, with winter, it dispersed across the country, all the while providing reinforcement drafts for the brigade in Korea.

Building up the army so quickly inevitably created problems. Contractors working at Camp Petawawa in 1951 had 'bought' construction equipment from several officers and men. The minister ordered an independent investigation of the specific case and any broader implications. The report, prepared by George S. Currie of Montreal, a close aide to Colonel Ralston in the Second World War, pointed to serious breaches in accounting practices at Petawawa and, in a charge that haunted Claxton and the army for years to come, said that horses had been put on the payroll under the names of workers. The scam had enriched a few corrupt contractors and soldiers and, to the public, it all sounded like extravagant waste. The army's standing was not helped by Currie's charge that there were serious shortcomings in the Department of National Defence – 'a general breakdown in the system of administration, supervision and accounting.'[54]

That exposure was serious enough, but questions of manpower and reinforcements also came to assume importance. Although there was no overall shortage of volunteers for the army, there was little public interest in or support for the war – a conflict in a far-off land that few Canadians cared about. The Adjutant-General calculated in May 1952 that, by September, the brigade could expect to be 374 infantry understrength. Particularly acute was a shortage of francophone infantrymen and junior officers. At one point eighteen English-speaking subalterns had to be posted to the Van Doos in Valcartier to bring the battalion there up to strength, and the proportion of francophones in the army was far lower than in the population at large. In December 1950 French Canadians made up just over 12 per cent of the army, though in the infantry 26 per cent of officers and 20 per cent of other ranks were franco-phones.[55] Dealing with the problem required asking soldiers to volunteer for a second tour of duty with the 25th Brigade.

This request concerned the army leadership. There had been almost no public opposition among Québécois to Canadian soldiers going to war in Korea, the godless Communist enemy finding little favour in the province. Probing opinion polls, however, registered substantial unease among franco-phones at the dispatch of troops overseas to Korea and Europe, and Montreal's nationalist and isolationist newspaper *Le Devoir* predictably argued against any military commitments. Ottawa remained confident that it could carry the province in a public fight and had even made preparations to impose conscription at once should war break out with the Soviet Union. Everyone from St Laurent on down believed that this move would be accepted readily in Quebec. Brooke Claxton told a journalist friend confidentially that 'with this Prime Minister ... we can do anything in Quebec.'* Perhaps, but an opinion poll that asked French Canadians about conscription for Korean service found 83 per cent opposition to the idea.[56]

The army brains trust, past and present, still wanted compulsory service. Retired General Harry Crerar made speeches across the country calling for conscription; more seriously, Simonds, the CGS, told Claxton in May 1951 that, without it, Canada could not meet its commitments in the event of a major war. There were already problems in maintaining the units in Korea, a national registration would take time, and specialists were certain to be in short supply. Claxton indicated that if it became necessary, he would support conscription. Happily, it never became necessary.[57]

With the Korean War in stasis, the Secretary-General of the United Nations, Trygve Lie, called for a cease-fire on June 1, 1951. The Chinese

---

* The Americans were less confident than the government. In a 1952 report, one State Department officer wrote that 'Canada is not likely to catch up to the average NATO country's mobilization in relation to population because conscription is one of the most serious, deep-rooted political issues between French and English Canada.' Memo to Officer in Charge of Commonwealth Affairs, nd, attached to Memo, Assistant Secretary of State for European Affairs to Secretary of State, November 19, 1952, *Foreign Relations of the United States, 1952–1954* (Washington, 1986), vol. 6: 2055.

expressed interest, and discussions began on July 10 at Kaesong on the 38th parallel. The two sides, sometimes meeting regularly, sometimes not, talked for two more years. The soldiers, competent at their jobs, inevitably became more cautious. Who wanted to get killed while the peace talks were under way? But as no conclusion came, the men almost forgot that the Kaesong talks were going on.

The Chinese, however, were unafraid to hit the UN's Jamestown Line. On November 2, 1951, the enemy attacked the 25th Brigade, first striking the 2 Royal Canadian Regiment in its positions on Hill 187. The eerie bugles sounded and wave after wave of infantry hit the RCR positions, cutting off one platoon. The platoon commander, Lieutenant E.J. Mastronardi, and two soldiers set up a rearguard while the rest of the platoon retreated to the main company position. The Chinese attack ceased only when artillery smashed the position. But now the Chinese had brought artillery forward and, in attacks through November, they used it. Communist troops hit the PPCLI four times on November 4, but failed to dent their lines. On November 23 it was the Van Doos' turn and, although a neighbouring American unit retreated, Lieutenant-Colonel Jacques Dextraze, a much-decorated Second World War hero, ordered his men to hold fast. Directing artillery and tank fire at the Chinese, he led his men in repelling four attacks. The next morning the Chinese struck once more behind a heavy artillery concentration. They carried mats to help them cross the Canadians' barbed wire, and there was always another enemy soldier to take the place of one killed. A Van Doos' platoon from 'D' Company had to retreat, but again artillery halted the Chinese. The company held its position and, the next morning, the enemy was gone. The Van Doos had lost sixteen killed, forty-four wounded, and three missing in four days of hard fighting. Lieutenant Gérard Bélanger of the Van Doos wrote home after this struggle in a despairing vein. 'If we continue to lose men at this rate, the Battalion will be decimated in a few weeks ... We're living like rats and we'll probably die like rats,' he said. '... I haven't slept since yesterday morning. So much for the glorious life of a platoon commander.'[58]

The Korean War held few attractions for Canadian soldiers, whatever the fictional Private Jacket Coates might have thought. With the exception of 'Katcoms,' Korean Augmentation to Commonwealth soldiers who served with Canadian units, and those who worked as porters for the Canadians, the Koreans were 'gooks' and largely despised. The country was disease-ridden and smelled of human feces, which were widely used in farming. Stories continue to persist, some possibly true, of how Canadians pitched grenades into roadside huts indiscriminately or killed prostitutes rather than pay them. In a war of great cruelty, such atrocities seemed almost incidental.

Politics reared its head for the Canadians when, in May 1952, American commanders ordered a company of the RCR to duty at Koje-do, a prisoner-of-war camp largely taken over and run by Communist cadres. This order violated Canada's condition that its troops be kept together; it also upset Ottawa that Canadian soldiers had been pitched into a situation that many believed the Americans had badly bungled. The Canadian company did its brief tour at Koje, then returned to its regiment, but not before relations between Washington and Ottawa and the Canadian and American military became strained.[59] The head of the Canadian Military Mission in Tokyo, Brigadier A.B. Connelly, lost his job as well because he had not resisted the Koje assignment.

In April 1953 the 25th Canadian Infantry Brigade went into the line in the old positions on the Jamestown Line, this time with the 3rd Battalions of the RCR, the Royal 22e Régiment, and the PPCLI. Historian David Bercuson has argued forcefully that these battalions were 'less ready for combat than their predecessors ... unprepared in doctrine, untrained in tactics, and woefully ill-equipped to fight a defensive war.' (Others have suggested the 1st Battalions were worse still.) The officers lacked professional knowledge, the NCOs did not know the capabilities of their weapons, and the soldiers' weapons handling was poor. The new brigade commander was Brigadier Jean-Victor Allard, a highly respected wartime commander.[60]

Chinese patrolling became especially active after the new battalions went into the line, and Allard concluded that the enemy knew his brigade was very green. On May 2 the brigade commander sensed a coming attack and hurried to brace his troops. It fell on 3 RCR, and heavy artillery fire pinned the Canadians in their trenches as the enemy drew nearer. The Chinese penetrated into two platoons' lines, throwing grenades into the trenches; all that drove them off was Canadian artillery firing directly on the RCR trenches. Four thousand shells smashed the enemy, and the surviving Canadians moved to the adjacent platoon's position. Not until the early morning of May 3 could the RCR and the Van Doos retake the lost ground. Twenty-six Canadians died, twenty-seven suffered wounds, and eight became POWs. The Chinese had taken their dead and wounded with them when they retreated.

This episode was the last major Canadian action of the war. On July 27 the armistice at last came into force. The 25th Canadian Infantry Brigade had taken more than 1500 casualties: 312 killed in action, dead of wounds, or missing and presumed dead; 1202 wounded; and 33 POWs. There were 94 non-battle fatalities.

Nominally a UN operation, Korea in fact was an American-led coalition struggle against communism. The United States forces suffered 33,629 fatal casualties, the heavy price of global leadership. The South Koreans, fighting to preserve their independence, lost 325,000 soldiers and hundreds of thousands of civilians. North Korean and Chinese casualties remain unknown, but certainly were very heavy. The war had ended in a draw, but the communist attempt to take over South Korea by force of arms had failed. For Canada, the Korean 'police action' was a relatively small commitment, though the soldiers who were killed were just as dead as if it had been a war. The nation's unpreparedness in 1950 and hasty assembly of a contingent were, unfortunately, in the Canadian tradition. So, too, was the good performance of the soldiers in action.

In the eyes of Western capitals, the major Soviet threat in 1950 lay in Europe. The invasion of South Korea had persuaded the United States and its allies that Western Europe was in great danger from the USSR and its satellites, and they transformed NATO from a loose alliance into a close military coalition. Ottawa shared this assessment and, deciding to do its part, the St Laurent government announced on January 30, 1951, that it was going to assign or earmark troops for the NATO integrated force. This force was under the Supreme Allied Commander in Europe (SACEUR) and was to fight alongside other NATO formations, not in national isolation. Whether Canadian troops would go to Europe was not yet stated and would not be until May 4, when Claxton told Parliament that Canada intended to station a brigade group in the British sector of Germany, backed up by two more in Canada – in effect, a divisional commitment to NATO. As reinforcements, Canadian planners believed the country could send an armoured division within thirty days, a third division within six months, and a fourth after sixteen months.[61] The commitment of a brigade by a nation that had never before sent troops abroad in peacetime marked a major change in policy. For a start, the pledge demanded a major expansion of the Active Force, one substantial enough to put the Reserve in the shade. The regulars were now, without question, Canada's main defence force.

This NATO commitment was largely the work of General Charles Foulkes, General Guy Simonds, and General Dwight Eisenhower. In February 1951 the new Chairman of the Chiefs of Staff Committee, Foulkes, had thought of transferring the part of the brigade group training for Korea at Fort Lewis, Washington, to NATO, but the Americans would have none of that while the fighting continued. Canada therefore had to send a newly raised brigade to Europe, but where? Foulkes advised Canada to adopt American weaponry, in large part because he wanted access to American supply lines; for this reason, he proposed to station the Canadian brigade with the Americans. The U.S. Army Chief of Staff agreed. Foulkes's judgment, even though it flew in the face of history, was made on the basis of military necessity: the Americans could provide more and better assistance to Canada than the British. In the end, Canada's NATO brigade used a mix of American and British weapons, and supply posed no problems.

Foulkes and Simonds worked together on how to raise the brigade for NATO service and decided to recruit it as part of the Active Force. Recruiting began on May 7. For its part, NATO's military headquarters (the Supreme Headquarters of the Allied Powers in Europe, or SHAPE) assumed that the brigade was to be stationed with the Americans, much as the RCAF wanted to post its fighter squadrons to work with the U.S. Air Force in Europe. British representatives at SHAPE became upset that a Commonwealth country was not to be under British command, and their concerns became the subject of Anglo-Canadian political discussion. If Foulkes was an Americanist, the anglophilic Simonds was not, and he began to weigh in on the side of those who favoured having Canada's NATO brigade serve with the British Army of the Rhine. Even if the brigade used American equipment, Simonds said, it could easily be supplied in northern Germany. The argument pitted general against general, and the pro-British against the pro-American in the government. Eisenhower, the first Supreme Allied Commander in Europe, produced a very Canadian compromise: the brigade group would go to the British zone, while the RCAF's fighter squadrons would serve with the Americans.[62] Over the 1950s, probably as Simonds had anticipated, the brigade's equipment became more British and less American.[63]

The creation of the NATO brigade, soon to be named the 27th Canadian Infantry Brigade Group, was chaotic. Simonds's preferred method, conscription, was a political non-starter, so the CGS turned to the Reserve Force and proposed that six battalions be created out of fifteen existing regiments, each of which would provide two companies. The composite infantry battalions were to be called the 1st and 2nd Canadian Infantry, 1st and 2nd Canadian Rifle, and 1st and 2nd Canadian Highland Battalions, and the officers and men would wear their Reserve regiment badges. This arrangement would provide enough infantry for two brigades, one to be held in Canada and intended to rotate with the NATO brigade overseas. The regiments selected, including the Seaforth Highlanders, the Queen's Own Rifles, the Carleton and Yorks, and the Fusiliers Mont-Royal, the sole francophone unit, all had strong traditions and excellent war records. An armoured squadron, to be equipped with the British-made Centurion Mk. 3 tank, came from the Royal Canadian Dragoons of the Active Force, but the artillery battery in each of the brigades was to be provided by the Reserve. Many of the brigade's support units were to be raised in the same fashion from the militia. In the event of war, Simonds planned to make each company the nucleus of a battalion, thereby giving Canada two divisions. The composite battalions took form in the Reserve regiments' home towns and enlisted only the fittest of men – a sharp contrast with the way the Special Force had been raised the year before. The term of enlistment was one year for married men and two years for single men. The soldiers could engage for up to three years and re-engage beyond that.[64]

Recruiting generally went well. Almost all the Reserve units involved found little difficulty in meeting their quotas. Training soon began for the 27th Brigade in Valcartier, Quebec, and initially proved to be a difficult task. Most of the veterans were rusty, and those who enlisted off the street or from the Militia's ranks had much to learn. The plan called for collective training to take place in Germany, and in November and December 1951, under the command of Brigadier Geoffrey Walsh, the men set sail for Europe and quickly moved into quarters at Hannover. The men of the rotational brigade trained where they were raised until, in the summer of 1952, they moved to

Camp Borden, then Valcartier, Camp Ipperwash on Lake Huron, and finally to Wainwright.

The brigade faced the usual shakedown problems in Germany. One problem was the food: 'Brit rations. Camouflaged bully beef. Camouflaged brussel [*sic*] sprouts. They'd do anything to camouflage it,' one soldier recalled, 'but it was the same old garbage.' It took a near-revolt to persuade brigade headquarters to bring in better cooks and improve the food to North American standards.[65] In the field, soldiers still ate the British compo rations their predecessors had hated in Sicily.

Worse than the rations, Hannover was an unlovely, unfriendly industrial town, and relations with the local citizenry were difficult at best. Prostitutes preyed on the troops, described as naive by military police and gulled by 'the amount of sinful temptations which abound in Germany today.'[66] The CGS soon asked that the Canadian brigade be moved to Soest, Werl, and Hemer-Iserlohn, smaller towns with fewer temptations, and this transfer took place in 1953. Many of the men of the brigade, despite the greater care exercised in recruiting them, turned out to be less than perfect gentlemen, with substantially less battle experience than had been expected, and there was a high rate of desertion. Because no families had been allowed to come to Germany (though some came unofficially), there were higher-than-usual rates of military crime, drunkenness, and male-female troubles with the Germans. Moreover, the Reserve units proved unable to provide replacements for their companies, a problem when some of the married soldiers took their release. Why, then, preserve the direct link to the militia?

That was Simonds's view, and he proposed that the army's organization be rationalized. He wanted fifteen infantry battalions: three for Korea, three for NATO, three for home defence, and six for rotation. His plan called for six regular infantry regiments: the PPCLI, the Van Doos, and the RCR, the existing regular regiments, and the Queen's Own Rifles, the Black Watch, and the Canadian Guards. Guards? The QOR and the Black Watch had links to the militia units that had raised companies, but the army had never had regular Guards units. Simonds argued that the composite infantry battalions ought not to perpetuate a specific geographical region, so he suggested a four-battalion Canadian Guards regiment, including one bilingual battalion. Although this scheme seemed to many a retrograde colonial step, Simonds got his way and the new organization came into effect in October 1953.[67] All the men were now regulars on the same terms of service, liable to be deployed anywhere the government chose. Eventually, 2 RCR, 2 PPCLI, and 2 Royal 22e Régiment went to NATO in October and November 1953 to serve in what was now to be called the 1st Canadian Infantry Brigade. In 1955 the 2nd Brigade, made up of the first battalions of the three regiments, took over the NATO role; in 1957, it was the 4th Brigade's turn. Although it had 1200 fewer men than the 2nd Brigade, the 4th was much stronger than its predecessors because it included a complete armoured regiment, an attempt to give the brigade more punch and make it more self-sufficient. The infantry also began to carry the army's new rifle, the FN C1, using the NATO standard 7.62 mm cartridge. In 1957 the army also finally built permanent married quarters in the Soest area. Canada was in NATO for the long haul.

For the 27th Brigade, the first to be deployed in Europe, the immediate task was to complete its training to face a Soviet attack, seen in NATO and Western capitals as a real possibility. NATO forces were heavily outnumbered in Europe compared with the Russians and their satellites. In the early 1950s the USSR had more than 300,000 soldiers in East Germany alone and enjoyed a fifteen to one advantage in aircraft. (The RCAF's Air Division of Sabres was a very large proportion of NATO air power.) The Russians' capacity to reinforce their troops quickly was also greater than the West's, though NATO planning in 1952 called for a fifty-division force before the end of that year,[68] and early Allied estimates put a Russian army on the English Channel ten days after a war began. As time passed and as NATO strength and effectiveness slowly improved, the Allied strategy altered to fighting in front of and on the Rhine.

For the Canadian brigade in northern Germany, directly in the path of any invasion from the east, the prospects in war were not good. The Canadians were to advance to a defensive position on the Weser River and, when retreat became necessary, to put up a final defence on the Rhine in front of Düsseldorf. Despite optimistic statements to the contrary by NATO and Canadian generals, the brigade's situation was perilous. The Canadians trained themselves strenuously for their task, however, improving their defensive capacities daily. Realistic exercises combined the Canadians with the British, Dutch, Belgians, and, soon, the Germans. They required the creation of standard operating procedures, good liaison, and learning how to fight in situations where the enemy was all but certain to have the advantage of numbers on the ground and in air superiority. In the circumstances of the early and middle 1950s, when conventional forces mattered and battlefield nuclear weapons had yet to appear in any army in quantity, the Canadian brigade was important to NATO. About half the size of a British division, made up of regulars rather than conscripts, the Canadians provided one-sixth of the British Army of the Rhine's strength. In terms of quality, the Canadians easily equalled or bettered anything their allies could provide. The commander of the BAOR in 1957 called the brigade 'the best fighting formation in the world.'[69] It may even have been true. LCol Ike Kennedy, at the time a young gunner, recalled: 'I thought we were better than anyone else ... despite the lack of equipment ... we all believed we were the best little (and we considered ourselves big) army in the western world. In fact, my recollection was that we didn't know we were badly equipped!' Certainly the Canadians thought themselves infinitely superior soldiers to the Americans and much better than the British, whose ranks were full of National Service conscripts. In 1957 the Canadian brigade became one of the main elements of the BAOR's forward defences, the force intended to absorb the first shock of a Soviet attack.[70]

No time limit had been put on the Canadian commitment to NATO – a good thing, as the Cold War showed few signs of ending. Josef Stalin's death in 1953 stirred hopes of peace briefly, but the crushing of an East German revolt, the emergence of a bellicose Nikita Khrushchev as leader, the brutal smashing of the Hungarian Revolution of 1956, and repeated Russian efforts to harass the Allies out of West Berlin kept the pot at the boil.

The Liberal government in Ottawa seemed prepared for the long haul. Times were good, the economy was booming, and the Active Force, with 49,000 officers and men, was at its highest strength ever. In 1954 the CGS created the First Canadian Division with headquarters at the new Camp Gagetown in New Brunswick under Major-General John Rockingham, while a skeleton Second Division headquarters existed quietly in central Ontario. Rockingham was a superb fighting soldier, not a good organizer,[71] but his division ran all-arms exercises, as did the brigades in Canada. There were almost no troops stationed in the north, which no one any longer expected to be an arena of active land operations, but the army ran occasional exercises there. Most of the General Staff's work in Canada aimed at preparing the army for operations in Central Europe. For the first and only time in its history, the regular Canadian Army was well trained, well equipped,* and ready to fight the battle that, the officers and men believed, had to be fought sooner or later. The army had great respect for Soviet military capabilities, but as NATO's effectiveness and strength grew, the Canadian Army confidently believed that it and its allies could prevail.

Recruits still joined for the traditional reasons – adventure, patriotism, and escape – and still trained in the old-fashioned and time-honoured ways. Basic training took place in a regimental depot, heavy on drill and indoctrination into the peculiar mores of the regiment. New soldiers pounded the parade square, practised on the rifle range, did daily physical jerks, and bonded with their mates. They memorized the regiment's battle honours, learned all about the customs of the service, and, at the end of six months, the recruits were deemed fit to be posted to a unit. There, advanced training occurred, in barracks in winter and on exercises in summer.

Soldiers lived in quarters in their camps. The majority were still housed in tarpaper and wood H-huts built in the Second World War, but the lucky ones were accommodated in new barrack blocks that provided large two-person rooms and could house a company. Men ate simple high-calorie food cafeteria-style, but NCOs had their own mess, as did the officers. Bases included canteens, chapels, playing fields and gyms, and medical and dental facilities, and most had Permanent Married Quarters for officers and NCOs. Ordered, stable, conservative, the old army, as David Bercuson described it, was heavily British in origin, especially the officer corps.[72] The army of the 1951–65 era, the golden age of Canadian military professionalism and, for most of those years, the only period in peacetime in which it received adequate funding, was also very efficient. The fact that professionalism, funding, and efficiency came together should surprise no one.

The credit for Canada's part in this development largely belonged to Guy

---

* Except for clothing. In the field in summer, soldiers wore bush clothes, which were adequate enough, though multi-hued depending on how often they had been washed. There were no winter field uniforms, and soldiers wore U.S. Army field jackets. On exercises, black coveralls were the usual dress, the sloppiest uniform in any army at any time. Until the army introduced combat clothing in the mid-1960s, Canadian soldiers looked as though they had been kitted out by a second-hand clothing store. I am indebted to LCol J.P. McManus for reminding me of this sad state of affairs.

Simonds. Under his able direction, the Regular Army had increased in size in a few short years. He reorganized Army Headquarters into the centre for policy and planning, in effect creating the nation's first true General Staff, and he decentralized as many other functions as possible to the army's five commands in Canada. Responsibility and power lay with the commands, which could even play a role in the recruiting and training of officers and men. 'The effect was electric,' George Kitching recalled: 'it was no longer necessary to get the approval of highest authority to carry out some low level manoeuvre. Initiative was encouraged at all levels and rewarded.'[73]

Contrary to Canadian myth, peacekeeping was not invented at Suez in November and December 1956. What was created by Suez was the idea that Canadian soldiers were natural-born peacekeepers, the ideal military to be interposed between warring nations in the service of peace. Certainly before 1956, and for years afterwards, the army leadership was a reluctant participant in peacekeeping efforts, pleading insufficient personnel and too few specialists. There were manpower shortages, but the reason for the army's reluctance was the conviction that peacekeeping was a distraction from the real task: preparing to fight the Soviet Union on the north German plain.

The first UN request for Canadian peacekeepers came in December 1948. The United Nations wanted forty officer observers to patrol the demarcation line in Kashmir between India and Pakistan. The tiny Active Force had no interest in this assignment, but the Secretary of State for External Affairs persuaded the Defence Minister to try to find reservists to do the job. In February 1949 four Reserve Force officers went to Kashmir, followed in July by four more. In early 1950 Active Force officers took over the task, although a reservist, the able Brigadier H.H. Angle, was the Chief Military Observer of the UN Military Observer Group in India-Pakistan. Angle died in an air crash in July 1950, the first of the 109 Canadians to die on peacekeeping duties over the next half-century.

The next UN request came in 1953, when the UN Truce Supervisory Organization (UNTSO), an observer team trying desperately to maintain the increasingly shaky peace between Israel and its Arab neighbours, asked for four Canadians. In early 1954 four regular officers went to the Middle East and, later that year, Major-General E.L.M. Burns, the former commander of

I Canadian Corps in Italy in 1944, was named Chief of Staff of UNTSO. 'I had the feeling,' Burns wrote later of this difficult job, that 'I was trying to stop a runaway truck on a steep hill by throwing stones under the wheels.' Two Canadian officers with UNTSO suffered serious injuries in a land-mine explosion in 1956; a Jordanian sniper later killed one of the same officers, Lieutenant-Colonel George Flint of the PPCLI.

Peacekeeping was also a task outside the United Nations. In 1954 the long war between the French and communist-nationalist guerillas in Indochina ended. The Great Powers brokered a deal at Geneva that created the independent countries of Laos, Cambodia, and Vietnam, although the latter, intended to be united, was in reality divided into a Communist North and a non-Communist South. To supervise the disengagement of forces and the repatriation of refugees, and to try to preserve peace, Britain, China, the United States, and the USSR in July called for the creation of three International Commissions for Supervision and Control and, without consultation, proposed Communist Poland, neutral India, and democratic Canada as members.

Stunned by this request from Geneva, Ottawa believed it had no choice but to agree. The commitment was very large – 150 military officers and diplomats from the Department of External Affairs – and the army had the task of finding eighty-three officers, including three major-generals, and thirty-one other ranks, almost all bilingual, for the three commissions. The mission proved difficult, the Poles following the party line, the anti-colonialist Indians tilting towards the communists, and the Canadians trying with less and less success to be genuinely independent and unbiased. The effort at impartiality had disappeared in frustration by 1955 and, although the commissions for Laos and Cambodia met with substantial success, that for Vietnam turned into a morass.[74] Many of the Canadians who served in Vietnam returned home bitterly anti-communist. None admired the South Vietnamese government, but the North Vietnamese communists' viciousness and the Poles' open partiality and deliberate obfuscation embittered everyone. As a result, many Canadian soldiers and diplomats had no hesitation in passing on any information they gathered to the Americans.[75]

These three peacekeeping efforts in the old Indochina were little known by Canadians primarily because they occurred on the edge of the main area of East-West confrontation. The Suez Crisis, outside the arena though it was, became a major global issue because it embroiled the Great Powers. It was also a partisan political question in Canada because it directly involved Britain and France and deeply angered the United States.

The issues were complex. The 1950s saw the rise of decolonization as countries in Asia, Africa, and the Middle East sought to go their own way. Indonesia had broken away from the Netherlands, India and Pakistan from Britain, and French Algeria was in open rebellion against Paris. The Cold War let the Soviet Union, preaching anti-colonialism to all who would listen, offer military and financial aid to the new nation-states. Egypt's President, Colonel Gamal Nasser, tried to play East against West in his efforts to develop his country, but in 1956, in frustration at being stonewalled in his requests for funding by the West, he nationalized the Suez Canal. This move infuriated Britain and France, which owned the canal and relied on it to get their oil from Saudi Arabia, Iran, and Iraq. London and Paris colluded with Israel in arranging that the Israelis would invade Egypt, and the British and French would intervene to 'protect' the canal. Ideally, Nasser's regime would fall as a result of the military attack, restoring the *status quo ante*. While proclaiming their intention not to use military force, the British and French built up forces in the Mediterranean. In the last week of October 1956, while the Soviet Union brutally crushed the revolt in Hungary, Israel invaded Egypt's Sinai Desert. A joint British-French ultimatum with a twelve-hour time limit was handed to the Israelis and Egyptians on October 30; it called for the cessation of fighting and for Israel to halt its forces 10 miles from the canal. As planned, Jerusalem agreed, but Cairo refused. With Nasser's rejection of the ultimatum, the British and French began air and sea operations against Egypt, belatedly putting soldiers on the ground on November 5. Between the three attackers, Egypt's military forces were all but neutralized.

At the United Nations and in Washington and Ottawa, there was fury at these events, which, to many observers, smacked of nothing so much as nineteenth-century colonialism. The British had lied to Ottawa about their intentions and misled the Americans, the latter a particularly delicate matter because the U.S. presidential elections were in their last few days. The attack had also let the Soviet Union escape much of the condemnation it truly merited for its bloody, repressive actions in Hungary. Canada's primary objectives in the crisis were to restore Anglo-American relations, preserve NATO, help the British and French extricate themselves from the mess they had created, and move the intractable Middle East problem towards a solution. At the United Nations on November 1, Lester Pearson, the Secretary of State for External Affairs, proposed that the Secretary-General 'begin to make arrangements with Member Governments for a United Nations force large enough to keep these borders at peace while a political settlement is being worked out ... My own government would be glad to recommend Canadian participation in such a United Nations force.'[76] This idea and Pearson's subsequent role in creating the United Nations Emergency Force (UNEF) won him the 1957 Nobel Peace Prize.

Ottawa dispatched three military staff planners to New York to work with Secretary-General Dag Hammarskjöld's planning staff. The CGS, Lieutenant-General Howard Graham, also went to New York for consultations. Quickly the UN headquarters decided to make General Burns, who was in the immediate area with UNTSO, the commander of the new mission. Several of his officers began to provide assistance and lay the groundwork. In New York, UN member countries lined up to offer infantry battalions. In Canada, however, public opinion sharply divided on the Canadian role in the crisis, many painting Nasser as a new Hitler and others decrying Anglo-French stupidity. Anti-Americans denounced the St Laurent government for supporting a position favoured by the United States, which had sharply criticized the Israeli-Anglo-French aggression. But on the idea of a peacekeeping force itself, there seemed only public support. The question was simple: How was Canada to participate?

The infantry battalion selected to form the heart of the Canadian commitment to UNEF was the 1st Battalion of the Queen's Own Rifles of Canada, a Regular Force regiment based in Calgary. To Canadians' utter astonishment, especially because of Pearson's role in the crisis, the Egyptians objected. The Canadian flag was the Red Ensign with a Union Jack in the corner, and the soldiers of the Queen's Own Rifles wore British-pattern uniforms. They spoke English, and their very name was British: in the immediate aftermath of the invasion, how could Egyptians not see them as the enemy who had invaded their country from the air and sea? Was there another Canadian battalion that could go? General Graham wrote in his memoirs of his quandary: 'Other available units, like the Princess Patricia's, the Royal Canadian Regiment, the

Black Watch (Royal Highlanders), and the Royal 22nd Régiment, would all have had the same effect ... because of the implication that they were British.'[77] Pearson actually told the Egyptian Ambassador to the United Nations on November 12: 'We had even been careful to exclude from the [Queen's Own Rifles] force any Canadians with noticeably English accents.'[78] It required extraordinary efforts by General Burns, Dag Hammarskjöld, and the Canadian Ambassador in Cairo, Herbert Norman, to persuade the Egyptians to allow Canada to contribute not the 1 Queen's Own Rifles but the logistical support UNEF needed to function. Egypt grudgingly announced its acceptance of Canada on November 17, and Burns duly provided a face-saving letter to Pearson asking that Canada provide UNEF with 'administrative elements.' The government was off the hook, and the disappointed Queen's Own returned to barracks. By November 22 almost three hundred logistics specialists were *en route* to the Middle East. In December, Canada agreed to provide a signals squadron, a field workshop, two transport platoons, an armoured reconnaissance squadron, and an RCAF communications squadron. The Canadian contingent then numbered more than one thousand men, one-sixth of UNEF's entire force.[79]

The extraordinary Suez Crisis demonstrated that, whatever Canadians might think, in some parts of the world they carried historical baggage. Canada had in sorrow and anger condemned Britain and France for their actions and proposed a way out of the crisis. But the imperial link was a drawback to the Egyptians for perfectly understandable reasons. Even so, Cairo agreed to let the Canadians join UNEF because the army, providing the great bulk of the contingent, was one of the few remotely acceptable nations with the capacity to offer administrative support for a force that simply could not function without it. Canada's military history and its overseas army commitments enabled it to provide logistical and communications support.

For the decade UNEF functioned in Egypt before Nasser ejected it just prior to the 1967 Arab-Israeli War, duty there was infinitely boring, in squalid conditions, and completely without glamour. One junior officer with the Royal Canadian Dragoons reconnaissance squadron wrote in 1962 that it was 'a funny thing coming off the desert – everyone feels like a big party and has a tremendous itch to shoot up the local police post.'[80] Another posted in the Canal Zone noted that 'boredom is a place much like Port Said.'[81] The frus-

trations of service in UNEF were severe, in other words, and it was a rare soldier sent there who did not envy the Queen's Own its good fortune in not
being allowed to participate.[82]

The crisis affected the army in other ways as well. First, Pearson's Nobel
Peace Prize made Canadians into the world's leading believers in peacekeeping. Every world crisis after 1956 saw Canadians demanding that their troops
bring peace to the world. This pressure literally forced the Diefenbaker government to send peacekeepers to Lebanon in 1958 and to the Congo in 1960–
64.* Second, Egyptian complaints about the Queen's Own Rifles marked the
first time that many Canadians realized that the army's British-pattern uniforms and regimental names might send an unintended message. The seeds of
the unification of the armed forces and a distinctive Canadian military uniform may have been sown in November 1956. Finally, Pearson's interest in a
distinctive Canadian flag, one without a Union Jack, began to grow. Suez was
part of Canada's belated coming of age.[83]

The Diefenbaker government that came to power with a minority government
in 1957 and a huge majority the next year† did not agree that Canada had
acted properly during the Suez Crisis. John Diefenbaker was firmly anti-communist, but he had strong anti-American and pro-British attitudes that soon
became matters of political import. His Minister of National Defence, General George Pearkes, a Victoria Cross winner in the Great War and a division
commander in the Second, shared some of Diefenbaker's attitudes, though the
Chairman of the Chiefs of Staff Committee, General Foulkes, had been one of
his wartime officers and was able to move the Minister when he deemed it
necessary.

Foulkes persuaded Pearkes and Diefenbaker to sign the North American
Air Defence Agreement with the United States in 1957, something that the
RCAF had long wanted. By the late 1950s the Soviet Union had demon-
strated its ability to place satellites in orbit. To defence planners, this meant

---

* Post-Suez peacekeeping will be examined in chapter 10.
† Military voters (and Permanent Married Quarters polling stations at almost all bases in Canada) in the
  1957 and 1958 elections, as in every election between 1949 and 1968, gave the Liberals absolute majori-
  ties. See J.L. Granatstein, 'The Armed Forces Vote in Canadian General Elections, 1940–1968,' *Journal
  of Canadian Studies* 4 (February 1969): 6ff.

that North America, already vulnerable to a Russian bomber attack, might face intercontinental ballistic missiles armed with nuclear warheads. As part of a Canadian response to this new strategic situation, Foulkes played a key role in persuading the government to cancel the hugely expensive Avro Arrow interceptor and to purchase a variety of weapons systems for the forces, all of which required nuclear weapons to be truly effective.

For the army, this decision meant the acquisition of a battery of Honest John nuclear rockets for the NATO brigade in 1960.[84] Beginning in 1954, the NATO brigade had been training to fight on a nuclear battlefield, and the tempo of preparation picked up as the 1950s wore on. Canadian troops went to Nevada and marched through the desert where nuclear weapons had just been detonated. Their leaders discounted radiation's effects, if they knew them, and soldiers confidently believed that, if they were prepared, they could live in and fight a nuclear war. Staff College sand table exercises and field training exercises in Canada and in NATO by 1960–1 anticipated that both sides would use tactical 'nukes' in profusion in any war in Germany.[85] If this was the case, the army brass maintained, the brigade had to have nuclear weapons at its disposal, subject to all the rules NATO and the United States, the provider of the warheads, might impose on their use. A medium range (38 kilometres maximum) surface-to-surface rocket with 2, 20, or 40 kiloton warhead yields, the Honest John apparently could be fired with a conventional warhead, but its only effective use came when using its nuclear payload. The rocket fuel for the missile required heating for one to two full days before launch, making quick response completely impossible.[86]

The question of whether Canada should accept the warheads for this weapon and for others Canada had purchased for its armed forces provoked a major crisis with the United States from 1960 to 1963, when Diefenbaker fell from power. The military found itself aligned with the United States, increasingly angry at the Progressive Conservative government's stalling on the warheads. Pearkes wanted the nuclear weapons, as did his successor, Douglas Harkness. Diefenbaker and Howard Green, the Secretary of State for External Affairs, did not. The Departments of National Defence and External Affairs were also at odds, the khaki (and sky-blue and dark-blue) suits bitterly opposed to the striped pants. For the first time, the military almost unanimously agreed that the Americans were right, its government wrong. The

1962 Cuban missile crisis erupted with Canada's nuclear weaponry still unready, and the military's anger at the government was palpable. As important, the prospect of nuclear war made defence the dominant political question in Canada. Since 1949 there had been broad support in Canada for participation in NATO and cooperation with the United States in defence. But the nuclear debate made glaringly obvious that the consensus on defence had broken down, and in the fallout in 1962–3 the Progressive Conservative government tore itself to pieces.[87] The Honest Johns did not get their warheads until Diefenbaker was gone and the Liberals under Lester Pearson had come to power.

If the defence consensus had broken down, so too had the booming economy. It was Diefenbaker's misfortune that his government took power in 1957, just as the postwar boom ended. Unemployment and deficits rose, and the government tried to hold the line on spending. Drawing a huge portion of the national budget, defence took a hit. For the army, the result was delays in procurement decisions and the curtailment of training. The re-equipment of the NATO brigade was a relatively low priority for the Tory government, and the forces in Canada were even further down the list. For a soldier to get a pencil or a few sheets of paper by 1962 was a major feat, and exercises at Camp Borden found officers and soldiers training in broken-down jeeps without tops in pouring rain.[88] The situation was not as bad for the brigade in NATO. The three battalions of the brigade were mechanized, and in 1962 the armoured regiment received reconnaissance helicopters that greatly increased the brigade's effectiveness. Most of the army's first cadre of helicopter pilots and technicians had trained in the United States, an initiative of General Graham, Simonds's successor as CGS.[89] Graham believed that the main concern of the army was the defence of North America, something demanding much closer liaison with the Americans, but the only army commitment to this role while he was CGS was 3500 troops. 'We were at this time ... dependent on our neighbour to the south to come to our aid in the event of a hostile encroachment or attack upon Canadian territory,' he said.[90] In 1962 government officials apparently considered bringing the NATO brigade home,[91] a decision it decided to defer. Canada's days as a major player in the alliance seemed to be ending. If, despite the quality of the brigade in Germany, Canada did not matter much in NATO, and if NATO did not matter to Canada,

Canadian military professionalism and the army's era of peak efficiency were in jeopardy.

The situation was even worse for the Reserve Force by the end of the Diefenbaker government. During the early 1950s, its strength reaching 40,000, the militia had begun to rebuild its units, and new equipment filtered down from the Active Force. A major study in 1954 recommended a reaffirmation that the Reserves remained the basis of wartime mobilization. It also proposed that the Reserve's name be changed to Canadian Army (Militia), and that of the Active Force to Canadian Army (Regular), a recommendation that was quickly implemented. The historic process of consolidating units also proceeded once more, and some historic names disappeared. The Carleton and York Regiment, for example, amalgamated with the North Shore Regiment and became the Royal New Brunswick Regiment.[92] But as the Soviet Union built up its bomber force and the threat of missile attack on North America increased, was there still a place for mobilization planning for a large war, or were forces in being all that was required? If the latter, was there a role for the Militia at all?

By 1957 the Militia was beginning to hear about its duty to assist the nation's Civil Defence organization in dealing with nuclear attack; by 1958 this support was policy, and Ottawa reduced the number of training days for which it would pay from sixty to forty-five a year. Reservists (and regulars too) spent much training time on National Survival courses, learning how to tie knots and erect ladders in ways that might be useful in rescuing civilians from piles of radioactive rubble. Snakes and ladders, soldiers called it, jeering that these activities were not real soldiering. The Militia leadership objected, but the CGS was unmoved. 'I asked them to think about conditions as they were ... and then to think about the type of war we were likely to have to fight in the future, rather than to continue to think in terms of conditions and types of war in the 1930s and 1940s,' General Graham said. The Militia 'had to change [its] thinking ... to fit the new set of circumstances.'[93]

Graham had begun his career as a militiaman in the Hastings and Prince Edward Regiment, but, despite his best efforts, he failed to mollify the Militia. Recruiting dried up except for those enlisted off the streets for special short National Survival courses, a measure designed to fight unemployment more than to train soldiers. Some units tried to continue 'real' training without pay and on their own time. The National Survival training emphasis fell away within five years, but the Militia never truly recovered. The Liberals, in December 1963, reduced the Militia's authorized strength to 32,000, eliminated regiments wholesale, and amalgamated others. The army 'footprint' across Canada began to disappear, especially in rural areas and small towns where armouries were shut down. By 1965 the Militia's role began to be reshaped to the provision, not of units, but of officers, specialists, and soldiers on an individual basis 'to fill gaps' in the Regular force.[94] At March 31, 1970, Militia strength was 19,343.

At roughly the same time, the Department of National Defence decided to eliminate the Canadian Officers Training Corps in the country's universities. With the Vietnam War spurring anti-war demonstrations on U.S. campuses and with some of that sentiment spilling over the border, this step likely seemed prudent. The Militia was shrinking; many, if not most, COTC graduates did not want to enter the reserves; and the COTC cost money. The result was a small cash saving and a serious blow to the long-term prospects of the army. Killing the COTC ensured that 'the new members of the civilian leadership elites in Canada have had no military experience.' This, said Colonel B.S. Macdonald, 'is probably the biggest and most profound [reason for] the low level of public support for Canadian defence spending at the beginning of the 21st Century.'[95]

The army's reserve had all but been pronounced irrelevant. General Graham had told the Militia leaders that reserve funding had to be cut 'as funds were needed for the Regular forces to be properly equipped to meet our commitments.'[96] However true this was, the gap in training and efficiency between the Regulars and the reserves, manageable in the interwar period when the Permanent Force was tiny and as ill-equipped as the Militia, had become a chasm by the beginning of the 1960s. After a decade of intense professionalism and major overseas commitments, the Regular army, whatever its serious problems and growing concerns about the Diefenbaker government and its (lack of) policies, was a finely tuned, well-trained force. The militiamen, condemned by government policy to clean up the cities after nuclear explosions, seemed increasingly irrelevant in an era when forces in being were all that mattered to the army leadership.

The army and the other services viewed the coming of the Liberals to power in April 1963 with great relief. The nuclear weapons the military wanted arrived when the Liberals quickly implemented their promises to honour Canada's commitments to NORAD and NATO. But the euphoric feelings lasted only a short time, as Lester Pearson's Defence Minister, Toronto Member of Parliament Paul Hellyer, proved to have a mind of his own. Hellyer wanted to do things in different ways, and he looked to his own brief wartime career for ways to fix what he believed to be wrong. As a young airman in the closing stages of the Second World War, Hellyer had been mustered out of the RCAF just at the time the army was in the throes of the conscription crisis of 1944. When he joined the army, he had to repeat his basic training.[97] This time-wasting experience and lack of coordination between the services made a deep impression on Hellyer, who believed that he could make the Department of National Defence run more smoothly if the interservice barriers could be removed. The Prime Minister, some believed, also remembered the Suez difficulties over the Queen's Own Rifles and supported Hellyer's plans.

Brooke Claxton, the Minister from 1946 to 1954, had held similar views on the virtues of coordination and integration. Claxton ran all three services under a single ministry, and he created the post of Chairman of the Chiefs of Staff in 1951 to help coordinate the services and to give the Minister advice on 'the fulfillment of a single defence policy.'[98] The structure worked. RMC became a tri-service institution; the military's padres, legal services, and dental and medical services were coordinated; and one service or another operated various functions for the other two. The process continued under George Pearkes, Diefenbaker's first Defence Minister, as procurement of food and postal services became tri-service.[99] To go beyond this point in the face of entrenched habits and traditions required a minister with rare determination. Hellyer proved to be that man.

The military was in difficulty in 1963. Combined personnel strength remained at approximately 120,000, but the defence budget of $1.57 billion was down substantially from 1956–7. There was almost no money – just 13.3 per cent of the defence budget – available for new equipment, a situation that naturally produced rivalry among the three services for whatever funds could be found.[100] Canada might soon have the 'best dressed, best fed, best paid, but worst equipped military force in the world,'[101] one of Hellyer's aides said. The brigade group with NATO (and those in Canada too) lacked armoured personnel carriers, and the troops could not operate effectively without them on either the non-nuclear or the nuclear battlefields. (This deficiency was not remedied until 1965–8, when the army began to get M-113 armoured personnel carriers; the artillery, self-propelled 155 mm guns; and the brigade acquired an independent anti-tank unit with a variety of anti-tank weapons.) The air force in NATO could not provide close support for the brigade, and the navy had little or no capacity to transport troops to reinforce the brigade in the event of war. The three services' war plans were uncoordinated, each the product of different 'general staffs' with different assumptions. This situation was wholly unsatisfactory, the Minister believed with good reason, and he prepared a draft White Paper on Defence in late 1963 for Cabinet consideration in early 1964.[102]

To Hellyer, Canada's defence priorities were three: collective security through the United Nations, collective security through NATO, and the defence of North America. One could quarrel with the order but not the priorities. What was different in Hellyer's approach was his determination to reshape defence policy on Canadian foundations and to have this strategy determine defence structure. The alliances in which Canada participated still remained, but Canada could and should be able to decide how it organized itself to best meet its commitments.

This priority was the basis of Hellyer's plan to integrate the three services. The Minister proposed to replace the three service chiefs and service councils with a single Chief of the Defence Staff and an integrated Defence Staff at a renamed Canadian Forces Headquarters.[103] He argued that this organization would save money by eliminating triplication, pushing the funds available for capital expenditure from 13.6 per cent in the 1964 defence budget back up to 25 per cent. Operationally, Hellyer pledged to make no major change to the Canadian roles in NATO (other than to provide a battalion from Canada for the new Allied Mobile Force designed to fight in Norway),[104] NORAD, or in UN peacekeeping. Indeed, he proposed to increase Canadian capacity by creating an 'intervention force' capable of operating anywhere, a force with a new focus on mobility and firepower. The most favourable of the service heads to this integration plan was Lieutenant-General Geoffrey Walsh, the army's Chief of the General Staff. Some Ministers had their doubts, but the Pearson Cabinet approved the White Paper on March 25, 1964, including Hellyer's sentence that integration 'will be the first step toward a single unified defence force for Canada.'[105] Parliament accepted the necessary legislation in July 1964. The new Chief of the Defence Staff was to be in place in June 1965.

The Minister then moved to implement his plan. He told the military's senior officers in August 1964 that he wanted a single recruiting system, a single basic training organization, and full integration at headquarters and in the commands. 'If in achieving these objectives,' Hellyer said bluntly, 'a single unified Defence Force for Canada is clearly the logical end result, then such a unified Defence Force will be established.' As a start, Hellyer announced a cut of 10,000 men, an arbitrary 20 per cent reduction in the 50,000 personnel employed on support roles. He added that Canadian Forces Headquarters in Ottawa was to be cut by 30 per cent (including two NCOs from his own office, his way of showing he was serious), and the reductions were to be accomplished by giving those leaving the forces a cash payment, a so-called golden bowler. Army strength, 49,760 in 1963, was to decrease to 46,264 in 1965 and 40,192 in 1968.

The personnel cuts let Hellyer live up to his promise of new equipment. The army acquired armoured personnel carriers (it took Hellyer's direct intervention to get this purchase through),[106] new self-propelled artillery, and modern mortars; the navy got supply ships; and the air force gained more air transport capability. The intervention force might just be a reality. At Canadian Forces Headquarters, new organizations took shape: a single comptroller-general and a unified pay system, a single personnel branch, a single logistics branch, and a single technical services branch. The public relations branches combined, as did construction engineering, intelligence, and communications, while the trades structure was simplified. These major achievements saved personnel and dollars, though the initial period was confused and confusing.[107]

The second stage of integration tackled the military's operational commands. Instead of eleven commands in the army, navy, and air force, there would be six functional commands: Mobile Command, in effect the army and tactical air units; Maritime Command, the navy and air anti-submarine operations; Air Defence Command; Air Transport Command; Training Command; and Material Command. Mobile Command grouped together the brigades in Canada, CF-5 tactical air fighters, light transport aircraft, and helicopters. The objective was to be ready for deployment quickly anywhere in the world. Mobile Command was intended to do peacekeeping and to be able to fight limited conventional wars. The brigade in NATO, though not formally part of Mobile Command, *de facto* belonged to it. All this made some sense, though Canada had never before operated by itself with all its services fighting together, and was in place on paper by 1965.[108] However, implementing the ministerial orders and making the reconstructed military function effectively took much longer.

Hellyer pressed ahead. In November 1964, Major-General George Kitching recalled, the Minister summoned all the general officers to a meeting 'and addressed us as if we were a group of immigrants.'[109] It was time to unify the forces, to eliminate the army, navy, and air force, and to create a new force with a common rank structure and 'new' traditions. The battle lines emerged quickly on such questions as uniforms, rank titles, and badges. Lieutenant-General Robert Moncel, the Vice Chief of the Defence Staff, put it candidly at a meeting of the Defence Council in December 1965 with the Minister. It was a matter of 'if, when and how ... we should not rush into unification with a few notes on the back of a cigarette package ... we must know where we are going. We will be getting down immediately to practicalities – issues of badges, caps, ranks, careers, etc.' Moncel was an able officer with distinguished wartime service, and he pointed to the problems that troubled the army. It was one thing to have 'a single designation which would encompass multiple families that do certain things ... It was possible to perpetuate the single bits that have no civilian counterpart and retain the great names that go with them. The Corps names were meaningful to personnel and should be retained.'[110]

To Hellyer, such matters of 'buttons and bows' were supremely unimportant. To soldiers who lived – and sometimes died – in a system of regiments and corps and who prized the distinctions, these issues had real importance. Soldiers believed their regiment was the best – unique, a family, a band of brothers – and many believed that Hellyer intended to do away with all regimental names and distinctions, not just those of the logistical and support corps such as the Royal Canadian Ordnance Corps and the Royal Canadian Electrical and Mechanical Engineers. Many also feared that he proposed to create a 'jack of all trades' military, where one day a man could be on ship, the next day flying, and the third in a tank. This was ludicrous and not at all what

Hellyer wanted, but so bitter had the military's mood become by the mid-1960s that many expected the worst of the Minister.

Nor did Hellyer worry much about the career plans of the senior officers. Moncel expected to succeed Air Chief Marshal Frank Miller as Chief of the Defence Staff, but Hellyer, after Moncel's speech at Defence Council, knew that the General was no supporter of unification. Instead, in 1966 the Minister fixed on Lieutenant-General Jean-Victor Allard, the commander of Mobile Command, as his choice for CDS. Allard, a francophone, was less likely to be wedded to the anglo customs and traditions of the army than Moncel, and he took the post, one of his intentions being to speed the bilingualization of the forces.[111] Allard understood that the changes involved in unification upset many, and he answered the critics by going full speed ahead as the only way for the military to overcome the difficulties of doubt and worry.[112] He was a charismatic leader, proven in battle, but few believed he was a good staff officer. 'He had brilliant ideas that changed every two weeks,' one general said, 'and he failed to organize a staff to keep *him* under control.'[113] For his part, Moncel retired, along with two of the most senior three-star (lieutenant-general or equivalent) officers. Hellyer agreed to dismiss them, thereby getting the officers their full pensions, but his charitable act only increased nervousness in the military dramatically.

As the pace of change accelerated in the forces, huge numbers of senior* and junior officers and senior NCOs left. 'I hope you won't think of me as a rat leaving a sinking ship,' Major-General Paul Bernatchez wrote to a friend in 1965, ' but I cannot take it any longer.'[114] Opponents of unification began to come to the fore, initially in the media and the navy.[115] In Toronto, some Reserve officers soon joined the fray, and a national group called 'TRIO' – the Tri-Services Identities Organization – took form as Hellyer's main opponent. The Militia, as a whole, hung back. Many of its officers were businessmen and feared Hellyer's wrath, while francophone officers liked Allard's commitment

---

* Between January 1, 1965, and August 30, 1966, twenty-eight army officers of brigadier rank or higher retired, most of them extremely unhappy with the pace of change and unification. See R.B. Byers, 'Structural Change and the Policy Process in the Department of National Defence: Military Perceptions,' *Canadian Public Administration* 16 (summer 1973): 220ff. In all, over an eighteen-month period after integration, 26,300 left the forces, with 13,142 departing prematurely. Desmond Morton, *Canada and War* (Toronto, 1981), 186.

to bilingualism. Many former other ranks also stayed out of TRIO in droves, viewing it as a senior officers' organization. TRIO had powerful supporters in the opposition parties and in the press, but public opinion polls showed substantial support for Hellyer's unification. The spirited resistance made Prime Minister Pearson wobble in his support for Hellyer, a difficult Minister at the best of times, although he did support the unification bill when it came before the House of Commons in November 1966. After a long struggle in committee, as the opposition was fed information by disgruntled navy officers and others, unification passed into law on April 25, 1967. It came into effect on February 1 the next year.

Ultimately, unification was a blow to the army's identity. By attacking the uniqueness of the service, by forcing administrative and logistics personnel into a tri-service identity, it weakened the army's sense of itself. Even though the infantry, armoured, and artillery regiments managed to keep their identities, unification struck at what remained of the Britishness of the force – as did Allard's appointment and his commitment to giving francophones a chance to function in their own language. At the same time, as senior officers resigned in a fury, it left those who took their place open to the charge of careerism. When the Canadian Forces new green uniform came into use early in 1968, it too was another blow at the army's identity.* This uniform, many said, 'was an attempt to cleanse the forces of their Britishness,' a trait deemed 'contrary to the cause of Canadian unity.'[116] Perhaps it was such an effort. Or perhaps, after Suez and Colonel Nasser's rejection of the Queen's Own Rifles, the Canadian Army had to become Canadian in look and feel and attitudes. Whatever the case, the times were changing, and the army did not like it at all.

From the early 1950s onwards, the Regular Army had enjoyed its peacetime professional peak. The regimental system, the parachute commitment, and especially the first-class brigade in Europe let soldiers know they belonged to a modern force that cherished its history and traditions. Budget cuts under Diefenbaker had begun to whittle away at this pride, and Hellyer's integration

---

* One of the first officers to wear the new uniform overseas, retired Major-General F.F. Worthington, told the press: 'The Germans especially seemed keen on it. "Now you Canadians will be recognizable – now you can look like yourselves and not like the British."' Quoted in Paul Hellyer, *Damn the Torpedoes: My Fight to Unify Canada's Armed Forces* (Toronto, 1990), 247–8.

and unification, together with the elimination of the names of corps and regimental uniform distinctions for budgetary and other reasons, weakened it even more. By the time unification came into effect, followed immediately by the accession to power of Prime Minister Pierre Trudeau, a leader who professed no interest in or understanding of defence issues, the army was adrift in a completely new era.

ten

PROFESSIONALISM UNDER SIEGE, 1968–2001

'Ours is not a divine mission to mediate,' the long-time diplomat and historian of Canadian foreign policy, John Holmes, wrote in 1984. 'Our hand is strengthened by acknowledged success,' he continued, 'but it is weakened if planting the maple leaf becomes the priority.'[1]

—✺—

All too often, Canadian participation in peacekeeping under the United Nations or other bodies has been shaped by this idea of 'planting the flag.' Canada was in every single peacekeeping operation until 1989 – and any government that refused a chance to join in seemed certain to suffer attack from the public and the press. The simple fact that these UN operations often made little sense, that Canadian troops were in short supply, or that the available soldiers were manifestly unsuited for the particular role never seemed to matter. Had not Mike Pearson won the Nobel Peace Prize in 1957? Surely some other foreign minister or prime minister could repeat his triumph.[2]

Throughout the Cold War, Canadians seldom asked 'Why Canada'? Why were the Canadian Forces seen as natural peacekeepers? By the 1990s, as manpower became scarce, as army units were overcommitted around the world, as troubles within the army mounted, a somewhat more realistic approach to long-term service abroad at last began to be followed.

These questions and many others came to the fore as the army struggled to survive the last third of the twentieth century. So long as the Cold War continued, the army knew its enemy and, within limits, understood what it was supposed to do. But once the Soviet Union crumbled into dust, the Warsaw Pact dissolved, and the Cold War ended, the army was left uncertain of its role. Paradoxically, overseas operations in the new world disorder increased at the same time as the government slashed defence budgets and force strength declined. Trouble was inevitable for the army, and it came, again and again.

What had gone wrong? The Canadian Forces as a whole and the army in particular were poked and prodded, studied by civilian management consultants, probed by inquiries and commissions, harried by parliamentary committees, and hacked and slashed at by bean counters. In the process, the professional military lost much of its confidence, as its equipment aged, its ethos crumbled, and its leadership, distracted and sometimes self-serving, became distrusted by the junior officers and other ranks. The Militia, short of funds and equipment and pressed to provide individual soldiers for duty with the Regular Force, became increasingly bitter at the professionals as its numbers shrivelled and its historic role of providing a base for mobilization disappeared. The wonder is that anything survived the strain, compounded as it was by the impact of huge budgetary and personnel cuts, unification, successive reorganizations, and the imposition of gender and racial quotas and bilingualism on an institution in crisis.

The culmination of a long process of disintegration came with a breakdown of discipline within regiments, a process demonstrated most clearly by the killing under torture of a Somali teenager during a peacekeeping operation in 1993. After Somalia and an abortive commission of inquiry, the army began the long process of reform in an effort to rebuild confidence in itself and with the public. This chapter attempts to put this prolonged crisis and the subsequent reforms into context.

Pierre Trudeau came to power in April 1968, an unlikely prime minister. Elected to Parliament only three years before, he had almost no political record. He was an intellectual, a doughty warrior against Maurice Duplessis in the Quebec of the 1950s, and a soldier in the increasingly sharp struggle against the *nationalistes* and separatism in Quebec. He was not a man with any interest in the armed forces or defence policy. Aside from a brief period in the Canadian Officers Training Corps when he was a student during the Second World War and inglorious service in a reserve regiment in wartime Montreal, he had no military experience. The military life, to him, was nasty, brutish, and short, and the armed forces stuffed full of dullards. He had written a vicious editorial in his magazine *Cité Libre* attacking Lester Pearson's support for the acquisition of nuclear weapons in 1963, he had criticized American involvement in the Vietnam War, and he believed that Canada's foreign and defence policy 'was largely its policy in NATO, through NATO.'[3] He also agreed with ministers such as Walter Gordon who, during the Pearson government, had questioned Canada's heavy NATO commitment. Europe had recovered since 1945, Gordon and others argued, and it made sense for the Europeans to bear the burden of defending themselves. To Trudeau and the NATO critics, if Canada owed Europe anything at all, it owed a demonstration of solidarity in the smallest military way possible: a few Canadians should be in Europe to be hostages to fortune, ready to die in any European war. A war against the USSR in all likelihood would quickly become general nuclear war, and one Canadian was as good a symbol of support as a brigade. Or so Trudeau believed.

No one in government was overly surprised when Trudeau's Cabinet on May 15, 1968, decided to conduct a 'comprehensive review ... of Canada's armed forces policy, including alternative forces' structures and costing.' The review was announced on May 28 as Trudeau led his party into a victorious election: the new Trudeau government committed itself to 'take a hard look, in consultation with our allies, at our military role in NATO and determine whether our present military commitment is still appropriate to the present situation in Europe.'[4]

The review, predictably perhaps for one undertaken by bureaucrats, largely endorsed the status quo. When the Cabinet Committee on External Affairs and National Defence reviewed the first draft, Donald Macdonald, the President of the Privy Council, demanded that the paper consider the possibility of Canadian neutrality and urged a complete Canadian withdrawal from Europe. Trudeau did not want to go that far, but, unhappy with the bureaucratic paper, his Cabinet called in August for a full-scale review of defence and foreign policy, with all options to be explored. The bureaucracy was now beginning to be very concerned. The review continued, its details parsed elsewhere.[5]

In the autumn of 1968 the government made a major change to its NATO role. Canada had long been committed to sending two brigades to Europe in the event of war. Defence Minister Paul Hellyer's unified force, however, had grown 'lighter,' making it more difficult for the Canadian-based brigades to fight alongside heavily armoured, mechanized, nuclear-armed European and U.S. forces in NATO. Trudeau's government reduced the commitment to a single brigade, and then Hellyer's Associate Minister and subsequent successor as Minister, Léo Cadieux, ended the commitment to send reinforcements to NATO's central front in 1968.

Coming as this announcement did just weeks after the Soviet Union and its satellites invaded Czechoslovakia and crushed the 'Prague Spring,' this retrenchment was not well received by NATO. Instead of an additional brigade on the likely Soviet invasion route, Canada now pledged to contribute the Canadian Air/Sea Transportable Combat Group to either Norway or Denmark in the event of war. The CAST brigade was to include the Allied Mobile Force battalion previously promised to NATO. Initially, Canada planned to pre-position equipment in Norway, but the Norwegians feared this move might appear provocative to Moscow. Hence, Ottawa decided to deploy the brigade by air and sea from Canada. This role sounded plausible, but it was, given Soviet submarine and air strength, almost certain to be completely impracticable in wartime unless the navy had nuclear depth charges. The commitment, reduced in 1979 by Defence Minister Barney Danson after an exercise failed dismally, nonetheless continued in force until the Mulroney government finally ended it.[6]*

It is curious that the CAST decision was made while the defence review was under way. More significant is that, in March 1969, the Cabinet fought through the defence issues, Professor Trudeau conducting a seminar for his ministers. His foreign policy aide, Ivan Head, had produced a paper – in sharp

---

* The Allied Command Europe Mobile Force and the Canadian commitment to it continue to this day. Indeed, the commander of the 20,000-man force from seventeen nations in 2000 was a Canadian major-general. The Canadian contribution in late 2000 was 3 Royal Canadian Regiment, a battery from 2 Royal Canadian Horse Artillery, and 2 Service Battalion. *The Maple Leaf* 3, 22 (2000): 4.

distinction to the departmental review – that called for Canada's military, then numbering just above 101,000, to be reduced to 50,000 over the next decade and its forces limited to domestic duties, except for 1800 Canada-based troops assigned to NATO's Allied Command Europe Mobile Force. Nuclear weapons, including the Honest Johns, were to be abandoned. This plan obviously represented the Prime Minister's position, but so confused had the discussion in Cabinet become that officials had to meet to sort out the details. So too did Trudeau and Cadieux, who ultimately compromised on 'a planned and phased reduction' of Canadian forces in NATO.

Trudeau told Canadians on April 3, 1969, that his government's defence priorities were Canadian sovereignty, North American defence, NATO, and peacekeeping. For NATO, he said, the government intended 'to take early steps to bring about a planned and phased reduction of the size of the Canadian forces in Europe.'[7] The result, after much discussion in Canada and almost none in NATO, was that Cadieux, a loyal NATO soldier, told the assembled NATO defence ministers that Canada was going to cut its army and air force in Europe to 3500 men. After NATO representations and strenuous efforts by Cadieux, the force fell only to 5000, half the existing strength of the brigade and the air division in 1968.[8] The Canadian NATO contribution was to be co-located under a combined Canadian headquarters at Lahr, West Germany, a small town of 35,000 people near Strasbourg. Keeping the NATO cut to only 50 per cent was a rare and small victory for Cadieux, who, on June 23, 1969, had to tell the Canadian Armed Forces and the nation that Canada's military forces were to be cut by 20 per cent to just above 80,000. The Reserves would be slashed to 19,000. The Canadian Guards, the Queen's Own Rifles, the Black Watch, and the Fort Garry Horse all disappeared from the Regular Force, though third battalions were added to the Royal Canadian Regiment and the Princess Patricia's Canadian Light Infantry. The army also created two new French-language units, one artillery, one armour, and established the Canadian Airborne Regiment. For the next three years, the defence budget was fixed at $1.8 billion.

For the army, the new policy amounted to a disaster of the first order. The NATO force, the cutting edge of the land forces and, by 1968, a brigade almost perfectly designed to meet NATO's new strategy of flexible response, was to be only 2800 strong. A mechanized battle group with no nuclear weapons, the NATO force comprised two understrength battalions, each with three infantry companies, an armoured regiment of three squadrons, an artillery regiment, an engineer squadron, and a service battalion. The Honest Johns disappeared.[9] The renamed Canadian Mechanized Battle Group was to be located close to the Franco-German border, in deep NATO reserve. After consultation, NATO assigned the CMBG a counterattack role in support of American or German forces.[10]

General Sir John Hackett, the commander of the Northern Army Group in which the Canadians had served, said: 'I regarded the Canadian Brigade as one of the best elements in our front line defence ... one of the star items.' Now the brigade had been relegated to what Hackett called 'a third line, as it were, reserve capability in Lahr.'[11] The Combat Group's first commander, Major-General W.C. Leonard, later estimated that his men were good 'for about one and a half counterattacks.' In 1973 the CMBG's strength was increased to 3212, a small step forward. As Leonard added, his force still retained access to American and NATO nuclear support – Canada's nuclear virginity was completely spurious.[12] The NATO brigade, arguably Canada's best and most professional force, one respected by the nation's allies, had been gutted by the Trudeau government.

At the same time, rank inflation affected the army. The Chief of the Defence Staff who had put unification in place, General Allard, had also tried and failed to get his soldiers more pay. In response, he hit on the idea of making every trained private soldier a corporal and creating the new 'command' rank of master corporal. This scheme had the desired effect of generating more pay to the men, but unit commanders unanimously recommended against it because of its pernicious effects. The Canadian army quickly became the only army in the world with more non-commissioned officers than privates, with sergeants as section commanders, and a plethora of new warrant officer ranks. Over time, it also became known as an army with the highest number of generals per capita. At the beginning of the unification process in 1970 the army had 15 per cent of its strength in the officer ranks; by 1995 it had just above 20 per cent. In 1970 it had 64 per cent of its other ranks at corporal or below; in 1995 it had 69 per cent of its non-commissioned members at the rank of sergeant or below, with the sergeants having equivalent duties to the corporals of a quarter-century before.[13] Corporals' messes disappeared and sergeants' messes grew in size. For a time, one officer recalled, there were two classes of sergeants: 'real ones and Hellyer sergeants.'[14] Rank inflation had been pervasive and it spread like wildfire. Allard's intentions had been good, but the results were damaging.

If most Canadians thought of Canada as a perpetually peaceable kingdom immune from domestic insurrections and political violence, Pierre Trudeau did not. He had worried about the violence on the streets of Washington and Detroit in 1968, and he feared it might spill over into Canada. He believed that he understood Quebec well, and he likely was not wholly surprised by the events of October 1970. A cell of the Front de la libération de Québec kidnapped James Cross, the British Trade Commissioner in Montreal, on October 5 and issued a series of demands. Five days later, in what seemed a carefully coordinated plan, another FLQ cell seized Quebec Labour Minister Pierre Laporte on the front lawn of his Montreal house. Separatist terrorists had planted bombs at federal institutions and in mailboxes in Quebec for some years, resulting in a few casualties. But the October incidents seemed different, much more daring, much better planned. The provincial Liberal government of Robert Bourassa, shaken by the kidnappings, watched uneasily as students, labour militants, and separatists rallied and seemed poised to topple his government.

In Ottawa, Trudeau's government decided to intervene massively to prevent public opinion being swayed by the revolutionary rhetoric. On October 12 the government put up to 3000 troops on the streets of Ottawa to guard public buildings and the homes of senior political figures. Former prime minister John Diefenbaker travelled through Rockcliffe accompanied by armed soldiers, much to his amusement. Three days later, at federal urging, Premier Bourassa asked for the army's aid to the civil power. Battalions of the Van Doos responded quickly, moving to guard persons and property. At 4 a.m. on October 16 Trudeau invoked the War Measures Act, to deal with what he declared to be 'a state of apprehended insurrection.'

These actions stunned the country. Opinion polls in Quebec and across Canada showed more than 90 per cent support for the government response, which was aimed as much at the militants in Quebec as at the FLQ. Laporte's murder on October 17, just after the invocation of the War Measures Act, was a tragedy that hardened hearts across the nation. The police ultimately located the British trade commissioner at the beginning of December and, in exchange for his freedom, the kidnappers flew to exile in Cuba. Laporte's murderers received jail terms.

For the army, the crisis was an extraordinary series of events. Some officers at Mobile Command headquarters had been collecting intelligence on radical movements in Quebec for some time; others thought in terms of 'protracted revolutionary warfare' against groups such as the FLQ; and still others wanted an army that could undertake 'civic action' to deal with the revolutionaries.[15] Whatever the thinking that preceded the October crisis, planning and procedures faced a high-pressure test – and the army delivered. Ordered to deploy at 1:07 p.m. on October 15, a company from 2 Royal 22e Régiment helicoptered to Montreal within an hour. Truck convoys carried soldiers from Valcartier to Quebec City, Sherbrooke, and other towns. In Edmonton the Canadian Airborne Regiment's 1ère Commando Aeroporté left for Montreal within minutes of the deployment order; the next day, infantry from Camp Gagetown received similar orders. Competent, heavily armed soldiers patrolled the streets of Montreal, dealing sensibly with the public, almost all of whom, French- or English-speaking, seemed grateful for their presence.[16] 'The soldiers were funny,' one journalist recalled fifteen years later, 'so much smaller and younger than policemen, and they were not from Montreal so they looked lost in the city streets.'[17] Other units guarded hydro stations, protected air force bases where nuclear weapons were held, and patrolled small towns such as Drummondville, Trois-Rivières, and Sorel. In all, 7500 troops did service in Montreal and hundreds more across Quebec, a tour of duty that lasted to the end of 1970.

Military morale briefly soared after the army's very successful action during the crisis. Surely the Prime Minister now would recognize the utility of the armed forces, soldiers said. There were no indications that he did. At the same time, some public servants had worried that French-speaking troops might be susceptible to the blandishments of separatists and FLQ supporters. There was no sign of this collaboration either. One junior officer on the streets of Montreal in 1970, later a very senior officer, recalled that his francophone soldiers simply did not know what was involved and had no difficulty in obeying orders. Were a similar crisis to occur in the mid-1990s, however, he feared a different outcome.[18] During the Quebec referendum of 1995, that was also the view of a senior Chrétien Cabinet minister who was close to the situation. As it seemed that the 'oui' side might win on the day before the vote, National Defence Headquarters scrambled to put together contingency plans. 'I had no concern about the senior [francophone] officers,' the minister said, 'but I worried about the ill-educated, unilingual junior ranks who would have felt the call of the blood.'[19] Happily, Canada won.

The Defence Minister during the FLQ crisis of 1970 was Donald Macdonald, who had been appointed in September 1970. Only thirty-eight years old and just two years in Cabinet, Macdonald had favoured unification and a complete withdrawal of forces from Europe. He had also been open to the idea of Canadian neutrality. His appointment to the defence post, therefore, was seen as a harbinger of worse to come for the already reeling Canadian Armed Forces. In fact, Macdonald had been told by Trudeau that the 1969 decision on NATO forces was final and he was not to press for more cuts. The three-year budget freeze was also firm; even so, his task was to raise the forces' morale and to produce a new White Paper that charted a course for the future.

Macdonald released 'Defence in the 70s: White Paper on Defence' on August 24, 1971. The paper gave internal security a high priority, naturally enough in light of the FLQ crisis. Keeping order was a civil responsibility, but 'timely assistance from the forces' might be required. The Canadian Armed Forces also had a role to play in 'national development,' including assistance in natural disasters, which was normal, and in research, communications, and protection of the environment, which were not. To have national development cited as a key role in a Defence White Paper rattled the army. The White Paper confirmed that the defence of North America was the second priority, mainly an air force role, and reaffirmed the continuation of the existing NATO contribution: 'the Government has no plans for further reductions.' The CMBG in NATO, however, lost its Centurion tanks, their replacement being a 'light, tracked, direct-fire-support vehicle' that could be moved by air. What those vehicles were to do was unclear.

Peacekeeping was the final priority. Trudeau had no interest in the Pearsonian 'helpful fixer' role, and Macdonald agreed. Canada would take on peacekeeping only if the missions had realistic terms of reference, if all parties agreed on the purposes and roles, and there were prospects for success. Macdonald also announced the creation of a Management Review Group to examine the organization of his department, and he pledged to press bilingualism forward.[20] The White Paper gave little to the army beyond confirmation of what it had lost, although it received a good measure of praise from defence commentators. The commitment to bilingualism, however, was long overdue.

Canada's difficult wartime experiences in trying – and largely failing – to persuade French Canadians to volunteer for military service had, as we have seen, caused serious political and racial problems in Canada. Conscription exacerbated the communal tensions. How could the problem be fixed?

In 1946 Army Headquarters had asked Brigadier J.P.E. Bernatchez, a Royal Military College graduate, a Permanent Force officer of the Royal 22e Régiment, and one of three French-speaking brigadiers to hold field command during the war, to examine the situation of francophones in the army. Bernatchez's recommendations disappeared as the army slipped off the radar screen in an atmosphere of demobilization and retrenchment, and nothing was done other than to create a French-language recruit training school in 1949. The difficulties of recruiting in Quebec during the Korean War brought the problem back to the forefront as Ottawa at last began to realize that francophones saw the army as a wholly anglophone institution. Recruits came forward in appropriate numbers – approximately 27 per cent in the 1950s – but left the military sooner and in larger numbers. It was hard to rise in an army that could not offer courses in French to soldiers or officers. In 1951 francophones made up only 14 per cent of army officers and 21 per cent of the men.

Change was slow and hesitant. In 1952 Le Collège Militaire Royal de St-Jean opened as the third of the Canadian Services Colleges. One of those who pressed for CMR, Brigadier Jean Allard, was quite blunt in saying why the college was necessary: 'to avoid the problems that occurred during the mobilizations of 1914 and 1939.'[21] Aimed at producing functionally bilingual officers, CMR succeeded in attracting francophones wanting to join the forces (until the college was closed for budgetary reasons in the mid-1990s). The necessity to spend the last two years before graduation at RMC in Kingston, however, might have been a contrary pressure. Summer training was almost always offered in English only, another factor encouraging a high dropout rate.[22] The army did create a francophone artillery battery in 1954, but stupidly posted it to Picton, Ontario. A tank squadron, formed in 1957, was cut in the early 1960s, along with the battery.

Not until the Royal Commission on Bilingualism and Biculturalism, created in 1963, focused national attention on the Quebec-Canada situation did the mounting pressure begin to produce results. Prime Minister Lester Pearson declared in 1966 that there had to be proportionate francophone representation in the public service, and in 1969 the new government of Pierre Trudeau passed the Official Languages Act. Canadians now had the right to deal with their government in either of the nation's two official languages.

The military found itself caught up in the new mood. Various studies on implementing integration and unification also looked at bilingualism and reached widely varying conclusions. Even so, there seemed some willingness to consider change, and Hellyer and Léo Cadieux, his associate minister and later successor, determined to make the Canadian Forces more bilingual. The key figure in pressing change forward was General Jean-Victor Allard.

As Chief of the Defence Staff since 1966, Allard was personally committed to improving the French Canadian place in the forces. One of his first acts was to establish a task force under Colonel Armand Ross to recommend ways that francophones could have the same career opportunities as anglophones. Allard created a bilingualism secretariat,[23] and he insisted that francophones serve in all trades and ranks in numbers proportionate to their percentage of the population. In the early 1950s Allard had called for French-language units to be created in Quebec, but he had been unsuccessful in persuading his superiors.[24] Now he created French Language Units, or FLUs, in all three services and developed a program to train French-speaking recruits in their own language before their serving in FLUs.

But there were concerns in Prime Minister Pearson's office when Cadieux, just ten weeks into his post as Defence Minister, began to press for the creation of a concentration of FLUs in Quebec. The Minister wanted to base the Royal 22e Régiment, an artillery and an armoured regiment, and all associated combat and support units, as well as their French-speaking personnel, at Valcartier. But because *indépendantiste* sentiment in Quebec had received a huge fillip after President de Gaulle's 'Vive le Québec libre' speech in the summer of Centennial year, some officials had begun to worry about where Quebec was heading. Marc Lalonde, one of Pearson's aides, said: 'We should avoid very carefully the concentration of these French-speaking forces inside Quebec ... We have to think here of the problems that such a concentration could cause in the case of a very serious political upheaval in the Province of Quebec ... I don't want to sound unduly pessimistic,' Lalonde added, sounding just that, 'but we should avoid providing the Government of Quebec with a ready-made Army at its disposal.' Michael Pitfield, another key Privy Council Office official, added his concern that this was 'one of the most potentially dangerous decisions that the Federal government could ever take ... unilingual French-Canadian units concentrated in Quebec could – in the circumstances of our times, and with the trends that are likely to become even more powerful in the future – irrevocably lay the groundwork for an exceedingly dangerous situation.'[25] The FLUs nonetheless came into existence, announced by Cadieux on April 2, 1968, just days before Trudeau won the Liberal leadership. Based around the two Van Doos battalions and concentrated at Valcartier, just north of Quebec City, the army FLUs soon became the 5e Groupement de Combat. A French-language trades training school, dubbed 'Francotrain,' opened at Canadian Forces Base St-Jean.[26]

It was partially bad luck that Cadieux's cuts to English-speaking regiments took place at the same time as the FLUs came into being. The army was to have nine infantry battalions, with three regiments of three battalions, and some units disappeared from the Regular Army. That hurt, and the cuts created substantial bitterness among anglophones. As Desmond Morton put it, 'From being a virtual anglophone monopoly, the Canadian armed forces came, for a time, to resemble the country they served: two mutually resentful solitudes.'[27]

Cadieux and General F.R. Sharp, the new CDS, moved ahead nonetheless. In December 1969 the Defence Council accepted a ten-year plan to 'ensure that the Canadian Armed Forces reflect the linguistic and cultural values as well as the proportionate representation of both language groups.'[28] The next step came in June 1970, when the Trudeau Cabinet declared its intention to amend the National Defence Act to reflect the equality of the two official languages in the forces. A French-language section within Mobile Command was to be created and, to staff it appropriately, the government adopted a Royal Commission on Bilingualism and Biculturalism recommendation that 'qualified personnel who can exercise their duties in French be rapidly promoted.'[29] In February 1971 the CDS ordered that 'equal opportunity will be achieved by designating 28 percent of the existing rank structure at all levels and in all areas of responsibilities for francophone personnel.' By 1976 four in ten officers of the rank of lieutenant-colonel and above and 35 per cent of the remainder of the forces were to be functionally bilingual. Both ratios were scheduled to be increased substantially by 1980. The Canadian Forces impossibly precise plan called for a combined armed force of 83,000 to have 59,760 anglophones and 23,240 francophones. Precisely 33,347 personnel were to serve in English-speaking units 'manned at the national ratio of 72% anglophones / 28% francophones,' and 11,620 francophones were to serve in FLUs whose strength was to total 14,525.[30]

Because attrition rates for francophones remained high, the levels of bilingualism had to be cut back: after five years, 40 per cent of generals were to be bilingual, 30 per cent of officers, 20 per cent of senior non-commissioned officers, and 15 per cent of privates. To achieve that goal, recruitment was to aim at 50 per cent francophones for officers and 40 per cent for other ranks.

There were soon difficulties, as bilingual and francophone officers and NCOs achieved rapid promotion. Bypassed anglophones became bitter, while some francophones began to suspect that their promotions were based less on their military merit than on their mother tongue. Enforced bilingualism created real fury among those anglophones passed over for promotion. They watched angrily as what they believed were less-qualified francophones became majors or lieutenant-colonels before they did, or while vacancies went unfilled because no bilingual officer was available. Quotas create a dynamic of their own, and the consequences can be harmful. In 1971, for example, the newly created francophone armoured regiment, the 12e Régiment Blindé, was short of NCOs. The army advised corporals in Lord Strathcona's Horse to transfer to the 12e RB if they wanted to get promoted. Unilingual corporals, willing to learn French, stood an excellent chance of getting the promotions they could not in the LSH, or so it appeared. This 'corporals' mess' caused hard feelings all round, and it was replicated in other corps.[31] A report in 1973 by the Deputy Director General of Bilingualism and Biculturalism at Ottawa headquarters noted 'deviations' from the merit list, complaints from Commanding Officers that bilingualism interfered with unit efficiency by taking good soldiers away for language courses, and suggestions that the program was so rigid as to be harmful. The policy of promoting francophones and bypassing anglophones remained.[32]

The percentage of francophones in the military gradually increased towards the official goal of 28 per cent. In 1983, for example, it stood at 27 per cent, though there was still overrepresentation at the lower ranks and underrepresentation at the higher. At the same time, language training for anglophone and francophone officers increased, the object continuing to be a functionally bilingual officer corps – officers with the ability to speak to the troops in their own language. Translation of army manuals was stepped up (but was slow for technical manuals in particular), and memoranda could be submitted – and usually read – in either official language. These achievements all made for substantial progress, as was the Canadian Forces' decision in the late 1980s that, by 1997, functional bilingualism was to be a requirement for promotion to the rank of lieutenant-colonel and above.[33] As a Ministerial Committee on official languages in the armed forces noted in 1992, the object had to be to give francophones and anglophones the opportunity to have full careers in their own language and, above all, to have leaders who could lead in the language of their subordinates. Only in that way could effective Canadian operational forces result.[34]

For all its problems, and they were and are many, bilingualism had worked. Though sometimes, as one senior officer noted, bilingualism meant that 'like breasts, we had to have two of everything,'[35] the Canadian Forces had overcome the root causes of the difficulties that so troubled them until the late 1960s. The resulting army was a better reflection of the country's duality than almost any federal institution – indeed, better than any Canadian institution of any kind. As Morton put it after the bitterness had died down, 'Few any longer claimed that discipline or efficiency had been sacrificed' to serve bilingualism.[36]

The Management Review Group that Defence Minister Donald Macdonald created in 1971 was intended to study the department's organization to 'ensure effective planning and control.' The existing Department of National Defence was divided in two – the deputy minister controlled the money and the military controlled the operations, and sometimes neither side talked to the other. The result, depending on who was asked, was either that the military operated unchecked, or that it was hamstrung by its lack of financial control and internal rivalries over a steadily diminishing budget.

The Management Review Group had proposed, incredibly, that the deputy minister should outrank the Chief of the Defence Staff. But there were two new figures in the department – the deputy minister, Sylvain Cloutier, and the CDS, General Jacques Dextraze. They persuaded the Minister that a better solution would be for the deputy and the CDS to be equal in status, with a combined staff serving both. The deputy would have responsibility for management, and the CDS for operations. This division made sense, and it worked because Cloutier and Dextraze made it work, though the relationship between them was often full of cursing and shouting.*

In the integrated Canadian Forces Headquarters, however, civilian officers could outrank military officers, and managers, civilian or military, could outrank commanders. The resulting civilianization of the department – the dominance of managers over the military, and of military bureaucrats over operational commanders – had major long-term implications for the army and the other environments. As one student of military justice noted, the new integrated National Defence Headquarters created opportunities for more interaction between civilians and soldiers, but the department 'failed to delineate respective responsibilities in any legal or binding manner through amendments to the National Defence Act.'[37] Officers stayed in posts where civilians might have been more appropriate and, in some cases, the reverse was true. The result, as the head of the Defence Research Board, Dr O.M. Solandt, called it, was 'an act of mayhem committed in the name of administrative madness.'[38] Perhaps he overstated matters. What is certain is that civilians and military managers gradually gained more control over the operational side of the forces, a condition that likely reached its peak in the 1990s when Robert

---

* Dextraze could fight with his ministers too, but, 'sometimes when we reached an impasse,' Barney Danson, Minister of National Defence from 1976 to 1979, recalled, 'he would stand to attention. I was his superior and if I wanted something done he would treat it as an order and get on with the job.' 'Not Bad for a Sergeant: The Memoirs of Barney Danson' (unpublished manuscript), 210.

Fowler was deputy minister.[39] For the soldiers on the ground, the joke was that the traditional military challenge had to be altered. 'Halt. Who goes there?' And then, not 'Advance and be recognized' but 'Advance and be reorganized.'[40] The bean-counters and managers were in charge. To them, the armed forces were a corporation or a government department like any other, the 'in' management techniques of the day should prevail, and the era of business plans and of officers with MBAs was just around the corner.

These changes were compounded for the army by the effects of unification. The entire system of training changed, with basic recruit training for the three environments given at the Canadian Forces Base Cornwallis in Nova Scotia. Basic training, in other words, was to be the same for soldiers, sailors, and airmen, and for women. Concurrently, and in substantial part for fiscal reasons, bases were consolidated. The regimental garrisons largely closed down and units, including their air force and navy personnel, ordinarily operated within one force's organizational structure. Regimental messes, the heart of the units, disappeared, replaced by base officers' and NCOs' messes that had little life in them. Something tangible had been lost, and the impact compounded when more soldiers took to living 'on the economy,' renting accommodation in town. The differences between soldiers and civilians had begun to blur.

At the same time, at operational bases in Canada, an army brigade might have 'purple' tradesmen, so called because the support services were unified and no longer army, navy, or air.[41] So long as everyone wore the dark green uniform, this unified system appeared to the outsider to be functioning properly; once the three environments reverted to different uniforms in the mid-1980s, a parade at any base looked bizarre. Those in the system didn't need the different uniforms to know that the process wasn't working. Too often an air force or navy mechanic posted in to an army position did not know the equipment or have any idea how to function and survive in the field. The inevitable result was that support for the operational forces deteriorated, producing a 'significant decline in expertise and capability' for the land forces, or so one official study in 1985 reported.[42]

There were also too few men – just above 20,000 – for the tasks assigned to Mobile Command and the Lahr-based Combat Group. In particular, the army wanted a new tank to replace the twenty-year-old Centurions, something Macdonald's 1971 White Paper had discounted. To get this main battle tank required extensive lobbying by the CDS, aided by German Chancellor Helmut Schmidt, who worried over NATO's defences and persuaded Trudeau of the alliance's utility and importance. Dextraze preferred a U.S. tank, but the Americans were in the early stages of developing a new main battle tank, the newest British tank was too heavy, and the Canadians deemed the Germans' Leopard eminently satisfactory – which, of course, gratified Schmidt. Interested in securing an economic link with the European Community and personally friendly with the Chancellor, the Prime Minister agreed in 1976, despite the opposition of the new Finance Minister, Donald Macdonald. The army soon had 128 Leopards for $210 million. The NATO brigade received 86 tanks, giving it some teeth at last.

The budgetary problems were less easy to resolve. The freeze was to end in 1974, but Cloutier managed a breakthrough in 1973, winning approval for a 7 per cent increase in each year of a five-year period. The difficulty was that inflation was running in double digits, and DND's budget actually lost ground despite the increased funding. A Defence Structure Review in 1975 reaffirmed the military's priorities, but phrased them in terms of combat capability and committed the government to increasing capital expenditures in defence by 12 per cent a year for five years. This increase was enough to get the army 491 Cougar, Grizzly, and Husky wheeled armoured vehicles by 1982 and almost 3000 new 2½-ton trucks by 1984. There were also new anti-tank and anti-aircraft weapons and self-propelled 155 mm howitzers. In 1977 the Canadian Airborne Regiment became part of the new Special Service Force, based at Petawawa, and including 1 Royal Canadian Regiment, 8th Canadian Hussars, and 2 Royal Canadian Horse Artillery. The Special Service Force was a light, air-transportable force with airborne capability; because it was based close to Ottawa, some people thought it was intended for use in case of civil disturbances – a reasonable assumption given that the Parti Québécois was in power in Quebec City and threatening to hold a referendum on independence for Quebec. The remaining Combat Groups were redesignated as brigade groups, and the NATO brigade became 4 Canadian Mechanized Brigade Group.

By 1980–1, with the Soviets embroiled in Afghanistan, Ronald Reagan in power in Washington, and the Cold War going full blast, the pace of training for the NATO brigade picked up. The new equipment, slow in arriving, hampered the Canadians as they tried to play their small part in NATO. Alliance strategy had changed to fighting the so-called Air-Land Battle, which featured deep penetrations into Soviet and satellite territory. In some areas, such as air defence, however, 4 Canadian Mechanized Brigade Group remained woefully underarmed. To defend against aircraft and helicopters, soldiers had only hand-held Blowpipe missiles, 'little better than slingshots,' Peter Newman wrote. The air force's bases had their air defences provided by 40 mm Bofors anti-aircraft guns 'taken off the late and lamented HMCS *Bonaventure*,' the navy's aircraft carrier that was scrapped at the end of the 1960s.[43] Brigadier-General Richard Evraire, commanding the brigade from 1982 to 1984, recalled telling an American commander that his force 'was not equipped' for the new battle concept: 'the best use he could make of 4 Brigade was to make sure that it was in a fairly static defensive position with the possibility of counterattacking here and there, but not as an offensive weapon ... I know this did not please too many people,' Evraire said, 'but it was hardly the place to be untruthful.'[44]

The weakness of 4 Brigade was serious because, in 1982, the Soviet bloc had more tanks (42,500 to 13,000), more artillery pieces (31,500 to 10,700), more armoured personnel carriers (78,800 to 30,000), and more attack helicopters (700 to 400) than NATO. The disparities were alarming, and the NATO decision in 1979 to station land-based intermediate range missiles in Europe was a response to the arms imbalance that favoured the Soviets so heavily.

In the eyes of its allies, Canada was not pulling its weight in the alliance. This lag inspired continued efforts by Deputy Minister Cloutier, who had served previously in the Treasury Board and understood how the system could be made to work. He succeeded in 1978 in winning Trudeau's support for annual 3 per cent *after inflation* increases in the defence budget. Trudeau, in fact, did better than that and, by 1984, the Defence budget was $7.97 billion, up from $4.39 billion in 1980. Inflation had played its part in swelling the total budget figure and, according to Dr J.C. Arnell, a former Assistant Deputy Minister in the department, in 1980, 'Inflation was probably the main cause of any general decline in the Canadian Armed Forces.'[45]

The Progressive Conservatives under Joe Clark held power briefly in 1979–80, just long enough for Defence Minister Allan McKinnon, a Second World

War veteran and a peacetime Regular officer, to undertake a review of unification. The Tory victory had greatly pleased the armed forces, but the new government seemed more interested in trying to unscramble the unification omelette than anything else. The Defence view, shared by senior military officers and civilian officials, was that this complex issue was better left untouched, but McKinnon insisted and created his own Review Committee under businessman George Fyffe.[46] To the committee members' surprise, they discovered that unification was not universally detested in the forces and, surprisingly, they did not recommend its undoing. They did, however, call for a return to distinctive uniforms and more say at NDHQ for each of the environment chiefs to 'put the focus back on operations.' The committee delivered its report after the Liberals had returned to power in the 1980 election. A subsequent review of the Review Committee's report, ordered by Trudeau's next Defence Minister, Gilles Lamontagne, urged the department to give the environmental commanders more clout but refused to agree to spending money on new uniforms. That had to await the arrival of the Mulroney government in 1984.[47]

The Conservative government, in power until 1993, at first raised hopes for the army and then, when federal budget deficits mounted and the Soviet Union collapsed, it dashed them. Both in opposition and in the 1984 election campaign, Mulroney had promised to raise the strength of the forces by ten thousand, to increase defence spending by 6 per cent a year, to bump up capital spending, and to provide new uniforms for each of the three environments.[48] The first of these promises to be broken was that on funding. In November 1984 the Finance Minister cut $154 million from the defence appropriations left by his Liberal predecessor. At the same time, Mulroney's promise of additional funds – $190 million – also disappeared. That was a blow to Robert Coates, the new Defence Minister, but it did not stop him from proposing to give the three environments new and distinctive uniforms. The cost estimates ranged from $36 million to $100 million – difficult enough when funds were scarce, but particularly so when the CDS, General G.C.E. Thériault, believed that new equipment was a vastly more important priority. The Minister prevailed and presented 'the Coates of many colours' on February 7, 1985. The army retained the green winter uniform, but now had a tan summer uniform. Coates's career was cut short when he was forced to resign over a scandal a few days after the unveiling.[49]

Coates's successor as Defence Minister was Erik Nielsen, previously the Deputy Prime Minister, the enforcer of Progressive Conservative Party and caucus discipline, and vice-chair of the Cabinet's priorities and planning committee. Potentially the most powerful Defence Minister in years, Nielsen believed, as did his Prime Minister, President Ronald Reagan, and NATO, that the Soviet Union again posed a real threat to Western Europe. Just two weeks after his appointment, Nielsen announced that Canada would send an additional 1200 troops to NATO at a cost of $100 million a year. That commitment meant an extra squadron for the armoured regiment, an artillery battery, and an additional company for each of the two infantry battalions. For a time, the army was cock of the walk, but the 1986 budget brought everyone back to reality. Instead of Mulroney's promised 6 per cent, the Department of National Defence received 2.75 per cent in 1986–7 and 2.5 per cent in each of the following years. The proposed NATO troop increase was cut by a quarter and the Canadian Forces' overall strength increased only by 1752, a far cry from the promised ten thousand.

There was still some progress: Mobile Command, led by Lieutenant-General Charles Belzile, produced 'Corps 86,' a plan to restructure the army so that it had all the units essential to field a division and all the corps troops that would be required in the event of mobilization. There were some steps towards re-equipment, notably new trucks and jeeps, improved TOW (Tube launched, Optically guided, Wire controlled) anti-tank missiles with a thermal imaging sight, a new 5.56 mm rifle and machine gun, and low-level air defence guns and missiles. There were more and larger exercises in Canada in 1985: 14,000 troops took part in 'Rendezvous 85,' a six-week training exercise that tested fighting and support units to the fullest. As the army's Regular Force strength was only 22,500 and its Reserves 15,500, this exercise brought together a large part of the land forces. Professionalism demanded training, and training required exercises that tested commanders and soldiers at all levels. Belzile's army understood this need.

In June 1987, after a lapse of sixteen years, the department issued a new White Paper, a personal project for the new Minister, Perrin Beatty.[50] Marked by Cold War rhetoric that was already sounding outdated by the time the document came from the printers, *Challenge and Commitment: A Defence Policy for Canada* sounded good to the army. 'If our conventional forces are to deter,' it said, 'they must be able to defend. If they are to defend, they must be able to fight. To do that, we must maintain their readiness and provide for their sustainment.' The White Paper admitted that the Canadian Forces equipment was in 'an advanced state of obsolescence or ... already obsolete.' 'Rust-out' was a real difficulty that could only be met by increased resources, reduced commitments, or some combination of the two, and the Minister stated that the government had decided 'to alter some commitments ... while improving the effectiveness' of the others. In particular, Beatty pledged to increase the Reserves fourfold, creating additional brigades for the defence of Canada, and to consolidate the country's European commitments, notably by eliminating the CAST brigade role in Norway and pledging to send it to join 4 Canadian Mechanized Brigade, a new name, in a two-brigade First Canadian Division. The plan even included new tanks and the positioning of equipment in Germany for the Canada-based brigade. It sounded too good to be true – and most of it was.

The 1987 White Paper died from the combination of the Mulroney government's rapidly rising deficits and the beginning of perestroika and glasnost in Mikhail Gorbachev's Soviet Union.[51] In short order the Warsaw Pact disbanded, Eastern Europe's Soviet satellites turned into free nations, the two Germanies reunited, and the Union of Soviet Socialist Republics collapsed and splintered. The assumptions of an intensifying Cold War that had shaped Beatty's paper were gone by the early 1990s, and the budgetary crisis guaranteed that the Canadian Forces would not receive what he had promised. As early as 1989 the Defence department's annual report said flatly: 'No one seriously believes that the current Soviet leadership has any intention of attacking Western Europe or North America.'[52]

The end of the Soviet threat did not guarantee a peaceful world in an international situation suddenly freed from the heavy hand of Cold War politics. Canada itself was not exempt, and militants in many quarters had become dissatisfied with the pace of change. Some of these groups were soon pressing for radical action – as in the small Quebec community of Oka.

On March 1, 1990, Mohawks from the Kanesatake reserve set up barricades to protest Oka's decision to expand a golf course on land the Mohawks claimed as theirs. The Sûreté du Québec, the Quebec provincial police, arrived and, on July 11, after a long, increasingly tense process, the Sûreté stormed the barricades. One officer was shot and killed and the barricades remained in place. Four hundred Mohawks from Kahnawake now joined the protest and blocked the Mercier Bridge from Montreal to the south shore of the St Lawrence River. With tensions increasing daily, on August 7 the Quebec government called for the army to replace the Sûreté at the barricades. On August 27 Quebec City asked the army to take down the barricades. Using a combination of negotiations and escalating pressure, 2 RCR, aided by Cougar armoured vehicles from the 12e Régiment Blindé, did the job quickly at Kahnawake and reopened the bridge.

At Oka, however, a well-armed group of 200 masked and camouflaged Mohawk 'Warriors' refused to dismantle their barricades. The Warriors, armed with anti-tank weapons, AK-47 assault rifles, and sniper rifles, dug a trench system and, some feared, planted mines. The troops on the ground were from the 5e Brigade, based at Valcartier. Their orders were to prevail – with the minimum necessary force. With television crews on the scene each and every day, the army had to do its task in the full glare of publicity. Using the same combination of tactics that the RCR had employed, the 2 Royal 22e Régiment behaved with admirable restraint and professionalism, though it had plans ready to storm the barricades. On September 26 the Warriors gave up the game and dispersed. Oka had been a military victory, all the better for being a bloodless one. Peter Worthington, a journalist often critical of the army, wrote after the crisis that the army now 'is, literally, the world's expert in easing tense, volatile situations ... without fanfare or fuss, mostly on their own judgment and initiative.'[53]

The army also played a major role in eastern Ontario and Quebec during the huge ice storm of 1998. With power out and the hydro companies unable to cope, the army helped rebuild power lines, rescued trapped families, and shuttled supplies. This effort was substantial and it won the army much praise.

The Gulf War was another bloodless victory for Canada, though not for the invaded Kuwaitis or the Iraqis. The Iraqi invasion of Kuwait on August 2, 1990, led the United States to put together a huge coalition that ultimately fielded a force of more than a half-million. The Canadian contribution was three ships and a CF-18 fighter squadron; the army's was two airfield defence companies, a handful of air defence gunners to serve aboard the ships, and a field hospital. Although Headquarters Canadian Forces Europe prepared a plan for dispatch of a battle group, and Mobile Command simultaneously worked out a plan for a brigade group of three mechanized infantry battalions, an armoured regiment, and a reconnaissance squadron, Canada's land forces played no part in the ground war. There were logistical problems, time needed to train and transport troops to Saudi Arabia, and possibly even an aversion to casualties and a recognition that casualties might produce reinforcement problems. Ultimately, however, the real reason the Canadians did not participate in a major way on land was clear: the army had no troops it could send who could operate effectively with the coalition, and no modern equipment that could keep pace with the allies' main battle tanks. The Leopards, new in 1976, were all but obsolete by 1990. Realistically, after years of cutbacks, the army could do little – and even that, not very well.[54]

The Gulf War, with its massive air campaign preceding a lightning armoured strike led by American, British, and French forces, sent the Iraqis reeling back into their country. The coalition quickly liberated Kuwait and, while the Canadian fighters and ships did their part, the army's few soldiers on the scene did little other than patrol the boundaries of the airfield used by the air force's CF-18s. It was a humiliating display of impotence for a once-proud army.[55] The war also left a legacy of soldiers, sailors, and airmen ill with 'Gulf War syndrome,' something the military considered to be all but mythical in nature but unquestionably made service personnel very sick.[56]

Worse was to come. The Progressive Conservative budget of February 1992 made clear that all Canadian Forces would be out of Germany by 1994. Moreover, 4 Canadian Mechanized Brigade was not to be reconstituted in Canada, its infantry, artillery, and armoured units becoming Total Force units, a bastardized mix of 10 per cent Regular and 90 per cent Militia personnel. By the summer of 1993, 4 CMB was no more, after a Canadian NATO presence in Germany of forty-two years.[57] The unemployment rate in Lahr doubled and the estimated $400 million a year that the Canadians had pumped into the local economy disappeared with the pullout of the brigade and the air force.[58] Canada did retain the commitment to fly a brigade to Europe in case of emergency. The two additional brigades in Canada had the task of cooperating with United States forces in defence of North America. The army earmarked three battalion-sized battle groups for commitments to NATO, the Americans, and the United Nations.

The demise of the Conservative government in 1993 and the arrival of the Liberals under Jean Chrétien could have heralded change for the better. However, the new government's primary task was to get the national finances under control, so cuts hit every sector of government, including the Defence department. The government announced its plans to reduce Canadian Forces' strength from 75,000 to just above 66,000 by 1998 and to cut $7 billion out of the budget in that same period.[59]

The new government's emphasis on dollars reinforced the managerial and bottom-line ethos within the military. Officers now routinely produced business plans for their units; the business school jargon came to predominate; and planning, budgeting, and spending all became locked into an annual cycle of reporting that absorbed so much time and effort that little remained for soldiering. An army, one British writer said, 'does not march on its pay scales alone.' He added that if the army is turned into a monetary organization, a monetary mentality is the result.[60] A good leader has to be aware of the fiscal implications of what he does, but a budget planner is not necessarily an effective leader. A good army understands that operational effectiveness and cost effectiveness are not the same. Driven by funding shortfalls, the Canadian military regrettably lost sight of these truisms.

The government also launched a review of defence policy, sorely needed since the geopolitical assumptions underlying the 1987 White Paper had been overturned by world events. The 1994 Defence White Paper was the result. Long on rhetoric, short on specifics, the White Paper was notable for two things. First, it declared that domestic considerations, notably the parlous finances of the federal government, demanded that 'defence spending ... in real terms would be less than 60 percent of that assumed in the 1987 Defence White Paper.' Largely keeping this one promise, the Liberal government in fact slashed defence spending by 23 per cent between 1993 and 1998. Second, the 1994 paper maintained that Canada was to continue to field multipurpose combat-capable armed forces able to fight 'alongside the best, against the best.' At the same time, it hacked away at the capabilities that would permit this achievement. What the paper did do was to say that 'Canadians have a strong sense of responsibility to alleviate suffering and respond, where their efforts can make a difference.'[61] This human security agenda, later developed by Foreign Minister Lloyd Axworthy, or so Joe Jockel and Joel Sokolsky wrote, may have provided 'the only convincing intellectual basis' for the future of the Canadian Forces 'as a force that should be capable of overseas peacekeeping and combat operations.'[62]

For the army, the 1994 White Paper proclaimed that 'multi-purpose combat capabilities are now maintained to carry out a wide variety of domestic and international operations,' but not those at the high intensity level. It promised that the land forces would be 'adequately equipped,' in particular with new armoured personnel carriers. At the same time, force reduction was to continue, and the practice of 'contracting-out' services to civilian firms expanded. The last decade of the 1990s held little promise for the army and the Canadian Forces.

Women had played a role in the army since 1885, when nurses accompanied the expedition that defeated Riel's rebellion in the North-West. Women had again served with distinction as Nursing Sisters in the Boer War and the First World War. In the Second World War, the Canadian Women's Army Corps, with its personnel filling virtually every role except combat, and the Nursing Sisters once more served with distinction. Nursing Sisters provided medical care in Korea. Gradually, other military occupations became open to women, but in 1971 women still made up only 1.8 per cent of Canadian Forces personnel.[63] In 1973 the forces set a target of 8000 women by 1983. By 1974 women could serve in eighteen of twenty-seven officer classifications in the three environments, and in sixty-four of ninety-seven trades. Quotas limiting the number of women disappeared in that year and the next, and women made up 3.6 per cent of the Regular Force and 13.4 per cent of the Reserves. The department's annual report in 1974 proudly stated that 'most openings will be filled by the best applicant, male or female ... Enrolment qualifications for men and women have been standardized. Female recruits are receiving training almost identical to that of males, including weapons training on a trial basis. Women are now part of base duty staffs, and they serve on ... base defence forces.' Women soldiers also served in NATO and the United Nations Emergency Force (UNEF II) after 1975.[64]

The one glaring exception in which army women could not serve was in the combat or combat support trades. By 1978 women made up 6 per cent of the Regular strength of the Canadian Forces and 19 per cent of the Reserve Force.[65] The next year, the army ran trials to see if women could successfully be integrated into combat support roles – trials conducted with the Service Battalion and a Field Ambulance in 4 Canadian Mechanized Brigade Group in NATO and at the isolated Canadian Forces Station Alert in the Arctic. The results of the SWINTER (Servicewomen in Non-Traditional Roles and Environments) tests were not wholly satisfactory, one report stating bluntly that 'should women be placed in combat situations, more Canadians will likely die.'[66] Political imperatives had become more important than military ones, however, and the barriers began falling quickly.

In 1980 the first twenty-four lady cadets (so called to match the gentlemen cadets designation) entered the Royal Military College. There was tension, conflict, and some sexual harassment, but twenty-one graduated four years later to become Regular officers.[67] The first women graduates did not necessarily believe in quotas. 'It was rigorous training,' one of the graduates said, 'and it is not something that every woman is going to want to do. So to simply say "Well, you should have a 25-per-cent quota of women in the military" – there is not going to be 25 per cent of women out there that want to run through swamps and want to be carrying a pack around on their back ... it just isn't going to happen.'[68]

The inclusion of the Charter of Rights and Freedoms in the Canadian Constitution in 1982 nonetheless increased pressure across the country for quotas in many areas, and the army began to bring its practices into line. In 1986 the Chief of the Defence Staff created a special commission to examine the integration of women into combat roles, and the next year the army began recruiting women to support its Combat Related Employment of Women (CREW) trials. In 1989 a Canadian Human Rights Tribunal ordered that women be integrated into all military occupations by 1999.[69] One member of that tribunal, Colonel James Allan, disagreed with the majority, arguing that the tribunal had left the military with a 'nonsensical policy ... of trying to recruit women to the combat arms where most of them don't want to be.'[70] Perhaps mistakenly, the Department of National Defence had not sought exemptions to the Charter for the Canadian Forces after 1982,[71] and such tribunal decisions were only to be expected.

There was another point that few have considered. If the Charter and human rights legislation can be used to compel the army to make itself friendlier and more open to women, to oblige it to place women into all military specialties, women will also be used in war – if Canada should require it of its citizens. Conscription for men only would be as discriminatory as a male-only army in peacetime, and women could be assigned, like men, to any duty the army chose.

Whatever the tribunals and the Charter might say, studies and experience showed that peacetime recruitment and retention of women in the combat arms was difficult – perhaps so difficult that the army could never satisfy demands for equity. There were 6800 women in the Canadian Forces in 1998, but few in the combat arms. As one serving officer stated in 2001: 'This is *the* most sensitive issue in the military. The Forces have changed for the better because of the inclusion of women. But maybe some women don't want to serve because the notion of shooting people dead doesn't appeal to them.'[72] A parliamentary committee added that 'the physical strength and stamina required to meet the physical standards within the combat arms presents a considerable challenge to many women.' In 1998 only 90 of 400 women who volunteered for the combat arms successfully completed training.[73] The effect of such dismal results was the de facto lowering of standards. One retired officer said bluntly that if anyone denied that training standards had been lowered for women, 'that's a lie.' Physical tests, he added, are now 'gendered' and women are told they must meet the 'same standards as a 45-year-old man.'[74]

At the same time, there were also 'numerous social and psychological barriers' to women's success in training, a study by two female officers observed, not least 'the very fact that they are women in a male defined and male-dominated environment ... Perceptions of their ability and motivation are based, to a significant degree, on cultural (male) assumptions related to accepted, expected, and/or "appropriate" social and sexual behaviours and gender roles.'[75] As further studies conducted for the Chief of the Land Staff in 1998 demonstrated, 'a male dominated Combat Arms culture has provided an unwelcome and overall non-supportive environment for women.'[76] The Association for Women's Equity in the Canadian Forces charged in 2000 that women recruits had been forced to meet a higher training standard than that for men at the Land Forces Western Training Centre at Wainwright, Alberta.[77]

As a result of the 'overall non-supportive environment' in the army, all ranks by the end of 1998 were required to take sensitivity training in the SHARP program – Standard for Harassment and Racism Prevention. (Some service personnel also voluntarily participated in a Native Awareness Seminar at Camp Borden in 2001 that, according to the *Globe and Mail*, had thirty soldiers in a circle, 'crying, confessing and searching for [the] inner soldier.')[78]

But sensitivity training could not fix everything. There was harassment, unfortunately, and there was also rape. A series of sensational articles in *Maclean's* in 1998 pointed to widespread rapes, cover-ups, and a resulting high rate of women soldiers leaving the army.[79] The Chief of the Defence Staff, General Maurice Baril, told the magazine: 'Sometimes, it is not very pleasant to be expected to be an angel, but that is what the public is expecting. Society is asking us to be better, more professional.'[80] With reason, Baril pointed to poor discipline and even poorer self-discipline as the root of the problem. He created a toll-free sexual harassment line to handle complaints, while a Canadian Forces ombudsman, independent of the military chain of command, soon reported to the minister.[81] Critics of Baril's approach argued that the plethora of military 'social programs' and 'snitch' lines had undermined discipline by providing an acceptable way of bypassing the chain of command.

In October 1992 the Canadian Forces abolished restrictions on gay and lesbian recruits in the Canadian Forces. Before 1988 homosexuals had been barred, as the military refused to permit openly gay and lesbian men and women to serve. The Canadian Human Rights Act and the Charter put this policy in jeopardy and, though Canadian Forces personnel, according to surveys, were concerned about serving alongside homosexuals, court cases forced the military to adapt. The best the CDS, General John de Chastelain, could do was to say that 'inappropriate sexual conduct by members of the forces, whether heterosexual or homosexual,' would not be tolerated. In fact, a study in 2000 found that the army and the Canadian Forces had accepted this tolerant approach. The policy was 'not universally embraced,' according to two observers, but 'it does appear to be universally accepted.'[82]

The Canadian Forces in 1998 next established 'targets' – quotas in plain English – for visible minorities, the goal being to enlist roughly 25 per cent of recruits from non-white segments of the population. With non-whites constituting under 2 per cent of CF strength, the object was to make the army, as quickly as possible, approximate the percentage of visible minorities in the labour force – 9 per cent. This goal was in fact a requirement, since the Canadian Forces fell under the terms of the federal Employment Equity Act. Whether visible minorities wanted to join the Canadian Forces, any more than women wanted to join the combat arms, was unknown. Whether the failure to encourage more visible minorities to join was a result of military bias or of choice was completely unknown, but the governmental pressure to use the armed forces for social engineering purposes was unrelenting.[83]

Finally, in 2001, the Minister's Advisory Board on Canadian Forces Gender Integration and Employment Equity issued its report. Noting that the targets for recruiting were 28 per cent women, 9 per cent visible minorities, and 3 per cent aboriginal peoples, the board pointed to the 1997–2000 results, respectively 11.1 per cent, 2.5 per cent, and 1.8 per cent. It blamed the CF 'failure' on the culture of 'insensitivity, ignorance and biases inconsistent with and non-supportive of the CF desire to create a culture of inclusiveness and respect.' It reported that women officers' attrition rates in the combat arms were more than twice that of men and, for non-commissioned members, more than three times as high.[84] In his foreword, General Baril declared that the Canadian Forces were 'unequivocally committed to gender integration and employment equity,' and added that it was up to the chain of command to provide the leadership needed to create the appropriate climate and results.[85]

Some critics accused Baril of political expediency and of neglecting his duty to give the nation effective military forces, but the CDS was right. The CF leadership has no choice but to make gender and racial integration work in the peacetime Canadian Forces. Armies ultimately exist to fight wars, however, and whether Canada's gender-integrated, multiracial army will work in wartime, whether women infantry soldiers will be able to stand the stresses of battle, or will impair the operational efficiency of the men in their units, remains to be proven. The public is clearly in favour of the fullest measure of integration today, but how it will react tomorrow to the sight of women soldiers killed in combat remains unknown. Whether a sensitivity-trained military will attract the right kind of men as recruits is also unproven. But the issue is settled, however much old sweats may complain, and it is long past time for the army to turn the page and make it work.

The army also has to find some way to make the Militia work. The 1987 White Paper had proposed to increase the Reserves by 400 per cent and to have Militia work with Regulars in a 'total force,' pledges that largely disappeared along with most of the promises in that paper.[86] By 1995 the Militia had 133 units in 125 cities and towns, an authorized strength of 19,957, and an effective strength of 18,347. This was a far cry from the 50,000-strong Militia of 1914 and 1939, though it was more than the 15,000 of 1979. Some units had strengths under one hundred, much of it made up by company or squadron commanders and senior warrant officers.[87] There were many officers and few privates, much of the unit strength in junior ranks coming from students or the unemployed who saw Militia service as providing reasonable pay for training they considered adventurous and fun. But if there were other jobs offering better pay, as there were in the second half of the 1990s, recruits stayed away in droves and the partially trained left the unit.

While the Militia was suffering from declining numbers, the end of the Cold War increased the army's calls on it. With the Regular Force shrinking in size, reservists came to be called upon – indeed, relied upon – for augmentation of units. Carefully selected individual Militia soldiers went through a quick training process designed to enhance their physical fitness and military skills before they joined a Land Force unit to take a slot that would ordinarily have been a Regular's. By the mid-1990s some army units proceeding on peacekeeping operations in the former Yugoslavia had as much as 20 per cent of their strength from the Militia. Up to half the rifle-toting infantry, as opposed to specialists, could sometimes come from the reserves.

The Militia men and women who served with the Regulars ordinarily performed every bit as well as the regular soldiers, including those who fought in Croatia. The difficulty was that augmentation was not a satisfying role for the hometown Militia units. The unit commanding officers, the honorary colonels, and the veterans of the Second World War and Korea wanted their soldiers to return to the Militia unit after service overseas and become its future leaders; some did, but many joined the Regular Force or, burnt out and sometimes suffering from Post-Traumatic Stress Disorder, dropped out after their return to Canada. The senior officers also wanted their units to be the basis of mobilization, as they had been in 1939. The army, in fact, had no mobilization plan and saw almost no need for one. There was no war on the horizon by the 1990s and no scenarios at National Defence Headquarters that envisaged a national mobilization.* This rationale did not satisfy the Militia, which added increasingly bitter complaints that the regular units were siphoning off all the money and equipment.

There were elements of truth in this accusation. With the defence budget tight, with new equipment scarce, and with units heading overseas on peacekeeping and peace enforcement operations at a breakneck tempo, the hard-pressed Regular units had to be as well equipped as possible. The Militia understood the argument, but that did not stop the complaints, which led to demands for a separate Reserve budget. By 1995, when Defence Minister David Collenette appointed a Special Commission on the Restructuring of the Reserves led by the former Chief Justice of Canada, Brian Dickson, relations between the army and the Militia were poisonous.

The SCRR accepted some of the Militia arguments. It recommended that a mobilization plan be prepared and that the Militia's role in mobilization be recognized. At the same it saw the need for continued Militia augmentation of the regular army, if possible eventually by entire platoons and companies.[88] The commissioners worried that some Militia units were too understrength to train at a proper level and proposed that units be combined in such a way that they kept their identity but could train at platoon and company levels, something they had not been able to do in their shrunken state. The commissioners rejected the idea of a special Reserve budget, but urged the Defence Minister to guarantee four days' paid training time each month for units. They also demanded that the CF pay system, hitherto incapable of paying reservists on time and with accuracy, be made to work. And the commission urged that reservists' jobs be protected while they were on active service. The Canadian Forces Liaison Council, the employer support organization for the reserves, opposed any such guarantee.[89]

The response to the SCRR report could charitably be described as mixed. The Minister liked some of it, the generals in Land Force Command liked other parts, and the Militia rejected any idea of consolidation of units,

---

* Beginning in the late 1990s, the Canadian Forces College in Toronto ran an annual mobilization exercise for its Staff College students. The collected papers provided some groundwork for the mobilization planning that, by 2001, National Defence Headquarters at last had begun. See NDHQ, file 3120-1-110 (CLS), Land Force Defence Plan, LFDP 110 Mobilization General Plan, draft 11/12/01.

deplored the failure to recommend a separate Reserve budget, and remained unhappy with the commission's support for a Regular Force augmentation role for the Militia. The Militia, hard-line Reservists believed, had one role only: to serve as the basis for mobilization. The root difficulty was that Collenette was a Toronto Minister, as was Art Eggleton, another of his successors. Neither one could deal effectively with the Toronto honorary colonels who, even if the Militia was a pale reflection of its former glory, could still mobilize powerful political and social pressure. Doug Young, the New Brunswick MP who was Minister between the two Torontonians, might have been able to cut the Militia's Gordian knot, but he lost his seat in the 1997 general election.

While the Defence Department implemented many of the SCRR recommendations, the bitterness between the Regular Force and the Militia did not cease or ease. The Regular Army's troubles after the Somalia incident and the ensuing Somalia Inquiry also spurred some Militia advocates to suggest that the time had come to reduce the professionals to a status similar to that of the interwar period. Let the Regulars act as a training cadre for the citizen soldiers, they suggested, and, not knowing the history of the two groups, offered only a recipe for disaster in the future.[90]

As Canada went through a substantial and long-lived economic boom, Militia strength continued to decline. New studies examined the problem. The Hon. John Fraser, the chairman of the Minister's Monitoring Committee on Change, studied the reserves.[91] Land Force Headquarters conducted a Land Force Reserve Restructure (LFRR) process that produced plans to change the roles of many Army Reserve units (the term Militia again had gone into the discard) into specialist units that might be necessary in the event of mobilization. This latter study left the Reserve leadership so unhappy that it looked back to the failure to implement all the SCRR report as a missed opportunity. The Chief of the Land Staff from 2000, Lieutenant-General Mike Jeffery, made strenuous efforts to create peace and to open the books to show that the Regulars were not stealing the Reserve's money. He pledged that there would be no re-roling of units in the immediate future and proposed to employ a composite Militia company formed out of a single Militia brigade on overseas operations by the summer 2002 rotation to Bosnia, a promise that some feared might be impossible to fulfil.[92] Jeffery and his LFRR team, moreover, now aimed to *persuade* the Militia leadership that the Regular Force needed more specialists and to permit that leadership to assist in the decision-making that might close down existing regiments. This was the goal for Phase II of the Land Force Reserve Restructure plan. Defence Minister Art Eggleton, for his part, promised to see the long-sought mobilization plan drafted and to increase Army Reserve strength to 18,500 within five years. Meanwhile, the numbers had fallen to some 14,000, the lowest level in Canadian history.[93]

The one certainty in all this squabbling, occurring while both Regular and Reserve strengths sank, was that the Militia leadership had outlasted the army's. Needed change had once again been put off to the time when there might be a new Chief of the Land Staff and a new Defence Minister with different ideas. The former Vice Chief of the Defence Staff, Admiral Dan Mainguy, commented soberly 'that until the Regular Force Army and the Army Reserve get their squabbles sorted out, they will stay in trouble ... they really do need to learn to speak with one voice.'[94] The model, though he left it unsaid, was the Navy Reserve, which not only has a role but works closely with the Regulars.

The end of the Cold War let loose the nationalisms that had been suppressed for so long. Countries invaded their neighbours, ethnic genocides began, and peacekeepers found themselves in great demand. For Canada's small armed forces, the peacekeeping industry was the only growth sector in their small and declining economy.

Canada's real expertise in peacekeeping dated from 1956, when Lester Pearson brokered the creation of the United Nations Emergency Force. His Nobel Peace Prize proclaimed Canada's middle power role, and the public henceforth assumed that Canadian soldiers would, and should, serve on every future UN mission. Canadians could be found on UNOGIL, the observation group in Lebanon formed in 1958; in the Congo from 1960 to 1964; in West New Guinea in 1962–3; and in Yemen in 1963–4. This action was international do-goodism, and Canadians, who liked to think of themselves as especially moral and as different from the Americans, loved the attention their peacekeeping received. Perhaps because of the missionary impulse that had sent Canadian Christians around the world from the Victorian age, Canadians sometimes acted as if they were *the* world's moral superpower. And because the United States, as a genuine superpower leading the confrontation with the

Soviet Union and China, was no more acceptable in peacekeeping than the Russians or Chinese were, Canadians tended to believe they kept the peace while the Americans made war. As a graduate student put it succinctly and without much irony, 'the United States is to Violence as Canada is to Peace.' The complex subject of Canadian anti-Americanism was reinforced and sometimes fed by the national preoccupation with peacekeeping.[95]

Canadians forgot that the Canadian Forces frequently did their peacekeeping as a U.S. or Western surrogate. Canada was in Indochina after 1954 precisely because it was a Western democracy. It was also true that Canadians in peacekeeping often relied on the United States for airlift, logistics, and sometimes equipment. The Canadians who went to UNEF in 1956–7 travelled on Canadian aircraft or naval vessels, but, to cite only one example, the overall UNEF logistical effort relied on American bases in Italy. The examples were legion.

Early Canadian advocates of peacekeeping also neglected the fact that the armed forces, and especially the army leadership, disliked the duty. Manpower was always scarce, as far as the army was concerned, and peacekeeping took trained soldiers and softened them up with doing good. The army's main task, as its leaders saw it, was to be prepared to fight the Soviet Union in Central Europe. Its training and its doctrine all looked to that future war. Peacekeeping was a distraction, plain and simple. This view might have been, and likely was, shortsighted for the army leadership, but it existed.

There were signs of this attitude in 1960, when UN Headquarters in New York asked for Canadian troops for the force being created for service in the newly independent Congo. The huge central African nation had liberated itself from Belgian rule and immediately sunk into chaos. The request was especially difficult for the army because the UN's need was for 280 French-speaking and bilingual signallers, and they were in very short supply. Prime Minister John Diefenbaker and his Defence Minister were reluctant, but they had their hand forced by public opinion. How could Canada, the creator of peacekeeping, decline a UN request? The government gave in and sent 57 Signal Squadron, as well as some aircraft and staff officers who soon took over much of the operation. The Chief of Staff of the UN force in 1963–4 was Brigadier J.A. Dextraze, later Chief of the Defence Staff. If he was there, he ran the UN force![96]

The duty turned out to be hazardous. Unruly Congolese soldiers roughed up Canadian soldiers, scattered in penny packets across the vast Congo, because they automatically assumed that any French-speaking white was a Belgian. At Stanleyville, Congolese troops beat and jailed the signals detachment. Released, Captain J.B. Pariseau, the detachment commander, invited the local Congolese commander to dinner, told him that bygones would be bygones, and agreed that it was all a mistake. If there was a repetition, he added, then his men would fight, and the Congolese would be answerable to the Canadian Army.[97]

The Congo crisis gradually turned into an area of Cold War confrontation and developed into a war over the resources in Katanga province. It was the first peacekeeping war, and the Pearson government eagerly pulled its last fifty-six servicemen from this commitment in June 1964.[98]

The UN Cyprus force, created in 1964, was different. Canada provided an infantry battalion, a reconnaissance squadron, and a brigade headquarters, another large commitment from scarce resources. Unlike the Congo operation, the Canadian role was destined to last for three decades. In Cyprus, Greek- and Turkish-Cypriots lived anxiously with each other, and the two mother countries, both NATO members, came close to war. Canada's interests lay in preserving NATO and in doing a good turn for U.S. President Lyndon Johnson, who was desperate that the alliance's southern flank not fall apart. Efforts to create a Commonwealth or NATO peacekeeping force failed, and the UN Security Council in March 1964 called for a UN force. The army was quick off the mark, putting 1 Royal 22e Régiment and a reconnaissance squadron of Royal Canadian Dragoons on the ground within a matter of days. The Canadian arrival forestalled a Turkish invasion and temporarily stabilized the situation.[99] President Johnson was grateful enough, some suggest, to agree to the Canada–U.S. Auto Pact!

The Canadian contingent in the UN force in Cyprus had a difficult task initially, first trying to create and then patrol the Green Line that separated the Turkish- and Greek-Cypriots in the capital, Nicosia. They shuttled misplaced people across the line, tried to intimidate hothead gangs on both sides into coexistence, and watched warily as politicians in Greece and Turkey kept the Cypriot situation at the boil. By the early 1970s UNFICYP's force strength had been reduced by some 50 per cent, a reflection of the United

Nations' growing financial problems. When a Greek-Cypriot coup overthrew the government of Cyprus in 1974, Turkey invaded the island. The Canadians, now just over 500 troops from the Canadian Airborne Regiment, found themselves confronting their Turkish NATO allies, most notably at Nicosia airport, which the Canadians kept open despite Turkish threats. There were many instances of bravery, as Canadians rescued civilians under fire and soldiers helped wounded comrades at risk of their lives. The Canadians had two men killed and seventeen wounded during the 1974 crisis, a reminder that peacekeeping had its costs in lives. From 1974 onwards the UN force had to patrol a buffer zone running the 180 kilometre width of the island – an extraordinarily difficult task, especially in the immediate aftermath of the Turkish invasion.[100]

The other cost of peacekeeping, as Cyprus demonstrated all too well, was that it never ended.[101] The operation, begun in 1964, still continues, the parties no closer to a resolution than at the outset. Canada finally pulled out its troops in 1993, having lost twenty-seven dead in its thirty years service there. Some servicemen had done six, seven, or more tours in Cyprus. Some were reputed to have second families there. If all UN peacekeeping did was to freeze dangerous situations without resolving the conflict, then peacekeeping perhaps ought not to be the answer.

The Middle East was another area where freezing a crisis produced little resolution. In 1967 President Nasser of Egypt unceremoniously ordered the United Nations Emergency Force out of his country. Nasser responded to a calming statement by Prime Minister Pearson by calling him an 'idiot' and ordering the Canadian contingent out in forty-eight hours. Ottawa fortunately had aircraft at the ready and the Canadians left – just before Israel invaded on June 5. The Department of External Affairs drew the proper conclusion, one heartily shared by the army, when it noted that 'a peace-keeping operation such as UNEF is not an end in itself but a practical adjunct to peace-making ... a truce [is not] a satisfactory long-term settlement.' The humiliating expulsion from UNEF for the first time made Canadians realize that peacekeeping was not all beer and skittles.

It took another war in 1973 and another peacekeeping force, UNEF II, before the beginnings of peace in the Middle East could occur. Canadians served on the new UN force, providing most of the logistical support for

UNEF II through a Service battalion and a Signals squadron. Women served in both units, the first time they had deployed with a UN mission. UNEF II withdrew in 1979, after Egypt and Israel had at last reached a peace treaty.[102]

The experience in Egypt led the Canadian government to impose strict conditions – and to stick to them – when the United States, seeking to make its way out of the morass in Vietnam that had cost it so heavily, used the Paris peace talks as a forum to create a new International Commission of Control and Supervision in early 1973, this time to consist of Canada, Hungary, Indonesia, and Poland. The Trudeau government reluctantly agreed to send 240 officers and men and 50 diplomats to the ICCS for a two-month period and pledged to follow an 'open mouth' policy: if there was any interference and obstruction, the Canadians would say so. The ICCS bogged down quickly, as the Poles and the Hungarians, both members of the Warsaw Pact, proved unwilling to criticize North Vietnamese cease-fire violations. The ICCS helped to facilitate the United States withdrawal but achieved little else. Although Canada did extend the commitment by four months, it pulled the contingent out at the end of July 1973 over strong protests from Washington.[103] The war went on until the North Vietnamese won in 1975.

The futile Vietnam, Cyprus, and UNEF I peacekeeping operations marked the nadir of Canada's love affair with the concept. But they did not end the UN's efforts to persuade Canada to send troops on new missions. In 1974 Canadians went to the UN Disengagement Obserever Force on the border between Israel and Syria,[104] in 1986 to the Multinational Force and Observers created by the 1979 peace treaty to patrol the Israeli-Egyptian border, and in 1988 to the UN Iran-Iraq Military Observer Group, where they patrolled the lines between the two nations that had fought an eight-year-long war. The army provided fifteen observers and a 525-man signal group – which had to acquire its communications equipment from the United States and fly it into the area on United States Air Force C-5 Galaxies. In 1988 Canada also dispatched a handful of officer observers and anti-mine technicians to Afghanistan.[105] Women soldiers there played a very useful role: they could teach Afghan women the perils of mines and boobytraps, something Muslim law forbade male soldiers from doing.

Canada also provided army officers to the UN Observer Group in Central America in October 1989, a force designed to monitor Nicaragua's borders with its neighbours. ONUCA played a key role in achieving a ceasefire in the area and in demobilizing forces that had been disruptive. And, after the liberation of Kuwait by the American-led coalition in February 1991, Canada provided 300 soldiers to serve on the UN Iraq Kuwait Observation Mission. Some Canadians had fretted that Canadian participation, limited as it was, in the war against Iraq had doomed Canada's ability to be impartial and to serve on UN peacekeeping missions. The request for soldiers for UNIKOM, coming very soon after the war's end, showed that UN needs, not mythical impartiality, shaped the world organization's requests of Canada. Most of the Canadians in this UN force were engineers, who worked at clearing the tens of thousands of mines sown by the Iraqis.

There were literally dozens of other UN missions after the end of the Cold War. In the early 1990s there was a spirit of optimism, a sense that the world was now the United Nations' oyster, and UN activity extended everywhere. Some UN operations were tiny and benign; others were large and dangerous. There was a Secretary-General's Group in Afghanistan that had one Canadian; an election verifications mission in Haiti with eleven observers; the Angola Verification Mission with fifteen military observers; a mission for the referendum in Western Sahara with thirty-five observers; a European Community (not UN) Monitoring Mission in Yugoslavia with fifteen personnel; the UN Special Commission that searched for Iraq's weapons of mass destruction with, among others, a dozen Canadians; the UN Transitional Authority in Cambodia with 240 personnel;[106] and the UN Mission in El Salvador with up to fifty-five observers. There were additional missions in Rwanda, Haiti,[107] the Dominican Republic, Mozambique, Nagano-Karabakh, Guatemala, East Timor,[108] Eritrea, the Central African Republic, and on and on. A simple list runs to three pages with forty-six different missions. The smallest Canadian contribution was a single soldier, and the largest encompassed 1250.[109]

For a military that, early in the 1990s, was less than 80,000 personnel, for an army that was dropping rapidly in the late 1990s towards a total strength of 20,000, this range of commitments was unbearable. Soldiers all too frequently went on a deployment, usually for six months, returned home for six months, and were then sent abroad once more. The strain on service families, many already living in ramshackle married quarters (PMQs) and suffering the effects of low pay, was severe.[110] Drunkenness, wife battering, and divorce were frequent. Compounding matters was the fact that service in the former Yugoslavia or in Rwanda was frequently horrific, as murder, rape, and genocide were the order of the day and the UN forces were unable, unwilling, or too ill-armed to intervene. Soldiers discovered that the army provided little treatment for their Post-Traumatic Stress problems. '"You okay?" the doc asked each soldier,' Scott Taylor and Brian Nolan reported of soldiers returning from service in the former Yugoslavia in 1993. '"Yeah, I feel fine." "How about mentally? Do you think you can adjust okay?" "Yeah, I feel fine."'*[111] This perfunctory questioning was completely unsatisfactory in uncovering stress symptoms; so too was the fact that Veterans Affairs Canada did not consider peacekeepers to be veterans when they left the army.† There were mysterious illnesses in the former Yugoslavia as well, some said to be caused by American use of depleted uranium munitions or the filling of sandbags with radioactive-contaminated dirt by Canadians.

Undoubtedly, as army strength declined, the strains on all ranks increased. Most of the difficulties that befell the army in the 1990s sprang from the simple truth that the Canadian governments of Brian Mulroney and Jean Chrétien could not say no to the UN. Canada was a member of every peacekeeping operation until the late 1980s, and Canadians served on almost all the operations after that time. That the Nobel Peace Prize in 1988 was awarded to UN peacekeepers around the world made it harder to say no. Canadians seemed unanimously to believe that the prize was really theirs.

In retrospect, 1988 was the high point of peacekeeping, and the decline began soon after. In 1988 the UN had thirteen peacekeeping missions in the field; by the end of 1992 there were five more missions and, by late 1994, an additional seventeen operations with some 80,000 peacekeepers serving on them. Moreover, peacekeeping was morphing into Peace Support Operations,

---

* The real cause of PTSD was that too many of the units sent to the former Yugoslavia, for instance, had their ranks filled with 'augmentees' who, while they served well, lacked the regiment's support system. 'No trust, no knowledge, no first-name basis,' General Lewis Mackenzie put it, 'each guy just wanting to survive the six months.' 'The Minnow and the Whale: Will the Canadian Forces Be Rescued by US Defence Policy?' in D. Rudd et al., eds., *Playing in the 'Bush League': Canada–US Relations in a New Era* (Toronto, 2001), 76.

† In March 2001 Veterans Affairs Canada announced its intention to change the definition of 'veteran' to include those who had served in the former Yugoslavia and Rwanda. Extra benefits now will be made available.

a broader term that included the traditional 'first generation' UN operations, which, under chapter VI of the UN Charter, observed or interposed troops between states, and the 'second generation' operations that enforced peace under chapter VII, intervened to respond to gross violations of human rights or aggression, and tried to rebuild societies and create confidence through peace building.[112] The explosion of UN peacekeeping was too much too soon for the world body, and the UN failed disastrously in Somalia and Rwanda and came perilously close to complete failure in Bosnia. As one experienced Canadian peacekeeper put it, the UN's efforts were hampered by 'incompetent UN-appointed civilian mission commanders, "dead wood" bureaucrats sidelined to field appointments rather than blocking comfortable positions at UN headquarters in New York, inadequate mandates, and insufficient resources.'[113]

The members of the United Nations and the UN organization itself began a process of rethinking and retrenchment, and a more hesitant UN began to contract out peacekeeping to regional organizations or to the few countries willing to play a primary role. The United States, for example, took the lead in Haiti in 1996, pressing Canada to cooperate with it there. Inevitably, perhaps, as UN peacekeeping fell into difficulty, members of the Security Council began to disregard it. When the Security Council was unable to agree how to stop Serbian persecution of Kosovars in Kosovo, for example, NATO acted without its sanction. The Kosovo war, in which Canada participated, might have been illegal under international law; it was, however, moral and right. A few years earlier, when the small UN peacekeeping force in Rwanda, led by Canadian Major-General Romeo Dallaire, had to stand idly by while genocide all but destroyed a people, the UN averted its eyes.[114] The shame of Rwanda had led directly to the NATO action in Kosovo, and Canada dispatched 1375 soldiers to that territory in mid-1999 and kept them there for a year.

For a country like Canada that has always prided itself on its role as a moral superpower, the failures of peacekeeping stung. Canada has pressed hard for ways to improve the UN's rapid reaction capability[115] and has unsuccessfully promoted the establishment of a rapidly deployable mission headquarters. With the Nordic countries and the Netherlands, among others, it has also called more successfully for SHIRBRIG (a Multinational Stand-by Forces High Readiness Brigade), a joint quick-reaction UN peacekeeping force commanded by a mobile headquarters.* But Canada's understrength, underfunded army cannot do everything that the government might wish, and the United Nations is a weak reed at best.[116] The 1994 Defence White Paper put it clearly: 'Our resources are finite ... We will commit forces to such operations if suitable resources are available, and if our personnel can be appropriately armed and properly trained to carry out the task and make a significant contribution to the success of the mission.'[117] If only Canada had acted as the White Paper said.

The key peacekeeping operations of the 1990s for Canada's army were in the former Yugoslavia, where Canada found itself pursuing humanitarian and peace enforcement operations, and in Kosovo, intervening as part of a NATO-led war. With its volatile mixture of religions and nationalities, Yugoslavia had held together so long as the central government remained strong. But with the death of President Tito, the centre could not hold, and in 1991 the component provinces of the country began to break away – a process that seemed to demand the expulsion of everyone not of the same ethnicity or religion. The hub of the subsequent difficulties was in Croatia and Bosnia-Herzegovina, with their mixed populations of Muslim and Christian communities. The Western European Union tried and failed to broker peace or to create an intervention force, and the United Nations in 1992 created the UN Protection Force of twelve battalions and some supporting units to protect parts of Croatia. Canada reluctantly became involved at the outset, and a contingent, Canbat I, was put together from the RCR and the Royal 22e Régiment in the NATO brigade for service there. (For the first time an infantry battalion was specially created from existing units for long-term operational deployment.) Canada might be getting out of its NATO commitments in Europe, but, as the UNPROFOR commitment demonstrated, it was not getting out of Europe. At every opportunity the country's diplomats went to great lengths to spell this distinction out to the sceptical Europeans.[118]

---

* The UN Mission in Ethiopia and Eritrea (UNMEE) in 2000–1 represented an apparently successful try-out for SHIRBRIG. A Canadian company group served with a Dutch Marine battalion and provided the land force, while eight Canadian officers worked on the SHIRBRIG staff that formed the UN mission headquarters. The SHIRBRIG deployment was for six months only. *www.dnd.ca/eng/archive/2000*, 'Canadian Forces Peacekeeping contribution to ... UNMEE,' November 21, 2000; ibid., 'The Origins and Status of SHIRBRIG,' September 20, 2000.

UNPROFOR's headquarters were in Sarajevo in Bosnia-Herzegovina, while Canbat I operated in west Croatia, patrolling the zone of separation between Serbs and Croats. Their role was traditional peacekeeping, though perhaps more dangerous than most such missions. Meanwhile, Sarajevo, hitherto a successfully functioning city of mixed nationalities and religions, came under ferocious Serb attack. The Chief of Staff of UNPROFOR happened to be a Canadian, Brigadier-General (soon to be promoted to Major-General) Lewis MacKenzie, and he persuaded his superiors on the ground and in Canada to put Canbat I into the besieged city. In the face of Serb intransigence, the Canadians moved into Sarajevo to protect the airport and the road from the airfield to the city to order to keep UN and non-governmental organization aid efforts going.[119] It proved to be a difficult duty, in part because the soldiers faced the risk of being shot at, but also because it was horrifying to see civilians slaughtered. 'Two children were killed while talking to the soldiers in front of our headquarters,' one Canadian wrote. 'Children gather to receive candy and talk. Last night, the Serbs launched a mortar attack on the main street. The bombs land[ed] where the children were standing. Eight were injured and two dead.'[120] For his part, General MacKenzie emerged as a skilled communicator, and from Sarajevo he became the public face of UNPROFOR on the world's television screens – the best-known Canadian soldier since 1945. The media was the only weapon he had, and MacKenzie used it masterfully.

MacKenzie had, like most Canadian soldiers of his generation, spent a large portion of his career on peacekeeping duties in Egypt, Cyprus, Central America, and Vietnam. He understood that the United Nations was a terrible employer – disorganized and unable to supply its military servants with any regularity. The Canadian Forces knew this record too and regularly acted to get around the UN's problems – for example, by sending more armoured personnel carriers with the troops deployed on UNPROFOR than the UN wanted. The extent of the chaos in UNPROFOR surprised even the experienced MacKenzie. The political leadership paid no attention to military advice; supply contracts went to civilian firms that, quite sensibly, did not want their drivers to get shot while delivering goods to the soldiers in the field; and UN Headquarters too often chose military leaders on the basis of political correctness, not military competence. MacKenzie also found himself subject to spurious denunciations as a war criminal and a sexual predator by Croats and Bosnian Muslims because he allegedly favoured the Serbs. In fact, Mac-Kenzie was even-handed, denouncing all with impartiality for their brutality and lies.[121] (It was unfortunate for his reputation that he made paid appearances in North America for Serbian causes after he left the army in 1993.)

Meanwhile, the UN decided to upgrade its efforts, forming UNPROFOR II for Bosnia, with the mandate to protect humanitarian convoys and aid efforts. UNPROFOR II needed force at its disposal, but did not want to provoke the factions – not that they needed much to provoke them into violence – and horrific atrocities such as ethnic cleansing, a new term, proceeded apace. The Canadian government provided Canbat II, a mechanized infantry battalion of RCR in M-113 armoured personnel carriers with a squadron of Cougar armoured wheeled vehicles from the 12e Régiment Blindé. It took time for Canbat II to be allowed by the warring parties to enter Bosnia; when it did, the battalion deployed to Visoko, a dangerous junction point where Serbs, Croats, and Bosnian Muslims all jostled for control, each group fighting the other. The Cougars and the infantry struggled to get the aid convoys through the lines unscathed, a task sufficiently difficult that National Defence Headquarters in November 1993 decided that Canbat II should be reorganized into an armoured battle group. There were now two Cougar squadrons of the 12e Régiment Blindé, a mechanized infantry company of Van Doos and an engineer company. As was becoming the norm, Militia units supplied about one-sixth of the personnel of the armoured squadrons. The Cougars, which were in short supply in Canada, were taken from Militia Training Centres, effectively gutting Reserve Force training.

This added strength did little to deter the parties to the war. The Croats committed atrocities equal in savagery to the Serbs, but the Serbs especially were hostile to the Canadians, refusing to allow UN forces into their areas of control and hampering aid convoys on a regular basis. On two occasions Serbs took Canadians hostage, and once subjected the disarmed men to a mock execution. A major confrontation occurred when the Canadians, with British special forces, tried to drive Serb artillery, then busy shelling Sarajevo, out of the area. There was a tense, grossly unequal standoff between the undergunned Canadian Cougars and Serb M84 main battle tanks, but Canadian negotiating skill prevailed and the Serbs withdrew their guns.

By the summer of 1993 the strain on Canadian army manpower was becoming severe. Some argued that the two battle groups should be reduced to one, but in the end the decision was made to continue with two, though to cap force strength in the Former Yugoslavia at 2000. Future battle groups would have a maximum strength of just 750 men each, a decision guaranteeing that, should they face action, they would be severely understrength from the outset. Thus 2 PPCLI, stationed in the Medak pocket of Croatia after July 1993, had some difficulty in patrolling the Serb-Croat boundary, especially in areas that were under constant shellfire. On September 9 the Croats attacked the Serbs in force, not incidentally shelling the Canadian positions in the pocket, presumably to ensure that there would be no UNPROFOR interference. Under severe political pressure, the Croats pulled back, and the UN commander in the area ordered the well-equipped 2 PPCLI (in effect a composite Regular and Militia battalion) and two companies of heavily armed French soldiers to move into the contested area to guarantee the cease-fire.

The advance initially met with no opposition, but on September 15 the regiment came under heavy Croat fire for fifteen hours. The PPCLI's Commanding Officer, Lieutenant-Colonel Jim Calvin, subsequently negotiated safe passage for his unit. Before they left the Medak pocket, the Croats ethnically cleansed the area, raping women, killing men, and destroying buildings and livestock. A corporal with the regiment wrote that 'the Croatians have taken over a number of Serbian towns, after going there and butchering every living thing.'[122] The PPCLI had orders simply to gather evidence for future prosecutions, not to intervene. At one point, with TV media in attendance, Calvin denounced the Croat troops to their face for war crimes, and this incident forced a Croat withdrawal. In the largest Canadian action since the Korean War, 2 PPCLI had inflicted an estimated 130 casualties on the Croats without suffering any fatalities in its own ranks.[123]

The siege of Sarajevo continued, meanwhile, and there were additional horrific Serb atrocities at Srebrenica, which was surrounded by Serbs and, wrote one Canadian, was 'machine gunned, bombarded and mortared back to the last century.'[124] NATO talked of air strikes to hit at the Serbs in 1993, but although Serbs took 400 peacekeepers, including 55 Canadians, hostage in late 1994, little happened until the Croatians rolled over UN lines and struck at the Serbs in western Slavonia.[125] The Serbs in turn shelled Sarajevo. There were NATO airstrikes and the Serbs took 370 military hostages, literally using some (including a Canadian captain) as human shields to halt NATO's attacks. Emboldened, the Serbs swallowed Srebrenica and rounded up its 40,000 Moslems for disposal. Not until late August 1995, after a Serb mortar attack on Sarajevo caused carnage, did NATO unleash some 3000 sorties at Bosnian Serb positions.[126] At the same time, Bosnian Croats and Muslims launched an offensive that took back much of their lost territory. A settlement of sorts duly followed at Dayton, Ohio, in November.

In late 1995 NATO moved into the Former Yugoslavia in strength, creating the NATO Implementation Force. Pressured by its allies and with some reluctance, Canada sent a brigade headquarters, an infantry company, an armoured squadron, and other units, to a total strength of 1030. In 1996 NATO altered its Bosnia force into SFOR, the NATO Stabilization Force. This time Canada's contingent was 1242 strong, based on a mechanized battle group, and the Liberal government agreed to accept more front-line responsibilities and to cover a larger area of operations.* Finally, in 1999, Canadian aircraft participated in the Kosovo war, and Canada committed some 1300 troops to the Kosovo Force.[127] After matters calmed down (and before the Kosovars began agitating for independence and supporting their compatriots in Macedonia), Canada consolidated its troops in Bosnia, and in September 2000 Major-General Rick Hillier took command of NATO's 4000 soldiers in SFOR's Multinational Division Southwest – the first Canadian to hold such a position. The commitment in the former Yugoslavia seemed all but endless, and it was more than Canada's tiny army could sustain for long. This operation, like the briefer Gulf War commitment, also left soldiers with inexplicable illnesses, and the Canadian Forces did not always treat these medical complaints seriously or fairly.[128]

The Canadian participation in Somalia in 1993 was confused from the beginning. The east African nation, impoverished and war-torn, had no effective

---

* One soldier who had served in the early difficult days in Croatia told the *Globe and Mail* on November 11, 2000, that his present duty in Bosnia was not satisfying. 'At least I was doing the job of a soldier. I want to get away from this humanitarian-aid shit. We're just kind of the middle-men – we go out, talk to people, see what they need and relay it back to the other organizations.' Leah McLaren, 'War and Peace,' *Globe and Mail*, November 11, 2000.

government, no infrastructure, and clans fought with each other and ruled their own territories. Humanitarian organizations that tried to offer help often became easy prey for the clans. In 1992 the United Nations authorized the creation of a chapter VI peacekeeping force (UNOSOM) to protect the aid agencies and to try to disarm the clans. As with other chapter VI operations (most UN peacekeeping operations, in fact), force could be used only in self-defence. The Canadian contribution was to be the Canadian Airborne Regiment, a unit with three commandos, one each from the three regular infantry regiments, the PPCLI, the RCR, and the Royal 22e. The CAR was supposed to be an elite unit with quick reaction capability. For some of its soldiers, it was precisely that. For others, unfortunately, it became a dumping ground for problems that the infantry regiments preferred to dispose of to the CAR. Another difficulty, a serious one for the army as a whole, was that the three infantry regiments had distinctly different military cultures, followed different practices in the field, ran their own 'career managers' for officers and Non-Commissioned Members, and, in the case of the Royal 22e Régiment, spoke a different language. The three commandos fit together uneasily as a result of the army's regimental system.[129]

There were additional problems not of the CAR's making. For Somalia, the regiment had to reorganize itself into a mechanized infantry battalion. With every other infantry battalion either on peacekeeping duty, just back from overseas, or preparing to go, the CAR was all the army had on the shelf, so the airborne unit had to convert to another role. The regiment quickly learned to drive borrowed Grizzlies. But then, in December 1992, the United Nations, at the instigation of the United States, changed the definition of the force because UNOSOM, the initial UN force in Somalia, was clearly not working well. It would now be a chapter VII military intervention, authorized to use force – and expected to be obliged to use force – to restore peace, and it was to serve under U.S., not UN, command, as the Unified Task Force (UNI-TAF). As a result of this altered role, a squadron from the Royal Canadian Dragoons joined the operation. Because the RCD Cougars were not in good shape, the unit had to borrow parts from two other armoured regiments to make them fit for operations and add a Bison-mounted mortar platoon from the Royal Canadian Regiment. The jerry-built, ramshackle structure of the army in 1992–3 was all too apparent.

The Canadian armoured squadron flew on United States Air Force C-5s to east Africa in January 1993, arriving just after the Canadian Airborne Regiment. The RCD deployed to an area close to the Ethiopian border and north of Belet Uen, where the CAR set up camp. Conditions were rough, water was scarce, there was danger from landmines and occasional firefights, but through good management or good luck, the RCD missed the troubles that befell the CAR.[130]

Those troubles ultimately resulted in the disbandment of the CAR, the near-destruction of the army, the almost total discrediting of the profession of arms in Canada, and the worst blows the Canadian Forces had ever sustained in peacetime. Stationed in the desert near a scrubby town, the CAR ran its patrols through its designated areas, trying to bring a semblance of peace to the people. Subsisting on bottled water and U.S. MREs (Meals Ready to Eat) – manpower restrictions meant that no cooks were deployed with the CAR, condemning the men to eat from ration packs – living in dust, and pestered by flies and scorpions,* the Airborne Regiment did its work effectively. American senior officers – and Somalis in the immediate area – praised its work in fulsome terms. The Canadians dealt with local leaders to create a civil police, open schools, and repair damaged bridges.[131]

The regiment's difficulties arose when Somali thieves tried to get into the Canadian camp, searching for whatever weapons, equipment, or food they could find. Such thieves might simply be looking for loot, but they might also have been infiltrators who posed a genuine security threat. Many were caught, held overnight, and turned over to the local authorities. There were additional incidents that led the CAR's Commanding Officer to tighten camp security, and troubles with hostile crowds raised tensions for both the CAR and local Somalis. Some CAR officers took out patrols, without authorization, to attempt to hit back at unruly Somali elements; some such patrols put out bait in the form of food and water and waited for hungry Somalis to turn up. On

---

* A newly developed Canadian Theatre Activation Team, deployable in forty-eight hours and first used in the UN Mission in Ethiopia and Eritrea in 2001, can build a camp site in a few weeks, including facilities such as sewers, water, electricity, communications, gyms, hospitals, kitchen and mess, repair facilities, ammunition dumps, barbed-wire fences, and bunkers. Had such a TAT existed in 1993, the Somalia incidents might not have occurred. The 475 Canadians in UNMEE, half serving with a Dutch infantry battalion, were also using a new Tactical Command and Control Communications System that provided seamless communications. *National Post*, March 21, 2001, A15.

at least one occasion the bullet wounds on a dead Somali caught in an ambush suggested an execution. In addition, the squalour of their living conditions and the boredom of their situation led some soldiers to heavy drinking.[132] The beer ration was two cans per man per day, but anyone intent on getting drunk could easily find more. The CAR, and especially its 2 Commando, formed from the Princess Patricia's Canadian Light Infantry, seemed to be an accident waiting to happen.

On March 16, 1993, a sixteen-year-old Somali, Shidone Arone, fell into the hands of 2 Commando, caught redhanded in an attempted heist. Its officer commanding, Major Anthony Seward, had issued orders that deadly force was not to be used by the snatch patrol that had caught Arone. 'Abuse [anyone caught] if you have to, just make the capture,' he said. That was interpreted by platoon commander Captain Michael Sox to mean that his men could 'beat the shit out of the prisoners,' whatever Seward's original intent had been. The patrol captured Arone at 8:45 p.m., bound his hands behind his back, and took him to a bunker, where he was left under guard. Sometime after 10 p.m., Master Corporal Clayton Matchee, with the assistance of Trooper Kyle Brown, tortured, abused, and ultimately killed Arone. Brown photographed the process of torture, he and Matchee posing with Arone in the midst of his agony. At least eight soldiers looked into the bunker while this murder was under way; so disliked were Somalis by the Canadians that no one said a word. No officers intervened, no warrant officers responded to Arone's cries, although they must have heard them.[133] Matchee and Brown had both been in trouble before and had been included in 2 Commando for the Somalia operation despite the urgent warnings of their platoon commander and warrant officer.[134]

Within a few hours, word of the Somali's death made its way up the chain of command to Ottawa. Although the Canadian Forces created a board of inquiry in April 1993 to examine the Somalia mess, it concluded that misbehaviour by a few trouble makers had caused the difficulty. Some events thereafter seemed – to some – to have been covered up to protect Kim Campbell, the Defence Minister who had become a Progressive Conservative Party leadership candidate and was soon the Prime Minister, fighting an election. Matchee tried to hang himself shortly after the killing of Arone. He failed, though his brain functions were irreparably damaged. Brown was court-

martialed.[135] Demoted, Major Seward received a sentence of three-months'
imprisonment. Matchee's section commander, Sergeant Mark Boland, was
dismissed from the army. But that was only the beginning.

Early in 1994 a video made by CAR soldiers in Somalia, and subsequently
played on television, showed CAR soldiers tattooed with swastikas, drinking
beer, and uttering racist comments about the Somalis. As Lieutenant-Colonel
John English noted, 'For such behaviour to have occurred could only have
meant that senior commanders either never inspected or that they simply did
not comprehend ... That none of their subordinate officers or NCOs saw fit to
take correction attested to a cavalier approach.'[136] A second video, discovered
and broadcast in early 1995, showed members of the 1re Commando (from
the Royal 22e Régiment) of the regiment in thoroughly unpleasant hazing rit-
uals at Camp Petawawa in 1992; a third video, also broadcast in 1995, showed
equally disgusting incidents of hazing in 1994. The hazing likely was no worse
than that in a college fraternity initiation, however, and it had existed in the
army for decades. Appearing on the nation's TV screens after the media
accounts of the killing in Somalia, it flew in the face of the public's vision of
Canadian soldiers as the world's pre-eminent peacekeepers. Canadians
demanded a standard of behaviour higher than that exhibited by the CAR.
The firestorm of public reaction led to the inevitable end of the Canadian Airborne Regiment, ordered disbanded by Defence Minister David Collenette on
March 5, 1995. The Minister's decision was supremely political, but few serving officers, from the CDS, General John de Chastelain, on down, seemed
prepared to go to the wall to save the regiment. A once-proud elite unit, with a
great tradition dating back to the 1st Canadian Parachute Battalion that
jumped into Normandy on D-Day, had fallen apart, destroyed by the actions
of a few of its officers and men.[137] The regimental system itself came perilously close to being eliminated from the army.

What happened next tore the Canadian Forces asunder. The Liberal government appointed a Commission of Inquiry into the Deployment of Canadian Forces to Somalia on March 20, 1995. Of the three commissioners, chair
Judge Gilles Letourneau, Judge Robert Rutherford, and journalist and jour-
nalism professor Peter Desbarats, only Rutherford had any military experience. The commission's mandate was broad: the pre-deployment choice and

training of the CAR; the events in Somalia; and the post-deployment phase and the alleged cover-up of the Arone killing at National Defence Headquarters. Because of the commission's splenetic chair, who badgered witnesses and regularly exploded in front of the TV cameras, the inquiry's relations with the Department of National Defence and the Canadian Forces deteriorated to the point of open hostility. The commissioners clearly believed that the department was being dishonest, while the military found the commissioners ill-informed and uncomprehending. Senior officers saw the commission as a kangaroo court that, incredibly, devoted most of its time to an intensive investigation of who had altered a handful of press releases at NDHQ. In the process, the Chief of the Defence Staff, air force General Jean Boyle, had his career destroyed, in part at least by his own hand. The commission unquestionably found evasion of the spirit and letter of the Access to Information Act and some attempts to cover up information that might have damaged the reputation of the Canadian Forces and their political masters.

After two years and two extensions of its life, the commission's work was cut short by a new Defence Minister, Doug Young, in April 1997. The commissioners then blamed the Department of National Defence for their failure to complete their task, but, in the end, in their appallingly titled report, *Dishonoured Legacy*, they produced a host of generally sensible recommendations on leadership, accountability, discipline, personnel selection, training, rules of engagement, readiness, and operational planning.[138] In effect, the commissioners declared that no future force should leave Canada without proper equipment, training, a clear chain of command, and a full understanding of its role. Readers will recognize that preparation of this order has never yet happened in Canadian military history. Yet the commissioners were right: it should.

Where the Somalia Commission went wrong was in its attacks on individuals during its hearings, an attitude that suggested an absence of impartiality. This focus turned the inquiry into a media circus, one that did terrible harm to the reputation of the leaders of both the army and the Canadian Forces. The commissioners' strictures on individuals in their report made the damage worse. The inquiry offered adverse comments on seven generals, one colonel, two lieutenant-colonels, and one major, pronouncing them failures. The commissioners demonstrated little understanding that military-political decisions were often made with incomplete information and under pressure, and their report ended careers. Some deserved to have their careers derailed; others did not. All warranted more humane treatment, more understanding, from a supposedly impartial and dispassionate commission of inquiry.[139]

Additional commissions and inquiries came out of the Somalia affair. Former Chief Justice Brian Dickson led an inquiry into the military justice system[140] and, in January 1997, Minister Young commissioned four academics – three military historians and a political scientist – to offer recommendations on the armed forces.[141] The academics' mandate was broad: the management and command of the Canadian Forces; military ethos and discipline; the selection, promotion, and leadership of the officer corps; the place and role of civilians in the Department of National Defence; and responsibility and accountabilty. Their recommendations were many and various, but, strikingly, they all pointed to the poor education of the officer corps as a root cause of the problems. This author, in his paper for Young, noted that 'only 53.29 percent of officers have a university degree and only 6.79 percent have graduate degrees, most in technical areas. Almost a quarter of the officer corps has only a high school education.' In the United States, by contrast, virtually every officer has an undergraduate degree, most officers above the rank of major hold graduate degrees, and nine of ten general officers had graduate degrees. While education does not necessarily make officers better, it could and should broaden their perspective. 'Formal education is not a sufficient condition for good and effective military leadership,' one of Young's four academics, David Bercuson, wrote in 2001. 'Leaders are born, not made ... But once leaders have been identified and selected, then education is essential to reinforce their natural leadership abilities and to broaden their understanding of both the technological and the human contexts within which they must exercise that leadership.'[142] A military officer is not merely a technician of death, the American scholar Richard Gabriel has noted, but he must also be a humanist. Otherwise, a soldier becomes an automaton and courts moral disaster.[143] The Canadian Forces soon moved to make a university degree mandatory for officers, though allowing ample time for a transition.[144]

While these commissions and reports moved towards their conclusion, the Canadian Forces found themselves subjected to new pressures and scrutiny of a kind they had never before enjoyed. Absorbed with what was dubbed 'human security,' the Department of Foreign Affairs launched a successful crusade in 1996 to ban anti-personnel landmines around the world, a worthy goal to be sure, but not one on which the diplomats consulted the Canadian Forces in advance or listened to much during the course of the crusade. That Western armies ordinarily mark their minefields carefully did not seem to matter; that small armies like Canada's need mines to protect their lines in action against waves of enemy troops also mattered little. Weakened by the scandals arising out of Somalia, the Canadian Forces had little clout.[145] The land mines treaty came into effect on March 1, 1999.[146]

At the same time as the military's political powerlessness became obvious, journalists spent much time reporting on the armed forces in the press and on television. *Esprit de Corps*, a small magazine that proclaimed itself the voice of the Non-Commissioned Members of the forces, evolved into a vicious muckraking journal, gleefully trumpeting every sin, real and imagined, in the officer corps. Its editor, Scott Taylor, became a much sought after television commentator and author. In his book, *Tarnished Brass*, he said that, if a 'top-ranking soldier shows not only a blatant disregard for obeying regulations, but also a flagrant contempt for the negative impact such actions will have on his troops' morale, then the standard has been set for a morale meltdown.' Regrettably, there had been enough unsavoury incidents involving senior commanders to lend some of Taylor's scatter-gun charges credibility. Non-accountable funds were available to a few generals who spent freely, fiddled their expense accounts, enjoyed all but rent-free accommodation, and received free repairs to their private automobiles. Taylor was a scandalmonger, to be sure, but there were far too many scandals.[147] The ethical standard of some members of the officer corps was deficient. Senior officers cheated the system, exploited it for personal gain, and, in some cases, evaded responsibility for their actions. A retired air force colonel put it clearly in words that applied to all three services: 'There has been a demonstrated lack of ethical oversight, governance, supervision and leadership on the part of General Officers at NDHQ and elsewhere. This, coupled with a propensity to line their pockets with unbecoming perks and emoluments, creates a moral climate unsuitable for the leadership of armed forces. The troops are watching,' he concluded, 'and the troops know.'[148] Operating in a stressful time, underfunded, unsure of their role in the post–Cold War future, and generally unappreciated by the government and the Canadian public, the officer corps of the Canadian Forces had permitted the creation of both a moral and a morale disaster.*

Doug Young lost his New Brunswick seat in the general election in the spring of 1997. The Liberal government, through his successor as Defence Minister, Art Eggleton, accepted 132 of 160 Somalia inquiry recommendations[149] and a host of additional ones produced by the other commissions and reports, including those by the academic quartet. The department duly created an oversight committee under John Fraser, a former Progressive Conservative minister and Speaker of the House of Commons, to ensure their implementation,[150] all but guaranteeing that a 'cover your ass' syndrome became rampant through the officer corps. No one wanted to take a chance if the certain result was trouble with the oversight committee, Parliament, the Minister, or the media. The result, as Desmond Morton commented, was a 'whole mess of new directives, orders, regulations and rules for the already over-regulated Canadian Forces. Troops and their officers will spend thousands of hours studying ethics, accountability, gender discrimination and racism.'[151] Perhaps such supervision was necessary, but, more likely, better leadership and the existing Code of Service Discipline could have sufficed.

Certainly the results of a rule-based army operating in full view of the television cameras were entirely predictable. Officers and NCMs understood that the worst thing that could happen to their career was to be in the media. The unwillingness to show initiative developed and grew, the managers displaced the leaders, and the army turned inward, its élan drying up. Rules of Engagement for UN or NATO operations were legal documents, screened by the Judge Advocate General, and some soldiers reportedly claimed to be afraid to fire a weapon without first checking with the legal officers attached to almost

---

* The Canadian Forces would do well to put U.S. Senator John McCain's words into their handbooks. A much-decorated Vietnam POW, McCain, in his biography, *Faith of My Fathers* (New York, 1999), had this to say: 'An officer must not lie, steal, or cheat – ever. He keeps his word, whatever the cost. He must not shirk his duties no matter how difficult or dangerous they are. His life is ransomed to his duty. An officer must trust his fellow officers, and expect their trust in return. He must not expect others to bear what he will not ... For the obedience he is owed by his subordinates, an officer accepts certain solemn obligations to them in return, and an officer's obligations to enlisted men are the most solemn of all ... Any officer who stains his honor by violating these standards forfeits the respect of fellow officers and no longer deserves to be included in their ranks. His presence among them is offensive and threatens the integrity of the service.' Quoted in L.-E. Nelson, 'The Good Soldier,' *New York Review of Books*, October 21, 1999, 6–7.

all operations. So bad did the situation become that even the Canadian Forces noticed. In a 2001 report, *NCM Corps 2020*, the drafters stated bluntly: 'In recent years ... the development of a risk adverse [sic] organizational culture combined with the erosion of trust at all levels has led to a military environment that suppresses initiative and fosters micro-management.'[152]

New leadership was needed and the army's process of renewal began in September 1997, with the appointment of General Maurice Baril as the Chief of the Defence Staff. A quietly determined Van Doo, the fifty-four-year-old Baril had the good fortune to be out of Canada during the Somalia crisis and remained untainted by it. As CDS, he presided over what historian Dean Oliver called 'one of the most thorough and painful reassessments of military organization, training, law, and doctrine that this country has ever witnessed.'[153] Baril had been posted in New York as the military adviser to the UN's Department of Peacekeeping Operations then headed by future Secretary-General Kofi Annan. In this capacity he had dealt with Major-General Romeo Dallaire in Rwanda and received his telegrams warning of the coming genocide. Baril has spoken publicly only once of why he did not pass on Dallaire's key warning. The international community wasn't listening, he said: 'What difference would it have made if we had stuck up a copy of it on every telephone pole of New York City?'[154] He was regrettably right, even though he ought to have brought the message to his political masters, but clearly Dallaire does not blame Baril.[155] Dallaire's understanding of his friend's dilemma almost certainly ensured that Baril retained his prestige in Ottawa.

A quiet man, calm but intense, Baril presided with some success over the long period of recuperation within the Canadian Forces and the army. Just as the post-Vietnam era was a period of rebuilding for the U.S. Army, so too did Baril try to lead the Canadian Forces and the army through its Calvary. He preached transparency and openness, and he tried to live up to his words. He implemented a new focus on officer education at the staff colleges, at the Royal Military College, and at civilian universities across Canada, and during his tenure the army began to publish a professional journal, as did the Canadian Forces.* Dallaire had initiated these changes after his return to Ottawa as

---

* According to BGen Ernest Beno, how to encourage junior officers to write in these journals without 'fear of repercussions is a dilemma. How we get senior officers to give thought to the major issues and publish

Assistant Deputy Minister (Personnel), and then as Special Advisor to the CDS for Professional Development.

Although there were still some complaints of indifference, there was also a new effort to take care of soldiers who had been damaged by their overseas services. This initiative was again led by Dallaire, who courageously spoke publicly of his own stress-related problems and even appeared in a Defence Department video on Post-Traumatic Stress Disorder. 'I am in a valley at sunset,' Dallaire said to the *New York Times* of his recurring nightmare, 'waist deep in bodies, covered in blood. I am holding up my arms trying to get out. Each time it comes back the scene is worse. I can hear the rustle of bodies, and I am afraid to move for fear of hurting someone.'[156] Dallaire observed that in the 1990s, while Canada was at peace, the Canadian Forces were at war. And he was one of the casualties of that war.[157]

Baril made major efforts during his tenure to improve CF medical services and the quality of life of military families, who had been struggling for too long to make ends meet.[158] He also posted a major-general to work as a deputy corps commander with the U.S. Army, a type of experience simply unavailable in Canada. If Canada was to operate with the Americans, as it most certainly would, such postings were important.[159] Baril persuaded the government to provide pay raises for the troops† and, in his time as CDS, the army began to receive new equipment – from clothing to upgunned Leopard tanks and light armoured vehicles, including the highly sophisticated LAV-III armoured and Coyote reconnaissance vehicles. The CDS tried to create an atmosphere in which the military ethos was paramount and, despite continuing (if diminishing) troubles in the Canadian Forces, he made substantial headway. 'Ethical values,' he said, 'are the foundation of our profession.'[160]

Above all, Baril apparently won the government's consent to slow down

their thoughts is equally a problem.' Beno admits he has no answers, but is correct in saying that the 'consequences of not acting when problems are perceived [are] professional stagnation and the persistence of the problems.' Ernest Beno, *Training to Fight and Win: Training in the Canadian Army* (Kingston, Ont., 1999), 59–60.

† Before raises announced on March 1, 2001, pay for a private ranged from $23,616 to $34,692; for a sergeant from $45,588 to $47,488; for a lieutenant from $39,456 to $51,012; and for a lieutenant-colonel from $84,192 to $89,592. Martin O'Malley et al., 'What Our Soldiers Do ...' CBC News Online, March, 2001.

the perennial pellmell rush to join every peacekeeping operation and to accept long-term commitments. The UN itself, through the Brahimi Panel on United Nations Operations that reported in 2000, had suggested reforms that included a more robust peacekeeping posture. These changes meant more fighting, but the government did not seem to shy away from that.[161] On March 21, 2001, Defence Minister Eggleton announced that the government at last had begun to realize that the understrength Canadian Forces could no longer handle long-term missions. The new philosophy under consideration was 'get in quick, get out fast.' The Canadian Forces would 'deploy among the first and use their expertise to stabilize an area of operation. These forces are then relieved' and replaced by soldiers from less-experienced peacekeeping nations[162] The CDS had said much the same thing in 1999 when he announced his hope that Canadian soldiers would serve for six months over-seas and then remain at home for the next twenty-four months.[163] These statements, however, did not stop Eggleton from offering a substantial contri-bution to the war against al Qaeda terrorism in Afghanistan in late 2001. The CF's small JTF-2 anti-terrorism force deployed up to forty soldiers there in December and, at year's end, 3 PPCLI remained on standby to serve in a stabi-lization force, if required.

The root of the difficulty was that peacekeeping cost more money every year and there were too few troops to do it properly: Canada had sent 4500 troops on operations abroad in 1999, amounting in all to about 7 per cent of CF strength and close to 20 per cent of army strength, and 3328 in December 2001.* Even the lower figure was unsustainable for the long term.[164] In August 2001, when NATO pressed Canada to send troops into Macedonia in a desperate effort to prevent an all-out civil war, the only source of the

---

* As of the week of December 14, 2001, Canada had 1619 troops in the NATO Stabilization Force in Bos-nia, 3 with the mission in Macedonia, 3 with the UN Mission in Kosovo, 190 with the UN Disengage-ment Observer Force on the Golan Heights, 2 with the UN in Cyprus, 8 with the UN Truce Supervisory Organization in Jerusalem, 29 with the Multilateral Force and Observers in the Sinai, 5 with the UN Iraq-Kuwait Observer Mission, 5 with the UN Observer Mission in Sierra Leone, 6 with the UN Mis-sion in the Congo, and 8 with the UN Mission in Ethiopia and Eritrea. Almost all these troops were pro-vided by the army. There were 1443 participating in Operation Apollo, the Afghan war, mostly navy and air force, and additional forces were deployed on NATO duties at sea, in the air, and on small army train-ing missions, including 11 in Sierra Leone. (www.dnd.ca/menu/operations/index). Whether this total of 3328 included the JTF-2 deployment was unclear. At this point, 3 PPCLI was on seven-day standby for Afghanistan.

200 troops was from the contingent in Bosnia. One weak unit was raided to create a second one.[165] Thus, an in-out policy, with longer periods between deployments, was essential unless the army increased its budget or its strength – and neither appeared likely in the near future.* What the Canadian public might say if casualties were high in a robust Brahimi-style operation was unclear.

By June 2001, when Baril stepped down as CDS, the army's morale, while still fragile, in most respects was vastly better. Still, Baril and his Chief of Land Staff, Lieutenant-General Bill Leach, had been unable to make much headway in dealing with the critical weaknesses in budget, training, and personnel. The military budget was not truly rising, though the government offered the carrot of an additional $2.3 billion over four years in the 2000 budget and added $640 million more in the 2001 supplementary estimates. Only $350 million of the 2000 budget cash was new money for investment in equipment, and the supplementary funds covered expenses already generated. The December 2001 budget did nothing for the CF beyond paying most of the costs for the Afghan war deployment and providing $300 million in one-time funding for unspecified capital costs, a pittance that left the army's senior officers all but shattered.[166] The sad truth was that Canada's per capita defence expenditure, Luxembourg aside, remained the lowest in NATO, and defence as a percentage of government spending was only 8 per cent in 2001,[167] a far cry from 40 per cent in 1954 at the height of Cold War rearmament.

These numbers translated directly into serious declines in operational efficiency and readiness. Army training continued to be cut back, and the number of soldiers was dropping. Infantry battalions, for example, normally operated at about half strength. If the army was to retain its best professionals, there had to be training to keep a war-fighting capability. Both the SABRE brigade, a contingency mechanized brigade group that would be cobbled together from units in Canada in the event of a major crisis overseas, and the

---

* A poll reported in *Maclean's*, December 25, 2000–January 1, 2001, 30, noted that 82 per cent of Canadians want their country to be a peacekeeping leader. But when asked to choose between investing in a stronger military or funding housing for the homeless, 75 per cent opted for the latter, and 19 per cent for military upgrading. Comparative peacekeeping costs between 1979 Cyprus and 1999 Bosnia were staggeringly different: one corporal for a year: $45,208 and $65,488; clothing for a squadron, $33,240 and $178,752; a rifle $811 and $2011; vehicle costs for a squadron, $133,590 and $12,940,528. *Maclean's*, February 12, 2001, 26.

CANUS brigade, similarly structured and pledged to continental defence, had never trained together.[168] The rapid reaction battalion, promised to both NATO and the UN, could not be deployed in the pledged twenty-one days – unless the CF rented aircraft to move the unit and its equipment.[169] The three understrength brigades in Canada, their battalions having only three companies each, had not trained as brigades since 1992, and the brigade commanders had become general managers as much as or more than operational leaders. Not a single CF brigade commander had ever led all his troops on an exercise, a situation that was surely almost without parallel in a modern state.

Moreover, the brigades' logistical units, providing services on their bases and with an increasing portion of their duties contracted out to cheaper civilian firms, had begun to become static, increasingly incapable of operating in the field.[170] Civilian contractors also went to Bosnia in 2000 to provide logistics, communications, and engineering support services.[171] The rationale was not to save money – the civilians cost more than army personnel – but to spare scarce support specialists repeated deployments. In effect, even though military personnel were 'embedded' into each civilian-managed task in case a crisis demanded evacuation of civilian personnel, and an army specialist was on standby in Canada for each position in case of a crisis,[172] this arrangement was a de facto demilitarization of the army.

In a very real sense, the situation of the army in 2001 was not dissimilar to the dark days of the interwar years. In percentage of population terms, the Regular Army of 19,700 in 2001 Canada, with its population of 31 million, was not much larger than the 1939 Permanent Force of some 4500 in a Canada of 10 million.[173] If the Reserve Army (50,000 in 1939, compared with 14,600 in 2001) was added to the total, Canada's present situation was far worse.

But with personnel costs for the 58,500 members of Canadian Forces eating up 40 per cent of the DND budget, the forces faced a simple equation. Acquiring new equipment necessary for the modern high-tech battlefields of the present and future meant devoting more cash to procurement. In the absence of major new funding, the only place that money could be found was by reducing personnel costs – decreasing the numbers of soldiers – even further. After the budget of December 2001, it seemed all too obvious that the Chrétien government was unlikely ever to provide serious new money for defence, aside from occasional top ups for specific purposes.* So the choice was clear: modern equipment or a still smaller army. But how small could an army be and still be viable – two weak brigades? 15,000 men and women? 10,000? 5000? At what point did even the pretense of combat capability disappear?[174]

Other forces were also in play. Canadian Forces projections in 2001 showed effective military strength dropping as normal and early retirements occurred, and official estimates foresaw the military numbering under 46,000 by 2002–3, unless major steps were taken. Attrition, running at 8 per cent a year, was exceeding the 'production rate' of new personnel by more than two-to-one, and, to achieve stabilization, recruiting in each of the three years from 2001–2 to 2004–5 had to be above 7000 a year – if the ceiling of 58,500 was to be maintained.[175] Finding those numbers of suitable recruits was a challenge in a country where Canadian Forces' opinion surveys showed that no more than 1 per cent of the population had any interest whatsoever in the military. Most informed observers, and many senior officers, did not believe that the Canadian Forces could do it (though the recession of 2001–2 could increase the flow of recruits, always better in times of high unemployment). One sign of desperation was the decision, announced in June 2001, to raise the retirement age from fifty-five to sixty years.

The army faced problems of dollars, numbers, equipment, and roles as it looked ahead for the next twenty years. Would any Canadian government ever decide to finance an army equipped and able to fight? Could the army continue its efforts to overcome the problems that had brought it down in the 1990s? Could it overcome the mistrust between NCMs and officers and between junior and senior officers? Could it attract and retain first-class men and women and let them exercise their initiative as soldiers? Could it do this in a highly competitive job market? Could it get the modern and high-tech

---

* Prime Minister Jean Chrétien's comments on defence in 2001 year-end TV interviews held out scant hope for the Canadian Forces. The forces 'are well-equipped,' he said. 'My view is that we have restored the [defence] budget to the level it was when we had to make the cuts.' Officials in the DND, he added, 'always complain that they don't have enough money, but we have to adjust our policy in defence to the needs.' Chrétien also blamed defence industry lobbyists and generals with a '1939' mentality for the complaints. (*National Post*, December 21, 2001, A6.) For extremely supportive public attitudes to increases in defence spending, see the polls reported in *Maclean's*, December 31, 2001, 28–9, and in the *Globe and Mail*, December 28, 2001, A1.

equipment it needed to make itself fit to fight with the best and against the best? Was it to be a multipurpose military with a war-fighting capability or merely a jumped-up gendarmerie capable only of low-end operations? The answers to these questions would determine whether the Canadian army could rebuild and maintain into an uncertain future the professionalism it had sought to achieve in its modern history.

eleven

AFGHANISTAN AND THE REMAKING OF THE ARMY

What ultimately changed everything for the Canadian Forces and, in particular, the Canadian Army was 9/11. The al Qaeda attacks on New York and Washington on September 11, 2001, killed 2976, including 24 Canadians, and began what the George W. Bush administration labelled the war on terror. This led quickly to the American attack on Afghanistan and the ouster of the Taliban regime that had given al Qaeda a sanctuary and, in 2003, the American-led second Iraq War that toppled Saddam Hussein's regime. The Canadian government sent an infantry battalion to Afghanistan in 2002 for a six-month deployment and refused to participate in the Iraq War, instead sending troops back to Afghanistan, where they remained for most of the decade. The Afghan operations, changing from combat to a kind of low-level war and then full-out combat, along with the election of Stephen Harper's Conservative government at the beginning of 2006, focused attention on the Canadian Forces' condition and led to massive budgetary increases, additional personnel, and substantial upgrades of equipment. The war also resulted in many killed, wounded, and injured.

Al Qaeda's brilliantly planned and ruthlessly executed attacks brought Islamist terrorism to the forefront. Within days the United Nations and the North Atlantic Treaty Organization reacted; NATO's response was the first-ever invocation of Article V of the Treaty that declared an attack on one an attack against all. The United States quickly began operations against the Taliban government of Afghanistan that had sheltered al Qaeda and its leader Osama bin Laden. The Taliban government was already fighting against disaffected tribal factions labelled as the Northern Alliance, and the United States had ready allies. By early October, Canada had begun to plan for a substantial and expensive upgrading of its security apparatus and had promised to provide forces for the Americans' Operation Enduring Freedom or, as Ottawa labelled it, Operation Apollo.

The Chrétien government's military response was somewhat surprising. Ottawa had opened Canadian airspace to aircraft barred from the United States immediately after the 9/11 attacks, and a massive rally in support of the United States had taken place on Parliament Hill. But some of the media were quick to lay part of the blame for the al Qaeda attacks on the United States itself, and the prime minister's own remarks had tended in the same direction. Nonetheless, despite the prime minister's deeply cynical views – 'The Canadian Forces always claimed it needed more,' he wrote in his memoirs, 'but I wasn't sure that its self-interest was the same as the national interest'[1] – the government dispatched a substantial naval task force to the Arabian Sea, in December 2001 sent some forty Special Operations soldiers from the secretive JTF-2 unit, air resources, and early in 2002 deployed a 900-strong battle group based around the 3rd Battalion of the Princess Patricia's Canadian Light Infantry (PPCLI) to serve as part of the U.S. Army's 101st Airborne Division in Afghanistan. On November 14, 2001, the battle group had begun preparations for the nation's first war-fighting deployment since Korea, and its training was intensive. In Canada, the light infantry role was on the verge of being eliminated from the Army, the battalions converting to LAV IIIs, light armoured vehicles; in Afghanistan 3rd Battalion PPCLI would work in its traditional foot-pounding role. As Lieutenant-Colonel Pat Stogran, the Commanding Officer, noted, 'Our Patricias demonstrated the skills, knowledge and robustness demanded of Light Infantry, which our [infantry] Corps has been losing sight of with the introduction of the LAV.'[2]

The 3rd Battalion PPCLI was to serve for six months in theatre, frequently ranging far afield from its base at Kandahar Airfield into the rough and mountainous country near the Afghanistan-Pakistan border. It performed its tasks well, joining U.S. troops in operations against Taliban forces, notably on Operation Harpoon, where it sought out, regrettably without much success, suspected al Qaeda hiding places in elaborate cave complexes. The regiment's snipers in particular performed superbly on Operation Anaconda in the

Shah-i-Kot Valley in March 2002, impressing their U.S. counterparts with their astonishing and deadly accuracy at long range. One sniper, Corporal Rob Furlong, killed a Taliban fighter carrying a machine gun at 2430 metres (or 1.51 miles), then the longest recorded kill by a sniper.[3] But as Stephen Thorne reported in *Legion Magazine*, the U.S. commanders did not initially realize the Canadians' potential. The Americans 'didn't know that Canada's Army, while small and ill-equipped, is among the best-trained in the world,' able to do much more than similar U.S. infantry. One U.S. Army staff officer the next year told a sceptical American general who worried that a Canadian battle group would 'reduce his battle space' that '3 PPCLI was one of the most-disciplined and most capable infantry battalions he had seen in action in his career.'[4] In any case, the PPCLI battle group suffered no killed or wounded in operations.[5] However, on April 18 on a night firing exercise three miles from Kandahar Airfield a United States Air Force F-16 fighter mistakenly hit A Company with a 500 lb laser-guided bomb in a 'friendly fire' incident, killing four and wounding eight.[6]

The Army's basic equipment deficiencies had become quickly visible in Afghanistan. In contrast to the Americans' desert camouflage, for example, the Canadians wore temperate woodland–zone clothing, the standard green CADPAT camouflage uniform. Apparently, no one at NDHQ had ever contemplated that Canada might deploy troops to an arid territory.[7] Even more serious were the CF's endemic personnel shortages. The understrength 3rd Battalion PPCLI had to fill its ranks before deployment with a company's worth of soldiers from its sister 2nd Battalion, and after its six-month tour, the government did not want to replace the battle group. Canada was out of Afghanistan for good, or so it seemed.

The nation also stayed out of Iraq, where the Bush administration, fearing that Saddam had weapons of mass destruction, ranging from chemical weapons to nuclear weapons under development, and very anxious to remove him from power, tried for months but eventually failed to secure United Nations sanction to strike at Baghdad. With some Allied support, the United States proceeded nonetheless on March 20, 2003, attacking Iraqi installations from the air and quickly launching a land invasion. Jean Chrétien's Canada, its military strength at its nadir and with little to contribute in any case, declined to participate. Opinion in English-speaking Canada, most notably in Alberta, favoured joining in; public opinion in Quebec, then in the midst of a provincial election where all the leaders wore anti-war ribbons during a televised debate, was heavily opposed. Not wanting to give the separatist and anti-military Parti Québécois a boost, Ottawa decided to remain aloof for this and other reasons.[8]

Instead, in February 2003, shortly before the American assault on Saddam began, Canada suddenly and surprisingly decided to redeploy troops to Afghanistan. As Minister of National Defence John McCallum told the House of Commons, the CF was to send 1900 soldiers to Kabul for a six-month rotation beginning in August 2003 and would take command of the International Security Assistance Force (ISAF) in February 2004. General Rick Hillier later recalled that 'the driving force behind the decision was clearly not our [the CF's] readiness or ability to carry out the mission, but the political cover needed to allow Canada to say no to the U.S.' on Iraq.[9] McCallum himself indiscreetly confirmed this when he stated, 'The Afghanistan mission is it for Canada. [U.S.] Defence Secretary Donald Rumsfeld welcomed the initiative … [and] is fully cognizant of the fact that this mission limits the deployment of Canadian land forces to other parts of the world for well over a year.' One general at National Defence Headquarters resigned in protest, and the then-Chief of the Land Staff, Lieutenant-General Mike Jeffrey, later told CBC News that the government announcement on February 11, 2003, had been made against his advice and took him completely by surprise: 'I did not know … that the decision had been made to go.'[10]

The ISAF had been created by the United Nations Security Council on December 20, 2001, after a conference in Bonn, Germany, on how to re-establish government functions in Afghanistan. ISAF was to be led by European nations, not yet by the North Atlantic Treaty Organization, and it was ISAF under which Canada served. With only limited U.S. support, ISAF's initial task was to hold Kabul, the capital, and the immediately surrounding area to permit the creation of a transitional administration under a former Taliban supporter, Hamid Karzai. By August 2003, when Canadian troops reached Kabul, NATO had taken ISAF over, but it remained separate and distinct from the United States' Operation Enduring Freedom. From October (with UN Security Council concurrence), the alliance expanded its reach gradually over more of the country, still without strong American support since the United States remained tied up in Iraq. Although the war was one without moral ambiguity, NATO did not grasp control of the situation, its priorities remained muddled, and its member states fought for command posts but shied away from deploying troops, especially combat troops.[11] The situation was not helped by the incompetence and never-ending corruption of the Karzai transitional administration and the inadequacy of the Afghan police and the few trained personnel of the Afghan National Army. The Canadian government declined to permit its forces to operate outside Kabul.[12]

The CF contribution, Operation Athena, saw the dispatch of some 1900 troops to Kabul in the summer of 2003, the battle group organized around the 3rd Battalion of the Royal Canadian Regiment. What were these troops doing in Afghanistan? The battle group commander, Lieutenant-Colonel Don Denne, bluntly observed that whatever they were doing it was not peacekeeping: 'God, I hate it when they call us peacekeepers. We loathe the term, abhor it. Peacekeeping can turn into a general war situation in the snap of your fingers.'[13] Another officer shared this view: the term 'peacekeeping' offended soldiers for its 'associated expectations and clichéd images.' Peacekeeping 'suggests a passive non-invasive presence operating in a benign environment ... The reality is somewhat different.'[14]

The Canadians, based at their Camp Julien behind barbed wire and blast barriers, formed the largest part of a multinational brigade – commanded first by Brigadier-General Peter Devlin, a Canadian officer, with a largely Canadian-staffed brigade headquarters – that patrolled the Afghan capital while the Karzai regime tried to function. Initially Task Force Kabul was a low-level combat operation, there being relatively little Taliban resistance at the time, though the threat level had begun to increase, with improvised explosive devices (IEDs) and mines posing the main danger. The CF, for example, suffered four fatal casualties between 2003, when two soldiers died after their unarmoured Iltis jeep was destroyed by mines, and the end of 2005.[15] The engineering squadron commander at the time of the 2003 mine strike noted that it was 90 per cent certain that it had been a deliberate attack, not simply an explosion from a leftover mine from an earlier period. 'We found fragments of a TM57 AT (anti-tank) mine in the crater,' Major Keith Cameron wrote, '[and] found two additional fuzes and mine shipping plugs on the scene.' The area was supposed to have been cleared in 1998, so the likelihood of the Taliban targeting ISAF was high.[16] After the deaths, Lieutenant-Colonel Denne was asked if the sixteen armoured vehicles his battle group had available, rather than the sixty that had been assessed as needed, were sufficient. Had everything been done to get the contingent what it required, as the defence minister had said? Denne replied: 'Boy, that's a road I really don't want to go down.'[17]

The Task Force, the 3rd RCR replaced by a battle group from the Royal 22e Régiment after six months, was the largest ISAF contingent in the country. It mounted patrols, engaged in small-scale construction and reconstruction projects, and helped provide security for Afghanistan's 2004 elections, but its role was limited in part because approval had to be sought from Ottawa for participation in each and every larger operation.[18] Notably, soon after becoming Chief of the Land Staff (CLS), Lieutenant-General Rick Hillier became the ISAF commander in February 2004 for a six-month stint.[19] Hillier was a charismatic figure who won the devotion of his troops in every billet he filled.[20] He had commanded an armoured squadron in Germany and his regiment and a brigade in Canada, been deputy commander of the III U.S. Corps in Fort Hood, Texas, led a multinational division in Bosnia, and been the Army's deputy commander before becoming CLS. With this unrivalled experience, he was easily the best-qualified Canadian for the post in Kabul, even if it meant temporarily giving up his position as CLS to Major-General Marc Caron until his return. Based in Kabul, he established close relations with the Karzai regime, suggesting and then providing what became known as a Strategic Advisory Team to create the processes to deliver development aid, most of the planning assistance offered by Canadian officers.[21] Unfortunately, the West's development effort was half-hearted, and the failure in aid and the weaknesses of the Karzai transitional regime allowed the Taliban, very weak in 2004, to begin to regenerate.

Hillier's sharp mind and clear eye helped him assess the situation in Afghanistan. In an address in 2005, he pointed out that the strains on a Canadian serving in Kabul were severe: 'Among four million people in Kabul, 25–50 probably would want to kill you on a given day. Between 50 and 100 would probably be inclined to assist the 25–50, but four million wanted you there.' He went on to add: 'If you went to the gate of Camp Julien as a Canadian soldier and treated all four million like that first group, by week three they would all be trying to kill you.'[22] An activist and an officer with strong views, Hillier made his mark wherever he was.

As the brand new Chief of Land Staff, Hillier had already made an impact in Ottawa from the day he took over and shortly before he went to Kabul. As he recorded in his memoirs, he told the minister that the Army 'can do the mission in Afghanistan until August of '04,' or one year, 'but after that you've essentially got nothing, unless you're prepared to carry it on the backs of the soldiers,' or in other words, extend deployments well beyond the norm. The infantry battalions, their establishments intended to be 800-strong, had strengths of 450 to 500 or so, and the only way a battalion could be deployed was to cannibalize another one to fill out the platoons. In effect, the Army had become a 'plug and play' manpower pool. The choice for the government, Hillier said, was to do nothing after August 2004, to ruin the soldiers and their families, or to grow the Army. The latter was expensive and not something the Chrétien government could contemplate. The second option would cause a political storm. The first, cutting back in Afghanistan, was all that remained, and after August 2004, the Army in an operational pause, the deployment in Kabul dropped significantly in strength to some 700.[23]

Meanwhile, the American invasion of Iraq initially went well, Saddam fleeing into hiding and his rotten, brutal regime toppling. But widespread looting began at once, ministries and museums being pillaged by Iraqis, while the U.S. troops inexplicably stood by. Soon Saddam loyalists and other Islamist factions looted arms depots that had unforgivably been left unguarded, and guerrilla warfare began. Incredibly, the Bush administration seemed not to have had a workable plan for taking over after the battle, and Chrétien's decision to stay out began to look better and better. Moreover, the diversion of U.S. and Allied focus from Afghanistan to Iraq allowed the Taliban time to reform. That was to prove very costly, not least for the Afghan government, which never truly recovered.

Whether Canada's national interests had been served well by remaining aloof from Iraq was another question. Its economy remained heavily dependent on the U.S. market, and after 9/11 the border had become harder to cross for commercial vehicles, aircraft, and travellers. Did a refusal to join in the Iraq War help or hurt? Did the renewed Afghan commitment ease American worries that Canada was not a wholly reliable ally?

What was certain was that there was growing concern in some Canadian politico-military circles at the anti-American tenor of Chrétien's government, including some of its ministers, officials, and backbenchers, and at the weaknesses of the Canadian Forces. The defence budget in 2003 was just north of $11 billion, though the 2003–4 budget that year promised $800 million more for the next three years; the personnel strength of the CF was only 60,000 nominally, but in practice some 53,000 effectives; and the military's equipment – its aircraft, ships, and trucks, tanks, and guns – was rapidly becoming obsolete. Chretien's government had no interest in fixing matters. As a result, pro-defence groups such as the Conference of Defence Associations and the Council for Canadian Security in the 21st Century began to voice their critiques, and organizations like the C.D. Howe Institute, the Canadian Defence and Foreign Affairs Institute, the Institute for Research on Public Policy, the Canadian Council of Chief Executives, the Fraser Institute, and others began to publish articles and analyses on Canadian defence, foreign policy, Canada-U.S. relations, and associated problems.[24] This interest melded seamlessly into a growing public interest in Remembrance Day and the Tomb of the Unknown Soldier, dedicated in 2000, the construction of the new Canadian War Museum, opened in May 2005, and the public's sense that 'the greatest generation,' those who had fought and won the Second World War, was rapidly dying off. Peace groups published their contradictory reports, led by Maude Barlow's Council of Canadians and its many offshoots, but, by the end of 2003, the ground palpably seemed to be shifting.

The key to this changed attitude was the rise of Paul Martin to the prime ministership on December 12, 2003, after he successfully forced out Jean Chrétien. Hitherto the finance minister (and thus responsible for the budgets that had starved the CF during the Chrétien government), Martin was a bilingual businessman, the son of a powerful King-St Laurent-Pearson-Trudeau era cabinet minister and, by instinct, no supporter of defence. He largely shared the Liberals' attitudes to the Bush administration and the United States, opposed Canada's joining in missile defence with the Americans, and initially did little to begin the process of rebuilding the CF.[25] But public opinion, not least 'informed' opinion, was beginning to express the need to improve the CF in the post-9/11 era.

What appears to have moved Martin – or at least moved him sufficiently to telephone the lead author on the day it appeared – was the publication of a volume, *Canada without Armed Forces?* which appeared in December 2003 just days before he took office. Edited by Dr Douglas Bland, a retired Army lieutenant-colonel and professor in the Defence Management Studies Program at Queen's University, the book, published in cooperation with the Conference of Defence Associations, was devastating in its analysis. 'The next government will be caught up in a cascading policy entanglement initiated by the rapid collapse of Canadian Forces core assets and core capabilities,' Bland wrote. 'This problem will inevitably disarm foreign policy as Canada repeatedly backs away from international commitments because it lacks adequate military forces.' Because of personnel shortages and without new funding and new equipment, the authors argued, the air force would disappear between 2008 and 2013, and either the Army, its ranks holding 19,000, or navy would disappear as well. The defence budget was insufficient to operate, let alone rebuild, the military's ranks, the CF was top heavy with senior officers and bureaucrats, the training system was falling behind, and it took eight to twelve years to bring major pieces of equipment into service. Just as bad, there was no plan: since 9/11 there had been no review of the implications of the changed security situation on the CF and Canadian strategy.[26]

Stung, the Martin government set out to provide a plan. The driving force for change would come from an unlikely source. Toronto Member of Parliament Bill Graham had been named Chrétien's foreign minister in 2002, and, although he supported the Afghan War and Canada's commitment to it, he had seemed noticeably Axworthian in his approach, favouring soft 'values' over hard 'national interests.'[27] After the 2004 election, however, Graham became defence minister and represented the interests of his new portfolio well. One of his key tasks was to secure a new chief of the defence staff, General Ray Henault having been selected to fill the post of chair of the NATO Military Committee in Brussels. Graham interviewed the likely candidates, first talking to Rick Hillier, only recently back from Kabul, in November. The next month, having made up his mind, Graham took Hillier to Martin's home at 24 Sussex Drive in Ottawa, where the general, 'sketching and doodling ... describ[ed] the changes I wanted to make to the Canadian Forces.' As General Hillier wrote, 'I knew at the end of that breakfast meeting that I was going to become CDS.' He had already decided that he would accept the post 'only if there was a real commitment to support the changes necessary to rebuild the Canadian Forces.'[28]

His first task, even before he took over as CDS, was to begin drafting a new defence policy paper, the first in a decade, to be part of the new administration's International Policy Statement. Graham had been given an earlier draft that was, he and Hillier believed, a rehash of existing policy documents. What Hillier and Graham wanted now was a policy paper that promised change to make the CF 'effective,' 'relevant,' and 'responsive,' and that demanded reorganization, new equipment, and more people.

General Hillier gave an indication of his approach in his blunt remarks at the change-of-command ceremony when he took over as CDS on February 4, 2005, and turned to the prime minister to say: 'We'll probably never be able to give [the CF] enough money to have all the equipment that they need to do what we ask them, but we sure can give them too little, and that's what we're doing right now. Remember them in your budgets.'[29] The Martin Liberals did, after a fashion, when in April 2005, the government released its International Policy Statement, which was notably realistic, spoke clearly on Canadian national interests, and in a chapter on defence recognized both that the Canadian Forces would do expeditionary deployments into failed states in the future and that it was presently in a deplorable condition and required a transformation of its organization.*[30] The money for renewal was pledged, but unfortunately and characteristically for Martin's weakly led government, the bulk of the funding, $12.8 billion in new money, was to come in years four and five of a five-year plan. In other words, with Martin in a minority situation in Parliament after the election of June 28, 2004, the funding existed only in a political never-never land. As Hillier put it bluntly in his memoirs, the

---

* Hillier's transformation project remade the CF's structure. Four of his new commands affected the Army: Canada Command was responsible for operations at home and in North America; Canadian Expeditionary Force Command (CEFCOM) had charge of overseas operations, including Afghanistan; Canadian Special Operations Forces Command (CANSOFCOM) had charge, among other elements, of JTF-2, fighting in deepest secrecy against the Taliban; and Canadian Operational Support Command (CANOSCOM) was responsible for operational support in Canada and abroad. The new commands came into being on February 1, 2006. (David Pugliese, 'Military Has Too Much Overhead,' *Ottawa Citizen*, June 14, 2010; confidential source.) The commands absorbed substantial numbers of personnel into the new headquarters, including as many as 400 trained Army staff, a subject of later complaints. Among other things, the new structure made the service chiefs, including the Chief of Land Staff, force generators without responsibility for deployments. See Lieutenant-General (Ret'd) M.K. Jeffery, *Inside Canadian Forces Transformation: Institutional Leadership as a Catalyst for Change* (Kingston, 2009), and Philippe Lagassé, 'A Mixed Legacy: General Rick Hillier and Canadian Defence 2005–08,' *International Journal* (Summer 2009): 614–15.

Martin government 'couldn't organize themselves to spend [the funds] to achieve their goals and left it for the Conservatives to utilize.'[31] The Tories would do so.

What Martin, Graham, and Hillier did do, however, was to change dramatically the commitment in Afghanistan. As early as the fall of 2004 (some say as early as the autumn of 2003), Ottawa had begun planning to move the Canadian battle group out of Kabul. NATO and ISAF had intentions to expand operations over most of Afghanistan in 2006 and wanted Canada to assume responsibility for Regional Command West and to take the lead in Herat Province in western Afghanistan. Herat was a low-visibility task, however, and apparently no one in Ottawa wanted that. Instead, 'tough' Kandahar was the choice, the very opposite of low visibility, the city to which Canadians had first deployed in 2002, and the volatile heart of the Taliban.[32] With its big U.S. airbase, Kandahar could readily support a Canadian force logistically, as Herat could not. But Kandahar then was not under ISAF; instead, it was under the Americans' Operation Enduring Freedom and would be until the beginning of August 2006, making the shift in locale and command structure even more dramatic for a Liberal government that had never had any hesitation in playing the anti-American card with the Canadian public. At Hillier's insistence, the new deployment was to include a full battle group with attached sub-units, approximately 1900 soldiers, along with a Provincial Reconstruction Team (eventually 330 military, diplomats, and aid workers), making in all some 2200 soldiers.[33] And the task? It was to fight the new concept of the three-block war. Hillier described it by saying that 'if you are knocking something down in the conduct of operations, you had better be building the country up as you are doing it or you are wasting your time.'[34] And both building up and tearing down could be going on at the same time within a few city blocks. As Graham put it to Hillier and the prime minister, 'We're going to fight in the hills and make love in the cities. We're going to make sure the population's getting development and aid in the cities; we're going to make sure that the Taliban are going to be kept off-balance.'[35]

Prime Minister Martin, much more attuned to United Nations peacekeeping than to war fighting, wanted to keep open the possibility that the CF might send troops to Darfur in the Sudan, the locale of an internal civil war hardly susceptible to the balm of UN peacekeeping – or white Canadian

troops. He pressed Hillier for assurance that if Canada was called on to participate there, the CF could do the job. Hillier agreed, but he must have had his
fingers crossed when he did so. That the shrunken CF could not do this
simultaneously with a major commitment in Afghanistan should have been as
immediately clear to the prime minister as it must have been to the chief of
the defence staff; it should also have been obvious that Darfur might have
trapped Canadian soldiers in a bloody quagmire without a major logistical
base and with scant prospects of evacuation if besieged, given the CF's scant
air transport resources. Darfur was a blue beret pipedream – even if Canada
had never sent a single soldier to Afghanistan.[36]

But if some in government did not realize that Canada had slipped into a
war by moving to Kandahar, the defence minister was not one of them: Graham understood that this was no peacekeeping mission, and he took pains to
tell Canadians in his speeches that there would be casualties.[37] Still, neither
the minister nor the CDS anticipated major battles; instead the expectation
was for low-intensity combat. For Hillier, who remembered British and other
officers in Former Yugoslavia deriding the Canadian battalions (or Canbats as
they were abbreviated) as 'Can'tbats' because of the restrictions placed upon
them by Ottawa,[38] the task was for the battle group to fight well when it had
to, to restore the CF's reputation as a combat force, and to hit the Canadian
peacekeeping myth squarely between the eyes.* He also wanted to reconnect
the CF to the public, orchestrating a brilliant public relations campaign to
'Recruit the Nation.' The Kandahar deployment and its accompanying publicity would do all these things in spades, in effect creating a cultural shift for
the CF and the Canadian public. Hillier also understood that there could be
no aid, no development, without security. 'We knew the Afghan Army was
still developing. The Afghan police are even further behind. So, we were going
to have to … provide that security and stability.'[39]

By November 2005, the move to Kandahar was close to completion. The
Provincial Reconstruction Team had begun work in the city, and the bulk of
the Canadian personnel with their heavy equipment had moved from Camp

---

* The Chief of Land Staff, Lieutenant-General Andrew Leslie, shared much of this view, saying that the
  military had become 'completely and utterly risk averse. We have been consumed by bureaucratic efficiency, and become fixated on process and planning.' Quoted in J.L. Granatstein, *Whose War Is It?* (2nd
  ed., Toronto, 2008), 217.

Julien to new quarters on the huge Kandahar Airfield, the main U.S. base. The multinational brigade headquarters under Brigadier-General David Fraser, which was to control operations in Regional Command South, was preparing to deploy into the field in early March 2006. The incoming battle group based on the 1st Battalion of the Princess Patricia's Canadian Light Infantry, or Task Force Orion as it was called by its commanding officer Lieutenant-Colonel Ian Hope, was completing its pre-deployment training at Canadian Forces Base Wainwright, Alberta, and readying itself to move to Kandahar early in the new year. Task Force Orion, destined to engage in some of the heaviest fighting of the Afghan campaign, had three rifle companies (one of which came from the 2nd Battalion of the PPCLI) in LAV IIIs or other armoured vehicles, a Headquarters Company with snipers, a reconnaissance platoon, and a surveillance troop from 12e Régiment Blindé du Canada, a battery of newly purchased and highly accurate M-777 155mm howitzers from 1st Royal Canadian Horse Artillery, a Combat Engineer squadron, a Forward Support Group to handle logistics and maintenance, a military police platoon, and a Health Services Support company. There was also an Unmanned Aerial Vehicle troop, the UAVs first used in Kabul three years earlier. An able, tough-minded leader in his mid-forties with a quarter-century of service in the British and Canadian armies, including time spent in Kabul with General Hillier, Hope had co-located all his soldiers in one bivouac in training, decentralized his combat support assets, and worked to build cohesion in TF Orion.[40] However, the training plan, not set by the battle group, seemed geared to fighting a northwest European style of war, a cause of concern to senior officers, who expected low-level combat in Kandahar. As it turned out serendipitously, Task Force Orion's training proved not inappropriate for what it would face – combat against formed enemy units.[41]

It must be noted, however, that the 1st Battalion of the PPCLI was so understrength that it had to be augmented by a company from another battalion in the regiment and by the addition of approximately a hundred reservists, a trend repeated in even greater numbers in all future rotations. Moreover, the PPCLI, like all infantry battalions, had been stripped of its pioneers (in-unit engineers), its mortars, and its anti-tank capabilities. The key combat support units, such as the Combat Engineer Regiments and the artillery, were equally short of personnel. And in Afghanistan, 1st Battalion PPCLI would have no helicopter support of its own to draw on, forcing it to queue for resources from other national fleets. The Canadian Army had become a hollow shell of its former self – and it had been so for more than a decade.[42]

At the same time in Canada, the second – and last – of Paul Martin's elections was underway. In the final days of campaigning, Glyn Berry, a diplomat working with the Canadian Provincial Reconstruction Team, died in a suicide bombing in Kandahar on January 15, 2006. As Hillier noted later, his death led the Department of Foreign Affairs and International Trade and the Canadian International Development Agency to scale down participation in the PRT 'and set our operation in Kandahar back a minimum of two years.' The 3-D approach – defence, development, and diplomacy – worked together or not at all. 'The fact was that having the few civilians in the PRT confined to the reconstruction team's camp meant 3-D was a farce ... That meant that our soldiers had to do all the necessary tasks outside the wire.' Those tasks included training Afghan army and police, getting aid projects underway, rebuilding a road, and working with tribal elders on local governance.[43]

The Kandahar region was rough country, desert, mountains, and rocks, rivers and fertile ground. A triangular greenbelt extending east from Kandahar city was covered in ditches and walled villages, all but impenetrable by weaponry, and the vegetation was lush. As Colonel Hope wrote, many roads were roofed over by mulberry trees that 'dropped hundreds of mulberries into our [LAV] crew compartments – staining everything brownish-red, a colour very similar to the stains of dried blood.'[44] The main crops were opium poppy and grapes, the latter of which grew on raised furrows that were covered by the high vines. This made the terrain ideal defensive country, and it was here the resurgent Taliban chose to fight. Close to Kandahar and its markets, they had cover, water, and shade. The 200 trained enemy fighters *in situ* when Task Force Orion arrived knew the terrain intimately and could draw on local supporters to flesh out their ranks along with men coming north from the Taliban's safe havens in Pakistan, many of them foreign jihadists. By June 2006, Hope conservatively estimated that 400–600 enemy were located in his area; the next month, there were thousands of insurgents and local supporters. The Taliban were capably led, they planned their operations carefully, and their five-man teams, armed with AK-47s, rocket-propelled grenades (RPGs), machine guns, mortars, and an apparently limitless supply of IED-making equipment, were able to communicate by radio or cellphone with others to create a quick concentration. The Taliban even used their satellite telephones to adjust the fall of shot to make their mortaring of ISAF forces more accurate and deadly. When Canadian and other ISAF troops entered a Taliban kill zone, the jihadi response was to lay down heavy fire with the intent of isolating small parties that could be wiped out. When artillery or air support began to fall on them, the Taliban melted away quickly, dragging all of their killed and wounded with them.

Against the Taliban, Task Force Orion used its three companies of infantry and varying numbers of the Afghan National Army and Police. The Afghan National Police, largely Dari speaking, were neither well-trained nor reliable, and were almost uniformly hated by the local Pashtun population. The ANA, on the other hand, often had the people's high regard, and the small numbers in Hope's area were 'very brave during combat, loyal to those willing to suffer alongside them, quick on their feet, but simple in tactics.' Colonel Hope integrated ANA commanders into his planning and worked to provide escorts for their thin-skinned vehicles, artillery support, and medical evacuation for their wounded. 'In exchange, we were given promises that these soldiers would die for us; a promise that they fulfilled.' Also in Regional Command South were American, British, Australian, and Dutch troops.[45]

Colonel Hope quickly realized that his comparatively ponderous troops, riding their LAV IIIs, could not react quickly enough to the Taliban's moves. Deliberate plans based on hard intelligence were rarely possible in a counter-insurgency battle across a large area. Instead, he began to deploy his men and women into company and platoon Forward Operating Bases (FOBs) or Patrol Bases – in effect, 'living among the locals, in the face of the enemy, out of the back of the LAVs.'[46] Closer to the enemy, the Canadians could react more quickly, but logistical problems increased because the Task Force did not have its own helicopters; that meant that road resupply was the only – and danger-ous – option.

Task Force Orion began its operations in March 2006. For the next half-year, it was in almost continuous, costly firefights, the sub-unit commanders keeping up an aggressive tempo of operations in the face of IED strikes and suicide attacks. On March 4, Hope's own vehicle was hit in a suicide attack; the next day, one Afghan participant in a *shura*, a village meeting, struck Captain Trevor Greene, a reservist Civil-Military Cooperation [CIMIC] officer, on the head with an axe. One of Greene's soldiers shot the attacker, and Greene, grievously wounded, barely survived.[47]

Shortly afterwards, the new Conservative prime minister, Stephen Harper, paid his first visit to Afghanistan. In an address to the troops, he talked of how the struggle in Kandahar was in Canada's national interests. Then he added that 'standing up for these core Canadian values may not always be easy at times. It's never easy for the men and women on the front lines. And there may be some who want to cut and run. But cutting and running is not your way. It's not my way. And it's not the Canadian way. We don't make a commitment and then run away at the first sign of trouble.'[48] Harper's words, so different in tone from anything uttered by a Canadian leader for a half-century, resonated with the soldiers. They had less impact at home, where the war was not welcomed.[49]

Two months later, Colonel Hope's 'B' Company moved to clear the enemy out of the village of Pashmul and a fierce firefight erupted. One platoon fell into an enemy ambush and suffered casualties, including the death of gunner Captain Nichola Goddard, the Forward Observer Controller, whose LAV III was hit by at least two RPGs. Hope insisted that his sub-units be able to be covered by his own artillery, firing on the enemy for the first time since Korea; hence the need for artillery forward controllers who also coordinated helicopter and fixed-wing airstrikes and electronic warfare assets. 'I knew it was Nich before they told me,' Colonel Hope told journalist Christie Blatchford. 'I knew because on all ops up until that point, Nich was a constant on the radio, giving me incredible detail about what was happening ... She could synthesize everything.'[50] Some 500 metres away, 'C' Company heard of Goddard's death and fired at the Taliban with their LAV III chain guns. They then watched two precision-guided bombs from a USAF bomber overhead fall on a compound behind the tree line from which the Taliban had fired. 'You guys want to fuck with us,' Sergeant Mike Denine told journalist Chris Wattie, 'well, here you go.'[51] By every account an able officer, Goddard was the first female Canadian combat soldier ever to be killed in action, and her death drew an extraordinary public response at home. Her husband received the Memorial [Silver] Cross, making him the first male spouse to be so honoured.[52]

In fact, as the increasing numbers of dead from Afghanistan were returned to Canada, completely spontaneous demonstrations began. The aircraft carrying the caskets landed at the Air Force base at Trenton, Ontario, to be met by family members and political and military notables.[53] Then the cortège proceeded along Highway 401 to Toronto, where autopsies took place. Crowds lined the roads out of Trenton and then gathered on the overpasses along Highway 401, in August 2007 renamed the Highway of Heroes by the provincial government. The spectators carried flags and banners, saluting or applauding as the mournful cortège of hearses passed by. Even Toronto, liberal and strongly anti-war, named the parkway into the city centre its Route of Heroes. Soldiers at hockey games were spotlit and cheered, while Don Cherry, on *Hockey Night in Canada* shows, spoke movingly about each and every soldier killed in action. Civilian groups organized 'red Fridays,' wearing red to signify support for the CF. Others put 'I Support Our Troops' bumper stickers on their autos, and business leaders organized fund-raising dinners to support military families, wounded soldiers, and to send the children of dead soldiers to university. The outpouring of emotional support for the Canadian Forces was simply unprecedented in 'peacetime,' General Hillier's 'Recruit the Nation' campaign having achieved its ends. Hillier himself was the heart and soul of the effort. First, in every one of his many speeches he was funny, patriotic, and transparently sincere in the way he singled out soldiers, sailors, and airmen and airwomen in the audience who had been decorated for meritorious service. Wars to Hillier were not fought only by and for generals. It was the soldiers who did the hard, dirty work, and the CDS wanted Canadians to know this. The troops loved him for his obvious concern for them, and so did the people. He made sure that everyone understood that war was a costly business, and the extraordinary outpouring of respect and patriotism when the remains of those killed in Afghanistan return home is clear evidence that he succeeded.[54] In the world wars and Korea, Canadian dead were buried near where they fell; the Afghan War dead came home, giving Canadians the opportunity to bid farewell. And they did.

Task Force Orion, by now, in *Globe and Mail* columnist Christie Blatchford's phrase, was 'a killing machine,'[55] and it was soon to enter its most trying time. In mid-July, it fought in the Panjwai area against Taliban forces that had dug in and prepared to battle the Canadians for control. The PPCLI and its attached ANA elements seized control of the battlefield and inflicted heavy losses on the Taliban. Then the Task Force moved to relieve British troops besieged in Sangin and to put pressure on the enemy command in Helmand. Succeeding, the Task Force then received orders to re-take the towns of Nawa and Garmser on July 18. Lieutenant-Colonel Hope had no maps of the areas involved – rather less than he might have expected in the first decade of the twenty-first century – and his men had been in heavy action without cease. But Hope did an aerial reconnaissance, and he gathered his unit (and its 150 vehicles) for a briefing on the 120-kilometre route to Garmser, guiding them with his hand-sketched map. By dawn the town was in Canadian hands, and Nawa soon was too, the Task Force by this time 240 kilometres from its Kandahar base at the end of a long supply line.[56] This was an extraordinary feat of arms, marred only by casualties suffered in an attack on a convoy.

Then, at the beginning of August as Hope's unit began to hand over to the 1st Battalion Royal Canadian Regiment Battle Group, the Canadians went into action in Panjwai once more, fighting a costly action in Pashmul that cost four dead and eleven wounded. On August 3, an IED blew up a LAV III, and after the casualties had been evacuated by helicopter (Hope stopped the operation and evacuated his casualties, including his vehicle casualties to ensure no LAV IIIs fell into Taliban hands), the PPCLI moved to secure the area. Blatchford recorded that what they discovered stunned them: 'well-prepared firing points for IEDs, defensive positions around the bridge, an RPG with ammunition, spider (initiation) devices for bombs ... three more IEDs, some already half-buried in the soft ground.'[57] The enemy was very skilful, well-prepared, and capable of careful planning and tenacious fighting.

Nonetheless, Task Force Orion's action derailed a Taliban attack on Kandahar city, but led to a major assault on Panjwai District Centre on August 19. Defended by ANA and 'A' Company of 2nd Battalion PPCLI, just arrived in Kandahar and attached to the 1st Battalion RCR Battle Group, and supported by artillery and airpower, the attack failed at heavy cost to the Taliban. The victory, much of it fought in darkness, was characterized by Hope, who had been touring the area of operations before returning to Canada, as 'desperate and unplanned hard-fought actions' that brought this phase of the battle to a close. Task Force Orion's tour of duty had reached its end.[58] The PPCLI and its attached sub-units had suffered 10 per cent casualties in their six and a half months in Kandahar.

The soldiers of Task Force Orion, their incorporated reservists aside, were professionals. Some of the officers might have read histories of Afghanistan and tried to understand the historic conflicts and tribal divisions that had shaped the area. Not many soldiers did so. They went where their government sent them and did the job they had been given. They fought for their friends, their platoon, and their company, and for their regiment's honour, just as soldiers have always done. They fought to kill the enemy and to stay alive, and they fought to win. And win they did, but at a high cost.

But was the Task Force's work a success? The answer can only be 'yes, but ...' If the aim was to 'clear, hold, and build,' the Canadian Task Force defeated the Taliban every time it faced it in the field. But it had too few soldiers to hold the ground it cleared for very long, and in essence all it could do with its limited numbers was to disrupt the enemy's plans. It did this very effectively. But if the aim was to build and to win the population's allegiance and to guarantee them ISAF's protection, the Canadian PRT (and every other PRT in contested areas) failed in providing governance and development, in substantial part because, after Glyn Berry's death, the Kandahar PRT remained inside the wire in its camp.[59] The Taliban returned to the villages, frequently killed those who had helped the Canadians, and terrorized the rest by destroying schools or aid projects. The Task Force could put its finger in the dyke, but there was too much water, too many holes, to be plugged by a three-company unit. As Carl Forsberg wrote in a study for the Institute for the Study of War in Washington, DC, 'The Canadian battalion was too small to conduct sustained combat operations.' He was regrettably correct. ISAF ought to have put more troops into Kandahar earlier than 2010; if it had, the war might well have proceeded differently and the growth of the Taliban there have been checked.[60] If there had been more soldiers on the ground, development work might have been more effective. So, military success, yes, but also a failure in development.

There were other troops than the Canadians in the Afghan south. At one point in its half-year of fighting, Task Force Orion had a company of U.S. Army infantry under command, the first time this had occurred in action in more than a half-century. After working with both the British and the Americans in Helmand in July, Colonel Hope realized that 'at some point in the past decade we have had a fundamental shift in the culture of the Canadian infantry, making us identify most readily with American, and not British, infantry. Devil Company was easy to work with, reliable, and very professional ... they wanted to fight, unlike the soldiers of other allied countries who remained very risk-averse, too shy to stand and fight the Taliban.' 'When firing began,' Hope wrote, 'the American leaders demonstrated decisiveness and tenacity, and the American soldiers performed battle drills quickly and with great effect.'[61]

This was a marked shift in attitude, one that Hope was not alone in forming. Privately, after the experience of hard fighting in 2006, some of the most senior Canadian officers were harshly critical of the British and Dutch.[62] That risk-averse countries with troops in Afghanistan stirred bitterness was not surprising. The French refused to shift troops to Kandahar where there was combat; the Germans operated under caveats that forbade their troops to fight at night; and other countries sought safe billets and imposed similar restrictions. NATO's participation in the war, therefore, was less than wholehearted, and there was continuing harsh commentary among Canadian senior officers, politicians, and media on how NATO had let the West – and Canada – down. Indeed, many officials and officers at National Defence Headquarters and even some at Foreign Affairs and International Trade by mid-2010 had begun to question if NATO any longer had any utility for Canada given the caveats and constraints members had imposed on the use of their forces in Afghanistan. If Canada had been a better NATO ally over the past forty years, had not unilaterally cut its commitments in 1969 and 1993, and had not applied its own caveats on the employment of its forces in Former Yugoslavia (where the 'Can'tbats' slur that so offended General Hillier had originated), such ahistorical complaints would have had more force.[63] Even so, that the Dutch might be criticized was not particularly unexpected; that the British could be was. That the Americans were praised by Canadian soldiers was also unusual, so much so that it had to be genuine.[64]

Of course, not all Americans, and not all Canadians, were instinctively courageous. Hope wrote later that 'once we had found the enemy, we needed to fix him with fires and finish him in close-quarter combat.' This was never easy because it was against human nature to stay within 100–150 metres of the enemy. 'The majority of soldiers when fired upon for the first time would seek to disengage back to the "last safe place" they had occupied.' Only 'true fighters' resisted this urge, those 'men and women predisposed to keep fighting regardless of violence and danger; those who repressed fear … because of an overwhelming desire to beat the enemy; those who truly wanted to hunt the enemy and make him the victim. I would estimate that there were only 6 or 7 such individuals in every forty-man platoon.'[65] Those were the fighting leaders, the soldiers Hope relied on, as he again discovered a truth known to all commanders in every war. Hope said later in an address to cadets at the Royal Military College: 'Leadership's place is on the ground; it is out front with your soldiers. If it is not there, they will not take that last 100 yards of deadly ground.'[66]

The 1st Battalion of the Royal Canadian Regiment Battle Group, led by Lieutenant-Colonel Omer Lavoie, now carried the action forward in Panjwai, yet again a centre of Taliban strength. After fighting there so vigorously in the summer heat, the undermanned Canadians had left Panjwai, allowing the Taliban to re-establish themselves. Now the enemy wanted to test ISAF and the new battle group of Canadians. Once again, they had to be driven out in Operation Medusa, which put some 1400 Canadian, coalition, and ANA soldiers on the contested ground and ran through the first two weeks of September 2006. The enemy had not done well against the 1st Battalion PPCLI, but the Canadians had nonetheless departed; now the Taliban would mass in even greater numbers, hold the ground, and look for another fight. The ISAF plan, developed by General Fraser, called for U.S., Dutch, Afghan, Danish, and Canadian forces to clear the eastern Panjwai District, and on September 2, the civilians prudently having fled the area, artillery and air bombardment began to hit Taliban positions. The RCR advanced the next day, crossing the Arghandab River, almost immediately losing four men in two deadly incidents as they fought against well-dug-in Taliban (using Soviet-style defensive tactics, said one Canadian officer) in large numbers.[67] But the pressure on the Taliban continued day and night, the LAV IIIs effectively using their powerful chain guns. The Battle Group's run of bad luck continued on September 4, when a United States Air Force A-10 close support aircraft, called in by the RCR to attack a Taliban position, mistakenly fired on 'C' Company, killing one and wounding more than thirty men. The company stayed in the fight, but it had lost all four of its warrant officers and the company commander in three days.[68]

The ISAF forces now used their firepower to hammer the Taliban and to force the enemy to revise its plan. Instead of holding the ground, the enemy found itself forced to withdraw under pressure. General Fraser said later that 'the Taliban fighters tried to bug out one night. Not many made it out.'[69] There were arguments from the battle group commander about Fraser's changes to his plan and some heated discussions between Canadian officers and a U.S. colonel from the 10th Mountain Division.[70] Such things happen, but what is most important is that ISAF's Canadian-led brigade achieved its aim of clearing the eastern Panjwai by the middle of September, claiming more than one thousand of the enemy killed. All that remained of the Taliban were cells of suicide and roadside bombers, the usual Taliban, in other words, but there were enough of those to result in a steady toll of killed and wounded. And the Taliban controlled the ground once the RCR left the area. On the other hand, the Taliban would not take on the Canadians again in a major set-piece battle. The enemy had discovered that, though it could inflict casualties and thus help to weaken home-front morale in Canada, it could not win such a fight.

The soldiers of Task Force Orion and the 1st Battalion RCR Battle Group might fairly claim to have saved Kandahar in the biggest battle of the war thus far. They might even claim to have prevented the fall of Afghanistan to the Taliban. Certainly General Fraser did.[71] That might overstate matters, but not by much. As Major Bill Fletcher, a company commander in 1st Battalion PPCLI, told Chris Wattie, 'The boys did their job and we accomplished our mission. I truly believe we improved the overall situation and did a hell of a lot for Canada's reputation both militarily but also on the world stage.' Fletcher could not forget that seven of his soldiers had been killed. 'I cannot help but believe that they died doing their duty and moving forward, taking the fight to the enemy. I take comfort in that, but still wish I could have brought everyone back alive.'[72]

Could heavy armour reduce the casualty lists? Ottawa apparently thought so, dispatching a squadron of Leopard C2 battle tanks to Afghanistan; by the beginning of December, the tanks had deployed to a Forward Operating Base in Panjwai and were almost immediately using their guns against the enemy. Tanks had been on the way out of the Canadian Forces, their fate determined by General Hillier, himself an armoured officer. But the Afghan war brought them back because their ability to move cross-country – while the LAV IIIs got stuck in culverts – gave genuine advantages. Then their big 105 mm guns could fire High Explosive Squash Head rounds with precision against enemy compounds, and their heavy armour offered protection against mines.[73] The results of Operation Medusa in particular led Ottawa to increase troop strength with more artillery and engineers. They also eventually led National Defence Headquarters to purchase up to one hundred more Leopard C2A6 tanks in Europe, to press the government to acquire Chinook helicopters (the CF's Chinooks had been sold to the Dutch by the Mulroney government in the early 1990s) to reduce the toll imposed by road movement, and, to protect the Chinooks, to send light Griffon helicopters armed with machine guns to Kandahar. The air strength amounted to 450 personnel. Similarly, the increasing Taliban use of ever-more-powerful IEDs that could destroy LAV IIIs and severely damage even the Leopards forced the government to acquire specialized anti-mine armoured vehicles, including South African-made Nyalas and the Husky, an IED 'bird dog.'[74] Sometime earlier (August 2005), the Army began providing the wonderfully named 'Omelets' or OMLTs – small Operational Mentor and Liaison Teams – to work in the field with ANA *kandaks* (battalions) and to offer tactical and training advice. By May 2010, the Army had 180 officers and non-commissioned members working with the 1st Brigade, 205th Corps of the Afghan National Army.[75]

The new equipment and roles led to increases in the Canadian contingent's strength, raising it to 2800 (including personnel based at Camp Mirage, the Air Force's staging base in a Gulf state). The Harper government in Ottawa spared no expense in providing what the Canadians in Afghanistan required. It is probably fair to say that, after 2006, there was nothing that the troops needed that was not provided. It is also probably correct to say that this had not been the case in any Canadian Forces operation at home or abroad since 1945.

The war, however, had become increasingly unpopular in Canada. In late February 2006, the *Globe and Mail* published the results of a Strategic Counsel opinion poll on Canada's role in Afghanistan. When asked whether they would vote to send troops there if they were a Member of Parliament, 27 per cent said yes and 62 per cent said no. Those in favour were then asked if they would change their minds if the deployment might result in significant casualties. Thirty-one per cent said they would. In other words, only a small number of Canadians wholeheartedly supported Canada's present mission in Kandahar, and successive opinion polls showed support declining over time.[76]

Why? The reason was likely the persistent and popular perception that the only role for the Canadian Forces was peacekeeping. In December 2007, Bob Rae, not yet a Member of Parliament from Toronto but already the de facto Liberal foreign affairs critic, reflected this attitude when he suggested that the Harper government's policy would lead to Canada being 'essentially engaged in a counterinsurgency campaign in Afghanistan, and I think that's extremely unwise … I don't think that's where people want to be. I think they want to see us in a peacekeeping role. I think they want to see us in a peacemaking role.'[77] That Paul Martin's government had put the CF in Kandahar only a year and a half earlier mattered not.

Additionally, many Canadians saw Afghanistan as an American war, a direct response to the al Qaeda terror attacks of 9/11. That may have been correct in 2002, when the aim was to drive from power the Taliban government that had sheltered al Qaeda. But the aim of the war had shifted to assisting an elected government, weak and corrupt as it may have been, to establish itself in the face of attacks from Taliban remnants. At the same time, much effort was put into educating girls and helping women, alongside development projects big and small. Nation-building, in other words. Unfortunately, none of this appeared to matter to Canadians. Afghanistan might have been authorized by the UN and NATO, but it was still the Americans' war, President George W. Bush's war, and automatically increasing numbers believed it must be wrong.[78] (Nor would it matter to Canadians after January 2009, when Afghanistan became the popular Barack Obama's unpopular war.) Nonetheless, the minority Harper government pushed a motion through Parliament (with a vote of 149 to 145) in the spring of 2006 to approve the Afghan mission and its continuance beyond the original end-date of February 2007 to 2009. The Liberals were badly divided in their caucus, 24 supporting the government (including acting leader Bill Graham and leader-in-waiting Michael Ignatieff), and the rest opposed; the NDP and Bloc Québécois voted against the extension.

As might have been expected, the casualties in the summer and fall of 2006 in the Panjwai and after, though they initially boosted support, over time helped increase the opposition in Canada, and the debate over what Canada should do grew more heated through 2007 as the battle group rotations regularly proceeded from Canada to Kandahar.[79] Late in 2007, the government appointed an independent panel, chaired by former Liberal deputy prime minister John Manley, to advise on the mission's role and character after the beginning of 2009. Manley's report, released in early 2008,[80] warned against a precipitate withdrawal but pointed to the requirement for more coalition assistance to the hard-pressed Canadians in Regional Command South. The government's response, negotiated behind the scenes with the still-divided Liberal Opposition in February and March 2008 and the incorporation of Liberal amendments into the government motion, brought the Liberals and Conservatives together. The result was agreement to extend the Canadian combat role in Kandahar into 2011 but to end it thereafter. The text of the resolution directed 'the government of Canada [to] notify NATO that Canada will end its presence in Kandahar as of July 2011, and, as of that date, the redeployment of Canadian Forces troops out of Kandahar and their replacement by Afghan forces [will] start as soon as possible, so that it will have been completed by December 2011.'[81]

The decision to maintain Canadian combat forces in Afghanistan to 2011 meant that the cycle of training, deployment, and recuperation post-deployment continued for the Army. With only nine battalions of infantry and with all the battalions still understrength, the strain on the sharp end was severe. A unit would train intensively for up to six months before moving to Kandahar, including a stint at the Canadian Manoeuvre Training Centre at CFB Wainwright, where they would live in Afghanistan-like conditions, train with the full suite of weapons and vehicles they would have in theatre, and deal with 300 Afghan-Canadians role-playing as villagers and Taliban;[82] it would then spend at least six months in Kandahar, and after its departure spend time decompressing, first for five days in Cyprus, and then in Canada before beginning the pre-deployment phase once again.[83] With only some 20,000 men and women all told in 2006, the Army was simply too small to sustain this pace – and it was wearing down its officers and warrant officers, some of whom might have completed four or five Afghanistan tours by 2011. A good case could be made that the Army could not readily sustain the Kandahar mission after 2011.[84]

Then there were emergency deployments – a terrible earthquake in Haiti in January 2010 led Ottawa to scramble to dispatch the CF, including a Royal 22e Régiment battalion that had been intended to proceed to pre-deployment training for Afghanistan, engineers from CFB Gagetown, a logistics battalion, helicopters, a field hospital, and the DART, the CF's Disaster Assistance Response Team. A massive deployment of 4000 CF personnel, most from the Army, to provide security for the Vancouver 2010 Olympics and another large deployment, again mainly soldiers, for the G8-G20 meetings in Ontario also absorbed personnel and money.[85] Strong efforts to recruit more soldiers eased the manpower situation somewhat – there were 22,800 in the Army by mid-2010, an increase of some 3,000 over the last four years – but unexpectedly high retirements tended to negate the impact of the new soldiers, especially as those leaving tended to be the most experienced and highly skilled.[86] The regular Army and the CF generally remained almost wholly unsuccessful in recruiting in ethnic communities;[87] the reserve forces were doing substantially better. Nonetheless, among new recruits there was a waiting list to join the infantry.[88]

To keep up its battle group strength, the Army turned to the reserves, looking to Militia units to provide from 15 to 25 per cent of the soldiers on each deployment and likely a higher percentage of infantry section soldiers. The underfunded, under-resourced Militia managed this, even though its total strength ranged only from 16,000 to 21,500 over the course of the Kandahar deployment, a figure that failed to take into account the impact of a staggeringly high 25 per cent turnover rate each year. Still, the reservists, trained to regular force standards before deployment, did extraordinarily well in action. Their performance as part-time professionals did much to ease the long-standing grievances between the regulars and the Militia, and if the reservists returned to their units (many joined the regular force), they brought their much-needed learned professionalism with them.[89]

None of this expansion in strength would have been possible without a bigger defence budget. The Martin government had begun the process, as we have seen; the Harper government pressed ahead with it, expanding the envelope dramatically and pushing the budget for the Department of National Defence above $20 billion a year and increasing the Army's spending by 50 per cent in the four years from 2006.[90] Some of this was the costs of the war, costs that were estimated by the Office of the Parliamentary Budget Officer to range from a low of $13.92 billion to a high of $18.14 billion from 2001 to 2011.[91] Government figures were substantially lower, but the cost of combat operations in Afghanistan to 2008 was estimated to be some $7 billion.[92] In any case, while defence expenditures might be expected to decline after the 2011 withdrawal, much had been spent on infrastructure and equipment. The Army received or had on order new tanks and armoured vehicles, guns, trucks, night vision gear, and had been promised the refurbishment of its hard-used LAV IIIs.[93] Air force equipment – the four giant CC-17 transports that had been acquired because Harper's first defence minister Gordon O'Connor made their acquisition a personal priority[94] – made the movement of troops easier (and cheaper), and the often-promised but yet to be ordered Joint Support Ships for the navy, though still a long way off, could make small deployments easier to support. There were always problems, delays, and political games underway, but the Conservative government unquestionably did more for the Army and the entire CF than any government since that of Louis St Laurent.

The grinding, brutal war took an increasing toll year by year. In 2002, Canada lost four soldiers; in 2003 two; in 2004 and 2005 one each year; in 2006 thirty-six; in 2007 thirty; in 2008 thirty-two; in 2009 thirty-two. To the end of August 2010, in all 152 Canadian soldiers had been killed in the fighting,[95] some two-thirds being infantry and most of the dead killed in IED strikes. The numbers of wounded, released by DND only once a year in an all-too-apparent effort to keep the numbers hidden from public view, were 529 as of February 2010. The injured numbered 913. It seems clear that the CF was not prepared for casualties on this scale, its medical services having shrunk over the last decades.[96] Not included in those statistics were soldiers suffering from post-traumatic stress disorder (PTSD). Almost 38,000 Canadians had served in Afghanistan to 2010. Some 8200 CF men and women (not all but most with Afghan service) were receiving treatment for PTSD, a very high percentage indeed.[97] And, as always, the pain of losses was spread unevenly across Canada. 'Who fights and dies for Canada?' a journalist asked. 'Young white men,' said Douglas Bland of Queen's University, 'that's who fights.' He was right, notwithstanding that three women had been killed in action along with six visible-minority soldiers. The great majority of the killed were white males between twenty and thirty-nine years in age, most having been raised in small towns, with a high proportion (more than one in five) from eastern Canada. The six biggest metropolitan areas in the country comprised 45 per cent of the population but accounted for only 20 per cent of the dead. Toronto had lost four soldiers, the same as tiny Truro, NS; Vancouver had one killed.[98] The war's human costs fell heaviest on Canada's economically laggard areas, but wherever they fell, they were substantial and increasing.

The reasons were clear. 'The enemy pays local children to fly homemade plastic-bag kites whenever a patrol passes nearby,' journalist Adam Day wrote of the 1st Battalion PPCLI deployment in October 2009, 'and then illiterate men manage to kill Canadians with $10 bombs. The Canadian Forces have satellites and laser-guided weapons and officers with PhDs. It's not clear who has the advantage. The enemy has a straight-up goal – to get foreigners out of their country – and they have all the time in the world to do it.'[99] The chief menace that faced the soldiers, now living in the villages alongside the Afghan people and trying to win their trust and cooperation, was the improvised explosive device (IED): 'The IEDs are everywhere, all the time, and after a while the whole thing feels like a high stakes and very unfunny game of minesweeper. The black calculations are constant and unsettling, any tiny choice or unnoticeable decision may mean the difference between life and destruction.'[100]

And while making those tiny, unnoticeable decisions, the Canadians, much as the Princess Pats in Salavat in Panjwai District in October 2009, adapted their tactics to the changing tempo of the counter-insurgency war, trying to win the hearts and minds of the Afghans and to gain trust and secure intelligence, none of them being able to speak the local language. It was a tough job as year by year, month by month, the Taliban increased its attacks on ISAF troops and Afghan civilians loyal to the Kabul government; perhaps it was an impossible task. Certainly the ideas of victory over the enemy that had been heard in 2005 had been replaced by a more cautious tone. In April 2008, when he was asked how he would categorize an ISAF success, Stephen Harper said: 'It depends what you mean by "success." If you took the definition of success which could be Afghan forces able to ensure a western equivalent security environment, maybe that's a 20–25-year task. If you're saying Afghan forces able to manage the day-to-day security in most of the country, we think that's an objective that, if we put our focus and determination towards, is achievable in a much shorter timeframe.'[101] That did not sound much like success; certainly it was not victory.

On the other hand, the Manley Independent Panel report of 2008 let Canada pressure NATO to find more troops to serve with the battle group in Kandahar. In the end, a U.S. battalion stepped in, as the Americans, their Iraq commitment beginning to lessen, stepped up their role in Afghanistan. This was a help in Kandahar, but it was still too few troops to fight the Taliban in a large populous province the size of New Brunswick. Brigadier-General Jonathan Vance, a successful Canadian commander for nine months in 2009 (and reappointed in 2010 when his successor was recalled to Canada for having an affair with a corporal on his staff), was blunt in saying that 'between 2006 and 2009 there was a small effort in Kandahar, mostly Canadian. We did not have the capacity to do everything that needed to be done to achieve success through counter insurgency. All we could do is not lose.' Vance went on to assess the Taliban as having a problem: 'They don't have a plan. It's not a particularly good insurgency. They have a safe haven [in Pakistan] and an exhausted population, but they are not driving toward unseating the government or forcing out the "infidels" … They absolutely don't have the military capacity to challenge the government or the security forces. All they can do,' said Vance, 'is be a spoiler.'[102]

Vance also told a Canadian journalist writing for *Harper's* in 2009: 'We were facing the worst-case scenario in 2006 – a conventional takeover by Taliban forces. The Canadian battle groups had been able to hold the insurgency more or less at bay.' But he admitted that the life of the average Kandahari had become less secure as the Taliban began to tighten their grip on Kandahar city. 'I don't have the capacity to make sure someone doesn't rip their guts out at night.' Vance added that he knew some of the Afghan security officers he dealt with were drug-dealing entrepreneurs. 'Yes,' he said. 'We are completely aware that there are a number of illicit activities.' One high-ranking officer 'runs effective security ops that are designed to make sure that the business end of his life runs smoothly, and there is a collateral effect on public order,' he said. 'Ideally, it should be the other way around. The tragedy of Kandahar is that it's hard to find that paragon of civic virtue.'[103]

That was true, but complicating matters was the undeniable fact that the Taliban had time on their side. President Barack Obama's surge in U.S. troops, putting another 30,000 troops into the field, including a large number into Kandahar, was cause for optimism in Vance's opinion, and deservedly so, except that Obama had pledged to begin bringing some troops back from Afghanistan in 2011. If the Taliban could survive for two or three more years – and despite Special Operations and UAV attacks targeting the enemy leadership, there was little reason to believe they could not – they might be in a position to capitalize after the Dutch left on August 1, 2010, the Canadians in 2011, and when the United States and other eager-to-withdraw nations began their own pull-outs. After a July 2010 conference in Kabul that looked forward to the Afghan government assuming responsibility for its security by 2014, for example, Britain's coalition government was quick to express the conviction that it would be out of Afghanistan by that date.

At the same time the flood of American troops brought to Kandahar province by the surge – and Canada's decision to pull all its combat troops from Afghanistan in 2011 – led the United States to take the helm in Regional Command South on July 15, 2010, and, moreover, to assume responsibility for Kandahar city, hitherto under a Canadian officer. A one-star Canadian general after November 2010 would command only the Canadian battle group and a single U.S. battalion with responsibility for Panjwai District, and the U.S. general in command in the region would have 21,000 troops, including the Canadians, reporting to him. 'Somebody new has come to play in our ballpark [and] it's the big-leaguers,' said Douglas Bland, chair of Defence Management Studies at Queen's University. 'We had ownership of the whole place. The victories and defeats were clearly identifiable as Canadian. That's changed.'[104] Still, with the United States in charge, the command structure was clear, perhaps for the first time in the long war.[105] Indeed, the U.S. military was in charge in all of Afghanistan, creating the first clear chain of command for the ISAF forces.

Other things had changed as well. A huge controversy developed in Canada in 2007 and peaked in 2009 and 2010 over the treatment of Taliban and suspected Taliban taken prisoner by Canadian troops. After revelations of the maltreatment of prisoners by American troops in Iraq, there was no desire in Ottawa to hand over captives to the U.S. forces. The CF had no interest (nor the resources to do so) in setting up its own prison facilities in Afghanistan, and NATO failed in its effort to get its contributing members to create an alliance system. Thus the decision was made and codified in an agreement in mid-December 2005 (negotiated by the two governments but signed by General Hillier because Canada was in the midst of an election and no minister was prepared to come to Afghanistan at the time) to let the Afghans receive and interrogate the detainees captured by the CF, holding those it believed to be Taliban.[106] The usual Afghan ways of treating prisoners verged on the brutal; the main point differentiating the Afghan government from its enemy was that the government's jailers did not kill all their prisoners all the time. No one seriously suggested that Canadian soldiers had brutalized prisoners, but some Canadians, most identifiably against Canadian participation in the war, quickly alleged that, by handing captives over to torturers in 2006 and after, the CF had made itself complicit in war crimes.[107] To the CF leadership, understandably enough, such charges amounted to a disservice to the CF and the country. One senior officer wrote privately: 'We are being picked apart by several whose agenda is to manipulate disjointed info[rmation] to discredit and cause a change of policy: a strategy known as Lawfare!' 'The media,' the general continued, 'is not only complicit but encouraging the agenda.'[108] There was little doubt that the aim of most critics was to get Canada out of Kandahar and, indeed, out of any future military operations except the most benign blue beret forms of UN peacekeeping. The government in 2007 had strengthened its 2005 agreement with the Afghan government, ensuring that Canadian officials could visit detainees to ensure they were not ill-treated.[109]

Nonetheless, abuse in Afghan prisons almost certainly continued. One Canadian who strongly supported the war wrote confidentially from his base in Kabul that Canada had 'screwed up, learned the lessons the hard way and then tried to fix the problem.' What should have been done, he went on, was to 'admit the mistakes, explain that Afghanistan is a sovereign state ... and then tell people what we're doing to make a horrid system a little less horrid.' Unfortunately no politician 'simply stood up and sucked it up.'[110] The result was that the detainee torture issue became a political football in Canada, kept going by media leaks and revelations and documents from an officer in the Department of Foreign Affairs and International Trade who had served in Afghanistan.[111] The officer's testimony was flatly contradicted by other military and Foreign Affairs officials, but it is likely fair to say that, while the Canadian public was divided, almost all the Opposition in Parliament believed the charges. In the winter and spring of 2010, so heated did the issue become that the detainee issue came close to toppling the minority Harper government before the Speaker of the House of Commons brokered a deal for the examination and clearance of hitherto heavily redacted documents by a panel of senior judges and their eventual study by a parliamentary committee. What the outcome might be was unclear at the time of writing.

Other issues roiled the waters. A Canadian infantry officer, Captain Robert Semrau, served in an OMLT advising an Afghan battalion. In an operation on October 19, 2008, in Helmand Province, an air attack grievously wounded a Taliban fighter. Semrau allegedly considered the Taliban's wounds to be mortal and, following what he described as the soldier's code that such a fighter should be put out of his misery, shot and killed him. Months later, Semrau was court-martialled and charged with murder and other offences against Canadian military law.[112] This case divided public (and military) opinion, but in July 2010, the court martial found him not guilty of the most serious charges but guilty of disgraceful conduct. In October, Semrau's sentence was handed down: reduction in rank to 2nd lieutenant and dismissal from the Canadian Forces. An able soldier by every reckoning, Semrau saw his military career ended.

So too in all likelihood was the career of Brigadier-General Daniel Ménard, the commander of Canadians in Afghanistan in 2010. National Defence Headquarters recalled Ménard to Ottawa in May when it learned that he was having an affair with a married female corporal on his staff.[113] Army orders forbade sexual liaisons in the field,[114] and Ménard, the officer charged with enforcing discipline on Canadian troops, had made his own position completely untenable. Curiously, many civilian commentators in a Canada that understood very little of the military saw nothing wrong with Ménard's conduct; virtually every ex-military commentator understood that discipline had to be enforced and that those whose task it was to do so had to set the example.[115] Ménard would be charged with obstruction of justice and conduct to the prejudice of good order and discipline; he, more than Captain Semrau, ought to have been charged with disgraceful conduct. His case remained unresolved at the time of writing. So too did that of the senior

Canadian officer in Haiti, Colonel Bernard Ouellette, who also was relieved of his command several weeks after Ménard, the charges against him also involving sex (though not with a military subordinate) and a loss of morale among those under his command.[116]

Such cases, along with the arrest of an Air Force colonel on murder and sex crimes charges, called the qualities of the CF senior officer corps into question with the public at a time of high stress for the military. The torture allegations left no stain on the Army; the sexual escapades of senior officers besmirched personal reputations and suggested an utter foolishness and lack of discipline that gave reason for doubting qualifications for high command; and Captain Semrau's actions were seen as ultimately moral by many; certainly very few condemned his actions outright. But the reality is that those who are tasked with leading Canadians into battle must be disciplined. An Army without discipline is a mob; Army leaders without discipline themselves cannot enforce it on their soldiers. To its credit, the CF and Army leadership moved promptly and properly to ensure that discipline in the field was maintained.

But what seemed clear by late summer 2010 was that the Canadian Army's combat commitment in Afghanistan was going to end the next year. The Chief of the Land Staff, Lieutenant-General Andrew Leslie, stated publicly that 'no one has suggested to me that we are staying past 2011. As such we currently do not have any plans or even any line diagrams on a blank sheet of paper for post 2011. This is the will of Parliament.'[117] The parliamentary resolution of 2008 had directed that end date but also contained a very large loophole. The resolution had called for ending the combat commitment in Kandahar, not necessarily in all Afghanistan. In other words, the government could end the Kandahar mission but replace it with a role elsewhere in Afghanistan. If that loophole had been deliberately crafted, Prime Minister Harper did his very best through late 2009 and 2010 repeatedly to interpret the resolution to mean that Canada would completely end its military role in Afghanistan, including the battle group, military participation in the Provincial Reconstruction Team, and the OMLTs by the dates specified in the resolution. In November 2010, however, apparently facing strong pressure from the country's NATO allies, the Prime Minister completely reversed course and announced that Canada would keep trainers in Afghanistan but 'behind the wire' in non-combat roles until 2014. The Liberal opposition seemed willing to accept this continuation of the mission. How this shift in policy would play out was unclear, but Canada apparently would stay in Afghanistan.[118]

twelve

CONCLUSION

'This Government took office with a firm commitment to stand up for Canada,' Prime Minister Stephen Harper said in introducing his government's 'Canada First Defence Strategy' (CFDS) on May 12, 2008. He continued:

> Fulfilling this obligation means keeping our citizens safe and secure, defending our sovereignty, and ensuring that Canada can return to the international stage as a credible and influential country, ready to do its part. Rebuilding the Canadian Forces into a first-class, modern military is a fundamental requirement if we are to deliver on these goals ... Supported by predictable, long-term funding, the Strategy not only delivers increased security for Canadians, but also significant economic benefits for citizens across the country. By unveiling a detailed plan for the future replacement of key equipment fleets, we are providing Canadian industry the opportunity to more effectively meet defence procurement requirements, and to position themselves for global excellence.[1]

Brief and lacking much of the necessary detail as it was, scarcely meriting the name of a 'strategy,' the CFDS nonetheless committed the government to a host of acquisitions, including four CC-177 strategic lift aircraft, seventeen C-130J Hercules tactical lift aircraft, and sixteen Chinook helicopters, all of genuine usefulness for the Canadian Expeditionary Force Command and the Army. The CFDS also pledged that the Army was to receive a fleet of 2300 medium and heavy trucks and up to one hundred new Leopard C2A6 tanks, and there was a promise of a new fleet of land combat vehicles and systems. All this was promising indeed; so too was the pledge to increase the regular Canadian Forces to 70,000 and the reserves to 30,000, many of whom would be in the Land Forces.

The heart of the CFDS was the government's commitment to long-term and stable funding, intended as a twenty-year plan. When the Conservatives came to power in early 2006, the defence budget was some $14.5 billion. In May 2006 the new government stated it would 'increase the National Defence budget base by $5.3 billion over 5 years.' This meant that by 2011–12 defence spending would be approximately $20 billion, which, deducting the extraordinary costs of the Afghan War, it will almost certainly reach. (The main estimates for 2010–11, still including war costs, posited defence expenditures of $21.1 billion.)[2] The budget of February 2008 subsequently stated that beginning in 2011–12 the automatic annual increase in defence spending would be 2 per cent per year until 2028, a plan that suggested that by 2028 the defence budget would be some $28 billion, although the figure offered by Prime Minister Harper after his CFDS speech was $30 billion. Without question, the Harper pledge held out the prospect of a larger, stronger, and much better-equipped Canadian Forces and Army.[3] The difficulty, of course, was and is that no government can commit its successors to following a twenty-year plan. Global financial crises, political upheavals around the world and in Canada: all could conspire to reduce, or possibly increase, defence spending. Certainly there was nothing to suggest that if the Liberals, New Democrats, or Bloc Québécois formed a government on their own or in coalition that the Harper defence spending plans would remain intact.

And the Harper government itself was having difficulty meeting the fiscal problems caused by the 2009 recession. The defence equipment acquisitions announced so confidently in the Canada First Defence Strategy in 2008 were in many cases in process of being either reduced in quantity or cost, delayed, or shelved.[4] Events had conspired in 2010 to stall plans announced for 2028. That said, the minority Harper government continued to allocate more money to defence than many had believed possible.

Adding to the difficulties was the confusion in defence procurement, which has, if anything, worsened in the last several years in part because of the government's urgent need (and success) to re-equip the Canadian Forces so it could fight effectively in Afghanistan. The CF's procurement system remained short of project managers, and the dead weight of Public Works and government regional development policies continued to hang over every equipment acquisition. There was the regrettably strong opposition to the Department of National Defence in key agencies of government – in the Privy Council Office, the Prime Minister's Office, Foreign Affairs, Finance, and Public Works – opposition that focused on the huge demands for funding to purchase expensive equipment. How much better if the money could be spent on daycare or MPs' or public servants' pensions or subsidies to discourage tobacco growers – at least that seemed to be the attitude. To the credit of Harper and his finance minister, the urgent needs of the CF continued to be addressed, but no one could confidently predict the immediate, let alone the long-term, future. That hitherto supportive organizations such as the C.D. Howe Institute had begun to call for money-saving changes to CF pensions and for limits to military spending to a rate not exceeding inflation and population growth was a portent of change.

At a time of war and stress on the military's personnel and equipment, none of this makes any sense, but it is a clear indication of coming problems. The St Laurent government of the 1950s pushed defence spending to over 7 per cent of gross domestic product; the current government, for all its efforts, has raised defence spending to just under 1.2 per cent of GDP. The Conference of Defence Associations' financial analyst, Colonel Brian Macdonald, estimates that even with the projected growth, defence spending may fall below the present 1.2 per cent level in the next decade.[5]

As the list of cancelled, delayed, deferred, and stalled training and defence projects grew, so too did the delays in increasing CF regular and reserve personnel to achieve the numerical targets set by the CFDS. The pledge of 70,000 regulars and 30,000 reservists, itself rather less than the CF really needed, continued to be pushed further into the future. At the same time, the number of CF headquarters and their staffs continued to increase,[6] while strength at the sharp end held steady at best, leaving Canada with an increasingly fragile military. The number of combat arms personnel was much lower than needed, the number of infantry remaining especially short, and the Army was forced to continue its practice of cannibalizing one battalion to man the next. The rising rate of retirements of key personnel showed no sign of slow-ing, and many junior leaders were also opting out. The CF openly acknowledged that it was losing the race with the changing demographics of Canada as it tried to fill its ranks. There were still small numbers of visible minorities recruits and of men and women enlisting from the urban centres, which remained the drivers of Canada's population growth. The Maritimes cannot continue to carry the CF forever.

The immediate problems for the CF were pressing, not least for what the Chief of the Land Staff from 2006 to 2010, Lieutenant-General Andrew Leslie, bluntly called 'the hollow Army.' One report, signed by Leslie and leaked to Brian Stewart of the Canadian Broadcasting Corporation, stated that the Army 'is now operating beyond its capacity,' a direct result of the Afghan War. 'The Afghanistan mission is particularly taxing on Army capabilities and the current operations tempo is not sustainable,' Leslie's report said. His key concern was an 'Army leadership deficit,' as many officers and warrant officers left the Army, a loss compounded by a shortage of military trainers to ready troops for combat. The situation, in turn, was made more serious by the military's shortage of technicians. The Chief of the Defence Staff, General Walter Natynczyk, conceded that there were problems: 'It's tough right now because we don't have enough soldiers on the ground to do the job,' he said, adding that some in the military are tired: 'the senior NCOs and officers especially.' And then, as Stewart's article pointed out, there were problems in keeping the Army's equipment going. The Army recently estimated it would need $5 billion to spend on new armoured and transport vehicles, and a good part of that was simply to replace or repair equipment broken or worn out in Afghanistan. The government moved to meet this need in 2010. But Leslie's 'hollow Army' report revealed that an extraordinary 35 to 60 per cent of vehicles were off-road for repair at any one time – and there were not enough personnel to repair them.[7] These were serious problems that could only be resolved with a period of rest and recuperation for the Army, something that will be possible only after the withdrawal from Afghanistan.[8]

But there are positive signs. While some officers and warrants are leaving the Army, those who remain after their Afghan service have had their leadership tested in battle. Very simply, the Army leadership cadre for the next twenty years will be better prepared than at any time in the past half-century. At the same time, the war had turned the Army into one of the most digitally advanced in the world. General Leslie explained:

We're not perfect, but when you go into a brigade or battlegroup headquarters, it's crude in the sense that it is a rough wood building, but it closely resembles the bridge of The [USS] Enterprise [on *Star Trek*], where you have huge screens on which real-time feeds from UAVs or aircraft or helicopters are portrayed. Most of the communications happens digitally, with updates on positioning right down to the vehicle level, with information and secret reports being transmitted right down to combat team and platoon, with feedback and amendments happening automatically. The model for this is actually a combat information centre on a frigate. It is essentially the same approach with the same awareness, information feeds, sequencing and queuing of work and responsibilities. We've learned an enormous amount in the last three years. We're at the cutting edge right now.[9]

However, the impact of the war in Afghanistan on Canadians has had its consequences. First, the cost in killed and wounded, the expenditure of blood and treasure, the extraordinary wear and tear on equipment, have been high, and the war has been and continues to be unpopular even though support for the troops is unprecedented. Some critics of the war, especially those most strongly affected by the allegations that Canadians had handed over Taliban suspects to torture at Afghan government hands, talk about how people abroad ask what happened to the kinder, gentler Canada of the Chrétien/Axworthy years and frequently portray Canada as having lost influence in the world. Gerald Caplan, an NDP-leaning commentator on public affairs, noted: 'My country seems to be slipping away in front of my very eyes. Our proud identity, our cherished core values – never mind the vast gap between aspiration and achievement – are being turned upside down ... Peacekeeping is out, warriors are in. Preventing war is out, killing scumbags is in.' The distinguished writer Erna Paris said in the Ottawa *Citizen* at the end of 2009 that this moment 'may be seen by future historians as the marker moment when the fragile underpinnings of contemporary Canadian identity began to unravel.'[10] Maude Barlow, the National Chair of the Council of Canadians, added her voice to the lamentations in an article entitled 'Ashamed to Wear the Maple Leaf.' It is, she began, 'time to accept an unpleasant reality: Canada's international reputation as a progressive middle power is gone. Instead, our country is increasingly seen as a human rights-denying eco-outlaw that has lost its way and its special status as a standard bearer for a better world.

This change is largely the doing of Prime Minister Stephen Harper and the ideology that has motivated him and his mentors for decades.' She concluded: 'I am personally ashamed of my country as I travel internationally. In a world calling out for new models of justice, conflict resolution and environmental stewardship, Canada could be playing such a powerful role as it has done in the past. Stephen Harper with a majority frightens me.'[11]

Let us stand back a moment and analyse matters. First, Canada has been, is, and will remain a small nation that, to be blunt, does not matter very much in the great game of nations. We have been a good ally through the last century, doing our duty for the right causes and paying a heavy price for doing so. We have done peacekeeping well and persuaded ourselves that this military task said something important about our character, especially when we used it to contrast Canadians' kinder, gentler ways with the more aggressive and bumptious actions of our great neighbour to the south. There is some truth in this self-characterization, but it is not ordinarily recognized abroad as anything more than preening. We are no moral superpower now – and never were except in our own minds.

The Afghan 'torture' affair, which was treated with extraordinary seriousness in Canada in 2009–10, had little to do with torture and much to do with political and bureaucratic spinning. The major case on display involved a suspect Taliban taken prisoner by Canadian troops in 2006 and handed over to Afghan security authorities, who hit the man with shoes, an Islamic insult, and then beat him. Whatever else this was, it was not torture, and the Canadian soldiers duly took the prisoner back. No one suggested that the Canadian military tortured anyone or behaved with anything other than exemplary correctness. To be sure, the Canadian government did not act so well. The defence minister dumped on the Foreign Affairs official who testified about alleged torture, the government spinning madly to keep up with the opposition that disguised its obvious desire to get Canada out of Afghanistan now and not in 2011 behind holier-than-thou execrations of the government and pious assertions that they really supported the troops.

Canada's reputation has not been harmed by this incident, except in the eyes of those who never wanted the nation to be in Afghanistan or Kandahar or to cooperate militarily with the United States in the first place. The government's tactics have been clumsy, but reputation exists in the eye of the beholder. Friends and enemies abroad, if they knew anything at all of this story, must have been greatly puzzled by the clamour in the media here. Curiously, many who go abroad or talk to visitors from Europe or Asia hear a different story. 'Canada's back,' people say. The Harper government, building on the lead given by Paul Martin's administration, has begun to rebuild the Canadian Forces, buying equipment, propounding a defence strategy, and trying to recruit more men and women. The defence budget is up by some 50 per cent in a few years, and, indeed, people notice – allies in NATO, for one, and in the United States for another. 'Friends that have stood by us' – that was how most U.S. soldiers and officials looked at Canada now.[12]

Canadian soldiers, their casualties regrettably heavy in relative terms, have performed well in action in Afghanistan. The government spent billions to ensure that the troops had everything they needed – no more unarmoured Iltis jeeps – by way of specialized equipment. Canada will almost certainly have left the battlefield by the end of 2011, but the Canadian Forces have re-established their military credibility there. The sorry tale of Canada's Army as peacekeeper and nothing else – the reality of the 'Can'tbats,' as the British called the Canadian battalions serving in Former Yugoslavia in the mid-1990s – is gone, except in the minds of the critics of anything and everything military. This matters.[13]

But the mindset of most Canadians remains fixated on peacekeeping as the only role, the correct role, for Canada and the Canadian Forces. In that sense, Gerald Caplan is correct. The public views the Afghan War as an aberration. This was immediately apparent in 2006 as Canadian casualties in Kandahar began to increase. 'We have strayed from our traditional role as peacekeepers,' said one letter writer in the *Toronto Star*.[14] Another writer from Vancouver, seemingly unaware that Canada had participated in the Great War, the Second World War, Korea, the Gulf War, the Kosovo intervention, among others, observed that 'Our role in the world has always been one of peacekeeping. How and why did we deviate from this honourable role?'[15]* Writing in Toronto's *Now* weekly, columnist Paul Weinberg noted that Canadians are having difficulty 'trying to absorb the sudden historic shift in mandate introduced by stealth by the Liberals.' In the fiftieth anniversary year of peacekeeping, he

---

* Peacekeeping, wrote Desmond Morton, 'is the great morale builder. It is the only thing the public think the military are any good for. It is a distraction from the military role, but it is unfortunately the one every one out there will put as priority one.' 'What Is to Be Done? Canada's Military Security in the 1990s,' *Peace and Security* (Summer 1990): 5.

wrote in 2005, 'our troops are knee-deep in U.S.-controlled counter-insurgency' in Afghanistan.[16] A letter writer from Victoria echoed and expanded that theme, arguing that the role of Canadians in Afghanistan is 'to support an interventionist American foreign policy in order to create an environment safe for the unimpeded exploitation of Central Asian energy resources.'[17] And New Democratic Party leader Jack Layton, and indeed all his Members of Parliament, have never failed to refer to Canada's 'traditional' role as a peacekeeper when wondering why the nation was involved in Kandahar. The NDP's then-defence critic Bill Blaikie said, 'I do not think we have paid sufficient attention to the departure or the significance of the change in the role of the Canadian military that our activity in Afghanistan represents.'[18]*

Clearly, large numbers of Canadians have come to believe that traditional United Nations peacekeeping is their métier.[19] Peacekeeping is portrayed on Canadian coins and bills, and the peacekeeping monument in Ottawa is the only government military memorial to have been erected since the Second World War. The very idea of peacekeeping has its place in the nation's values, in its sense of itself: 'Canada: The World's Peacekeeper,' a CBC News online article trumpeted.[20] 'Peacekeeping is an important aspect of Canada's national heritage,' says the Department of Foreign Affairs on its website, 'and a reflection of our fundamental beliefs.'[21] More popularly put, 'Canadians keep the peace; Americans fight wars': this Canadian myth now appears to be accepted as gospel truth from St John's to Vancouver. Canadians proudly cite Lester B. Pearson's Nobel Peace Prize for his role at the United Nations in stabilizing the Suez Crisis of 1956. They look at the Nobel Peace Prize that went to United Nations peacekeepers in 1988 and say, loudly, that it was really for Canada's soldiers. They assume that, in contrast to their superpower neighbour, they are uniquely moral in global affairs. We are the good guys in white hats or, at least, blue berets. Canadians are nature's middlemen, innately neutral, helping to bring peace to the globe.[22] If only the Americans would let us.

---

* In an online discussion, *Globe and Mail* reporter Michael Den Tandt, just back from Afghanistan, noted that 'Canadians have developed a comforting mythology over the years that says the American military are warlike and aggressive, whereas our soldiers are peacekeepers. This is nonsense,' he said. The U.S. in Afghanistan is doing humanitarian work just like the Canadians. 'By the same token, Canadian troops are deployed in an offensive role, not just defensive ... That means shooting and killing. That's part of what soldiers – all soldiers, including Canada's – do.' Online discussion, www.globeandmail.ca, March 1, 2006.

It was perceptions like these that had led Prime Minister Paul Martin to think of sending Canadian troops to Darfur in 2005 and some in the Departments of Foreign Affairs and National Defence to look to the Congo in 2009 and 2010 as a locus for post-Afghan deployment. That Darfur and the Congo are horrible human tragedies is beyond doubt, and more needs to be done to end the horror. But not by Canadian troops. Canada is a white, Western nation, and this is not a plus in either the Congo or Darfur. Canada's troops require the infrastructure and logistics of Western armies – helicopters, trucks and armoured vehicles, gasoline and maintenance, food and reasonable levels of accommodation, all operating from secure bases. This was available in Afghanistan because the United States created and operated a huge base in Kandahar on which the CF could piggyback. But there are no such bases in the deserts of Darfur or the jungles of the Congo, and the CF is too small and too cash-poor to sustain a small Canadian force. And without such bases there is no way to maintain a Canadian contingent or, just as important, to extricate it in the event of major troubles. Those who assume that peacekeeping is by definition always bloodless do not know their history – Canada has lost some 122 personnel on its peacekeeping missions[23] – or understand the conditions in the bloody African conflicts where peacekeeping troops have been repeatedly attacked. The best Canadian aid would be the provision of equipment – as the CF has already done to help African Union peacekeepers function in Darfur – or money.[24]

Canada is a nation without much sense of its history, but it is nonetheless surprising that the events of the last half-century have been so misunderstood. Major-General (ret'd) Lewis MacKenzie correctly told CBC Radio's *Cross Country Checkup* that Canada was 'never a peacekeeping nation. We aren't and we never will be. At the height of our peacekeeping reputation in the '60s, '70s, and '80s, when we had about 1,500 troops in the Golan Heights, Cyprus, etc., we had 10,000 troops as part of the NATO force armed with nuclear weapons, surface-to-surface missiles, F-104s, air-to-ground missiles, waiting for the Soviet hordes to come across the border.'[25] At the same time, much of Canada's air force patrolled the north against Soviet bombers and participated in NORAD, an air defence alliance with the United States. Peacekeeping was a sideline, nothing more, but it captured the public's mind. The Afghan War and the revelation that Canadians could and would fight well dealt the peacekeeping mythology a mighty blow, but there can be no doubt that it lives on.

The implications of these attitudes for the Canadian Forces are clear enough. Either the military buys into the peacekeeping mythos, as some of its soldiers do, or it tries to stay a professional military, as do most officers and other ranks. There are ways to square the circle, to be sure. A professional army can do anything from the most benign blue beret peacekeeping to fighting a war; a peacekeeping military can only do peacekeeping; and someday the public is bound to recognize the benefits in having a real army at hand. Some Canadians – those who support the Afghan War – already have. And the soldiers? The Hillier approach has probably flushed the peacekeeper-only soldiers out. The Canadian Army once again has become a truly professional military, and the Harper government has provided the equipment to foster this approach for the next few decades.

This does not mean that Canada should not do peacekeeping when the conditions are right. The government should be willing to offer military assistance to peace operations if key conditions are met first. There must be a strong political will to act at the United Nations Security Council. The host nation(s) must agree to accept foreign soldiers on their soil and demonstrably want to resolve the crisis. There must be a clear exit strategy or a withdrawal date stated in advance by the UN or by the Canadian Parliament. The CF must be able to do the job, and the mission must serve Canada's national interests. Above all, the troops must always be deployed with the equipment, training, and in the required numbers to achieve the operation's ends. Only if those conditions are met should the government of Canada ever send its men and women abroad for peacekeeping.[26] The critical test for every government is to be able to resist a public clamour to participate if the conditions are not met, as they could not have been for either Darfur or the Congo. Canada's professional army will always be able to do a peacekeeping job if these conditions are satisfied – and anything else it might be tasked to do.

What might that be? First, there is no requirement that Canada do anything. We need not fight another war simply to employ the Army, anymore than we must take on a peacekeeping mission. An army can sit and train and do so for years without losing its edge. Second, it would help in determining what the country was to do with its army if it knew what it wanted to do. The 'Canada First Defence Strategy' declared the basic task of the Canadian Forces to be the defence of Canada. That is the correct priority, and there will be challenges aplenty to our sovereignty in the coming years. But what else must the CF do? What role should Canada play in the hemisphere, in Asia, in the world? Does Canada have an obligation to do its share of the global heavy lifting that is often required? What is the foreign policy into which the military must fit? The reality is that the government has no idea what Canadian foreign policy is or should be, beyond the realization, as Eugene Lang and Eric Morse noted, 'that Canada is incapable militarily, diplomatically, and politically of acting outside a multilateral coalition.'[27] That is certainly so; thus the first requirement is that the government know what it wants – and what it does not want – to do. Once that is decided, the Army must prepare itself to carry out the tasks, whatever they may be. And if the government cannot decide or leaves matters up to events to determine its course of action (which is, after all, the Canadian way), then the Army must be flexible and must train for a range of contingencies ranging from benign peacekeeping through peacemaking and peace enforcement to counterinsurgency operations and all-out war. That is pretty much what the Canadian Army has been doing and likely will continue to do because that is what professional soldiers do. They train to be ready for whatever their government orders. They present their hypotheses of future actions to the politicians and, depending on how persuasive they are in making their case, the government buys them equipment and adjusts their personnel numbers. If they get it right, they do well on operations; if they get it wrong, large numbers of Canada's youth will die. Our record of forecasting has not been stellar, but happily Canadian soldiers have proved able to adapt and improvise and fight well if they are properly led.

The key is professionalism. The argument of this book is that a professional army is a necessity for Canada if we wish to prevent high casualty tolls, and nothing that has happened in the decade since *Canada's Army* first appeared has changed this situation. Instead, the Afghanistan War confirmed the requirement for professionalism, and the nation's soldiers demonstrated this professionalism in action, as chapter 11 has shown. That the Army survived the bleak years of the 1990s verged on the miraculous, and this was due to the professionalism of its leaders. Now Canadian soldiers and the government must work together to enhance the professionalism of the Army and to ensure that the next time we fight we will again do well.

Military professionals are experts with specialized and superior knowledge and skill, mastered through continuous study and practice and capable of being tested against measurable standards. Their task is the management of violence, the ordered application of force. In wartime, this expertise means learning how to apply technical skills on the battlefield, how to employ tactics and strategy to defeat the enemy. In peacetime, military expertise requires that soldiers study and draw the appropriate lessons from military history, identify and master the use of the weapons and equipment needed for future conflict, and prepare a doctrine based on those weapons and on the capabilities of likely enemies.

Military professionals belong to a corporate culture and believe that their members form a group separate and distinct from civil society. Just as doctors are trained to believe they have sacred obligations, so soldiers believe that only they are qualified to judge the competence of those in the military profession. The military has its own educational system and controls its content, it has its own regulations to govern promotion, and it has its own hierarchy and traditions. As a corporate body, soldiers also have their own code of ethical conduct, and they must follow it in their personal and military behaviour.

Finally, the military profession has a sense of responsibility to the state. As a responsible professional, the soldier serves the state and, because the soldier controls deadly force, this responsibility is all important. In a democracy like Canada, the soldier accepts, acknowledges, and understands that the political power has the supreme authority and the ultimate responsibility. The government lays down policy, and the soldier follows it. In return for this unquestioning obedience, which may involve risk to life, the government has the duty to produce sensible policies to ensure the nation's security. The army can agree or disagree about these policies, but it has the responsibility to obey its political masters and not to assume that its judgment should supersede that of the elected leaders. A responsible soldier will offer advice, but will accept the decisions of the government; if the soldier cannot do so, the duty is to resign. Cooperation and trust are part and parcel of a responsible soldier's role, in other words. Responsibility also implies that the military professional owes an obligation to offer selfless service and to care for the troops and the national interest.

The United States Military Academy summed up its concept of professionalism in its motto 'Duty, Honor, Country.' The Royal Military College of Canada's motto is 'Truth, Duty, Valour,' and the present Canadian Forces' watchwords are 'Duty, Integrity, Discipline, Honour.'[7] All these mottoes express much the same sentiments, though it is likely significant and disheartening that the Canadian formulations omitted 'Country.' A Canadian military professional cannot share the public's angst about Canadian identity and the internecine Quebec-Canada struggles. The professional's task, the army's task, is to serve Canada, first and last.[28]

This book has tried to demonstrate why military professionalism has not been a hardy perennial in Canada. Before the Great War, the concept scarcely existed within the Permanent Force, and it was scorned by the ministers and the people, both of whom believed devoutly in the Militia myth. During the 1914–18 war, professionalism gradually developed in the crucible of battle, and, by the time of the Hundred Days, the Canadian Corps was as efficient an army as existed anywhere. In the interwar years a few officers struggled to keep up with their profession, but the state did not keep its share of the bargain by providing the necessary tools to implement a sound defence policy. It took time and cost lives, therefore, before professionalism could develop again in the Second World War. By 1945, however, the First Canadian Army had become a superior and professional force, 'the best little army in the world,' as Lieutenant-Colonel John English called it. The heyday of post-1945 professionalism unquestionably came in the period from the creation of NATO and the Korean War through to the mid-1960s. The army was well led, well trained, and well equipped, confident in its leaders and its prowess. But once again the government failed to keep its part of the bargain,[29] and unification, budget cuts, personnel reductions, bilingualism, social engineering, and a failure to renew equipment gradually broke down morale and sapped professionalism. The crisis of the 1990s did not have to occur as a result of Somalia, but it was bound to happen.

The crisis affected the Land Force Reserve too. No one any longer believes the myth that the Militia alone can defend Canada, but the Army Reserve has proved itself by the way it has provided its soldiers to backfill regular force units in operations ranging from Former Yugoslavia to Afghanistan. With additional training before deployment, reservists performed as well in action as regulars. The only problem is that there are not enough reservists to form the basis for a mobilization, should that become necessary once more, nor enough to allow Militia units to undertake proper training on their own. The government's bargain with the citizen soldier is less binding than that with the professional, but our political leaders have failed to fulfil their obligation to provide a sensible policy and the means to carry it out. The nation needs an Army Reserve to be the military footprint in communities large and small; it needs a Militia to provide the units that will be necessary if Canada ever needs to fight in a large war.

In this age of global terrorism, the Army must confront the idea of wars abroad and troubles at home. The ever-increasing lethality of the battlefield and the constant growth in intelligence-gathering and -processing capacity have changed the way soldiers operate now and in the future. The requirement for an educated officer corps and soldiery is now an imperative. Technical training is essential, continuous learning is necessary, as is the ability of officers and soldiers to understand the world around them. Not many Canadian soldiers will know how to speak Pashtun or Dari if Canada returns its combat forces to Afghanistan after 2011, for example, but it is not too much to expect that officers posted to Kandahar have read and understood histories of Afghanistan, past and present, as well as military studies of counter-insurgency tactics. The requirement for a well-educated, thinking Army is clear.

None of this will matter, however, if Canadian governments shirk their duty or neglect the national interest. The basic task of government must be to protect the Canadian people and the nation's territory and to maintain domestic order. We also have the obligation to assist in the defence of North America, the Western hemisphere, and our treaty allies. As a democratic state, Canada also has the duty – if it chooses to accept it – to work with its friends to advance the cause of freedom abroad, even though such actions will sometimes cause divisions at home. Canada need not enter into optional conflicts; protecting our people, territory, and our immediate neighbours, however, is not an option, and the government must always maintain sufficient force to be able to do so. It goes without saying that at some points in Canada's very recent past, these requirements have been neglected. Our governments cannot forget about them again in the globalized world of terror in the twenty-first century.

A well-trained, well-equipped army remains the nation's insurance policy.

We pay the premiums to achieve the protection it can provide when needed. If there is any lesson in our history, no one should doubt that a Canadian army will once more be needed to fight to protect this nation. Far better to have the skilled professionals on hand and a trained militia when that eventuality occurs than to try yet again to create them from nothing. On the new battle-fields of this century, nothing less will suffice.

NOTES

1 The Militia Myth: Canadian Arms to Confederation

1 George T. Denison, *Soldiering in Canada* (Toronto, 1900), 88.

2 Egerton Ryerson, *The Loyalists of America and Their Times: From 1620 to 1816* (Toronto, 1880), 2: 471. See also S.F. Wise, *God's Peculiar Peoples* (Ottawa, 1993), chap. 8.

3 Quoted in J. Mackay Hitsman, *The Incredible War of 1812* (Toronto, 1965), 93.

4 See Carl Benn, *Historic Fort York, 1793–1993* (Toronto, 1993).

5 Quoted ibid., 93, 137; J.L.H. Henderson, ed., *John Strachan: Documents and Opinions* (Toronto, 1969), 32ff.

6 H.P. Biggar, *The Works of Samuel de Champlain*, vol. 2: *1608–1613* (Toronto, 1925), 98–9.

7 Quoted in Hitsman, *The Incredible War of 1812*, 138. See Carl Benn, *The Iroquois in the War of 1812* (Toronto, 1998).

8 The usually sensible J.R. Miller argues in *Skyscrapers Hide the Heavens: A History of Indian-White Relations in Canada* (Toronto, 1991), 60–1, that the ethnocentric British and French simply failed to understand the ritual significance of the aboriginals' practices of torture and cannibalism. Moreover, he says more usefully, both European powers encouraged scalping by offering bounties.

9 G.F.G. Stanley, *New France: The Last Phase, 1744–1760* (Toronto, 1968), 147ff. In this book I have chosen to use the spelling 'guerilla.'

10 Quoted in D. Gillmor and P. Turgeon, *Canada: A People's History* (Toronto, 2000), 1: 76. Compare P.M. Malone, *The Skulking Way of War: Technology and Tactics among the New England Indians* (Baltimore, 1991).

11 Ian McCulloch, '"Within Ourselves …" The Development of British Light Infantry in North America during the Seven Years' War,' *Canadian Military History* 7 (spring 1998), 41ff.

12 See W.J. Eccles, *Canada under Louis XIV, 1663–1701* (Toronto, 1964), 187ff.; Jay Cassel, 'The Militia Legend: Canadians at War, 1665–1760,' in Yves Tremblay, ed., *Canadian Military History since the 17th Century* (Ottawa, 2001), 59ff.

13 C.P. Stacey, *Quebec, 1759* (Toronto, 1959), 146–7. Montcalm could have learned, for many of the officers in French regiments were *Canadiens* of the *noblesse*. See Dale Miquelon, *New France, 1701–1744: 'A Supplement to Europe'* (Toronto, 1987), 240–1. Montcalm's remains, held by the Ursulines in Quebec, were reinterred in the fall of 2001 with those of a thousand French and British soldiers at the cemetery of the Quebec General Hospital.

14 On the Seven Years' War and the battle for Quebec, see the splendid maps in the *Historical Atlas of Canada*, vol. 1 (Toronto, 1987), plates 42–3.

15 Fred Anderson, *Crucible of War: The Seven Years' War and the Fate of Empire in British North America, 1754–1766* (New York, 2000), 344.

16 William Gray, *Soldiers of the King: The Upper Canadian Militia, 1812–1815* (Erin, Ont., 1995), 26–7. Gray's book of facts on the Upper Canadian militia is very useful.

17 The most recent account is Barry Wilson, *Benedict Arnold: A Traitor in Our Midst* (Montreal, 2001), chaps. 7–9.

18 W.B. Turner, *British Generals in the War of 1812* (Montreal, 1999), 28. See also *Ten Years of Upper Canada in War and Peace: Being the Ridout Letters* (Toronto, 1890), 128; Jean Pariseau and Serge Bernier, *Les Canadiens français et le bilinguisme dans les forces armées canadiennes*, tome 1: *1763–1969* (Ottawa, 1987), chap. 1; and J.R. Grodzinski, 'The Project of Conquering This Province Is Premature: Battle of the Chateauguay, 26 October 1813,' *Army Doctrine and Training Bulletin* 1 (November 1998): 28ff. The best account of Châteauguay and Crysler's Farm is Donald Graves, *Field of Glory: The Battle of Crysler's Farm, 1813* (Toronto, 1999). See also the entry on de Salaberry in the *Dictionary of Canadian Biography*, vol. 6 (Toronto, 1987), 341ff.

19 Quoted in Hitsman, *The Incredible War of 1812*, 162–3.

20 Pierre Berton, *Flames across the Border, 1813–1814* (Toronto, 1981), 218ff. An early history is Benjamin Sulte, *Histoire de la milice canadienne-française, 1760–1897* (Montreal, 1897).

21 J. Mackay Hitsman, *Safeguarding Canada, 1763–1871* (Toronto, 1968), 79–81.

22 Ibid.; Turner, *British Generals in the War of 1812*, n. 48, 195–6.

23 Donald Graves, *Where Right and Glory Lead! The Battle of Lundy's Lane, 1814* (Toronto, 1997), 68–9.

24 George Sheppard, *Plunder, Profit, and Paroles: A Social History of the War of 1812 in Upper Canada* (Montreal, 1994), 5. See also Jane Errington, *The Lion, the Eagle, and Upper Canada* (Kingston, 1987), chap. 4.

25 Turner, *British Generals in the War of 1812*, 71.

26 Hitsman, *The Incredible War of 1812*, 239.

27 Sheppard, *Plunder, Profit, and Paroles*, 95–7.

28 David Facey-Crowther, *The New Brunswick Militia, 1787–1867* (Fredericton, 1990), 27–8, 32–3.

29 The British raised two battalions of Royal Canadian Volunteers in 1795. These 'provincial corps' were regulars committed to the defence of Upper and Lower Canada. The Volunteers were disbanded in 1802. See Carl Benn, 'The Volunteers,' *The Beaver* (June–July 1999), 33ff.

30 Facey-Crowther, *The New Brunswick Militia, 1787–1867*, 66ff., 111–12.

31 Hitsman, *The Incredible War of 1812*, 110–11.

32 For a graphic presentation of the campaigns of 1812–14, see *Historical Atlas of Canada*, vol. 2 (Toronto, 1993), plate 22.

33 Hitsman, *Safeguarding Canada*, 112.

34 Allan Greer, *The Patriots and the People: The Rebellion of 1837 in Rural Lower Canada* (Toronto, 1993), 301ff.

35 See Donald Graves, *Guns across the River: The Battle of the Windmill, 1838* (Np, 2001).

36 See Wayne Kelly, '"Black Troops to Keep an Intelligent People in Awe!" The Coloured Companies of the Upper Canadian Militia, 1837–1850' (MA thesis, York University, 1996); Wayne Kelly, 'Canada's Black Defenders,' *The Beaver*, April–May 1997, 31–4.

37 Arthur Doughty, ed., *The Elgin–Grey Papers, 1846–1852* (Ottawa, 1937), 1: 126.

38 Ibid., 1: 268.

39 Quoted in Hitsman, *Safeguarding Canada*, 158. Much of the material here on the post-Rebellions period is based on Hitsman's fine account and on C.P. Stacey, *Canada and the British Army, 1846–1871* (Toronto, 1963), chap. 5ff.

40 A perfect example, expressed in tones that suggest politicking was completely natural, can be found in Denison, *Soldiering in Canada*, chap. 4ff.

41 B. Tennyson and Roger Sarty, *Guardian of the Gulf: Sydney, Cape Breton, and the Atlantic Wars* (Toronto, 2000), 78ff.

42 Denison, *Soldiering in Canada*, 169; Facey-Crowther, *The New Brunswick Militia, 1787–1867*, 109.

43 Hitsman, *Safeguarding Canada*, 180.

44 J.B. Wilson, '"That Vast Experiment": The New Brunswick Militia's 1865 Camp of Instruction,' *Canadian Military History* 6 (autumn 1997): 39ff.

45 Facey-Crowther, *The New Brunswick Militia, 1787–1867*, 121ff.

46 Denison, *Soldiering in Canada*, 98.

47 *Historical Atlas of Canada*, 2: plate 24, shows the British military presence – and its monetary costs – in British North America to 1871.

48 W.T. Barnard, *The Queen's Own Rifles of Canada, 1860–1960* (Toronto, 1960), 17–18.

49 Brian Reid, '"Prepare for Cavalry!" The Battle of Ridgeway,' in Donald Graves, ed., *Fighting for Canada: Seven Battles, 1758–1945* (Toronto, 2000), 166.

50 Douglas McCalla, 'Upper Canadians and Their Guns: An Exploration via Country Store Accounts, 1808–61' (unpublished paper, 2000), suggests that, for farmers by mid-century, 'firing a gun was an occasional more than a routine part of life.' How much more occasional was it for urban residents? It should not be surprising that the militia fired off their ammunition quickly.

51 Quoted in Reid, '"Prepare for Cavalry,"' 177. The account in Barnard, *The Queen's Own Rifles of Canada, 1860–1960*, 21–3, sees no sign of a precipitate retreat by the Queen's Own. Desmond Morton, *The Canadian General: Sir William Otter* (Toronto, 1974), 24ff., is a balanced account focused on the adjutant of the Queen's Own.

52 Reid, '"Prepare for Cavalry,"' 183.

2 Making an Army: Beginnings

1 Quoted in H.V. Nelles, *The Art of Nation-Building: Pageantry and Spectacle at Quebec's Tercentary* (Toronto, 1990), 210.

2 See Joseph Lehmann, *The Model Major-General: A Biography of Field-Marshal Lord Wolseley* (Boston, 1964), chap. 6.

3 A.B. McCullough, 'Gunner Jingo: Thomas Bland Strange, 1831–1925,' *Alberta History* 48 (winter 2000): 2ff.

4 See R.A. Preston, *Canada's RMC: A History of the Royal Military College* (Toronto, 1969).

5 Stephen Harris, *Canadian Brass: The Making of a Professional Army, 1860–1939* (Toronto, 1988), 23–4.

6 Walter Stewart Collection, Walter Stewart Diary, March 30, 1885 (available at www.mala.bc.ca).

7 Quoted in Bob Beal and Rod Macleod, *Prairie Fire: The 1885 North-West Rebellion* (Edmonton, 1984), 174.

8 Desmond Morton and R.H. Roy, *Telegrams of the Northwest Campaign, 1885* (Toronto, 1972), 53.

9 Ibid., xxx–xxxi.

10 Ibid., li.

11 Stewart Diary, May 9, 1885.

12 Ibid., May 12, 1885. The commander of A Battery with Middleton, Capt. James Peters, took photographs of the campaign, apparently the first combat photographs by a Canadian. See O. Cooke and P. Robertson, 'James Peters, Military Photography and the Northwest Campaign, 1885,' *Canadian Military History* 9 (winter 2000): 23ff.

13 See Beal and Macleod, *Prairie Fire*, 258ff.; George Denison, *Soldiering in Canada* (Toronto, 1900), chap. 23; Stewart Diary, May 11, 1885.

14 R.G. Haycock, *Sam Hughes: The Public Career of a Controversial Canadian, 1885–1916* (Waterloo, 1986), 18.

15 Harris, *Canadian Brass*, 27.

16 Desmond Morton, *The Canadian General: Sir William Otter* (Toronto, 1974), 142.

17 Roger Sarty, *Silent Sentry: A Military and Political History of Canadian Coast Defence, 1860–1945* (Toronto, 1982), 61ff.

18 Harris, *Canadian Brass*, 28ff.

19 Between 1904 and 1908 British officers and officials concerned themselves with Canada's defences against the United States and the unhappy state of the militia. See Public Record Office (PRO), London, War Office Records, WO106/40-B1-8, Lt-Col. H.J. Foster, 'A Study of the Strategical Considerations Affecting the Invasion of Canada by the United States,' 1904; PRO, Cabinet Records, CAB 5/102918, CID 24C and 25C, June 1905; WO 106/40-B1-20, 'The Conditions of a War between the British Empire and the United States,' January 1908. I am indebted to Dr Roger Sarty for drawing these documents to my attention.

20 See Ian McCulloch, 'Yukon Field Force, 1898–1900,' *The Beaver*, October–November 1997, 4ff.

21 See Carman Miller, *Painting the Map Red: Canada and the South African War, 1899–1902* (Montreal, 1993), chap. 3; P. Stevens and J. Saywell, eds., *Lord Minto's Canadian Papers* (Toronto, 1981), xxxiv ff.

22 For an account of PEI N/S Georgina Pope, see B. Beck and A. Townshend, 'The Island's Florence Nightingale,' *The Island* 34 (fall/winter 1993): 1ff.

23 National Archives of Canada (NA), J.S. Willison Papers, C.F. Hamilton to Willison, November 11, 1899.

24 Miller's is by far the best account of the composition of the RCR and subsequent contingents.

25 Tom Wallace Papers, Tom to Mother, October 27, 1899. (In possession of Dr W.R. Young, to whom I am most grateful.)

26 Quoted in Pierre Berton, *Marching as to War: Canada's Turbulent Years, 1899–1953* (Toronto, 2001), 35.

27 NA, G.R.D. Lyon Papers, Diary, November 2, 1899.

28 C.F. Hamilton, quoted in J.L. Granatstein and David Bercuson, *War and Peacekeeping: From South Africa to the Gulf – Canada's Limited Wars* (Toronto, 1991), 50.

29 Wallace Papers, Tom to Len, January 7, 1990.

30 Brian Reid, *Our Little Army in the Field: The Canadians in South Africa, 1899–1902* (St Catharines, 1996), is the best account of Canadian actions in South Africa.

31 Directorate of History, National Defence Headquarters, 77/559, Diary of J.A. Perkins, February 28, 1900 [mistakenly entered as February 8].

32 The Dutton Advance Collection, Douglas McPherson to Mamie, March 3, 1900 (available at www.mala.bc.ca).

33 Diary of J.A. Perkins, February 28, 1900.

34 NA, F.S. Lee Papers, Lee to parents, February 28, 1900.

35 Quoted in C. Pulsifer with H. Wright, '"It's just like the resurrection": The Boer Surrender to the Canadians at Paardeberg,' *Canadian Military History* 9 (winter 2000): 49. Berton, *Marching as to War*, 49ff., somehow gets the Paardeberg story wrong.

36 S.M. Brown, *With the Royal Canadians* (Toronto, 1900), 223.

37 Morton, *Canadian General*, 201.

38 See Stevens and Saywell, *Lord Minto's Canadian Papers*, 233ff.

39 For a sample of the strained relations between Otter and his 2 i/c, Major Lawrence Buchan, see Serge Durflinger, 'Otter's Wound and Other Matters: The "Debate" between ... Otter and ... Buchan,' *Canadian Military History* 7 (autumn 1998): 55ff.

40 Willison Papers, Hamilton to Willison, May 25, 1900.

41 Quoted in Granatstein and Bercuson, *War and Peacekeeping*, 76.

42 On the Strathconas, see *Strathcona's Horse: South Africa, 1900–1901* (Calgary, 2000); Samuel Steele, *Forty Years in Canada* (Toronto, 1972); and R. Stewart, *Sam Steele: Lion of the Frontier* (Toronto, 1979).

43 The best account of Leliefontein is by Brian Reid '"For God's sake ... save your guns!" Action at Leliefontein, 7 November 1900,' in Donald Graves, ed., *Fighting for Canada: Seven Battles, 1758–1945* (Toronto, 2000), chap. 4.

44 Morton, *Canadian General*, 221.

45 John A. English, *National Policy and the Americanization of the Canadian Military* (Toronto, 2001), 7.

46 Berton, *Marching as to War*, 78; Harris, *Canadian Brass*, 66ff.

47 See Stevens and Saywell, *Lord Minto's Canadian Papers*, 474ff.

48 PRO, Cabinet Records, Cab5/10298, 'The Militia Act, 1904,' January 25, 1904.

49 There is a succinct account in Desmond Morton, *A Military History of Canada* (Toronto, 1992), 122ff. See also Mark Moss, *Manliness and Militarism: Educating Young Boys in Ontario for War* (Toronto, 2001).

50 Ibid., 146.

51 See Roger Sarty, *The Maritime Defence of Canada* (Toronto, 1996), 31ff.; Barry Gough and R. Sarty, 'Sailors and Soldiers: The Royal Navy, the Canadian Forces and the Defence of Atlantic Canada, 1890–1918,' in M. Hadley et al., eds., *A Nation's Navy: In Quest of Canadian Naval Identity* (Montreal, 1996), 116ff.

52 The British nonetheless created a Dominions' Section in the Directorate of Staff Duties. See R.A. Preston, *Canada and 'Imperial Defense'* (Toronto, 1967), 458–61.

53 Harris, *Canadian Brass*, 35ff.

54 See Haycock, *Sam Hughes*, 155ff.

55 Glimpses of militia efficiency can be found in John Swettenham, *McNaughton*, vol. 1: *1887–1939* (Toronto, 1968), 21ff.; Daniel Dancocks, *Sir Arthur Currie: A Biography* (Toronto, 1985), 17ff.

56 David Love, *'A Call to Arms': The Organization and Administration of Canada's Military in World War One* (Winnipeg, 1999), 37ff.

57 See Jean Pariseau et Serge Bernier, *Les canadiens français et le bilingualisme dans les forces armées canadiennes*, tome 1: *1763–1969* (Ottawa, 1987), chap. 2.

58 Desmond Morton, 'French Canada and the Canadian Militia, 1868–1914,' *Social History* 3 (1969): 35.

59 Desmond Morton, *Ministers and Generals: Politics and the Canadian Militia, 1868–1904* (Toronto, 1970), 49–50.

60 Preston, *Canada's RMC*, 58–62, 69–70; Serge Bernier, 'A Century of Copping Out: The Canadian Government and the Francophones in Canada's Armed Forces (1867–1967),' in *The Army and the Nation* (Gagetown, NB, 1998), F4-2/5.

61 Morton and Roy, *Telegrams of the Northwest Campaign*, lxxviii–lxxix; Beal and Macleod, *Prairie Fire*, 281–2.

62 Desmond Morton, 'French Canada and War, 1868–1917: The Military Background to the Conscription Crisis of 1917,' in J.L. Granatstein and R. Cuff, eds., *War and Society in North America* (Toronto, 1971), 90–1. A useful analysis of the social composition of the Quebec militia is in J.Y. Gravel, *L'Armée au Québec* (Montreal, 1974).

63 R.A. Rutherdale, 'The Home Front: Consensus and Conflict in Lethbridge, Guelph and Trois-Rivières during the Great War' (PhD dissertation, York University, 1993), 35–7.

64 Bernier, 'A Century of Copping Out,' F4-2/5; Morton, 'French Canada and War,' 93.

3 A Militia under Arms: Sam Hughes's Army

1 Ralph Connor, *The Major* (Toronto, 1929), 338.

2 See Daphne Reid, ed., *The Great War and Canadian Society: An Oral History* (Toronto, 1978), chap. 5; Daniel Dancocks, *Welcome to Flanders Fields* (Toronto, 1989), 32ff.

3 Ronald Haycock, 'The Proving Ground: Sam Hughes and the Boer War,' *Journal of Canadian Studies* 16 (fall–winter 1981): 14ff.

4 See *Official History of the Canadian Forces in the Great War, 1914–1919*, vol. 1: *Chronology, Appendices and Maps* (Ottawa, 1938), 11–13 [cited as *Official History Documents*].

5 Stephen Harris, *Canadian Brass: The Making of a Professional Army, 1860–1939* (Toronto, 1988), 93–4.

6 *Alberta in the 20th Century*, vol. 4: *The Great War and Its Consequences* (Edmonton, 1994), 11, 16.

7 Robert Rutherdale, 'The Home Front: Consensus and Conflict in Lethbridge, Guelph, and Trois-Rivières during the Great War' (PhD dissertation, York University, 1993), 37–8.

8 Hughes in House of Commons, January 26, 1916, quoted in *Official History Documents*, 13.

9 John Macfie, *Letters Home* (Meaford, Ont., 1990), 1.

10 See Jeffery Williams, *Princess Patricia's Canadian Light Infantry* (London, 1972), chap. 1; Jeffery Williams, *First in the Field: Gault of the Patricias* (St Catharines, Ont., 1995), chap. 7.

11 *Official History Documents*, 58.

12 Col. A.F. Duguid, *Official History of the Canadian Forces in the Great War, 1914–19*, vol. 1: *Aug. 1914–Sept. 1915* (Ottawa, 1938), 52 [cited as *Official History*]; Macfie, *Letters Home*, 2.

13 A.M.J. Hyatt, *General Sir Arthur Currie: A Military Biography* (Toronto, 1987), 20.

14 On the Valcartier process, see Ronald Haycock, *Sam Hughes: The Public Career of a Controversial Canadian, 1885–1916* (Waterloo, 1986), 183–5.

15 Bill McAndrew, 'Canadian Officership – An Overview' (unpublished paper, March 2000), 5.

16 Hyatt, *Currie*, 25; Haycock, *Hughes*, 188–9.

17 G.W.L. Nicholson, *Canadian Expeditionary Force, 1914–1919* (Ottawa, 1962), 22–4; *Official History*, 70–1.

18 *Official History Documents*, 159–60; *Official History*, 145–7.

19 *Official History Documents*, 122–3.

20 Henry Borden, ed., *Robert Laird Borden: His Memoirs*, 2 vols. (Toronto, 1938), 2: 465.

21 Macfie, *Letters Home*, 11.

22 John Swettenham, *McNaughton*, vol. 1: *1887–1939* (Toronto, 1968), 37.

23 *Official History Documents*, 158.

24 Macfie, *Letters Home*, 29.

25 *Official History Documents*, 235ff.

26 Swettenham, *McNaughton*, 1: 44–5.

27 *Official History*, 254.

28 F.G. Scott, *The Great War as I Saw It* (reprinted Ottawa, 2000), 37–8.

29 Tim Cook, *No Place to Run: The Canadian Corps and Gas Warfare in the First World War* (Vancouver, 1999), 24ff.

30 Swettenham, *McNaughton*, 1: 45–6.

31 Bill Rawling, *Surviving Trench Warfare: Technology and the Canadian Corps, 1914–1918* (Toronto, 1992), 17, 38ff. There is a good account of the Ross's history and problems in *Official History Documents*, 75ff.

32 Dancocks, *Flanders*, 297.

33 *Official History*, 307.

34 Rawling, *Surviving Trench Warfare*, 37–8.

35 John Swettenham, ed., *Valiant Men: Canada's Victoria Cross and George Cross Winners* (Toronto, 1973), 35.

36 *Official History Documents*, 279 [Sam Hughes in House of Commons]. See also Tim Travers, 'Currie and 1st Canadian Division at Second Ypres, April 1915: Controversy, Criticism and Official History,' *Canadian Military History* 5 (autumn 1996): 7ff.

37 Daniel Dancocks, *Sir Arthur Currie: A Biography* (Toronto, 1985), 51–2.

38 *Official History Documents*, 296.

39 Albert Edward Roscoe Collection, Roscoe to Mrs C. Bateman, May 13, 1915 (available at *www.mala.bc.ca*).

40 Richard Holmes, *The Western Front: Ordinary Soldiers and the Defining Battles of World War I* (London, 2000), 62.

41 Desmond Morton, *Silent Battle: Canadian Prisoners of War in Germany, 1914–1919* (Toronto, 1992), 26–8. Morton gives a total 1410 POWs at Ypres, but he seems to count captured wounded who subsequently died and are usually listed as 'died of wounds.' This figure is more than the entire total for 1915 given in Jonathan Vance, *Objects of Concern: Canadian Prisoners of War through the Twentieth Century* (Vancouver, 1994), 254.

42 Macfie, *Letters Home*, 30–1.

43 Grace Morris Craig, *But This Is Our War* (Toronto, 1981), 28.

44 There is a detailed and painstaking analysis of the 5000 or so men who joined the 22nd Battalion throughout the war in Jean-Pierre Gagnon, *Le 22ᵉ Bataillon* (Ottawa and Quebec City, 1986) , 72ff., 206ff., and tables.

45 Harris, *Canadian Brass*, 98.

46 D.P. Morton, 'The Limits of Loyalty: French Canadian Officers and the First World War,' in E. Denton, ed., *Limits of Loyalty* (Waterloo, 1980), 90.

47 John F.T. Saywell and John T. Saywell, '*Just Canadians': The Story of Our Family* (Parksville, BC, and Toronto, 1975–98), unpaginated.

48 Morton, *Silent Battle*, 87, demonstrates that one Mohawk POW was singled out by his captors and brutalized. Hughes may have been right.

49 J.L. Granatstein and J.M. Hitsman, *Broken Promises: A History of Conscription in Canada* (Toronto, 1977), 48n. See also James Dempsey, 'The Indians and World War One,' *Alberta History* 51 (1985): 1ff.; James Dempsey, *Warriors of the King: Prairie Indians in World War I* (Regina, 1999), and the review of this book by P.W. Lackenbauer in the on-line *Journal of Military and Strategic Studies* (winter 2000–spring 2001).

50 National Archives of Canada (NA), Robert Borden Papers, Memorandum, November 1, 1915, f. 31606.

51 Nicholson, *Canadian Expeditionary Force*, 546.

52 Granatstein and Hitsman, *Broken Promises*, chap. 2.

53 Ibid.

54 See Gagnon, *Le 22e Bataillon*, passim; Desmond Morton, *When Your Number's Up: The Canadian Soldier in the First World War* (Toronto, 1993), 60ff.; Jacques Michel, *La participation des canadiens français à la Grande Guerre* (Montreal, 1938); Mason Wade, 'Olivar Asselin: 2,' in R.L McDougall, ed., *Canada's Past and Present* (Toronto, 1965), 166ff.; Desmond Morton, 'The Short, Unhappy Life of the 41st Battalion, CEF,' *Queen's Quarterly* 71 (winter 1974): 70ff. See also *Historical Atlas of Canada* (Toronto, 1990), plate 26.

55 See J.M. Bliss, 'The Methodist Church and World War I,' *Canadian Historical Review* 49 (September 1968): 217–18; R.M. Bray, '"Fighting as an Ally": The English-Canadian Patriotic Response to the Great War,' *Canadian Historical Review* 61 (June 1980): 147ff.; Pierre van Paasen, *Days of Our Years* (New York, 1946), 64–5.

56 These numbers are from David Love, *'A Call to Arms': The Organization and Administration of Canada's Military in World War One* (Winnipeg and Calgary, 1999), 77. Morton, *Number's Up*, 58, states that 258 battalions were authorized, plus the RCR and PPCLI. Deciding what to count as a battalion is not simple, so both Morton and Love could be right.

57 Harris, *Canadian Brass*, 109–10.

58 Love, *'A Call to Arms,'* 90–3.

59 Ibid., 93–4; R.H. Roy, *For Most Conspicuous Bravery: A Biography of Major-General George R. Pearkes through Two World Wars* (Vancouver, 1977), 30–1.

60 J. Harold Becker, *Memoir of John Harold Becker, 1894–1956: World War I Recollections* (Minneapolis, 1998), 24.

61 See Harris, *Canadian Brass*, 113ff.

62 Nicholson, *The Canadian Expeditionary Force*, 211; Desmond Morton, *A Peculiar Kind of Politics: Canada's Overseas Ministry in the First World War* (Toronto, 1982), especially chap. 5.

63 Quoted in Harris, *Canadian Brass*, 120.

64 Rawling, *Surviving Trench Warfare*, 42.

65 E.L.M. Burns, *General Mud: Memoirs of Two World Wars* (Toronto, 1970), 15.

66 See the account in Sandra Gwyn, *Tapestry of War* (Toronto, 1992), 143–6.

67 See Rawling, *Surviving Trench Warfare*, 48ff.

68 Nicholson, *The Canadian Expeditionary Force*, 137.

69 Macfie, *Letters Home*, 47.

70 Tim Cook, '"More a medicine than a beverage": "Demon Rum" and the Canadian Trench Soldier of the First World War,' *Canadian Military History* 9 (winter 2000): 7ff.

71 John Ellis, *Eye-Deep in Hell: Trench Warfare in World War I* (Baltimore, 1989), 153. See also S. Buckley and J.D. McGinnis, 'Venereal Disease and Public Health Reform in Canada,' *Canadian Historical Review* 63 (September 1982): 338ff.

72 Deborah Cowley, ed., *Georges Vanier: Soldier. The Wartime Letters and Diaries, 1915–1919* (Toronto, 2000), 126.

73 Morton, *Number's Up*, 139ff.

74 The comment was made to me in an interview. See also Claude Bissell, *The Young Vincent Massey* (Toronto, 1981), 101–2.

75 Craig, *But This Is Our War*, 52.

76 There is a good account by a 31st Battalion soldier in R.H. Roy, ed., *The Journal of Private Fraser* (Ottawa, 1998), 112ff.

77 Ibid., 138.

78 NA, RG 150, acc. 1992-3/166, file 9137-12, Snider file. I am indebted to Patrick Brennan for passing this reference on to me.

79 Quoted in Hyatt, *Currie*, 55.

80 Jeffery Williams, *Byng of Vimy* (London, 1983), 115.

81 See Ian McCulloch, '"Batty Mac": Portrait of a Brigade Commander of the Great War, 1915–1917,' *Canadian Military History* 7 (autumn 1998): 11ff.

82 See Norm Christie, *For King and Empire: The Canadians at Mount Sorrel* (Ottawa, 2000).

83 'Malcolm Smith Mercer,' *Dictionary of Canadian Biography*, vol. 14 (Toronto, 1998), 756–7.

84 N.M. Christie, ed., *Letters of Agar Adamson* (Ottawa, 1997), 184. See also Williams, *Byng*, 110ff.

85 Much the best account of censorship is Jeffrey Keshen, *Propaganda and Censorship during Canada's Great War* (Edmonton, 1997). Compare I.H.M. Miller, *Our Glory and Our Grief: Torontonians and the Great War* (Toronto, 2001), for a different interpretation of what the homefront knew.

86 See Joanna Burke, *An Intimate History of Killing* (London, 1999).

87 For a contrarian view of the treatment of shellshock, see Ben Shephard, *A War of Nerves: Soldiers and Psychiatrists, 1914–1994* (London, 2000).

88 Patrick Brennan, 'Reluctant Warriors: Battalion Commanders in the CEF, 1915–18' (unpublished paper).

89 Pat Barker, *Another World* (London, 1999), 151.

90 A.B. Godefroy, *For Freedom and Honour* (Ottawa, 1998), passim; D.P. Morton, 'The Supreme Penalty: Canadian Deaths by Firing Squad in the First World War,' *Queen's Quarterly* 79 (fall 1972): 345ff. The government announced on December 11, 2001, that, while it would not pardon those executed in the Great War, it would inscribe the names of twenty-three in the Book of Remembrance. Desmond Morton properly described this as

'self-indulgent rubbish' that shifted blame to those ordering the executions. *National Post*, December 12, 2001. See also *Globe and Mail*, December 22, 2001.

91 Cited in a letter from LGen Henri Tellier to Robert Tooley, March 29, 1990. I am grateful to Gen Tellier for letting me see this correspondence.

92 Patrick Brennan, 'Surviving Open Warfare: Success and Failure in the Canadian Corps, 1918' (unpublished paper).

93 Susan Mann, ed., *The War Diary of Clare Gass* (Montreal, 2000), 124.

94 Williams, *Byng*, 127.

95 Based on an interview with Byng's Chief of Staff, quoted in Ian McCulloch, 'Bungo and the Byng Boys,' *The Beaver* (December 1996–January 1997), 22.

96 Harris, *Canadian Brass*, 119.

97 Brennan, 'Reluctant.'

98 See Burns, *General Mud*, 64–6.

99 Data from Love, 'A Call to Arms,' 76–7.

100 Hughes to Mrs Cowan, July 13, 1916, attached to Patricia Cowan to Canadian War Museum, June 11, 2000.

4 Becoming Professional: Arthur Currie's Army

1 'On the Wire,' from Robert W. Service, *Rhymes of a Red Cross Man* (Toronto, 1917), 79.

2 R.C. Brown and Desmond Morton, 'The Embarrassing Apotheosis of a "Great Canadian": Sir Arthur Currie's Personal Crisis in 1917,' *Canadian Historical Review* 60 (spring 1979): 41ff.

3 Currie receives full and fair treatment in Robin Neillands, *The Great War Generals on the Western Front, 1914–1918* (London, 1999), especially 147–8, 400–5, 519–20.

4 Dean Oliver, 'A Day at Beaumont Hamel,' St John's *Telegram*, November 12, 1998. See also *Historical Atlas of Canada*, vol. 3 (Toronto, 1990), plate 26, which graphically demonstrates street by street the impact of the war on St John's.

5 Archie MacKinnon Letters (Toronto), MacKinnon to his sister, August 15, 1916. Privately held.

6 R.H. Roy, ed., *The Journal of Private Fraser* (Ottawa, 1998), 193.

7 Hart Leech Collection, Leech to mother, September 13, 1916 (available at *www.mala.bc.ca*). Leech died in the attack.

8 Roy, ed., *The Journal of Private Fraser*, 207–8.

9 Serge Bernier, *The Royal 22e Regiment* (Montreal, 2000), 47–9.

10 MacKinnon Letters, MacKinnon to his sister, September 27, 1916.

11 R.H. Roy, *For Most Conspicuous Bravery: A Biography of Major-General George R. Pearkes, V.C., Through Two World Wars* (Vancouver, 1977), 45ff.

12 On Haig, about whom much has been written, see Tim Travers, *The Killing Ground: The British, the Western Front and the Emergence of Modern Warfare, 1900–1918* (London, 1990), chaps. 4–5.

13 The numbers of Nursing Sisters are uncertain. The likely correct figure here is from

G.W.L. Nicholson, *The Official History of the Canadian Army: Canadian Expeditionary Force, 1914–1919* (Ottawa, 1962), 546. Other figures range up to 3141, with 2504 serving overseas.

14 See Jennifer Trewartha, 'The Sweet Escape,' *Legion* (May/June 2001), 24ff., for the letters of stretcher bearer Pte Thomas Harris of the 6th Field Ambulance in 1917.

15 See Roy, ed., *The Journal of Private Fraser*, 314–15, for Private Fraser's progress to treatment after being wounded at Passchendaele. Another readily available source is the Harry Morris Collection, Morris to Lillian, Mother and Son, April 5, 1917 (available at www.mala.bc.ca).

16 Sir Andrew Macphail, *Official History of the Canadian Forces in the Great War, 1914–19: The Medical Services* (Ottawa, 1925), chap. 18; *Report of the Ministry: Overseas Military Forces of Canada, 1918* (London, nd), 391–3.

17 John F.T. Saywell Papers (in possession of Dr John Saywell, Toronto), Mabel to Saywell, January 9, 1918 [1919]. Mabel was secretary to the GSO of Military District No. 12. 'He doesn't do anything except draw his pay,' she said of the GSO, 'but I do the D[istrict] O[fficer] C[ommanding]'s job too, so have my time pretty well taken up.'

18 Desmond Morton, *When Your Number's Up* (Toronto, 1993), 181.

19 See Bill Rawling, *Death Their Enemy: Canadian Medical Practitioners and War* (Np, 2001), chap. 3.

20 See Herbert Bruce's *Politics and the C.A.M.C.* (Toronto, 1919), and his memoir, *Varied Operations* (Toronto, 1958), chap. 5. Sir Andrew Macphail's effective counterattack is in *Official History*, chap. 13.

21 These units are listed on the walls of Currie Hall at the Royal Military College, where each element of the corps is detailed. Currie Hall was designed as a memorial to the corps and to honour its first and only Canadian commander.

22 See Arnold Warren, *Wait for the Waggon: The Story of the Royal Canadian Army Service Corps* (Toronto, 1961), chaps. 5–6; David Love, 'A Call to Arms': The Organization and Administration of Canada's Military in World War One* (Winnipeg and Calgary, 1999), 108ff.

23 Tim Cook, '"A Proper Slaughter": The March 1917 Gas Raid at Vimy Ridge,' *Canadian Military History* 8 (spring 1999): 7ff.; Andrew Godefroy, 'A Lesson in Success: The Calonne Trench Raid, 17 January 1917,' ibid., 25ff.

24 John Swettenham, *McNaughton*, vol. 1: *1887–1939* (Toronto, 1968), chap. 4. See also Leslie W.C.S. Barnes, *Canada and the Science of Ballistics, 1914–1945* (Ottawa, 1985), 37ff.

25 P.H. Brennan and T.P. Leppard, 'How the Lessons Were Learned: Senior Commanders and the Moulding of the Canadian Corps after the Somme,' in Yves Tremblay, ed., *Canadian Military History since the 17th Century* (Ottawa, 2001), 135ff.

26 Bill Rawling, *Surviving Trench Warfare: Technology and the Canadian Corps, 1914–1918* (Toronto, 1992), 76ff.

27 Ibid., 89ff.; Daniel Dancocks, *Sir Arthur Currie: A Biography* (Toronto, 1985), 84ff.

28 C.P. Stacey, 'The Staff Officer: A Footnote to Canadian Military History,' *Canadian Defence Quarterly* 20 (1990): 25–6; Stephen Harris, *Canadian Brass: The Making of a Professional Army, 1860–1939* (Toronto, 1988), 128–30; John A. English, *National Policy and the Americanization of the Canadian Military* (Toronto, 2001), 8–9

29 Swettenham, *McNaughton*, 1: 90.

30 The Dutton Advance Collection, Lieut. Stuart Kirkland to John Kirkland, May 10, 1917 (available at www.mala.bc.ca).

31 Private Ronald MacKinnon Letters (Toronto), MacKinnon to his father, April 6, 1917. Privately held. MacKinnon was killed in the attack. See also the 13th Battalion's Captain Ian Sinclair in Gordon Reid, ed., *Poor Bloody Murder* (Oakville, Ont., 1980), 149.

32 F.G. Scott, *The Great War As I Saw It* (Ottawa, 2000), 117.

33 Pierre Berton, *Vimy* (Toronto, 1986), 20.

34 E.L.M. Burns attributed the difficulties of the 11th Brigade to casualties suffered in an abortive large-scale raid, on February 28–March 1, 1917, which eliminated experienced leaders. *General Mud* (Toronto, 1970), 38ff.

35 See Victor Wheeler, *The 50th Battalion in No Man's Land* (Ottawa, 2000), chap. 8.

36 N.M. Christie, ed., *Letters of Agar Adamson* (Ottawa, 1997), 274.

37 Deborah Cowley, ed., *Georges Vanier: Soldier. The Wartime Letters and Diaries, 1915–1919* (Toronto, 2000), 190.

38 Nicholson, *Official History*, 284. Currie was very reluctant to let Garnet Hughes have a division. He once wrote that the Fifth Division had been 'created solely' so Hughes 'might be made a Major General.' Barbara Wilson, 'The Road to the Cobourg Court Room,' *Canadian Military History* 10 (summer 2001): 70.

39 See Ian McCulloch, '"Batty Mac": Portrait of a Brigade Commander in the Great War, 1915–1917,' *Canadian Military History* 7 (autumn 1998): 11ff.

40 Dancocks, *Sir Arthur Currie*, 101ff.

41 Brown and Morton, 'The Embarrassing Apotheosis of a "Great Canadian,"' 58–9; A.M.J. Hyatt, *General Sir Arthur Currie* (Toronto, 1987), 74–5.

42 Shane Schreiber, *Shock Army of the British Empire: The Canadian Corps in the Last 100 Days of the Great War* (Westport, Conn., 1997), 11–12.

43 Swettenham, *McNaughton*, 1: 101–2.

44 Dean Oliver, 'The Canadians at Passchendaele,' in Peter Liddle, ed., *Passchendaele in Perspective: The Third Battle of Ypres* (London, 1997), 260.

45 M.G. Millman, ed., 'Letters Home, 1915–1918' (unpublished manuscript), 61, 74.

46 See J.E. Hahn, *The Intelligence Service within the Canadian Corps, 1914–1918* (Toronto, 1930); Dan Jenkins, 'The Other Side of the Hill: Combat Intelligence in the Canadian Corps, 1914–1918,' *Canadian Military History* 10 (spring 2001), 7ff.

47 Timothy Findley, *The Wars* (Toronto, 1977), 78.

48 John Swettenham, *To Seize the Victory: The Canadian Corps in World War I* (Toronto, 1965), 185.

49 See Robin Prior and Trevor Wilson, *Passchendaele: The Untold Story* (New Haven, 1996), 172–3. For a succinct description of the tactical situation, Oliver, 'Passchendaele,' 255ff., is the best Canadian account.

50 Swettenham, *McNaughton*, 1: 111–13; Neillands, *The Great War Generals*, 402; Bill Rawling, *Technicians of Battle: Canadian Field Engineering from Pre-Confederation to the Post–Cold War Era* (Toronto, 2001), 30.

51 R.H. Roy, *Sherwood Lett: His Life and Times* (Vancouver, 1991), 38–9.

52 Christie, ed., *Letters of Agar Adamson*, 309.

53 Andrew Wilson Collection, Wilson to wife, November 14, 1917, and Diary, November 10–11, 1917 (both available at www.mala.bc.ca). The letter was published in the Rosetown, Saskatchewan, *Eagle*, on December 13, 1917.

54 Sandra Gwyn, *Tapestry of War* (Toronto, 1992), 420–1.

55 J.L. Granatstein, *The Ottawa Men: The Civil Service Mandarins, 1935–1957* (Toronto, 1998), 113.

56 J.L. Granatstein and J.M. Hitsman, *Broken Promises: A History of Conscription in Canada* (Toronto, 1977), 49ff.

57 Nicholson, *Official History*, 546.

58 Dancocks, *Sir Arthur Currie*, 122.

59 National Archives of Canada (NA), Arthur Currie Papers, vol. 2, telegram, 3 December 1917; A.M.J. Hyatt, 'Sir Arthur Currie and Conscription,' *Canadian Historical Review* 50 (September 1969): 292–3.

60 See Granatstein and Hitsman, *Broken Promises*, 80–1; Desmond Morton, 'Polling the Soldier Vote: The Overseas Campaign in the Canadian General Election of 1917,' *Journal of Canadian Studies* 10 (November 1975): 39ff.

61 Saywell Papers, Saywell to Mollie, December 10, 1917.

62 Barbara Wilson, ed., *Ontario and the First World War, 1914–1918* (Toronto, 1977), lxiv.

63 D.P. Morton, 'The Limits of Loyalty: French Canadian Officers and the First World War,' in E. Denton, ed., *Limits of Loyalty* (Waterloo, 1980), 95–6.

64 Nicholson, *Official History*, 551–3.

65 Ibid., 382ff. For the diary of a Fifth Division machine gunner who went to France in March 1918, see David P. Beatty, *Memories of the Forgotten War: The World War I Diary of Private V.E. Goodwin* (Port Elgin, NB, 1988).

66 This account is based on Schreiber, *Shock Army of the British Empire*, 19ff.

67 Harris, *Canadian Brass*, 138; Desmond Morton, *A Peculiar Kind of Politics: Canada's Overseas Ministry in the First World War* (Toronto, 1982), 152ff.

68 *Report of the Ministry ... 1918*, 333–4.

69 John A. English, *The Canadian Army and the Normandy Campaign: A Study of Failure in High Command* (New York, 1991), 15.

70 J.R. Grodzinski and M.R. McNorgan, '"It's a charge, boys, it's a charge!" Cavalry Action at Moreuil Wood, 30 March 1918,' in Donald Graves, ed., *Fighting for Canada: Seven Battles* (Toronto, 2000), 241ff.

71 Nicholson, *Official History*, 381. See also Stephen Harris, 'From Subordinate to Ally: The Canadian Corps and National Autonomy,' *Revue Internationale d'Histoire Militaire* 51 (1982): 109ff.

72 See the letters and diary accounts in Cowley, *Vanier*, 208ff., and the useful monthly casualty totals in Rawling, *Surviving Trench Warfare*, app. B.

73 Janice McGinnis, 'The Impact of Epidemic Influenza: Canada, 1918–1919,' *Canadian Historical Association, Historical Papers 1977*, 121–2.

74 See Andrew Horrall, '"Keep a-fighting! Play the Game": Baseball and the Canadian Forces during the First World War,' *Canadian Military History* 10 (spring 2001): 27ff.

75 J.R. Mutchmor, *Mutchmor: The Memoirs of James Ralph Mutchmor* (Toronto, 1965), 52.

76 See Duff Crerar, *Padres in No Man's Land* (Montreal, 1995).

77 The best source for the amount of time spent on sports, shows, bath-houses, and the 'University' is the Major McFarland Memoir (unpublished manuscript, nd), passim. Privately held. See also *Report of the Ministry ... 1918*, 473ff.; E.A. Corbett, *Henry Marshall Tory* (Toronto, 1954), chap. 13. On Innis, see Gwyn, *Tapestry of War*, 373.

78 'Diary of Michael Duggan, August 1916–April 1917,' manuscript copy in possession of John Fulford, Toronto, to whom I am most grateful for its loan.

79 Brennan and Leppard, 'How the Lessons Were Learned,' 4–5.

80 C.J.B. Monroe, ed., *Memoir of John Harold Becker, 1894–1956: World War I Recollections* (Minneapolis, 1998), 161.

81 McFarland Memoir, 79. Tim Cook, *No Place to Run: The Canadian Corps and Gas Warfare in the First World War* (Vancouver, 1999), is indispensable.

82 Rawling, *Surviving Trench Warfare*, 216ff.

83 Paul Kennedy, 'Britain in the First World War,' in A.R. Millett and W. Murray, *Military Effectiveness*, vol. 1: *The First World War* (Boston, 1988), 69–70. Compare John Lee, 'The SHLM Project: Assessing the Battle Performance of British Divisions,' in P. Griffiths, ed., *British Fighting Methods in the Great War* (London, 1996), 175ff. This appraisal of Canadian, compared with British, performance is not a unanimously held view among military historians, but it is one I believe very strongly.

84 Hyatt, *General Sir Arthur Currie*, 120.

85 See J. McWilliams and R.J. Steel, *Amiens: Dawn of Victory* (Toronto, 2001).

86 Hyatt, *General Sir Arthur Currie*, 198–9.

87 Cowley, *Vanier*, 243–4. There is a good account of the August 8 operation in Roy, *Pearkes*, 70ff.

88 Veterans Affairs Canada, www site, Wartime Letter from Captain Bellenden S. Hutcheson, nd. There is another quite extraordinary account of this action in the Becker memoir, 169ff.

89 Roy, *Lett*, 44–5.

90 English, *National Policy and the Americanization of the Canadian Military*, 11.

91 Joseph Pope, ed., *Letters from the Front, 1914–1919* (Toronto, 1993), 132.

92 Swettenham, *To Seize the Victory*, 222. The best account of the Canal du Nord operation is Schreiber, *Shock Army of the British Empire*, chap. 6.

93 Patrick Brennan, 'Surviving Open Warfare: Success and Failure in the Canadian Corps, 1918' (unpublished paper).

94 Denis Winter, *Haig's Command: A Reassessment* (London, 1992), 141.

95 G.L. Cook, 'Sir Robert Borden, Lloyd George, and British Military Policy, 1917–1918,' *Historical Journal* 14 (1971): 385.

96 Nicholson, *Official History*, 475. See Will R. Bird, *Ghosts Have Warm Hands* (Ottawa, 2000), 120.

97 See Desmond Morton, *Silent Battle: Canadian Prisoners of War in Germany, 1914–1919*

(Toronto, 1992), and Jonathan Vance, *Objects of Concern: Canadian Prisoners of War through the Twentieth Century* (Vancouver, 1994). I use Vance's figures, since they are the more recent.

98 Tim Travers, *How the War Was Won: Command and Technology in the British Army on the Western Front, 1917–1918* (London, 1992), 172–3.

99 See The North Shore Archives Collection, Archie Keat to mother, November 11, 1918 (available at www.mala.bc.ca).

100 Burns, *General Mud*, 81.

101 Frank C. Cousins Collection, Cousins to Nellie, November 11, 1918 (available at www.mala.bc.ca).

102 John Macfie, *Letters Home* (Meaford, Ont., 1990), 187.

103 Ibid., 200; *Historical Atlas*, vol. 3, plate 26, shows the 46th Battalion from Saskatchewan with more than 90 per cent casualties among the 5374 who served in its ranks.

104 John A. English, *Marching Through Chaos: The Descent of Armies in Theory and Practice* (Westport, Conn., 1998), 62–3.

5 Losing Professionalism: The Interwar Years

1 Tony Foster, *Meeting of Generals* (Toronto, 1986), 62.

2 For the measure of Currie's fury at these charges and at the lukewarm defence of him offered by the Borden government, see Barbara Wilson, 'The Road to the Cobourg Court Room,' *Canadian Military History* 10 (summer 2001): 67ff.

3 Directorate of History and Heritage, National Defence Headquarters, Pope Biography file, Notes of Interviews with Lieutenant-General Maurice Pope, July 5 and 27, August 23, 1977.

4 *Report of the Department of Militia and Defence ... 1920* (Ottawa, 1921), 11.

5 See E. Gibson and G. Kingsley Ward, *Courage Remembered* (Toronto, 1989), chaps. 7–8.

6 For an account of the pilgrimage by 8000 veterans and their families to Vimy for the dedication of the monument, see David P. Beatty, *The Vimy Pilgrimage, 1936* (Amherst, NS, 1987).

7 See *The Return of the Troops: A Plain Account of the Demobilization of the Canadian Expeditionary Force* (Ottawa, 1920).

8 Desmond Morton and Glenn Wright, *Winning the Second Battle: Canadian Veterans and the Return to Civilian Life, 1915–1930* (Toronto, 1987), 111; Desmond Morton, 'Kicking and Complaining": Demobilization Riots in the Canadian Expeditionary Force, 1918–19,' *Canadian Historical Review* 61 (September 1980): 334ff.

9 Clifford Bowering, *Service: The Story of the Canadian Legion, 1925–1960* (Ottawa, 1960), 3–4.

10 Quoted in James Eayrs, *In Defence of Canada*, vol. 1: *From the Great War to the Great Depression* (Toronto, 1964), 43.

11 H.M. Urquhart, *Arthur Currie* (Toronto, 1950), 284.

12 Daniel Dancocks, *Sir Arthur Currie: A Biography* (Toronto, 1985), 194ff. Dancocks appraises the warmth of Currie's welcome home differently. See also J.C. Hopkins, *The Canadian Annual Review ... 1919* (Toronto, 1920), 33ff.

13 Urquhart, *Arthur Currie*, chap. 22.

14 Robert Sharpe, *The Last Day, The Last Hour: The Currie Libel Trial* (Toronto, 1988).

15 See Jonathan Vance, *Death So Noble: Memory, Meaning and the First World War* (Vancouver, 1997).

16 See Dagmar Novak, *Dubious Glory: The Two World Wars and the Canadian Novel* (New York, 2000), chap. 2.

17 The most recent account is M.W. McCue, 'Robert Borden's Siberian Adventure,' *The Beaver* 81 (December 2000–January 2001): 25ff.

18 On the intervention, see Eayrs, *From the Great War to the Great Depression*, chap. 1; Roy MacLaren, *Canadians in Russia, 1918–1919* (Toronto, 1976); John Swettenham, *Allied Intervention in Russia, 1918–1919, and the Part Played by Canada* (Toronto, 1967).

19 Stephen Harris, *Canadian Brass: The Making of a Professional Army, 1860–1939* (Toronto, 1988), 143ff.

20 Desmond Morton and Glenn Wright, 'The Bonus Campaign, 1919–21: Veterans and the Campaign for Re-establishment,' *Canadian Historical Review* 64 (June 1983): 147ff.

21 Quoted in Eayrs, *From the Great War to the Great Depression*, 68. For the tenor of GWVA attitudes, see Hopkins, *The Canadian Annual Review ... 1919*, 618ff.

22 See J.L. Granatstein and J.M. Hitsman, *Broken Promises: A History of Conscription in Canada* (Toronto, 1985), 106ff.

23 Quoted in Eayrs, *From the Great War to the Great Depression*, 65.

24 John Swettenham, *McNaughton*, vol. 1: *1887–1939* (Toronto, 1968), 186–7; Serge Bernier, *The Royal 22e Regiment, 1914–1999* (Montreal, 2000), 77ff.

25 *Report of the Department of Militia and Defence ... 1921* (Ottawa, 1921), 21.

26 National Archives of Canada (NA), G.W.L. Nicholson Papers, vol. 3, Gunners II drafts file, Simonds's notes on chapters 1–2, nd.

27 Harris, *Canadian Brass*, 143.

28 Desmond Morton, *The Canadian General: Sir William Otter* (Toronto, 1974), 355. See Army Headquarters, Directorate of History Report No. 22, 'The Reorganization of the Canadian Militia, 1919–20,' January 31, 1949. This report is available on line through the Department of National Defence, Directorate of History and Heritage www site.

29 Swettenham, *McNaughton*, 181–2.

30 *Report of the Department of Militia and Defence ... 1922* (Ottawa, 1922), passim.

31 Granatstein interview with MGen A. Bruce Matthews, April 25, 1991. Copies of my interviews are held in the Directorate of History and Heritage, National Defence Headquarters.

32 Strome Galloway, *The General Who Never Was* (Belleville, 1981), 25.

33 Letter, A.A.G. Smith to Granatstein, January 4, 1994.

34 Arnold Warren, *Wait for the Waggon: The Story of the Royal Canadian Army Service Corps* (Toronto, 1961), 129–30.

35 Eayrs, *From the Great War to the Great Depression*, 309.

36 The best recent accounts are in David Mackenzie, *Arthur Irwin: A Biography* (Toronto, 1993), chap. 8, and Patrick Brennan, *Reporting the Nation's Business: Press-Government Relations during the Liberal Years, 1935–1957* (Toronto, 1994), 35ff.

37 See Howard Graham, *Citizen and Soldier: The Memoirs of Lieutenant-General Howard Graham* (Toronto, 1987), 100ff.

38 University of Victoria Archives, LCol J.C. Cave interviews, August 14 and 24, 1978; Dominick Graham, *The Price of Command: A Biography of General Guy Simonds* (Toronto, 1993), 40.

39 University of Victoria Archives, Brig S.E.E. Morres interview, June 12–19, 1979.

40 Granatstein interview with MGen C.B. Ware, February 24, 1992.

41 Foster, *Meeting of Generals*, 58ff.

42 Larry Worthington, *'Worthy': A Biography of Major-General F.F. Worthington* (Toronto, 1961), 148ff.

43 Swettenham, *McNaughton*, 270ff.

44 Worthington, *'Worthy,'* 141–2.

45 Eayrs, *From the Great War to the Great Depression*, 124ff.

46 NA, G.P. Vanier Papers, vol. 4, file 4–14, Gen. Fiset to Governor General's secretary, July 11, 1922; University of Victoria Archives, Brig G.R. Bradbrooke interview, May 22, 1980.

47 Granatstein interview with MGen W.J. Megill, January 18, 1992.

48 For example, Guy Simonds Papers (private collection), Prewar box, Camberley Papers.

49 See M.A. Pope, *Soldiers and Politicians: The Memoirs of Lt.-Gen. Maurice A. Pope* (Toronto, 1962), 53ff.

50 Ibid., 98ff.; J.L. Granatstein, *The Generals: The Canadian Army's Senior Commanders in the Second World War* (Toronto, 1993), 14ff.

51 J.H. Lutz, 'Canadian Military Thought, 1923–1939: A Profile Drawn from the Pages of the Old Canadian Defence Quarterly,' *Canadian Defence Quarterly* 9 (1979): 40ff.

52 On Burns between the wars, see his *General Mud: Memoirs of Two World Wars* (Toronto, 1970), chap. 6.

53 The articles are in the *Canadian Defence Quarterly* 15–16 (April 1938–July 1939). See also Graham, *The Price of Command*, 34–6, and J.W. Hammond, 'The Pen before the Sword: Thinking about "Mechanization" between the Wars,' *Canadian Military Journal* 1 (summer 2000): 95ff.

54 See W.J. McAndrew, 'Canadian Doctrine: Continuities and Discontinuities' (unpublished paper 2001), 11ff.

55 This same conclusion appears in B. Horn and M. Wyczynski, 'E.L.M. Burns: Canada's Intellectual General,' in B. Horn and S. Harris, eds., *Warrior Chiefs: Perspectives on Senior Canadian Military Leadership* (Toronto, 2001), 148–50.

56 United States National Archives, RG 165, Military Intelligence Division Correspondence 1917–41, box 1769, item 2694-36, LCol G.T. Perkins, 'Canadian Trip (June 1926)'; USNA, State Department Records, 8420.20 MID Reports/5/6, 'Canada Combat Estimates,' 1 July 1939.

57 Granatstein interview with LGen W.A.B. Anderson, May 21, 1991.

58 N. Hillmer and W.J. McAndrew, 'The Cunning of Restraint: General J.H. MacBrien and the Problems of Peacetime Soldiering,' *Canadian Defence Quarterly* 20, 2 (1990): 45ff.

59 Harris, *Canadian* Brass, 152ff.

60 *Report of the Department of Militia and Defence ... 1921*, 6.

61 R.A. Preston, 'Buster Brown Was Not Alone: American Plans for the Invasion of Canada, 1919–1939,' *Canadian Defence Quarterly* 3 (1974): 47ff.; R.A. Preston, *The Defence of the Undefended Border: Planning for War in North America, 1867–1939* (Montreal, 1977), chap. 8; Floyd Rudmin, 'Blind-Eye Behaviour: A Cognitive History of Canadian Avoidance of American Threats, 1910–1990' (paper presented to the Organization for the Study of the National History of Canada conference, 1995); Floyd Rudmin, *Bordering on Aggression: Evidence of US Military Preparations against Canada* (Hull, QC, 1993).

62 The plan is printed in Eayrs, *From the Great War to the Great Depression*, as Document 1, 323ff.

63 Ibid., 70ff.

64 See Pope, *Soldiers and Politicians*, 82–3, 93.

65 See Gregory Johnson, 'Canada and the Far East during the 1930s,' in J. Schultz and K. Miwa, eds., *Canada and Japan in the Twentieth Century* (Toronto, 1991), 113ff.; Roger Sarty, "Entirely in the Hands of the Friendly Neighbour': The Canadian Armed Forces and the Defence of the Pacific Coast, 1909–1939,' in Sarty, *The Maritime Defence of Canada* (Toronto, 1996), 79ff., and 'Mr King and the Armed Forces: Rearmament and Mobilization, 1937–1939,' ibid., 110ff.

66 Granatstein and Hitsman, *Broken Promises*, 124–5; C.P. Stacey, *The Military Problems of Canada* (Toronto, 1940), 100ff. See, generally, James Eayrs, *In Defence of Canada*, vol. 2: *Appeasement and Rearmament* (Toronto, 1965), chap. 5.

67 Cited in G.N. Hillmer, 'Defence and Ideology: The Anglo-Canadian Military "Alliance" in the 1930s,' in B. Hunt and R. Haycock, eds., *Canada's Defence* (Toronto, 1993), 87.

68 Stephen Harris, 'Or There Would Be Chaos: The Legacy of Sam Hughes and Military Planning in Canada, 1919–1939,' *Military Affairs* 46 (1982): 124; C.P. Stacey, *Six Years of War*, vol. 1: *Official History of the Canadian Army in the Second World War* (Ottawa, 1955), 31.

69 Harris, *Canadian Brass*, chap. 9.

70 House of Commons, *Debates*, March 30, 1939, 2605ff.

71 Harris, *Canadian Brass*, 186; P.D. Dickson, 'The Education of a Canadian General: Harry Crerar between the Two World Wars' (paper presented at the Canadian Historical Association annual meeting, 1990).

72 J.L. Granatstein, *Canada's War: The Politics of the Mackenzie King Government, 1939–1945* (Toronto, 1990), 9.

73 Data as of March 31, 1939, from the *Report of the Department of National Defence ... 1939* (Ottawa, 1939), 40, 70; C.P. Stacey, *Canada and the Age of Conflict*, vol. 2: *1921–1948* (Toronto, 1981), 219–20.

74 Stacey, *Six Years of War*, 35.

6 McNaughton's Army: The Long Wait

1 Earle Birney, *Turvey* (Toronto, 1976), 138–9. On the Canadians in the United Kingdom, see C.P. Stacey and Barbara Wilson, *The Half-Million: The Canadians in Britain, 1939–1946* (Toronto, 1987).
2 Stacey and Wilson, *The Half-Million*, 209.
3 J.L. Granatstein, *Canada's War: The Politics of the Mackenzie King Government, 1939–1945* (Toronto, 1990), 10–11.
4 C.P. Stacey, *Six Years of War*, vol. 1: *The Canadian Army in the Second World War* (Ottawa, 1955), 42–3.
5 National Archives of Canada (NA), W.L.M. King Papers, Diary, September 19, 1939.
6 Chris Vokes, *Vokes: My Story* (Ottawa, 1985), 63.
7 W.J. McAndrew interview with Brig I.S. Johnston, June 1980.
8 Granatstein interview with William Young, December 17, 1991. An RMC graduate, Young was the son of MGen J.V. Young, an ex-cadet and Master-General of Ordnance, 1942–5. His view was shared widely in my interviews. Copies of my interviews are held in Directorate of History and Heritage, National Defence Headquarters.
9 Stacey, *Six Years of War*, 54–5.
10 J.L. Granatstein, *The Generals: The Canadian Army's Senior Commanders in the Second World War* (Toronto, 1993), chap. 9.
11 David Bercuson, *The Patricias: The Proud History of a Fighting Regiment* (Toronto, 2001), 152.
12 Greg Cook, 'Nobody had nothing ...' *The New Brunswick Reader* (November 6, 1999), 8. One excellent account of the years of preparation is George Blackburn, *Where the Hell Are the Guns? A Soldier's Eye View of the Anxious Years, 1939–44* (Toronto, 1997).
13 Based on LGen Henri Tellier, 'Out of Context Notes: Profile of a Soldier,' April 23, 1996. I am grateful to Gen Tellier for letting me see this piece.
14 W.J. McAndrew, 'Canadian Officership: An Overview,' in B. Horn and S. Harris, eds., *Generalship and the Art of the Admiral: Perspectives on Canadian Senior Military Leadership* (St Catharines, Ont., 2001), 62n.
15 Granatstein, *The Generals*, 61–2.
16 Granatstein interview with Col J.A. Calder, May 4, 1992.
17 John Swettenham, *McNaughton*, vol. 2: *1939–1943* (Toronto, 1969), chap. 1; Granatstein, *Canada's War*, 42–3.
18 Granatstein interview with Brig. Jack Christian, May 31, 1991.
19 C.P. Stacey, *Canada and the Age of Conflict*, vol. 2: *1921–1948* (Toronto, 1981), 291.
20 Dominick Graham, *The Price of Command: A Biography of General Guy Simonds* (Toronto, 1993), 51–2.
21 Granatstein interview with MGen J.D.B. Smith, September 14, 1991.
22 J.A. English, 'Reflections on Canadian Generalship in World War II,' F.F. Thompson lecture, RMC, 1985, 12.
23 Granatstein interview with LGen Robert Moncel, October 6, 1991.

24 There is a good account in Howard Graham, *Citizen and Soldier: The Memoirs of Lieutenant-General Howard Graham* (Toronto, 1987), 116ff.

25 For the background to Ogdensburg, see R.D. Cuff and J.L. Granatstein, *Ties That Bind: Canadian-American Relations in Wartime from the Great War to the Cold War* (Toronto, 1977), 98ff.

26 Ben Dunkelman, *Dual Allegiance* (Toronto, 1976), 56; Eddie Goodman, *Life of the Party: The Memoirs of Eddie Goodman* (Toronto, 1988), 18.

27 See Bill Rawling, *Technicians of Battle: Canadian Field Engineering from Pre-Confederation to the Post-Cold War Era* (Toronto, 2001), 148.

28 There was serious concern about venereal diseases among the United States forces that garrisoned Newfoundland from 1941. See the extraordinary, not to say bizarre, document found by Peter Neary, '"A grave problem which needs immediate attention": An American Report on Venereal Disease and Other Health Problems in Newfoundland, 1942,' *Newfoundland Studies* 15 (1999): 81ff.

29 Granatstein, *Canada's War*, 208ff. See also F.W. Gibson and B. Robertson, eds., *Ottawa at War: The Grant Dexter Memoranda, 1939–1945* (Winnipeg, 1994), 227ff.

30 John A. English, *National Policy and the Americanization of the Canadian Military* (Toronto, 2001), 17.

31 See E.L.M. Burns, *Manpower in the Canadian Army* (Toronto, 1956) – still the best study on this subject.

32 House of Commons, *Debates*, June 18, 1940, 854.

33 NA, A.G.L. McNaughton Papers, vol. 227, CC7/Crerar/6, Crerar to McNaughton, August 8, 1940. See Daniel Byers, 'Mobilising Canada: The National Resources Mobilization Act, the Department of National Defence, and Compulsory Military Service in Canada, 1940–1945,' *Journal of the Canadian Historical Association* 7 (1996): 175ff. For a full study of the civilian and military mobilization process, see Michael Stevenson, *Canada's Greatest Wartime Muddle: National Selective Service and the Mobilization of Human Resources during World War II* (Montreal, 2001).

34 J.L. Granatstein and J.M. Hitsman, *Broken Promises: A History of Conscription in Canada* (Toronto, 1985), 147.

35 Ibid., p. 153. The government, it should be noted, did not want Japanese Canadians or Chinese Canadians in the forces. See Patricia Roy, 'The Soldiers Canada Didn't Want: Her Chinese and Japanese Citizens' (paper presented to the Canadian Committee on the History of the Second World War Conference, 1977). For detail on Canadian Indians' largely negative attitudes to compulsory service, see Michael Stevenson, 'The Mobilization of Native Canadians during the Second World War,' *Journal of the Canadian Historical Association* (1996).

36 See Ruth Pierson, '"Jill Canuck": CWAC of All Trades ...' Canadian Historical Association, *Historical Papers*, 1978, 106ff.; Pierson, 'The Double Bind of the Double Standard: VD Control and the CWAC in World War II,' *Canadian Historical Review* 62 (1981): 31ff. In *'They're Still Women After All': The Second World War and Canadian Womanhood* (Toronto, 1986), Pierson argues weakly that the wartime experience did not advance the equality of

women. Compare Terry Copp, 'The Role of Jill Canuck,' *Legion* (October 1996), 16–17. On women and the Veterans Charter, see Peter Neary and J.L. Granatstein, eds., *The Veterans Charter and Post–World War II Canada* (Montreal, 1998). Generally, see Barbara Dundas, *A History of Women in the Canadian Military* (Montreal, 2001), *Equal to the Challenge: An Anthology of Women's Experiences During World War* II (Ottawa, 2001), and the Directorate of History, Army Headquarters Report No. 15, 'The Canadian Women's Army Corps, 1941–46,' which is available on line through DND's Directorate of History and Heritage www site.

37 R.H. Roy, 'Morale in the Canadian Army during the Second World War,' *Canadian Defence Quarterly* 16 (autumn 1986): 44.

38 For a 'fictional' but deadly accurate account, see Ralph Allen, *The High White Forest* (New York, 1966), 234ff.

39 See Daniel Byers, 'Canada's "Zombies": A Portrait of Canadian Conscripts and Their Experiences during the Second World War' (unpublished paper, 1997), which provides a statistical analysis of NRMA soldiers and detail on the pressures to go 'active.'

40 NA, Department of National Defence Records, file HQS 20–6, vol. 2, Adjutant-General to Minister, November 27, 1941.

41 Harry Jolley Papers (in possession of Carol Sures, Annapolis, MD), Jolley to Mr and Mrs L. Geller, May 1, 1942.

42 Pierre Berton, *Starting Out: The Days of My Youth, 1920–1947* (Toronto, 1993), 208–9.

43 There is one very valuable study by Terry Copp and Christine Hamelin, 'Le Régiment de Maisonneuve: A Profile Based on Personnel Records,' *Canadian Military History* 8 (autumn 1999): 17ff., that indicates the varied types of francophones who enlisted.

44 J.V. Allard, *Mémoires du Général Jean V. Allard* (Boucherville, QC, 1985), 54–5.

45 See Jacques Gouin, *Lettres de Guerre d'un Québécois, 1942–1945* (Montreal, 1975), 17ff.

46 Granatstein, *Generals*, chap. 9.

47 Jean Pariseau and S. Bernier, *Les Canadiens français et le bilingualisme dans les forces armées canadiennes*, tome 1: *1763–1969* (Ottawa, 1987), 106.

48 P.E. Trudeau, *Memoirs* (Toronto, 1993), 32ff. See J.L. Granatstein, 'The Contrarian, 1919 to 1949,' in *Trudeau Albums* (Toronto, 2000), 10ff.

49 See Allard, *Mémoires*, 72ff., for a sensitive account of an able francophone officer's reasoning on the plebiscite. Military voters in Canada voted 84 per cent Yes; overseas, only 72 per cent did so. Stacey, *Six Years of War*, 123.

50 For more detail, see Granatstein and Hitsman, *Broken Promises*, chap. 5, and Granatstein, *Canada's War*, chap. 6.

51 Patricia Roy et al., *Mutual Hostages: Canadians and Japanese during the Second World War* (Toronto, 1990), 63. The autumn 2001 issue of *Canadian Military History* is devoted to the Hong Kong expedition and includes academic articles and contemporary documents.

52 Granatstein interview with MGen H.A. Sparling, 18 April 1991.

53 S.R. Elliot, *Scarlet to Green* (Toronto, 1981), 375.

54 Newsletter of the Friends of the Canadian War Museum 12 (January 2001).

55 There is a good account in G.S. MacDonell, *This Soldier's Story (1939–1945)* (Nepean, Ont., 2000), 32ff.

56 Brereton Greenhous, *'C' Force to Hong Kong* (Toronto, 1997), 80. General Maltby's postwar report predictably put the blame for the defeat on the Canadians.

57 MacDonell, *This Soldier's Story*, 39ff.

58 William Allister, *Where Life and Death Hold Hands* (Toronto, 1989), 35.

59 Roy et al., *Mutual Hostages*, 68.

60 J.L. Granatstein and Desmond Morton, *A Nation Forged in Fire* (Toronto, 1989), 46.

61 On the POWs, see Roy et al., *Mutual Hostages*, chaps. 3 and 7; Georges Verreault, *Journal d'un prisonnier de guerre au Japon, 1941–1945* (Sillery, QC, 1993); on the postwar prosecutions of Japanese war criminals, see Patrick Brode, *Casual Slaughters and Accidental Judgments: Canadian War Crimes Prosecutions, 1944–1948* (Toronto, 1997), chaps. 9–10. See also Charles Roland, *Long Night's Journey into Day: Prisoners of War in Hong Kong and Japan, 1941–1945* (Waterloo, 2001).

62 Stacey, *Six Years of War*, 461ff.

63 D.R. Williams, *Duff: A Life in the Law* (Vancouver, 1984), 236. Williams is very harsh on Duff, the government, and the military, too much so in my view. See also Carl Vincent, *No Reason Why* (Stittsville, Ont., 1981), 87ff. Vincent's thesis is obvious from his title, but he fails to understand the political realities.

64 See Tony Foster, *Meeting of Generals* (Toronto, 1986), 262ff. The troops that were used, the 13th Canadian Infantry Brigade, were largely NRMA conscripts, who could be employed anywhere in North America. One regiment, the reconstituted Winnipeg Grenadiers, staged a brief near-mutiny. Ibid., 272.

65 Granatstein, *Generals*, 34ff.

66 C.J.V. Murphy, 'The First Canadian Army,' *Fortune* (January 1944): 164.

67 For a serio-comic description of Montgomery's inspection of the South Saskatchewan Regiment, see Reginald Roy, *Sherwood Lett: His Life and Times* (Vancouver, 1991), 104–5. See also Wallace Reyburn, 'Over There,' *Maclean's*, December 1, 1941.

68 Geoff Hayes, 'Pondering Canada's Army Leadership in War and Peace,' in Y. Tremblay, ed., *Canadian Military History Since the 17th Century* (Ottawa, 2001), 213ff.; W.J. McAndrew, 'Canadian Officership: An Overview' (unpublished paper, March 2000), 7ff.

69 Imperial War Museum, Trumball Warren Papers, Montgomery to Warren, April 25 and June 1, 1942; NA, H.D.G. Crerar Papers, vol. 8, 958C.009 (D182), Montgomery's Notes on Beaver IV, May 13, 1942. On Montgomery and the Canadians, see Nigel Hamilton, *Monty*, vol. 1: *The Making of a General, 1887–1942* (London, 1987), especially chaps. 12–15.

70 Granatstein interview with Trumball Warren, May 27, 1991. Warren showed me a handwritten letter from Montgomery on January 1, 1969, making this statement.

71 Swettenham, *McNaughton*, 2: 172.

72 Granatstein interview with MGen M.B. Hoffmeister, March 2, 1992.

73 In the MGen Bert Hoffmeister scrapbooks (in possession of Mr Rod Hoffmeister in West Vancouver, BC), there are two cartoons of Major Hoffmeister in 1940 dreaming up duties to keep his men occupied. I am indebted to Major Doug Delaney for giving me copies.

74 Roy, 'Morale,' 40; Terry Copp, 'The Fifth Canadian Infantry Brigade, 1944–45: A Profile of Other Ranks Based on Personnel Records' (paper presented to the American Military Institute, Durham, NC, 1991), supports some of these statistical generalizations.

75 See Jeffrey Keshen and David Mills, '"I am preparing for the day it ends": The Wartime Communication of Canadians,' in D. Vogel and W. Wette, eds., *Andere Helme – andere Menschen?* (Essen, 1995), 257ff.

76 Alexander Ross, *Slow March to a Regiment* (St Catharines, Ont., 1993), 101.

77 For a critique of battle-drill training, see John A. English, *The Canadian Army and the Normandy Campaign: A Study of Failure in High Command* (New York, 1991), chap. 5. For a more nuanced treatment, see David Bercuson, *Battalion of Heroes: The Calgary Highlanders in World War II* (Calgary, 1994), 35ff.

78 For a brief account of Dog, see Bercuson, *Battalion of Heroes*, 33–4.

79 Granatstein interview with LCol Peter Bennett, September 6, 1991.

80 Crerar Papers, vol. 8, 958C.009 (D182), Montgomery to Crerar, May 30, 1942; Graham, *Citizen and Soldier*, 66.

81 Crerar Papers, vol. 2, June 3 and April 16, 1942. See also English, *The Canadian Army*, chap. 6.

82 Granatstein, *Generals*, 32. On Montgomery and Dieppe, see Hamilton, *Monty*, chap. 16.

83 A. Robert Prouse, *Ticket to Hell via Dieppe* (Toronto, 1982), 8.

84 CBC–TV produced a DVD, 'Dieppe,' in 2001 that includes 1962 TV interviews with Mountbatten, Montgomery, and Roberts, among others.

85 Brian Villa, *Unauthorized Action: Mountbatten and the Dieppe Raid* (Toronto, 1990), argues that Mountbatten did not have authority to mount the raid. The case is strong but completely circumstantial. The best overall account, though weak on the political background, is Denis Whitaker and Shelagh Whitaker, *Dieppe: Tragedy to Triumph* (Toronto, 1992). For a splendid dissection of Mountbatten's role and responsibility, see Andrew Roberts, *Eminent Churchillians* (London, 1994), 65ff.

86 Graham, *Citizen and Soldier*, 292ff.

87 Terence Robertson, *The Shame and the Glory: Dieppe* (Toronto, 1962), 288.

88 Canadian War Museum, C.C.I. Merritt file (file 47), Col Merritt to D. Glenney, July 9, 1996.

89 On the South Sasks, see Cecil Law, 'Operation Jubilee,' *This Country Canada* (summer 1992), 42ff., which is based on after-action interviews with survivors. Merritt died in July 2000. See his obituary in the *National Post*, July 18, 2000.

90 Whitaker, *Dieppe*, 242–4.

91 Ibid., 257.

92 Ibid., 254.

93 There is a superb letter on the raid by Brigadier Sherwood Lett, printed in Roy, *Sherwood Lett*, 110–12. Lett maintained that his communications with most of his units ashore was good.

94 G.W.L. Nicholson, *Canada's Nursing Sisters* (Toronto, 1975), 129.

95 Robertson, *The Shame and the Glory*, 379–80.

96 Charles Roland, 'On the Beach and in the Bag: The Fate of Dieppe Casualties Left Behind,' *Canadian Military History* 9 (autumn 2000): 7ff.

97 Letter, A.A.G. Smith to Granatstein, January 4, 1994.

98 W. Young interview. Young was Crerar's ADC at the time.

99 Roy Jenkins, *Churchill: A Biography* (New York, 2001), 692, suggests that 'the main result – maybe the main purpose – of this action was to take the edge off the mounting obstreperousness among idle Canadian troops ... and to demonstrate how difficult was a landing on a fortified coast.'

100 Bill McAndrew, 'Leadership' (unpublished paper, 1995), 10.

101 Quoted in C.P. Stacey, *A Date with History* (Ottawa, 1983), 103. Stacey's account of the raid, from his perspective as Army Historian, is most interesting.

102 Ross Munro, *Gauntlet to Overlord* (Toronto, 1946), 207.

103 See Bercuson, *Heroes*, 47–8.

104 For a good account by one officer, see Strome Galloway, *Bravely into Battle* (Toronto, 1988), 85ff.

105 Granatstein, *Generals*, 103ff.; Paul Dickson, 'The Hand That Wields the Dagger: Harry Crerar, First Canadian Army Command and National Autonomy,' *War & Society* 13 (October 1995): 113ff.

106 Liddell Hart Centre, King's College, University of London, Viscount Alanbrooke Papers, file 3/A/VIII, Notes on My Life, 653. Swettenham, *McNaughton*, vol. 2, chap. 10; J.N. Rickard, 'The Test of Command: McNaughton and Exercise "Spartan," 4–12 March 1943,' *Canadian Military History* 8 (summer 1999): 22ff.; and English, *The Canadian Army*, 144ff., are the best studies of McNaughton during Spartan. A. Danchev and D. Todman, eds., *Field Marshal Lord Alanbrooke: War Diaries, 1939–1945* (Berkeley, Cal., 2001), is the published version of Alanbrooke's diaries.

107 Public Record Office, War Office Records, WO 106/4226, 'Comments by C-in-C Home Forces,' March 1943. There is a good, brief account of Spartan and the weaknesses it revealed in David French, *Raising Churchill's Army: The British Army and the War against Germany, 1919–1945* (Oxford, 2000), 209–11.

108 Bercuson, *Heroes*, 48.

109 Granatstein interview with Brig P.A.S. Todd, May 8, 1991.

110 English, 'Generalship,' 13–15. See the Directorate of History, Historical Officer Canadian Military Headquarters Report No. 94, 'GHQ Exercise Spartan March 1943,' May 12, 1943, available on line through the Department of National Defence, Directorate of History and Heritage www site.

111 Confidential interview, October 16, 1991, with two officers, one an artillery brigadier, the other a Service Corps colonel.

112 Granatstein, *Generals*, 74ff.

7 Into Battle: Sicily and Italy, July 1943–June 1944

1 Quoted in D.G. Dancocks, *The D-Day Dodgers: The Canadians in Italy, 1943–1945* (Toronto, 1991), 382–3. There are other versions. See Anthony Hopkins, *Songs from the Front and Rear: Canadian Servicemen's Songs of the Second World War* (Edmonton, 1979), 110.

2 On Salmon, see George Kitching, *Mud and Green Fields* (Langley, BC, 1986), 140ff.; Granatstein interview with LGen Geoffrey Walsh, May 24, 1991. Copies of my interviews are held in the Directorate of History and Heritage, National Defence Headquarters.

3 Chris Vokes, *Vokes: My Story* (Stittsville, Ont., 1985), 140–1.

4 For descriptions of many of Simonds's officers, see Richard Malone, *A Portrait of War, 1939–1943* (Toronto, 1983), 152.

5 On the Ram, see E.R. Nurse, 'Canada's Wartime Tank Program: The Development of the Ram' (MA thesis, York University, 1995). Canada, Nurse says, 'was unable to build a combat-ready tank. All the political will in the world and vast amounts of money could not compensate for the lack of an adequate design staff and a general understanding of what was needed to successfully build tanks in Canada.' Ibid., 144.

6 Farley Mowat, *And No Birds Sang* (Toronto, 1979), 90.

7 Vokes, *Vokes*, 95.

8 Mowat, *And No Birds Sang*, 106.

9 Robert McDougall, *A Narrative of War* (Ottawa, 1996), 24.

10 Kitching, *Mud and Green Fields*, 167.

11 See Strome Galloway, *Bravely into Battle* (Toronto, 1988), 139.

12 Ibid., 170; Howard Graham, *Citizen and Soldier: The Memoirs of Lieutenant-General Howard Graham* (Toronto, 1987), 158ff.; Dominick Graham, *The Price of Command: A Biography of General Guy Simonds* (Toronto, 1993), 88ff. There is a different account in W.J. McAndrew's interview with Brigadier Ian Johnston, June 1980.

13 Stephen Fochuck, *'Remembering': Lennox and Addington Veterans of World War II and the Korean Conflict* (Napanee, Ont., 2001), 33.

14 Mowat, *And No Birds Sang*, 127ff.

15 Ibid.; George McElroy, 'Assoro: Canadians in Battle in Sicily 1943,' *The Beaver* 74 (April/May 1994): 4ff.

16 See W.J. McAndrew, 'Fire or Movement? Canadian Tactical Doctrine, Sicily – 1943,' *Military Affairs* 51 (July 1987): 140ff.

17 Graham, *Simonds*, 94ff., offers a defence of Simonds.

18 Serge Bernier, *The Royal 22e Régiment* (Montreal, 2000), 122.

19 McDougall, *A Narrative of War*, 59–60.

20 C. Sydney Frost, *Once a Patricia* (St Catharines, Ont., 1988), 165ff.; for a Nursing Sister's account of Italian service, see Doris Carter, *Never Leave Your Head Uncovered* (Waterdown, Ont., 1999), chaps. 9ff.

21 Bill Rawling, *Death Their Enemy: Canadian Medical Practitioners and War* (Np, 2001), chap. 7. See also Jean Portugal, *We Were There: The Army – 5* (Shelburne, Ont., 1998).

22 J.T.B. Quayle, *In Action: A Personal Account of the Italian and Netherlands Campaigns of WWII* (Abbotsford, BC, 1997), 142–3.

23 See Gregory Blaxland, *Alexander's Generals: The Italian Campaign, 1944–45* (London, 1979), 23. For detail on the decision to add the division and corps headquarters, see G.W.L. Nicholson, *The Canadians in Italy, 1943–1945* (Ottawa, 1957), 340ff.

24 Bill Rawling, *Technicians of Battle: Canadian Field Engineering from Pre-Confederation to the Post-Cold War Era* (Toronto, 2001), 127.

25 Graham, *Simonds*, 190.

26 Mowat, *And No Birds Sang*, 221.

27 See Quayle, *In Action*, for a full account. Sterlin, killed a few days later, was shamefully awarded only a Mention in Dispatches for the defence of Sterlin's Castle.

28 Vokes, *Vokes*, 142.

29 Galloway, *Bravery into Battle*, 166.

30 Jean V. Allard, *Mémoires du Général Jean V. Allard* (Boucherville, Qué., 1985), 97.

31 Bernier, *The Royal 22e Régiment*, 136ff.

32 Terry Copp, *No Price Too High: Canadians and the Second World War* (Whitby, Ont., 1996), 134.

33 Nicholson, *The Canadians in Italy*, 315.

34 The fullest account is Mark Zuehlke, *Ortona: Canada's Epic World War II Battle* (Toronto, 1999).

35 McDougall, *A Narrative of War*, 143.

36 W.J. McAndrew interview with MGen Bert Hoffmeister, nd, 69.

37 There is a first-class account of Ortona by a Three Rivers Regiment trooper in E.R.M. Griffiths, *Dare to be True: An Odyssey of Hope and* Challenge (Ottawa, 2000), 128ff. See the German account by Carl Beyerlein, 'Parachute Engineers in Combat, Ortona 1943,' *Canadian Military History* 8 (autumn 1999): 47ff.

38 See Saverio Di Tullio, *1943: The Road to Ortona* (Ottawa, 1998), which is an extraordinarily accurate comic book written from the point of view of Ortona's civilians.

39 See Durnford's diary entry in McDougall, *A Narrative of War*, 154–6.

40 Quoted in Zuehlke, *Ortona*, 347.

41 McAndrew interview with MGen Hoffmeister; J.L. Granatstein, *The Generals: The Canadian Army's Senior Commanders in the Second World War* (Toronto, 1993), 196.

42 C.P. Stacey, *A Date with History: Memoirs of a Canadian Historian* (Ottawa, 1983), 131.

43 On battle exhaustion, see Terry Copp and Bill McAndrew, *Battle Exhaustion: Soldiers and Psychiatrists in the Canadian Army, 1939–1945* (Montreal, 1990), and Farley Mowat, *My Father's Son* (Toronto, 1992), 13ff., which treats fear with impressive frankness.

44 Quoted in Copp and McAndrew, *Battle Exhaustion*, 63. Mowat, *And No Birds Sang*, 236ff., offers testimony to the condition of the Hasty Ps at this time.

45 A.E. Pawley, *Broadcast from the Front: Canadian Radio Overseas in the Second World War* (Toronto, 1975), 62.

46 This was Vokes's view. McAndrew interview with MGen C. Vokes, June 1980.

47 Quoted in Bill McAndrew, *Canadians and the Italian Campaign, 1943–1945* (Montreal, 1996), 76.

48 For hindsight, see B. Greenhous, 'Would It Not Have Been Better to Bypass Ortona Completely? A Canadian Christmas, 1943,' *Canadian Defence Quarterly* 19 (April 1989): 51ff.

49 M.H. Rimer Collection, Trooper M.H. Rimer to parents, December 15, 1943 (available at

www.mala.bc.ca); Harry Jolley Papers (in possession of Carol Sures, Annapolis, MD), Jolley to Mr and Mrs L. Geller, December 17, 1943.

50 John Marteinson and Michael McNorgan, *The Royal Canadian Armoured Corps: An Illustrated History* (Toronto, 2000), 118ff.

51 Ibid., 201–2.

52 See Nicholson, *The Canadians in Italy*, 355ff.

53 See Kitching, *Mud and Green Fields*, 183–4.

54 See Granatstein, *The Generals*, 160–3.

55 See ibid., chap. 5.

56 Granatstein interview with MGen J.D.B. Smith, September 14, 1991.

57 See Granatstein, *The Generals*, 196–7.

58 Quoted in Douglas Delaney, 'The Apprenticeship of a Battlefield General: Bert Hoffmeister's Early Development as a Commander' (graduate paper, Royal Military College, 2001), 59.

59 See Stanley Scislowski, *Not All of Us Were Brave* (Toronto, 1997), 112ff., for a good account of the Perth Regiment.

60 Kitching, *Mud and Green Fields*, 186ff. The 1st Armoured Brigade's units did not often work with the First Canadian Division after Ortona because of a conflict between General Vokes and Brigadier Wyman. The brigade ordinarily supported British units and earned a high reputation. Marteinson and McNorgan, *The Royal Canadian Armoured Corps*, 178.

61 Fred Cederberg, *The Long Road Home* (Toronto, 1989), 87.

62 Barry Rowland, *The Padre* (Scarborough, Ont., 1982), 53.

63 Granatstein interview with MGen H.A. Sparling, April 18, 1991; McAndrew interview with MGen Hoffmeister, 79–80; McAndrew interview with MGen A.E. Wrinch, June 1980.

64 W.J. McAndrew, 'The Canadian Army and Allied High Command in the Second War' (unpublished paper), 15.

65 Blaxland, *Alexander's Generals*, 28–9.

66 See Farley Mowat's description in *My Father's Son*, 87, and E.L.M. Burns's account in *General Mud: Memoirs of Two World Wars* (Toronto, 1970), 138–9. The fullest, most recent account is Mark Zuehlke, *The Liri Valley: Canada's World War II Breakthrough to Rome* (Toronto, 2001). The title is more than slightly misleading.

67 Dancocks, *The D-Day Dodgers*, chaps. 11–12, provide a good account.

68 See Major Harry Pope's account in *La Citadelle*, February 1986, printed in English in *Canadian Military History* 2 (autumn 1993): 65ff.

69 See Burns, *General Mud*, 148, for his comment on this probe.

70 McDougall, *A Narrative of War*, 177.

71 David Bercuson, *The Patricias: The Proud History of a Fighting Regiment* (Toronto, 2001), 220ff.

72 McDougall, *A Narrative of War*, 192ff., has letters and accounts by Seaforths treating this battle.

73 Strome Galloway, *The General Who Never Was* (Belleville, Ont., 1981), 200. See John Ellis,

One Day in a Very Long War (London, 1998), 393ff., on the 48th Highlanders' doubts and eventual success.

74 Granatstein interview with Col Clement Dick, May 7, 1991.

75 McAndrew interview with Brig Johnston.

76 Imperial War Museum, Viscount Montgomery Papers, BLM 97/22, Leese to Montgomery, June 11, 1944.

77 Ellis, *One Day*, 443; Granatstein interview with MGen J.D.B. Smith, September 14, 1991.

78 Marteinson and McNorgan, *The Royal Canadian Armoured Corps*, 190.

79 For an account by a Strathconas' troop commander blinded when his tank was destroyed, see John Windsor, *Blind Date* (Sidney, BC, 1962), 46ff. See Ellis, *One Day*, 403.

80 Peter Stursberg, *The Sound of War: Memoirs of a CBC Correspondent* (Toronto, 1993), 173–4.

81 McAndrew interview with MGen Hoffmeister, 88

82 Rowland, *The Padre*, 73.

83 Harold Russell, 'The 24th Canadian Field Ambulance,' *Canadian Military History* 8 (winter 1999), 70.

84 John Gregory Dunne, 'The Hardest War,' *The New York Review of Books*, December 20, 2001, 51.

85 Copp and McAndrew, *Battle Exhaustion*, 81ff. See their table 2, illustrating differences in regimental battle exhaustion cases. The Royal 22e Régiment had the highest ratio of NP cases to battle casualties; the Loyal Edmonton, the least. There is no easy explanation for the differences between units. The Royal 22e also had much the highest rate of courts-martial in the 1st Division between 1940 and 1945, something perhaps attributable to the regiment's desire to keep a high standard of discipline. See correspondence between Robert Tooley and LGen Henri Tellier, January 14–March 29, 1990. I am grateful to Gen Tellier for letting me see this material.

86 Cited in Modris Eksteins, 'The Convictions of Our Courage,' *Globe and Mail*, October 7, 2000, D3.

87 Granatstein, *The Generals*, 134ff.; National Archives of Canada, Peter Stursberg Papers, vol. 28, E.L.M. Burns file, Burns interview, May 16, 1978. For an overview, not always accurate, see Blaxland, *Alexander's Generals*, especially 165–6.

88 Mowat, *My Father's Son*, 92.

8 Into Battle: Northwest Europe and Italy, June 1944–May 1945

1 Donald Pearce, *Journal of a War* (Toronto, 1965), 170–1.

2 Terry Copp is the leading Canadian proponent of this view, and I accept his arguments – in large part. See his forthcoming *Fields of Fire: The Canadians in Normandy*, which he kindly allowed me to read in mss. See also Terry Copp and Robert Vogel, *Maple Leaf Route*, 5 vols. (Alma, Ont., 1983–88), which use text, photographs, and maps to tell the story of Canadians in Northwest Europe in an innovative, effective fashion.

3 Adrian Preston, 'Canada and the Higher Direction of the Second World War, 1939–1945,' *RUSI Journal* 110 (February 1965): 28ff.

4 The official army history is C.P. Stacey, *The Victory Campaign: The Operations in North-West Europe, 1944–1945* (Ottawa, 1960). See also Jeffery Williams, *The Long Left Flank: The Hard Fought Way to the Reich, 1944–1945* (Toronto, 1988), and R.H. Roy, *1944: The Canadians in Normandy* (Toronto, 1984). The newest account, harsh on Canadian performance, is Russell A. Hart, *Clash of Arms: How the Allies Won in Normandy* (London, 2001).

5 Gerald Clark, *No Mud on the Back Seat: Memoirs of a Reporter* (Montreal, 1995), 60.

6 See Dan Hartigan, *A Rising of Courage: Canada's Paratroops in the Liberation of Normandy* (Calgary, 2000).

7 Copp, *Fields of Fire*, 'D-Day,' ms 10–11.

8 Charles Martin, *Battle Diary* (Toronto, 1994), 4–6; Jean Portugal, *We Were There: The Army*, vol. 2 (Shelburne, Ont., 1998), chap. 16.

9 See Portugal, *We Were There: The Army*, vol. 4, chap. 30.

10 Based on accounts by Wesley Alkenbrack, 'The Sixth of June,' 'The Guns We Used,' and 'First Deployment of the 14th Fd Regt RCA Immediately after the Landing.' Mr Alkenbrack lives near Napanee, Ont., and Professor Jerry Tulchinsky passed me his accounts.

11 Portugal, *We Were There: The Army*, vol. 2, 908.

12 Copp, *Fields of Fire*, 'D-Day,' ms 17.

13 See Terry Copp, ed., *Montgomery's Scientists: Operational Research in Northwest Europe* (Waterloo, Ont., 2000), chaps. 3–4.

14 For a contemporary account of Shermans vs Panthers, see L.S.B. Shapiro, 'Tank Battle,' *Maclean's*, September 15, 1944.

15 The best account of Meyer is Tony Foster, *Meeting of Generals* (Toronto, 1986). On Meyer's murders, see Howard Margolian, *Conduct Unbecoming: The Story of the Murder of Canadian Prisoners of War in Normandy* (Toronto, 1998); Ian Campbell. *Murder at the Abbaye* (Ottawa, 1996); and Patrick Brode, *Casual Slaughters and Accidental Judgments* (Toronto, 1997). See also B.J.S. Macdonald, *The Trial of Kurt Meyer* (Toronto, 1954), 187, which details Meyer's acquittal on charges of murdering POWs taken at Authie.

16 Eddie Goodman, *Life of the Party: The Memoirs of Eddie Goodman* (Toronto, 1988), 26. See also Gwilym Jones, *To the Green Fields Beyond* (Burnstown, Ont., 1993), 94.

17 D. Shaugnessy, 'Some Thoughts about Harold L. Green of the Scout Platoon, the RHLI,' *Canadian Military History* 10 (winter 2001), 74.

18 Terry Copp interview with Brig D.G. Cunningham, October 1982, 11.

19 Quoted in Bill McAndrew et al., *Normandy 1944: The Canadian Summer* (Montreal, 1994), 56.

20 M. McNorgan, 'Black Sabbath for the First Hussars: Action at Le Mesnil-Patry, 11 June 1944,' in D. Graves, ed., *Fighting for Canada* (Toronto, 2000), 281ff.

21 For Simonds's tactical ideas in July 1944, see 'General Simonds Speaks: Canadian Battle Doctrine in Normandy,' *Canadian Military History* 8 (spring 1999): 69ff.

22 Quoted in Clark, *No Mud on the Back Seat*, 65.

23 J.A. Snowie, *Bloody Buron* (Erin, Ont., 1984), 71–2.

24 For the sole study of a Canadian brigade, see Terry Copp, *The Brigade: The Fifth Canadian Infantry Brigade, 1939–1945* (Stoney Creek, Ont., 1992).

25 The most sensitive study of the ground the Allies fought over in Normandy is Marc Milner, 'Reflections on Caen, Bocage and the Gap: A Naval Historian's Critique of the Normandy Campaign,' *Canadian Military History* 7 (spring 1998): 7ff. See also Copp, *Fields of Fire*, 'The Battles for Caen,' ms 21. A superb account of the Normandy battles is George Blackburn, *The Guns of Normandy: A Soldier's Eye View, France 1944* (Toronto, 1995).

26 Mary Jo Leddy, *Memories of War, Promises of Peace* (Toronto, 1989), 107.

27 See Bill McAndrew, 'The Canadians on Verrières Ridge: A Historiographical Survey,' in D. Bercuson and S. Wise, eds., *The Valour and the Horror* (Toronto, 1994), 128ff.

28 Douglas Delaney, 'The Apprenticeship of a Battlefield General: Bert Hoffmeister's Early Development as a Commander' (graduate paper, Royal Military College, 2001), especially 53.

29 John A. English, *The Canadian Army and the Normandy Campaign: A Study of Failure in High Command* (New York, 1991), 251.

30 See Denis and Shelagh Whitaker, *Victory at Falaise: The Soldiers' Story* (Toronto, 2000). On Montgomery and the Gap, see Nigel Hamilton, *Monty*, 2: *Master of the Battlefield, 1942–1944* (London, 1987), chap. 14.

31 Granatstein interview with LGen S.F. Clark, February 24, 1992. Copies of my interviews are available at the Directorate of History and Heritage, National Defence Headquarters.

32 Carlo D'Este, *Decision in Normandy* (New York, 1994), 290.

33 For Simonds's role in the great battles of July and August 1944, see Graham, *Price of Command*, chap. 10. A much less hagiographic judgment is in English, *The Canadian Army and the Normandy* Campaign, book 2.

34 McAndrew, *Normandy 1944*, 132.

35 The first account to tie the formation and execution of the air plan into Totalize is Jody Perrun, 'Missed Opportunities: First Canadian Army and the Air Plan for Operation Totalize, 7–10 August 1944' (MA thesis, Carleton University, 1999).

36 Granatstein interview with LCol Don Mingay, June 6, 1991.

37 See the rather bleak assessments of the RAF's effectiveness in the bombing in Copp, *Montgomery's Scientists*, Reports Nos. 8 and 14, 95ff.

38 For the RAF's explanation for the disaster, see Henry Probert, *Bomber Harris: His Life and Times* (Toronto, 2001), 298–9.

39 See George Kitching, *Mud and Green Fields* (Langley, BC, 1985), chap. 14.

40 Granatstein interview with LCol Peter Bennett, September 6, 1991.

41 On Simonds in Tractable, see the over-the-top analysis by R. Jarymowycz, 'General Guy Simonds: The Commander as Tragic Hero,' in B. Horn and S. Harris, eds., *Warrior Chiefs: Perspectives on Senior Canadian Military Leaders* (Toronto, 2001), 124ff. Two excellent regimental histories should be read: on Major Currie and the South Albertas at Falaise, see Donald Graves, *South Albertas: A Canadian Regiment at War* (Toronto, 1998), chaps. 9–10; on A/Major Martin and the Argyll and Sutherland Highlanders, see R.K. Fraser, *Black Yesterdays: The Argylls' War* (Hamilton, 1996), 238ff.

42 Graves, *South Albertas*, 146–7.

43 There is a good account by Kitching in an interview with R.H. Roy in the University of Victoria Archives, Accession 82–5, box l, f. l, nd.

44 Williamson Murray and Allan Millett, *A War to Be Won: Fighting the Second World War* (Cambridge, Mass., 2000), 432.

45 For some British and American views, see J.L. Granatstein, *The Generals: The Canadian Army's Senior Commanders in the Second World War* (Toronto, 1995), 146. This book is not the place for an examination of subsequent historiography, but Canadian historians especially have been harsh on Simonds. Uncharacteristically, I come down in the middle: Simonds was the best Canadian commander, even though he made errors.

46 Again, see Milner, 'Reflections,' 7ff.

47 W.J. McAndrew, 'The Soldier and the Battle,' in J.L. Granatstein and Peter Neary, eds., *The Good Fight: Canadians and World War II* (Toronto, 1995), 134ff.; McAndrew, 'Canadian Doctrine: Continuities and Discontinuities' (unpublished manuscript, nd).

48 Bill McAndrew, *Canadians and the Italian Campaign* (Montreal, 1996), 117.

49 Quoted in J. Marteinson and M. McNorgan, *The Royal Canadian Armoured Corps: An Illustrated History* (Toronto, 2000), 206.

50 Quoted in McAndrew, *Italian*, 120.

51 S. Scislowski, *Not All of Us Were Brave* (Toronto, 1997), chap. 6.

52 Quoted in McAndrew, *Italian*, 122.

53 J.A. English, 'Reflections on the Breaking of the Gothic Line' (unpublished manuscript [1983?]).

54 National Archives of Canada (NA), M.H.S. Penhale Papers, vol. 1, Vokes to Penhale, November 2, 1944.

55 Quoted in W.J. McAndrew, 'Canada and the Italian Campaign,' in P.D. Dickson, ed., *1943: The Beginning of the End* (Waterloo, Ont., 1995), 79.

56 McAndrew, *Italian*, 156.

57 Terry Copp, 'The March to the Seine,' *Legion*, March–April 2000, 37.

58 Granatstein, *The Generals*, 112.

59 See Terry Copp and R. Vogel, '"No Lack of Rational Speed": 1st Canadian Army Operations, September 1944,' *Journal of Canadian Studies* 16 (fall–winter 1981): 145ff.; T. Copp, '2nd Division in September 1944,' *Legion* (May/June 2001), 39ff.

60 Pearce, *Journal of a War*, 133.

61 Denis and Shelagh Whitaker, *Tug of War: The Canadian Victory That Opened Antwerp* (Toronto, 1984). For the larger picture of which the Scheldt battle was part, see Nigel Hamilton, *Monty*, vol. 3: *The Field-Marshal, 1944–1976* (London, 1987), chap. 4.

62 This was Simonds's view. See US Army Military History Institute, Carlisle, Pa, OCMH Collection, WWII Supreme Command box, folder: Interviews, 'The Supreme Command,' interview by F.C. Pogue with Brig David Belchem and LGen Simonds, February 20, 1947.

63 Terry Copp, 'The Battle North of Antwerp,' *Legion*, September–October 2001, 41.

64 Granatstein interviews with Brig G.E. Beament, May 24, 1991, and LGen Geoffrey Walsh, May 24, 1991.

65 See John Ellis, *One Day in a Very Long War* (London, 1998), chap. 2.

66 Portugal, *The Army*, vol. 4, 2000ff.

67 J.A. Roberts, *The Canadian Summer: The Memoirs of James Alan Roberts* (Toronto, 1981), 100.

68 Copp, 'Battle North of Antwerp,' 41.

69 Ibid., 43.

70 George Blackburn, *The Guns of Victory: A Soldier's Eye View, Belgium, Holland, and Germany, 1944–45* (Toronto, 1996), 100.

71 Stephen Fochuck, *'Remembering': Lennox and Addington Veterans of World War II and the Korean Conflict* (Napanee, Ont., 2001), 160.

72 Beament interview.

73 David Bercuson, *Battalion of Heroes: The Calgary Highlanders in World War II* (Calgary, 1994), 184ff.

74 J.L. Granatstein and J.M. Hitsman, *Broken Promises: A History of Conscription in Canada* (Toronto, 1985), 210. Beginning in March 1944, Canada sent 673 junior officers to the British Army, which was desperately shorthanded. To judge by the nominal roll, substantial numbers were francophone. See W.I. Smith, *Code Word Canloan* (Toronto, 1992), 308ff. For a memoir, see R.F. Fendick, *A Canloan Officer* (Nauwigewauk, NB, 2000).

75 NA, W.L.M. King Papers, Diary, October 26, 1944.

76 NA, Privy Council Office Records, Cabinet War Committee minutes, August 3, 1944.

77 Granatstein and Hitsman, *Broken Promises*, 212–13; on Stuart, see Granatstein, *The Generals*, chap. 8.

78 See Whitaker, *Tug of War*, chap. 10. Terry Copp studied personnel records of men killed in action in the 5th Brigade and discovered that most were not remustered or untrained. ('The Fifth Canadian Infantry Brigade, 1944–45: A Profile of Other Ranks Based on Personnel Records' [paper presented at American Military Institute 1991]. There is a clear difference between received wisdom and the records that needs to be explored further, though records do not measure the quality of training and should not be taken at face value. Poor training was not only a Canadian problem. See John Ellis, *On the Front Lines* (New York, 1990), 304ff. The first public charges of untrained reinforcements at the front were made on September 19, 1944, by artillery Major Conn Smythe, owner of the Toronto Maple Leafs. See Douglas Hunter, *War Games: Conn Smythe and Hockey's Fighting Men* (Toronto, 1996), 136ff.

79 See David French, *Raising Churchill's Army: The British Army and the War Against Germany, 1919–1945* (Oxford, 2000), 148–9.

80 McAndrew in Granatstein and Neary, *The Good Fight*, 133.

81 See J.L. Granatstein, *Canada's War: The Politics of the Mackenzie King Government, 1939–1945* (Toronto, 1990), chap. 9.

82 On McNaughton as minister, see John Swettenham, *McNaughton*, vol. 3: *1944–1966* (Toronto, 1969), chaps. 2–3.

83 Queen's University, T.A. Crerar Papers, Memorandum, A.D.P. Heeney to Cabinet, November 6, 1944.

84 C.P. Stacey, *Arms, Men and Governments: The War Policies of Canada, 1939–1945* (Ottawa, 1970), 471.

85 King stoutly maintained that there had been a revolt, as he told Grant Dexter of the *Winnipeg Free Press* in January 1945. Queen's University Archives, Grant Dexter Papers, Memorandum, January 9–10, 1945.

86 See R.H. Roy, *For Most Conspicuous Bravery: A Biography of Major-General George R. Pearkes V.C.* (Vancouver, 1977), chap. 12.

87 Pearce, *Journal of a War*, 160.

88 Donald Graves, '"If only we had the wisdom of our generals": The Kapelsche Veer, 26–31 January 1945,' in D. Graves, ed., *Fighting for Canada* (Toronto, 2000), 319ff. The Dutch army teaches this action in its staff college as a 'how-not-to' lesson. Bodies from Kapelsche Veer continue to be found: see *Globe and Mail*, April 28, 2001, A14, and *National Post*, July 12, 2001, A3.

89 Granatstein, *The Generals*, 188.

90 Granatstein interview with MGen W.J. Megill, January 18, 1992.

91 R.F. Anderson, '1st Canadian Parachute Battalion in the Ardennes: A Personal Account,' *Canadian Military History* 8 (autumn 1999): 59ff.

92 See Denis and Shelagh Whitaker, *Rhineland: The Battle to End the War* (Toronto, 1989).

93 Roberts, *The Canadian Summer*, 109.

94 Whitaker, *Rhineland*, 145.

95 Graves, *South Albertas*, 272.

96 Granatstein interview with Col Clement Dick, May 7, 1991.

97 Bercuson, *Battalion*, 236–7.

98 Alexander Ross, *Slow March to a Regiment* (St Catharines, Ont., 1993), 212ff.

99 Granatstein interview with Peter Hertzberg, December 19, 1991. Hertzberg was GSO III in the Fifth Canadian Armoured Division. McAndrew interview with Col Clement Dick, May 26, 1980.

100 Roberts, *The Canadian Summer*, 122.

101 Alex Morrison and Ted Slaney, *The Breed of Manly Men: The History of the Cape Breton Highlanders* (Toronto, 1994), 320ff.; Daniel Byers, 'Operation "Canada": 5th Canadian Armoured Division's Attack on Delfzijl, 23 April to 2 May 1945,' *Canadian Military History* 7 (summer 1998): 35ff.

102 John M. Gray, *Fun Tomorrow: Learning to Be a Publisher and Much Else* (Toronto, 1978), 312.

103 Michiel Horn, 'More Than Cigarettes, Sex and Chocolate: The Canadian Army in the Netherlands, 1944–1945,' *Journal of Canadian Studies* 16 (fall–winter 1981): 159; David Kaufman and M. Horn, *A Liberation Album: Canadians in the Netherlands, 1944–45* (Toronto, 1980).

104 Canadians suffered a higher percentage of fatalities in the armed forces than the United States and France did. See *Historical Atlas of Canada*, vol. 3 (Toronto, 1990), plate 47.

105 Roberts, *The Canadian Summer*, 144.

106 Granatstein interview with LGen Robert Moncel, October 6, 1991.

107 J.A. English, *Lament for an Army: The Decline of Canadian Military Professionalism* (Toronto, 1998), 44.

108 Farley Mowat, *My Father's Son* (Toronto, 1992), 256.

109 Graves, *South Albertas*, 329.

110 Harry Jolley Papers, Jolley to Mr and Mrs. L. Geller, May 17, 1945. See also Barry Rowland, *The Padre* (Scarborough, Ont., 1982), 20–1, and the Dominion Institute's *www.thememoryproject.com*, which has a huge collection of V-E Day stories.

111 Gnr J.P. Brady, 'Jottings from a Record of Service in the North West Europe Campaign,' in Gregory Johnson, *Lac La Biche Chronicles: The Early Years* (Lac La Biche, Alta., 1999), 297.

112 Goodman, *Life of the Party*, 36.

9 The Professional Army, 1945–68

1 Herbert Fairlie Wood, *The Private War of Jacket Coates* (Toronto, 1966), 78–9. Wood served in Korea and was the army official historian of the war.

2 See J.A. English, *Lament for an Army: The Decline of Canadian Military Professionalism* (Toronto, 1998), chap. 4.

3 See John A. English, *National Policy and the Americanization of the Canadian Military* (Toronto, 2001), 30–1.

4 J.L. Granatstein, *The Generals: The Canadian Army's Senior Commanders in the Second World War* (Toronto, 1993), 202; C.P. Stacey, *Six Years of War*, vol. 1: *Official History of the Canadian Army in the Second World War* (Ottawa, 1955), 510ff.

5 See the account of one junior officer's training for the Pacific Force in Lloyd Dennis, *Marching Orders: A Memoir* (Toronto, 1988), 247ff.

6 Dean Oliver, 'When the Battle's Won: Military Demobilization in Canada, 1939–1946' (Ph D dissertation, York University, 1996), 353; Stacey, *Six Years of War*, 431ff.

7 See Peter Neary and J.L. Granatstein, eds., *The Veterans Charter and Post–World War II Canada* (Montreal, 1998).

8 Kurt Loeb, ''The Boys of Summer': A Personal Account of the Canadian Berlin Battalion, June–July 1945,' *Canadian Military History* 8 (autumn 1999): 69ff.

9 C.P. Stacey, *Arms, Men and Governments: The War Policies of Canada, 1939–1945* (Ottawa, 1970), 65; Peter Kasurak, 'Pawn in the Game of National Politics: Origins and Fortunes of the Canadian Army Occupation Force, 1943–46,' *Canadian Defence Quarterly* 5 (winter 1975): 41ff.; Mary Halloran, 'Canada and the Origins of the Post-War Commitment,' in M. MacMillan and D. Sorenson, eds., *Canada and NATO: Uneasy Past, Uncertain Future* (Waterloo, 1990), 1ff.

10 David Kaufman and Michiel Horn, *A Liberation Album: Canadians in the Netherlands, 1944–45* (Toronto, 1980), 137.

11 James Eayrs, *In Defence of Canada: Peacemaking and Deterrence* (Toronto, 1972), 62–3.

12 John M. Gray, *Fun Tomorrow: Learning to Be a Publisher and Much Else* (Toronto, 1978), 328.

13 National Archives of Canada (NA), Privy Council Office Records, box 18, file D-19-D, 'Minutes of Special Meeting of Ministers of National Defence and Chiefs of Staff, June 25, 1945'; ibid., vol. 3895, file N-2-13-9, 'Strategic Factors Affecting Canada's Post-War Military Requirements,' July 5, 1945; J.L. Granatstein and J.M. Hitsman, *Broken Promises: A History of Conscription in Canada* (Toronto, 1985), 246ff.

14 NA, W.L.M. King Papers, Diary, August 2, 3, 1945.

15 H.F. Wood, *Strange Battleground: Official History of the Canadian Army in Korea* (Ottawa, 1966), 17–18.

16 *Canada's Defence: Information on Canada's Defence Achievements and Organization* (Ottawa, 1947), 16–17.

17 Sean Maloney, 'The Mobile Striking Force and Continental Defence, 1948–1955,' *Canadian Military History* 2 (August 1993).

18 *Canada's Defence*, 16–17.

19 John Marteinson et al., *We Stand on Guard: An Illustrated History of the Canadian Army* (Montreal, 1992), 334ff. See the memo by the Chargé in Canada to Director of the Office of British Commonwealth and Northern European Affairs, April 24, 1953, in *Foreign Relations of the United States, 1952–1954* (Washington, 1986), vol. 6: 2080: 'In theory there is an airborne brigade in Canada ... but its personnel are scattered, the unit is seriously undermanned, and it lacks the aircraft to become operational.'

20 See R.A. Preston, *Canada's RMC: A History of the Royal Military College* (Toronto, 1969), chaps. 13–14.

21 Pierre Coulombe, 'Social and Cultural Composition of the Canadian Armed Forces,' in H. Massey, ed., *The Canadian Military: A Profile* (Toronto, 1972), 157.

22 Quoted in John English, *The Canadian Army and the Normandy Campaign: A Study of Failure in High Command* (New York, 1991), 97–8.

23 NA, H.D.G. Crerar Papers, vol. 4, 958C.009 (D179), Crerar to Murchie, July 5, 1945.

24 On Foulkes's career, see Granatstein, *Generals*, 173ff.

25 Quoted in Eayrs, *In Defence of Canada: Peacemaking and Deterrence*, 61.

26 On Foulkes as Chairman of the Chiefs of Staff, see Sean Maloney, 'General Charles Foulkes: A Primer on How to Be CDS,' in B. Horn and S. Harris, eds., *Warrior Chiefs: Perspectives on Senior Canadian Military Leaders* (Toronto, 2001), 219ff.; Douglas Bland, *Chiefs of Defence: Government and the Unified Command of the Canadian Armed Forces* (Toronto, 1995), 50ff.

27 English, *Lament*, 48; Granatstein interview with Col Robert Raymont, May 23, 1991. Raymont was Director of the Joint Staff in Ottawa and worked closely with Foulkes. Copies of my interviews are held in the Directorate of History and Heritage, National Defence Headquarters.

28 'Canadian Defence Planning,' a speech in the House of Commons, June 24, 1948 (published in pamphlet form).

29 See C.P. Stacey, *Canada and the Age of Conflict*, 2: *1921–1948* (Toronto, 1981), 406ff.; Lawrence Aronsen, 'American National Security and the Defense of the Northern Frontier, 1945–1951,' *Canadian Review of American Studies* 14 (fall 1983): 259ff.

30 *Canada's Defence Programme, 1949–50* (Ottawa, 1949), 23–4.

31 See R.D. Cuff and J.L. Granatstein, *American Dollars, Canadian Prosperity* (Toronto, 1978), 220–1.

32 *Canada and the Korean Crisis* (Ottawa, 1950), 34.

33 Robert Bothwell, 'The Cold War and the Curate's Egg,' *International Journal* 3 (summer 1998): 416–17.

34 For the diplomacy involved in the Korean decision and the dispatch of troops, see G. Donaghy, ed., *Documents on Canadian External Relations*, 16: *1950* (Ottawa, 1996), 61ff.

35 Wood, *Strange Battleground*, 24.

36 Foulkes apparently neglected to include reinforcements, an oversight caught by the Vice CGS, MGen Howard Graham. Howard Graham, *Citizen and Soldier: The Memoirs of Lieutenant-General Howard Graham* (Toronto, 1987), 220.

37 Wood, *Coates*, 5.

38 Wood, *Strange Battleground*, 29–30. On Claxton's role, see David Bercuson, *True Patriot: The Life of Brooke Claxton, 1898–1960* (Toronto, 1993), 213ff.

39 J.L. Granatstein, 'The American Influence on the Canadian Military, 1939–1963,' in B.D. Hunt and R.G. Haycock, eds., *Canada's Defence: Perspectives on Policy in the Twentieth Century* (Toronto, 1993), 132ff.

40 J.L. Granatstein and David Bercuson, *War and Peacekeeping: From South Africa to the Gulf–Canada's Limited Wars* (Toronto, 1991), 111.

41 John Melady, *Korea: Canada's Forgotten War* (Toronto, 1983), 63–4.

42 Ibid., 117. There are good maps of this engagement and virtually all Canadian military campaigns from Champlain to Kosovo in Mark Zuehlke and C. Stewart Daniel, *The Canadian Military History Atlas* (Toronto, 2001).

43 Ted Barris, *Deadlock in Korea: Canadians at War, 1950–1953* (Toronto, 1999), 85.

44 Pierre Berton, *Marching as to War: Canada's Turbulent Years, 1899–1953* (Toronto, 2001), 560.

45 See David Bercuson, *The Patricias: The Proud History of a Fighting Regiment* (Toronto, 2001), 257ff.; Barris, *Deadlock in Korea*, chap. 5.

46 Ibid., 106–7.

47 David Bercuson, *Blood on the Hills: The Canadian Army in the Korean War* (Toronto, 1999), 130ff.

48 Robert Peacock, *Kim-Chi, Asahi and Rum: A Platoon Commander Remembers Korea, 1952–1953* (Np, 1994), 20–2.

49 Wood, *Strange Battleground*, 260.

50 For a largely U.S. view of the Chinese, see K. Mahoney, *Formidable Enemies: The North Korean and Chinese Soldier in the Korean War* (Novato, Cal., 2001).

51 Harry Pope died in 2000. His memoirs, which include much on Korea, have not been printed in English, but were published in the Royal 22e Régiment's *La Citadelle* in twenty-six parts between 1986 and 1993, including Pope's paper on patrolling that led to his setting up the school.

52 Wood, *Strange Battleground*, 17–9.

53 Quoted in Melady, *Korea*, 84.

54 Cited in Bercuson, *True Patriot*, chap. 12.

55 Royal Commission on Bilingualism and Biculturalism, 'Armed Forces Historical Study,' mimeo, nd; Eayrs, *In Defence of Canada: Peacemaking and Deterrence*, 130ff.

56 Queen's University Archives, T.A. Crerar Papers, Grant Dexter to Crerar, nd, enclosing memo, February 22, 1951; Granatstein and Hitsman, *Broken Promises*, 252ff.; Blair Fraser, 'Conscription!' *Maclean's*, March 15, 1951, 18ff.; J.I. Gow, 'Les Québécois, la guerre et la paix,' *Canadian Journal of Political Science* 3 (March 1970): 88ff.

57 NA, Brooke Claxton Papers, Simonds to Claxton, May 9, 1951; ibid., C.M.D[rury] to Claxton, June 19, 1951; ibid., telegram, Claxton to J.W. Pickersgill, November 11, 1951. Simonds made off-the-record pro-conscription speeches that leaked to the press and caused trouble. Granatstein interview with Col Robert Raymont, May 23, 1991; Dominick Graham, *The Price of Command: A Biography of General Guy Simonds* (Toronto, 1993), 252ff. After he retired, Simonds attacked Canada's defence policy in 'Where We've Gone Wrong on Defence,' *Maclean's*, June 23, 1956, 22ff.

58 Bercuson, *Blood*, 161; Jon Halliday and Bruce Cummins, *Korea: The Unknown War* (London, 1990), 179.

59 The best account of Canada–US relations in the Korean War period is Denis Stairs, *The Diplomacy of Constraint: Canada, the Korean War, and the United States* (Toronto, 1974). Compare R.S. Prince, 'The Limits of Constraint: Canadian–American Relations and the Korean War, 1950–51,' *Journal of Canadian Studies* 27 (winter 1992–3): 129ff. On Koje, see Bercuson, *True Patriot*, 235ff., and Melady, *Korea*, chap. 14.

60 Bercuson, *Blood*, 222–3. For a contrary view, see B. Greenhous's review of Bercuson's book in *Canadian Military Journal* 1 (spring, 2000): 77.

61 Sean Maloney, *War without Battles: Canada's NATO Brigade in Germany, 1951–1993* (Toronto, 1996), 20.

62 The best account is David Bercuson, 'The Return of the Canadians to Europe: Britannia Rules the Rhine,' in MacMillan and Sorenson, 15ff. Bercuson notes a number of errors in James Eayrs, *In Defence of Canada: Growing Up Allied* (Toronto, 1980), but Eayrs's account remains valuable. For the diplomacy involved in getting troops to NATO, see G. Donaghy, ed., *Documents on Canadian External Relations*, 17: *1951* (Ottawa, 1996), 733ff.

63 See Peter Archambault, 'British Weapons, Canadian Dollars: Equipping Canada's Military, 1945–1953,' paper presented to Canadian Historical Association, 1994.

64 Bercuson, 'Return,' 22–3. See the Directorate of History, Army Headquarters Report No. 51, 'The 27th Canadian Infantry Brigade Group, February 1951–May 1952,' May 6, 1952. This report is accessible on-line through the Directorate of History and Heritage www site.

65 Maloney, *War without Battles*, 96–7.

66 Ibid., 50.

67 In 1956 the army disbanded two of the Guards battalions and created a new armoured regiment for the Regular Force, the 1/8th Canadian Hussars (Princess Louise's); one squadron was primarily francophone. A fourth Regular armoured regiment, the Fort Garry Horse, was created in 1958, providing an armoured regiment for each brigade. John Marteinson

and M. McNorgan, *The Royal Canadian Armoured Corps: An Illustrated History* (Toronto, 2000), 359.

68 *Documents on Canadian External Relations*, 18: *1952* (Ottawa, 1990), 718.

69 Maloney, *War without Battles*, 109; D.J. Bercuson, 'Canada, NATO, and Rearmament, 1950–1954: Why Canada Made a Difference (But Not for Very Long),' in J. English and G.N. Hillmer, eds., *Making a Difference: Canada's Foreign Policy in a Changing World Order* (Toronto, 1992), 103ff.

70 LCol I.M. Kennedy to author, May 2, 2001. See Roy Rempel, *Counterweights: The Failure of Canada's German and European Policy, 1955–1995* (Montreal, 1996), chap. 6.

71 George Kitching, *Mud and Green Fields: The Memoirs of General George Kitching* (Langley, BC, 1986), 289.

72 David Bercuson, *Significant Incident: Canada's Army, the Airborne, and the Murder in Somalia* (Toronto, 1996), 60–1.

73 Kitching, *Mud and Green Fields*, 293.

74 One memoir by a Canadian in Laos in the early days of the Commission is LCol J.E.G. de Domenico, *Land of a Million Elephants: Memoirs of a Canadian Peacekeeper* (Burnstown, Ont., 1997). For academic studies, see Douglas Ross, *In the Interests of Peace: Canada and Vietnam, 1954–73* (Toronto, 1984); R. Thakur, *Peacekeeping in Vietnam: Canada, India, Poland and the International Commission* (Edmonton, 1984).

75 See James Eayrs, *In Defence of Canada: Indochina: Roots of Complicity* (Toronto, 1983); Paul Bridle, 'Canada and International Control Commissions in Indochina, 1954–72,' *Behind the Headlines* (1973). There are also taped interviews with four Cambodia Commission members at the Canadian War Museum Archives, Oral History Project, 'Canadian Delegation – Cambodia, International Commission for Supervision and Control (Indochina) 1954.'

76 *The Crisis in the Middle East, October–December, 1956* (Ottawa, 1957), 9–10.

77 Graham, *Citizen and Soldier*, 234.

78 G. Donaghy, ed., *Documents on Canadian External Relations*, 22: *1956–1957, Part I* (Ottawa, 2001), 246.

79 See ibid., 248ff., for excellent detail on the fluctuating negotiations over the Canadian commitment of troops. See especially Ambassador in Egypt to Ottawa, December 4, 1956, 293–4.

80 Letter to author, 1961, from an RCD lieutenant.

81 Letter to author, 1962, from an RCASC captain.

82 Alastair Taylor et al., *Peacekeeping: International Challenge and Canadian Response* (Toronto, 1968), 118ff.; Granatstein and Bercuson, *War and Peacekeeping*, 198.

83 NA, L.B. Pearson Papers, vol. 62, file 306 Conf., Kent to Pearson, April 7, 1964; Granatstein interview with L.B. Pearson, 1970.

84 See John Clearwater, *Canadian Nuclear Weapons: The Untold Story of Canada's Cold War Arsenal* (Toronto, 1998), chap. 5, and Donaghy, *Documents, 1956–1957*, 1186–8, for military views on nuclear weapons for Canadian forces in early 1957.

85 Between 1957 and 1961, as an army officer cadet at Camp Borden, I received this kind of

training. In 1960–1, as a fourth-year cadet at RMC, I saw a sand-table exercise at the Canadian Army Staff College that planned for the explosion of at least a dozen NATO and Warsaw Treaty Organization tactical nuclear weapons over a two-day period in the Canadian brigade's area of operations.

86 Isabel Campbell, 'Canadians in Northern Germany – 1951–64,' *Vanguard* 4, 2 (1998): 8.

87 J.L. Granatstein, *Canada, 1957–1967: The Years of Uncertainty and Innovation* (Toronto, 1986), chap. 5.

88 Author's personal experience.

89 Kitching, *Mud and Green Fields*, 296.

90 Graham, *Citizen and Soldier*, 230.

91 Maloney, *Korea*, 164–5.

92 W.A. Morrison, *The Voice of Defence: The History of the Conference of Defence Associations ... 1932–1982* (Ottawa, 1982), 121ff.; English, *Lament*, 51–2.

93 Graham, *Citizen and Soldier*, 240.

94 Marteinson, *We Stand on Guard*, 410–13.

95 Brian Macdonald, 'Thinking Outside the Box: Radical Questions about Canadian Defence Planning,' in D. Rudd et al., eds., *Advance or Retreat: Canadian Defence in the 21st Century* (Toronto, 2000), 82.

96 Graham, *Citizen and Soldier*, 240.

97 Paul Hellyer, *Damn the Torpedoes: My Fight to Unify Canada's Armed Forces* (Toronto, 1990), 3–4.

98 Bercuson, *True Patriot*, 160ff.; R.L. Raymont, 'The Evolution of the Structure of the Department of National Defence 1945–1968,' a report to the Task Force on Review of Unification of the Canadian Armed Forces, November 30, 1979.

99 University of Victoria Archives, George Pearkes Papers, [R.H. Roy] Interview with Gen Charles Foulkes, June 5, 1967.

100 Royal Commission on Government Organization, Report 20: Department of National Defence (Ottawa, 1962), pointed at triplication of services in the DND and prefigured some of the Hellyer changes.

101 William Lee, 'Integration of the Armed services: Why and How,' *Commentator* 9 (January 1965): 18.

102 See Hellyer, *Damn the Torpedoes*, chap. 2; Douglas Bland, *The Administration of Defence Policy in Canada, 1947 to 1985* (Kingston, Ont., 1987), chap. 4.

103 See Bland, *Chiefs*, chap. 3.

104 Joseph Jockel, *Canada and NATO's Northern Flank* (Toronto, 1986), 20–1.

105 Granatstein, *Canada, 1957–1967*, 222ff. The White Paper is readily available in Douglas Bland, ed., *Canada's National Defence, 1: Defence Policy* (Kingston, Ont., 1997), 57ff.

106 Hellyer, *Damn the Torpedoes*, 112.

107 NA, Paul Hellyer Papers, 'Background to the White Paper'; Commodore Robert Hendy Papers (Toronto), Hellyer to Downham, September 30, 1966; Vernon Kronenberg, *All Together Now: The Organization of the Department of National Defence in Canada,*

1964–1972 (Toronto, 1973), 29ff.; David Burke, 'The Unification of the Armed Forces,' *Revue internationale d'histoire militaire* 51 (1982): 302ff.

108 Kronenburg, *All Together Now*, 68ff.; Marteinson, *We Stand on Guard*, 406ff.

109 Kitching, *Mud and Green Fields*, 309.

110 Hellyer Papers, vol. 7, 'Summary Record of the Discussion at Defence Council,' December 21, 1965. See also Moncel's comments before the House of Commons Standing Committee on National Defence, *Minutes*, 1967, 1304ff.

111 Hellyer, *Damn the Torpedoes*, 159–60; Jean V. Allard, *Mémoires du Général Jean V. Allard* (Boucherville, Que., 1985), chaps. 13–14; Bland, *Chiefs*, 84ff.

112 Committee *Minutes*, 1967, 1769.

113 David Burke, 'Hellyer and Landymore: The Unification of the Canadian Armed Forces and an Admiral's Revolt,' *American Review of Canadian Studies* 8 (autumn 1978), 11.

114 Quoted in Kitching, *Mud and Green Fields*, 310.

115 See Directorate of History, National Defence Headquarters, file 80/225, folder 115, D.J. Beattie, 'Perceptions of Unification, 1966–1967,' a paper prepared for the Task Force on the Review of Unification of the Canadian Forces; R.S. Malone, 'Defence Forces Integration,' a pamphlet reprinted from the *Winnipeg Free Press*, August 1966.

116 For instance, John Hasek, *The Disarming of Canada* (Toronto, 1987), 146.

10 Professionalism under Siege, 1968–2001

1 John Holmes, 'Most Safely in the Middle,' *International Journal* 39 (spring 1984): 384.

2 See David Pugliese, 'Nobel Fever,' *Saturday Night*, May 1997, 52ff.

3 Bruce Thordarson, *Trudeau and Foreign Policy* (Toronto, 1971), 71.

4 Paul Hellyer Papers (Toronto), Cabinet notes, May 15, 1968; Office of the Prime Minister, Press Release, May 29, 1968.

5 See J.L. Granatstein and R. Bothwell, *Pirouette: Pierre Trudeau and Canadian Foreign Policy* (Toronto, 1990), chap. 1.

6 See Joseph Jockel, *Canada and NATO's Northern Flank* (Toronto, 1986), 20ff.; Granatstein interview with Adm Richard Leir, September 24, 1987. Copies of my interviews are in the Directorate of History and Heritage, National Defence Headquarters. The brief account in Barney Danson, 'Not Bad for a Sergeant: The Memoirs of Barney Danson' (unpublished manuscript), 241–43, is very good.

7 Granatstein interview with Hon. Léo Cadieux, December 9, 1987; *Globe and Mail*, April 4, 1969.

8 See Marilyn Eustace, *Canada's Commitment to Europe: The European Force, 1964–1971* (Kingston, Ont., 1979).

9 Sean Maloney, *War without Battles: Canada's NATO Brigade in Germany, 1951–1993* (Toronto, 1997), 236ff.

10 Ibid., 291ff.

11 Ibid., 242–3.

12 Granatstein interview with MGen W.C. Leonard, June 15, 1989.

13 David Bercuson, *Significant Incident: Canada's Army, the Airborne, and the Murder in Somalia* (Toronto, 1996), 81.

14 LCol J.P. McManus to author, June 9, 2001.

15 See Dan G. Loomis, *Not Much Glory: Quelling the F.L.Q.* (Toronto, 1984); Sean Maloney, '"A Mere Rustle of Leaves": Canadian Strategy and the 1970 FLQ Crisis,' *Canadian Military Journal* 1 (summer 2000): 73ff.

16 J.O. Dendy, 'The Canadian Armed Forces and the "October Crisis" of 1970: A Historian's Perspective,' paper presented at the XIV International Military History Colloquium, Montreal, August 1988; John Gellner, *Bayonets in the Streets: Urban Guerilla at Home and Abroad* (Don Mills, Ont., 1974), chap. 4; Maloney, 'Rustle,' 80ff.

17 Lysiane Gagnon, 'A dark flirtation with history,' *Maclean's*, October 21, 1985, 7.

18 Confidential interview.

19 Ibid.

20 *Defence in the 70s: White Paper on Defence* (Ottawa, 1971); Granatstein interview with Hon. Donald Macdonald, April 5, 1988. See J.L. Granatstein, 'Preparing for the Millennium: The Trudeau and Mulroney Defence and Foreign Policy Reviews,' in C. Remie and J. Lacroix, eds., *Canada on the Threshold of the 21st Century* (Amsterdam, 1991), 487ff.

21 Serge Bernier, 'Hail to the Artist! The Art of Command and General Jean V. Allard,' in B. Horn and S. Harris, eds., *Warrior Chiefs: Perspectives on Senior Canadian Military Leaders* (Toronto, 2001), 286.

22 Jean Pariseau et Serge Bernier, *Les Canadiens français et le bilingualisme dans les forces armées canadiennes*, tome 1: *1763–1969* (Ottawa, 1987), 158ff.; J.Y Gravel, 'La fondation du Collège Militaire Royal de St Jean,' in Gravel, *Le Québec et la guerre* (Montreal, 1974).

23 See Armand Letellier, *DND Language Reform: Staffing the Bilingualism Programs, 1967–1977* (Ottawa, 1987).

24 Bernier, *Les Canadiens français*, 286.

25 National Archives of Canada (NA), L.B. Pearson Papers, N4, vol. 32, file 043.6 Pers. and Conf., Cadieux to Prime Minister, November 27, 1967; Lalonde to Prime Minister, December 5, 1967; Pitfield to Prime Minister, March 1, 1968. Compare Jean V. Allard, *Mémoires du Général Jean V. Allard* (Boucherville, Qué., 1985), chap. 14.

26 There is a detailed account of FLUs, Francotrain, and all subsequent events in Serge Bernier and Jean Pariseau, *French Canadians and Bilingualism in the Canadian Armed Forces*, vol. 2: *1969–1987* (Ottawa, 1994).

27 Desmond Morton, *A Military History of Canada* (Toronto, 1992), 258.

28 Gen F.R. Sharp, 'Bilingualism Policy in the CAF,' CDS Policy Directive, February 27, 1970.

29 Quoted in Gerald Porter, *In Retreat: The Canadian Forces in the Trudeau Years* (Ottawa, nd), 21.

30 Directorate of History, National Defence Headquarters, Jean Pariseau Papers, Briefing to CDSAC by DGOM on Plan and Goals to Increase Biculturalism in the Canadian Armed Forces, November 17, 1971.

31 Porter, *In Retreat*, 114ff. See 'Some Questions and Answers on French Language Units,' *Canadian Forces Bulletin* 6 (October 1971).

32 Porter, *In Retreat*, 24–5.

33 Tom Sloan, 'National Defence: Defending One's Country in One's Own Language,' *Language and Society* 30 (spring 1990): 6–7.

34 *Report of the Ministerial Committee on Official Languages in the Department of National Defence and the Canadian Armed Forces*, November 13, 1992.

35 MGen Leonard interview.

36 Morton, *Military History of Canada*, 259.

37 Chris Madsen, *Another Kind of Justice: Canadian Military Law from Confederation to Somalia* (Vancouver, 1999), 123; Douglas Bland, 'Institutionalizing Ambiguity: The Management Review Group and the Reshaping of the Defence Policy Process in Canada,' *Canadian Public Administration* 30 (winter 1987): 527ff. See also Douglas Bland, *The Administration of Defence Policy in Canada, 1947 to 1985* (Kingston, Ont., 1987), 62ff.

38 Quoted in Bercuson, *Significant Incident*, 72.

39 Adm Lynn Mason, 'The Organization of the Department of National Defence,' paper prepared for the Council on Canadian Security in the 21st Century, 2 (available on www.stratnet.ucalgary.ca/ccspapers).

40 P.D. Manson, 'The Restructuring of National Defence Headquarters – 1972–73,' *Canadian Defence Quarterly* 3 (winter 1973–74): 8.

41 Bercuson, *Significant Incident*, 75.

42 Pariseau Papers, file NDHQ S 1/85, 'The Impact of Integration, Unification and Restructuring on the Functions and Structure of National Defence Headquarters,' July 31, 1985.

43 Peter Newman, *True North: Not Strong and Free* (Toronto, 1983), 56.

44 Quoted in Maloney, *War without Battles*, 385.

45 NA, Department of National Defence Records, category VII, book 5, Arnell submission to Fyffe task force.

46 See Sid Tafler, 'How Bureaucrats Beat McKinnon,' Montreal *Gazette*, December 27, 1980.

47 Pariseau Papers, file 84/331, vol. 5b, 'Results of the Review Group on the Report of the Task Force on Unification of the Canadian Forces,' August 31, 1980; Granatstein and Bothwell, *Pirouette*, 250–2.

48 D. Bercuson et al., *Sacred Trust? Brian Mulroney and the Conservative Party in Power* (Toronto, 1986), 230–1.

49 See Erik Nielsen, *The House Is Not a Home* (Toronto, 1989), 248ff.

50 On the White Paper, see N. Michaud, 'Bureaucratic Politics and the Making of the 1987 White Paper,' in N. Michaud and and K. Nossal, eds., *Diplomatic Departures: The Conservative Era in Canadian Foreign Policy, 1984–93* (Vancouver, 2001), 260ff.

51 See N.M. Ripsman, 'Big Eyes and Empty Pockets: The Two Phases of Conservative Defence Policy,' in ibid., 100f.

52 Quoted in John Marteinson et al., *We Stand on Guard: An Illustrated History of the Canadian Army* (Montreal, 1992), 443. The 1987 White Paper is printed in Douglas Bland, *Canada's National Defence: vol. 1: Defence Policy* (Kingston, Ont., 1997), 183ff.

53 Quoted in J.L. Granatstein and D. Bercuson, *War and Peacekeeping: From South Africa to the Gulf – Canada's Limited Wars* (Toronto, 1991), 232; David Charters, 'From October to Oka: Peacekeeping in Canada, 1970–1990,' in D.R. Jones, ed., *Military Aid to Civil Authorities in the Anglo-Saxon Tradition* (1993), 376ff.; and C. Beauregard, 'The Military Intervention in Oka: Strategy, Communication and Press Coverage,' *Canadian Military History* 2 (spring 1993): 23ff.

54 See Maloney, *War without Battles*, 448ff.

55 See the official account: J.H. Morin and R.H. Gimblett, *Operation Friction: The Canadian Forces in the Persian Gulf* (Toronto, 1997), and D.E. Miller and S. Hobson, *The Persian Excursion: The Canadian Navy in the Gulf War* (Clementsport, NS, 1995).

56 See, for example, *Maclean's*, February 21, 2000, 52–4.

57 See Roy Rempel, *Counterweights: The Failure of Canada's German and European Policy, 1955–1995* (Montreal, 1996), chap. 8; Maloney, *War without Battles*, 480.

58 *Maclean's*, July 30, 2001, 21.

59 Hon. D. Collenette, 'National Defence: Budget Impact' (Ottawa, 1994).

60 Quoted in Bercuson, *Significant Incident*, 76.

61 The White Paper is printed in Bland, *Canada's National Defence*, 293ff. See also A. Morrison and S. McNish, eds., *The Canadian Defence Policy Review* (Toronto, 1994).

62 J. Jockel and J. Sokolsky, 'Lloyd Axworthy's Legacy: Human Security and the Rescue of Canadian Defence Policy,' *International Journal* 56 (winter 2000–1): 5.

63 'Manpower in Canada's Armed Forces,' *First Report of the Sub-Committee on National Defence of the Senate Standing Committee on Foreign Affairs*, January 1982, 37.

64 *Defence 1974* (Ottawa, 1975), 79.

65 *Defence: 1978 in Review* (Ottawa, 1979), 96–7.

66 *Defence 1984* (Ottawa, 1985), 92–3; Maloney, *War without Battles*, 389. Barney Danson noted that he was 'taken aback by the attitude of some women's groups ... Were we opening the door to allowing women to kill in war?' 'Not Bad for a Sergeant,' 248.

67 *Ottawa Citizen*, November 22, 1999, A3.

68 Ibid.

69 Lieutenant K.D. Davis, 'Chief Land Staff Gender Integration Study: The Regular Force Training and Employment Environment,' Personnel Research Team, National Defence Headquarters, September 1997, 1.

70 Quoted in *National Post*, December 4, 1999, B7.

71 This recommendation was made in 'Manpower in Canada's Armed Forces,' 38–9.

72 *Globe and Mail*, March 24, 2001, A17.

73 'Manpower in Canada's Armed Forces,' 38–9.

74 *Globe and Mail*, March 24, 2001; *Ottawa Citizen*, October 21, 2000. For a comparison of 1980s and 1990s training standards, see Annex A in Conference of Defence Associations, *Caught in the Middle: An Assessment of the Operational Readiness of the Canadian Forces* (Ottawa, 2001).

75 Lieutenant K.D. Davis and Virginia Thomas, 'Chief Land Staff Gender Integration Study: The Experience of Women Who Have Served in the Combat Arms,' Personnel Research

Team, National Defence Headquarters, January 1998, abstract. See also Sheila Hellstrom, 'Women in the Canadian Armed Forces: A Work in Progress,' in J. Hanson and S. McNish, eds., *The Military in Modern Democratic Society* (Toronto, 1996), 91ff.

76 DND Transcript 'Army Diversity and Gender Integrated Program,' June 17, 1998.

77 *Ottawa Citizen*, May 24, 2000, A5.

78 *Globe and Mail*, March 27, 2001, A3.

79 See especially *Maclean's*, May 25, June 1, 8, July 13, and December 14, 1998.

80 Ibid., June 8, 1998, 29.

81 Madsen, *Another Kind of Justice*, 152.

82 A. Belkin and J. McNichol, 'Homosexual Personnel Policy in the Canadian Forces,' *International Journal* 56 (winter 2000–1): 73ff.

83 For a positive interpretation on this process, see C. Dandeker and Donna Winslow, 'Challenges to Military Culture from Living in the 21st Century,' in D.M. Hayne, ed., *Governance in the 21st Century* (Toronto, 2000), especially 213ff. A perfect example of modern CF inclusiveness was the consecration of the new colours of the Royal Military College on September 29, 2001, where representatives of eight religions – including a Zoroastrian – participated.

84 See *National Post*, April 9, 2001, A5, for Minister Eggleton's comments on barriers to women infanteers' success rates at Camp Wainwright.

85 *Minister's Advisory Board on Canadian Forces Gender Integration and Employment Equity* (Ottawa, 2001).

86 Desmond Morton, paper presented to Conference of Defence Associations Institute, January 28, 1993.

87 *Report of the Special Commission on the Restructuring of the Reserves* (Ottawa, 1995), 27, 109ff. This author was a member of the commission, as was LGen Charles Belzile.

88 The SCRR ideas on mobilization largely came from LGen Belzile. See his paper, 'Canada's Response: Mobilization and a New Army Structure,' in B. Macdonald, ed., *Tactics and Technology* (Toronto, 1986), 27ff.

89 *Report of Special Commission*, passim; Canadian Forces Liaison Council booklets.

90 The tenor of the debate is in J. Hanson and P. Hammerschmidt, eds., *The Past, Present and Future of the Militia* (Toronto, 1998). See also T.C. Willett, *A Heritage at Risk: The Canadian Militia as a Social Institution* (Boulder, Col., 1987).

91 *In the Service of the Nation: Canada's Citizen Soldiers for the 21st Century* (Ottawa, 2000).

92 The Army Lessons Learned Centre's Analysis Report 9903, 'Reserve/Regular Integration Analysis,' January 2000, says flatly that the provision of formed or composite reserve sub- or sub-sub-units is 'not feasible.' The full text is available through *www.army.dnd.ca*.

93 A packet of documents on Land Force Reserve Restructure, issued October 6, 2000, including a Minister's announcement, a Government Policy Statement, 'The LFRR Strategic Plan and the Reserve Soldier,' and 'Backgrounder Documentation.' LGen Jeffrey's 'Land Forces Reserve Restructure Strategic Plan' is dated September 2000. These documents are available on the DND website.

94 D. Mainguy, 'A View from outside the Army,' *DANN National Network News* 8 (spring 2001): 32.

95 See Jeff Koloze, 'United States Is to Violence as Canada Is to Peace,' Conference of Defence Associations Institute, First Annual Graduate Student Symposium, Ottawa, 1998, 75ff.; J.L. Granatstein, *Yankee Go Home? Canadians and Anti-Americanism* (Toronto, 1996), especially chap. 7. There are a series of reports on peacekeeping operations in Directorate of History, Canadian Forces Headquarters Reports, available through the Directorate of History and Heritage website.

96 Sean Maloney, '"Mad Jimmy" Dextraze: The Tightrope of UN Command in the Congo,' in Horn and Harris, eds., *Warrior Chiefs*, 303ff.

97 Granatstein and Bercuson, *War and Peacekeeping*, 219.

98 Alastair Taylor et al., *Peacekeeping: International Challenge and Canadian Response* (Toronto, 1968), 147ff.; Trevor Findlay, *The Blue Helmets' First War: Use of Force by the UN in the Congo, 1960–64* (Clementsport, NS, 1999). See also Brian Urquhart, 'The Tragedy of Lumumba,' *New York Review of Books*, October 4, 2001, 4ff. On the contradictions in 1960s peacekeeping, see David Lenarcic, 'A Case of Double Vision: Canadian Peacekeeping Policy in the 1960s,' paper presented to the Canadian Historical Association, 1995.

99 Taylor et al., *Peacekeeping*, 169ff.

100 See Lewis MacKenzie, *Peacekeeper: The Road to Sarajevo* (Vancouver, 1993), chaps. 4, 5, and 8, for a good account of Cyprus service, and Robert Burns, 'A Hot Night in the Zone,' *Legion*, May/June 2001, 27ff.

101 MGen J.A. MacInnis, 'Cyprus – Canada's Perpetual Vigil,' *Canadian Defence Quarterly* 19 (August 1989): 21ff.

102 See MacKenzie, *Peacekeeper*, chap. 7; W.H. Porter, 'United Nations Emergency Force II,' *Canadian Defence Quarterly* 19 (August 1989): 48ff.

103 G.D. Smith, 'Truce Supervision in Indochina, 1954–1973,' *Canadian Defence Quarterly* 19 (August 1989): 34ff.; P. Dai, 'Canada's Reluctant Participation in the International Commission for Control and Supervision in Vietnam in 1973,' *Canadian Yearbook of International Law* 11 (1973): 244ff.

104 W.A.D. Yuill, 'The United Nations Disengagement Observer Force,' *Canadian Defence Quarterly* 19 (August 1989): 28ff. Nine Canadian servicemen serving in UNEF II died when a Syrian SAM shot down their UN-marked aircraft in August 1974 – the worst single disaster to Canadian arms on peacekeeping service.

105 D.S. Leslie and R.G. Elms, 'United Nations Good Offices Mission in Afghanistan and Pakistan,' *Canadian Defence Quarterly* 19 (August 1989): 51ff

106 R. Maxwell, 'Clearing Cambodia,' *Legion*, March/April 2001, 20ff.

107 Wayne Shields, 'Coping with Chaos in Haiti,' *Legion*, September/October 2000, 32ff.

108 Jessica Blitt, 'OP Toucan and Beyond: Contradictions in Canadian Policy in East Timor,' *CISS Strategic Datalink* 87 (March 2000).

109 See the list in Joseph Jockel, *The Canadian Forces: Hard Choices, Soft Power* (Toronto, 1999), 18ff.

110 According to the Kingston *Whig-Standard*, May 11, 2001, 6, the 760 PMQs without insulation in Kingston needed $15 million in repairs, but only $1.5 million was budgeted. Across Canada, $300 million was required, but rents for soldiers were still increasing in September 2001.

111 Scott Taylor and Brian Nolan, *Tested Mettle: Canada's Peacekeepers at War* (Ottawa, 1998), 116.

112 Allen Sens, 'From Peacekeeping to Intervention: Expeditionary Capabilities and the Canadian Force Structure Debate,' paper prepared for the Council for Canadian Security in the 21st Century, 2–3 (available on www.stratnet.ucalgary.ca/ccspapers).

113 MGen Lewis Mackenzie, review of *Why Peacekeeping Fails* in *International Journal* 56 (winter 2000–1): 176.

114 See Carol Off, *The Lion, the Fox, and the Eagle: A Story of Generals and Justice in Rwanda and Yugoslavia* (Toronto, 2000), 29ff.

115 See the government paper, *Towards a Rapid Reaction Capability for the United Nations* (1995).

116 See J.L. Granatstein, 'What's Wrong with Peacekeeping?' in M.J. Tucker et al., eds., *Canada and the New World Order: Facing the New Millennium* (Toronto, 2000), 45ff.; Rosemary Righter, *Utopia Lost: The United Nations and World Order* (New York, 1995); William Shawcross, *Deliver Us from Evil: Peacekeepers, Warlords, and a World of Endless Conflict* (New York, 2000).

117 See Bland, *Canada's National Defence*, 293ff.

118 See M. Tessier and M. Fortmann, 'The Conservative Approach to International Peacekeeping,' in Michaud and Nossal, eds., *Diplomatic Departures*, 113ff.

119 See Maloney, *War without Battles*, 475ff.

120 Letter, July 16, 1992, in J. Snailham, *Eyewitness to Peace: Letters from Canadian Peacekeepers* (Clementsport, NS, 1998), 12.

121 See MacKenzie, *Peacekeeper*. For a contrary view of MacKenzie, see Off, *The Lion, the Fox, and the Eagle*, 153ff. Another Canadian general, MGen J.A. MacInnis, was deputy commander of UNPROFOR. See his 'Peacekeeping and Postmodern Conflict: A Soldier's View,' *Mediterranean Quarterly* 6 (spring 1995): 29ff.

122 Letter of September 20, 1993, in Snailham, *Eyewitness to Peace*, 30.

123 David Bercuson, *The Patricias: The Proud History of a Fighting Regiment* (Toronto, 2001), 293ff.; Lee Windsor, 'Professionalism under Fire: Canadian Implementation of the Medak Pocket Agreement, Croatia 1993,' *Canadian Military History* 9 (summer 2000): 23ff. The Croatian general in command of the operation, Rahim Ademi, surrendered to the UN war crimes tribunal in The Hague in July 25, 2001; a second general was also indicted. PPCLI vets of Medak and senior Canadian commanders there in 1993 expressed great pleasure at Ademi's surrender and some were to testify against him. *National Post*, July 26, 2001, A3; July 27, 2001, A11.

124 Letter, February 12, 1994, in Snailham, *Eyewitness to Peace*, 39.

125 For a splendid account of one event – the role of PPCLI Major Pat Stogran in April 1994 as a UN military observer in saving the Muslim town of Goradze from Serbian ethnic cleansing – see *National Post*, January 12, 2001, B1.

126 See Norman Hillmer and Dean Oliver, 'The NATO–United Nations Link: Canada and the Balkans, 1991–1995,' in Gustav Schmidt, ed., *A History of NATO: The First Fifty Years* (Basingstoke, UK, and New York, 2001).

127 See the essays by LGen R. Henault and BGen J. Caron in B. Horn and S. Harris, eds., *Generalship and the Art of the Admiral: Perspectives on Senior Canadian Military Leadership* (St Catharines, Ont., 2001); Ivan Fenton, 'Canada's Role in Kosovo and KFOR,' in D. Rudd et al., *Future Peacekeeping: A Canadian Perspective* (Toronto, 2001), 15ff.; and four articles in *Canadian Military Journal* 1 (spring 2000): 41ff.

128 See *Maclean's*, August 9, 1999, 12ff.; *Maple Leaf* 2 (July 28, 1999): 1. The CDS issued an extensive information kit on August 13, 1999.

129 See, for example, Dan Loomis, *The Somalia Affair* (Ottawa, 1996), 459; James Davis, *The Sharp End: A Canadian Soldier's Story* (Vancouver, 1997), 49–50; and R. Ameral, *Eat Your Weakest Man* (Calgary, 2000).

130 J. Marteinson and M. McNorgan, *The Royal Canadian Armoured Corps: An Illustrated History* (Toronto, 2000), 402–3.

131 See M.A. Arush, 'Canada and Somalia in the 21st Century: An Overview of the Performance of the Canadian Armed Forces in Somalia,' *Strategic Datalink* 60 (February 1997), and C.S. Oliviero, 'Operation "Deliverance": International Success or Domestic Failure?' *Canadian Military Journal* 2 (summer 2001): 51ff.

132 One soldier, Robert Prouse, kept a journal, published in the *Ottawa Citizen*, July 15–16, 2000.

133 See G. Shorey, 'Bystander Non-Intervention and the Somalia Incident,' *Canadian Military Journal* 1 (winter 2000–1): 19ff.

134 Bercuson, *Significant Incident*, 227.

135 On Brown, see the ineffective apologia, Peter Worthington and Kyle Brown, *Scapegoat: How the Army Betrayed Kyle Brown* (Toronto, 1997).

136 John English, *Lament for an Army: The Decline of Canadian Military Professionalism* (Toronto, 1998), 4.

137 The best account with full context is LCol Bernd Horn, *Bastard Sons: An Examination of Canada's Airborne Experience 1942–1995* (St Catharines, Ont., 2001), chaps. 7–9. Horn acknowledges the problems but rues the disappearance of the CAR and its capabilities. See also Bercuson, *Significant Incident*; Donna Winslow, 'Rites of Passage and Group Bonding in the Canadian Airborne,' *Armed Forces and Society* 25 (spring 1999): 429ff.; and Peter Haydon, 'The Somalia Inquiry: Can It Solve Anything?' *Strategic Datalink* 62 (February 1997).

138 The commission's report, research studies, transcripts, and documents are available on CD-ROM: *Information Legacy: A Compendium of Source Material from the Commission of Inquiry into the Deployment of Canadian Forces to Somalia* (Ottawa, 1997). There are paper versions as well. Among the most valuable reports are J.-P. Brodeur, *Violence and Racial Prejudice in the Context of Peacekeeping*; Donna Winslow, *The Canadian Airborne Regiment in Somalia: A Socio-Cultural Inquiry*; Douglas Bland, *National Defence Headquarters: Centre for Decision*; and Allen Sens, *Somalia and the Changing Nature of Peacekeeping: The Implications for Canada* (Ottawa, 1997).

139 See especially Peter Desbarats, *Somalia Cover-Up: A Commissioner's Journal* (Toronto, 1997).

140 *Report of the Special Advisory Group on Military Justice and Military Police Investigation Services* (Ottawa, 1997).

141 See J.L. Granatstein, 'A Diary of the Defence Review, 1997,' *International Journal* 52 (summer 1997): 524ff.

142 D.J. Bercuson, 'The Current State of Canadian Military Education,' a paper presented to the Society for Military History, Calgary, May 2001.

143 Quoted in J.L. Granatstein, 'A Paper Prepared for the Minister of National Defence,' March 25, 1957. The other academic papers were by D.J. Bercuson, Albert Legault, and Desmond Morton, and they were grouped with several other pamphlets into Young's Report to the Prime Minister.

144 *The Maple Leaf* 2, 22 (1999): 20

145 See David Lenarcic, *Knight-Errant? Canada and the Crusade to Ban Anti-Personnel Land Mines* (Toronto, 1998); J.R. English, 'The Land Mine Initiative: A Canadian Initiative?' in A. Cooper and G. Hayes, eds., *Worthwhile Initiatives? Canadian Mission-Oriented Diplomacy* (Toronto, 2000), 23ff.; *National Post*, March 13, 1999.

146 On human security, see especially F.E. Hampson et al., eds., *The Axworthy Legacy: Canada among Nations, 2001* (Toronto, 2000), passim.

147 Scott Taylor and Brian Nolan, *Tarnished Brass: Crime and Corruption in the Canadian Military* (Toronto, 1996), chap. 4.

148 Quoted in Granatstein, 'A Paper Prepared,' 10. See also Bland, *National Defence Headquarters*, 66–7, and *Ottawa Citizen*, October 19, 2000.

149 'A Commitment to Change: Report on the Recommendations of the Somalia Commission of Inquiry,' October 1997.

150 The oversight committee's reports were published in several volumes as *Minister's Monitoring Committee on Change in the Department of National Defence and the Canadian Forces* (Ottawa, 1998ff.).

151 *Ottawa Citizen*, October 21, 1997, A17. A new CF 'ethos statement' was approved in August 1997. See Vincent Rigby, 'The Canadian Forces and Human Security: A Redundant or Relevant Military?' in Hampson et al., *The Axworthy Legacy*, 57–8.

152 First draft of *NCM Corps 2020: Detailed Strategic Guidance and Vision for the Professional Development of the CF Non Commissioned Members Corps* (Ottawa, 2001), I-21.

153 Dean Oliver, 'The Canadian Military after Somalia,' in F. Hampson and M. Molot, eds., *Canada among Nations 1998: Leadership and Dialogue* (Ottawa, 1998), 99.

154 *National Post*, June 23, 2001, A4.

155 Off, *The Lion, the Fox, and the Eagle*, 96–7. See also D.G. Anglin, 'Rwanda Revisited,' *International Journal* 56 (winter, 2000–1): 168.

156 *New York Times*, October 8, 2000.

157 Professor Peter Neary, who heard Dallaire make this statement, passed the comment to me.

158 For example, CDS' appearance before House of Commons, Standing Committee on National Defence and Veterans Affairs, Minutes June 4, 1998, and the committee's 'Moving Forward: A Strategic Plan for Quality of Life Improvements in the Canadian

Forces,' October 1988. See two books on military wives: Dianne Collier, *Hurry Up and Wait: An Inside Look at Life as a Military Wife* (Carp, Ont., 1994), and D. Harrison and L. Laliberté, *No Life Like It: Military Wives in Canada* (Toronto, 1994).

159 See Allan English, 'The Americanization of the Canadian Officer Corps: Myth or Reality,' in B. Horn, ed., *Contemporary Issues in Officership: A Canadian Perspective* (Toronto, 2000), 181ff.; *Globe and Mail*, February 22, 2000, A18.

160 Gen Maurice Baril, 'The State of the Profession of Arms in the Canadian Forces,' XVth Annual Seminar, Conference of Defence Associations Institute, January 29, 1999.

161 See Grant Dawson, 'In Support of Peace: Canada, the Brahimi Report, and Human Security,' in Hampson et al., *2001*, 294ff; D. Bratt and E. Gionet, 'Evaluating the Brahimi Report,' Canadian Institute of Strategic Studies *Strategic Datalink* 96 (May 2001).

162 *National Post*, March 22, 2001, A1; *Maclean's* , June 25, 2001, 26.

163 Quoted in Jocelyn Coulon, 'Le Canada et les operations de paix: Un engagement a redefinir,' paper prepared for the Council on Canadian Security in the 21st Century,' 3 (available on www.stratnet.ucalgary.ca/ccspapers).

164 Sens, 'From Peacekeeping to Intervention,' 3. See the chart, Annex C, attached to the Vice-Chief of the Defence Staff's paper, 'Rethinking the Total Force: Aligning the Defence Team for the 21st Century,' on the VCDS website, February 16, 2000.

165 *National Post*, August 23, 2001; D. Bercuson, 'What it takes to be a good NATO partner,' *National Post*, August 24, 2001.

166 Email from Executive Director, Conference of Defence Associations, July 16, 2001; email, Executive Director, CDA, to Hon. John Manley, November 26, 2001. On the 2001 budget, see *Globe and Mail* and *National Post*, December 11, 2001, and author's confidential interviews with senior officers.

167 In U.S. dollar terms, Canada spent $7.5 billion a year, which placed it seventh in NATO, just ahead of Spain, Greece, and the Netherlands, but well behind Italy and Turkey. *National Post Business*, January 2002, 74.

168 Jockel, *Canadian Forces*, 44ff.

169 Joe Varner, 'Canadian Rapid Reaction Capabilities Limited,' *DANN National Network News* 7 (fall/winter 2001): 21.

170 See *Ottawa Citizen*, October 17, 2000; Ray Crabbe, 'Alternate Service Delivery,' paper prepared for the Council for Canadian Security in the 21st Century' (available on www.stratnet.ucalgary.ca/ccspapers).

171 *Maple Leaf* 3 (June 14, 2000): 1.

172 C. MacLean, 'Contractor Support Program,' *Vanguard* 2 (2001): 24ff.

173 Evidence of the CLS, LGen M. Jeffery, to House of Commons Standing Committee on National Defence and Veterans Affairs, May 17, 2001. Text provided by Confederation of Defence Associations. The CDA report, 'Caught in the Middle,' gives the 19,700 figure.

174 See Jim Hanson, 'A Smaller, Better Equipped Army,' *Canadian Institute of Strategic Studies Bulletin* 12 (winter 2000): 7ff.

175 'Addressing the Military Personnel Challenge,' Unclassified Briefing to RMC Board of Governors, February 26, 2001. See also *An Honour to Serve: Annual Report of the Chief of the Defence Staff, 2000–2001* (Ottawa, 2001), 22–3, and Annex D; D. Pugliese, 'Forces'

Toughest Battle: HR,' *Ottawa Citizen*, October 17, 2000; and C. Ankerson and L. Tethong, 'Birds in Hand: The Need for a Retention-Based Strategy for the CF,' *Canadian Military Journal* 2 (summer 2001): 43ff.

11 Afghanistan and the Remaking of the Army

I am greatly indebted to Col (Ret'd) George Petrolekas, Col (Ret'd) Alain Pellerin, and Dr David Bercuson for their comments on this chapter.

1 Jean Chrétien, *My Years as Prime Minister* (Toronto, 2007), 303.
2 [3 PPCLI] Commanding Officer's page on www.angelfire.com/wizard/apollo0/.
3 Michael Friscolanti, 'We Were Abandoned,' *Maclean's*, May 15, 2006.
4 Confidential document.
5 Stephen J. Thorne, 'The Caves and Graves of Tora Bora,' *Legion Magazine* (July–August 2003).
6 Michael Friscolanti, *Friendly Fire: The Untold Story of the U.S. Bombing That Killed Four Canadian Soldiers in Afghanistan* (Mississauga, ON, 2005). A useful and detailed account of the 3PPCLI role can be found in a DND Backgrounder, 'The Canadian Forces' Contribution to the International Campaign against Terrorism,' BG-02.001p, January 7, 2004, at www.forces.gc.ca.
7 General Rick Hillier, *A Soldier First: Bullets, Bureaucrats and the Politics of War* (Toronto, 2009), 267.
8 A number of exchange officers from the CF with U.S. and UK forces did serve in Iraq. For his account, see Chrétien, *My Years*, 306ff. On Quebec attitudes, consistently against increased defence spending, more recently anti-U.S. and always anti-imperialist, and very cautious about military deployments abroad, see Jean-Sébastien Rioux, *Two Solitudes: Quebecers' Attitudes Regarding Canadian Security and Defence Policy* (Calgary, 2008).
9 Hillier, *A Soldier First*, 263.
10 Quoted in J.L. Granatstein, *Whose War Is It? How Canada Can Survive in the Post-9/11 World* (Toronto, 2007), 91–2. A lengthy defence of the government decision to stay out of Iraq – one that completely fails to mention the compensatory Afghan redeployment – can be found in the memoir by Chrétien's key aide, Eddie Goldenberg, *The Way It Works* (Toronto, 2006). Similarly silent is Chrétien, who adds that by taking command of ISAF in Kabul, 'we were going to get our soldiers into a more secure place where their assignment was closer to traditional peacekeeping.' *My Years*, 305.
11 Hillier, *A Soldier First*, 288ff.
12 Chrétien, *My Years*, 305.
13 J.L. Granatstein, *Who Killed the Canadian Military?* (Toronto, 2004), 173–4.
14 Maj Tom Mykytiuk, 'Company Command in the Three Block War: November Company – Task Force Kabul, Roto 0 – Operation Athena,' in Col. Bernd Horn, ed., *In Harm's Way: On the Front Lines of Leadership. Sub-Unit Command on Operations* (Kingston, 2006), 141–2.
15 See the chart of casualties by nation at 'Operation Enduring Freedom,' www.icasualties.org. The total killed between 2003 and the end of 2005 was 248, of whom 199 were American.

16 Maj. Keith Cameron, 'Afghanistan Diary,' *Veritas* [RMC Club] (December 2003).

17 Quoted in Granatstein, *Who Killed,* 174n.

18 Hillier, *A Soldier First,* 308.

19 See Hillier's account (ibid., 269–70) of how this occurred.

20 Confidential email.

21 See Colonel Mike Capstick, 'A Year in Kabul: Strategic Advisory Team-Afghanistan,' *On Track* (autumn 2006): 13–14; Christie Blatchford, 'Small Strategic Team Making Big Difference,' *Globe and Mail,* May 8, 2006. The SAT was killed despite the Karzai government's desire to keep it going. As one informed Army officer noted privately: 'Everyone from desk officers at DFAIT to DM level in PCO to at least one Ambassador in Kabul tried to torpedo it and, in time, succeeded. The hole left has still not been filled.' Confidential email and confidential documents. At its root, this was a conflict between the CF and NDHQ vs Foreign Affairs, with the Privy Council Office also anxious to constrain military influence. NATO was urged to pick up the SAT after Canada's team was terminated, but nothing came of this in 2008 (confidential document). Not until General David Petraeus took over in 2010 and de facto created a NATO SAT with 'senior strategic partners' (general officers or civilian equivalents) working directly with Afghan ministers did action occur. One Canadian observed: 'Think of the years of impact and influence we lost when we permitted rivalries to destroy the first iteration of the SAT' (confidential email).

22 General R.J. Hillier, 'Setting Our Course,' in D. Rudd, et al., eds., *Implementing Canada's Defence Policy Statement* (Toronto, 2005), 67.

23 Hillier, *A Soldier First,* 273–4. See also DND Backgrounder, 'Canadian Forces Commitment to Afghanistan to Date,' BG-05.012, May 16, 2005, at www.forces.gc.ca.

24 See, for example, J.L. Granatstein, *The Importance of Being Less Earnest: Promoting Canada's National Interests through Tighter Ties with the U.S.* (Toronto: C.D. Howe Institute, 2003); D. Stairs, et al., *In the National Interest: Canadian Foreign Policy in an Insecure World* (Calgary, 2003); J.L. Granatstein, 'A Friendly Agreement in Advance: Canada-U.S. Defence Relations,' *The Border Papers* [C.D. Howe Institute] (Toronto, 2002); and the Conference of Defence Association papers, available at http://www.cda-cdai.ca/cdai/uploads/cdai/2008/12/defencepolicy_2004.pdf and http://www.cda-cdai.ca/cdai/uploads/cdai/2008/12/nationatrisk_2002.pdf.

25 See, e.g., Dan Gardner, 'Martin Moved from Hawk to Dove at the Drop of a Writ,' *Ottawa Citizen,* June 26, 2004.

26 Douglas Bland, ed., *Canada without Armed Forces?* (Kingston, 2003), xii and passim. See also the extensive coverage of the Bland book in *National Post,* December 3, 2003. I am grateful to Dr Bland for letting me see his forthcoming Claxton Paper, *Let Sleeping Dogs Lie* (Kingston, 2010), which analyses the DND response to his book and other reports critical of governmental defence policies. Bland notes that when told that Martin had telephoned him, one senior DND official threw his notepad across his office.

27 See my *Importance of Being Less Earnest,* 5ff.

28 Hillier, *A Soldier First,* 322. See Douglas Bland, 'Hillier and the New Generation of Generals: The CDS, the Policy, and the Troops,' *Policy Options* (March 2008): 58ff. Not all was

praise for the CDS. See, e.g., Gerald Caplan, 'War and Peace Are Too Important to Leave to Generals,' *Toronto Star,* March 9, 2006.

29 Hillier, *A Soldier First*, 324–5.

30 *Canada's International Policy Statement: A Role of Pride and Influence* (Ottawa, 2005). For a varied group of assessments, see D.J. Bercuson and D. Stairs, eds., *In the Canadian Interest? Assessing Canada's International Policy Statement* (Calgary, 2005).

31 Hillier, *A Soldier First*, 350.

32 Confidential interview.

33 The best account of the decision to dispatch a full battle group is Bill Schiller, 'The Road to Kandahar,' *Toronto Star*, September 9, 2006. On the PRT's role and work, see Peter Pigott, *Canada in Afghanistan: The War So Far* (Toronto, 2007).

34 Hillier, 'Setting Our Course,' 71–2.

35 Hillier, *A Soldier First*, 344. On the shift from Kabul to Kandahar and the manoeuvring in the government and bureaucracy that achieved it, see Janet Gross Stein and Eugene Lang, *The Unexpected War: Canada in Kandahar* (Toronto, 2007). Others, however, including Hillier's memoir, argue that the decision to go to Kandahar was in train before he became CDS. Some strongly suggest it came out of DFAIT, not DND, or at the very least out of cooperation between the two departments and, moreover, that the United States knew before Hillier became CDS that Canada would go to Kandahar. Another source maintains that a move to Kandahar was first suggested by a DFAIT official at a meeting in Kabul as early as October 2003. The new tasking had to be meaningful, the official argued, and it could only be so if it was seen to be difficult. At the time, Hillier (and others) preferred that Canada assume responsibility for operating and defending Kabul's airport. Confidential emails.

36 Schiller, 'Road to Kandahar'; Stein and Lang, *Unexpected War*, 178ff. On Afghanistan vs Darfur, see Rob Huebert, 'The Debate between the Canadian Commitment to Afghanistan and the Sudan: The Need to Consider All Costs!' *Calgary Papers in Military and Strategic Studies (*2007), 1ff.; Peter Langille, 'Web-Exclusive Comment,' www.globeandmail.ca, April 27, 2006; James Travers, 'Peacekeeping Pledge Broken,' *Toronto Star*, May 11, 2006. The CF did send the former CLS, Lieutenant-General Mike Jeffrey, to Darfur to study the situation. As a result APCs were sent to the African Union peacekeepers, along with military advisers.

37 See my 'The End of the Hillier Era,' *Ottawa Citizen,* April 16, 2008.

38 Hillier, *A Soldier First*, 158–9.

39 Schiller, 'Road to Kandahar'.

40 Ian Hope, *Dancing with the Dushman: Command Imperatives for the Counter-Insurgency Fight in Afghanistan* (Kingston, 2008), 22–3. Hope had some difficulties with tactical decisions flowing down the chain of command, and he argued vigorously with Brigadier-General David Fraser. His book (152ff.), along with some articles published in *Legion Magazine,* put these – not unusual in Canada's military, past or present – battlefield disagreements into the public domain. See Adam Day, 'The Battle for Panjwai, Parts 1–3, *Legion Magazine* (September 2007–January 2008). Hope had the benefit of detailed 'lessons learned' that

had been collected by a Canadian officer who had extensively interviewed a battalion commander in the U.S. Army's 10th Mountain Division on his experiences in southeast Afghanistan (confidential document). The key lesson was 'I believe we will have to trust commander's judgments on the ground like we never have before,' a judgment that LCol Hope appears to have believed was not followed, or so the conclusions of his book suggest.

41 Confidential email. Conflicts over the training regimen at CFB Wainwright were sharp enough that the CDS and CLS went to the base in January 2006 to meet with the battle group's officers and warrants to thrash out the problems.

42 Ibid.

43 Hillier, *A Soldier First*, 388ff.

44 Hope, *Dancing with the Dushman*, 27

45 Ibid., 28ff.

46 Ibid., 55. Using the lessons learned in Kandahar, the Army produced its first manual on *Counter-Insurgency Operations* (Ottawa, 2009) in February 2009. On the manual, see Adam Day, 'The Army's New War,' *Legion Magazine* (May-June 2009): 34ff.

47 For good reportage on the very early stages of TF Orion, see Mitch Potter, 'War: Canadian-Style,' *Toronto Star*, March 12, 2006, D1–12.

48 'Address by the Prime Minister to the Canadian Armed Forces in Afghanistan, 13 March 2006,' on www.pm.gc.ca/eng/media.asp?id=1056.

49 See, e.g., Rick Salutin, 'Welcome to the Quagmire,' *Globe and Mail*, March 17, 2006.

50 Christie Blatchford, *Fifteen Days: Stories of Bravery, Friendship, Life and Death from Inside the New Canadian Army* (Toronto, 2007), 170.

51 Chris Wattie, *Contact Charlie: The Canadian Army, The Taliban and the Battle That Saved Afghanistan* (Toronto, 2008), 109–10. The 2010 edition of this book altered the subtitle to 'the Battle for Afghanistan,' presumably a reflection of the difficult fighting. Noted in David Pugliese's 'Defence Watch' blog, July 26, 2010, on the *Ottawa Citizen* website.

52 On Captain Goddard, see Valerie Fortney, *Sunray: The Death and Life of Captain Nichola Goddard* (Toronto, 2010), and also Goddard's 'Reflections and Letters Home,' *Veritas* (November 2006): 11ff. By late July 2010, two more women were killed in action and another died from non-battle causes in Afghanistan.

53 The way in which Canadians killed in action would be received at Trenton – with or without press coverage – was a source of controversy in early 2006. See my 'Honouring the Dead without Hypocrisy,' a column distributed by the Council for Canadian Security in the 21st Century, April 27, 2006; Bill Curry, 'Ottawa Fails Fallen Soldiers, Critics Say,' *Globe and Mail*, April 25, 2006.

54 See my 'End of the Hillier Era.'

55 Blatchford, *Fifteen Days*, 2.

56 See the account by Task Force Orion's logistics commander John Conrad, *What the Thunder Said: Reflections of a Canadian Officer in Kandahar* (Toronto, 2009). For an account by a combat engineer troop commander in Task Force Orion, see Captain Nathan Price, 'Five Hectic Days: An Account from Afghanistan,' *Veritas* (November 2006): 17ff.

57 Blatchford, *Fifteen Days*, 20.

58 Hope, *Dancing with the Dushman*, 129ff.

59 Confidential interview.

60 Carl Forsberg, *The Taliban's Campaign for Kandahar* (Washington, 2009), esp. 27ff.; confidential emails.

61 Hope, *Dancing with the Dushman*, 127. A fine account and meditation on the courage of U.S. soldiers in Afghanistan is Sebastian Junger, *War* (New York, 2010).

62 Confidential interviews.

63 'Report on Conference of Defence Associations Institute–Canadian Defence and Foreign Affairs Institute NATO Strategic Concept study discussion at NDHQ, 21 June 2010.' A retired senior diplomat privately noted that the public servants most responsible for getting Canada into the Afghan war 'as the going got tough … arranged to remove themselves, some through comfortable ambassadorships abroad … Many of those they left behind to run the war had no business being in the jobs they were given.' Confidential email. For comment on NATO, see Paul H. Chapin, *Security in an Uncertain World: A Canadian Perspective on NATO's New Strategic Concept* (Ottawa, 2010); Doug Saunders, 'The Hollow Shell That Is NATO,' *Globe and Mail*, July 3, 2010.

64 Confidential interviews.

65 Hope, *Dancing with the Dushman*, 97–8.

66 Ian Elliot, 'Colonel Shares His War Stories,' *Kingston Whig-Standard*, reprinted on *eVeritas*, RMC Club blog, February 16, 2009, www.everitas.rmcclub.ca/?m=200902&paged=2.

67 A document made public by Wikileaks.org, one of more than 75,000 released at once on July 26, 2010, indicated that the four Canadians had been killed in a friendly fire incident. This was instantly denied by Ottawa, by soldiers involved, and by relatives of the killed soldiers. Juliet O'Neill and K. Laidlaw, 'Canadian Deaths May Have Been Friendly Fire: File,' *National Post*, July 27, 2010; Juliet O'Neill, 'Bombshell Claim That Friendly Fire Killed Canadian Soldiers Unravels,' *Montreal Gazette*, July 28, 2010. For the Soviet tactics comment, see Adam Day, 'Operation Medusa: The Battle for Panjwai,' Part 3, *Legion Magazine* (January–February 2008).

68 The best accounts of Operation Medusa are in ibid., Parts 1–3, *Legion Magazine* (September–October 2007 to January–February 2008), and in Mitch Potter, 'What Really Happened When Canadians Died in 2006 Firefight with Taliban,' www.thestar.com, July 28, 2010. Potter's and Day's (Part 1) accounts both note that a 1000-lb bomb bounced through the Canadian lines but did not explode. A second bomb that hit the Taliban let the RCR disengage (confidential email). Both authors properly attribute the four killed RCR to enemy fire on September 3, 2006, not to friendly fire. General Fraser briefed the North Atlantic Council on September 6, 2006, during Medusa and indicated that some 2500 Taliban had been killed in the last few months (including 200–300 in the last week) but reinforcements continued to arrive; hard-core Taliban would fight to the death, he said, as opposed to 'Taliban-for-hire' who were fighting for pay. Fraser also indicated how short of troops he was, with only one platoon in reserve. Confidential document.

69 Quoted in Stein and Lang, *Unexpected War*, 219.

70 Day, 'The Battle for Panjwai,' Part 3.

71 Stein and Lang, *Unexpected War,* 219.

72 Wattie, *Contact Charlie,* 293. On Canada's reputation, see my 'Canada's Reputation: Dead and Gone? Or Renewed and Influential?' Canadian Defence and Foreign Affairs Institute *Dispatch* (spring 2010). Major Fletcher received the Star of Military Valour. See his account, 'On Commanding in Battle,' *Veritas* (July 2007): 12ff.

73 David Pugliese, 'The Return of the Leopard,' *Ottawa Citizen,* July 8, 2006. See esp. Captain John Kim, 'The Role of Armour in the All-Arms Battle,' *Veritas* (summer 2010): 18ff.

74 In mid-2006, Ottawa announced $17 billion in new spending for the CF, including strategic and tactical airlift, new helicopters, and new trucks. Bruce Campion-Smith, 'Drones on Military Wish Lists,' *Toronto Star,* July 4, 2006.

75 For a good account of an OMLT in action, see Sean Maloney, 'Panjwayi Alamo: The Defence of Strongpoint Mushan,' *Canadian Military History* (summer 2009): 47ff.

76 Opinions varied sharply across the country. An Ipsos-Reid poll in August 2007 found 51 per cent support for the mission with 72 per cent support in Alberta and 35 per cent support in Quebec. *Ottawa Citizen,* August 25, 2007. Another Ipsos poll in August 2010 (*Vancouver Sun,* August 5, 2010) found almost 80 per cent of Canadians wanting an end to the mission in 2011 and 81 per cent expressing pride in the troops. Only one in three wanted to keep trainers in Afghanistan after 2011. See also the U.S. Army War College Strategic Studies Institute's C.A. Miller, *Endgame for the West in Afghanistan* (Carlisle, PA, 2010), 70ff.; David Bercuson, 'The War Where Public Opinion Marched Out the Door,' *Globe and Mail,* August 13, 2010; Kim Nossal, 'Making Sense of Afghanistan: The Domestic Politics of International Stabilization Missions in Australia and Canada,' a paper presented to Association for Canadian Studies in Australia and New Zealand, July 2010.

77 Bob Rae, quoted on www.globeandmail.ca, December 23, 2007.

78 See my 'Wake Up! This Is Our War, Too,' *Globe and Mail,* February 28, 2006.

79 On the 2007 campaign, see Lee Windsor et al., *Kandahar Tour: The Turning Point in Canada's Afghan Mission* (Mississauga, ON, 2008).

80 Report of *The Independent Panel on Canada's Future Role in Afghanistan* (Ottawa, 2008).

81 The motion passed on March 13, 2008, by a vote of 198 to 77, the NDP and Bloc Québécois opposing. There was scant time for debate, and this may have increased the opposition to the motion. See Hon. William Graham, 'Afghanistan: Challenges and Opportunities for Canada's Foreign Policy,' *General Sir William Otter Papers,* No. 1/08, Royal Canadian Military Institute, May 25, 2008.

82 Major-General Stuart Beare, 'The Nature of Combat,' *Veritas* (November, 2006): 22. On CMTC, see Adam Day, 'Training for Kandahar,' *Legion Magazine* (July–August 2006): 42ff.

83 There is a very good account of pre-deployment training in Windsor et al., *Kandahar Tour,* chap. 3.

84 Brian Stewart, 'Military Brass Bite Their Tongues over the "Hollow Army,"' www.cbcnews.ca, June 30, 2009; Jeff Davis, 'Army Hurting from Afghan Mission: Generals,' *Embassy* (March 2009).

85 Gen Walt Natynczyk, 'Projecting Power,' *FrontLine Defence* (May–June 2010): 10ff.

86 Army strength is difficult to state precisely because many regular and reserve soldiers serve outside the Army. Nonetheless, official figures from Army sources (confidential emails) showed 22,636 regulars and 21,556 reservists as of June 30, 2010. Figures provided simultaneously from another Army source broke down the reservists by category: 13,930 Class A reservists (i.e., ordinary Militia members), 6239 Class B reservists (i.e., Militia on full-time employment with the Army or on leave), and some 400 Class C reservists (those deployed overseas). The numbers provided unfortunately do not coincide for the two sources. There were in addition 4258 Rangers in the north and isolated areas, some 4000 men and women in training destined for but not yet in the Army, and thousands of regular and reserve soldiers employed in new headquarters and staffs in Ottawa and elsewhere and, e.g., in Canadian Special Operations Forces Command. These reservists and regulars are not counted in the Army totals. Civilians directly supporting the Army numbered 5621.

87 Hillier, 'Setting Our Course,' 75–6, 79. See Jungwee Park, 'A Profile of the Canadian Forces, Statistics Canada, *Perspectives* (July 2008).

88 Juliet O'Neill, 'Army Overflowing with Recruits but Air Force Short,' Canwest News Service, May 31, 2010.

89 See, inter alia, my 'The Search for an Efficient, Effective Land Force Reserve,' *Canadian Military Journal* (summer 2002): 5ff., and J.L. Granatstein and Charles Belzile, *The Special Commission on the Restructuring of the Reserves 1995: Ten Years Later* (Calgary, 2005). It is worth noting that some reservists – the half who were not students – brought civilian skills to Afghanistan that could, if they were properly employed by their superiors, be of use in development work. The Army unfortunately did not try to catalogue available skills.

90 Mitch Potter, 'Canadian Army Well-Prepared for Future Roles, Thanks to Afghan Mission, Top Commander Says,' *Toronto Star,* June 15, 2010.

91 Office of the Parliamentary Budget Officer, *Fiscal Impact of the Canadian Mission in Afghanistan* (Ottawa, October 9, 2008). Cf. David Perry, 'At What Price Freedom? What the War in Afghanistan is Costing the Canadian Forces,' *On Track* (winter 2007): 8ff.

92 David Perry, "Canada's Seven Billion Dollar War: The Cost of Canadian Forces Operations in Afghanistan," *International Journal* (summer 2008): 703.

93 See 'Canada Looks to Upgrade Its Armor,' *Defense Industry Daily,* July 9, 2009.

94 Confidential email.

95 See the table for Operation Enduring Freedom on www.icasualties.org. ISAF soldiers killed numbered just under 2000 at mid-2010.

96 A very useful account of the decline of CF medical services is Gary H. Rice, *A Sketch of Military Medicine in Canada, 1867–2009* (Carleton Place, ON, 2009).

97 General Roméo Dallaire's memoir of his time in Rwanda and after, *Shake Hands with the Devil* (Toronto, 2003), made PTSD understandable to the public, Army, and government.

98 Graeme Hamilton, 'Who Fights and Dies for Canada?' *National Post,* November 7, 2009.

99 Adam Day, 'The Struggle for Salavat,' Part 2: 'First Platoon against the Ropes,' *Legion Magazine* (May-June 2010): 26. A fine account of a 2nd Battalion Royal Canadian Regiment operation in 2007 can be found in Sean Maloney, 'Incursion at Howz-e Madad: An Afghanistan Vignette,' *Canadian Military History* (winter 2008): 63ff.

100 Adam Day, 'The Struggle for Salavat,' Part 3: 'The Shadowy World of Counter-Insurgency,' *Legion Magazine* (July–August, 2010): 25; Part 4: 'Hearts and Minds on the Line,' (September-October, 2010): 30ff. Day's reporting from Afghanistan is among the very best.

101 Michael Byers, 'Canada's Quagmire: The Steady Stream of Maimed or Killed Soldiers Is but One of Many Increasingly Disturbing Parallels between Afghanistan and the Vietnam War,' *Ottawa Citizen*, June 4, 2008. For more on Byers's views, see Michael Valpy, 'This Is Stephen Harper's War,' *Globe and Mail*, August 18, 2007.

102 'The Brian Stewart Interview: Brigadier-General Jonathan Vance,' *Munk Monitor* (spring 2010): 10.

103 Matthieu Aikins, 'The Master of Spin Boldak,' *Harper's*, December 2009, 62.

104 Murray Brewster, 'U.S. Surge Bumps Canada Command in Kandahar,' Canadian Press, June 13, 2010.

105 See Colonel Ian Hope, 'Unity of Command in Afghanistan: A Forsaken Principle of War,' a paper for the Strategic Studies Institute, United States Army War College (November 2008) http://www.StrategicStudiesInstitute.army.mil/.

106 'Arrangement for the Transfer of Detainees between the Canadian Forces and the Ministry of Defence of the Islamic Republic of Afghanistan,' December 18, 2005, www.forces.gc.ca/site/operations/archer/agreement_e.asp; confidential emails and confidential documents. James Travers, 'Who's Watching the Generals,' *Toronto Star*, April 26, 2007, was wrong in his interpretation of events.

107 See, e.g. Prof. Michael Byers's effort to have Minister O'Connor and General Hillier come before the International Criminal Court: www.ceasefire.ca/?p=3157; www.rideauinstitute .ca/file-library/Byers-Schabas-letter -to-ICC-3-Dec-2009.pdf.

108 Confidential emails.

109 'Arrangement for the Transfer of Detainees between the Government of Canada and the Government of the Islamic Republic of Afghanistan,' May 3, 2007 (see note 106).

110 Confidential emails.

111 For much of the detainee documentation, see Aaron Wherry, 'The Colvin Encyclopedia,' www.macleans.ca, December 6, 2009. For commentary, see Christie Blatchford, 'From Screams to Whimpers on Afghan Detainees,' *Globe and Mail*, April 30, 2010, and Michael Den Tandt, 'No Longer about Abuse,' *Toronto Sun*, April 30, 2010. Journalist Matthew Fisher, a veteran war correspondent, delivered the Kesterton Lecture at Carleton University on March 31, 2010. He remarked that 340 media had been embedded with the CF in Afghanistan since 2006, creating 'a revolving door' that led to superficial reporting almost completely uninformed on military issues. See also Robert Bergen, *Censorship; the Canadian News Media and Afghanistan: A Historical Comparison with Case Studies*. Calgary Papers in Military and Strategic Studies (2009); and Captain (N) Chris Henderson, 'Reporting Live from Kandahar,' *Canadian Military Journal* (summer 2006): 85ff.

112 Kathryn Carlson, '"An Act of So-called Mercy": Semrau Case Hinges on "Soldier's Pact,"' *National Post*, July 7, 2010. See especially Michael Friscolanti, 'A Soldier's Choice,' *Maclean's*, May 24, 2010, 20ff.; Friscolanti, 'Capt. Robert Semrau, Ethics, and the "Soldier's Pact,"' *Maclean's*, July 26, 2010.

113 Susan Pigg, et al., 'Grounding a Rising Military Star: Ousted General Faces Potential Court Martial over Alleged Relationship with Female Soldier,' *Toronto Star,* May 31, 2010.

114 'Military's No-Sex Fight in War Zones Called Unwinnable,' Canadian Press, June 5, 2010.

115 See, for example, Daniel Dale, 'What's Wrong with Making Love and War? The Case of Brig.-Gen. Daniel Ménard Raises the Question Anew,' *Toronto Star,* June 4, 2010.

116 On Ouellette, see Steven Chase, 'Canadian Colonel in Haiti Removed,' *Globe and Mail,* July 9, 2010.

117 'The State of the Canadian Army: An Interview with Lieutenant-General Andrew Leslie, Chief of the Land Staff,' *On Track* (autumn 2009): 11. The CDS's order to plan the pullout, 'CDS Directive for the End of the Current Mandate and Redeployment from Kandahar by December 2011,' dated August 7, 2009, was duly declassified and released publicly.

118 Campbell Clark and Bill Curry, 'Harper's turnaround: PM says he felt he had to extend Afghan mission,' *Globe and Mail,* November 12, 2010.

12 Conclusion

1 'A Message from the Prime Minister,' *The Canada First Defence Strategy* (Ottawa, May 12, 2008), 1.

2 Colonel Brian MacDonald, 'Defence Budget 2010/11,' Conference of Defence Associations, *CDA Commentary,* May 19, 2010.

3 Col. Brian MacDonald, 'The Canada First Defence Strategy of 2008 and the 20 Year Budget,' ibid., July 28, 2008; Elinor Sloan, 'Canada First Defence Strategy,' Canadian Defence and Foreign Affairs Institute paper, 2008, on www.cdfai.org. For comparative purposes, see Bill Robinson, 'Canadian Military Spending,' Canadian Centre for Policy Alternatives, *Foreign Policy Series* (December 2009).

4 Lieutenant-General (ret'd) George Macdonald, *The Canada First Defence Strategy – One Year Later* (Calgary, 2009).

5 Brian MacDonald, 'Canada First Defence Strategy.'

6 In mid-2010, Lieutenant-General Andrew Leslie left his post as Chief of the Land Staff to head a 'Transformation' team, one of its main tasks being to reduce the numbers in the various Command headquarters. See David Pugliese, 'Lt.-Gen. Andrew Leslie to Begin Work on Transformation Review This Month,' Defence Watch, *Ottawa Citizen* blog, August 4, 2010.

7 Brian Stewart, 'Military Brass Bite Their Tongue over "The Hollow Army,"' www.cbcnews .ca, June 30, 2009.

8 Jeff Davis, 'Army Hurting from Afghan Mission: Generals,' *Embassy* (March 2009); Murray Brewster, 'New Army Chief Cites Need to Regroup after Afghan Mission,' *Globe and Mail,* June 22, 2010.

9 Chris Thatcher, 'Mission Tested: Preparing the Army for 2021,' *Vanguard* (March–April, 2009).

10 Gerald Caplan, 'Oh-oh Canada,' *Globe and Mail*, December 4, 2009. See also Erna Paris, 'The Canada We Thought We Lived in,' *Ottawa Citizen*, December 23, 2009; James Travers, 'Kandahar, Copenhagen Sully Reputation,' *Toronto Star*, December 22, 2009.

11 Maude Barlow, 'Ashamed to Wear the Maple Leaf,' *Globe and Mail*, January 5, 2010.

12 Louise Mercier-Johnson, 'Canada's Army after Afghanistan,' *FrontLine Defence* (March–April 2010): 31.

13 See my 'Canada's Reputation: Dead and Gone? Or Renewed and Influential?' Canadian Defence and Foreign Affairs Institute *Dispatch* (spring 2010), also published in an abbreviated form (alongside the Barlow piece cited above) in *Globe and Mail*, January 5, 2010.

14 Ted Schmidt, *Toronto Star*, March 15, 2006.

15 Akbar Javer, *Vancouver Province*, March 8, 2006.

16 'Thumbs Down,' *Now*, March 16–22, 2005, 22–3.

17 Peter Martin, *Victoria Times-Colonist*, April 2, 2006. A useful, brief analysis of 'War: 101. Is It War or Peacekeeping?' by Lewis MacKenzie is in *Frontline Canada* (March/April 2006): 46.

18 An unidentified blogger (www.soapbox22.blogspot.com/2006/04/Layton-spins-yet-again .html) dissected NDP leader Layton's words on Afghanistan from May 2005 to April 2006 and pointed out that he had said nothing against the mission until the election campaign (*Halifax Chronicle-Herald*, December 9, 2005); indeed, he had neither participated in nor attended the 'take note' debate on Afghanistan in Parliament on November 15, 2005. The NDP position in the take-note debate was given by Bill Blaikie (see his remarks on www.billblaikie.ca/ndp.php/nationaldefence).

19 The preference for 'traditional' peacekeeping is well documented. See Lane Anker, 'Peace-keeping and Public Opinion,' *Canadian Military Journal* (summer 2005): 23ff. A poll done for the Canadian Forces by Ekos in late winter 2004–5 found 57 per cent in favour of 'traditional peacekeeping' and only 41 per cent favouring 'peacemaking' that would involve fighting. Mike Blanchfield, 'Canadians Oppose Tough New Role,' *Ottawa Citizen*, August 17, 2005. For public opinion in the 1990s, see also Pierre Martin and Michel Fortmann, 'Support for International Involvement in Canadian Public Opinion after the Cold War,' *Canadian Military Journal* (autumn 2001): 43ff., and Don Munton, 'Defending the Canadian Public,' *Canadian Military Journal* (autumn 2003): 25ff.

20 'Canada: The World's Peacekeeper,' www.cbcnews.ca, last update, October 30, 2003.

21 'Canada and Peace Support Operations' (March 1, 2006), www.dfait-maeci.gc.ca/ peacekeeping/menu-en.asp.

22 See Sean Maloney, 'From Myth to Reality Check: From Peacekeeping to Stabilization,' *Policy Options* (September 2005): 40ff.

23 Robert Smol, 'Lest We Forget the Cost of Peacekeeping' (July 14, 2009), www. cbcnews.ca.

24 Confidential emails. See my 'Defining Canada's Role in Congo,' *Globe and Mail*, April 7, 2010, and 'Peacekeeping If Necessary, But Not Necessarily Peacekeeping,' *Globe and Mail*,

May 26, 2010. On the changes in peacekeeping today, see Jocelyn Coulon and Michel Liégeois, *What Happened to Peacekeeping? The Future of a Tradition* (Calgary, 2010).

25 Quoted in Chris Cobb, 'A Nation of Warriors?' *Ottawa Citizen*, March 26, 2005.

26 See my 'Canada as a Peacekeeper Again,' *Globe and Mail,* May 26, 2010.

27 Eugene Lang and Eric Morse, 'What Next for Canada's Tough New Army?' Royal Canadian Military Institute, *Sitrep* (May–June 2010): 8; confidential emails.

28 J.L. Granatstein, 'Army Professionalism,' in J.L. Granatstein, *The G.G. Simonds Lectures on Canadian Army Heritage, 1997–98* (Kingston, Ont.: Canadian Land Forces Command and Staff College, 1998). See also Dean Oliver, 'Canadian Military Professional Development: The Way Ahead,' Conference of Defence Associations Institute, *The Profession of Arms in Canada: Past, Present and Future* (Ottawa, 1999), 63ff.

29 See Douglas Bland, 'Parliament's Duty to Defend Canada,' *Canadian Military Journal* 1 (winter 2000): 35ff.

A SELECTED BIBLIOGRAPHY OF
SECONDARY SOURCES

This bibliography lists the books I have used most, not all the books I have read or referenced in the notes. In particular, it omits almost all non-Canadian and standard works. For this new edition, it does contain recently published titles, some of whose judgments I have not been able to incorporate into the text because of the exigencies of modern publishing. What I can say is that had I been able to do so, all these works would have been used in shaping *Canada's Army*.

Allard, J.V. *Mémoires du Général Jean V. Allard*. Boucherville, Que., 1985

Allister, William. *Where Life and Death Hold Hands*. Toronto, 1989

Anderson, Fred. *Crucible of War: The Seven Years' War and the Fate of Empire in British North America, 1754–1766*. New York, 2000

Beal, Bob, and Rod Macleod. *Prairie Fire: The 1885 North-West Rebellion*. Edmonton, 1984

Beatty, David P. *Memories of the Forgotten War: The World War I Diary of Private V.E. Goodwin*. Port Elgin, NB, 1988

– *The Vimy Pilgrimage, July 1936*. Amherst, NS, 1987

Benn, Carl. *The Iroquois in the War of 1812*. Toronto, 1998

Bercuson, David J. *Battalion of Heroes: The Calgary Highlanders in World War II*. Calgary, 1994

– *Blood on the Hills: The Canadian Army in the Korean War*. Toronto, 1999

– *The Patricias: The Proud History of a Fighting Regiment*. Toronto, 2001

– *Significant Incident: Canada's Army, the Airborne, and the Murder in Somalia*. Toronto, 1996

– *True Patriot: The Life of Brooke Claxton, 1898–1960*. Toronto, 1993

Bercuson, David J., and S. Wise, eds. *The Valour and the Horror*. Toronto, 1994

Bernier, Serge. *The Royal 22e Regiment*. Montreal, 2000

Berton, Pierre. *Starting Out: The Days of My Youth, 1920–1947*. Toronto, 1993

Blackburn, George. *The Guns of Normandy*. Toronto, 1996

– *The Guns of Victory*. Toronto, 1997

– *Where the Hell Are the Guns?* Toronto, 1995

Bland, Douglas. *The Administration of Defence Policy in Canada, 1947 to 1985*. Kingston, ON, 1987

– *Chiefs of Defence: Government and the Unified Command of the Canadian Armed Forces.* Toronto, 1995

Blatchford, Christie. *Fifteen Days: Stories of Bravery, Friendship, Life and Death from Inside the New Canadian Army.* Toronto, 2007

Blaxland, Gregory. *Alexander's Generals: The Italian Campaign, 1944–45.* London, 1979

Burke, Joanna. *An Intimate History of Killing.* London, 1999

Burns, E.L.M. *General Mud: Memoirs of Two World Wars.* Toronto, 1970

– *Manpower in the Canadian Army.* Toronto, 1956

Campbell, Ian. *Murder at the Abbaye.* Ottawa, 1996

Carroll, Michael K. *Pearson's Peacekeepers: Canada and the United Nations Emergency Force, 1956–67.* Vancouver, 2009

Cassar, George H. *Hell in Flanders Fields: Canadians at the Second Battle of Ypres.* Toronto, 2010

Cederberg, Fred. *The Long Road Home.* Toronto, 1989

Christie, Norm, ed. *Letters of Agar Adamson.* Ottawa, 1997

Clearwater, John. *Canadian Nuclear Weapons: The Untold Story of Canada's Cold War Arsenal.* Toronto, 1998

Conrad, John. *What the Thunder Said: Reflections of a Canadian Officer in Kandahar.* Toronto, 2009

Cook, Tim. *At the Sharp End: Canadians Fighting the Great War 1914–1916.* Toronto, 2007

– *No Place to Run: The Canadian Corps and Gas Warfare in the First World War.* Vancouver, 1999

– *Shock Troops: Canadians Fighting the Great War 1917–1918.* Toronto, 2008

Copp, Terry. *The Brigade: The Fifth Canadian Infantry Brigade, 1939–1945.* Stony Creek, ON, 1992

– *Cinderella Army: The Canadians in Northwest Europe 1944–1945.* Toronto, 2006

– *Fields of Fire: The Canadians in Normandy.* Toronto, 2003

– *Montgomery's Scientists: Operational Research in Northwest Europe.* Waterloo, ON, 2000

– *No Price Too High: Canadians and the Second World War.* Whitby, ON, 1996

Copp, Terry, and Bill McAndrew. *Battle Exhaustion: Soldiers and Psychiatrists in the Canadian Army, 1939–1945.* Montreal, 1990

Copp, Terry, and Robert Vogel. *Maple Leaf Route.* 5 vols. Alma, ON, 1983–8

Cowley, Deborah, ed. *George Vanier: Soldier. The Wartime Letters and Diaries, 1915–1919.* Toronto, 2000

Craig, Grace Morris. *But This Is Our War.* Toronto, 1981

Dallaire, Roméo. *Shake Hands with the Devil: The Failure of Humanity in Rwanda.* Toronto, 2003

Danchev, A., and D. Todman, eds. *Field Marshal Lord Alanbrooke: War Diaries, 1939–1945.* Berkeley, CA, 2001

Dancocks, Daniel. *The D-Day Dodgers: The Canadians in Italy, 1943–1945.* Toronto, 1991

– *Sir Arthur Currie: A Biography.* Toronto, 1985

– *Welcome to Flanders Fields.* Toronto, 1989

Davis, James. *The Sharp End: A Canadian Soldier's Story.* Vancouver, 1997

Dawson, Grant. *'Here Is Hell': Canada's Engagement in Somalia.* Vancouver, 2007

Delaney, Douglas. *The Soldiers' General: Bert Hoffmeister at War.* Vancouver, 2005

Denison, George T. *Soldiering in Canada.* Toronto, 1900

D'Este, Carlo. *Decision in Normandy.* New York, 1994

Dickson, Paul, ed. *1943: The Beginning of the End.* Waterloo, 1995

Dickson, Paul D. *A Thoroughly Canadian General: A Biography of General H.D.G. Crerar.* Toronto, 2007

Dundas, Barbara. *A History of Women in the Canadian Military.* Montreal, 2001

Duguid, A.F. *Official History of the Canadian Forces in the Great War, 1914–1919.* Vol. 1: *Text*; vol. 2: *Documents.* Ottawa, 1938

Dunkelman, Ben. *Dual Allegiance.* Toronto, 1976

Eayrs, James. *In Defence of Canada.* 5 vols. Toronto, 1964–83

Ellis, John. *Eye-Deep in Hell: Trench Warfare in World War I.* Baltimore, 1989

– *One Day in a Very Long War.* London, 1998

Engen, Robert. *Canadians Under Fire: Infantry Effectiveness in the Second World War.* Montreal, 2009

English, John A. *The Canadian Army and the Normandy Campaign: A Study of Failure in High Command.* New York, 1991

– *Lament for an Army: The Decline of Canadian Military Professionalism.* Toronto, 1998

– *Marching through Chaos: The Descent of Armies in Theory and Practice.* Westport, CT, 1998

– *National Policy and the Americanization of the Canadian Military.* Toronto, 2001

English, J., and N. Hillmer, eds. *Making a Difference: Canadian Foreign Policy in a Changing World Order.* Toronto, 1992

Facey-Crowther, David. *The New Brunswick Militia, 1787–1867.* Fredericton, 1990

Fischer, David Hackett. *Champlain's Dream.* New York, 2008

Foster, Tony. *Meeting of Generals.* Toronto, 1986

Fowler, William M., Jr. *Empires at War: The Seven Years' War and the Struggle for North America 1754–1763.* Vancouver, 2005

Fraser, D.K. *Black Yesterdays: The Argylls' War.* Hamilton, ON, 1996

French, David. *Raising Churchill's Army: The British Army and the War against Germany, 1919–1945.* Oxford, 2000

Friscolanti, Michael. *Friendly Fire: The Untold Story of the U.S. Bombing That Killed Four Canadian Soldiers in Afghanistan.* Mississauga, ON, 2005

Frost, Sydney. *Once a Patricia.* St Catharines, ON, 1988

Gagnon, Jean-Pierre. *Le 22e Bataillon.* Ottawa and Quebec, 1986

Galloway, Strome. *Bravely into Battle.* Toronto, 1988

– *The General Who Never Was.* Belleville, ON, 1981

Gibson, E., and Kingsley Ward. *Courage Remembered.* Toronto, 1989

Goodman, Eddie. *Life of the Party: The Memoirs of Eddie Goodman.* Toronto, 1988

Graham, Dominick. *The Price of Command: A Biography of General Guy Simonds.* Toronto, 1993

Graham, Howard. *Citizen and Soldier: The Memoirs of Lieutenant-General Howard Graham.* Toronto, 1987

Granatstein, J.L. *Canada 1957–1967: The Years of Uncertainty and Innovation.* Toronto, 1986

– *Canada's War: The Politics of the Mackenzie King Government, 1939–1945.* Toronto, 1990

– *The Generals: The Canadian Army's Senior Commanders in the Second World War.* Toronto, 1993

– *Who Killed the Canadian Military?* Toronto, 2004

– *Whose War Is It? How Canada Can Survive in the Post-9/11 World.* Toronto, 2007

Granatstein, J.L., and David Bercuson. *War and Peacekeeping: From South Africa to the Gulf – Canada's Limited Wars.* Toronto, 1991

Granatstein, J.L., and Robert Bothwell. *Pirouette: Pierre Trudeau and Canadian Foreign Policy.* Toronto, 1990

Granatstein, J.L., and Robert Cuff, eds. *War and Society in North America.* Toronto, 1971

Granatstein J.L. and Norman Hillmer. *Battle Lines: Eyewitness Accounts from Canada's Military History.* Toronto, 2004

Granatstein, J.L., and J.M. Hitsman. *Broken Promises: A History of Conscription in Canada.* Toronto, 1977

Granatstein, J.L., and Desmond Morton. *A Nation Forged in Fire.* Toronto, 1989

Granatstein, J.L., and Peter Neary, eds. *The Good Fight: Canadians and World War II.* Toronto, 1995

Granatstein, J.L., and Dean F. Oliver. *The Oxford Companion to Canadian Military History.* Toronto, 2011.

Gravel, J.Y. *L'Armée au Québec.* Montreal, 1974

Graves, Donald. *Field of Glory: The Battle of Crysler's Farm, 1813.* Toronto, 1999

– *South Albertas: A Canadian Regiment at War.* Toronto, 1998

– *Where Right and Glory Lead! The Battle of Lundy's Lane, 1814.* Toronto, 1997

– ed. *Fighting for Canada: Seven Battles, 1758–1945.* Toronto, 2000

Gray, Hub. *Beyond the Danger Close: The Korean Experience Revealed: 2nd Battalion Princess Patricia's Canadian Light Infantry.* Calgary, 2003

Gray, John. *Fun Tomorrow: Learning to Be a Publisher and Much Else.* Toronto, 1978

Gray, William. *Soldiers of the King: The Upper Canadian Militia, 1812–1815.* Erin, ON, 1995

Gwyn, Sandra. *Tapestry of War.* Toronto, 1992

Halliday, Hugh A. *Valour Reconsidered: Inquiries into the Victoria Cross and Other Awards for Extreme Bravery.* Toronto, 2006

Halliday, Jon, and B. Cummins. *Korea: The Unknown War.* London, 1990

Hamilton, Nigel. *Monty.* 2 vols. London, 1987

Hanson, J., and P. Hammerschmidt, eds. *The Past, Present and Future of the Militia.* Toronto, 1998

Harris, Stephen. *Canadian Brass: The Making of a Professional Army, 1860–1939.* Toronto, 1988

Hart, Russell. *Clash of Arms: How the Allies Won in Normandy.* London, 2001

Hasek, John. *The Disarming of Canada.* Toronto, 1987

Haycock, R.G. *Sam Hughes: The Public Career of a Controversial Canadian, 1885–1916.* Waterloo, ON, 1986

Hayes, Geoffrey, et al., eds. *Vimy Ridge: A Canadian Reassessment.* Waterloo, ON, 2007

Hellyer, Paul. *Damn the Torpedoes: My Fight to Unify Canada's Armed Forces.* Toronto, 1990

Hillier, Rick. *A Soldier First: Bullets, Bureaucrats and the Politics of War.* Toronto, 2009

Hillier, R.J., and Colonel Bernd Horn. *No Ordinary Men: Special Forces Missions in Afghanistan.* Toronto, 2009

Hitsman, J. Mackay. *The Incredible War of 1812.* Toronto, 1965

– *Safeguarding Canada, 1763–1871.* Toronto, 1968

Hope, Ian. *Dancing with the Dushman: Command Imperatives for the Counter-Insurgency Fight in Afghanistan.* Kingston, ON, 2008

Horn, B., ed. *Contemporary Issues in Officership: A Canadian Perspective.* Toronto, 2000

Horn, B., and S. Harris. *Generalship and the Art of the Admiral: Perspectives on Canadian Senior Military Leadership.* St Catharines, ON, 2001

– eds. *Warrior Chiefs: Perspectives on Senior Canadian Military Leadership.* Toronto, 2001

Humphries, Mark O., ed. *The Selected Papers of Sir Arthur Currie: Diaries, Letters, and Report to the Ministry, 1917–1933.* Waterloo, ON, 2008

Hyatt, A.M.J. *General Sir Arthur Currie: A Military Biography.* Toronto, 1987

Iarocci, Andrew. *Shoestring Soldiers: The 1st Canadian Division at War, 1914–1915.* Toronto, 2008

Isitt, Benjamin. *From Victoria to Vladivostok: Canada's Siberian Expedition, 1917–19.* Vancouver, 2010

Jockel, Joseph. *Canada and NATO's Northern Flank.* Toronto, 1986

– *The Canadian Forces: Hard Choices, Soft Power.* Toronto, 1999

Johnston, William. *A War of Patrols: Canadian Army Operations in Korea.* Vancouver, 2003

Kaufman, D., and M. Horn. *A Liberation Album: Canadians in the Netherlands, 1944–45.* Toronto, 1980

Keshen, Jeffrey. *Propaganda and Censorship during Canada's Great War.* Edmonton, 1997

Keshen, Jeffrey. *Saints, Sinners and Soldiers: Canada's Second World War.* Vancouver, 2004

Kitching, George. *Mud and Green Fields.* Langley, BC, 1986

Lehmann, Joseph. *The Model Major-General: A Biography of Field-Marshal Lord Wolseley.* Boston, 1964

Lenarcic, David. *Knight-Errant? Canada and the Crusade to Ban Anti-Personnel Land Mines.* Toronto, 1998

Loomis, Dan G. *Not Much Glory: Quelling the F.L.Q.* Toronto, 1984

– *The Somalia Affair.* Ottawa, 1996

Love, David. *'A Call to Arms': The Organization and Administration of Canada's Military in World War One.* Winnipeg, 1999

MacDonell, G.S. *This Soldier's Story (1939–1945).* Nepean, ON, 2000

Macfie, John. *Letters Home.* Meaford, ON, 1990

Mackenzie, David, ed. *Canada and the First World War: Essays in Honour of Robert Craig Brown.* Toronto, 2005

MacKenzie, Lewis. *Peacekeeper: The Road to Sarajevo*. Vancouver, 1993

– *Soldiers Made Me Look Good: A Life in the Shadow of War*. Vancouver, 2008

MacLeod, D. Peter. *Northern Armageddon: The Battle of the Plains of Abraham*. Vancouver, 2008

Madsen, Chris. *Another Kind of Justice: Canadian Military Law from Confederation to Somalia*. Vancouver, 1999

Malcolmson, Robert. *Capital in Flames: The American Attack on York, 1813*. Montreal, 2008

Malone, P.M. *The Skulking Way of War: Technology and Tactics among the New England Indians*, Baltimore, 1991

Malone, Richard. *A Portrait of War, 1939–1943*. Toronto, 1983

Maloney, Sean. *War without Battles: Canada's NATO Brigade in Germany, 1951–1993*. Toronto, 1996

Maloney, Sean M. *Canada and UN Peacekeeping: Cold War by Other Means, 1945–1970*. St Catharines, ON, 2002

Mann, Susan, ed. *The War Diary of Clare Gass*. Montreal, 2000

Margolian, Howard. *Conduct Unbecoming: The Story of the Murder of Canadian Prisoners of War in Normandy*. Toronto, 1998

Marteinson, John, et al. *We Stand on Guard: An Illustrated History of the Canadian Army*. Montreal, 1992

Marteinson, John, and Michael McNorgan. *The Royal Canadian Armoured Corps: An Illustrated History*. Toronto, 2000

Martin, Charles. *Battle Diary*. Toronto, 1994

McAndrew, Bill. *Canadians and the Italian Campaign, 1943–1945*. Montreal, 1996

– *Normandy 1944: The Canadian Summer*. Montreal, 1994

McDougall, Robert. *A Narrative of War*. Ottawa, 1996

McWilliams, J., and R.J. Steel. *Amiens: Dawn of Victory*. Toronto, 2001

Miller, Carman. *Painting the Map Red: Canada and the South African War, 1899–1902*. Montreal, 1993

Millett, A.R., and W. Murray, eds. *Military Effectiveness*. Vol. I: *The First World War*. Boston, 1988

Morin, J.H., and R.H. Gimblett. *Operation Friction: The Canadian Forces in the Persian Gulf*. Toronto, 1997

Morton, Desmond. *The Canadian General: Sir William Otter*. Toronto, 1974

– *A Military History of Canada*. Toronto, 1992

– *Ministers and Generals: Politics and the Canadian Militia, 1868–1904*. Toronto, 1970

– *A Peculiar Kind of Politics: Canada's Overseas Ministry in the First World War*. Toronto, 1982

– *Silent Battle: Canadian Prisoners of War in Germany, 1914–1919*. Toronto, 1992

– *When Your Number's Up: The Canadian Soldier in the First World War*. Toronto, 1993

Morton, Desmond, and J.L. Granatstein. *Marching to Armageddon*. Toronto, 1988

Morton, Desmond, and R.H. Roy, eds. *Telegrams of the Northwest Campaign, 1885*. Toronto, 1972

Morton, Desmond, and Glenn Wright. *Winning the Second Battle: Canadian Veterans and the Return to Civilian Life, 1915–1930*. Toronto, 1987

Mowat, Farley. *And No Birds Sang*. Toronto, 1979

– *My Father's Son*. Toronto, 1992

Murray, W., and A. Millett, *A War to Be Won: Fighting the Second World War*. Cambridge, Mass., 2000

Neary, Peter, and J.L. Granatstein, eds. *The Veterans Charter and Post–World War II Canada*. Toronto, 1998

Neillands, Robin. *The Great War Generals on the Western Front, 1914–1918*. London, 1999

Newman, Peter C. *True North: Not Strong and Free*. Toronto, 1983

Nicholson, G.W.L. *Canadian Expeditionary Force, 1914–1919*. Ottawa, 1962

– *The Canadians in Italy, 1943–1945*. Ottawa, 1957

Off, Carol. *The Ghosts of Medak Pocket: The Story of Canada's Secret War*. Toronto, 2004

– *The Lion, the Fox, and the Eagle: A Story of Generals and Justice in Rwanda and Yugoslavia*. Toronto, 2000

Okros, Alan, et al. *Between 9/11 and Kandahar: Attitudes of Canadian Forces Officers in Transition*. Kingston, ON, 2008

Owens, Bill. *Lifting the Fog of War*. New York, 2000

Pariseau, Jean, and Serge Bernier. *Les Canadiens français et le bilingualisme dans les forces armées canadiennes*. 2 vols. Ottawa, 1987–94

Patterson, Kevin, and Jane Warren, eds. *Outside the Wire: The War in Afghanistan in the Words of Its Participants*. Toronto, 2007

Peacock, Robert. *Kim-Chi, Asahi and Rum: A Platoon Commander Remembers Korea, 1952–1953*. Np, 1994

Pearce, Donald. *Journal of a War*. Toronto, 1965

Pigott, Peter. *Canada in Afghanistan: The War So Far*. Toronto, 2007

Pope, Joseph, ed. *Letters from the Front, 1914–1919*. Toronto, 1993

Pope, M.A. *Soldiers and Politicians: The Memoirs of Lt.-Gen. Maurice A. Pope*. Toronto, 1962

Porter, Gerald. *In Retreat: The Canadian Forces in the Trudeau Years*. Ottawa, nd

Portugal, Jean. *We Were There*. 7 vols. Shelburne, ON, 1998

Preston, R.A. *Canada and 'Imperial Defense.'* Toronto, 1967

– *Canada's RMC*. Toronto, 1969

– *The Defence of the Undefended Border: Planning for War in North America, 1867–1939*. Montreal, 1977

Prior, Robin, and Trevor Wilson. *Passchendaele: The Untold Story*. New Haven, 1996

Quayle, J.T.B. *In Action*. Abbotsford, BC, 1997

Rawling, Bill. *Death Their Enemy: Canadian Medical Practitioners and War*. Np, 2000

– *Surviving Trench Warfare: Technology and the Canadian Corps, 1914–1918*. Toronto, 1992

– *Technicians of Battle: Canadian Field Engineering from Pre-Confederation to Post–Cold War*. Toronto, 2001

Reid, Brian A. *No Holding Back: Operation Totalize, Normandy, August 1944*. Toronto, 2005

– *Our Little Army in the Field: The Canadians in South Africa, 1899–1902*. St Catharines, ON, 1996

Report of the Ministry: Overseas Military Forces of Canada, 1918. London, nd

Rickard, John N. *The Politics of Command: Lieutenant-General A.G.L. McNaughton and the Canadian Army 1939–1943*. Toronto, 2010

Rioux, Jean-Sébastien. *Two Solitudes: Quebecers' Attitudes Regarding Canadian Security and Defence Policy*. Calgary, 2005

Roberts, J.A. *The Canadian Summer: The Memoirs of James Allan Roberts*. Toronto, 1981

Robertson, Terence. *The Shame and the Glory: Dieppe*. Toronto, 1962

Roy, Patricia, et al. *Mutual Hostages: Canadians and Japanese during the Second World War*. Toronto, 1990

Roy, R.H. *1944: The Canadians in Normandy*. Toronto, 1984

– *For Most Conspicuous Bravery: A Biography of Major-General George R. Pearkes through Two World Wars*. Vancouver, 1977

– *Sherwood Lett: His Life and Times*. Vancouver, 1991

– ed. *The Journal of Private Fraser*. Ottawa, 1998

Sarty, Roger. *The Maritime Defence of Canada*. Toronto, 1996

– *Silent Sentry: A Military and Political History of Canadian Coast Defence, 1860–1945*. Toronto, 1982

Schreiber, Shane. *Shock Army of the British Empire: The Canadian Corps in the Last 100 Days of the Great War*. Westport, CT, 1997

Scislowski, Stanley. *Not All of Us Were Brave*. Toronto, 1997

Scott, F.G. *The Great War As I Saw It*. Ottawa, 2000

Sharpe, Robert. *The Last Day, The Last Hour: The Currie Libel Trial*. Toronto, 1988

Shawcross, William. *Deliver Us from Evil: Peacekeepers, Warlords, and a World of Endless Conflict*. New York, 2000

Sloan, Elinor. *Security and Defence in the Terrorist Era*. Montreal, 2005

Smith, W.I. *Code Word Canloan*. Toronto, 1992

Spooner, Kevin A. *Canada, the Congo Crisis, and UN Peacekeeping, 1960–64*. Vancouver, 2009

Stacey, C.P. *Arms, Men and Governments: The War Policies of Canada, 1939–1945*. Ottawa, 1970

– *A Date with History: Memoirs of a Canadian Historian*. Ottawa, 1983

– *The Military Problems of Canada*. Toronto, 1940

– *Quebec, 1759*. Toronto, 1959

– *Six Years of War*, vol. 1: *Official History of the Canadian Army in the Second World War*. Ottawa, 1955

– *The Victory Campaign: The Operations in North-West Europe, 1944–1945*. Ottawa, 1960

Stacey, C.P., and Barbara Wilson. *The Half-Million: The Canadians in Britain, 1939–1946*. Toronto, 1987

Stein, Janice Gross, and Eugene Lang. *The Unexpected War: Canada in Kandahar*. Toronto, 2007

Swettenham, John. *Allied Intervention in Russia, 1918–1919, and the Part Played by Canada*. Toronto, 1967

– *McNaughton*. 3 vols. Toronto, 1968–69

– *To Seize the Victory: The Canadian Corps in World War I*. Toronto, 1965

Taylor, A., et al. *Peacekeeping: International Challenge and Canadian Response*. Toronto, 1968

Tennyson, B., and Roger Sarty. *Guardian of the Gulf: Sydney, Cape Breton, and the Atlantic Wars*. Toronto, 2000

Thordarson, Bruce. *Trudeau and Foreign Policy*. Toronto, 1971

Travers, Tim. *How the War Was Won: Command and Technology in the British Army on the Western Front, 1917–1918*. London, 1992

– *The Killing Ground: The British, the Western Front, and the Emeregence of Modern Warfare, 1900–1918*. London, 1990

Turner, Wesley. *British Generals in the War of 1812*. Montreal, 1999

Urquhart, H.M. *Arthur Currie*. Toronto, 1950

Vance, Jonathan. *Death So Noble: Memory, Meaning and the First World War*. Vancouver, 1997

– *Objects of Concern: Canadian Prisoners of War through the Twentieth Century*. Vancouver, 1994

Villa, Brian. *Unauthorized Action: Mountbatten and the Dieppe Raid*. Toronto, 1990

Vokes, Christopher. *Vokes: My Story*. Ottawa, 1985

Watson, Brent. *Far Eastern Tour: The Canadian Infantry in Korea, 1950–1953*. Montreal, 2006

Wattie, Chris. *Contact Charlie: The Canadian Army, the Taliban, and the Battle that Saved Afghanistan*. Toronto, 2008

Wheeler, Victor. *The 50th Battalion in No Man's Land*. Ottawa, 2000

Whitaker, Denis, and Shelagh Whitaker. *Dieppe: Tragedy to Triumph*. Toronto, 1992

– *Rhineland: the Battle to End the War*. Toronto, 1989

– *Tug of War: The Canadian Victory That Opened Antwerp*. Toronto, 1984

– *Victory at Falaise: The Soldiers' Story*. Toronto, 2000

Williams, Jeffery. *Byng of Vimy*. London, 1983

– *The Long Left Flank: The Hard Fought Way to the Reich, 1944–1945*. Toronto, 1988

Wilson, Barbara, ed. *Ontario and the First World War, 1914–1918*. Toronto, 1977

Windsor, John. *Blind Date*. Sidney, BC, 1962

Windsor, Lee, et al. *Kandahar Tour: The Turning Point in Canada's Afghan Mission*. Mississauga, 2008

Winter, Denis. *Haig's Command: A Reassessment*. London, 1992

Wood, H.F. *The Private War of Jacket Coates*. Toronto, 1966

– *Strange Battleground: Official History of the Canadian Army in Korea*. Ottawa, 1966

Wood, James. *Militia Myths: Ideas of the Canadian Citizen Soldier*. Vancouver, 2010

Worthington, Larry. '*Worthy': A Biography of Major-General F.F. Worthington*. Toronto, 1961

Zuehlke, Mark. *Ortona: Canada's Epic World War II Battle*. Toronto, 1999

Zuehlke, Mark. *The Gothic Line: Canada's Month of Hell in World War II Italy*. Vancouver, 2005

– *Holding Juno: Canada's Heroic Defence of the D-Day Beaches, June 7–12, 1944*. Vancouver, 2005

– *Juno Beach: Canada's D-Day Victory, June 6, 1944*. Vancouver, 2004

– *On to Victory: The Canadian Liberation of the Netherlands, March 23–May 5, 1945*. Vancouver, 2010

– *Operation Husky: The Canadian Invasion of Sicily, July 10–August 7, 1943.* Vancouver, 2008
– *Ortona: Canada's Epic World War II Battle.* Vancouver, 2002
– *Terrible Victory: First Canadian Army and the Scheldt Estuary Campaign, September 13, November 6, 1944.* Vancouver, 2007.

ILLUSTRATION CREDITS

Photographs

Author's Collection: Reunion Dinner, 1922

Canadian War Museum: Parade of volunteers in Rosetown, SK, in August 1914 (CWM 19810649-028 p. 4); Loading the First Contingent and its equipment aboard ship in September 1914 (CWM 19800038-001 p. 45a); Gas attack on the Somme (CWM 19700140-077); Canadians put together bridge over the Yser, near Ypres, in 1916 (CWM 19800038-001 p. 34b); Convalescent hospital in Britain (CWM 19720144-008 p. 20b); Two soldiers cook their rations over an improvised stove in 1915–16 (CWM 19820549-020 #3); Amputees and other wounded sit in the sun at Yonge and Carlton streets in Toronto, 1916 (CWM 19800471-005).

City of Toronto Archives: Canadian Armoured Fighting Vehicle School, Camp Borden, Ont. (CTA SC266-61431); Ontario Regiment, Oshawa, Ont., May 4, 1945 (CTA G&M100525).

Department of National Defence: Herbie cartoon; Soldiers trudging across a valley, March 1951 (DND SF840); Soldiers at 1953 armistice in Korea (DND SF8001); Peacekeepers in the Sinai (DND ME733); Patrolling soldier in Cyprus (DND IXC 88-342); Canadian soldiers under fire in Cyprus (DND CYP74-123-35 and DND CYP74-123-36); Lieutenant-Colonel Pierre Daigle, Oka, Que. (DND ISC 90-741); Canadian Cougar, Bosnia (DND, Canadian Cougar 2, photo by Sgt France Dupuis); Reconnaissance platoon in East Timor (DND tim00-037-19, photo by Sgt France Dupuis).

Glenbow Archives: Canadian Women's Army Corps recruit, Vermilion, Alta. (NA-2624-9).

Grip P. and P.: Illustration of the Battle of Duck Lake.

Minister of Public Works and Government Services: Mission briefing in Afghanistan (ISD02-3014, photo by Sgt Gerry Pilote); Conducting perimeter security in Kandahar (IS2005-0448, photo by MCpl Robert Bottrill); LCol Ian Hopes arrives in Afghanistan (KA2006-R106-0025a, photo by MCpl Ken Fenner); Canadian soldiers in Helmand province, Afghanistan (AS2006-0311a, photo by Sgt Dennis Power).

National Archives of Canada: Railway engine transported volunteers to the battle at Ridgeway (NA C2611); Crowds hailing the volunteers on Montreal's Champs de Mars. (NA C653); Colonel Wolseley's camp at Prince Arthur Landing (NA William Armstrong I-18); 1885 North-West Rebellion, militiamen on ferries (NA C4592); General Frederick Middleton visiting wounded after Batoche (NA C3453); Winnipeg cheering the departure of its first contingent to South Africa (NA C12272); The Royal Canadian Regiment's role at Paardeberg was hailed, as in this contemporary illustration (NA C22006); Wounded RCR lie on the ground waiting treatment after Paardeberg (NA C6097); The arid, stony terrain sometimes gave scant cover to the RCR (NA C24606); Prisoners were taken at Paardeberg (NA C24627); Men of the 5th Canadian Mounted Rifles, en route to South Africa in 1902 (NA PA 16427); Major-General Sir Sam Hughes, Canada's Great War Minister of Militia and Defence (NA); Major George Pearkes, wearing the ribbon of the Military Cross (NA PA2364); Home front poster (NA C95281); Walking wounded' from Hill 70 in August 1917 at a field kitchen. (NA PA1596); Montreal recruitment scene (NA PA129610); Dieppe, August 1942 (NA C14160); Canadian Sherman tank during the Italian campaign (NA PA144103); Seaforth Highlanders enjoy their 1943 Christmas dinner (NA PA152839); Men of the Third Canadian Division, awaiting the order to go on June 5, 1944 (NA PA129053); Generals Rod Keller of the Third Canadian Division and Harry Crerar (First Canadian Army) on July 1, 1944 (NA PA132916);General Guy Simonds, II Canadian Corps, and Defence Minister J.L. Ralston in October 1944 (NA PA136762); Tanks of the Fort Garry Horse operate near Beveland on October 30, 1944 (NA PA138429); Trucks, half-tracks, and jeeps in the Hochwald forest, Germany (NA PA138353); South Saskatchewan Regiment near Groningen, The Netherlands (NA); Canadian soldiers meet Russian officer (NA PA 150930); Shipload of soldiers, home, after victory (NA PA112367); Brigadier John Rockingham briefs some of his officers during the Korean War (NA PA133340); The Canadians during the Korean War with Second World War weapons (NA PA179973); A weary soldier loads a Bren gun magazine while KATCOMs look on (NA PA136761); Bunkers during the Korean War (NA PA140790); Soldier in Vietnam with the Canadian contingent in the International Control Commission (NA PA151200).

RCMP Archives: General Middleton's troops in 1885.

Toronto Star: Macpherson cartoon.

Toronto Telegram **Collection, York University Archives:** CEF liberation of Mons, Belgium.

Maps

All maps reprinted by permission of the Directorate of History and Heritage, Department of National Defence: *The Armed Forces of Canada*, Goodspeed (1967): Map 1: The Western Front, 1914–1918: Canadian Operations; Map 5: The Raid on Dieppe, 19 August 1942; Map 6: Italy, 3 September 1943–25 February 1945; Map 7: Victory in Europe and D-Day. *Canadian Expeditionary Force, 1914–1919*, Nicholson (1962): Map 2: Ypres: The Gas Attack, 22 April 1915; Map 3: Vimy Ridge: 9–12 April 1917; Map 4: Passchendaele, 26 October–10 November 1917. *Normandy 1944: The Canadian Summer*, McAndrew (1994): Map 8: The Closing of the Falaise Gap, 17–21 August 1944. *Strange Battleground*, Wood (1966): Map 9: Invasion and Counter Stroke, Chinese Communist Intervention 1950; Map 10: Kapyong.

INDEX